W9-ADK-910

UNDERSTANDING EXCEPTIONAL PEOPLE

COLLEEN J. MANDELL
Department of Special Education
Bowling Green State University

EDWARD FISCUS
Department of Special Education
Bowling Green State University

UNDERSTANDING EXCEPTIONAL PEOPLE

WEST PUBLISHING COMPANY
St. Paul   New York   Los Angeles   San Francisco

Copyediting: Carol Pritchard-Martinez, Stuart Kenter
Design: Janet Bollow
Technical art: John Foster
Cover and text illustrations: Jen-Ann Kirchmeier
Production coordination: Janet Bollow Associates
Composition: Hansen & Associates

COPYRIGHT © 1981 By WEST PUBLISHING CO.
50 West Kellogg Boulevard
P.O. Box 3526
St. Paul, Minnesota 55165

All rights reserved

Printed in the United States of America

Library of Congress Cataloging in Publication Data

Mandell, Colleen J.
    Understanding exceptional people.

    Bibliography: p
    Includes index.
    1. Exceptional children—Education.   I.   Fiscus,
Edward D., joint author.   II.   Title.
LC3965.M275   371.9   80–27076
ISBN 0–8299–0394–1

CREDITS

pages 41-42 Reprinted with permission of THE EXCEPTIONAL PARENT magazine. Copyright © 1973 Psy-Ed Corporation, Room 700, Statler Office Building, Boston, Massachusetts 02116.

page 75 From A. W. Carroll, "The Classroom as an Ecosystem," *Focus on Exceptional Children* 6 (4), 1974, p. 7. Copyright Love Publishing Company.

page 88 From *Developing and Implementing Individualized Education Programs*, A. P. Turnbull, B. B. Strickland, and J. E. Brantley, Charles E. Merrill Publishing Co., 1978.

page 119 From *Parenting Learning-Problem Children: The Professional Educator's Perspective*, E. Edge, B. J. Strenecky, and S. I. Mour, 1978. Reprinted by permission of the National Center for Educational Media and Materials for the Handicapped.

page 155 Copyright © 1976 *Human Behavior* magazine. Reprinted by permission.

page 161 From "Making Better Use of Support Services," E. Gallay and G. J. Bensberg, *School Shop*, Vol. 37, No. 8, 1978, p. 56.

page 162 Mann-Goodman-Wiederholt: TEACHING THE LEARNING-DISABLED ADOLESCENT. Copyright © 1978 by Houghton Mifflin Company. Used by permission.

page 184 "Cipher in the Snow" by Jean Mizer in *Today's Education*, November, 1964.

page 224 From EXCEPTIONAL CHILDREN IN THE SCHOOLS, Second Edition, edited by Lloyd M. Dunn. Copyright © 1963, 1973 by Holt, Rinehart, and Winston, Inc. Reprinted by permission of Holt, Rinehart, and Winston.

page 228 *Speech Correction: Principles and Methods*, 6th edition, C. Van Riper. Prentice-Hall, Inc., 1978.

page 241 (a) *Teaching and Learning Strategies for Physically Handicapped Students*, M. L. Calhoun and M. Hawisher, University Park Press, 1979, p. 183. (b) From McDonald, E. and Schultz, A., "Communication Boards for Cerebral-Palsied Children," *Journal of Speech and Hearing Disorders*, Vol. 38, 1973.

page 244 Kim Von Wert and Kevin Settlage, "Patience Key to Instructing Deaf Children," *The BG News*, June 3 and 4, 1980.

page 248 *Hearing in Children* © 1978, page 12, J. L. Northern and M. P. Downs. The Williams and Wilkins Co., Baltimore.

page 297 Adapted by permission from *Mental Retardation in School and Society* by Donald L. MacMillan. Copyright © 1977 by Little, Brown and Company (Inc.).

page 312 "The Profoundly Retarded: A New Challenge for Public Education," R. E. Luckey and M. R. Addison, *Education and Training of the Mentally Retarded*, October, 1974, Vol. 9, No. 3, p. 125.

page 333 Lerner: CHILDREN WITH LEARNING DISABILITIES, 2nd edition. Copyright © 1976 Houghton Mifflin Company. Used by permission.

page 357 From "Patterns of Aggression, Withdrawal, and Immaturity," H. C. Quay in *Psychopathological Disorders of Childhood*, John Wiley and Sons, Inc., 1978.

(continued following index)

371.9
M27

84-2266
6981544

To Julie and Steven

CONTENTS IN BRIEF

CONTENTS

The objective of this text is to provide students preparing to become teachers with a comprehensive foundation for understanding the needs and potential within every exceptional child and youth in America. Hopefully, this understanding will result in the positive, yet realistic, attitude necessary for developing appropriate and effective educational programs for exceptional students.

"Special education" for exceptional students is rapidly evolving into the provision of a special education for all children and youth. The importance of identifying individual differences in learning characteristics and developing appropriate individualized educational programs has become widely accepted. Many exceptional students can be successfully educated in regular school and classroom settings. However, the successful integration of exceptional children is dependent upon all teachers, not just those preparing to become teachers of special education classes. All teachers need to become knowledgeable of the characteristics of exceptional children and of the common concerns involved in the provision of appropriate, individualized educational programs. This text is suited for all students who are preparing to become teachers, as well as for those teachers who are currently teaching and desire to broaden their knowledge of exceptional children and special education.

It is not assumed that students reading this text have any background in special education or exceptional children. Several techniques are utilized in an attempt to make the information, understandings, and concepts come alive for the reader. Case Studies are used extensively to describe the individuality of particular exceptional children and adults and, at the same time, to review common concerns and issues in special education as they pertain to children with particular characteristics. Applications, included at the end of each chapter, provide more concrete and detailed discussions of particular areas of interest and issues introduced within the chapter. Many of the application topics are related to educating exceptional learners in the classroom.

In order to develop the broad perspective required by students who are preparing to become teachers, this text includes extensive discussions of many common concerns relative to teaching exceptional children, as well as descriptions of various exceptionalities. Section I provides the reader with a background in the critical areas related to all exceptional children and youth. Included are: information on the important influence of litigation and legislation; assessment and placement procedures; the development of individual educational programs; perspectives of the parents and families of exceptional children; considerations in providing programs for the very young, as well as the adolescent exceptional student; and current issues, strategies, and techniques utilized by those who teach exceptional children and youth.

Section II reviews and describes the characteristics, educational programming, and issues associated with each exceptionality. A categorical format is utilized for these descriptions to enhance communication and in consideration for common prevailing practices. When reading the chapters on the various exceptionalities, the reader already will have acquired from the content of Section I a knowledge of variables related to developing the potential within every exceptional student.

PREFACE

ACKNOWLEDGEMENTS

We gratefully acknowledge the contributions of many fine professionals and parents who assisted in the development of this book: Deborah Speece, Jennifer McCord, David Marchman, Julie Fiscus, William Moroney, and Kari Joyce with research; Chris Semington and Katherine Crates with content contributions; and Norma Morris, Barbara Wensel, Sharon McDonald, and Betty Coggin with manuscript preparation.

The conscientious efforts of the following reviewers provided us with many valuable comments and insightful suggestions:

Leroy Aserlind University of Wisconsin, Madison	Alonzo E. Hannaford Western Michigan University
Grant Bitter University of Utah	Jean R. Harber Indiana State University
Lanthan D. Camblin James Madison University, Virginia	Gerald Hasterok University of Southern California
William Caskey East Tennessee State University	Charles M. Ireland Southeast Missouri State
Laurence J. Coleman University of Tennessee	Leo J. Schmidt California State University, Fullerton
Wietse de Hoop Eastern Kentucky	Chriss Walther University of Utah
Shirley E. Forbing San Diego State University	E. H. Williams University of Southern California

A special thanks to Janet Bollow and her staff for their expertise in editing and designing the book.

A very special thanks to the editoral staff at West Publishing Company. Their "no problem" attitude provided us with continuous support throughout the preparation of this book.

COLLEEN J. MANDELL
EDWARD D. FISCUS

UNDERSTANDING
EXCEPTIONAL PEOPLE

CONTENTS

FULFILLING THE MANDATE

1

The rights of exceptional children and youth to receive an appropriate education have been mandated, an act that results in major changes within our educational system. Teachers, as well as parents and other professional personnel, are challenged with the responsibility of providing exceptional children with an appropriate education. Never in the history of our nation's schools has the role of the teacher been so exciting, nor has it ever before encompassed the potential for influence and change that it does today and will tomorrow. This book has been written to assist those professionals in preservice and in-service training who accept the challenge of educating exceptional children and who seek to further develop and define their own role in this regard.

Teacher training programs across the United States are being revamped to include, at least on an introductory level, information about exceptional people. In the past, only students studying to be special educators took courses related to handicapped children. Society's attitude had been to generally ignore handicapped persons or to provide them with separate educational opportunities that were not always equal to regular educational programs. Yet, exceptional children have always existed within our society.

The educational system in the United States reflects the changes occurring in American society. Our educational system tends to maintain changes that have already been initiated by other institutional and societal forces. Many of these forces impacting on the education of exceptional children led to the passage of **Public Law 94-142** (PL 94-142) in 1975. This influential and significant legislation codified the right of all handicapped children to a free, appropriate education. It thus accelerated a concern throughout the educational establishment

Many handicapped students are now being educated in regular classrooms.

that will continue for many years. As a result of this mandate, preservice and in-service teacher education programs now require their students (regardless of the area of specialty) to take courses that focus on the characteristics and needs of exceptional children, as well as on common considerations in special education.

An analysis of attitudes toward exceptional people throughout recorded history suggests that societal attitudes are strongly related to the religious, political, and social occurrences of particular eras. For example, when primitive people were forced to concentrate on providing for their own most basic needs, they could give little attention to the plight of a minority group such as the handicapped. Yet, with increased technology and relatively stable economic conditions, a general social awareness (evidenced, for example, by the civil rights movement) emerged during the twentieth century. With this intensified emphasis on individual worth, **parent advocacy groups** organized for a single cause—to obtain quality education for their exceptional children. The right to a free, appropriate education for the handicapped was thus effectuated through the legal and judicial systems. Teacher training programs, as mentioned, responded to this change in attitude. And, as another consequence, every effort is now being made to educate both the handicapped and nonhandicapped in the same classroom.

DEFINITION OF TERMS

Frequently, the terms "disabled," "handicapped," and "exceptional" are used interchangeably to refer to the same individual. Yet, they are often defined differently. A child is identified as **exceptional** if he or she is atypical, if performance deviates from what is expected. Broader in scope than "disabled," "exceptional" includes not only those people who have limitations, but those whose performance excels or goes beyond normal expectations. A **disability** refers to either a total or partial behavioral, mental, physical, or sensorial loss of functioning. All disabled people are exceptional; the reverse, however, is not true. Whereas a disability or exceptionality is within an individual, a **handicap** refers to the environmental restrictions put on a person's life as a result of his or her disability or exceptionality.

Illustrating the distinction among "disability," "exceptionality," and "handicap" is the case of a six-year-old boy, James, who has spina bifida, which is failure of the spinal column to close. In this disability, the degree of paralysis and loss of body function is related to the severity of the defect. James has limited use of his legs and no bowel or bladder control. Despite these physical limitations, he is able to attend a regular first-grade class because he is mobile with crutches. Regarding academic potential, James has been identified as intellectually gifted. His school made arrangements to have his diapers changed with minimum disruption to the school day. However, he is handicapped physically because of environmental barriers such as stairs. Yet, ingenuity helps him surmount many physical obstacles. For instance, at Halloween James dressed up as Dracula, but trick-or-treating from house to house posed a problem, since he tires easily on crutches. The solution was to pull him in a wagon decorated as a coffin, which added realism to the costume and circumvented his physical limitations.

The degree to which an exceptional person can participate in normal activity and benefit from the learning process depends on a variety of factors not necessarily related to the impairment. The forces that operate to increase the variability among handicapped individuals include:

- Family reaction, which involves parents' and siblings' acceptance of the disability, and their willingness to deal with the problem
- Time of intervention
- Appropriateness of educational programs offered
- Support services available, and the degree of social acceptance in the community

In James's case, all of the factors were handled in a positive way. His mother and medical professionals have provided expert support and care since his birth; the school psychologist works closely with James's teachers to normalize his school environment; and a community worker from a children's services agency works with the medical professionals, James, and his mother to aid him in acquiring self-help skills, such as diaper changing and behavior control.

Thus, if James were to be labeled, his profile would read:

Label	Corresponding Behaviors
Exceptional	Deviates from the norm regarding physical performance (below average) and intellectual performance (above average)
Disabled	Unable to walk; unable to control bowels and bladder
Handicapped	Cannot move physically throughout his environment without assistance or modifications; requires educational program for the academically talented. (Although giftedness is not considered a handicap according to federal interpretation, it is the authors' opinion that the gifted are handicapped in the sense that their superior abilities, for the most part, are not developed in most traditional educational programs.)

PREVALENCE

Prevalence refers to the number of children at any specific time who are identified as handicapped. If we say that the prevalence of handicapped children is 7 percent, we are saying that at this particular point in time 7 percent of our population of children is handicapped (MacMillan, 1977).

Although the handicapped include approximately 35 million citizens in the United States, the focus of this discussion is on handicapped children and adolescents. Exceptional children who are eligible by law for services through special educational placements are categorized as follows: mentally retarded, deaf and hard of hearing, speech impaired, visually impaired, emotionally disturbed, orthopedically and other health impaired, and learning disabled. Figure 1-1 depicts the prevalence of handicapped children in these various categories.

These figures do not include all exceptionalities; for example, the gifted and talented, the abused and neglected, and the bicultural populations are not accounted for. These children can often be legitimately labeled as handicapped when their classroom performance is observed. But because of poor reporting of abuse and neglect, lack of a national mandate to identify and serve the gifted and talented, and disagreement on defining the bicultural population, it is extremely difficult to estimate how many children fit into any one of these categories.

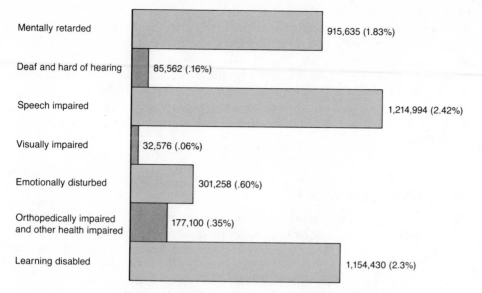

Mentally retarded	915,635 (1.83%)
Deaf and hard of hearing	85,562 (.16%)
Speech impaired	1,214,994 (2.42%)
Visually impaired	32,576 (.06%)
Emotionally disturbed	301,258 (.60%)
Orthopedically impaired and other health impaired	177,100 (.35%)
Learning disabled	1,154,430 (2.3%)

Number of children, ages 3–21, 1978–1979 school year

FIGURE 1-1 Prevalence of handicapped children receiving special education and related services, ages 3 to 21, school year 1978–1979, as reported by state agencies to the U. S. Office of Education and published in *Education Daily*, August 3, 1979, Education News Service Division, Capitol Publications, Inc., Washington, D. C.

In 1976, the National Advisory Committee on the Handicapped estimated that almost half (over 3½ million) of the handicapped children and youth in our country (ages 0 to 19) were not having their educational needs met. In 1979, however, after the identification and reporting procedures required by PL 94-142 were instituted, the numbers of children identified as handicapped were significantly below the previously estimated prevalence level. The previous 1976 estimate of almost 8 million exceptional children accounted for nearly 12 percent of the child population. The updated prevalence figures, however, indicated a prevalence of just under 8 percent, which is between 3 and 4 million handicapped children. This drop in prevalence was even more substantial in some specific categories. For example, the number of children identified as emotionally disturbed in 1979 was 301,258, or 0.60 percent, whereas the earlier estimate of 2 percent, or 1,310,000, was over four times greater.

The more sophisticated (and probably more accurate) reporting procedures of the Bureau of Education for the Handicapped seem to indicate that earlier prevalence estimates were in error, generally. Despite the improved counting procedures, several factors continue to complicate the task of devising accurate prevalence data and to cloud the resultant statistics. Definitions of handicapping conditions that are too broad and ambiguous confuse and impair prevalence counts. Likewise, the problem of classification in more than one handicapping category creates counting problems. So, too, does the fact that each school district interprets various handicapping definitions differently based on the needs of the children within the context of that particular school system. For example, what is considered a learning disability in one district may be called an underachievement in another and accordingly be handled in a different way. In some communities, the stigma of the handicapped label is so great that parents may refuse to have their child evaluated. Or, if evaluated, refuse to have a son or daughter subjected to special education services. These children, while handicapped, would not appear in prevalence figures, which represent children enrolled in special education programs.

Regarding the accuracy and acceptance of the more current lower estimate of handicapped children and youth in America, Meyen and Moran (1979) caution that "if the data are in error, then the consequences are serious in that potentially large numbers of handicapped children and youth are not receiving an appropriate education" (p. 26).

DEGREE OF DISABILITY

Analysis of significant variables related to successful learning by exceptional children indicates that the severity factor of the disability is critical. It is important to recognize that exceptional categories or labels are actually umbrella terms, each with its own specifically related characteristics. However, not all individuals identified with a particular label will exhibit all related characteristics.

Table 1-1 compares the learning and behavioral characteristics of three nine-year-olds recognized as having learning disabilities. The term **learning disabilities** refers to those children who display a significant discrepancy between

TABLE 1-1 Comparison of Three Nine-Year-Old Students Diagnosed as Learning Disabled

Marc

Strengths	*Weaknesses*
■ Well respected by peers	■ Easily distracted—cannot attend to an academic task for more than five minutes
■ Attempts all tasks presented	
■ Responds to social reinforcement	■ Sight vocabulary of approximately 30 words
■ At grade level in math	■ Cannot discriminate short vowel sounds
■ Good motor skills, excels in organized sports	■ Cannot discriminate consonant sounds in final and medial positions

Louise

Strengths	*Weaknesses*
■ Reading word attack and comprehension skills at grade level	■ Unable to plan and organize; e.g., rarely remembers to turn in homework
■ Good memory abilities	■ Refuses to participate orally in large group instruction
■ Understands basic addition and subtraction concepts	■ Verbal expression is limited to phrases
■ Responds well to one-to-one instruction with teacher	■ Lacks understanding of following math concepts: time, multiplication, fractions, measurement
■ Good vocabulary	■ Isolates self from school-related peer activities

Truman

Strengths	*Weaknesses*
■ At grade level in math	■ Poor fine motor skills; e.g., manuscript and cursive writing are unintelligible
■ Reading two years above grade level	
■ Relates well to peers and adults	■ Difficulty in performing gross motor tasks successfully, especially those requiring eye-hand coordination
■ Recognizes "writing problems" and perseveres at getting written tasks completed	

estimated learning potential and demonstrated academic achievement. The students' profiles indicate, for the most part, that the only commonality they share is the same label. Because each student's learning style and capabilities are unique, a prognosis of perceived success should be based on specific information obtained from an individualized assessment battery. Prognosis should not rely on a diagnostic label. Parent support and involvement, early intervention, and the development of an appropriate educational program are external but interrelated variables that help determine to what degree the exceptional child reaches his or her learning potential. These common considerations are described and discussed in Section I of this text.

EDUCATING TEACHERS

Since handicapped citizens can no longer be denied opportunities simply because they are disabled, attitudes toward accepting them into the mainstream of life must be developed. An important vehicle for eradicating misconceptions and faulty stereotypic images is education. The goal of any beginning text on exceptional people should be to introduce educators to the exceptional population from a positive, yet realistic, perspective. In order to best provide educators with fundamental information about exceptional people, this text is divided into three sections: Common Considerations, Exceptionalities, and The Future. This last section examines the direction of special education, which you, the reader, will assist in guiding.

Knowledge of Common Considerations

The interplay of family, intervention, assessment, education, and support services has a profound influence on the lives of the handicapped. These factors can be positive, as in James's case, or negative. Because they play such an important part in the lives of all exceptional people (regardless of the specific handicapping condition), these elements are addressed in Section I. Chapter 2 describes legislative mandates and legal precedents that paved the way for appropriate services to exceptional persons; Chapter 5 addresses important family issues related to exceptional children; Chapters 3, 4, and 8 are concerned with educational matters —assessment, development of relevant educational programs, and teacher education; Chapters 6 and 7 delineate a wide range of educational services, from early identification and early childhood programs to programs for handicapped adolescents and adults. All these facets are critical in developing the maximum potential of exceptional children.

The only factors not obviously impacting the lives of exceptional chidren are litigation and legislation. However, without legal mandates the other aspects would be permissive, that is, suggested rather than required. By understanding the evolution of current laws affecting handicapped children, the reader can more fully appreciate the significance of the concepts and ideals discussed in Chapters 3 through 8.

Section I of this text is structured to provide the reader with a frame of reference when studying the exceptionalities presented in Section II. By gaining knowledge of the many variables intrinsic to an exceptional person's world, one can better comprehend the individual differences in people who have the same disability.

There is more to working with exceptional people than teaching methods and a cognitive grasp of specific handicapping conditions with their corresponding behavior characteristics. It is not only necessary to realize how people are different, but also how they are the same. Exceptional persons have the same needs as those without disabilities. Themes found throughout the case studies (which introduce each of the exceptionality chapters) include a sense of belonging, a feeling of productivity, and a need for a personal identity apart from the disability. The route to these goals may differ for disabled persons, but the finish line is the same for all.

Knowledge of Exceptionalities

Many educators view the practice of tagging children with an exceptional label negatively. They believe that the label frequently becomes a scapegoat; that is, the child is not learning because he or she is retarded, or blind, or deaf, and so forth. Failure becomes the fault of the student. However, labeling a student with a specific exceptionality can be a positive procedure. It can help get that student into an appropriate learning environment.

The long-standing issue of labeling effects is one of the most controversial in the field of special education. The work of Rosenthal and Jacobsen (1968) demonstrated the negative effects of labels on the teacher's perceptions of children's activities. These researchers postulated that teacher expectancies based on labels established a **self-fulfilling prophecy** effect (that is, the child becomes what the teacher thinks he or she is). Subsequent research, however (MacMillan, Jones, and Aloia, 1971), has failed to substantiate the existence of this self-fulfilling prophecy effect, the strong stigmatization involved, and the validity of the original research conclusions. Reschly and Lamprecht (1979) reported the results of a study involving classroom teachers, pupils, and the labels of normal, gifted, and mentally retarded. They concluded "that teachers ultimately form expectations on the basis of the child's actual behavior. Labels may exert a significant effect on a teacher's expectancies only if other information is unavailable. The wise teachers who for a long time have been telling us 'You can't teach labels, you must teach children' have explicitly made this generalization" (p. 57).

Current federal guidelines, however, require identification, labeling, and classification of children into specific handicapping condition categories as a prerequisite for receiving special educational services. Thus, the controversies over labeling and the related issue of classification are likely to continue. Most special educators agree that a particular label or classification has little value in educating exceptional children, since each child is unique. What is useful (and even required if the child is to learn effectively) is an evaluation of the child's relevant learning characteristics. Such a functional assessment is necessary for achieving success with or without the label, which is often medically determined.

Although labels carry the positive effect of allowing handicapped children to be eligible for special education programs, educators still need to remain aware that determining a special education category does not solve the exceptional child's problems. The next step—planning and implementing an individualized program based on a careful analysis of the child's unique learning strengths and weaknesses—is much more important to and critical for the child's ultimate success in learning.

Knowing the causes, developmental patterns, behavioral characteristics, and educational alternatives associated with specific exceptionalities will help educators to:

- Recognize and dispel their own negative stereotypic images associated with particular groups of exceptional persons. (For example, a common fallacy is that blind persons, because of their handicap, cannot be contributing members of society. Another is that gifted persons tend to have a higher than normal rate of mental and emotional instability.)
- Screen and refer any of their students who may benefit from an alternative placement whether it be special education and/or support services and/or regular class placement.

A word of caution is in order concerning material in Section II. Remember that not all persons within a given category have the same educational, emotional, and social needs. In order to maintain a sense of individuality while studying group behaviors, each exceptionality chapter is introduced by a case study. These serve as a means for the reader to expand knowledge and understanding of the common considerations discussed in Chapters 2 through 8. The reader can then critically evaluate the significance of issues, concepts, and concerns by applying the concepts learned earlier within the context of the lives (case studies) of various exceptional people.

With appropriate education, blind people, as well as other handicapped people, can be active, contributing members of society.

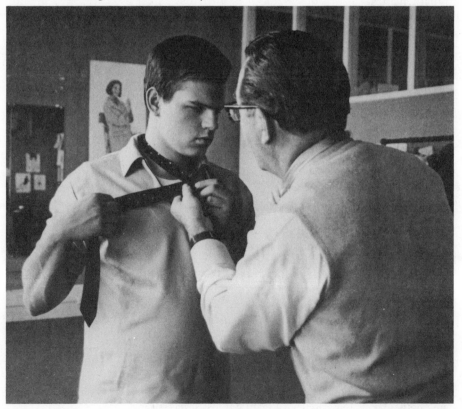

Case Studies

The following case studies show how different factors have influenced the lives of three handicapped people. Their stories may evoke a variety of reactions, including humor, rage, sympathy, and pity. It is suggested that each case study be read twice—once to judge initial feelings and, then, to determine how family, time of intervention, educational programming, and support services helped or hindered the exceptional person's development. The second step will help the reader begin to understand the complexities of an exceptional person's world, which is one of the goals of this text.

The case studies are told from different points of view—by a parent or directly by the handicapped person. These and other case studies in this text are authentic; they are about real people. To honor privacy, however, names have been changed and identifying details omitted to assure anonymity. The first case study involves a young woman with a severe problem in using any form of language (including numbers and words) through written expression.

Sharon

DISABILITY: Specific Learning Disability
DEFINITION: "...a disorder in one or more of the basic psychological processes involved in understanding or in using language spoken or written which may manifest itself in an imperfect ability to listen, think, speak, read, write, spell, or do mathematical calculations" (*Federal Register*, December 29, 1977, part 3). The learning disabled population characteristically demonstrates poor academic achievement in relation to expected potential.

I came to the attention of the school system when I was in third grade and still could not read. Although I excelled in math verbally, I was unable to put my thoughts on paper. The school thought I was lazy and immature and that I would read when I was ready. My parents did not believe this so they took me to the institute where my mentally retarded brother received training. After three months of testing, the institute diagnosed a learning disability and gave my parents a special diet plan and a structured motor therapy program for me in addition to regular trips to the institute. My parents discontinued the program because it did not seem to help.

In the beginning of fifth grade I was placed in the program for educable mentally retarded (EMR) students without my mother's knowledge. The room was carpeted but contained no desks, chairs, or books. The students simply drew pictures on the chalkboard and we had different teachers all the time. The teachers just babysat. My mother did not find out for a long time because we received report cards just like everyone else. I did not want to tell her because it was fun in that class. When my mother found out, she went to the school and insisted that I be tested and placed in a regular classroom. After a great deal of resistance from the school, I was tested in academic areas and again the report indicated that I was a "lazy" child because I excelled in math even though I "refused" to write anything down. I would not admit that I could not write. I would rather have people think that I was nasty than dumb. Being thought of as stupid has been a lifelong fear.

Although I did enter a regular fifth-grade classroom, it turned out to be a nightmare rather than the answer. The teacher despised me. She hit me with a yardstick when I lost my place in reading and smacked me in the face. One day I ran away from school and hid in the field and not even the police could find me. When I got home and realized my mother knew, I just pretended that I got lost at recess time.

After spending the rest of the year in an EMR class, I was placed in a regular sixth-grade classroom. The school allowed this because I had won first prize in a story contest by dictating a story to my mother. My mother explained to the teacher that I had to be taught differently and responded differently than other kids. She did not use the term learning disabled, but understood completely what I needed. That teacher never called me "stupid." I learned how to read a little and how to write in cursive writing, but I still could not print. The sixth-grade teacher spent many hours working with me and suggested testing by the school psychologist as well as a learning disability class to my mother, but we moved before the testing could begin.

By the time I was in junior high school, I had become a professional at cheating and conning the teacher. I learned that it did not matter what you knew, just what grade was on your paper. I learned as much as I could by listening in class. During tests I copied from people sitting near me. I often made up entire books for book reports, including the cover design. When the teacher asked to see the book, I pretended I lost it, but I usually got A's. Sometimes they caught me cheating but I just pretended that I did not care. In science I was good at conducting and making up my own experiments. I was the first to volunteer for activities but I had difficulty turning in written work. I was a cheerleader and on the track, swimming, basketball, and gymnastics teams. In the 11th grade, I became involved with a bad group of kids and got in trouble. Those students accepted me for what I was. The students I associated with were dropouts and flunkies. It was a "tough" bunch of girls who often skipped school and I followed along. I wrote notes for them and forged their mothers' signatures. By then I was good at copying handwriting. I was expelled from school for being involved in a fire. I was really just a bystander. That group of people that I associated with did not care how I did academically.

After school I fell in love and got married. All I wanted to do was be a housewife and be taken care of, but my husband encouraged me to get my high school diploma. The school psychologist determined that I was severely learning disabled and read at the kindergarten level. Through tutoring, which included reading tests to me and taping books, I earned my degree in six months. College became a goal, so to receive additional remedial work the high school counselor advised me to contact the Bureau of Vocational Rehabilitation (BVR), a state agency that provides funds for handicapped persons. Because learning disability was not on BVR's list of acceptable handicaps, I had to provide evidence of abnormal brain waves by obtaining a brain scan. I finally received tutoring and applied to college.

My skills in conning, which helped me survive during my secondary schooling, were put to use again. I applied to college as a blind student, but they caught me when they asked if I would be using a dog or a cane, so I applied as a special student instead. I felt that I should qualify for the same books and tutoring as blind students because I am "blind" when it comes to reading and paperwork. The college wanted an IQ test. The person giving the test insisted that I write by myself and that the test be timed. It takes a great deal of time for me to write words down. My IQ turned out to be borderline retarded. The college sent a letter to BVR concerning my low IQ, and stated that I was illiterate. I was denied admission. BVR suggested remedial tutoring for two years and said that if I learned to read, maybe I could take another test, achieve a normal IQ score, and maybe the school would accept me. I found a tutor and was tutored for one and a half years. I progressed rapidly and took another IQ test that required writing but it was not timed and other compensations were given. This time my IQ was quite high. The tutor notified BVR that I would have no trouble with any course in college. I applied to a different school because the people in the admissions office of the first college laughed at me. I interviewed with people in the admissions office and they had me talk to the dean of education. I am currently enrolled at a private university in the College of Education. I use a tape recorder, talking books, textbooks on tape, and any other resources I can get my hands on. I plan to someday teach teenaged pupils with learning and behavioral disorders.

Maybe I should feel bitter about the way I was treated by the educational system, but I think the experience taught me a lot about the kind of teacher I want to become. A major problem was negative attitudes—mine and the teachers'. I used to think that teachers were trying to make things difficult. In math, for example, the "less than" and "greater than" signs looked the same to me and I thought teachers decided what was correct depending on their particular mood each day, and I had no patience with moody teachers. I argued with them and corrected them often. I simply stopped trying when teachers said, "You can do better!" I admit that I was very vindictive and tried to hurt people who hurt me, but no teacher should rely on school records in determining how to deal with a student. I started every year fresh until I sensed the negative attitude of the teacher.

Including parents in the teacher/child relationship is so important. My mother accepted me 100 percent; I wish my teachers could have listened to her more carefully. In fact, I did not realize how different I was until I left my family. Teachers have the ability to make parents proud of their children. As a teacher, I will strive to have my students realize that their personal and emotional growth is as important as intellectual growth. If you hate the person you are, what you learn doesn't seem to matter.

Points for Consideration

- Sharon's parents were not sure what her problem was. Nonetheless, they tried various remedies, and they provided such a strong, positive base of support for her that she did not realize she was different until she interacted more frequently with persons outside her family.
- School personnel had great difficulty in understanding Sharon's disability and in deciding what to do to help her. She was in grade three before being recognized as different. She was misidentified as mentally retarded and often thought of as lazy.
- Sharon's abilities were quite high in some areas and extremely low in others during her public school career. While her mother recognized these differences and knew how to cope with them, she was not involved significantly in educational decisions. This extreme variation in Sharon's skills continued to confuse persons working with her.
- Sharon's learning disability triggered coping behaviors on her part that were negativistic and inappropriate. She refused to write, refused to admit her problems, and decided she would rather be known as nasty than as dumb. Later she learned to copy, cheat, and con the teacher in order to obtain passing grades. As a teenager, the behaviors paralleled those of other youths who didn't care about her academic achievement but accepted her as she was. Further social and behavioral troubles followed her association with her inappropriately behaved peers.

The next case is told by another young adult, Linda, who is blind. The nature of her disability allowed intervention much earlier than was the situation for Sharon, but early intervention did not prove to be the most important factor.

Linda

DISABILITY: Blindness (or Severe Visual Impairment)
DEFINITION: (Educational) Requires the use of Braille to read and learn. (Legal) "...visual acuity for distant vision of 20/200 or less in the better eye, with best

correction; or visual acuity of more than 20/200 if the widest diameter of field of vision subtends an angle no greater than 20 degrees" (*National Society for Prevention of Blindness Fact Book*, 1966, p. 10).

I have been blind since birth. My mother's labor was induced in the seventh month of pregnancy and afterward I was given high levels of oxygen, which damaged my eyesight. This was a common practice around the early 1950s and no one knew the hazards involved.

I went to kindergarten in a public school. I really liked it and had a smart teacher who let me do things. When they were doing things I could not do, she would never let me sit there; she would give me something else to do. She let me work with the calendar which had names of the days in heavy cardboard. That is how I learned the days of the week. Or else she'd have me play with clay or fingerpaint. I was really happy in public school. In the afternoons I went to class, and in the mornings my mom would teach me Braille with a pegboard.

Although my mother wanted me to continue in the public school system, the principal and superintendent said it would be impossible to teach me. A school in a nearby metropolitan area had a teacher for the blind, but they would not accept students from outside the city. The only option available at that time was to attend a school for the blind away from home.

Living in an institution was a negative emotional experience for me. I was separated from my mother and never had the opportunity to argue with my brothers and sisters or do any of the other things considered normal in growing up. The people at the institution acted like they owned me. They would get very upset when my mother took me home on weekends and would tell me not to tell her anything that happened at the institution. I told her for a while, but, afterwards, the institution folks would be so angry with me that I withdrew and became quiet.

School was very boring. Although I was talented musically, my skills were never developed at the institution. I am ashamed to say that I graduated from that institution. The only valuable thing I learned was to depend only on myself.

I attended a small private college for one year but had to drop out for financial reasons. I majored in music and held a C average. I often think the grades were given to me. I took a typing job and then decided to try college again.

My adjustment to college and life away from the institution has not been easy for me. Developmentally and emotionally, I have always been about two years behind. I struggle to become an independent person and not the "blind girl" in somebody's class. Each blind person is different, and sighted people often do not realize this. I feel fortunate that I have a roommate who won't laugh at me when I talk about strange things. Although I have learned to be more responsible for myself by living on campus, I resent the dormitory and long for a home. I guess this is because I have lived in a dorm for 18 of my 25 years.

My most urgent need at this time is to find a competent, optimistic advisor to help me plan my career. In the past, I have been given tests of every conceivable form, from psychological to employment, but it is people, not test scores, that will help me. Some counselors in the institution told me that I was unrealistic to want to pursue music. I cannot accept that. I know a blind lady who is a radio newsbroadcaster and the radio station installed a teletype machine in Braille. Obviously the aid I seek is not impossible or unrealistic. I need an advisor who believes in me as much as I believe in myself.

Points for Consideration

■ Linda is a young woman struggling to achieve independence as all young persons do. Her struggle, however, is unique in that in order to lose the image of the "blind girl," she needs the support of someone with sight. Unfortunately, sighted persons frequently stereotype blind persons and fail to recognize them as individuals.

■ While the public school and her mother were able to initially cooperate in implementing Linda's education, she was placed at a young age in an institution in order to receive an appropriate education. The absence of a normal family life while growing up; the development of feelings such as boredom, mistrust of institutional authorities, and unfulfillment of talent; and the subsequent withdrawal behavior resulted in an overall negative emotional experience.

■ While Linda has adapted to her disability very well and attained her public school education, her difficulties are not over. She continues to face problems and make adjustments as she has all through her life.

The parents in the next case study describe their reactions to giving birth and living with a child having **Down's syndrome**. This condition is caused by a chromosome abnormality resulting in mental retardation, severe medical problems, and abnormal physical appearance, including slanted eyes, thick tongue, and short, stocky build.

Jonathan

DISABILITY: Moderate Mental Retardation related to Down's Syndrome
DEFINITION: "Mental Retardation refers to significantly sub-average general intellectual functioning existing concurrently with deficits in adaptive behavior and manifested during the developmental period" (Grossman, 1973, p. 5).

I was alone in the hospital and my son was 24 hours old when the doctor, a general practitioner, came to talk with me. I asked how my baby was and the doctor hesitated. "Mongoloid" flashed in my mind but the doctor said "Down's syndrome," which I did not understand. My intuition was correct; mongoloid is the layman's term for a person with Down's syndrome, a chromosomal defect. The doctor hoped he was wrong but the pediatrician said there was little doubt. A chromosome test would be done for confirmation.

My reaction was total disbelief and negativism. How could this happen? After all, I had already given birth to two healthy, normal boys. I remembered seeing a 30-year-old Down's syndrome man who was loud and ill-mannered. Mike, my husband, was thinking of the future. Would Jonathan always be dependent on us? His birth changed our entire perspective on life.

Those first few weeks can only be described as a crisis. Jonathan was born on May 24, Mike was receiving his doctoral degree June 9, and a positive diagnosis took eight days. In addition to dealing with our personal feelings, the general practitioner said we had to decide if we would keep him or put him in an institution. Luckily, we found out about a mental health facility that could counsel us, and Mike gathered information during the first few days, assuming that the tests would confirm Down's syndrome.

Jonathan had so many medical problems. He was close to death very often during the first six months. At the six-week checkup, a heart murmur was found. This was almost as big an emotional blow to me as the original diagnosis. At that point, Mike was expecting almost anything.

We moved when Jonathan was three months old. He was hospitalized for five weeks with pneumonia two months later. After returning home, Jonathan deteriorated and had total heart failure on the left side. Digitalis, a heart stimulant medication, cleared up the problem. He received open-heart surgery at three years to repair a dime-sized hole known medically as a ventricular septal defect.

Jonathan's first three years were emotionally draining for me, as it was a 24-hours-a-day, 7-days-a-week job. We had fantastic support, though, along the way. When we first moved, our neighbor was a nurse who had a brain-damaged child. She was a tremendous help because she had a very positive attitude toward Down's syndrome. We have found that through a willingness to talk about it we have met others who have had the same experience. It really helps to keep those channels of communication open.

When Jonathan was born we explained to our oldest son, Tommy (seven years old), that Jonathan would not learn or grow up as fast as other children. Ned was only three years old at the time so we answered his questions as they came along. Since Jonathan's heart surgery, we treat him like the other children and try not to give him special considerations. Tommy and Ned have a great relationship with Jonathan. Kids congregate at the house and include him in everything.

Jonathan has been in a school environment of some type since he was two years old. He now attends a preschool class at a school for moderately retarded children (sometimes called trainable mentally retarded). He was functioning so much better that the teachers wanted to place him in the developmentally delayed class, which is a bridge to regular class placement. He needed to be tested for the placement and only got an IQ score of 34, but 50 is the cutoff for the class. The testing conditions, however, were horrible. A busy cafeteria with many distractions was the setting. The principal, who had often observed Jonathan in the classroom, also agreed that the developmentally delayed class was the best placement for him, despite his low IQ score. When I met with the teacher, she reported that the IQ test score had somehow disappeared from his file. Thus, the placement decision would be based on observed classroom behavior. To date, Jonathan is doing well in the developmentally delayed class.

The future is brighter now that people have become more accepting and understanding of retarded people. Mike has changed jobs and we are hopeful that Jonathan can learn the trade (carpentry) and will be able to work with his father. We are concerned about his education. It is easy to keep him safe and protected at his present school, but

Like other preschoolers, Down's syndrome children enjoy play activities.

sending him to a public school where attitudes are not as positive is a bit frightening. The school system has classes for retarded children in the elementary school but after that there are no special classes. It is disturbing that he can go to elementary school and then have no program at the junior and senior high school level. We hope by the time he reaches that level, programs will have changed.

Points for Consideration

■ The confusion, disbelief, and emotional strain that Jonathan's parents experienced at his birth have not disappeared. His physical problems and the difficulties in determining the most appropriate educational placement for him continue to stimulate emotional crises and impact upon the family.

■ While cooperation exists between Jonathan's parents and school personnel, the issue of what educational placement is best for him is not clear-cut or easy to decide. Testing procedures appear to be ambiguous and even interfering at times.

■ It is unlikely that Jonathan will be able to continue his current level of progress if appropriate educational programs are not available for him as he matures. The positive effects of early intervention may be lost in the negative aftermath of the school's failure to follow up.

■ Exceptional persons have a significant impact on their families. How their families respond and adapt to their presence greatly influences their development. Parents are often faced with very difficult, emotionally draining questons, such as, "Should we consider placement in an institution?" "Should we investigate another special clinic?" and "What can we do to help assure that our child will have continuous opportunities for educational progress?" Answers are not easily supplied.

Society, in general, and schools, in particular, are improving greatly in providing appropriate responses to the expressed needs of exceptional children and their families. The present direction is positive and the future bright. However, how much we accept the challenges of teaching exceptional children determines how bright their future becomes.

APPLICATION OF KNOWLEDGE

An application will be presented at the conclusion of each chapter of this book. The topics were selected primarily on the basis of two criteria. First, they identify current trends and issues related to exceptional persons; and, second, because the topics are broad in scope, they expand and apply the reader's knowledge about exceptional persons in the educational arena as well as in other aspects of life.

A widely accepted fact is that a transfer of learning occurs more readily when information is relevant and can be easily applied in other settings. So, each application functions as a bridge between the abstract and the concrete. Chapter concepts are applied, for the most part, to situations and events that the reader has either experienced or probably will experience. By studying relevant, realistic applications it is hoped that the reader will develop an awareness of exceptional people as human beings. Topics were selected to help dispel some of the mystique and curiosity frequently associated with exceptional people. Table 1-2 lists chapter and application titles.

TABLE 1-2 Chapter and Application Titles

17

FULFILLING THE MANDATE

Chapter Title	Application Title
1 Fulfilling the Mandate	Opportunities for Active Involvement with Exceptional Persons
2. Arriving at the Mandate	Extending the Rights of Exceptional Persons
3. Assessment and Placement	Diagnosis vs. Prognosis
4. Individualized Education Program	The IEP—A Vehicle for Developing Communication between Teachers
5. Parent and Family Perspectives	Parent/Teacher Interaction
6. Young Exceptional Children	Transdisciplinary Teaming—An Alternative for Young Handicapped Children
7. Exceptional Adolescents and Adults	Vocational Rehabilitation
8. Professional Preparation	Individualizing Instruction in the Regular Classroom
9 The Visually Impaired	Teaching the Blind—Conceptual Learning and the Arts
10. The Speech and Language Impaired	Communication Boards—An Alternative to Silence and Isolation
11. The Hearing Impaired	Beyond High School—Educational Opportunities for the Deaf
12. The Orthopedically Handicapped and Other Health Impaired	Integration—Preparing All Students
13. The Mentally Retarded	Human Sexuality and Mental Retardation—A Continuing Controversy
14. The Learning Disabled	Peer Tutoring—Who Benefits the Most?
15. The Behavior Disordered	Changing Behavior
16. The Gifted and Talented	Developing Creativity in the Classroom
17. The Bicultural	Achieving Bicultural Awareness—A Two-Way Endeavor
18. The Abused and Neglected	Prevention—Alternative Approaches
19. Looking to the Future	Learning and Teaching in the Future

SUMMARY POINTS

■ PL 94-142 in 1975 established the right of all handicapped children to a free, appropriate education. Society, as well as teacher training programs throughout the county, increasingly recognizes the existence of exceptional persons and the roles of all teachers in providing an appropriate education for all children.

■ The terms "disabled," "handicapped," and "exceptional," while often used interchangeably, are different. With increased awareness and services to the disabled population, many will face fewer handicaps in the classroom and in society.

■ Accurate prevalence figures on the number of handicapped children in our country have been difficult to obtain due to broad, ambiguous categories and overlapping definitions.

■ Categories of exceptionality are broad, and not all persons labeled in the same category will share all of the same characteristics. The degree of disability and handicap of individual children within categories is an important factor.

■ Because PL 94–142 requires identification and categorization of handicapped children in order for them to receive special educational services, the controversy over labeling continues.

REVIEW QUESTIONS

1. Define "disabled," "exceptional," and "handicapped." How do they relate to each other?
2. Why is it difficult to obtain accurate prevalence data?
3. Identify common considerations relative to exceptional children in general. Why are they critical factors for developing the maximum potential of exceptional persons?
4. List the advantages and disadvantages of labeling. Do you think this practice is justifiable?
5. What similar needs and goals run through all three case studies despite their obvious individual differences?

OPPORTUNITIES FOR ACTIVE INVOLVEMENT WITH EXCEPTIONAL PERSONS

Re-integrating handicapped persons into the mainstream of society cannot be accomplished without the cooperation and active involvement of our nonhandicapped citizens. Advocate groups ensure the physical and psychological well-being of handicapped persons by pursuing their legal and social rights as well as providing psychological and medical services for them. Becoming an advocate, however, may not be the first active step to take for a person wishing to become involved with the handicapped and their special education. Many opportunities exist for pre-service and in-service students who desire to volunteer to assist and concomitantly learn about exceptional persons. A few of these opportunities are highlighted below.

SPECIAL OLYMPICS

In 1968, the Joseph P. Kennedy, Jr., Foundation created the Special Olympics to emphasize the accomplishments of mentally retarded persons. The Special Olympics allow the mentally retarded to develop their physical and mental health through training and through athletic competition with themselves and others. This promotes year-round fitness. Special Olympic events are held at the local, state, and national level (every four years). They usually include opening and closing ceremonies, a fair, a victory dance, educational and recreational clinics, and demonstrations for coaches and athletes as well as the athletic events themselves. These activities promote overall self-confidence and positive attitudes in mentally retarded persons.

Currently there are over 15,000 Special Olympic games, meets, and training programs being conducted year-round in all states and in many foreign countries. Nearly 200,000 volunteers acting in roles including organizers, coaches, trainers, timers, judges, presenters of ribbons, meal supervisors,

chaperones, and huggers (persons who stand at the end of the race and give each participant a warm hug as they complete the event) are responsible for the success of the Special Olympics.

Special Olympic participants must be at least eight years old, but there is no upper age limit, with persons as old as seventy having competed. In order to assure positive attitudes, confidence, and better self-images in the mentally retarded, athletes are grouped by ability as well as by age, providing for a better chance for a successful experience.

Those persons interested in learning more about the Special Olympics and how they can help develop cooperation, self-discipline, sportsmanship and a larger degree of independence in mentally retarded persons can contact their local or state Special Olympic Committee or the Joseph P. Kennedy, Jr., Foundation, 1701 K Street, N.W., Suite 205, Washington, D.C. 20006.

Special Olympic events provide handicapped youths with opportunities for physical, personal, and social growth.

STUDENT COUNCIL FOR EXCEPTIONAL CHILDREN (SCEC)

The Student Council for Exceptional Children (SCEC) is an international student organization related to the parent professional body, the Council for Exceptional Children (CEC). SCEC has chapters at many colleges and universities across the country. These chapters promote high professional standards, improve professional programs dealing with exceptional children and youth, promote programs for attracting students into the profession of special education, and disseminate information regarding the educational needs of exceptional children. SCEC chapters implement volunteer service projects with exceptional children in the local community, sponsor meetings for professional growth, raise community awareness of the needs and abilities of exceptional children through week-long campus activities, and assist summer camp programs for exceptional children. Several SCEC chapters now participate in the Family Play To Grow Program (sponsored by the Joseph P. Kennedy, Jr., Foundation) which is aimed at helping families learn how to better assist their handicapped children through family play activities.

Students interested in and concerned with the education of exceptional children and youth may join SCEC and, as such, be an integral part of CEC. In this capacity, they are then able to participate fully in the organization decision and policy making. They also receive the benefit of CEC's many professional publications, including their professional journal, *Exceptional Children*.

Further information and materials related to SCEC can be obtained by contacting the Council for Exceptional Children, 1920 Association Drive, Reston, Virginia 22091.

YOUTH NARC

Youth NARC is a division of the National Association for Retarded Citizens (NARC) organized in 1967 for young persons who desire to help the mentally retarded. More than 20,000 members, ages 13 to 25, provide direct personal services to mentally retarded individuals through 43 state and 600 local associations. Types of involvement include taking mentally retarded children on outings —to the park, the zoo, the movies; planning dances and parties; serving in babysitting programs for parents of mentally retarded children; and serving as special friends to mentally retarded persons. More information about Youth NARC may be received by contacting a local Association for Retarded Citizens, or Youth NARC, 2709 Avenue E East, P.O. Box 6109, Arlington, Texas 76011.

A VERY SPECIAL ARTS FESTIVAL

The National Committee on Arts for the Handicapped has estimated that only about 12 percent of all handicapped children enrolled in our nation's schools participate in arts programs. In order to reverse this lack of arts participation by handicapped children, this Committee is developing Very Special Arts Festivals in all states. These festivals include performances, demonstrations, exhibitions, and workshops by special students and their teachers in the area of dance (square, modern, jazz), music (instrumental, vocal), theater arts (drama, puppets, readings), visual arts (paintings, drawings, sculpture, crafts), and film/media (film, video, slides).

Information on the Very Special Arts Festival can be procured by contacting teachers of the arts in public schools and/or the state departments of government in your state responsible for education and related services to handicapped children and youth.

Opportunities for assisting and learning about exceptional persons abound in modern-day society. From the few described here, it is clear that student volunteers have a wide variety of activities and situations to choose from. Volunteers may choose involvements that match their own skills and aptitudes or they may accept the challenge of learning new knowledge and skills right along with the exceptional persons with whom they are working. From tutor to coach to hugger, the opportunities are there for those will accept the challenges.

1. Which of the opportunities described in this application do you think you personally would like to participate in? What skills and strengths do you have that would particularly suit you for this opportunity?
2. What other potential opportunities for working with and learning about handicapped persons exist in your community?
3. What benefits do you think may accrue to nonhandicapped persons as a result of their active involvement with handicapped persons?

SUGGESTED READINGS

Meyen, E. L., and Moran, M. R. "A Perspective on the Unserved Mildly Handicapped." *Exceptional Children*, 45 (April, 1979), 526–530.

Rosenthal, R., and Jacobsen, L. *Pygmalion in the Classroom: Teacher Expectations and Pupils' Intellectual Development*. New York: Holt, Rinehart, and Winston, 1968.

I

COMMON CONSIDERATIONS

CONTENTS

2

ARRIVING AT THE MANDATE

Each exceptional person is unique. If we are to succeed in assisting exceptional children and youth (no matter what their label or category), we must regard them as individuals. There are, however, several considerations relevant to all exceptional people. The issues of assessment, educational program development, intervention strategies, support services, and family perspectives are vitally important for those who desire to learn more about these groups.

This chapter describes the influential litigation and legislation that affected the education and well-being of exceptional children and youth during the 1970s. The culmination of these historic events was the passage of the Education for All Handicapped Children Act of 1975, Public Law 94-142 (PL 94-142).

PERSPECTIVES

The goals and objectives of education only reflect the values of a society at any given time; education usually does not initiate change. The catalysts for change in the status of handicapped persons throughout the 1960s and 1970s were the legislative and court systems.

Legislative enactments and judicial decisions of the 1970s regarding the rights of the handicapped have nurtured a developing positive climate for exceptional persons within our society. Human rights, once denied the handicapped, are now more fully accorded them. Society's attitude toward meeting the needs of exceptional people has thus undergone a major shift.

The general emphasis on human rights in our own country and others, along with the advocacy of children's rights (symbolized in the United Nations' International Year of the Child in 1979) have extended the climate of concern for the welfare and civil rights of all human beings. The United Nations' Declaration of Rights of the Child includes, among others, the right to affection, love, and understanding, the right to a free education, and the right to special care, if handicapped. This international decree parallels the American credo of human rights for all citizens, handicapped or not.

Indeed, in the minds of many Americans the ultimate goal of the equal rights movement has been reached. Members of our society are beginning to view exceptional people as citizens first and as handicapped second. The recently gained status of exceptional persons has had a positive effect; many people now overtly acknowledge the individuality of the person. Characterizations of handicapping conditions that have long masked the humanness of the exceptional person are beginning to fade. We are nearing a time when, in the words of Pope John Paul I, "The system is for man, not man for the system."

The terms "legislation" and "litigation" are often confused. **Litigation** is a process that occurs through the court system. It involves an individual or a small group of people filing a suit against another group, usually the majority. The suit represents a complaint against the status quo—for example, racial discrimination or exclusion from school. If the suit is won, it affects only those individuals who filed the complaint. Or, it can be a class action suit. For example, a parent of a mentally retarded child sues a school system on behalf of all mentally retarded children in the area for excluding them from classes. If the court ruled in favor of the plaintiff in this case, the outcome would affect all retarded citizens.

Legislation refers to laws or bills which are enacted by a majority vote of lawmakers. Often these laws are developed after much litigation has occurred.

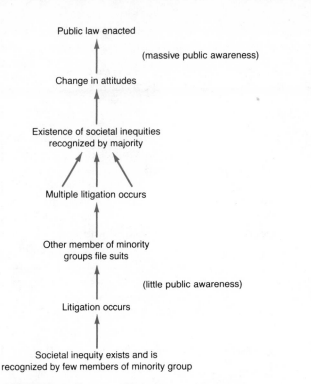

FIGURE 2-1 Process of litigation and legislation.

For example, various plaintiffs may have filed suits on behalf of the learning disabled population having been denied an appropriate education, or because the physically handicapped were denied access to certain buildings, and/or because the visually impaired were unfairly denied employment. When sufficient evidence exists that a change in attitudes is occurring (in this case regarding the rights of exceptional people), then the lawmaking body reacts. It may pass a law that mandates change in past practices or circumstances. This cycle of events is presented in Figure 2-1.

LITIGATION

In the early 1970s, parents and professionals challenged a number of state laws that had limited the rights of the handicapped. These actions were primarily based on the Fourteenth Amendment to the U.S. Constitution, which guarantees equal protection of the law to all citizens. Advocates for the handicapped argued that if a state provides education or any other such service for some of its residents, then the services must be available to all residents. This concept was clearly upheld in 1954 in the Supreme Court's *Brown* v. *Board of Education* decision, which addressed the question of *de jure* segregation based on race permitted by the separate-but-equal doctrine of *Plessy* v. *Ferguson*. In the *Brown* decision, the court stated that "in the field of public education the doctrine of separate but equal has no place." It was held that separate facilities were inherently unequal, and that racial segregation violated the equal protection of law guaranteed by the Fourteenth Amendment. The decision, in part, reads as follows:

> In these days it is doubtful that any child may reasonably be expected to succeed in life if he is denied the opportunity for an education. Such an opportunity, where the state has undertaken to provide it, is a right which must be made available to all on equal terms (*Brown v. Board of Education of Topeka*, 1954).

The roots of important subsequent legislation can be found in the *Brown* decision. The social climate was ready. By granting rights to other minorities, the court set the stage for extending those rights to the handicapped.

Parents of handicapped children were basically concerned with two problems. First, in many states, existing laws did not permit certain children with severe handicaps to receive educational services. Second, the interpreting and implementing of state laws often provided inappropriate special education services for their children. The resolution of this litigation eventually resulted in the right to an appropriate education; the right to **due process** of law, which guarantees handicapped children and their parents a hearing prior to placement in special education programs; and the right to a nondiscriminatory evaluation. These rights became part of the "law of the land" with the passage of PL 94-142.

Right to an Appropriate Education and Due Process

Pennsylvania Association for Retarded Citizens (PARC) v. Commonwealth of Pennsylvania Perhaps the most influential litigation on establishing the right to an appropriate education and to due process of law for handicapped children was the 1971 case of the *Pennsylvania Association for Retarded Citizens (PARC) v. Commonwealth of Pennsylvania*. For many years, school-age children in Pennsylvania, and other states, had been excused from attending public schools if they had been determined to be uneducable, untrainable, or otherwise unable to profit from presence at public schools. In effect, this excuse for noncompliance with Pennsylvania compulsory attendance laws rendered retarded children ineligible to receive school services.

In the suit, PARC filed two charges claiming the state's laws unconstitutional under the equal protection clause of the Fourteenth Amendment. The first charge stated that excluding severely mentally retarded children from public education denied them their equal protection rights. This practice was, therefore, unconstitutional. Secondly, the suit charged that the rights of retarded children had been violated by the lack of due process. That is, children were assigned to special programs for the mentally retarded without either appropriate notice to the parents or the opportunity for hearings.

A decision on the charges was not rendered in the *PARC* case because a **consent agreement** was reached by the parties in 1972. This consent agreement decreed, in part, the following:

1. Within 90 days the state was to locate and identify all retarded children of school age not in school and to begin teaching them no later than September, 1972.
2. It provided for medical and psychological evaluation for all children previously excluded to determine the "most appropriate placement."
3. Every child located and evaluated was to be placed in a free public program "appropriate to the child's capacity."
4. All children in special classes for the mentally retarded were to be reevaluated to determine the proper placement.

5. The State Department of Education was required to submit a plan describing the range of programs available, what was needed to assure all retarded children the appropriate program, and arrangements for financing these programs and recruiting teachers (MacMillan, 1977, pp. 287–288).

The signed consent agreement established the right to an education for retarded children between the ages of 6 and 21 in Pennsylvania. Although the term "most appropriate placement" was not defined by the court, it was indicated that placement in a regular school program was to be preferred over placement in a special program.

The *PARC* consent agreement also decreed the use of a full due-process hearing. This hearing was intended for any child referred for evaluation of suspected mental retardation, and for whom a change in educational program was anticipated. The due-process terms stated in the consent decree include: the right to prior notice to parents; an impartial hearing officer's examination of the evaluation materials, documents, and witnesses used in making the school's recommendations; provisions for requesting and obtaining an independent evaluation; and the provision for a hearing prior to implementing the school's recommendation. Thus, the *PARC* case confirmed the right of retarded children to full, due process of law.

Marlega v. Board of Directors of the City of Milwaukee Earlier litigation involving the exclusion of children in Wisconsin in 1970 established guidelines for due-process hearings; however, the case did not receive the publicity, nor have the impact, of the *PARC* case. Procedures established in *Marlega v. Board of Directors of the City of Milwaukee* required due-process hearings to include the following:

1. Specification of the reasons for recommending exclusion
2. A hearing prior to the exclusion
3. The right of the child to be represented by counsel as well as the right to confront and cross-examine the witnesses
4. A stenographic record of the hearing
5. A written final decision that specifies the reason for exclusion
6. A specification of alternatives available to the child within public education (Cohen and DeYoung, 1973, p. 273).

The specifications outlined in these procedures certainly have had an impact upon subsequent legislative standards for due process in PL 93-380 and PL 94-142. In addition, the last point recognizes the responsibility of the public schools for the education of *all* children. It seems to share the philosophy of **least restrictive environment** espoused in PL 94-142 and Section 504 of the Rehabilitation Act of 1973. This principle states that handicapped children should be educated with no more segregation or restriction than is absolutely necessary.

Mills v. Board of Education of the District of Columbia This 1972 case was similar to the *PARC* litigation. Several parents from the District of Columbia filed a class action suit on behalf of all handicapped children excluded from the District's public school system. Included were not only the mentally retarded, but some children who had been labeled hyperactive, emotionally disturbed, incorrigible, and physically handicapped. In the *Mills* decision, the court ordered that all District of Columbia school-age children be provided with an appropriate, free education regardless of their handicap or its severity. The court refused to accept the lack of sufficient funds as an excuse for not providing the children's education. Also, the judge condemned the practice of excluding, expelling, or suspending pupils from school without prior hearing and review. He ordered the school district to establish legal due-process procedures so that no child could be assigned to, or transferred to or from, a special education program without the opportunity for a full due-process hearing. The decision also affirmed the children's and parents' rights in the hearings. These include the right to be represented by counsel, to examine the child's school records, to compel the attendance of school officials who may have evidence to offer, to cross-examine witnesses, and to introduce evidence of their own.

Following the *Mills* decision, local school districts reconsidered the procedures that were used in the evaluation process and, in particular, the steps in making the initial referral. Establishment of and adherence to a more formal set of due-process requirements were achieved.

Clearly, then, the PL 94-142 rights of due process and the right to an appropriate education had legal precedents in earlier litigation on behalf of handicapped children—*PARC* v. *Commonwealth of Pennsylvania* and *Mills* v. *Board of Education of the District of Columbia*.

Right to a Nondiscriminatory Evaluation

Another critically important right mandated in PL 94-142 is the right to a **nondiscriminatory evaluation**. This legislative mandate originated in the 1960s with the concern of special educators about the problems of classification and labeling in education. It was alleged that categorical labels in many cases created a stigma that became more of a handicap to the child's success than his or her original condition. Labeling was also thought to often establish a self-fulfilling prophecy which damaged the child's interaction with others and which could ultimately affect his or her school progress (Mann, 1960).

During this period, many researchers questioned the reported over-representation of minority group children in special education programs. For example, Mercer (1973) studied the mentally retarded in California. This study found many more black and Mexican-American children in classes for the mentally retarded than would have been expected, based on their proportions in the community's total population. Dunn (1968) summarized and described the problems of special class placement for the mildly retarded. Dunn's clear and emphatic statement of the issues stimulated educators to focus critical attention on the effectiveness and appropriateness of special classes.

Diana v. *State Board of Education*   In this climate of concern over testing and placement of children in special education programs, a suit was filed in California in 1970. This suit was brought on behalf of nine Mexican-American pupils enrolled in classes for the mentally retarded. In this case, *Diana* v. *State Board of Education*, it was charged that the pupils had been tested and placed in special education on the basis of inappropriate tests. The Stanford-Binet Intelligence Scale and the Wechsler Intelligence Scale for Children were developed using white, middle-class children as the norm group. Both of these tests had been used in the testing, which had been conducted in English. When all nine of the Hispanic children were retested with the same tests in Spanish (their predominant language), seven of them scored IQs high enough to make them ineligible for the educable mentally retarded classes. It was argued, therefore, that these children were not mentally retarded, but instead had been misclassified because of their cultural difference.

The suit also charged that the children had received poor education in the special classes and had been caused irreparable injury due to the stigma of such a placement. The agreement, settled out of court, focused on the use of individual intelligence tests with minority children. It stipulated that future intelligence testing would be conducted in the child's primary language, that all Mexican-American students in classes for the educable mentally retarded would be re-evaluated, that compensatory education should be provided for those children found to have been misclassified, that immediate efforts should be undertaken by psychologists to develop and standardize an appropriate intelligence test, and that provisions should be made for prior explanation to parents of the testing/placement process in the parents' primary language.

Larry P. v. *Riles*   A parallel California case, *Larry P.* v. *Riles* (1972), involved the inappropriate testing and subsequent placement of six black pupils. The suit charged that the pupils had been misclassified as educable mentally retarded. It further charged that this misclassification had been made on the basis of testing procedures that ignored differences between the cultural background of the black students and the white, Anglo, middle-class culture base of the tests. The court concluded that a racial imbalance did exist in the classes for the educable mentally retarded in the San Francisco Unified School District. It attributed this imbalance to use of an inappropriate classification device—the individually administered intelligence test. The court found that IQ test results could negatively affect

IQ test scores can no longer be the only criteria for placement in a special education program.

teacher perceptions and expectations and thereby could lower the pupils' academic performances. Continued use of inappropriate intelligence tests with black pupils was therefore denied.

In response to the *Diana* and *Larry P.* case agreements, state education agencies began to require testing procedures that considered many different sources of information and data for deciding placements. Also, other factors began to prevail across the country: parents became deliberately involved in reviewing their children's evaluations, and professional teams were utilized to classify students.

Throughout the 1970s, the relationship between the litigation supporting the educational rights of the handicapped and the state legislation providing appropriate education for handicapped pupils is apparent. A 1975 Council for Exceptional Children survey of state laws indicated that of the 48 states having passed legislation for the educational rights of handicapped children by that time, 37 had adopted their mandates since 1970 (Abeson and Ballard, 1976). Litigation efforts on behalf of exceptional children had obviously not gone unnoticed by lawmakers nationwide.

LEGISLATION

The Constitution of the United States nowhere mentions education or describes the functions that the federal government is to have in relation to it. Furthermore, the Tenth Amendment declares that any issues not designated in the Constitution are to be dealt with either by the individual states or by the people themselves. This inherent ambiguity has caused much confusion and inaction between federal government processes and the developing system of education in the United States. This lack of progress has been especially noticeable in the education of exceptional children. Until the mid-twentieth century, the federal government remained almost entirely removed from the concerns of the handicapped. Responsibility in this area was left in the hands of state legislators, who, in their turn, also neglected their young handicapped citizens.

Early Legislation

The earliest federal legislative support for special education was laws providing funds that created college and university training programs for special education personnel. In 1961, Congress passed an important act, PL 87-276, which funded a limited, university-level program designed to train students to teach deaf children. Follow-up legislation was subsequently enacted in 1962—PL 87-258 and PL 87-715, which additionally funded developing programs (and the training of educators) for deaf children. The year 1963, however, yielded the first major federal legislation for the handicapped. This law, PL 88-164, entitled the Mental Retardation Facilities and Community Mental Health Centers Act, expanded previous legislation passed in 1958 (PL 85-926). It provided financial assistance to universities for training professionals to become teachers of exceptional children. Also, funds were supplied for developing research projects and innovative study plans that would enhance the educational experiences of handicapped children. As a result of this legislation, many classes for exceptional children throughout the country were either initiated or enlarged.

Legislation in the late 1960s furnished yet more funds for improving educational opportunities for exceptional children. PL 89-750 (Title VI) provided grants for states to originate, expand, and/or improve programs specially designed for handicapped children from preschool through secondary levels. PL 90-247 created regional resource centers that would assist teachers of handicapped children. This law also initiated a program to intensify the recruiting of personnel to work with the handicapped, and to utilize the most recent innovations in educational methodology. In addition, through further grants, this act encouraged media programs to be developed that could include all handicapped children (Carey, 1971).

In the 1970s, however, the equal rights movement for the handicapped gained strength with the passage of new, broader legislation, with several important court rulings, and with the establishment of certain state and federal executive branch educational agencies (whose concern was with exceptional children). One of the first bills enacted in 1970 was PL 91-230, which made more grants available, trained more personnel, broadened all existing programs, and, for the first time, included children with learning disabilities who had previously been barred from these programs. Another legislative landmark was established when PL 92-424 was passed. This law, pertaining to Head Start, mandated "...that no less than 10 percent of all enrollment opportunities must be filled by handicapped children" (LaVor, 1972, p. 249). The Head Start program, which administers to children between the ages of three and five years, had previously excluded all handicapped children.

The 1973 Rehabilitation Act, or PL 93–112, became a controversial issue because some critics of the bill believed it to overlap far too much with previous legislation. This controversy marked the first time any bill dealing with the handicapped had not met with unanimous approval in Washington. PL 93–112 provided for programs for the severely handicapped; it made relevant, practical research mandatory in order for states to receive expanded federal services; it established the Rehabilitation Services Administration, which became responsible for all research, training, and services; and it reaffirmed the notion of developing an individualized program for each handicapped pupil (Soeffing, 1974). With this act the federal government had recognized the broad needs of handicapped persons living in our society.

Public Law 93–380

In 1974, PL 93–380, Education of the Handicapped Amendments, which amended and extended the Elementary and Secondary Education Acts of 1965, was passed by Congress. Historically, PL 93–380 represents a statement of our country's policy on the equality of educational opportunity for all. In this landmark legislation, Congress established the rights of handicapped children as described here by Bonham (1975, p. 7):

> In recent years the federal and state courts, state legislators and state executives have been increasingly upholding the principle that these children are legally and morally entitled to a free appropriate public education. It is to this end that this Amendment is addressed. For it establishes for the first time in federal policy that handicapped children are entitled to an appropriate free public education.

The basis for many of the requirements for due process later established in PL 94–142 were outlined in PL 93–380. Procedural safeguards were included, such as prior notice to parents when a proposal for a child's educational placement is being considered, the opportunity for parents to obtain a due-process hearing, and the right of the parent to obtain an independent educational evaluation. Also, this act led the way by calling for the assurance that children with handicaps would be educated in the same classroom with nonhandicapped children.

From pre-1975 surveys, and through 1975 committee hearings on the extension of PL 93–380, Congress discovered that the special needs of exceptional children were still not being completely met. As a result, Congress resolved that the federal government must aid the states and localities to a greater degree to establish an equal educational opportunity for all children (Crawford, 1978; Abeson and Zettel, 1977). The law subsequently enacted was a culmination of rapidly evolving legislative trends and attempts. PL 94–142, or the Education for All Handicapped Children Act of 1975, finally guaranteed, with strong financial backing, the right of handicapped children to a free, appropriate education.

Public Law 94–142 — Education for All Handicapped Children Act of 1975

The Education for All Handicapped Children Act (PL 94–142) was signed on November 29, 1975. This event marked the dawn of a new era in the history of the education of exceptional children in the United States. Indeed, a major change in the total education program offered in America's public schools had begun. This signing also was the climax of a host of societal forces that had begun in the mid-twentieth century and matured in the 1970s. The overwhelmingly positive vote for the final version of PL 94–142 in both houses of Congress (404 to 7 in the House, and 87 to 7 in the Senate) testifies to the American public's acknowledgement of its handicapped members, and of the rights of exceptional children to an equal educational opportunity.

In the preface of PL 94–142, Congress outlined its "Statement of Findings and Purpose" as follows [*Public Law 94–142*, 1975, Section 3, (b), (1)–(5)]:

> The Congress finds that (1) there are more than eight million handicapped children in the United States today; (2) the special education needs of such children are not being fully met; (3) more than half of the handicapped children in the United States do not receive appropriate educational services which would enable them to have full equality of opportunity; (4) one million of the handicapped children in the United States are excluded entirely from the public school system and will not go through the educational process with their peers; (5) there are many handicapped children throughout the United States participating in regular school programs whose handicaps prevent them from having a successful educational experience because their handicaps are undetected.

Clearly, legislators recognized the multifaceted nature of the existing problems confronting our nation's handicapped children. First, it was apparent that the number of children who were handicapped learners was, indeed, significant. Second, Congress realized that the difference between educational needs and the fulfillment of those needs for handicapped children amounted to a national scandal.

> ...because of the lack of adequate services within the public school system, families are often forced to find services outside the public school system, often at great distance from their residence and at their own expense; developments in the training of teachers

and in diagnostic and instructional procedures and methods have advanced to the point that, given appropriate funding, state and local educational agencies can and will provide effective special education and related services to meet the needs of handicapped children; state and local educational agencies have a responsibility to provide education for all handicapped children, but present financial resources are inadequate to meet the special educational needs of handicapped children [*Public Law 94–142*, 1975, Section 3, (b), (6)–(7)].

Members of Congress came to understand, in part, the hardships that inadequate educational programs for exceptional children placed on the parents of these children. They also recognized the responsibility of state and local school districts to provide meaningful and appropriate educational experiences for handicapped children. Also, Congress saw that the educational technology was now available, both diagnostically and instructionally, to provide these services. The major obstacle to overcome at this time was funding, even though appropriations and processes had been specified by Congress to overcome this problem.

...and it is in the national interest that the Federal Government assist State and local efforts to provide programs to meet the educational needs of handicapped children in order to assure equal protection of the law. It is the purpose of this Act to assure that all handicapped children have available to them...a free appropriate public education which emphasizes special education and related services designed to meet their unique needs, to assure that the rights of handicapped children and their parents or guardians are protected, to assist States and localities to provide for the education of all handicapped children, and to assess and assure the effectiveness of efforts to educate handicapped children [*Public Law 94–142*, Section 3, (b), (9) and (c)].

One related service outline in PL 94–142 is speech therapy.

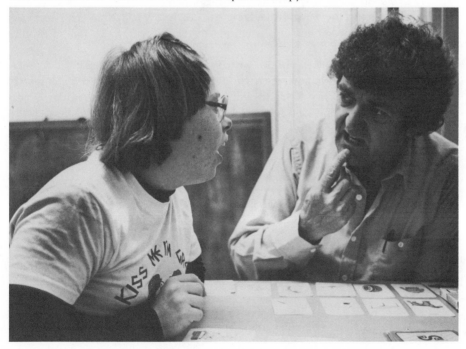

With this purpose, Congress established a major role for the federal government in assisting the states and the local school districts with their efforts to provide special educational services for exceptional people. The passage of PL 94–142 represents a major further expansion of the ever-growing capacity of the federal government in the field of education.

Exceptional children considered handicapped under PL 94–142 include those with mental retardation, hearing impairments and deafness, speech impairments, visual handicaps, serious emotional disturbances, orthopedic and other health impairments, multiple handicaps, and specific learning disabilities. Children and youth between the ages of 3 and 21 are included except when this age range conflicts with existing state laws.

The right of handicapped children to an education (as called for in PL 94–142) means that children can no longer be labeled as uneducable and excluded from public schools. The excuses that have always been offered by school districts for such exclusion are no longer legally acceptable. These include lack of program facilities, the child's inability to learn, lack of funding, and the severity of the handicapping condition. Further, those handicapped children who require special education are not to be banned from participating in other school services and programs. This provision includes the right to take part in all course offerings, such as vocational education courses (which previously had been denied to many children and youth with handicaps). This provision also states that it is the right of parents not to be required to bear the costs of their handicapped child's education under certain circumstances. It must be determined (by recommendation of the public school and/or by the results of impartial hearings) that their child requires educational programming in a private or public setting necessitating such costs as the payment of tuition, board and room, and transportation.

Congress also noted public school failure in the lack of appropriate educational services for many handicapped pupils *already* attending public schools. To remedy this problem of inappropriate educational planning, Congress included a written document, the **individualized education program** (IEP) for each identified handicapped child. Implementing of the IEP is the legal responsibility of the local school district.

The IEP proclaims the important principle of using the least restrictive environment for educating handicapped children. Each IEP requires a statement of "...the extent to which such child will be able to participate in regular educational programs" [*Public Law 94–142*, 1975, Section 4, (c), (19)]. The Act also recognizes the heterogeneity of the educational needs of exceptional learners. It specifies that a continuum of programs and services be provided for pupils with handicaps. Each state, in response to PL 94–142, must assure the federal government that regulations have been developed, insuring that

> ...to the maximum extent appropriate, handicapped children, including children in public and private institutions or other care facilities, are educated with children who are not handicapped and that special classes, separate schooling, or the removal of handicapped children from the regular education environment occurs only when the nature or severity of the handicap is such that the education in regular classes with the use of supplementary aids and services cannot be achieved satisfactorily [*Public Law 94–142*, 1975, Section 612, (5) (b)].

The public schools can no longer decide special education placements based on the availability or unavailability of a variety of program options. The least restrictive environment principle does not mean that all exceptional children will be educated in regular classrooms. Also, it does not mean that all pupils with handicaps will be placed in self-contained special classes or even in special education programs. What it *does* mean is that, in determining the most appropriate setting for a handicapped child, educators must select the program alternative that will be the least restrictive *relative to the normal school processes*. This placement decision assumes that each school system is capable of providing a variety of special programs if it is determined that the appropriate education for handicapped children cannot be achieved satisfactorily in regular classes.

The right to a nondiscriminatory evaluation (addressed previously by PL 93–380) is a major component of PL 94–142. This right now exists because of the long history of injustices concerning improper placement of racial and cultural minority group children in special education programs. It is virtually impossible to assure that the decisions reached in formulating the IEP are appropriate if the data collected to make those decisions are suspect. Following are the guidelines this component has established to evaluate pupils with handicaps [*Public Law 94–142*, 1975, Section 612, (5) (c)]:

1. ...materials and procedures for evaluations will be selected and administered so as not to be racially or culturally discriminatory...
2. ...materials or procedures shall be provided and administered in the child's native language or mode of communication...
3. ...no single procedure shall be the sole criterion for determining an appropriate educational program for a child

The latter requirement outlaws the practice of deciding placements based on a single test score, a method widespread across America in the early history of special education programs. No longer can the results of a single intelligence test be used for special education placement. The other two requirements attempt to ensure that evaluation activities focus on measuring the variables of concern. Differences in children's racial and cultural backgrounds, their language, and their manners of communication are to be accounted for in the evaluation process.

Congress included a section in PL 94–142 addressing the handicapped child's right to due process of law. Problems in communication and misunderstandings with families of children with handicaps led to certain legal decisions. These established procedural safeguards for use in the identification and placement procedures of local school districts. This component ensures that all rights included in PL 94–142 will be utilized by those parties concerned with the education of handicapped children: namely, the children themselves, their parents, and the public schools. These specific procedures are outlined as follows (Abeson and Zettel, 1977, pp. 125–126):

1. Written notification before evaluation. In addition, the right to an interpreter/translator if the family's native language is not English (unless it is clearly not feasible to do so).
2. Written notification when initiating or refusing to initiate a change in educational placement.
3. Opportunity to present complaints regarding the identification, evaluation, placement, or the provisions of a free appropriate education.
4. Opportunity to obtain an independent educational evaluation of the child.
5. Access to all relevant records.

   6. Opportunity for an impartial due process hearing including the right to:
   a. Receive timely and specific notice of the hearing.
   b. Be accompanied and advised by counsel and by individuals with special knowledge or training with respect to the problems of children with handicaps.
   c. Confront, cross examine, and compel the attendance of witnesses.
   d. Present evidence:
      (1) Written or electronic verbatim record of the hearing.
      (2) Written findings of act and decisions.
   7. The right to appeal the findings and decision of the hearing.

With PL 94–142, the applications for which due process was recognized as important were extended. From the procedures for identifying, evaluating, and placing (as in PL 93–380), applications were broadened to also include establishing procedures for providing a free, appropriate education for the child. Including this additional consideration gives families as well as school districts the opportunity to review and change (if appropriate) educational program decisions. If fully implemented, these due-process requirements will protect handicapped children from errors in classification and from failure to receive an equal educational opportunity. They also should establish the necessary positive channels of communication between parents and school personnel needed to maintain successful educational practices for handicapped children. The evolution of the basic rights of PL 94–142 from earlier litigation is displayed in Figure 2-2.

Important requirements in PL 94–142 not described within the discussion of the basic rights include:

1. extensive child identification procedures;
2. assurance of full service and provision of a timetable;
3. maintenance of programs and procedures for comprehensive personnel development, including in-service training;
4. policies and procedures that guarantee and protect the confidentiality of evaluation data and other information; and
5. the assurance of a surrogate to act for any child either when the parents are unknown or unavailable, or when a child is the ward of the state.

The latter requirement ensures that handicapped children without parents will have access to due process and will not be penalized in the provision of an appropriate educational program.

In order to apply for funds under PL 94–142, states must submit an appropriate implementation plan to the U.S. Commissioner of Education. Likewise, local school districts must submit similar plans to their respective state education agencies to receive special education funding. All plans must include a guarantee that all the rights of handicapped children and their parents will be upheld. In addition, each plan must describe all facilities, personnel, and services related to the education of the handicapped (Ballard and Zettel, 1978).

Section 504 of PL 93–112 — The Rehabilitation Act of 1973

In 1974, PL 93–112, the Rehabilitation Act of 1973, discussed earlier, was amended to provide a broader base for implementation. Section 504 states that

> no otherwise qualified handicapped individual in the United States...shall, solely by reason of his handicap, be excluded from the participation in, be denied the benefit of,

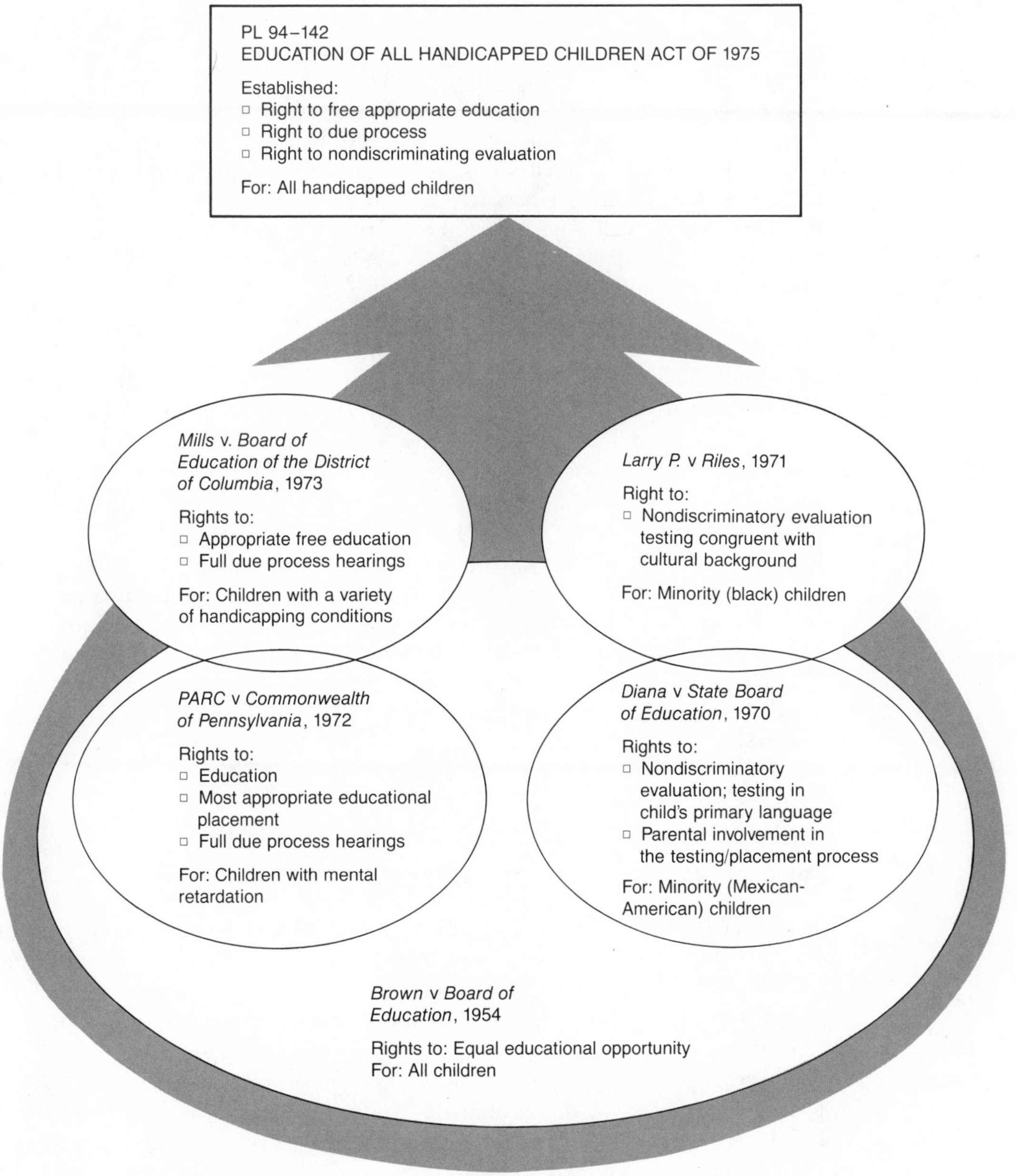

PL 94–142
EDUCATION OF ALL HANDICAPPED CHILDREN ACT OF 1975

Established:
☐ Right to free appropriate education
☐ Right to due process
☐ Right to nondiscriminating evaluation

For: All handicapped children

Mills v. *Board of Education of the District of Columbia*, 1973

Rights to:
☐ Appropriate free education
☐ Full due process hearings

For: Children with a variety of handicapping conditions

Larry P. v *Riles*, 1971

Right to:
☐ Nondiscriminatory evaluation testing congruent with cultural background

For: Minority (black) children

PARC v *Commonwealth of Pennsylvania*, 1972

Rights to:
☐ Education
☐ Most appropriate educational placement
☐ Full due process hearings

For: Children with mental retardation

Diana v *State Board of Education*, 1970

Rights to:
☐ Nondiscriminatory evaluation; testing in child's primary language
☐ Parental involvement in the testing/placement process

For: Minority (Mexican-American) children

Brown v *Board of Education*, 1954

Rights to: Equal educational opportunity
For: All children

FIGURE 2-2 Litigation as the foundation for rights mandated in PL 94–142.

or be subject to discrimination under any program or activity receiving Federal financial assistance [*Public Law 93–112*, Section 504, Section 7, (6)].

This amendment prohibits discrimination in health, welfare, and the other social services; in the employment of handicapped persons; and in admissions to post-secondary educational programs. Sub-part D relates to preschool, elementary, and secondary education. Its provisions have been closely coordinated with PL 94–142, and it requires a free, appropriate education for each handicapped child in the most appropriate setting. This law stipulates in Section 504, that no handicapped person in our country should be denied the benefit of any activity or be discriminated against in any program that receives federal funds. Section 504 also requires that programs and services offered by schools, agencies, and businesses that receive federal funds be accessible to handicapped persons. "All new facilities must be constructed so as to be readily accessible and usable from a program standpoint by all handicapped children" (Ballard and Zettel, 1978, p. 460). Since almost all state and local educational agencies receive some form of federal financial assistance, the rules and regulations of Section 504 have almost nationwide applicability.

Section 504 parallels PL 94–142 in many respects, and following the due-process requirements of PL 94–142 is a primary way by which school districts can comply with Section 504. Therefore, to violate the standards of PL 94–142, in most cases, means to also violate Section 504. This, in turn, could lead to the loss of all federal financial assistance, not just those funds forthcoming because of PL 94–142. Since most school districts rely on some form of federal funding, Section 504 is likely to be recognized historically as the civil rights law that ensured the implementation of PL 94–142.

Federal and state laws have been powerful forces for change in providing for a free, appropriate education for all handicapped children. They have also served to protect the rights of those children, and to provide a system for the accountability of the programs and services offered. If these laws are to be implemented effectively, however, parents, professionals, and those pro-handicapped activist groups who stimulated the legislation must continue to arouse the public consciousness.

IMPLEMENTATION OF PL 94–142

On October 1, 1977 (the beginning of Fiscal Year 1978), the American system of education entered a new era. The implementation of the full service requirements of PL 94–142 by September 1, 1980, represented an ideal to some observers. To others, it represented the fulfillment of the dreams of too many years. To still others, PL 94–142 was a temporary swing of the pendulum, the product of societal forces gone awry. In truth, the Education of All Handicapped Children Act is, as we have seen, the culmination of American educational, social, and political trends and forces. These have long-established roots in the consciousness of our country. The civil rights movement of the 1960s—a catalyst of concern for human rights and needs—led to the recognition of the rights of persons with handicaps and, indeed, its effects are still in evidence today. The past two decades have witnessed the trends of including and integrating the handicapped within our schools in particular. Changes in our society on behalf of exceptional people include: (1) the increase in financial support to local schools for developing special education services; (2) the productive questioning of the entire testing, labeling, and placement process; (3) continued growth in the political awareness and effectiveness of parent organizations; (4) advances in educational technology; and (5) the commitments of our judicial and legislative systems to the rights of handicapped children. Our society currently favors individual rights in preference to the needs and rights of the larger group.

Interaction with handicapped children can be a valuable part of the nonhandicapped child's education.

Implications for Nonhandicapped Children and Youth

Educators, anthropologists, and psychologists currently speculate that nonhandicapped children may, in fact, be unfairly deprived if their opportunities to interact and be educated with handicapped children are limited. The following reflections from Lisa Blumberg (who was born with cerebral palsy) in her article, "The Case for Integrated Schooling" (1973, p. 17) attests to the positive, two-sided nature of these associations.

> The disabled child is not the only one who benefits when he attends a regular school. Nondisabled children will be far less likely to build up misconceptions about the disabled if they have them as classmates. People who have gone to school with a visibly disabled person and who have seen him experience much of what they have experienced and seen him respond to things in almost exactly the same way as they have will be far less prejudiced than someone who has never had real contact with anyone disabled.
>
> Many of my college friends tell me that they were uneasy with me when they first met me. I resent this, but I cannot really blame them because I am the first person with an obvious physical disability most of them have ever known. It is no wonder that they are at first as unsure of my reactions as they would be of a Martian's. However, if throughout school they had had one or two disabled children in their classes, I think they would have been far more comfortable in relating to me or to any other disabled person.
>
> Exposing nondisabled children to children with physical or sensory disabilities can only make them more accepting of all kinds of people. It will provide them with living proof that people with limitations in some areas do have talents and abilities. I think that prejudice against the disabled will only begin to be eliminated when significant numbers of disabled children go to school side by side with nondisabled children.
>
> I am glad I have attended regular schools. I believe that sending a disabled child to a regular school is good for the child, for the others in his classes, and, indirectly, for

disabled people as a whole. It is the goal of many people to someday see persons with disabilities fully integrated into society. What better and more necessary place to start than in the schools?*

Implications for School Personnel

As we have seen, court case decisions and legislative mandates have established the principles, rules, and regulations for implementing the education of handicapped children. So that the promises of these legislative initiatives are carried out, much effort and direction must come daily from those on the firing line. In other words, if PL 94–142 is to be implemented successfully, then teachers, administrators, special support personnel, and parents must know and carry out their own responsibilities under the mandates as effectively as possible.

The potential impact of PL 94–142 on organizational change is great. In fact, many local school districts have been, or will be, forced to redefine their values and goals for educating all children in the community. For some school systems this situation offers an opportunity to take giant, positive steps toward improving their total educational program. For others, this challenge represents a threat to be ignored, passively resisted, or counterattacked. How each state and local school agency actually implements PL 94–142 will depend largely upon the leadership of the educators and the parents involved at the local level. The understanding and acceptance of the role of advocate by professional educators and by parents is a difficult but necessary step.

The implications of effectuating PL 94–142 have been numerous for both teachers and school administrators. First, teachers have found that extra demands have been made on their already crowded schedules. IEP conferences before and after school hours and during free periods are not uncommon. A second (and related) implication is the increased demand for cooperative planning, not only among educators, but also with parents. Improved sophistication in communication and conferencing skills is a must for teachers and administrators. Also, teachers have been required to relearn or upgrade existing skills in administering and interpreting assessment procedures, developing instructional objectives from the annual goals of IEPs, and organizing classrooms for individualized instruction. Some special education teachers complain that the increased paperwork leaves little time to teach the handicapped child. Finally, teachers, parents, and administrators alike will have to accept the role changes that the current mandates demand. The first step in responding appropriately to these changes is to become acquainted with the rights and responsibilities of everyone involved. The second step is to share that knowledge positively.

The implementation of PL 94–142 and the achievement of mandated goals cannot be accomplished by special educators alone.

> What will happen inside the schoolhouse door will largely depend upon members of this population who have had little or no exposure or knowledge about exceptional children. Above all, the entire school community needs to become sensitized to the fact that handicapped children are first children, and second children with special learning needs [Abeson and Zettel, 1977, pp. 126–127].

*Reprinted with permission of the EXCEPTIONAL PARENT magazine. Copyright © 1973, Psy-Ed Corporation, Room 700, Statler Office Building, Boston, Massachusetts 02116.

It is hoped that this text will facilitate the implementing of education for all children by enhancing the reader's knowledge of, and sensitivity to those we call exceptional or handicapped learners.

The poet Carl Sandburg once said that "there is always that saving minority —even when the majority gets bamboozled—there are always those few people who still keep the dream..." (Segal, 1978, p. 135). Many legal victories have been won and precedents established. Likewise, many legislative mandates have been accomplished. Totally successful implementation of these achievements, however, while in sight, has not yet been realized. What Americans, whether as students, professionals, citizens, or simply human beings, choose to do about implementing "the dream" will make the difference.

SUMMARY POINTS

- The roots of current legislation regarding the handicapped can be traced to persistent parent advocacy groups and related litigation.
- Two landmark decisions affecting handicapped children's rights to an education are *PARC* v. *Commonwealth of Pennsylvania* and *Mills* v. *Board of Education of the District of Columbia*. Whereas the former focused on the rights of retarded citizens, the *Mills* decision included all handicapped children in the District of Columbia.
- Decisions rendered in the *Larry P.* v. *Riles* and *Diana* v. *State Board of Education* cases protected minority pupils' rights to appropriate testing and placement.
- In the early 1960s, PL 87–276, PL 87–258, and PL 90–247 centered on developing professional training programs to teach the handicapped. Also in that decade Title VI funds (PL 89–750) became available for developing programs for handicapped children and youth.
- PL 92–424 mandated the inclusion of handicapped preschoolers into Head Start programs, which previously had denied handicapped children educational opportunities in an integrated environment.
- The first bill dealing with handicapped persons that did not receive unanimous support by our nation's lawmakers was PL 93–112 (Rehabilitation Act of 1973).
- PL 93–380 reflected Congress's recognition that all children have the legal right to equal educational opportunities.
- The most significant piece of legislation affecting the handicapped is PL 94–142, which signified the federal government's commitment to the handicapped.
- PL 94–142 mandates a free, appropriate public education for all our nation's handicapped. This landmark legislation specifies the process and guidelines that local schools are to follow in guaranteeing the rights of the handicapped student and his or her parents.
- PL 94–142 requires that each state submit a state plan outlining its procedures for compliance.
- Section 504 of the Rehabilitation Act safeguards handicapped persons' rights by prohibiting their discrimination or exclusion in any federally funded program or activity.

■ Section 504 of PL 93–112, the Rehabilitation Act of 1973, is the motivational force behind the implementation of PL 94–142. Violations of Section 504 and PL 94–142 could lead to a cutoff of federal funds.

■ Implications of PL 94–142 for school personnel are many and far-reaching. Additional time is required of teachers, principals, and other personnel in order to assist in the planning and implementing of specified guidelines.

■ Teachers have had to upgrade their skills in assessment, in developing instructional goals and objectives, and in organizing classrooms for individualized instruction. If the promises mandated in PL 94–142 are to be fulfilled, all school personnel—not just special educators—must learn the skills and develop the attitudes that are necessary to the successful implementation of new programs.

REVIEW QUESTIONS

1. Distinguish between litigation and legislation. How are these two phenomena related in the history of the rights of handicapped persons?

2. One outcome of court rulings and legislative mandates has been increased participation of handicapped people in the mainstream of society. What recognizable changes have schools, businesses, cultural, and government facilities made that have increased your awareness of the handicapped?

3. List the court cases that have influenced the development of federal legislation for handicapped persons. How do the results of each case relate to the specific provisions of PL 94–142?

4. Identify the significance of both PL 93–380 and Section 504 of the Rehabilitation Act. What is the relationship of each to PL 94–142?

5. List the specific provisions of PL 94–142. In your opinion, what implications does implementation of these provisions have for teachers and administrators?

6. Do you agree that nonhandicapped children and youth lacking interactive and educational opportunities with handicapped children may be unfairly deprived? Support your position.

EXTENDING THE RIGHTS OF EXCEPTIONAL PERSONS

The recent accomplishments in human rights for handicapped persons through litigation and legislation are truly signficant achievements. For many—especially the handicapped—the battle has been won; the goals have been reached. While much has been accomplished by the enactments of PL 94–142 and Section 504 of the Rehabilitation Act of 1973, and while PL 94–142 is "...a permanent statutory authority with no expiration date" (Ballard and Zettel, 1978, p. 461), the struggle over defining the rights of handicapped persons continues. Some educators have questioned whether the federal government will fulfill its commitment to the handicapped by appropriately funding the implementation of PL 94–142.

NEED FOR CONTINUED ADVOCACY

Since PL 94–142 "...is complaint oriented, and enforcement will depend heavily on the vigilance of parents and other advocates" (Ballard and Zettel, 1978, p. 459), the continued advocacy for the human rights of handicapped persons is a necessity. With regard to developmental disabilities (mental retardation, cerebral palsy, epilepsy, and autism), states are required to establish organizations to guard the rights of their handicapped persons. For example, the Ohio Association for Protection and Advocacy for Persons with Developmental Disabilities is funded by the federal government. Its purpose is to serve as a watchdog over the rights of handicapped Ohioans as they interact with social systems and agencies.

The federal government has also attempted to help persons with disabilities help themselves. An example is a grant of $95,000 to aid in establishing the magazine *Mainstream*, which is the only publication of its kind produced by and for handicapped persons. This publication, which continues to receive some federal funding, serves as a means of training persons with handicaps. It teaches publication and clerical skills in training sessions lasting from three to four months. Over 300 disabled persons have received job training through this publication operation. The vast majority of these have found regular job placements after their training was completed.

Societal organizations and governmental bodies continue to wrestle over the implementation of the rights of handicapped persons. Within most religious organizations the movement to accommodate and provide for disabled persons seems slow. In local neighborhoods, residents continue to utilize zoning laws to resist the establishing of group or halfway homes for handicapped persons.

The question of whose rights should take precedence has not been decided conclusively. The issues of the rights of the individual versus the rights of the community, the rights of the minority versus those of the majority, and the rights of the parents versus those of their children are ongoing concerns. Since decisions made on the issues of human rights influence the quality of life (and sometimes even the existence of life) they are to be addressed thoughtfully and seriously.

THE RIGHTS OF THE INDIVIDUAL: WHO SHOULD BE PULLING THE STRINGS?

In the late 1970s, a state supreme court in the western United States ruled that the parents of a 13-year-old mentally retarded boy (with Down's syndrome) had the right to decide whether or not their child should have surgery to correct a congenital heart defect. In effect, the court said that in such matters of life or death the family has the right to decide the fate of minors who will not be able to live a "life worth living."

The retarded youth had resided in a small private facility for several years. His teachers testified in court that he had made "exceptional progress." When the parents were told that heart surgery was required in order to arrest further debilitation and ultimately prevent death, they elected to forego the surgery. They were afraid that if their son were to outlive them, he would be institutionalized for the rest of his life. They felt that it would be better if he were not allowed to live.

Despite the boy's excellent progress and the argument that his parents should not have the right to determine his fate, the courts, after appeals were heard, decided in favor of the parents' rights.

In another case, a young woman brought suit for 33 million dollars, listing as defendants her parents, the state in which she was born, a state institution for the mentally retarded, the hospital where she was born, and the physician who delivered her. The lawsuit charged that the young woman's parents placed her unlawfully in a state institution for the retarded. She thereby claimed to be deprived of experiencing the natural love and affection of a family life.

Shortly after she was born with an exposed spinal cord, her parents placed her in a state institution for the retarded; they told their relatives that the baby had died. When the daughter and mother met again 14 years later, the mother refused to acknowledge to other family members and relatives that the daughter was alive. This young woman and her preschool-age son survive on Social Security payments. She claims that because she is of average intelligence, her commitment to the state institution for the mentally retarded was equivalent to illegal imprisonment.

In the next decade, a greater number of similar cases involving the rights of children, their parents, and society are likely to fill the courts. The issues will not be easy to decide. They never have been. But in the years to come, we, as individuals and as a society, must continue to struggle with these issues. We must develop even better understandings of exceptional persons, their families, and their rights.

1. What events are currently taking place in your community that may be results of the continuing struggle to more clearly describe the issues concerning human rights for handicapped persons? What role do you play (or could you play) in these events?
2. Why do you think that religious organizations have been slow to make adequate accommodations for handicapped persons? What other barriers, besides physical ones, might be preventing disabled persons from joining religious organizations?
3. Should parents have the right to make decisions regarding the quality of life (or even the existence of life) for their handicapped children without interference from others? Why do you think some parents have taken the position that their handicapped child is better off dead, either in fact or by virtue of being forgotten in an institution?
4. In your opinion, why are the issues concerning the human rights of handicapped persons so difficult to resolve?

SUGGESTED READINGS

Abeson, A. "Movement and Momentum: Government and Education of Handicapped Children," *Exceptional Children*, 39 (September, 1972), 63–66.

Abeson, A., and Zettel, J. "The End of the Quiet Revolution: The Education of All Handicapped Children Act of 1975." *Exceptional Children*, 44 (October, 1977), 114–128.

Bonham, S. J., Jr. "Public Law 93–380: A Bill of Rights for the Handicapped." *Focus on Exceptional Children*, 7 (September, 1975), 1–8.

Irvin, T. "Implementation of Public Law 94–142." *Exceptional Children*, 43 (November, 1976), 135–137.

Weintraub, F. J., Abeson, A., Ballard, J., and LaVor, M., eds. *Public Policy and the Education of Exceptional Children*. Reston, Va.: Council for Exceptional Children, 1976.

3

CONTENTS

ASSESSMENT AND PLACEMEMENT

PL 94–142 has mandated that all handicapped children and youth be provided with an appropriate, individualized education in the least restrictive environment. The first step in planning and implementing individual educational programs involves completing a nondiscriminatory multifactored assessment. Data collected in this stage determine whether or not the pupil is handicapped and, if so, what type of program placement is most appropriate.

This chapter discusses the purposes of assessment, the mandated requirements of assessment, the identification procedures, the process of multifactored assessment, the functions of the assessment team, and some special considerations in identification, assessment, and placement.

PURPOSE OF ASSESSMENT

"Tom is inattentive, lazy, and slow; I doubt whether he should even be in school."

"Al seems to be daydreaming most of the time and never completes his assignments. I doubt if he'll ever amount to much of anything!"

These statements, or similar ones, are not unusual. Over the years, such statements have often echoed from the walls of teachers' rooms around the country. At times, they have even been heard during parent/teacher conferences. When we realize that the "Tom" referred to here is Thomas Edison and that "Al" is Albert Einstein, these "off the cuff" remarks take on new significance. How could these famous, outstanding persons have been so misjudged in school? The potentials of many less famous and less talented people have been masked by the educational system. These are among those children and youth often labeled as handicapped.

The aim of our educational system is to aid all children, including those with handicaps. Specifically, education strives to abet the development of children—to prepare them to achieve their own goals and to be optimally functioning members of society. Factors that inhibit functioning must be identified and assessed. Only then can meaningful and appropriate educational plans be devised and implemented. Each student is an individual with unique learning strengths and weaknesses. We must thus design unique learning programs that are based upon assessment data. Such programs will ensure that every child, despite handicaps or restrictions, will have the opportunity to develop his or her potential.

From a practical standpoint, if problems can be identified and treated when a person is young, much of the high cost of long-term treatment may be avoided. In many cases, early identification, assessment, and placement are forms of prevention; emergent behaviors are more readily remedied than are learning difficulties that have firm roots in long-established learning patterns.

The purpose of assessment in special education is twofold:

- To determine eligibility for special educational services. (If a child is identified as needing special services, then the team specifies which category of special education service is appropriate.)

- To determine an effective instructional program. (Specific teaching and learning strategies are outlined in an individualized educational program.)

This latter purpose is the most difficult to respond to effectively.

Classroom teachers have traditionally been very concerned with how children with learning problems can be helped. Considerations included the questions of what diagnostic category the child should be placed in, and with what diagnostic term the child should be labeled. Prior to the passage of PL 94–142, there was a definite trend away from categorization and toward identification of children's learning strengths and needs. This emphasis was agreed to be highly relevant for developing educational programs to help exceptional learners overcome or cope with their specific learning difficulties.

Since the passage of PL 94–142, a renewed stress on assessment to determine eligibility for special services has come into being. Funding for special education programs is based on the number of children identified as handicapped. A child must be identified as handicapped in order to become eligible to receive individualized special education services. So assessment for the purpose of identifying and labeling has again become primary.

While the requirement that the child fit into one of the handicapping conditions has certainly brought about a renewed emphasis on labeling, it has done so within an entirely different assessment framework. Early assessment often ends with the assigning of a diagnostic label. However, professionals operating within the new system of assessment required by PL 94–142 recognize that labels are not particularly useful in devising effective instructional techniques. If strengths and weaknesses are to be located and individualized programs developed, assessment procedures must go far beyond categorization of handicapping conditions. In other words, determination of eligibility for special education services is necessary; it is not, however, sufficient for completing a comprehensive educational assessment and developing an individualized educational program (IEP).

ASSESSMENT REQUIREMENTS UNDER PUBLIC LAW 94–142

PL 94–142 includes these requirements for educational assessment:

1. Every child referred as suspected of having a handicapping condition must have a thorough individual assessment.
2. Assessment procedures, including tests and other evaluations, must not discriminate against pupils because of cultural differences, ethnic differences, or handicapping conditions.
3. Assessment information used to develop individualized educational programs must come from a variety of sources, using a variety of procedures.
4. No single test or procedure can be used as the sole criterion for determining the pupil's educational program.
5. Due process, guaranteeing the rights of children and their parents, must be followed in conducting the assessment.
6. Children identified as handicapped and placed in special education programs must be re-evaluated every three years. Such re-evaluations employ assessment procedures paralleling those of the original identification, placement, and programming sequence.

PL 94–142, then, requires that local school districts use evaluation and assessment procedures for determining: (1) the existence of a handicapping condition; (2) eligibility for special education services; and (3) the most appropriate educational program.

Although these steps of the assessment process are sequential (and provide information to answer distinct questions), they are not separate entities. Rather, they are interrelated steps in the overall process of educational assessment and programming, which has as its purpose the development and maintenance of appropriate educational programs for exceptional children. The original assessment provides the basis for planning instruction; the instructional program, in turn, becomes the vehicle for further assessment and possible redetermination of educational goals. Figure 3-1 depicts the overall educational assessment/ programming process. In this chapter, the first two stages—information-gathering

FIGURE 3-1   Educational assessment/program planning cycle.

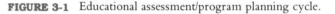

IDENTIFICATION: SCREENING AND REFERRAL

1. Might this child be "handicapped?"
2. Should this child be referred for further assessment to determine eligibility for special services?
3. What modifications can be made in this child's school program to facilitate learning?

RE-EVALUATION

1. Formal re-evaluation is required every three years.
2. An ongoing, continuous monitoring process is part of every child's instructional program.
   a. Does this child continue to require special education services?
   b. How can the child's program be modified to become more appropriate?

MULTIFACTORED ASSESSMENT BY A MULTIDISCIPLINARY TEAM

1. Is this child handicapped?
2. Does this child require special services?
3. What type of program(s) service(s) would be the most beneficial?
   a. What are the child's strengths?
   b. What teaching strategies are the most useful?
   c. What is the child's level of competence in various academic and social areas?

INDIVIDUAL EDUCATION PROGRAM: PLANNING AND IMPLEMENTATION

1. What are the child's current levels of performance?
2. What annual goals and short-term objectives should the child's program address?
3. What special education services are to be provided?
4. To what extent will the child be able to participate in regular class programs?
5. What evaluation criteria will be used and what is the schedule of monitoring activities to be used in determining whether the goals and instructional objectives are being met?

for identification and information-gathering for placement—are discussed. The educational programming process is reviewed in Chapter 4.

To design appropriate programs for handicapped pupils, a wide variety of professional personnel must be involved in the assessment procedures. However, the regular classroom teacher remains the most important link in the entire process for many handicapped children. The regular classroom teacher must be involved in both the initial and subsequent stages of the assessment process. Otherwise, sound planning and appropriate programming and placement are not possible. As identification procedures are initiated and information gathered for making decisions, the regular classroom teacher is clearly in a pivotal position to respond to these critically important questions:

1. Is this child handicapped?
2. Is the child in need of special education and/or related services?
3. What type of educational program could best meet this child's needs?

IDENTIFICATION: SCREENING AND REFERRAL

The first stage in developing appropriate individualized programs to help exceptional children is identification. Before a child is informally assessed to determine the need for, and the type of, special educational services, he or she must be identified as being a potentially handicapped person. The professional who most often must attempt to answer the question, "Might this child be handicapped?" is the regular classroom teacher. Besides the child's parents, there is probably no one else who knows the child's behavior better. Therefore, the teacher is probably the best qualified to raise the question of the presence of a handicapping condition. Before implementing an identification and screening process in a classroom, in a school building, in the total school district, in the community, or even nationwide, certain factors should be considered. Those persons or agencies responsible for the process should be able to respond in the affirmative to these three questions raised by Salvia and Ysseldyke (1978):

1. Is the problem identified or pinpointed by the screening process appropriate and important for the educational well-being of the child being screened?
2. Is the screening and identification process going to be followed up by an assessment and diagnosis?
3. Is there an available treatment or program designed to correct or modify the problem following assessment and diagnosis?

Child Find

PL 94–142 requires that all states and local school districts conduct—within their jurisdiction—drives to identify all the handicapped persons through age 21. This process is referred to as Child Find. States and school districts have conducted extensive publicity campaigns to notify the public of the need to identify all handicapped children and youth in order to be able to provide appropriate educational programs and services. Figure 3-2 shows, for example, a leaflet and a brochure widely distributed in Ohio to contact all who could possibly identify handicapped persons. Other publicity efforts include newspaper articles, radio

How to give handicapped children a chance.

Project Ohio
The Ohio Division of Special Education

Project Ohio Referral Form

Name of child ______ Age ____ Sex ____ School district of residence ______

Address ______ City,State,Zip ______

Telephone of parent or guardian ______ Is child in school? Yes ____ No ____

Has child been in a Special Education program or received any related service? Yes ____ No ____

What other agencies have been contacted? ______

Nature of the child's problem ______

Name of person referring ______ Relationship to child ______

Name of parent or legal guardian ______ Signature ______

Address ______ City,State,Zip ______

Mail to: The Ohio Division of Special Education, 933 High Street, Worthington, Ohio 43085

Please mark your envelope "Confidential."

Every handicapped child in Ohio is entitled to an appropriate education.

Education prepares the handicapped to become productive, contributing adults.

Services are available to identified handicapped children:

- **EVALUATION** and **DIAGNOSTIC SERVICES** for ages birth through 21
- **EDUCATIONAL PROGRAMS** suited to the individual for ages 5 through 21

Also, many school districts and agencies offer programs to handicapped children under 5.

If you know a child who may be handicapped and is not in school . . .

CONTACT YOUR LOCAL SCHOOL DISTRICT

or write
The Ohio Department of Education
Project Ohio
933 North High Street
Worthington, Ohio 43085
or call collect
The Ohio Department of Education
614-466-8854
Sponsored by the
Ohio Department of Education

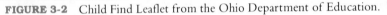

FIGURE 3-2 Child Find Leaflet from the Ohio Department of Education.

and television announcements, telephone contacts, and personal visits, such as door-to-door canvasses. The Child Find is similar to the identification, referral, assessment, and program placement process that is conducted in the schools; it is, however, broader in scope.

Screening in the Local School District

In the last several years many local school districts have organized district-wide and/or building-wide screening procedures, particularly at the prekindergarten and pre-first-grade levels. Generally, the purpose is to identify areas of difficulty in the child's early school years as a way of preventing future (and usually more complex) problems. But there are inherent difficulties with the process. First, identifying a young child as being different in some way—even if only by picking the child out for further study—may be initiating a self-fulfilling prophecy. Descriptions of learning and behavioral problems are often quite relative. What if a teacher with low tolerance for these problems decides that a particular child is a "different" type of learner? That child could, over a period, possibly become "different." This result might be otherwise had this child been placed in

Handicapped children deserve a chance...and the law guarantees them an education.

Every child in the country is entitled to an education. Without exception. Not only is it an American tradition—it's the law of the land.

"Every" child includes "handicapped" child—and that's what this folder is all about.

Handicapped children—regardless of type of handicap, regardless of severity of handicap—must receive full educational opportunities. They are guaranteed the right to achieve their full potential in intellectual, social and career development.

But there's a first step:
Find the child.

That may not be as easy as it sounds. Because of their handicaps, these children may be out of the community mainstream. Sometimes they're not in school.

Congress has acted on this problem. The finding of handicapped children was given high priority—"Child Find" is the name it's been given. The states are required (in the Education of the Handicapped Act, P.L. 93-380) to develop methods for finding children not receiving an education. This folder is one of the methods being used in Ohio. It's the first step towards giving a handicapped child—perhaps your child—free and appropriate educational services.

It's their right—according to law.

Educational handicaps of children.

Which children are we talking about? A definition or two might be in order.

We're looking for children not receiving an education. By children, we mean children up to and including 21 years of age. This includes both pre-schoolers (age to 5 years) and school-age children (ages 6—21).

"Handicap" includes such disabilities as:

Hearing impairments

Physical or orthopedic impairments

Visual impairments

Learning disabilities

Behavioral handicaps

Mental retardation

Speech or language impairments

Other health impairments, such as epilepsy or cardiac illness

Other severe or multiple handicaps

Not every handicap is listed. So if your child suffers from a handicap not shown above—and especially if he or she is not attending school or receiving an education—please respond. We want to find the children.

We want to give every child a chance.

How Project Ohio helps handicapped children.

Project Ohio locates handicapped children. Once they're found, they can receive a start towards an education, towards a more meaningful and productive life.

Their start can come through you. If you are the parent or legal guardian of a handicapped child, get in touch with us. We can help—but we must first find the child.

How the program works.

What happens after we find the handicapped child? First we notify the local school district in which the child resides. They, in turn, contact the parent.

The child's particular problems and needs are professionally evaluated. After this comprehensive assessment, an educational program is developed for the child. Instruction is tailored to the specific needs of the child and is based on such factors as the nature of the handicap, the level of education attained, the ability to learn new skills and so on.

For example, a child who can hardly see might receive the services of an orientation and mobility instructor, school psychologist and work-study coordinator—in addition to instructional services for the appropriate school level and such optional services as supplemental tutorial and reader help.

To help the child get started...To help the child achieve the fullest potential.

If you are the parent or legal guardian of a handicapped child not receiving an education, please respond. You can call the toll-free number: 800-282-8830. Or, fill out and return the Project Ohio referral form on the reverse side of this panel. If you know of such a child, you can help by passing this folder along to a person responsible for rearing the child.

Help us find the child—for the child's sake.

---

the class of another teacher with a broader definition of "normal" behavior. In this situation the same child would be less likely to assume a deviant posture.

Second, there has often been no organized follow-up (further formal assessment) of those children identified as "high risk." Without the individualized follow-up, errors during the screening process (such as saying a child is learning handicapped when he or she is not) will likely go unnoticed. This consideration is highly important. Most screening programs, to be maximally effective, initially identify more children as possibly having learning handicaps than actually do. Third, many districts screen prior to organizing remedial programs. It would be less risky *not* to identify children as possibly handicapped if there were no established programs to aid them.

Screening by the Classroom Teacher

The key to a successful screening program is the classroom teacher. Teachers are accustomed to employing observation skills to analyze the academic and social behavior of their pupils. Cartwright and Cartwright (1974) suggest that there are seven areas of pupil behavioral differences that teachers should observe daily. These are:

FIGURE 3-3 Warning signs of possible learning handicaps.

1. Information processing, storage, and retrieval problems (e.g., forgets quickly)
2. Language problems (e.g., runs words together in speech)
3. Perceptual–motor problems (e.g., poor handwriting)
4. Speech problems (e.g., stuttering, articulation errors)
5. Vision problems (e.g., tilting of head to one side)
6. Hearing problems (e.g., frequently asks teacher to repeat directions)
7. Social/emotional problems (e.g., overly aggressive with peers)

Figure 3-3 depicts some of the behavioral characteristics associated with these categories.

Two basic questions for teachers determining which children in their class may have learning handicaps are:

1. Which children demonstrate behavioral patterns that seem to be interfering with their learning progress? For example, children who experience difficulty in paying attention or who display such anxiety that they cannot complete their assignments are candidates for further evaluation.

2. Which children cannot achieve basic reading, writing, speaking, and arithmetic at the level expected in that particular grade? Those children who stand out due to academic deficiencies (e.g., a third-grader who cannot use consonant blends in word pronunciation) are likewise candidates for further evaluation.

The teacher may choose screening checklists and/or rating scales as part of the observational process. Figure 3-4 is an example of a rating scale used by educational personnel to identify possible learning handicaps. Teachers should also consult available school records in gathering information about a child. Reviewing a child's cumulative file might provide valuable information by answering the following questions (Moran, 1978):

1. Has a previous teacher or other professional considered referring this child for assessment before?
2. Does the child's earlier grade pattern provide any clue as to when the academic problems began?
3. Does the grade pattern in early years correlate with the child's attendance history?
4. Has the child attended so many different schools that continuity of instruction has been disrupted?
5. Are past standardized test results available for comparison with the child's current academic attainment?

Another source of valuable information for the teacher is the child's written assignments. Knowledge can be obtained by analyzing the written assignments

Classroom observations can provide teachers with meaningful information on a daily basis.

SCREENING INSTRUMENT FOR LEARNING AND BEHAVIOR DISABILITIES

Child's Name _____ Evaluator's Name _____

Date of Birth _____ Teacher _____ Grade _____

School _____ School Phone No. _____ Date _____

Directions: In rating child, rate him/her in relation to his own abilities. Please rate each and every statement by placing an (X) in the appropriate square after the statement. For a behavior that occurs very seldom an (X) may be placed under 1 or 2. For a behavior that occurs occasionally but not on a regular basis an (X) may be placed under 3 or 4. For those behaviors that occur often and on a regular basis, a rating of 5 or 6 may be used. If the statement does not apply to the student, place an (X) in the N/A (Not applicable) column.

ACADEMIC BEHAVIOR RATINGS

READING

	Seldom		Occasionally		Often		N/A
	1	2	3	4	5	6	
1. Understands what he or she reads							
2. Understands what others read		X					
3. Reads well orally		X					
4. Has good sight vocabulary		X					
5. Has good word attack skills		X					

Reading grade level achievement: Above Average_____ At Average_____ Below Average_____

Reading achievement according to child's ability: Above Average_____ At Average_____ Below Average_____

ARITHMETIC

	Seldom		Occasionally		Often		N/A
	1	2	3	4	5	6	
1. Knows number facts appropriate to his or her ability				X			
2. Understands relationship of symbol to amount				X			
3. Can work "story or thought" problems		X					
4. Attacks arithmetic problems logically			X				

Arithmetic grade level achievement: Above Average_____ At Average_____ Below Average_____

Arithmetic achievement according to child's ability: Above Average_____ At Average_____ Below average_____

LANGUAGE

	Seldom		Occasionally		Often		N/A
	1	2	3	4	5	6	
1. Expresses ideas well orally		X					
2. Expresses ideas well in written form	X						
3. Tells stories in sequence			X				
4. Speaks clearly						X	

58

FIGURE 3-4 Example of a rating scale used in identifying learning problems.

WRITING	Seldom		Occasionally		Often		N/A
	1	2	3	4	5	6	
1. Forms letters correctly			X				
2. Letters are properly sequenced (no reversals)			X				
3. Copies material correctly			X				
4. Has good spacing, size, and alignment			X				
5. Written work neatly done			X				

GENERAL	Seldom		Occasionally		Often		N/A
	1	2	3	4	5	6	
1. Follows oral directions well	X						
2. Follows written directions well	X						
3. Completes assignments	X						
4. Quality of work is consistent	X						
5. Classroom comments are often relevant			X				
6. Works well independently					X		
7. Participates well in group activities	X						

SOCIAL BEHAVIOR RATINGS	Seldom		Occasionally		Often		N/A
	1	2	3	4	5	6	
1. Stays in seat		X					
2. Does assigned seat work		X					
3. Participates in group activities			X				
4. Volunteers verbal responses			X				
5. Tidy		X					
6. Attends to tasks	X						
7. Alert		X					
8. Attentive		X					

Additional Comments: _____

_____
_____
_____
_____
_____
_____
_____
_____
_____
_____

in-depth, beyond just checking for correct and incorrect responses. In this manner, clues to a pupil's organizational abilities, sequencing skills, ability to follow directions, and fine-motor skill level may be ascertained.

Regardless of the techniques used, teachers should be aware that biases can sneak into their observations and interpretations. Observation should be considered only as part of a total information-gathering system. By continually cross-checking their own observations with information from other sources (such as formal and informal tests), and by contrasting their views with the perception of others, teachers can control the influence of personal bias.

Following the initial screening of a child with a handicapping condition, the teacher may choose from these alternatives:

■ Refer the child to the assessment/placement team for a formal assessment
■ Consult with other professional personnel regarding the problems and try to make curricular and instructional modifications within the existing classroom —postpone referral pending the outcome
■ Continue to gather information, with the assistance of support personnel, postponing referral until more data has clarified the situation
■ Decide there really was not a problem after all, and maintain the child under the current conditions

If a teacher decides to refer a child for formal assessment, a preassessment parent conference is required by law. However, parent involvement at the earlier information-gathering stages may be appropriate in many cases. It would certainly facilitate the entire identification and placement process.

In completing a referral to the multidisciplinary assessment team, the teacher combines all the information from the screening and observational process and presents it to the team in written form. Although referral formats vary, most school districts have established procedures for making referrals through school principals.

MULTIFACTORED ASSESSMENT

If the classroom teacher's attempts to modify conditions in the classroom fail to meet the pupil's needs, a referral to the multidisciplinary assessment/placement team is appropriate. There are procedural safeguards built into PL 94–142 that apply to providing nondiscriminatory assessment. These require local school districts to conduct evaluations and place pupils into special education programs using the following guidelines outlined in the *Federal Register* (May 4, 1977, p. 22682):

1. Tests and other evaluation materials have been validated for the specific purpose for which they are used and are administered by trained personnel in conformance with the instructions provided by their producer.
2. Tests and other evaluation material include those tailored to assess specific areas of educational need and not merely those designed to provide a single general intelligence quotient.
3. Tests are selected and administered so as to ensure that when a test is administered to a student with impaired sensory, manual, or speaking skills, the test results accurately reflect the student's aptitude or achievement level or whatever other factor the test purports to measure, rather than reflect the student's impaired

sensory, manual, or speaking skills (except where those skills are the factors that the test purports to measure).

Clearly, the evaluation procedures mandated by PL 94–142 require assessment personnel in local school districts to use the highest degree of test technology available in a professionally competent manner. No longer is the IQ score alone sufficient. Also, a child's performance on a test of intelligence, or any other test, should reflect the purpose of that test—not a handicapping condition (i.e., a child with a hearing loss may score relatively low on a standard intelligence test because of the sensory impairment, not because of low intelligence). To do otherwise would greatly increase the risk of misinterpretation, poor decision-making, and misplacement.

Composition of the Assessment/Placement Committee

The assessment/placement committee should include the following professionals:

- Teachers (either the one who has made the referral or the receiving teacher, or both) who will be responsible for implementing the committee's decisions
- School psychologists and/or other child evaluators responsible for providing information for making decisions about the child's educational programming
- Principals or other administrative personnel responsible for providing support for implementing the program decisions

The child's parents may choose not to participate as members of the committee, or they may wish to become actively involved. Whatever they choose, they have

Assessment information from many professionals assists in developing an appropriate educational plan.

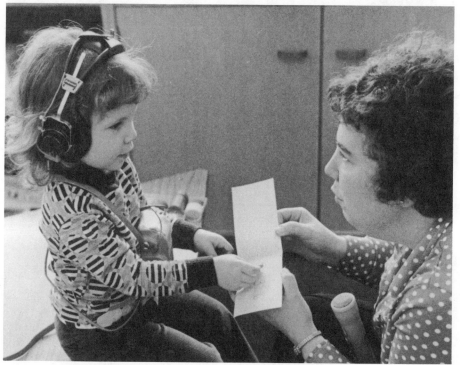

the right under due process to give or withhold their consent at any of the following points: before standardized tests are administered; before a special educational placement is implemented; or before any major changes are made in the pupil's educational program. Many local schools have found active parent participation helpful for several reasons:

- Understanding of the child's and the family's needs is greatly enhanced by the information that parents can provide
- Successfully implementing the child's program (as outlined by the committee) often depends upon parental cooperation
- If the parents are committee members and attend the meetings, they are more likely to comprehend how the committee works; thus, unnecessary delays in developing the child's individualized program may be avoided

The multidisciplinary nature of the assessment team yields assessments preferable to previous procedures. First, utilizing information from diverse sources tends to make committee conclusions less likely to be biased. Independent assessment of performance areas more thoroughly describes the child's handicapping condition as well as provides a deeper understanding of current functioning, including the child's particular strengths and weaknesses. In addition to sharing responsibility for the actual assessment, the team also shares responsibility for any liabilities that may result from their decision. Thus, open communication among team members is critical. The desire to embrace and respect the perspectives of professionals in one's own and other disciplines is a necessary ingredient for successful team functioning.

Professionals on the Team

Figure 3-5 shows various professionals who serve as assessors on special education placement committees. Which disciplines are represented depends on the needs of the child and the conditions of the referral.

Areas of Assessment

Despite the involvement of mixed professionals in a multidisciplinary evaluation team, a nonbiased assessment can only occur when information is gathered on several aspects of the child's total functioning. Educational decisions based on a single aspect of the child's functioning (e.g., intellectual) is inappropriate. Such decisions are potentially harmful to the child and to the educational program as well. A multifactored evaluation includes information about the child's functioning in these domains:

- Physical growth and development, including medical history and status
- Cognitive and academic functioning, including intellectual ability, achievement levels, and communication/language skills
- Social/emotional development, including **adaptive behavior** (a person's ability to adequately adjust to the environment) and self-help skills
- Fine- and gross-motor skills
- Perception and sensory-motor skills
- Vocational interests and skills

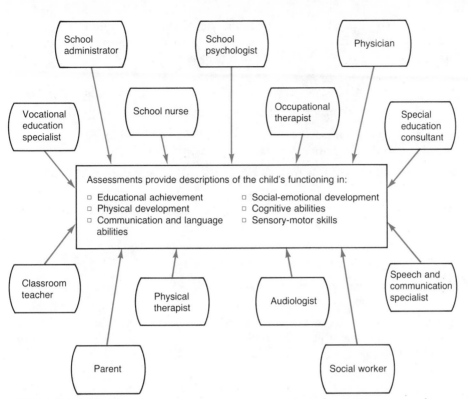

FIGURE 3-5 Multidisciplinary assessment team provides information on several aspects of children's functioning.

Sources of Information

The final criterion for a nonbiased assessment is that information should be gathered from a variety of sources using a variety of procedures. Procedures and data sources commonly employed by members of the assessment team include:

- Interviews—with parents, teachers, and other persons who know the child
- Observations—of the child in a variety of settings, including the classroom, the playground, and the home, and during different times of the day
- Review of records—including medical and health related, and records of previous school performance, both academic and behavioral
- Psychoeducational testing—including formal and informal instruments and procedures

Psychoeducational testing has been for some time a concern of professionals interested in special education programs. The use of **formal, norm-referenced tests** (which allow for comparison of scores and require standardized procedures of administration), particularly tests of intelligence, has been abused. Children were often labeled as having one handicapping condition or another based on a single IQ test. Because norm-referenced tests often resulted in a de-emphasis on developing an appropriate individualized program for pupils, educators began to use **informal tests** which are teacher-made and are not based on group comparisons. These instruments allowed them to pinpoint more precisely the academic strengths and weaknesses of individual children. More recently, educators have reorganized the legitimate role of formal tests in combination with informal tests as part of a complete assessment process.

FORMAL TESTING   Formal testing, or standardized testing, is useful in the total assessment/placement program for many reasons; it provides:

- An objective summary of the child's skill levels as compared with other children in the normative population
- A quantitative description of the child's skill levels (e.g., percentiles, grade equivalents, etc.)
- A basis for deciding whether more specific, detailed assessment is needed and in what areas

INFORMAL TESTING   Informal testing provides:

- Information that can verify, expand upon, or disallow data gathered previously through formal testing
- Specific information about what academic or social behaviors and tests the child can and cannot perform, which identifies the child's academic strengths and weaknesses
- Information that can serve directly as a basis for developing relevant educational strategies
- A process for continually monitoring the child's progress, based on an analysis of the child's responses to instructional strategies

MULTIFACTORED ASSESSMENT TEAM — CASE STUDY REPORT

A child suspected of having a handicapping condition is referred to the placement team. The team then determines eligibility for special services and how the educational program and related services should be designed. The responsibility for gathering and interpreting information about the child is given to a multidisciplinary team of professionals. An example of a team report, combining the assessment results, is provided in the next section.

David F. is a third-grader. The assessment/placement committee became aware of his problem when the school psychologist and the special education consultant were contacted by his regular teacher, Ms. Speece, after the Christmas holidays. She described his current and past behavior and asked for suggestions to help him in the classroom. Even though the modifications she made in David's program seemed to be having a positive effect on his academic progress and his behavior, she was still concerned that David would not be ready for fourth grade. Therefore, she referred David for assessment in order to evaluate his problems more precisely. Mr. and Mrs. F. were advised of the referral at a preassessment conference. They agreed with school personnel on the need to investigate David's problems more thoroughly. The completed referral form is shown in Figure 3-6.

Special Programs for Handicapped Children

Pupil Referral Form

Child's Name _David F._

Child's Age _9 years 2 mos._ Date of Birth _2/18/70_

Referred by _Mrs. Diane Speece_ _teacher_
                                        (position)

1. What problems, academic and/or behavioral, have you observed with
    this child?
    David has already been retained once in grade 3
    and is likely to fail again. His overall academic work
    is poor and he depends heavily upon his classmates to
    help him complete his written assignments, although they
    frequently are not handed in.

2. What circumstances or conditions are typically related to the problem
    described?
    David's main difficulty seems to be with reading, since
    most of his other subject matter work depends on it.
    Homework assignments, as well as class assignments,
    are often incomplete.

3. What curricular modifications or strategies have you used in trying
    to solve the problem?
    I've cut back in the amount of problems or work that I
    present to him at any one time (as suggested by
    Mr. Parks and Mr. Johnston). The accuracy of his works
    has improved somewhat, but he still is not completing
    enough of the required work.

4. What strengths does this child demonstrate?
    He's a good, cooperative, loving boy with a good
    sense of humor. He gets along well with his
    classmates. I'm afraid if his work continues to
    decline, his attitude and his relations with his
    peers may decline also.

Diane Speece
Signature of Referral Agent

FIGURE 3-6 Pupil referral form for special education program for handicapped children.

On the basis of referral information, a thorough diagnostic evaluation was recommended. The assessment team's report is presented below. The instruments used in this case were selected specifically for this child; a different set of instruments might be chosen in another child's case.

DATE: 4–25–79
PUPIL: David F.
DATE OF BIRTH: 2–8–70
SEX: Male
SCHOOL: Emerson Elementary

PARENTS: Ralph and Esther
AGE: 9 years, 2 months
GRADE: 3
TEACHER: Ms. Speece

I.   REASON FOR REFERRAL: David's teacher reports that he is continuing to experience difficulties in most school subjects, but particularly in reading, even though he is repeating the third grade this year. Mr. Marsh, the school principal, reports that David's frequency of behavioral difficulties on the playground and at lunch have increased this year. Mrs. F., David's mother, indicates that both she and her husband have noted a decrease in David's interest in school this year and an increasing reluctance on his part to discuss his school problems or activities with them.

II.   ASSESSMENT TECHNIQUES/INSTRUMENTS:

Wechsler Intelligence Test for Children-
Revised (WISC–R) (Parks, 4–10–79)

Bender Visual Motor Gestalt Test
(BVMGT) (Parks, 4–10–79)

Woodcock Reading Mastery Tests—
Form A (Johnston, 4–5–79)

Gray Oral Reading Test—Form A
(Parks, 4–12–79)

Peabody Individual Achievement Test
(PIAT) (Parks, 4–12–79)

Informal Reading Inventory (Speece,
4–2–79)

Classroom (Parks and Speece, 4–9–79)

Playground (Recess) (Parks, 4–9–79)

Adaptive Behavior Inventory for Children
(ABIC) (Nelson, 4–10–79)

Devereux Elementary School Behavior
Rating Scale (Speece, 4–10–79)

Health History Inventory (Speece,
4–11–79)

Physical Dexterity Tasks (Nelson,
4–11–79)

Sociocultural Scales (Nelson, 4–10–79)

Teacher Interview (Parks, 4–9–79)

Parent Interview Observations (Nelson,
4–10–79)

Cafeteria (Lunch) (Johnston, 4–11–79)

III.   OBSERVATIONS:

A.   *During Assessment*: All examiners noted David was extremely polite and cooperative during the assessment sessions. David's concentration suffered during the WISC-R when he was unable to complete more difficult items. He typically became excited and made comments such as "I don't think I can get this one; this is too hard!" As the difficult items continued, David began looking around the room and commenting on various items in the room. This behavior increased on those items that were timed. All examiners indicated that David tended to inquire frequently about the correctness of his responses and his overall test performance, saying things like, "Did I get that right?" and "How am I doing; not so good, huh?"

B.   *Classroom*: Ms. Speece and Mr. Parks both indicate that David's general classroom behavior is cooperative and purposeful. He relates well to his classmates in both large- and small-group instructional situations. He has difficulty in completing and submitting his written assignments, both those to be completed in class and those assigned as homework. In class, he frequently relies on classmates for assistance in finishing his seatwork assignments.

C. *Playground and Lunch*: In both environments, which are less structured than his classroom, David seemed to "cut loose." His recess play consisted mainly of running from one group of students to another, laughing and shouting. At lunch, he was reprimanded twice during a 35-minute period for talking too loud and not staying in his seat. He responded to correction cooperatively and without hesitation. Ms. Speece reported that both behaviors are typical of reports from the playground and cafeteria supervisors all year.

IV. ASSESSMENT RESULTS:

A. *Physical Development*: David's birth was reported by Mrs. F. to be normal. David had the typical childhood diseases with no serious injuries or illnesses except for a chronic ear infection that caused him to miss 45 days during his first-grade year. Although he developed language and motor skills appropriately, Mrs. F. reports that he was a "very active" young child. When a report from David's nursery school teacher confirmed her observations of his "overactivity," she took him to the family physician who recommended a trial with medication to "slow him down." A report from the physician, Dr. Gold, indicates that David is currently in sound physical health with a "somewhat higher-than-average activity level." David's chronic ear condition is no longer evident, and normal hearing and vision are apparent. While medication to lessen David's hyperactivity is not recommended at this time, Dr. Gold has asked that Mrs. F. and school personnel keep him informed of David's school progress. Vision and hearing screenings in October, 1978, indicate no difficulties in these areas. His performance on the Physical Dexterity Tasks indicates no "at risk" areas. David's performance on the Bender Gestalt is within the average range for a child of his age. The examiner noted, however, that as the designs became more difficult to draw, David became restless and his attention began to wander.

B. *Cognitive Development*: On the WISC-R, David scored within the average range of intellectual ability on the verbal scale, the performance scale, and on the full scale. The following scores were obtained on the WISC-R subtests (an average score is indicated by a scaled score of 10 on each subtest):

Verbal Score	Scaled Score	Performance Score	Scaled Score
Information	10	Picture completion	11
Similarities	12	Picture arrangement	12
Arithmetic	9	Block design	13
Vocabulary	13	Object assembly	10
Comprehension	11	Coding	8
Digit span	8	Mazes	10

No subtest scores were significantly below average, although a difference of five scale score points between David's highest subtest performance, vocabulary, and his lowest, digit span and coding, indicates some disparate functioning. Results of the administration of the sociocultural scales indicate that David falls within the cultural background of the WISC-R normative population. His Estimated Learning Potential (ELP) is within the average range of intelligence as measured by the WISC-R.

C. *Social/Emotional Development*: On the Adaptive Behavior Inventory for Children (ABIC), David scored in the "at risk" category for the "nonacademic school roles" subtest but not in the remaining five areas—family, community, peer relations, self maintenance, and earner/consumer. David's scores on the Devereux Elementary School Behavior Rating Scale completed by his teacher, Ms. Speece, indicate scores in the categories of impatience and achievement anxiety that are significantly above the average score for that category. The interview with Mrs. F. reveals that at home David is often impatient, and there are indications of anxiety, especially when he is asked to attempt new tasks that are difficult for him to accomplish readily.

D. *Educational Performance*: A review of the school records indicates that David's academic achievement was marked by "average" to "low average" performances in grades one and two. Last year in grade three, his school achievement declined to "below average" in all subjects except arithmetic, in which he maintained a "high C" grade for the year. So far this year, David's performance has improved, but his grades in all subjects except math are still below average. On the Peabody Individual Achievement Test (PIAT), David obtained the following scores:

	Grade Equivalent
Mathematics	4th grade-8th month
Reading recognition	3rd grade-8th month
Reading comprehension	3rd grade-5th month
Spelling	4th grade-0 month
General information	5th grade-3rd month

David's performance indicates a level of understanding of general information which is at a high average for his age group. On the other hand, his performances in reading (word) recognition and reading comprehension are significantly below expectations for his age, although not for his current grade placement. Further assessment in reading, using the Woodcock Reading Mastery Tests, the Gray Oral Reading Test, and an informal reading inventory, indicates the following levels of performance and discrepancies:

1. David has an independent reading level of early grade one and is at late first- to early second-grade instructional level.
2. David's reading comprehension skill level and his listening capacity level are above the level of expectation considering his weak word attack skills. Even when he is not able to pronounce the words, he can understand enough of the story from contextual clues to respond to questions of fact. His overall scores on tests of oral reading ability are influenced greatly by the large amount of time he requires.
3. David's word attack skills are on the second-grade level. He demonstrates difficulty in pronouncing consonants and consonant blends in the initial (e.g., *sh*ut) and final (e.g., ba*th*) positions. He has much difficulty with three-letter initial blends (e.g., *spr*ing). Although he can correctly pronounce all the short and long vowels in isolation, he has much difficulty applying phonetic rules (e.g., a single *e* at the end of the word makes the preceding vowel long). David demonstrates difficulty in pronouncing vowels in the medial position (e.g., he said "clumb" for "climb").
4. David's level of sight word recognition is below the third-grade level.

V. DATA INTERPRETATION, PUPIL'S STRENGTHS AND WEAKNESSES:

A. *General Ability Level*: David functions within the average range of intellectual ability, although his true potential may have been somewhat disguised by his apparent level of anxiety during the test administration. His relatively high scores on vocabulary and block design indicate a potential for "above average" intellectual functioning.

   B. *Relative Strengths*:
      1. Arithmetic computation (PIAT)—However, David's classroom performance in math is somewhat hindered by his difficulties with story problems, which often require reading skills beyond his current level of functioning
      2. General understanding of concepts expected of his age group through listening and awareness
      3. Cooperative and friendly with peers
   C. *Relative Weaknesses*:
      1. Attending to tasks that approach his instructional frustration level
      2. Word attack skills and use of phonetic rules
      3. High level of anxiety related to some academic tasks, particularly reading

VI. ELIGIBILITY RECOMMENDATIONS: It is recommended that David not be enrolled in a special educational program at this time; the following plan is, however, suggested to help him.
   A. David's teacher, the special education (learning disabilities) consultant, and the school psychologist should meet to modify and improve the procedures implemented earlier this year to help David complete his assignments more often. This team should devise plans for offsetting David's poor reading ability. These plans should include David's parents because they are actively involved with his difficulties in completing his homework assignments. This team should also consider devising a plan, with the cooperation of the playground and cafeteria aides, for improving David's behavior in those settings.
   B. Consideration should be given to enrolling David in the small-group remedial reading program and the summer reading program at the school, and to modify his classroom reading instruction to meet his specific deficiencies more directly.
   C. David should be referred to the school counselor for help in dealing with his school-related anxieties. The school counselor, David's teacher, and his parents are encouraged to involve David in some nonacademic school activities (e.g., scouting, choral group, athletics, band, craft groups, etc.) in an attempt to keep up his interest in school while his academic difficulties are being remediated.
   D. It is recommended that David be advanced to grade four for next year. It is the opinion of the assessment team that David's reading difficulties may well have begun as a result of limited reading instruction in first grade (David was absent for 45 days). Even though his health and attendance have improved markedly since then, he is beginning to develop an emotional overlay relative to continual frustration with his academics.
   E. A formal reassessment at the end of the first semester of the next school year is recommended. Continual monitoring by the classroom teacher is anticipated. David's fourth-grade teacher should be advised and assisted by the psychologist and the special education consultant throughout the first semester. Following the formal reassessment at the end of the first semester next year, consideration may again be given to enrolling David in a special education program.

INTERVENING VARIABLES IN TESTING

Teachers and other professionals must be aware of the intervening variables (outlined in Table 3-1) that influence the output, or test score, in assessment situations. The assessment and placement team must recognize these and other

Table 3-1 Possible Variables Influencing Assessment Results

Input	Intervening Variables	Output

1. Inherited abilities
2. Environmental background
  ■ Cultural background
  ■ Formal training
  ■ Experience with similar tests or assessment procedures
  ■ General health and special handicaps
	1. Personality
	  ■ Achievement motivation
	  ■ Interest in test or procedures
	  ■ Anxiety
	2. Situational demands
	  ■ Perceived importance of test and procedures
	  ■ Morale of the pupil
	  ■ Physical condition of pupil when being assessed
	  ■ Environmental interference
	  ■ Influence of the tester
	
	3. Test/assessment demands
	  ■ Specific abilities required
	  ■ Speed of response required
	  ■ Misleading items
	
	4. Random variation
	  ■ Guessing
	  ■ Clerical errors
		Assessment results, test scores

Adapted from: Goslin, D. A. *The Search for Ability.* New York: Russell Sage Foundation, 1963.

variables that may influence assessment outcomes. When adequate consideration is given to the situational demands, the test demands, the personality characteristics of the child, and the resulting interactions among these variables, interpretation and use of the results will be more authentic and effective.

EFFECTS OF LABELING

A major concern in the assessment process is the frequent confusion between the pupil's learning problem in school and the assignment of a diagnostic label. If the planning and implementation of the individual education program (IEP) is to be successfully conducted, it must be based on a thorough analysis of the pupil's needs, strengths, and weaknesses—not on a brief diagnostic label. During the past decade, the concern over the traditional reliance upon categorical labels in special education came to the fore simultaneously with the passage of PL 94–142. Societal pressures and attitudinal changes led to the legislation that guaranteed the right to a free, appropriate, public education for all handicapped children. In order to receive their rights to an education, however, these children must be identified. They must, in fact, be labeled as handicapped before special education and related services can be provided to them. The issues of categorization, the labeling process, and the advantages versus the disadvantages of labeling are still crucial matters, and will be for many years to come. One of the disadvantages of labeling in special education is the possibility of setting into motion a self-fulfilling prophecy (e.g., we say a child is mentally retarded; therefore, we treat the child as less capable and, recognizing our perceptions, he or she behaves in the expected, mentally retarded manner; the child has become what we have said).

Because this factor and other problems potentially accrue in the use of labels, it is extremely important that the assessment team be aware of the ramifications of mistakes in judgment when deciding "to label or not to label." In this regard, discussing some mistakes made in the diagnostic labeling process in two different professional situations is in order. Physicians recognize that if they are going to err it is best to do so by misdiagnosing patients to have a disease when, in fact, they have none. Incorrectly diagnosing a person as having tuberculosis and calling the patient tubercular has far less drastic ramifications than missing the disease completely. Failing to recognize tuberculosis and thus not treating the patient's condition could be a tragic mistake.

In education, on the other hand, it would seem to be a far less serious error for the assessment team to decide that a particular pupil is *not* handicapped when he or she, in fact, is. The pupil would continue in a regular program of studies and would, most likely, be screened for potential learning problems at some later time. If, however, a pupil is mistakenly thought to be handicapped when he or she is not, there is then a real danger that this child may perceive himself or herself as others do (i.e., as having an internal deviancy or disease), thereby activating the self-fulfilling prophecy. In three years, at the next required assessment period, the pupil may indeed be "handicapped."

Several other disadvantages of the traditional labeling process are summarized in the following list.

■ Labeling detracts from, and may limit the development of, appropriate individualized programs for handicapped children. If the assessment/placement team is mainly concerned with selecting the most appropriate label, they may think that their job ends with designating a category. This attitude leaves the more difficult and important job of designing an individualized educational program uncompleted.

■ Labels, once assigned, are difficult to remove. Pupils labeled and placed in a specific categorical program often remain there despite changes in their conditions. Even if they are later removed from the placement, their special status tends to remain with them and may influence their futures.

■ Labeling and subsequent categorial placement limits the opportunities for normal children to become familiar with pupils with handicaps. This lack of opportunity for interaction may lead to undesirable patterns of communication and involvement between handicapped and nonhandicapped pupils as they grow to adulthood.

■ Labeling tends to establish conditions for mistakes in assessment of minority group children. For example, the so-called **six-hour retarded** pupil, who is viewed as mentally retarded during the 6-hour school day but not during out-of-school time, has often been misplaced in special education programs for the mentally retarded. These pupils, from minority backgrounds, were labeled retarded in school, but at home and in their neighborhoods they performed their social roles quite well.

■ Labeling inevitably implies that the problems reside within the person being labeled. This minimizes the significance of societal and environmental factors. Thus, possibilities for remediation of the person's environment may be overlooked. This omission takes on added significance when we consider the possible implications that changes in the environment could have for a larger number of persons, handicapped and nonhandicapped alike. Many needed changes in the community (and in schools and teachers, in particular) have gone unrecognized because of the belief that the problem lies within the makeup of the handicapped individual.

Despite the negative connotations of labeling, the process continues and is emphasized under PL 94–142. Although labeling has many adverse effects, it also has advantages, such as:

■ Labeling allows advocate groups interested in specific handicapped persons to be extremely cohesive, thereby furthering their general and political persuasiveness and influence. Thus, labeling permits the recognition of specific needs. To remove labels may, in fact, weaken the effectiveness of a well-organized group by diffusing its focus.

■ Labeling facilitates organizing and administering special programs for persons with handicaps. The legislative reform, which has spawned so many positive developments, probably would not have been possible without the focus provided by the categorical labels. Indeed, the communication of ideas so necessary to legislative decision-making is itself made easier because labels exist.

■ Labeling by category facilitates research into the causes of particular handicaps and thereby promotes the development of additional preventative measures and treatment programs.

Although we should consider the positive aspects of labeling, the fact remains that in the past too much emphasis on labeling led to misplacement and inappropriate educational programming. Labels in and of themselves are not very useful in designing effective educational programs. Thus, in order to plan appropriate educational strategies, the assessment/placement team must concentrate on analyzing the handicapped learner's functioning and needs.

TRENDS AND ISSUES

Educational assessment has become intimately related to the teaching/learning process. It now emphasizes observations, informal and criterion-referenced tests, and analyses. This focus has brought the assessment and evaluation process back into the classroom as well as into direct contact with the specific criteria being utilized. Figure 3-7 depicts how educational assessment is integral to the instruc-

FIGURE 3-7   The instructional process.

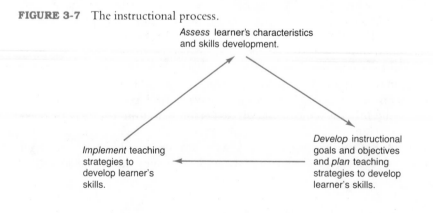

Assess learner's characteristics and skills development.

Implement teaching strategies to develop learner's skills.

Develop instructional goals and objectives and *plan* teaching strategies to develop learner's skills.

A thorough assessment includes observing the student outside the classroom.

tional process. Without this essential step, the goals, planning, and implementing of teaching strategies are likely, at least, to be less relevant than they should be and, at worst, to be totally ineffective.

Educational assessment has adopted a much broader outlook on children as learners interacting with their learning environments. This widened perspective includes not only involving parents, but also professionals from a range of disciplines. Those responsible for assessment have long recognized that interpreting children's behavior is risky if the situation and environment are not also considered. Children demonstrating learning difficulties can be classified as those whose difficulty is caused by (1) factors within themselves; (2) factors in the environment; and (3) factors created by a combination of the personal and environmental. If we believe in these three categories, then we recognize the fallacy of looking solely within the child for the solution to academic and/or social problems.

Ecological Assessment

The process of **ecological assessment** emphasizes the pupil's interaction with the educational environment. Analyzing how the child affects the learning environment (and vice versa) has been recognized as being more appropriate than analyzing the child as an isolated learner. Various elements in the school environment maintain (even initiate) particular behaviors. Different models have been developed to analyze these elements. Whatever procedure is used, however, the following factors should be included for assessment: teacher/pupil interactions, school climate, classroom climate, curriculum/pupil interaction, pupil/peer interactions, and variables of significance that may exist outside the school setting (Wallace and Larsen, 1978).

Once the teacher decides which school personnel and settings should be included in the assessment, procedures and instruments can be chosen. Systematic observations, rating scales, checklists, and sociometric devices can be used in answering such questions as:

■ Does the pupil appear to learn best individually or in group activities?
■ Do both teachers and pupils seem to be sensitive to each other's needs?
■ What percentage of time is spent on academic tasks? on social tasks? on behavioral learning objectives?
■ During what period of the school day does the pupil seem to do best?
■ By what means does most information reach the child? from the teacher? through individual study? by interaction with peers?

Figure 3-8 shows a classroom observation checklist from Carroll's (1974) model of ecological assessment. This checklist is designed to record and assess the classroom levels of individualization, group activity, interpersonal relations, and creativity.

After analyzing the multidimensional information gathered on pupils interacting with their learning environments, assessment teams can then recommend modifications for that environment. That is, they can make suggestions to reduce the negative, and enhance the positive, interactional effects.

Another trend in the field of assessment involves improving the quality of the norm-referenced tests used in placement decisions, especially those concerning children from racial or cultural minorities. One such instrument—the System of Multicultural Pluralistic Assessment (SOMPA)—has been used extensively in recent years. The SOMPA is designed to circumvent the problems associated with past inappropriate measures used in making placement decisions for minority group children.

System of Multicultural Pluralistic Assessment (SOMPA)

Dr. Jane Mercer, professor of sociology at the University of California, Riverside, developed the SOMPA. Mercer conducted extensive studies with populations of the mentally retarded during which she observed the phenomenon of the "six-hour retarded child." These are children who perform poorly in school but quite capably at home and in the community.

The SOMPA can be used with children aged 5 through 11, and was standardized on large populations of children from Black, Mexican-American and Caucasian backgrounds. The various tests of the SOMPA are subsumed under a medical model, a social systems model, and a pluralistic model. The tests included are the Physical Dexterity Tasks, the Health History Inventory, the Bender Visual Motor Gestalt Test, the Socio-Cultural Scales, the Adaptive Behavior Inventory for Children, and the Wechsler Intelligence Scale for Children-Revised (WISC–R). The SOMPA requires a multidisciplinary team approach to assessment. It attempts to answer the following questions:

■ Is there anything in this child's physical or biological makeup that we should be concerned about?
■ How does the child fit into various aspects of the social system as perceived by the parent?
■ What is this child's learning potential?

The child's learning potential can be ascertained by an Estimated Learning Potential (ELP) score. The ELP is determined by comparing the child's WISC–R IQ

CLASSROOM OBSERVATION CHECKLIST

Date _____ Time _____ Teacher _____ Observer _____ Learner _____

date/time   date/time   date/time
1st observation (10 min.) _____ **2nd observation** _____ **3rd observation** _____

Checklist may be used for the following: a) math lesson   b) reading   c) spelling   d) social studies
Rating scale: 1) none   2) little   3) some   4) occasionally   5) usually   6) to a great extent

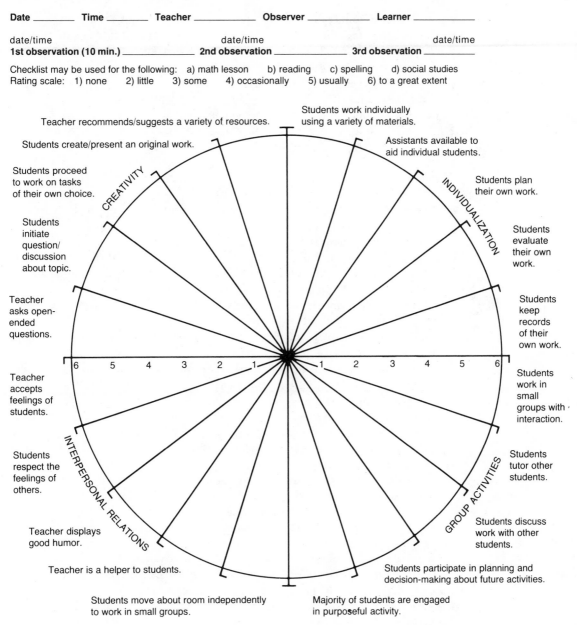

FIGURE 3-8   Classroom observation checklist. (From A. W. Carroll, "The Classroom as an Ecosystem," *Focus on Exceptional Children*, (4), 1974, p. 7. Copyright Love Publishing Company.

with the scores achieved by other children from the same ethnic and sociocultural background. Thus, the elements of cultural difference and learning potential have been differentiated from the issue of level of intellectual performance as measured by an IQ test.

The SOMPA was designed primarily as an assessment instrument to make placement decisions. It has, however, also proven useful in developing individual educational programs by helping to specify pupil's strengths and weaknesses.

SUMMARY POINTS

■ The purposes of assessment in special education include determining the influence the outcomes of assessment procedures, and (b) the advantages and ing charactersitics. These are ascertained so that an appropriate individual educational program can be planned and implemented.

■ PL 94–142 specifically outlines the assessment process and procedures that local schools must follow. It does so in order to identify a pupil as handicapped and to determine eligibility for special education services.

■ Each state is mandated to conduct a Child Find in order to identify all handicapped persons from birth through 21 years of age.

■ All teachers should be trained to administer screening instruments. They should be able to interpret these along with other data which would assist in identifying potentially high-risk students.

■ Multifactored assessments are conducted by a team of professionals. Selection of professionals to conduct a thorough assessment depends upon the needs of the student being assessed.

■ Sources of assessment information include: interviews with parents, teachers, and others; observations of the child in a variety of settings; reviews of the child's records (including academic, behavioral, and medical); and tests (formal and informal) administered to quantify the pupil's academic, cognitive, affective, and perceptual abilities.

■ A multifactored assessment gathers information on several areas of a pupil's functioning, including physical growth and development, cognitive functioning, academic achievement levels, communication and language skills, social/emotional development, fine- and gross-motor skills, and perception and sensory-motor skills.

■ Teachers and other professionals involved in the assessment and placement process must, among other things, be aware of (a) the many variables that influence the outcomes of assessment procedures, and (b) the advantages and disadvantages of labeling.

■ Before the multifactored assessment starts, the referred student's parents or guardians must be notified. They are required to give their consent.

■ Compared to past procedures, the multidisciplinary assessment approach provides a more complete, accurate picture of a pupil's learning and behavior strengths and weaknesses.

■ The practice of labeling has advantages and disadvantages. Critics claim that the label can replace the child's individuality or can become an excuse for explaining why the handicapped pupil is not learning.

■ The recent emphasis on ecological assessment (including assessment of the teacher/pupil interactions, pupil/curriculum interactions, and pupil/peer interactions) is a significant area of concern for the future.

REVIEW QUESTIONS

1. Define multifactored assessment. How can multifactored assessment procedures help overcome some of the pitfalls and misjudgments experienced historically in education?

2. Classroom teachers can provide valuable information to the assessment team. List ten warning signs that may indicate either a learning or behavior handicap.
3. Differentiate between formal and informal testing. What kinds of information can be provided by each?
4. Identify five factors that could influence a pupil's assessment results. What practices can professionals apply to minimize the effects of these variables?
5. Which position do you support regarding labeling? Why?
6. Define ecological assessment. Why is it an important concept to consider when assessing and placing pupils in special education programs?

DIAGNOSIS VS. PROGNOSIS

Every day each of us assesses a situation, a person, an event, or an object. Then we decide something based upon our assessment, no matter how informal it is. If we analyze our decisions, especially the more important ones, we discover that they are often predicated on what we think *might* happen—we predict the future with information received through assessment. For example, a friend invites you to select a puppy from a litter of two championship pups. After an informal, visual inspection of the two puppies, you notice that the small, brown, spotted one appears to be weak, inactive, and avoids contact with people. So you choose the more active pup, who affectionately nips at your heels. Two years later, you learn that the person who bought the runt has raised a lovable, prize-winning show dog. How could this have happened? Certainly, based upon your first evaluation, this would be highly improbable, if not impossible. Perhaps the buyer, from an expert's perspective, evaluated or saw something in the runt that you, as a casual observer, missed.

As professionals, we become involved in the assessment process to obtain more information about exceptional children. Usually, our diagnosis is based upon symptoms reported as scaled scores, percentiles, grade equivalents, and so forth. Then the educational program is planned and implemented.

Too often, the professional assumes that the behavior is static—that is, it stays at the same level or continues at the same pace. Only when we recognize the complexity of the learning process can we avoid one of the major pitfalls of the assessment process—prognosis. Prognosis is foretelling the future based upon symptoms and behavior patterns identified as a result of the diagnostic process. Unlike diagnosis, prognosis becomes a legitimate reason to label a child and then pigeonhole that child into a program. Ultimately, it limits the exceptional child's options for a more meaningful and normal life.

The following anecdote clearly illustrates how diagnosis can easily be interpreted into a prognosis.

Marty is a happy, sociable child diagnosed as having Down's syndrome, a type of mental retardation (see Chapter 13). Last year, at age 4½, he expressed no interest in and had few, if any, skills in working with letters or numbers; for example, Marty was unable to discriminate numbers and could not count from one to five. His teacher concluded that he probably would never learn even the most basic abstractions of the number system. At the end of last year's program, an individualized IQ test was administered to Marty. The resulting IQ score was 34. This score was later identified as the reason why Marty was not learning, and why he probably would not be able to learn abstractions.

This year, at age 5½, Marty is called the "number lover." He really enjoys learning, especially about how to use numbers. Marty and his father have developed several rather sophisticated number games. Now, he can count in sequence from 1 to 20, has one-to-one correspondence to about 12, and understands the concepts of greater than and less than. Marty is beginning to transfer these abstractions to his daily life. In the area of reading, he can read and discriminate the first and last names of his classmates. In addition, he is developing a sight-word vocabulary. Marty is now ready to learn and wants to learn. In retrospect, Marty seems to have had more faith in himself than the professionals did.

What caused this dramatic turnabout in Marty? It is quite probable that Marty was not ready to learn certain things last year. Perhaps his neurological system just was not mature enough to process the abstractions when he was four. However, from a developmental perspective, he *was* ready to learn them at age five. Exceptional children are no different from their nonimpaired peers in that all children go through sequential stages of development. The stakes are too high for professionals to assume that because a child did not learn in the past, learning will not occur in the future.

What are the implications for professionals?

■ First, any diagnostic data (i.e., test results, observations), no matter how valid they appear to be, should be interpreted as measuring one's performance at a particular point in time. In addition, there are a variety of variables (e.g., degree of security, awareness and understanding of what is being asked, physical comfort or discomfort) that may influence performance. Therefore, the professional can conclude only that under this set of circumstances, this child performed at this particular level at this point in time.

■ Second, if professionals follow the above-recommended format, they will avoid assuming that diagnosis is synonymous with prognosis. This does not mean that future objectives and goals, based upon professional judgment, should not be specified. On the contrary, professionals should predict learning outcomes, but only with flexibility and with the awareness that the rate and amount of learning is unique for each person.

■ Third, since learning styles are highly individualized, educators cannot assume that because one has not learned yet, learning will not occur later. A teacher's perceptions of a student's potential will affect that student's self-perceptions. If you think students can learn and you allow them to learn at their own rate, then they are more likely to view themselves as learners.

DISCUSSION POINTS

1. Think about a time during your educational career when you were tested. What effect did the test results have on your subsequent school experiences? What effects could the results have had?
2. Think about your own learning style and abilities. How much do you know about your own learning pattern and abilities? Do you know enough to make a prognosis regarding your future progress in your chosen career? What are some of the variables that you should consider?
3. Think about the influence that others have on your perceptions of yourself. Have your perceptions of your learning abilities ever been influenced by teachers, parents, or significant others? Do you have more confidence in your abilities in courses or subjects where the teacher perceives you as having the ability to learn and expects you to learn?

SUGGESTED READINGS

Functions of the Placement Committee in Special Education: A Resource Manual. Washington, D.C.: National Association of State Directors of Special Education, 1976.

Salvia, J., and Ysseldyke, J. E. *Assessment in Special and Remedial Education.* Boston: Houghton-Mifflin, 1978.

Smith, R. M., Neisworth, J. L., and Geer, J. G. *Evaluating Educational Environments.* Columbus, Ohio: Charles E. Merrill, 1978.

Wallace, G., and Larsen, S. C. *Educational Assessment of Learning Problems: Testing for Teaching.* Boston: Allyn and Bacon, 1978.

Writing Individualized Assessment Reports in Special Education: A Resource Manual. Washington, D.C.: National Association of State Directors of Special Education, 1978.

4

THE INDIVIDUALIZED EDUCATION PROGRAM

CONTENTS

As discussed in previous chapters, the major components of Public Law 94–142 are nondiscriminatory testing, individualized education programs, least restrictive environment, due process, and parent participation. Mandating change in existing educational practice for the handicapped is one thing; however, problems may occur in trying to implement legal change within the educational arena. Although these components are interrelated, it is the individualized education program (IEP) tenet that documents, in writing, the other provisions of the law. The IEP is meant to safeguard the appropriateness, delivery, and evaluation of educational programs for each handicapped child identified as needing special education.

The necessity for procedural safeguards becomes evident when past practices for the majority of handicapped students are reviewed. Once placed in a special education program most students spent the remainder of their educational careers there. In essence, special education was a one-way journey; few students were returned to the regular classroom (Gallagher, 1972).

DEFINITION

The term *individualized education program* (IEP) can be defined as follows:

> *Individualized* means that the program must be addressed to the educational needs of a single child rather than to a class or group of children. *Education* means that the program is limited to those elements of the child's education that are specifically special education and related services as defined by the act. *Program* means that the individualized education program is a statement of what will actually be provided the child, as distinct from a plan that provides guidelines from which a program must subsequently be developed (Abeson and Weintraub, 1977, p. 5).

The IEP identifies only those parts of the curriculum that require special education or related services. These services can be provided in any type of educational setting. For example, Holly may be required to spend three hours per week in a resource room to develop reading skills, and also to receive some special math instruction in the regular classroom. Both the reading and the special instruction in math are the only instructional areas that would be documented on the IEP. The remaining instructional periods in the regular classroom (social studies, spelling, art, etc.) are not mentioned in the IEP since they do not require special education or services. Thus, both the regular classroom and resource room teachers should have a part in the IEP development.

The IEP need not be restricted to academic areas. Depending upon each student's needs, it may refer also to social adjustment, vocational education, physical education, and adaptive behavior skills. These areas are often particularly important when dealing with handicapped children, since the handicap frequently affects every facet of a child's life. For example, Jim, aged 14, is physically handicapped, was denied admittance into any school program, and has been in a homebound instruction program. As a result of PL 94–142, however, a multifactored assessment was conducted that revealed he is functioning normally, has good verbal skills, and is performing academically on grade level. Thus, it is recommended that Jim be placed in a regular classroom. But because Jim has never attended school, he does not have the appropriate social skills for interacting with his peers. Therefore, the development of positive social interaction skills would be included in his IEP.

The law requires that an IEP must be completed prior to the beginning of the next school year for each already-identified handicapped child. However, for those children identified during the school year as needing special education, the IEP may be developed and implemented at any time. The IEP must be reviewed on an annual basis to determine if any changes are necessary, depending upon the student's progress or lack of progress. This review protects the handicapped student from being locked into a program for the remainder of his or her academic career.

DEVELOPING THE IEP

After the multifactored assessment, the multidisciplinary evaluation team meets to discuss all the information gathered. At this time, the data is classified and documented in relation to program planning. If the multidisciplinary committee recommends that a child receive special education, an IEP committee is appointed (based on the multifactored assessment information). Also, the parents are notified in writing of the evaluation results and of the importance of their role in developing the IEP.

Ideally, the IEP process should be divided into two stages: (1) the development of the Total Service Plan; and (2) the development of the Individualized Instructional Plan (IIP). The Total Service Plan is the end product of the IEP committee's work and, specifically, should include the following information:

- The student's current level of performance
- Goals to be met by the end of the school year
- Short-term objectives that are steps in achieving the annual goals
- Documentation of particular special education and other related special services to be provided
- Identification of specific materials and instructional methods
- Documentation of specific persons who will implement the recommended program
- Estimation of the time the child will spend in a regular education program
- Tentative dates for initiating services and an estimate of their duration
- Evaluation procedures and schedules for the child's mastery of short-term objectives (on a yearly basis at minimum)
- Identification of IEP committee members' roles and their signatures on the IEP

This information will enable teachers and administrators to provide the child with his or her educational needs in the quantity and quality determined necessary by the IEP committee (Torres, 1977; Turnbull, Strickland, and Brantley, 1978). See Figure 4-1 for a sample Total Service Plan.

The **Individualized Instruction Plan** (IIP) is developed by the special education teacher on the basis of information documented in the Total Service Plan (which services as a *general* representation of the student's educational needs). It is thus imperative that the receiving teacher(s) be on the IEP committee. The IIP describes the specific instructional program needed to achieve the annual goals listed in the Total Service Plan. Compare Figure 4-2, a sample IIP, with the corresponding Total Service Plan in Figure 4-1. PL 94–142 mandates that a Total Service Plan—commonly referred to as the IEP—be documented for each han-

School District

Name and Number: Summit

School Building: Mead Elementary

Name of Student: Stuart Williams

Date of Birth: 9–20–69 **Age:** 12 **Grade:** 6

Hours per Week in Regular Classroom: 32

Summary of Present Levels of Student Performance:

WRAT (Aug. 1981)
Reading   3.6
Spelling   3.8
Math   5.8

Program Goals	Special Education and/or Support Services	Professional Person(s)	Hours Weekly	Methods and Materials	Objective Evaluation Criteria
Reading ■ Will increase reading comprehension skills ■ Will increase knowledge of CVCV patterns and digraphs	resource room	Mr. Davis	4	Adapted material from SRA reading series	Adapted test material from reading text (90% accuracy)
Spelling ■ Will increase spelling skills emphasizing the use of plurals, prefixes, and suffixes	resource room	Mr. Davis	4	Teacher made multisensory material	Weekly teacher made test (100% accuracy)
Science ■ Will be able to understand concept of classification and will be able to conduct an experiment	resource help to the regular classroom	Mr. Davis Davis Mr. Johnson	3	Adapted science material Use of peer tutor	Unit test to be given orally (80% accuracy) Successfully complete an experiment (100% accuracy)

Description of Placement Recommendations:
Placement in resource room for one period a day, four days a week.

Starting Date: September 5, 1981

Ending Date: June, 1982

Review Date: June, 1982

Date of Placement Committee Meeting: 9–1–81

Placement Committee Members Present:

Position	Signature
Mr. Davis, (resource teacher)	
Ms. Fine, (school psychologist)	
Mr. Johnson, (regular teacher)	
Mr. & Mrs. S. Williams, (parents)	
Mrs. Taggart, (principal)	

FIGURE 4-1 Sample total service plan.

Name of Student: Stuart Williams

Resource Teacher: Mr. Davis

Date: From Sept. 5 to Sept. 8

Program Goals	Instructional Objectives and Techniques	Criteria for Evaluation	Reinforcement
Will increase reading comprehension skills	After reading a short story, will identify the main character(s) and the main idea	Teacher-made questions (100% accuracy)	Earn two minutes of free time to be taken at end of hour in the resource room
	When reading a short story will identify the sequence of events	Teacher-made material (80% accuracy)	Same as above
	Will answer multiple choice question on the literal interpretation of a short story	Teacher-made questions (100% accuracy)	Same as above

Weekly program changes (outline any IIP changes made in weekly instruction): _____

_____

_____

_____

FIGURE 4-2 Sample individual instructional plan.

dicapped child in need of special education. However, local school systems unfortunately are not required to expand the Total Service Plan into an IIP.

Format of the IEP

According to federal law, state and local education agencies may use any desired format for an IEP as long as it includes the required information mentioned earlier. Each local school system should evolve its own standard format for IEPs. Such a format should be used by all schools in the system, thus ensuring consistency from grade to grade and from level to level. A standard format also provides uniformity in monitoring the IEP.

Information other than that required by federal law may also be included in the IEP. Some states, for example, require additional items, such as a procedural checklist, a student's schedule, a list of IEP committee members, relevant test information, health information, special materials needed, and the specifications of the persons responsible for teaching the objectives. One or all of these items may be included, depending on the decision of the local school system. At any rate, adding such information would make the document more complete and provide more structure in implementing the IEP.

IEP Committee Members and Their Roles

PL 94–142 mandates that the following individuals be on the IEP committee (Turnbull, Strickland, Brantley, 1978, p. 125):

1. The student's teachers
2. A person, other than the child's teacher, who has responsibility for providing or supervising special education
3. The student's parents
4. The student, if appropriate
5. An evaluation expert, if the student is being considered for special education placement for the first time

If the child has been identified as having unique needs, other professionals knowledgeable in the necessary areas can be invited to the IEP meeting.

CHAIRPERSON   The person representing the local school system should chair the IEP meeting. The role of the chairperson is crucial to the functioning of the IEP committee. As a leader, whoever fills this position must organize the meeting, communicate with parents, and guarantee that the law is followed. This person should have the leadership skills necessary to conduct the meeting and should possess a thorough knowledge of the resources and the programmatic options available within a school system. As the spokesperson for the local educational agency, a major duty of the chairperson is to present the program recommendations to the parents. Other responsibilities of the chairperson include guaranteeing that the IEP follows the guidelines mandated by PL 94–142 and that IEP committee members are present at the meeting.

TEACHERS   Ideally, both the referring teacher and the prospective, or receiving, teacher should be present at the IEP meeting. Although not directly involved with implementating the IEP, the sending (referring) teacher is responsible for reporting to the committee on the student's past or present performance. This information should include details of specific programs in which the student is enrolled, results of conferences with parents and student, and a review of the student's academic and social strengths and weaknesses. The sending teacher should also present the committee with teaching materials and methods that have been successful in the past. These should be thoroughly discussed. This information provides the background from which the committee can draft recommendations regarding the student's program.

Unlike the referring teacher, the receiving teacher is directly involved with the development and implementation of the IEP. The receiving teacher uses his or her expertise and the information from the referring teacher to determine the feasibility of committee recommendations. The receiving teacher also locates special resources or services, if they are needed. For example, if a child requiring an adapted typewriter is to be placed in a regular teacher's classroom (receiving teacher), that teacher must be responsible for locating and obtaining that equipment. Or, suppose a visually impaired child is to be placed in both a resource room and a regular classroom. Then, both receiving teachers should be familiar with the special procedures for having the student's assignments available in Braille, if the use of Braille has been included in the IEP.

EVALUATION EXPERTS   If a student is being considered for special education placement for the first time, then an evaluation expert, such as a psychologist, must be on the IEP committee. This professional's job is to synthesize and interpret all relevant diagnostic and evaluation data from the multifactored assessment process and, further, to communicate this information to other committee members. Which expert or experts are to be on the committee usually depends upon the child's unique needs. For example, an adolescent with a neuromotor disorder resulting in limited physical functioning would require a vocational rehabilitation specialist and a physical therapist on the IEP committee.

PARENTS   The parents have a legal right to attend and participate in the IEP meeting. It is their responsibility to ask pertinent questions in such areas as programming and placement. And it is the responsibility of the other IEP committee members to respond to these parental concerns with candor. They should also make the parents feel comfortable participating in the committee's procedures. If parents believe that their rights or the rights of their child have been violated or denied, they can request an impartial hearing. In such cases, an impartial hearing officer is appointed by the local education agency to resolve such issues. Only when full cooperation and communication occurs among all committee members will the meetings run smoothly and the IEP be implemented successfully.

Along with prior notice of the IEP meeting, parents should also be informed that they may bring others to represent or support their views. Such additional people may include an attorney, an educator who is familiar with special programs, or a friend who can assist the parents in making decisions. The local school system may proceed with the IEP meeting without parent involvement only after making documented attempts to contact and encourage parents to attend. At least three attempts should be made to involve parents. Telephone calls, home visits, and written correspondence are recommended methods of contact. The law requires that all contacts be made in the parents' native language. For example, if the parents speak Spanish, a Spanish interpreter must relay the information; if a parent is deaf, a translator must be available to ask the parent to participate on the IEP committee via signing or other techniques. To be protected legally, the local school system must document all communication efforts with the parents; copies of letters or records of other attempts must be specified. See Figure 4-3 for a sample documentation form.

STUDENT   If appropriate, the student may be present at the IEP meeting. This decision, however, is usually left to the parents. If the student is no longer a minor, he or she may not only make the decision regarding attendance, but also other decisions involved in the IEP process. Should a student choose to attend, great care should be taken to clearly explain all decisions and their implications.

Functions of the Committee as a Whole

The IEP committee must first determine a method for making decisions, assign responsibilities to each member, and develop a timetable for planning and placement. The committee is also responsible for gathering the information needed to

FIGURE 4-3 Documentation for parental participation. (From *Developing and Implementing Individualized Educational Programs*, A. P. Turnbull, B. B. Strikland, and J. C. Brantley, Charles E. Merrill Publishing Co., 1978.)

Child's Name: _____ Address: _____

Parent(s) Name(s): _____ _____

Phone: _____ _____

Please check the appropriate spaces and provide the appropriate information to indicate the actions taken to satisfy the requirements of PL 94–142.

Part I: Parental Consent

Parental consent must be obtained, in writing, a reasonable time before:
 (i) Conducting a preplacement evaluation; and
 (ii) Initial placement of a handicapped child in a program providing special education and
    related services.
    [Section 121a.504 (b)]

                                                                         Dates

____1. Parental consent was obtained in writing.   _____

____2. Parental consent was refused.   _____

____3. Actions taken: _____   _____
                              _____   _____
                              _____   _____
                              _____   _____

Part II: Notification of Assessment Results

Parents must receive written notice of their child's assessment results, which meets the requirements of Section 121a.505.

____1. Notification, in writing, sent to parent(s)   _____
____2. Notice received by parent(s)   _____
____3. Additional procedures used to   _____   _____
        notify parents: _____   _____
                                        _____   _____

Part III: Parent Participation in IEP Meeting

Each local educational agency shall take steps to ensure that one or both of the parents of the handicapped child are present at each meeting, or are afforded the opportunity to participate, including the schedule of the meeting at a mutually agreed-upon time and place. [Section 121a.345)]

                                                                         Dates

____1. Parent(s) notified of IEP meeting, in writing
____2. Alternate ways by which parent(s)   _____
        were notified of meeting: _____
                                    _____   _____
____3. Parent(s) attended the meeting   _____   _____
____4. Parents participated in meeting by: _____
            ____individual telephone call
            ____conference telephone call   _____

88

_____5. The meeting was conducted on _____
at _____.

_____6. These steps were taken to ensure that the
parents understood the proceedings of the
meeting:

    _____arrange for an interpreter for parents
who are deaf or whose native language
is other than English

    _____other: _____

                                            _____

_____7. Parent(s), who so requested, received a copy
of the child's IEP

Part IV: Documentation Procedures

In the event of parent refusal to participate in the IEP meeting, the local educational agency must have a record of its attempts to arrange a mutually agreed-upon time and place. [see Section 121a.345 (d)]

A mutually agreed-upon time and place were not possible as verified by the following evidence:

_____1. Telephone calls made or attempted.

date	time	who called	result

_____2. Correspondence sent and responses received (see attached copies).

_____3. Visits made to the parent(s)' home or place of employment.

date	time	who visited	where visited	result

make sound decisions. The information should include educational history, social/emotional functioning, and environmental factors. The committee then translates the evaluation findings into educational goals and objectives through the IEP. Clearly, much sorting of information and planning is necessary after the child is assessed and *before* the IEP is developed (Turnbull, Strickland, and Brantley, 1978).

It would benefit the IEP committee to follow an established procedure in developing an IEP. That way, all information can be considered and the best possible plan can be developed. Although each school system may have its own specified way of proceeding through the IEP process, all school systems must in their meetings go through the process outlined in Figure 4-4 and the following pages.

DETERMINE CURRENT LEVEL OF PERFORMANCE   The first step in developing the IEP is to review all the evaluation information from the multidisciplinary committee. After analyzing the data (especially that which states the student's performance in behavioral terms), the student's level of functioning can be determined. Also, any information that leads to labeling a student and the procedures used to determine the label should be reviewed; information regarding individual program planning should also be examined.

The IEP committee next determines which areas of the student's program require special education. The IEP committee should include current information, use clear and concise language, and identify specific skills when reporting performance levels. Both learning strengths and weaknesses should be discussed. The following are two examples of ways to state performance levels:

RHONDA: *Regarding knowledge of sound-symbol relations*
1. Knows all consonant sounds in initial, medial, and final word positions
2. Does not know short vowel sounds

MATTHEW: *Regarding comprehensive skills*
1. Can correctly interpret pictures
2. Can give factual recall information
3. Cannot answer inferential questions

ESTABLISH ANNUAL GOALS AND SHORT-TERM OBJECTIVES   After identifying the current level of performance and individual learning style, the IEP committee can specify the **annual goals** for the student; that is, it estimates the student's progress during one school year after the IEP is implemented. Often, annual goals are high-priority items recognized by both parents and educators as a result of reviewing assessment data. Because they are frequently the people closest to the student, the annual goals set by these adults are likely to reflect realistic expectations of student growth. Here are some examples of annual goals:

Susan will be able to:
1. Control her bladder
2. Dress herself (i.e., pants, shirt, socks, shoes, coat, hat; note that no clothing items included require buttoning skills)

David will be able to successfully:
1. Demonstrate one-to-one number correspondence from 1 through 10
2. Identify the basic colors

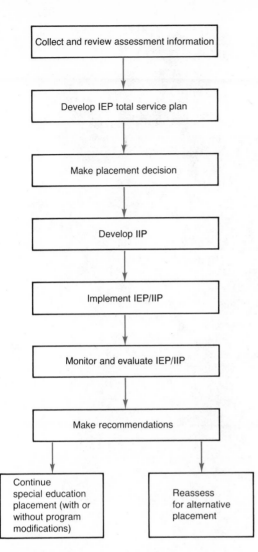

FIGURE 4-4   Functions of the IEP Committee.

Trisha will be able to:

1. Complete a job application
2. Pass the driver education course

Short-term objectives identify the intermediary skills between current levels of performance and perceived annual goals. It is important to state short-term instructional objectives in behavioral terms; that is, to indicate specific observable behaviors, and to list them sequentially. Benefits from writing annual goals and short-term objectives include improved student motivation, provision of accountability, developing of communication with parents, and more relevant teacher preparation (Hayes, 1977).

The following is an example of an annual goal and related short-term objectives. The example illustrates that the short-term objectives are sequentially and behaviorally stated tasks leading to the annual goal.

For some children, annual goals may focus on developing appropriate social skills.

EXAMPLE: If an annual goal for Rhonda is to master short vowel sounds, the following might be short-term objectives:

1. To be able to pick out the different vowel sound in a sound pattern (e.g., /e/, /e/, /a/, /e/) with 100 percent accuracy on five trials
2. To be able to pick out the different vowel sound in a pattern of words heard (e.g., cat, pan, fin) with 100 percent accuracy on five trials
3. To be able to identify the letter that corresponds to the different vowel sound heard in a pattern of words (e.g., swim, tin, mop, tip) with 100 percent accuracy

PROVIDE LIST OF SPECIAL EDUCATION AND RELATED SERVICES   A list of special education and related services to be provided to a student must appear in the IEP.

In reference to special education services, PL 94–142 (Section 121a.225) states that the IEP must include:

> A statement of specific educational services needed by the child (determined without regard to the availability of those services) including a description of (1) all special education and related services which are needed to meet the unique needs of the child, including the type of physical education program in which the child will participate and (2) any special instructional media and materials which are needed.

Special education refers to special instruction, and **related services** refers to support services, such as occupational therapy, transportation, and psychological services. The law also requires that the IEP specify when special education and related services will begin and what their duration will be. See Table 4-1 for a definition and list of related services.

ESTABLISH EVALUATION AND MONITORING PROCEDURES   Regarding evaluation, the IEP committee focuses on determining objective criteria, appropriate evaluation procedures, and monitoring the IEP. By including objective criteria in the short-term objectives, an evaluation system is built in.

Evaluation procedures should be determined according to the area being evaluated. Objectives in the academic domain may, for example, focus on the ability to recall information from last week's reading lesson or to recite multiplication tables. Standardized or informal achievement tests may be the most appropriate tool. Evaluating in the affective domain (attitudes, interests, and values) is more difficult. The psychomotor domain includes motor skills development, which may be evaluated by having the student demonstrate the physical activity stated in the objective. This might include tests that measure dexterity in mastering a new task or skills such as throwing a ball.

Evaluation information can be obtained from any or all of the following sources to determine if objectives were met:

■ Representative sample of student's classroom work
■ Teacher observation
■ Standardized test scores
■ Parent feedback
■ Checklist that correlates with short-term objectives written on the IEP

Monitoring provisions of services outlined in the IEP should also be conducted by the IEP committee. Two types of services exist: those provided on a one-time basis, and those provided on a continuing basis. Completion of a one-time service can merely be checked off the list of goals by noting the date of completion and follow-up. Monitoring a continuous service should include receiving or developing reports that state whether or not the service was provided, when and where, and the way the service was specified in the IEP.

LEAST RESTRICTIVE ENVIRONMENT

PL 94–142 does not specify exactly where special education and related services are to take place. However, the requirement of least restrictive environment must be adhered to in planning and providing for these services for the handicapped child. When considering program placement, the local school agency can choose from a continuum of educational settings. Every effort must be made to

TABLE 4-1 Listing and Definition of Related Services that May Be Documented in the IEP.
Source: From the *Federal Register* 42 (August 23, 1977).

§ 121a.13 Related services.

(a) As used in this part, the term "related services" means transportation and such developmental, corrective, and other supportive services as are required to assist a handicapped child to benefit from special education, and includes speech pathology and audiology, psychological services, physical and occupational therapy, recreation, early identification and assessment of disabilities in children, counseling services, and medical services for diagnostic or evaluation purposes. The term also includes school health services, social work services in schools, and parent counseling and training.

(b) The terms used in this definition are defined as follows:

(1) "Audiology" includes:

(i) Identification of children with hearing loss;

(ii) Determination of the range, nature, and degree of hearing loss, including referral for medical or other professional attention for the habilitation of hearing;

(iii) Provision of habilitative activities, such as language habilitation, auditory training, speech reading (lip-reading), hearing evaluation, and speech conservation;

(iv) Creation and administration of programs for prevention of hearing loss;

(v) Counseling and guidance of pupils, parents, and teachers regarding hearing loss; and

(vi) Determination of the child's need for group and individual amplification, selecting and fitting an appropriate aid, and evaluating the effectiveness of amplification.

(2) "Counseling services" means services provided by qualified social workers, psychologists, guidance counselors, or other qualified personnel.

(3) "Early identification" means the implementation of a formal plan for identifying a disability as early as possible in a child's life.

(4) "Medical services" means services provided by a licensed physician to determine a child's medically related handicapping condition which results in the child's need for special education and related services.

(5) "Occupational therapy" includes:

(i) Improving, developing or restoring functions impaired or lost through illness, injury, or deprivation;

(ii) Improving ability to perform tasks for independent functioning when functions are impaired or lost; and

(iii) Preventing, through early intervention, initial or further impairment or loss of function.

(6) "Parent counseling and training" means assisting parents in understanding the special needs of their child and providing parents with information about child development.

(7) "Physical therapy" means services provided by a qualified physical therapist.

(8) "Psychological services" include:

(i) Administering psychological and educational tests, and other assessment procedures;

(ii) Interpreting assessment results;

(iii) Obtaining, integrating, and interpreting information about child behavior and conditions relating to learning;

(iv) Consulting with other staff members in planning school programs to meet the special needs of children as indicated by psychological tests, interviews, and behavioral evaluations; and

(v) Planning and managing a program of psychological services, including psychological counseling for children and parents.

(9) "Recreation" includes:

(i) Assessment of leisure function;

(ii) Therapeutic recreation services;

(iii) Recreation programs in schools and community agencies; and

(iv) Leisure education.

(10) "School health services" means services provided by a qualified school nurse or other qualified person.

(11) "Social work services in schools" include:

(i) Preparing a social or developmental history on a handicapped child;

(ii) Group and individual counseling with the child and family;

(iii) Working with those problems in a child's living situation (home, school, and community) that affect the child's adjustment in school; and

(iv) Mobilizing school and community resources to enable the child to receive maximum benefit from his or her educational program.

(12) "Speech pathology" includes:

(i) Identification of children with speech or language disorders;

(ii) Diagnosis and appraisal of specific speech or language disorders;

(iii) Referral for medical or other professional attention necessary for the habilitation of speech or language disorders;

(iv) Provisions of speech and language services for the habilitation or prevention of communicative disorders; and

(v) Counseling and guidance of parents, children, and teachers regarding speech and language disorders.

(13) "Transportation" includes:

(i) Travel to and from school and between schools,

(ii) Travel in and around school buildings,

(iii) Specialized equipment (such as special or adapted buses, lifts, and ramps), if required to provide special transportation for a handicapped child.

provide the handicapped with an educational experience that is the least restrictive—that is, as much like a regular classroom setting as possible. The criteria for determining the least restrictive environment are the student's individual needs and the appropriateness of the educational setting for meeting these needs. Based on goals and objectives stated in the IEP, the least restrictive environment for some handicapped children may be the regular classroom; for others with more severe impairments, the most appropriate placement may, in fact, provide little or no contact with the nonimpaired population (Abeson, Bolick, and Hass, 1975).

Mainstreaming refers to the

> social and instructional integration of handicapped students in regular classes. It is not just their physical presence. Social integration involves peer relationships, an opportunity to gain status and acceptance, and feeling comfortable and secure as a full member of the classroom group with the corresponding rights and responsibilities of membership. . . . Instructional integration refers to the handicapped student being involved in the curriculum of the classroom. It means that appropriate instructional strategies are used to teach the student through individual, small group, and large group activities [Turnbull and Schulz, 1979, p. 56].

Thus, mainstreaming may be the least restrictive environment for some exceptional children.

The IEP must state where instruction will take place. When considering placement, every effort should be made to permit the handicapped child to attend a neighborhood school. Even if the IEP committee recommends academic instruction in a special education class, it might also recommend that nonacademic and extracurricular activities with nonhandicapped children would be the least restrictive environment for a particular child. For example, Susan's academic needs are met in a self-contained classroom; however, she receives personal typing and health instruction with her nonhandicapped peers.

A special services committee may be needed to monitor a student's placement to determine if it is, in fact, the least restrictive environment. This might be done for a variety of reasons. The school system may want to be assured that the student receives the proper amount of special education and is not limited by problems of accessibility. Or the committee may want to be reassured that the student's environment is not *too* unstructured. Some additional restrictions may possibly be necessary (even if only on a part-time basis) to make educational progress. Because PL 94–142 requires the removal of any architectural barriers in the school that could limit the full participation of handicapped students, the special services committee may want to inspect the buildings for this purpose.

A child's removal from a regular educational program to a special education program necessitates documentation. PL 94–142 requires (a) that the child's participation in regular education programs be described, and (b) that the type of educational placement outside the regular classroom be justified. Decisions to place a child in the least restrictive environment should be based on the student's capabilities, rather than on the handicapping label.

In deciding where to place a handicapped student, the *type* of placement should be specified rather than the name of the exact building (for example, intensive occupational therapy rather than Children's Hospital). Neither should placement be based on *existing* options alone. If the IEP calls for a unique placement or program, then the program must be located or created to meet the needs of the child. By leaving placement specifications somewhat open-ended, the child is guaranteed remediation at various locations rather than being limited by a vacancy in a particular institution or program.

If local school systems cannot provide suitable educational programs for handicapped children, the children may be referred to a private program. When the child is referred by the local school system, provisions must be made to ensure that the private program meets the specifications of PL 94–142. The financial obligation for the private program rests with the local school system, not with the parents.

Efficacy of Special Education

Children with special learning and behavior needs were originally grouped into self-contained, special education classrooms. This system was effectuated on the grounds that exceptional children would be removed from the competition, name-calling, and "pressure cooker" situations often believed to exist in the regular classroom. In addition, under this circumstance, instruction for these children would be specially designed for them. Therefore, they could learn faster and with a more positive attitude than in a regular class.

Dunn (1968), in a commentary on the efficacy of special education, questioned the validity of special education programs for the mildly retarded population. He also pointed out that many such programs included a disproportionate number of minority children. Based on research findings, the argument continued that for many exceptional children, learning in a self-contained, special classroom was no better, and sometimes less, than in a regular classroom (Goldstein, Moss, and Jordan, 1965; Smith and Kennedy, 1967; Bradfield, et al., 1973). One explanation is that the regular classroom environment (where there was probably more incentive to learn) enhanced the self-concepts of the handicapped children. However, since the research yields no unequivocal evidence for either position, the issue of justifying special education for the handicapped must remain unsettled, at least until more well-designed research studies are conducted. It is interesting to note that by including the principle of least restrictive environment in PL 94–142, the law actually supports the contemporary attitude that questions the validity of segregated special education services.

Service Delivery

In determining the least restrictive environment, the IEP committee can choose from various models of service delivery. In this choice, the degree of the handicapping conditions and the extent of needed support services are critical factors. Table 4-2 illustrates the placement options.

REGULAR CLASS   The least restrictive setting for exceptional students is full-time placement in the regular classroom environment. This type of educational setting allows for maximum interaction with the nonhandicapped population. While exceptional students are in regular classes, they may receive assistance from supportive services or supplementary instructional services. Following are examples of exceptional students placed full time in the regular classroom:

■ Although Caroline is visually impaired and considered legally blind, she
   spends her entire school day in a regular fifth-grade class. She uses the services

TABLE 4-2 Delivery of Service Options

Program Prototype	Interaction of Regular Teacher in the Program	Intensity of Need for Support Services	Degree of Severity of Handicapping Condition	Prognosis for Integration with Non-handicapped Peers	Degree of Students' Contact with Family
Regular class	—	Very low	Mild	—	High
Resource room	Very high	Low	Mild/moderate	Very high	High
Self-contained special class	Low/moderate	Moderate	Moderate	High	High
Special day school	Low	High	Severe	Moderate	High
Homebound short-term	High	Moderate	Mild/moderate health impairment	Very high	High
chronic	Moderate/high	Moderate/high	Severe health impairment	Low to high	High
Residential	Very low	Very high	Severe/profound	Very low	Very low

of peer tutors who read exams to her. In addition, she is involved in a supplementary support services program for mobility development on Saturday mornings.

■ All of Andrew's exceptional needs are met by his second-grade regular teacher. Although he has some learning problems that are related to his inability to read "like the other kids," Andrew's teacher has structured the classroom environment to meet his individual needs. As a result, Andrew does not receive any supplementary instructional services.

■ Tom spent two years in a self-contained, special classroom for children with behavior disorders. He is now placed full time in a regular eighth-grade class. All of Tom's teachers participated in an in-service program that was given by a behavioral consultant. The purpose of the in-service program was to provide Tom's regular teachers with information on alternative classroom-management techniques and strategies to be used in the regular classroom.

These three examples illustrate the variety of alternatives available for exceptional children and youth in the regular class environment:

■ The regular teacher may solely provide the prescribed program.

■ The regular teacher may provide the prescribed program with consultation services from specialists. In essence, the consultant gives direct in-service assistance to classroom teachers. Such in-service programs focus on, for example, identifying a target behavior, selecting and using assessment tools, structuring parent/teacher conferences, or developing alternative grouping strategies within the classroom.

■ The regular teacher may provide the prescribed program, while the student also directly receives supplementary assistance from other specialists, such as the resource room teacher or the speech therapist.

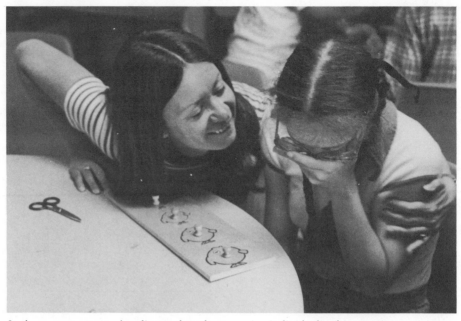

In the resource room, handicapped students receive individualized instruction.

When an exceptional student is placed full time in the regular class, the success of mainstreaming depends on the regular classroom teacher's attitude toward exceptional people as well as his or her knowledge and skill in individualizing instruction.

RESOURCE ROOM   The resource room may act to bridge the transition from the self-contained, special education class to the regular class. Since many handicapped children do not belong full time in either setting, they need an educational environment with the benefits of both types of classrooms. In the resource room, students can receive special education for part of the school day and spend the remainder of time in a regular class setting. The resource room concept can also be applied to regular students who have academic, perceptual/motor, language, or social/emotional problems that can be remediated in this type of setting.

The regular teacher usually provides most of the instruction; the resource room teacher provides diagnostic and tutorial services to the handicapped student in a specially staffed resource room. The resource room model may be adapted and restructured in the following ways:

■ The resource room teacher provides direct services to exceptional children by, for example, improving deficient reading comprehension skills, remediating fine motor skills, or concentrating on vocational skills.

■ The resource room teacher provides direct services to the regular classroom teachers who have exceptional children in their classrooms. Direct service could include helping one teacher develop alternative management strategies or assisting a group of teachers in developing individualized instruction techniques. The regular classroom teachers are directly involved with teaching students who have special learning and behavior needs.

■ The resource room teacher provides direct services to both regular classroom teachers and exceptional learners.

A model that requires the interaction of both the regular classroom and the resource room is more desirable than a model that provides services only to handicapped children because the special help to both the teacher and the student creates a mutual interest between the regular classroom teacher and the special education teacher. The services the resource teacher offers can vary from discussing educational problems to being present at parent/teacher conferences.

SELF-CONTAINED, SPECIAL CLASS   For students who need full-time help, the self-contained, special education class within the public school may be the least restrictive environment. This setting is usually used for moderately or severely handicapped students, although some mildly handicapped students may be included. The instruction in such classes is usually individualized for the entire day by a certified special education teacher.

SPECIAL SCHOOLS   If a neighborhood school with a special education class cannot supply special services, the student may be placed in a local, special day school. Frequently, educational services as well as other extensive support service needs are met. For example, if a student has a severe physical impairment that requires extensive daily therapy and an adapted physical environment, a school with an appropriately trained staff and equipment would be the least restrictive environment. For example, the St. Francis Achievement Center in Toledo, Ohio, is designed to meet the needs of children and youth with severe behavior disorders. The students enrolled in the Center come from many school districts within a large metropolitan area. They meet several times weekly with therapists and other specialists. Although this education environment allows for little interaction with the nonhandicapped peer group, it is the least restrictive environment for these students. Because of additional specialized staff and equipment, materials, etc., the special school is often better able to meet all the needs of the child than a self-contained public school classroom. Students who participate in day-school programs return to their families at the end of the day.

HOMEBOUND INSTRUCTION   Homebound instruction is an option for meeting the educational needs of children unable to attend school for an extended period of time. For example, for a child recovering from open heart surgery or an automobile accident, this service may be the most appropriate delivery system. It can be either temporary or continuous. Individual instruction is provided in the home by a certified teacher.

RESIDENTIAL FACILITY   Residential facilities may be required for severely and profoundly handicapped students if the local school system cannot meet their needs in the special education class or day school. Although the child receives 24-hour care, it is often difficult to create a "family" setting or environment for the handicapped. In the past, such institutions were large and situated in somewhat remote locations. However, community-based facilities are becoming more popular because they are designed to serve fewer students. Moreover, they are located closer to the student's family, thus allowing for frequent home visits. As in any other delivery service model, the IEP must be monitored.

Regardless of where a child is placed, whether in a regular class or a residential setting, it is the responsibility of the local school system to provide the services at no cost to the parents.

FACTORS RELATED TO SUCCESSFUL IMPLEMENTATION OF THE IEP

Successful implementation of the IEP depends on two issues: (1) attitudes toward exceptional people; and (2) appropriate training for teachers working with exceptional children. If these issues are not resolved, the possibilities for meeting the needs of exceptional students in the regular classroom are not good.

Attitudes and Training

The handicapped child in an integrated educational environment with nonhandicapped children is usually a new experience for everyone involved—the teacher, the nonhandicapped peer group, and the handicapped child. Because our society does not foster interactions with handicapped people, we tend to have negative perceptions of them. As a result, we form stereotyped images of the handicapped. For example, Ms. Breman, a fourth-grade teacher, was informed that Karen, a young blind girl, would be placed in her classroom in two weeks. During that two-week period, the teacher imagined all the tasks that Karen could not do. When Karen finally entered the class, Ms. Breman was surprised at Karen's ability to function independently in the classroom—her behavior did not resemble Ms. Breman's perceptions of what the visually impaired could do.

Zawadski (Birch, 1974, pp. 89–95) reported that regular teachers who had never been exposed to an educable mentally retarded (EMR) child had many concerns about integrating handicapped students with nonhandicapped students. Some apprehensions experienced by the regular teachers concerned:

1. Inappropriate classroom behavior
2. Curriculum
3. Negative behavior of regular class pupils toward an EMR child in the regular class
4. Problems of organization for instruction
5. Lack of teacher preparation and/or experience
6. Emotional problems of the EMR child
7. Negative attitudes of adults toward EMR children in regular classes
8. Lack of support services
9. Problems of physical defects
10. Safety
11. Inadequate assessment of achievement
12. Special health factor problems
13. Unfair grading policy of the school
14. Family problems of EMR children
15. Teacher liability

This list is representative of teacher concerns about the handicapped in general, not just the EMR. The attitude of the teacher can directly influence the success of any mainstreaming effort. Positive attitudes are the most effective ones for success. In addition to classroom influence, Zawadski also found that influence among teachers, administrators, and the community is reciprocal; that is, one's attitude tends to affect the attitudes of others.

Regular classroom teachers may sometimes feel inadequate regarding mainstreaming. This feeling may exist because the classroom teachers may receive little help from resource room teachers once the program has begun. The resource teacher would probably be more effective as a consultant to the regular teacher rather than directly teaching the handicapped child. However, many resource teachers are trained to deal only with handicapped children, not with other teachers. Since most teacher training programs tend to ignore communication skills with adults, no vehicle for communication is developed. Further, the effectiveness of the resource room program is decreased if the regular classroom teacher is not allowed input into the program. The loser is the mainstreamed student.

Regular classroom teachers tend to accept handicapped children more when they have close contact with them. In fact, many regular teachers were pleasantly surprised at the success of handicapped students mainstreamed into their classes. They commented that special education students were not different—and that some were better than the regular students (Birch, 1974). In a study by Johnston (1972), regular classroom teachers stated that having an educationally handicapped child in the class did not hinder progress. They also believed that these children were making greater academic advances. The presence and assistance of resource personnel in forming educational objectives made them more willing to work with the children.

Some studies indicate that negative attitudes can result from the labeling of exceptional children. Combs and Harper (1967) found that teachers made more negative responses to children who were labeled as exceptional than to exceptional children not so labeled. Foster, Ysseldyke, and Reese (1975) found the same response even though the handicapped children were exhibiting normal behavior.

Mandell and Strain (1978) measured teacher attitudes toward the integration of handicapped children into regular classrooms. Implications were that the teachers perceived a need for special methods and materials in teaching the handicapped children, thus reflecting a lack of confidence in their own abilities. Regular educators require assistance in developing realistic teaching techniques for exceptional learners.

Preparation for Integration

Preparing nonhandicapped students for integration with the handicapped should be an essential ingredient in curriculum planning. It is through positive experiences and constructive interaction that the handicapped will be accepted by their nonhandicapped peers. A study of children's attitudes toward the physically handicapped showed that nonhandicapped children's attitudes toward the physically handicapped become more positive after an integrative school experience. Before integration, able-bodied students thought the handicapped needed help. After integration, the physically handicapped were viewed as more capable of taking care of themselves. Thus, possibly the best preparation of nonhandicapped children is direct contact with handicapped children (Rapier, Adelson, Carey, and Croke, 1974).

Children learn from adults. If a teacher is looked upon as a "model" by students, that teacher's attitudes and beliefs can influence those of his or her pupils. If an integrated program is to be successful, the receiving teacher must believe that the handicapped student can fit into the academic and social environment of the classroom. Also, the regular and special education teachers should jointly plan classroom activities. This is important in order to develop the nonhandicapped students' sensitivity and awareness of the exceptional students' needs, strengths, and weaknesses. Finally, regardless of the kind of exceptionality, it is imperative that teachers skillfully prepare the exceptional student for entering an integrated learning environment.

SUMMARY POINTS

■ PL 94–142 mandates that an IEP be written for each handicapped person identified as needing special education and/or related services. No IEP is required for handicapped students able to be educated without special education instruction.

■ School districts may choose their own IEP format and may include additional information. However, the law lists specific data to be included in the IEP and specific procedural guidelines for developing the IEP.

■ The IEP must be reviewed annually to determine the appropriateness of the present program. The annual IEP review should prevent handicapped students from being locked into a special program.

■ Whereas the Total Service Plan identifies annual goals, the IIP lists specific short-term objectives for use in the classroom or in a related service setting. The IIP outlines instructional strategies, materials, and criteria for determining successful completion of each objective.

■ To comply with PL 94–142, the IEP committee must include an evaluation expert, the parents or guardians, the student (if appropriate), the student's teachers, and a representative of the local school system who is knowledgeable in the area of special education.

■ The IEP committee functions to determine a student's current level of performance, to identify annual goals and short-term objectives, to list special education and related services, and to establish a process for monitoring and evaluating the IEP.

■ Throughout the development of the IEP, the local education agency must document that appropriate efforts were made to include the student's parents or guardians in the IEP process. Regarding procedural safeguards, PL 94–142 specifies that if the parents or guardians are dissatisfied with either the document or the process, they have the right to an impartial hearing.

■ The IEP focuses on the total development of a handicapped student, not just on his or her academic growth. As indicated by the listing of related services, a handicapped student must, if he or she needs it, be provided with a wide range of services, including, but not limited to, psychomotor, cognitive, social, emotional, and medical service.

■ When determining the placement for a handicapped student, the IEP committee is mandated to select an educational setting that provides the least restrictive environment for that particular student.

■ Success in integrating handicapped students is related to the preparation of both regular and special educators. Teacher education programs, both at the preservice and in-service levels, may have to modify their curricula in order to furnish positive and realistic mainstreaming experiences for both handicapped and nonhandicapped students alike.

1. Under what circumstances might a parent or guardian request an impartial hearing?
2. Collect two different IEP forms from local school systems and examine their content. How does each compare with PL 94–142 guidelines? Is one preferable? If so, why?
3. Discuss the purpose and procedural rationale for including the IEP in PL 94–142.
4. What are some reasons that a school system might decide not to require an IEP?
5. Identify three learning activities or experiences that might help regular teachers develop more positive attitudes toward exceptional people.
6. Do you think that the IEP, specifically, and PL 94–142, in general, are examples of the federal government controlling public education? List advantages and disadvantages of such mandates.
7. Does your state require a prescribed IEP form?

THE IEP—A VEHICLE FOR DEVELOPING COMMUNICATION BETWEEN TEACHERS

The IEP can be a vehicle for developing effective communication among teachers and the success of its implementation is related to positive interaction. Thus, the IEP should be both a process for and a product of positive communication among professionals.

Because many exceptional children receive their education via the resource room, it is imperative that regular and resource room teachers communicate. Yet, too often, they talk at, rather than with, each other. A major cause for this lack of communication is the maintenance of traditional roles (Speece and Mandell, 1980).

The resource room teacher, assuming a superior role, is usually the giver of information. It is a widely accepted, but erroneous, belief that special educators are the only professionals capable of teaching exceptional children. Too often, the resource teachers transmit this sense of superiority to regular teachers, who then assume a passive receiving role when it comes to teaching exceptional children. These stereotyped roles inhibit effective communication.

The following conversation was overheard in a teachers' lounge. Ms. Stickles, the resource room teacher, and Ms. Calhoun, the regular third-grade teacher, are talking about Matthew, who is learning disabled. He spends 30 minutes in the resource room and the rest of the day in Ms. Calhoun's class. Both teachers are in the process of gathering information for Matthew's annual review.

MS. CALHOUN: Matthew just doesn't seem to be making it in my class.
MS. STICKLES: He's doing OK in my class.
MS. CALHOUN: Yesterday he forgot his homework. This morning he didn't have it again. I just don't know what to do...it takes him forever to get his paperwork done. [sigh]
MS. STICKLES: Boy! Those hyperactive or distractible kids! Tell me! I know, I have a whole room filled with LD kids. Somehow I manage. I've got to go now and work on my IEPs.
MS. CALHOUN: Speaking of IEPs, when did Mr. Winn [principal] say they were due? I'm not sure what information goes into an annual review.
[Ms. Stickles walks out and returns to her class.]

What really took place in this conversation was parallel talk, rather than a dialogue. After analyzing the comments, the following conclusions can be made:

■ Ms. Calhoun recognizes that Matthew is not learning in her class. If he is not learning, she probably feels that she is not a successful teacher. No one likes failure; this can result in frustration and/or anger. Her willingness to discuss Matthew is a plea for help.

■ Ms. Stickles' comments can be interpreted as maintaining a superior attitude. Not only is Matthew doing all right in her class, but she implies that she can teach a whole class of Matthews—in other words, she is a superior teacher.

■ The scenario ends with Ms. Stickles ignoring Ms. Calhoun's request for information on the IEPs. Although unintentional, Ms. Stickles may have cemented the barrier between the two. She leaves to return to her IEPs, and Ms. Calhoun remains feeling rebuffed and inept.

Who is responsible for bridging the communication gap? Since it is the resource room teacher who has the expertise, it is his or her responsibility to take the initiative in establishing rapport with other teachers. Special educators must learn to share their knowledge and skills. Matthew, who is typical of most children in resource rooms, spends more time with the regular classroom teacher. If the regular teacher is a failure, then these children are failing, too; no one is a winner.

The educational success of children with special needs is dependent upon interprofessional communication.

What can the resource room teacher do to facilitate communication?

■ *Accept the trouble-shooter role.* Since frustration produces anger, the resource room teacher should expect to be the target of the regular teacher's misplaced anger. If the resource teacher becomes defensive and angry, an opportunity for mutual cooperation may be lost. Therefore, it is important that the resource teacher recognize when the regular teacher is asking for help, even if it comes by way of a verbal attack.

■ *Be a good listener.* This is often difficult for teachers who usually do the talking. However, listening carefully to how, why, and what the regular teacher is saying can provide valuable information on that teacher's needs and priorities.

■ *Plan time for communication.* The resource and regular teachers must discuss their mutual concerns, plan programs, and evaluate progress. These discussions should be on an impersonal level. Their purpose is to solve problems, not belittle or scrutinize each other's teaching practices. Such discussions should be conducted on a positive note.

■ *Provide realistic suggestions.* What works in a classroom for 9 or 10 children may not work in a class of 25. The resource teacher can share ideas and demonstrate how materials can be adapted for the regular classroom.

■ *Recognize fallibility.* Although the resource teacher might be able to solve many problems, no one person can find the right solution all the time. By being open and honest, the resource teacher transmits a feeling of equality, rather than superiority. When this occurs, much can be accomplished (Hawisher and Calhoun, 1978; Lott, Hudak, and Scheetz, 1975; Wiederholt, Hammill, and Brown, 1978).

These recommendations for establishing an effective teacher partnership are also intended for regular teachers. They, too, must be good listeners, take an active part in the planning process, and be able to provide alternative methods in the regular classroom.

Keeping these suggestions in mind, let's reconstruct the previous dialogue. Now it might sound like this:

MS. CALHOUN: Matthew just doesn't seem to be making it in my class.

MS. STICKLES: I've noticed that Matthew is having difficulty in my class, too. What seems to be the problem?

MS. CALHOUN: Yesterday he forgot his homework. This morning he didn't have it again. I just don't know what to do...it takes him forever to get his seatwork done. [sigh] Does he hand in his homework for your class?

MS. STICKLES: Sometimes. But I really think you've hit upon one of Matthew's problems. Completing seatwork on time. Maybe we could sit down and try to think of some way to keep him on task.

MS. CALHOUN: Do you have any ideas?

MS. STICKLES: I saw a friend of mine who teaches fourth grade in another building. She gave me some ideas on how she uses individual contracts for her class of 28 students. Can you come by my class, or I'll stop by yours, after school today? I'll be working on my IEP evaluations, so any time is fine.

MS. CALHOUN: Okay. Listen, about those IEPs, I have some questions. Can we...?

MS. STICKLES: Sure!

In conclusion, the resource teacher's role is initially time-consuming, and one must realize that changes do not occur overnight. The myth that regular teachers cannot teach exceptional children will not be easy to erase. Only when communication is a two-way process can effective interdisciplinary efforts succeed and better meet the educational needs of exceptional children.

1. This application discusses techniques for resource teachers to facilitate communication. List several techniques that regular teachers could use to develop effective communication with resource teachers.
2. This chapter discusses three role options for the resource teacher. What are the major advantages and disadvantages of each approach? Which option was used in the application example?

SUGGESTED READINGS

Torres, S., ed. *A Primer on Individualized Education Programs for Handicapped Children*. Reston, Va.: Foundation for Exceptional Children, 1977.

Turnbull, A. P., Strickland, B. B., and Brantley, J. C. *Developing and Implementing Individualized Education Programs*. Columbus, Ohio: Charles E. Merrill, 1978.

Wiederholt, J., Hammill, D., and Brown, V. *The Resource Teacher: A Guide to Effective Practices*. Boston: Allyn and Bacon, 1978.

5

PARENT AND FAMILY PERSPECTIVES

CONTENTS

Each year the public school districts gain more knowledge concerning how to better plan and implement high quality, sophisticated IEPs for handicapped children. Successfully implementing those plans, however, depends upon the development of a parent/professional partnership. Frequently, this partnership does not exist, and the full potential of the IEP is thus never realized.

This chapter will discuss the parents and families of handicapped children and youth. Parental feelings, characteristics, problems, and concerns will be described. Methods of establishing cooperation and communication between parents and school personnel will be examined.

There is now a trend toward recognizing parents as partners in their child's educational process. Despite this emphasis, residual feelings that parents are to blame for the child's difficulties still exist. A generation ago, many psychologists and educators believed strongly that parents were the primary cause of most of their children's problems. This attitude naturally did not promote a positive climate for mutual trust and communication between parents and professionals. Rather, it led to a negative relationship characterized by distrust, suspicion, and defensiveness. When the parent was placed in the role of scapegoat, effective parent/professional teams did not usually result. Labeling parents and families often had negative effects similar to those experienced in categorizing handicapped children. These labels often isolated parents from teachers and from other professionals.

VIEWING PARENTS AND THEIR CHILDREN

Parental and family influences obviously play a key role in the social and academic development of the child. Thus, the family environment should be assessed to gain clearer insight into the child's development and current circumstances. The attitudes of their parents are extremely important in children's lives. Do the parents accept the child? Are they overprotective? Do they tend to ignore the child's problems? Professionals must recognize that in the past such questioning often led to both blaming and inappropriately labeling parents rather than to helping develop educational strategies for the child. Continued emphasis by professionals on examining families of exceptional children has at times led to biased views and mutual distrust. Professionals themselves may have been guilty of holding one set of expectations for parents of handicapped children and another for parents of normal children. Parents of exceptional children are often expected to perform with unrealistically high levels of parenting skill. The excerpts following (Cansler, Martin, and Voland, 1975) indicate that members of our society often perceive the behavior of parents of handicapped children differently. Regarding mothers and stress (p. 13):

> The working mother of normal children screams at the kids and breaks into tears after a horrid supper. She is said to be overworked and in need of a good night's rest. The working mother of a handicapped child does the same. She is said to be out of control emotionally and is urged to seek psychiatric help.

Regarding father's pride (p. 14):

> A father says that some day his beautiful daughter will be the first woman President. He, it is said, is prideful. Another father says that some day his beautiful daughter will walk. He, it is said, is unaccepting.

And on parents and schoolwork (p. 14):

> The parents of a normal child are told that because their child is having reading difficulty, it would be "nice" if they could work with him at home. The parents of an exceptional child are told that if they do not work with their child, he will not learn.

These examples are reminders to all professionals working with parents and families of handicapped children that parents are human beings and should be treated with understanding and respect.

WHY INVOLVE PARENTS?

The "Great Society" programs of the 1960s were aimed at providing comprehensive services to the poor and developing early childhood educational programs. They also stimulated research projects on the subject of interaction of family/parents and the child. These investigations demonstrated that parental involvement does make a difference in children's school performances. In educational programs where parental involvement was emphasized, the children scored significantly higher than comparison groups on achievement tests and intelligence tests (Nedler and Oralie, 1979). Through increased parental involvement, pupils' feelings of importance, their self-concepts, and their perceptions of their control over the environment improved. Subsequent improvement in their attitudes toward schoolwork made positive differences in their achievement levels (Rioux, 1978; Spencer, 1979).

Developing parent/teacher partnerships is also outlined within PL 94–142. This mandate includes these provisions for parent participation:

- Prior notice must be given to parents before any change in a current program is made (e.g., changes such as placement in special classes or the involvement of a resource teacher in the child's instructional program).

- Prior notice must be given to parents before any special education assessments are performed.

- Parents are to have full access to their child's school records.

- A surrogate parent may be assigned to use procedures on behalf of a child who is a ward of the state or whose parents are unknown or otherwise unavailable.

PL 94–142 has caused more attention to be paid to parents' rights. Parents are encouraged by the law to help plan their children's education. They must be invited to become a part of the team that formulates the children's IEP and have annual conferences with the teacher and other school personnel. Educators must be certain that the parents comprehend everything that transpires in these conferences, and they should make every effort to involve the parents in such activities. Also, before a child can be placed in a special program, the school must have the parents' consent. Parents must be included in team meetings that evaluate and assess the factors that influence these program decisions. Each local school district must make available to parents publications that explain their part in the special education process.

Sometimes, depending upon the severity of the handicap, goals previously set for the child need to be readjusted or abandoned. In these circumstances parents may be faced with the realization that their child might need constant attention for his or her entire life. Naturally, in many cases, initial reactions are strictly emotional —feelings of guilt and dismay—and questions such as "Why us?" are often expressed. Parents seek explanations for their having a handicapped child. Reasons such as marital discord, unusual sexual practices, use of drugs, and events occurring during pregnancy are among those felt by overwrought and anxious parents. In any event, the birth of such a child often produces high levels of guilt and anxiety.

A typical reaction of parents when they first learn of their child's handicap is cited by Schult (1975): "We feel utterly alone, helpless and convinced that no one else had ever faced this particular tragedy..." (p. 6). After the initial shock has subsided, the crucial concern is then the long-term reaction. This parental attitude is the most influential in the ongoing relationship with their child. It has the power to strengthen or weaken, to inspire or stifle. Will the parents overprotect the child from the outside world? Will they ignore the problem? Will they pity or truly accept the child?

Parents are typically afraid, no matter how positive their initial reaction was. They feel alienated from others; they think that no one else has a problem like theirs. They are suddenly confronted with problems they do not understand. Lack of knowledge often stimulates fear. Even full comprehension of their problems will not always alleviate the fear and pain involved in raising an exceptional child. In one case, the mother of a retarded child was herself a professional in the field of exceptional children. Despite her knowledge and skill in that area, she harbored many negative feelings that resulted from her interactions with the family and with others in her daily life. She reported that she was hurt by cold-shouldering neighbors who uttered subtle negative comments, and also by her family. Her sister, her father, her husband, and school and church officials all contributed to her problems (Michaelis, 1974).

In another case, the parents of a retarded child institutionalized at an early age seemed to forget that the child existed. Later, when state officials returned him to the community, the parents realized to their horror that they no longer wanted their son. This revelation was a devastating shock to them ("Case History: Who Shall We Sacrifice?" *Exceptional Parent*, 1975). Also, some parents express fear that the abnormality might be hereditary and will affect any unborn children. They are confused about where to place the guilt; they do not know who or what is actually responsible for their predicament. They wonder what their new responsibilities will be. *Will* they have to take care of the child for the rest of his or her life? What if one or both of the parents should die? They wonder how society, their friends, and their family will think of them. Will people see them differently? Will they be shunned? Or will they still be accepted into their family and their familiar circle of friends? (Schult, 1975).

Phillip Roos, who is both an active professional in special education and a parent of a handicapped child, views the anxieties that exceptional parents suffer as exaggerations of typical human problems. Raising a child with handicaps, however, tends to increase our awareness of these problems. He categorizes these conflicts and anxieties as follows (1978):

Like other children, the handicapped child has a need for being a part of everyday family life.

- *Loss of Self-Esteem*: Parents typically perceive their children as extensions of themselves. Therefore, if a child is defective, they may feel that their own self-worth is being questioned.
- *Shame*: Parents may sense the rejection and ridicule that others in society have for their child. The realization that their child is being laughed at may generate feelings of shame for which their feelings of love may provide only a partial protection.
- *Ambivalence*: All parents have mixed feelings at various times regarding their children. Children's inappropriate behavior may lead to the parents feeling resentment and anger. Parents may even wish that they never had the child. In turn, they may feel guilty for having these negative feelings. They may react to these mixed feelings with overprotection or rejection. For parents with handicapped children, these conditions are intensified.
- *Depression*: Parents of handicapped children, especially those with severe handicaps, may be very discouraged about the future. Parents may experience sorrow similar to that experienced when a loved one is lost.
- *Self-Sacrifice*: Some parents may react to having a handicapped child by adopting the martyr role. Total dedication to their exceptional child at great personal sacrifice may also involve neglect of other family members, siblings, and spouse.
- *Defensiveness*: Some parents may become extremely sensitive to remarks or actions that they think are critical of their child. Their responses to these perceived criticisms may involve resentment toward the other person and/or refusal to recognize the child's problems.

THE ELUSIVE GRIEVING PROCESS

The birth of a child into a family is ordinarily a time of stress as well as joy. It is also a time of high expectations (e.g., fulfillment in marriage and the beginning of an unlimited range of events, such as the first words, the first steps, and birthday parties). However, if the child is handicapped, many expectations are not met and the parents face a reality for which they had not been prepared. The stress is intensified.

The loss that parents experience after giving birth to a handicapped child has been described as the **elusive grieving process**, a phrase borrowed from Elisabeth Kübler-Ross's 1969 study of dying (Moses, 1979, 1978, 1977). The parents have dreamed and fantasized about experiencing unconditional love from the child and seeing him or her become someone important. They are disappointed, however, because very few of these dreams survive the birth of a handicapped child. The parents grieve at their loss and, because this grief goes unrecognized by our society, it is elusive. This process is automatic, and is absolutely necessary if parents are to "detach" themselves from what has been lost and thus avoid living in the past. This five-stage process (described in the following sections) should be acknowledged, but our society tends to frown on the sharing of grief resulting from these losses.

Stage One: Denial

Parents often refuse to believe the existence of a handicap, the permanence of it, or its impact on the life of the entire family. This denial process is positive and necessary. When catastrophe hits, we are unprepared to deal with the loss of personal omnipotence. We need time to gather enough ego strength to cope with things again. Denial is a mechanism that buys time to reorganize life. Denial will vanish when the environment becomes supportive and strengths are rebuilt. At this stage, the professional should offer an attitudinal framework that accepts the legitimacy of denial. Others who judge the denying parent create a tremendous pressure. If the professional lets the grieving person know that resisting the information is legitimate and reasonable, some of that pressure is alleviated. People will move through denial at their own rates, no matter what is done.

Stage Two: Guilt

Parents' guilt (which makes those around them feel uncomfortable) is manifested in one of three ways. The least common is displayed by having a concrete story that the parent caused the handicap by some specific past action. For example, the mother may believe that she is at fault because she did not take care of herself during pregnancy. A second form of guilt is seen in the belief that "bad things happen to bad people; therefore, I am bad." A third form—the most frequently found and the most difficult to deal with—resides in the belief that the impaired child is a just punishment for something that the parent has done.

Guilt forces the parents to work through their discomfort and to come to terms with the "whys" of existence. Parents ask themselves repeatedly why this has happened to them. This is a debilitating but necessary step. The professional accepts the pain and then keeps quiet and listens. Parents must be reassured that guilt is a human dilemma that needs to be shared. When you experience loss, you sometimes experience guilt. The parent does not need analytic interpretations but does need encouragement to feel the pain and to talk about it.

Stage Three: Depression

Depression—the next stage of the grieving process—is anger turned inward. Parents punish themselves because they cannot do what they want to do—that is, to make the child nonhandicapped. The professional often feels depression, too, for the same reason. Our culture holds that depression is pathological, and society is prone to reject the depressed person. While our society implies that normal people do not feel depressed, depression is often an appropriate reaction. Frequently when a person is feeling great pain and loss, no one in the world can "cure" the unhappiness. What should one do? The professional should offer these persons an environment where they can talk about their impotence and misery. The depression phase allows people to accept that which cannot be changed. It, too, will pass if parents are allowed to air their feelings.

Stage Four: Anger

Anger occurs on two levels. One is palatable, and the other is heinous. The palatable anger, which can be readily accepted, is often expressed as "why me?" The other is usually unspoken and frequently gets displaced onto the spouse, a sibling, or a professional. This silent anger is actually hatred for the handicapped child. Because this feeling is so ugly and primitive, parents often bury it deep within themselves and then turn with intense anger on the healthy sibling or the spouse. If someone can create an environment that will allow the parents to openly express this kind of anger, they will learn to accept it and to move on with their grief.

Stage Five: Bargaining

The last stage is bargaining, where the parent attempts to make a deal with science, with God, or with anyone. It is a "last ditch" attempt to cure the child.

Not all parents of handicapped children go through all five stages, and the intensity and duration of each stage varies from parent to parent. Teachers and other professionals should be aware that the process is often repeated at critical junctures of the child's and family's life cycle. Developmental milestones, such as reaching school age, attaining puberty, graduating from school, times when peers are getting married, and the parents' retirement trigger another recycling through the process. Each time, parents become more and more accepting of their own feelings. They continue to deepen their coping skills.

SIBLING REACTIONS

Gath (1974) found that older brothers and sisters are more affected by the presence of an exceptional child than younger siblings are. Sisters appear to be more affected than brothers because they are the ones expected to deal with the burdens of actual caring for the handicapped child. Also, studies have shown that the exceptional child's feelings about his or her family are typically less positive than those of the brothers and sisters.

Parents of the handicapped are also generally less satisfied with the effectiveness of their family life than parents with normal children. In some cases, normal siblings may attempt to avoid intimacy with the handicapped child by participating excessively in extracurricular activities outside of the home (Van der Veen and Novak, 1974). Of course, there are also families in which brothers and sisters of exceptional children assist with any treatments that might be required, play with the child, and protect him or her from the abuses and cruelty of others (Robinet, 1978). However, these siblings also may have special feelings concerning their family. It is often useful for parents and professionals to be sensitive to these matters in order to assist the brothers and sisters in their own efforts at judgment. Following are some concerns and feelings of siblings that are described in *Working with Families* (Cansler, et al., 1975, p. 105).

1. Siblings wonder what caused their brother's or sister's handicap and sometimes fear that something may be wrong with themselves.
2. Siblings sometimes feel that having to help take care of the handicapped child interferes with their own activities.
3. Siblings may want to talk with their parents about the handicapped child's problems but do not know how to bring up the subject.
4. Siblings may feel upset and angry that parents have to spend a lot of time with the handicapped child. Sometimes siblings try to get attention from the parents by acting like the handicapped child.
5. Some siblings feel that they have to work extra hard (in school, sports, etc.) to make up to parents for the handicapped child's deficiencies.
6. Siblings worry about how to tell their friends that they have a handicapped brother or sister and wonder whether their friends will make fun of them or the family for being different.
7. Siblings wonder whether they will be able to marry and have children.
8. Siblings may worry about whether they will eventually have to take care of the handicapped child; they may wonder whether they will be able to care for them if anything happens to their parents.

Professionals who understand these sibling concerns may be able to help the parents and the normal children in the family adjust.

REACTIONS OF THE EXTENDED FAMILY

Parents can find empathy, support, and guidance from the extended family, the community, and professionals. Grandparents, brothers and sisters of parents, as well as other relatives, can be very supportive at such times of crisis. In many communities, programs and workshops are conducted for training grandparents and other relatives to deal with the problems of handicapped children in families (Rhoades, 1975). In one case study, overzealous but well-meaning grandparents virtually took over the responsibilities of rearing their handicapped grandchild from their daughter, who resented such extreme and interfering attention. The daughter wanted to be allowed to raise her child at least semi-independently. The grandparents eventually released some of their hold on the handicapped child and redirected their energies to assist at a community residence for exceptional people. Even though in this instance grandparent participation was a problem, it is important to realize that "...elderly people represent an important bridge between the past and the future. They have lived long enough to see the recurring issues that are universal in all families. They are able to see that the decency of people survives the existence of problems. They are also able to provide their grandchildren, with or without disabilities, with unqualified acceptance" (*Exceptional Parent*, January/February 1974, p. 43).

For some grandparents, however, this acceptance proves to be difficult. Many tend to share the guilt feelings and fears of their son or daughter when an exceptional child is born. Some grandparents who are ordinarily eager to please are awkward and hesitant when confronted with such offspring. Many experience trouble adapting to the new situation, having never been exposed to such children or problems before. For some grandparents, avoiding the problem is one way of coping with it. Others attempt to overcome their discomfort through increased attempts at understanding.

COMMUNICATING WITH PARENTS OF EXCEPTIONAL CHILDREN

Establishing positive parent/professional partnerships depends greatly upon the ability of the professional to understand parents and to communicate effectively with them. Comprehending parents of exceptional children presupposes that one be aware of the many roles played by these parents. Communicating with parents effectively requires the use of a variety of information-sharing processes, including conferencing. A good grasp of the key factors in a counseling relationship can also aid in developing sound parent/professional communication.

Parental Roles

In working with parents of exceptional children, teachers receive parental-based information that will improve their teaching strategies. On the other hand, teachers also provide information to parents, which helps the parents to work effectively with the child at home. In order to facilitate this two-way communication, teachers and other professionals should respect the many roles that parents of handicapped children must play. While several of these roles are relevant to *all* parents, the responsibilities are intensified in the case of parents with exceptional children. These roles, described by Heward, Dardig, and Rossett (1979), are as follows:

- *Teacher*: Without systematic plans, children with learning handicaps do not learn as readily as their nonhandicapped peers. The extension of school teaching/learning processes into the home is essential for consistent, efficient learning. Also, some parents may be required to teach their handicapped children how to use certain prosthetic devices (artificial replacements of missing or defective parts of the body).
- *Counselor*: Exceptional children have the same anxieties and joys as other children. In addition, parents of these children are concerned about others' perceptions and possible rejection of them, the future of their children and their inability to participate in those tasks in which many of their age-mates are engaged.

Like all parents, parents of the handicapped child have a need to enjoy their children.

- *Behavior Manager*: Some exceptional children exhibit a wide range of inappropriate behaviors. Thus, parents often find themselves in the challenging position of helping these children to develop appropriate behavioral patterns to replace the aggressive, self-injurious, or inappropriate self-stimulating behaviors.
- *Parent of Nonhandicapped Siblings*: The relationship of parents to the handicapped child's siblings are often strained. The parent must help the brothers and sisters (a) to understand the exceptional child, (b) to assist in cooperative teacher/family instructing in the home, and (c) to respond appropriately to the jeers and queries of their peers.
- *Spouse*: Exceptional children often place a real strain on the parent-to-parent relationship. If home/school cooperative efforts are to be successful, both parents must agree with the plans. This means that parents must cement their own relationship to prevent it from being pulled apart by the critical issues involved in raising exceptional children.
- *Educator of Significant Others*: In addition to immediate family members, there are many others with whom the handicapped comes into contact. These significant others (e.g., neighbors, relatives, storekeepers) have an influence on the child's development too critical to leave to chance. The parent has the responsibility to educate these persons so that the child's progress is not inadvertently impaired by some random, inappropriate behavior on the part of others.
- *School/Community-Relations Person*: As we have discussed, parents of exceptional children have certain rights and responsibilities under the law. It is important for them to understand these rights and responsibilities and to act

One-Way	Two-Way
Advantages	
1. A great deal of reference material can be sent to parents	1. Opportunity for cooperative planning between parent and teacher
2. Updating on programs is frequent	2. Teacher has opportunity to perceive family interactions
3. Little time is necessary to dispense information	3. Follows the intent of PL 94–142
4. Written information can be referred to a later time	4. Helps involve the parent in the total education system
Disadvantages	
1. Little direct contact or interaction	1. Time consuming
2. Lack of parent-teacher involvement in planning and interaction	2. Parents may not be as informed because of time that elapses between conferences
3. Misunderstandings arise due to un-answered questions	3. Teachers not always trained in parent conferencing techniques
4. Teachers have little understanding of family interactions affecting the handi-capped child	4. Other school personnel and teachers do not always communicate the same information to parents

(From *Parenting Learning-Problem Children: The Professional Educator's Perspective*, D. Edge, B. J. Strenecky, and S. I. Mour, 1978. Reprinted by permission of the National Center for Educational Media and Materials for the Handicapped.)

accordingly. In doing so, they are quite likely to develop close relationships with the schools and, more broadly, with agencies and institutions within the larger community.

Information Sharing

Information sharing by schools and teachers with parents of exceptional children has traditionally followed the one-way model, the two-way model, or some combination thereof. While both models have advantages and disadvantages (as depicted in Table 5-1), the two-way system is preferred by those educators who are truly attempting to establish parent/school partnerships. Following this model, parents are able to participate in the development of the IEP by providing input, such as their observations of the child's developmental history and his or her behavior outside of the school. The two-way process fosters cooperation and the development of constructive programs. Overuse of the more traditional one-way model has led in the past to a breakdown in teacher/parent communication and the typical subsequent negative feelings (Edge, et al., 1978).

Conferencing

Those teachers and schools that follow the two-way model will establish a procedure for parent/teacher conferences. In planning and implementing these conferences, it is recommended that the teacher follow the general guidelines suggested by Cramer (1978):

I. Preparing for the Conference
   A. If you have had little or no experience with parent conferences, role-play a conference with a colleague or a friend to upgrade your confidence.
   B. Be sure that your communications, written or verbal, are friendly.
   C. Indicate in your invitation how much time is available for the conference.
   D. Prepare a folder that includes examples of the child's work, current accomplishments, etc. This folder may be taken home by the parent and should serve as a reminder to the parent or the child of the positive relationship between home and school.
   E. Prepare notes on particular concerns and commendations you wish to share with the parents.
   F. List goals and objectives for the conference to keep on target. Parents certainly may raise issues that need to be discussed, but your list of goals provides the basic framework and direction.
   G. Make sure that parents who arrive early have a comfortable place to wait.

II. Conducting the Conference
   A. Greet the parent warmly and begin the conference with an encouraging note about the child's progress.
   B. Listen carefully to the parent, accepting the expression of his or her feelings, ideas, and attitudes. This sincere interest does not mean you approve or disapprove, but that you do respect the parent and desire to form a partnership.
   C. Avoid educational jargon. If you cannot find a synonym for a specific, professional educational term, be sure to explain it.
   D. Avoid comparing the child to other children in school or to older brothers and sisters.
   E. At the conclusion of the conference, summarize the discussion and any steps for action that have been agreed upon. Make sure that your summary communicates your appreciation of the parent's ideas.
   F. Be sure the parent knows when you are planning to meet again and that you are available for a conference at other times, if necessary.

III. Follow-Up and Evaluation
   A. Devise plans for evaluation of each conference. List goals and objectives for planning strategies or plans of action over a period of time. This will help you to identify progress.
   B. Inform other teachers who need to be aware of the plans resulting from the conference and/or of any decisions reached.
   C. Carry out the plans agreed upon. Provide feedback to the parents before the next personal conference.

Counseling

At times, teachers working closely with parents (especially those of exceptional children) find themselves in the role of helper or counselor. While teachers are not expected to perform the duties of a professional psychological counselor, they are often the first professional with whom a parent is able to establish a trusting relationship. Parents frequently request referral to a professional counselor following the establishment of such a relationship. All teachers, therefore, should be aware of the characteristics of a good counselor so that they may incorporate them into their own helping style as they work with parents. Understanding these characteristics can also aid the teacher in subsequently deciding to refer the parents for additional help.

Stewart (1978) has suggested that a good counselor is one who: (1) is interested in people; (2) is accepting, trusting, and respectful; (3) is empathetic; (4) is able to establish rapport readily; (5) is honest and genuine; (6) is attentive; (7) behaves ethically; and (8) understands human behavior. Teachers who desire to establish positive relationships should analyze their behavior in terms of these characteristics and seek opportunities to develop these interpersonal skills.

PARENT GROUPS

As early as 1921, parents of handicapped children were organizing groups concerned with their special parenting problems. The most influential group at that time was the National Society for Crippled Children. In the 1930s, parent groups were predominantly self-help in nature with a strong focus upon health and welfare. The motivation for these early groups came mainly from professionals in the field. They saw a need for increasing parental understanding and linking parents together so the problems could be discussed and ideas exchanged. However, following World War II, parents began organizing themselves without professionals. What happened was that returning veterans with physical and psychological difficulties were being integrated into society. This acceptance soon generalized to other groups of handicapped people, such as exceptional children. The main force behind parental groups in the early 1940s and 1950s was located in two powerful national organizations that grew at phenomenal rates: the National Association for Retarded Children (now called the National Association for Retarded Citizens) and the United Cerebral Palsy Association (Cain, 1976).

Parent groups often began at the local community level. Parents initially gathered to talk about problems and about ways to help each other deal with their situations. The focus was mainly on their immediate needs. Eventually, discussions turned to societal conditions and effects on the rearing of handicapped children. Too few institutions, too little public awareness, uninformed legislators, and unpublicized technical accomplishments were identified as some of the crucial problems these parents faced. As a result, the parent groups evolved into formal organizations sponsoring activities aimed primarily at public awareness.

At first, the foremost targets were educational programs. Next, they attempted to inform legislators of the need for laws that would protect handicapped children and provide them with equal educational opportunity. Other priorities of these groups included teacher training programs, sheltered workshops, and parent educational services. Once these formal organizations were firmly established, they began to organize according to various types of handicaps (e.g., cerebral palsy, blindness, deafness). Initially, these organizations grew without help from professionals. An atmosphere of distrust existed between parents and professionals as the result of poor communication and bad experiences. However, as the organizations expanded, parents recognized the need for additional skilled personnel for fund raising, public relations activities, social work, and psychological services.

Gradually, with reluctance in some cases, parent groups and professionals began working together again. Parent organizations were striving to mobilize their resources on a united national level to raise funds to lobby governmental agencies (Cain, 1976). During the last generation, these parent groups, by pressuring legislative, judicial, and educational institutions, have accomplished a great deal. They have worked with affiliated groups as well as state and federal legislatures toward eliminating public apathy and establishing programs that serve the children who require special attention. They have been influencial in the widespread acceptance of public education programs for exceptional children.

Their lobbying has helped enact the landmark PL 94–142 and other similar legislation. Parent groups have also been active in litigation that led to changes in public laws. They were influential in establishing the President's Committee on Mental Retardation and the President's Committee on Employment of the Handicapped. (Names and addresses of parent and parent/professional organizations are listed in Appendix B.)

PARENT PROGRAMS

There are various types of parent groups concerned with different aspects of exceptional conditions. Groups are classified according to their specific purposes. For example, one group may be concerned almost entirely with providing education for parents. Therefore, the parents might choose to have a study group format for their meetings. Another might be interested in self-help associations where parents can communicate with and support each other. There are also groups that interact with professional volunteers who work with parents on remediation strategies.

The first few years in the handicapped child's life are often the responsibility of the parents alone. However, few parents are equipped to meet the challenges involved. Parent groups have formed as a direct result of these needs. A variety of programs available to assist parents and parent groups are referred to by various titles, including parent psychotherapy, parent counseling, parent training, parent education, parent seminars, educational counseling, group therapy, and group counseling.

These programs can be categorized in three broad, but not mutually exclusive, approaches to parent intervention: psychotherapy, counseling, and education. Psychotherapy concerns itself with remediation for parents, which might involve the reconstruction of the parents' personalities. Counseling basically involves identity clarification, guidance, suggestions for dealing with problems, and prevention of problems. Education embraces changes in the relationships between parent and child. Parents are trained to become change agents for remediation, for prevention of problems, and for helping their children develop to their maximum potential (Neisworth and Smith, 1978).

Excellent programs that require parent/teacher teams in the identification and teaching of children are offered before the child actually begins school. Programs such as "Parent Action in Childhood Education" (PACE) and "Parents are Effective Early Education Resources" (PEERS) call for regular teacher home visits to consult with and to instruct parents, as well as to check on the child's progress. Parents and teachers get together to discuss their objectives, which are generally implemented by the parents (Schoening, 1978; Crozier, 1976).

Such early education programs encourage the parents to begin at the preschool level to play an active part in the education of their children. Therefore, once a child enters school, parents are already familiar with teachers' behavioral objectives, and less time can be spent orienting parents to school methods. Also, identifying problems and placement can be facilitated through previous partial diagnosis of weaknesses in the child's learning styles. In any event, however, parents should be urged to participate in forming the child's educational program because of their knowledge, insights, and concerns. They should work as equals on teams with the teacher and other school personnel in all assessment procedures and placement decisions.

Parents should also know something about the areas in which their child is deficient. They might take courses at universities, read specialized books, or attend the various parent education programs offered in the community.

One such series—Systematic Training for Effective Parenting (STEP)—has been used in many study groups made up of parents of exceptional children, although most of the materials in the program are for all parents (Dinkmeyer and McKay, 1976). As Calvert (1971, p. 659) states:

> Active participation by family members in early education programs may well have an effect on the educational programs that handicapped children will encounter later, where typically the involvement of family members has been passive, peripheral, or even discouraged. The generation of parents experiencing active participation in...the many aspects of education may bring about a basic change in our total educational system.

Presently, there are many training programs for parents of exceptional children. These can be structured in the manner of STEP, or they can be professionally designed to meet a particular family's requirements. Parents can often take courses to help rear their special child. For example, in the field of sex education—an even more controversial issue for the handicapped—parents can go to school to learn how best to handle the questions of their children. Several studies (Hall, et al., 1973; Looft, 1971; Turner, 1970) have found that parents of exceptional children are very sensitive to their child's need for sexual knowledge, but prefer that it is received outside the home. The majority of parents who had educable mentally retarded (EMR) students in the Turner study felt that their child had no problem dealing with or adjusting to sex. Only one-third of the parents even discussed sexual issues beyond an explanation of birth. Many parents of disabled children tend to avoid such subjects; they feel their children might not lead sexually fulfilling lives, or even reproduce, when they become adults (Turner, 1970; Hall, et al., 1973). Parents need to play a larger role in the sex education of their children, in schools by helping to establish curriculum, and at home where they can effectively answer questions and help prepare the children for adulthood.

> If the parents...are to help their children to understand the fundamentals of growth, development, reproduction, and sexuality, it seems necessary that the parents must first know and understand their own sexuality. They must know enough to be able to read between the lines of...questions or actions and to determine what kind of information or parental behavior is needed... [Alcorn, 1974, p. 128].

Sex education is only one of the many subjects that needs to be understood by parents. In the past, many areas—such as sex education—have been neglected. Future parental education programs should recognize that parents can acquire knowledge about their children along with proper guidelines for instruction. As a result of these programs, parents should be better able to care for and understand their handicapped children, their problems, feelings, and goals (Hall, et al., 1973).

A unique example of the parent/educator partnership (and perhaps a sign that schools are attempting to establish new and creative methods of working with parents) is the "Dial-a-Teacher" program. This successful experimental program, established by the Philadelphia City Schools in 1979, provides pupils with the opportunity to receive help if they get stuck on homework assignments. Pupils can telephone the Dial-a-Teacher Assistance (DATA) line and request help on a wide range of subject area difficulties. The DATA line is answered by six to eight teachers from 5:00 to 8:00 P.M., Monday through Thursday. These subject-matter specialists also have reference books and textbooks readily available to quickly respond to questions.

The educators implementing DATA report a secondary benefit of the program: often the parent gets on the DATA line with the pupil and observes how the teacher tries to help the child solve the problem. By listening to the child/teacher interaction, parents gain a better understanding of how to help children without actually doing the work for them. Also, the parents may receive additional suggestions on how they can help the child at home with this and other homework assignments in the future. Thus, Dial-a-Teacher has established a three-way partnership among parent, child, and teacher. This linking serves to enhance the level of communication necessary to promote student achievement.

BUILDING POSITIVE RELATIONSHIPS

Parents of the handicapped often feel that professionals show insufficient empathy toward themselves and their disabled children. In a 1972 poll of subscribers conducted by the journal *Exceptional Parent*, 53 percent of all parents questioned felt that professionals understood their problems with their children "not too thoroughly" or "not at all." However, most of the parents (85 percent) felt that, as a whole, American society was becoming increasingly more aware of the problems of disabled children and their families (Ward and Reale, 1972, p. 29).

Professionals must be able to empathize with parents and speak to them in clear language, not educational and/or psychological jargon. They must not become immersed in statistics, but should realize that every child is an individual, not simply another case. Research has demonstrated that training programs for children where parents work with professionals often produce positive results. Professionals can train parents in behavioral principles. They can also help parents construct and apply a therapeutic program for their children or conduct group therapy for themselves. When professionals do this, they have been able to effect changes in children's speech dysfunctions, self-injurious behaviors, oppositional behaviors (such as tantrums and disobedience), and other antisocial, immature types of behaviors (Johnson and Katz, 1973). Parents, teachers, and other professionals must work together. Each can learn from the other about how best to work with the child, for each sees the child functioning under different circumstances.

Positive parent and professional interaction is a result of careful planning.

In order to build the type of relationships required in parent/teacher partnerships, Karnes (1977) offers the following suggestions, in addition to those required by law.

- Think of parents as teacher resources.
- Provide parents with the specific knowledge to meet their expressed needs.
- Involve parents directly in classroom activities.
- Utilize activities and teaching strategies that make sense to parents.
- Arrange to have parents of handicapped children work with parents of non-handicapped children.

A teacher/parent partnership should enable the parents to gain confidence in themselves. When parents realize that the teachers respect their knowledge and experience, the professional-knows-everything block to communication will be removed. Likewise, when the parent respects the teacher's expertise by trusting the teacher's judgment, another block to communication—distrust—is removed.

CONCLUSIONS

For teachers and administrators involved with the education of exceptional children, the question relative to working with parents should be, "What kind of partnership can we form?" rather than, "Can we form a partnership?" The latter has been answered for us. Professionals are required by federal and state laws to work with parents. The type of relationship, however, is very much open for consideration and planning. Is the parent/teacher relationship characterized by grudging cooperation, forced communication, and general dissatisfaction? Or is it a positive one in which teachers welcome the parents' help, are invigorated by the opportunities to interact, and become supportive partners? The future direction of the parent/professional relationship in the schools is up to educators. They have the opportunity to develop this rich, mainly untapped, natural resource. They also have the choice of ignoring the opportunity and, in effect, wasting the talents and ideas of many parents.

The message of the social ferment of the 1960s and 1970s was that Americans want to take part in the decision-making processes of institutions that serve the public. As consumers in local school districts in the 1980s, parents want to provide input to the policy-making process affecting the education of their children. Due process requires that teachers share their experience with parents; teacher/parent cooperation is needed in determining appropriate placement for exceptional children and is essential for practical and successful sharing of authority and decision-making (Reynolds and Rosen, 1976). The choice, then, of developing sincere partnerships with parents, rather than just polite rubber-stamp relationships, also carries with it the choice of influence and leadership. How well educators are able to develop this parent/professional partnership in special education may determine how well schools are able to implement this concept as general practice.

In the words of the Reverend Jesse Jackson, "Parents are the foundation of the educational process because they are the only elements of the system that can make anybody—students, teachers, and administrators—accountable" (Rubin, 1978, p. 2). Acting on this wisdom, professional educators *can* develop partnerships with parents thereby improving educational opportunities for all children.

SUMMARY POINTS

- Parent participation is mandated by PL 94–142. Parents have the right to be informed of any program plans being made for their child and to be given the opportunity to participate in the decisions being made regarding those plans. They also have the right to appeal any decision made. Notwithstanding the law, it is apparent that strong parent/teacher cooperation is necessary for the successful implementation of a pupil's education program.
- Like most parents, those of the handicapped are concerned about their child's progress in school. Frequently, they are unsure about their parental roles and responsibilities regarding the education of their child.
- In order to plan the best educational program, professionals must be aware of the handicapped child's home environment and family dynamics.
- Parents of handicapped children react in many different ways to their situation. Shame, loss of self-esteem, ambivalence, depression, defensiveness, denial, guilt, and anger are some of the reactions that are observed. Siblings, grandparents, aunts and uncles, cousins, and significant others are also affected. Their feelings and attitudes should also be noted by professionals.
- When parents initially learn of their child's handicap, they are frequently confused. A professional support system can assist parents in recognizing their feelings and can help parents in making decisions.
- When communicating with parents, whether through information sharing, conferencing, or counseling, school personnel should remember the various roles that parents of handicapped children play. The effective teacher recog-

nizes the commitment parents have to their child and welcomes parental knowledge and expertise.

■ Teacher/parent conferences should be two-way communication processes. Teachers and parents should share and learn from each other. Effective conferences are well planned in advance.

■ If communication between professionals and parents is limited to periodic conferences, the handicapped child's progress in the classroom will not be optimal.

■ Building positive relationships and true parent/teacher partnerships requires that teachers view parents as resources for teaching, involve parents in class activities, involve parents in setting goals and forming policies, utilize activities and teaching strategies that make sense to parents, and provide parents with information to meet their expressed needs.

■ Teachers must recognize that many parents of handicapped children feel confronted with crisis and are faced with many decisions. It is the teacher's responsibility to recognize such situations and to be familiar with community resources to which parents can be referred for counseling and/or other services.

■ Parent groups have played an important part in developing programs for exceptional children since the 1920s. They have been responsible for helping each other and their children, as well as aiding members of society to become aware of the needs and rights of persons with handicaps.

REVIEW QUESTIONS

1. Identify the rights that parents or guardians of handicapped children have as specified in PL 94–142.
2. Many parents interact with their child's teacher only on a disciplinary basis. List five activities that teachers could implement to facilitate more frequent and positive interaction with parents.
3. Parents are faced with many critical decisions throughout their child's development. Identify these and specify which professional(s) could assist in the decision-making process.
4. Parent groups and organizations have been influential in improving the lives of handicapped children. In which areas might they channel their efforts in the next decade?
5. What makes a parent/teacher conference successful? What barriers inhibit success?
6. Define the elusive grieving process and the teacher's role at each stage.

PARENT/TEACHER INTERACTION

Parents of handicapped children were asked for suggestions that would make beginning teachers more effective in their work. Several replied as follows:

- "Be honest; explain things, including the good and the bad sides."
- "Be sensitive to parents' feelings and give them as much information as you can."
- "Understand that most parents do care about their children and what happens; school is not a dumping ground or a babysitting service to them."
- "Offer suggestions to be used at home."
- "Set the example for the child; the teacher, like the parent, must model good behaviors."
- "Be open to parents' suggestions. Don't always be negative."
- "Have a lot of contact with parents."
- "Be sensitive to the child's needs and try to look at all aspects of the child."
- "Don't be afraid to ask that exceptional children work at home, but give them specific things to accomplish which are in tune with what is going on in the classroom."
- "Don't make premature judgments on the parents' learning potentials, thereby slowing down some learning that could be taking place."
- "Learn to relate to parents. Understand that their child is handicapped but that the parents are 'normal.' "
- "Help the child to feel important, to be 'top dog' in something."

Refined, all of these recommendations add up to cooperation and communication. In the following examples of parent/teacher interaction and cooperation these concepts are put into practice. In these cases, we see how cooperation and communication between parent and teacher help uncover real problems with the child's progress and help improve the educational process.

CASE 1
TEACHER ENLIGHTENS PARENT

During a parent/teacher program (designed to enhance interaction between parents and teachers in a school for mentally retarded children), a teacher described an effective toilet training program developed at the school. When an interested mother indicated her strong desire to have her own child toilet trained, the surprised teacher responded, "But your child *is* toilet trained." After the meeting, the enlightened parent and the teacher together devised strategies for implementing the school's toilet training program in the child's home. They also agreed to hold further conferences to explore other strategies to enhance the child's educational development (Turnbull and Turnbull, 1978).

CASE 2
PARENT ENLIGHTENS TEACHER

Mrs. Jones is the mother of eight children. Her oldest daughter Karen is 15 years old and attends classes for children with mental retardation. Mrs. Jones had been told during a parent conference that Karen was having extreme difficulty with picture and word identification tasks. At the invitation of Karen's teacher, Mrs. Jones returned to school during class time to observe. When the picture and word identification tasks were demonstrated in Mrs. Jones' presence, she noted that Karen had a sly smile on her face when the teacher asked her to complete the task. She knew that Karen was quite capable of teasing and making a game of the teacher's request.

Mrs. Jones suggested that Karen's teacher repeat the directions again. However, this time the teacher was requested to include a statement to Karen that this was a serious task and not a game. Karen was told to respond seriously. Following the new directions, Karen responded with 100 percent accuracy.

In these cases of mutual enlightenment, the observations and understandings of one significant person in a child's life were not enough. Both a well-trained professional and a veteran parent were hoodwinked by a child. In both instances, additional valuable time would have been lost had the parent/teacher communication not taken place. In both cases, the nature of the handicap was relatively severe and, thus, one would expect that the discrepancy in the child's functioning would be easy to detect. What happens with most children and youth with relatively mild handicaps and/or no handicaps? Is it possible that they, also, occasionally fool their teachers and parents? Could an established program of parent/teacher communication and cooperation enhance their educational progress?

DISCUSSION POINTS

1. Think about your own experiences as a student from elementary school to the present. What methods have been utilized, or attempted, by the school system (including your teachers) to establish and maintain communication between school and home? In what ways did your parents establish, or try to establish, cooperation between home and school?

2. In both of the cases presented in the application section, someone, either a parent or a teacher, was helped by receiving information from another. Both persons listened, understood, and learned from the experience, which they perceived as positive. Other persons, under similar circumstances, might have viewed the situation negatively; they might believe that they had made a mistake, were corrected, and were made to look foolish. With these feelings they might react defensively and break off further communication and cooperation. Can you remember situations when you had negative feelings rather than experiencing the intended positive outcomes? Describe the circumstances and the sequence of events to a friend. Ask them for their perceptions. Which aspects are similar to your viewpoint? Which are different? What might you do differently under similar circumstances next time? Under what types of conditions would you envision parents and teachers having mutual misperceptions and misunderstandings? What could a teacher do to attempt to lessen the possibility of misunderstandings and miscommunication?

SUGGESTED READINGS

Brown, S. L., and Moersch, M. S., eds. *Parents on the Team*. Ann Arbor: University of Michigan, 1978.

Croft, D. *Parents and Teachers: A Resource Book for Home, School and Community Relations*. Belmont, Ca.: Wadsworth, 1979.

Rutherford, R. B., and Edgar, E. *Teachers and Parents: A Guide to Interaction and Cooperation*. Boston: Allyn and Bacon, 1979.

Seligman, M. *Strategies for Helping Parents of Exceptional Chidlren*. New York: Free Press, 1979.

Swick, K. J., and Duff, R. E. *The Parent-Teacher Bond: Relating, Responding, Rewarding*. Dubuque, Iowa: Kendall/Hunt, 1978.

Turnbull, A. P., and Turnbull, H. R., III, eds. *Parents Speak Out: Views from the Other Side of the Two-Way Mirror*. Columbus, Ohio: Charles E. Merrill, 1978.

6

CONTENTS

YOUNG EXCEPTIONAL CHILDREN

The scope of the American special education scene has been greatly expanded. This has been due to the advent of such elements as parental involvement, appropriate education, individual education programs, multifactored assessment techniques, and integration of handicapped students with nonhandicapped peers. The strengthening of these services has occurred primarily in the elementary schools. Indeed, the primary and intermediate grades can be appropriately called the cradle of the special education movement.

Using grade schools as a pivot, educators have sighted both up and down the age continuum to target children who previously had been served inadequately or not at all. The focus of this chapter is on early childhood special education. Research and programs implemented during the early years of exceptional children's development are now of increasing interest to professionals.

The **early childhood period** refers to the age span from birth through age six, before formal, public education traditionally begins. For both researchers and parents, children in this age range are probably the most fascinating to study. Because the early childhood period is characterized by tremendous cognitive and physical growth, it can be appropriately subdivided into three age groups: infants (0 to 1½ years old), toddlers (1½ to 3 years old), and preschoolers (3 to 5 years old). These developmental periods lend themselves to a number of specific programs for exceptional children. Both in terms of quantity and quality, educators view the early childhood period as an appropriate starting point for educating children with special needs. Whether handicapped or developing normally, young children are very responsive to stimulating activities, and early childhood special education programs seek to adapt activities to aid exceptional youngsters in reaching developmental milestones.

Early intervention strategies and programs have been developed for many handicapping conditions. These have not, however, always been warmly embraced by child development and education professionals. The recent shift towards acceptance and promotion of early intervention can be understood by tracing the pioneer research on young children with special needs.

HISTORICAL PERSPECTIVE

The first research efforts in early childhood special education focused on retarded children. The successes with this group led to programs for children with other handicapping conditions.

The initial evidence supporting early intervention appeared during a chance observation by Skeels in the 1930s (Skeels and Dye, 1939). During his tenure as psychologist at an orphanage, Skeels found that two retarded infants removed from the orphanage to a home for retarded children seemed to be normal six months later. It appeared that the attention given to the babies by the retarded teenage girls in the home stimulated the infants' development. To gain more evidence, Skeels placed 13 other retarded infants (18 months old) in the home for the retarded and retested them two years later. The results indicated that these children gained an average of 28 IQ points, which changed their intellectual classification from "obvious mental retardation" to "normal." In contrast, a comparison group at the orphanage who did not receive extra attention had an average drop of 26 points. To determine if there were any lasting effects from the early exposure to stimulation or deprivation, Skeels located his original subjects

30 years later (Skeels, 1966). He found that all 13 members of the group who had received attention at an early age were self-supporting in adulthood. Of the 12 subjects who did not receive additional stimulation, 4 were in state institutions and the others were either unemployed or classified as unskilled laborers.

Dramatic as the first results were, Skeels' experiment was not highly regarded by his colleagues (Kirk, 1977). During the 1930s, American psychologists believed that intelligence was a purely inherited characteristic, which made it a static, unchangeable trait, much like eye color or bone structure. Skeels' work, however, prompted Kirk to further explore the issue of whether intelligence was strictly heredity-based or if it were related to environmental conditions as indicated by Skeels' research (Kirk, 1977). Kirk termed the controversy over the relative influence of hereditary and environment as the "nature-nurture" issue. In what later was to be regarded as a landmark study in early intervention, Kirk (1958) compared the intellectual growth of mentally retarded children participating in a preschool program with that of mentally retarded children receiving no additional stimulation. In general, he found that the preschool group experienced a gain in intellectual growth. Kirk maintained that although genetic factors may govern the absolute limits of one's intelligence, there are critical environmental factors that determine if the maximum or minimum potential will be realized. Thus, a child may be born with the capacity of obtaining a 70 to 110 IQ. But a deprived environment will most likely result in an IQ measurement of 70, while exposure to stimulating growth conditions such as varied experiences, words, and concepts will probably produce the 110 rating (Kirk, 1973). The role of heredity (nature) versus environmental (nurture) factors on intelligence is still a controversy today. The debate will probably continue until a definition of intelligence can be agreed upon, more reliable measurement tools are developed, and more studies are conducted using rigorous methodology and procedures.

Heber and his associates (Garber and Heber, 1973) stressed the concept of preventing rather than remediating the effects of mental retardation. An early intervention program known as the Milwaukee Project used a population of infants whose mothers had IQs of less than 75. The infants were divided into experimental and control groups. The experimental group received an infant stimulation and early education program; their mothers were taught child-rearing, homemaking, and employment skills. After five years in the program, the IQ scores of the children in the experimental group were about 30 points higher than those in the control group (which received no stimulation/education program at all). The researchers did recognize design limitations in the study. That is, the children could become test-wise after numerous test administrations. In addition, there are certain weaknesses associated with infant measurement, such as test reliability. However, the project was the only attempt to date to assess the long-range impact of early intervention with the goal of prevention in mind.

The knowledge that preschool stimulation programs could influence intelligence levels merged with other forces to make the 1960s a decade of tremendous growth for early childhood programs. During this time, Americans became more concerned with the social welfare of the poor. The realization that many low-income children were not successful in school gained national attention and eventually resulted in the establishment of services that counteract poverty conditions. In addition, books such as Benjamin Bloom's *Stability and Change in Human Characteristics* (1964) emphasized the preschool years as the most important time for maximum development of intelligence (Karnes and Teska, 1975; Safford, 1978).

These events led to the 1964 birth of Project Head Start, a federally funded program that provides health, nutritional, and developmental services to the nation's low-income four- and five-year-olds. This period saw the inception of many other early childhood projects that focused mainly on culturally diverse preschool children of varying ages (Weikart, 1967). The early intervention atmosphere in the mid-1960s was characterized by professional enthusiasm and, in retrospect, perhaps some unrealistic promises (Caldwell, 1974).

FEDERAL SUPPORT

Federal funding in the late 1960s spurred preschool programs serving not only the disadvantaged, but also handicapped children. Legislation passed in 1968—the Handicapped Children's Early Education Program—awarded federal grant money to public and private agencies to serve preschool handicapped children. Over 150 projects, known as the **First Chance Network**, were funded by the Bureau of Education for the Handicapped of the U.S. Office of Education. Two other pieces of legislation in 1974 and 1975 gave emphasis and funds to the preschool movement. The 1974 Education of the Handicapped Act (PL 93–380) centered on out-of-school handicapped children, including the early childhood population. The 1975 Education for All Handicapped Children Act (PL 94–142), provided $300-per-child incentive grants for every preschool handicapped child between the ages of three and five years who is provided services.

Federal legislation was vital in making early childhood special education a national concern. It is, however, the individual state's responsibility to give substance and support to early intervention. As with tax laws, federal educational directives have loopholes that allow states to avoid providing special services to young children. It is important to understand that, although PL 94–142 mandates that special education services must be provided for three- through five-year-olds, the mandate is only in effect if it is not in conflict with existing state laws.

Some states provide diagnostic services to this age group but do not require follow-up intervention programs. This inconsistency in state laws often frustrates and angers parents. The following incident illustrates this point.

Timothy was diagnosed at approximately six months of age as being legally blind by a pediatric ophthalmologist. When the parents asked what their program options were, they were informed that they had none. The father, a psychologist, asked the physician, "What do we do for the next 2½ years?" He was told, "Go home and wait."

In their state, although diagnostic services were provided for children from birth to age five, Timmy would have to wait. Intervention programs were only mandated for the three- to five-year-old handicapped population. Fortunately for Timmy, his mother had extensive special education background. She did research and planned a special sensory stimulation program for him at home. And waited.

EARLY INTERVENTION

In grades 1 through 12, it is often a relatively easy task to identify children who need special services. Teachers are the primary agents who identify children who are atypical in regard to learning, emotional well-being, or social skills. They can refer children suspected of having problems to the speech and language therapists, school psychologist, nurse, or other professional for further evaluation.

In comparison, children in the birth-to-five range do not receive these benefits because, generally, they are not enrolled in formal education programs. Thus, any systematic process for identifying exceptional young children in need of special services frequently must come either from preschool screening programs or from parental concern. Parents, the key people in the child's early life, need to be aware of normal developmental patterns, ranges of behavior, and sound health practices. Public awareness and, more specifically, parent education are the crucial factors in obtaining appropriate services for the exceptional young.

Process of Early Identification

The early identification procedure has four stages: (1) population/program definition; (2) screening; (3) diagnosis; and (4) intervention. This process is depicted in Table 6-1. Each stage depends upon the one preceding, although a child may enter the process at the diagnostic level by being referred directly by parents or agencies.

POPULATION/PROGRAM DEFINITION   The most difficult component to accomplish in the early identification chain may be the initial organization. As outlined in Table 6-1, many questions must be answered in order to establish the program's objectives. Without extensive planning, identification projects may lose focus, attempt to accomplish goals beyond the capabilities of available resources, or result in few children reaching the intervention level (Frankenburg, 1977).

A major issue in program planning revolves around devising a method to reach the target population. Zehrbach (1975) evaluated several methods of outreach, which included mass mailings to all parents of target children, contacting appro-

TABLE 6-1   The Early Identification Process

Steps	Activities	Outcome
1. Population/ Program Definition	a. Determine geographic region to be served b. Determine age group to be screened c. Describe problems to be identified d. Define pass/refer criteria e. Determine appropriate outreach method	Clear purpose for initiating screening program is identified
2. Screening	Administer appropriate tests, parent questionnaires, interviews	Children having potential problems referred for diagnosis
3. Diagnosis	Provide in-depth examination of suspected problem area by professionals	Confirmation or denial of problem —children with diagnosed problem receive intervention
4. Intervention	Implement appropriate treatment and/or educational plan based upon diagnostic information	Amelioration, remediation of identified learning and behavior deficit

priate professionals and agencies involved with children, media blitz, and personal surveys. Personal contact, such as telephone or house-to-house surveys, was the most effective technique in terms of the number of actual children reaching the screening stage.

SCREENING   Giving every preschool-age child a thorough medical, educational, and psychological examination is expensive. Thus, a method is needed to screen (or separate) potential high-risk children from those who appear to be developing normally. A diagnosis or prognosis should not occur at this point. The only purpose of a **screening** is to provide a quick, relatively easy, and inexpensive method of evaluating a large group of children and identifying those with possible problems.

A screening program may focus on one medical (or development) area, such as vision, or encompass a broader perspective. Speech, language, hearing, motor development, dental, and blood-lead level are other facets that can be screened in a young child. In situations where multiple areas are examined, the usual procedure involves screening stations wherein the child progresses from one station to the next. Trained volunteers and paraprofessionals conduct screening activities under the supervision of professionals.

The most critical aspect of a screening program occurs after the tests are evaluated. Follow-up services must determine if those children referred for further evaluation did in fact receive the necessary assistance. Contact with parents should be maintained to determine progress as well as any problems they may have in securing appropriate guidance.

Since screening instruments are not definitive, there will always be some error in separating normally developing children from those suspected of having problems. One of two events can occur: over-referrals (when children are identified and later found to have no problems), and under-referrals (children who pass but should have been identified). Medical screenings for defects in hearing, vision, and lead level in the blood are much more accurate than are screenings in developmental areas, such as cognitive, social, and emotional functioning (American Orthopsychiatric Association, 1978). This factor represents a major difficulty for those desiring to efficiently locate children with development problems. Further study is urgently needed in this area.

The federal government supported screening activities by legislating funds for a nationwide screening program. In 1967, the **Early and Periodic Screening, Diagnosis, and Treatment (EPSDT)** program provided comprehensive physical and developmental services to low-income children from birth to age 21. Because of problems in implementing EPSDT, another federal program—the **Child Health Assessment Program (CHAP)**—is under consideration and may soon be adopted. CHAP differs from EPSDT in the following ways (Moore, 1978):

- Children from low-income families not qualifying for welfare programs will be served, thus increasing the number of eligible children.
- Emphasis is put on interagency coordination to ensure that children receive needed services and do not get "lost in the system."
- Additional services, such as speech and language correction, and physical and ocupational therapy are included in the package.

Both programs extend beyond screening activities to include both diagnosis and treatment.

DIAGNOSIS   Diagnosis is the process of first determining if a problem exists, then defining the causes of the handicap, and finally developing a strategy to help the child and family deal with the problem (Cross, 1977). More in-depth information is required for a diagnosis than for a screening referral. This data is gathered by a range of professionals including doctors, social workers, educators, and psychologists. The necessity of a multidisciplinary approach depends on the nature of the suspected problem. If a child is referred from a vision screening, the most appropriate professional to evaluate the child would be an ophthalmologist or optometrist. Which professionals are to be a part of the diagnostic team is contingent upon the suspected handicap and varies for each case.

The diagnostic process uses standardized tests, careful observations of behavior, and family and medical histories as means of gathering information. The results are organized and interpreted to obtain a clear picture of the child's abilities and disabilities. Since both professionals and parents are involved in the diagnosis, both should participate in deciding the best program for the child.

INTERVENTION   At this level, the appropriate professionals work directly with the child. While diagnosis may confirm that a handicapping condition or medical problem exists, it is only the beginning of intervention. Important to intervention strategies is continual assessment of progress. For example, four-year-old Linda is diagnosed as having a significant language delay. Both individual and group therapy are identified on her IEP as needed special services. The speech and language clinician determines which therapeutic approach will be most beneficial for Linda. This clinician also designs motivating tasks and identifies the amount of time and attention the child can give to the tasks. In addition, the therapist plans activities that Linda's preschool teacher can implement on a daily basis. Consistent monitoring of behaviors provides information crucial to evaluating Linda's progress and to planning future programs for her.

ISSUES IN EARLY INTERVENTION

Several difficulties arise in implementing appropriate early intervention programs. For example, many intervention programs for young handicapped children have been too general in nature. That is, too often, once a child has been diagnosed as having a particular handicap, he or she is more or less lumped into a program without careful consideration of individual needs (Keogh and Kopp, 1978). Although handicapped preschoolers have benefited from initial intervention attempts, further investigations are needed in order to match the characteristics of exemplary programs to the needs of each child.

Assessment and measurement of children's growth as a result of program participation is another issue involved in early intervention programs. In grade school and secondary education one can more accurately assess progress in math, reading, spelling, or social studies since it can be gauged by standardized tests. Early intervention programs, though, are concerned with human development, which is much more difficult to quantify. Almost all attempts to document the success of early intervention have turned to intelligence quotient (IQ) gain as the sole criteria.

The issue is not that program developers think an IQ score is the only important outcome; in fact, the programs of the 1960s reviewed by Weikart (1967) all had goals related to social/emotional adjustment and positive self-concept. The crux of the matter, however, is how to reliably measure these concepts. Referring to this point, Caldwell (1974) stated that there have been "few dramatic developments in the field of measurement of human attributes in the past decade" (p. 495). Human attributes refer to happiness, mental health, self-concept, and attitudes. The difficulty in measurement is applicable to all ages. It is, nonetheless, more apparent in the context of early childhood programs, which tend to use tests measuring the child's affective and developmental growth as opposed to academic learning.

PROGRAM VARIABLES

Early childhood special education programs have varying emphases in curriculum, location of services, and the inclusion of nonhandicapped children. This section will describe different curricula, which will illustrate the degree of variety available in intervention approaches. Before differences are explained, common elements of these programs will be described.

Common Elements

An interdisciplinary approach to diagnosis and parent involvement are important factors in any successful program. Because the young children spend the bulk of their time with parents rather than with educators, parental influence cannot be

A thorough continuous assessment of the young handicapped child's learning potential requires the expertise of many professionals working together.

ignored. The Head Start program, for example, incorporates a parent-training component and gives parents a share of the responsibility in program operation. Inclusion of parents can reinforce the accomplishments made at a center-based program.

The **interdisciplinary** approach includes professionals from different fields of study. The purpose of incorporating such a wide range of backgrounds is to ensure that the best possible program has been developed for the child. It is virtually impossible for one person to have the expertise necessary to deal with all aspects of the life of a handicapped child and his or her family.

The team approach to problem-solving has another advantage: the sharing of knowledge and skills, which can further every staff member's competence. Of course, communication and cooperation are necessary; if a staff member remains completely loyal to one particular method or point of view, the system can come to a grinding halt.

Curriculum

Curriculum refers to the method of organizing what to teach, how to teach, and when to teach. As discussed previously, curriculum models are not well defined and may be indiscriminately applied to children with special needs. This is not surprising in light of the recentness of the early childhood movement. There are, however, basic models that give an idea of how programs differ. We will discuss three types of curricula: normal development, cognitive development, and behavioral. Table 6-2 shows some basic differences among these models. The differences listed under "Program Emphasis" should not be strictly interpreted. For example, the behavioral approach is characterized by an emphasis on academic learning, but does not necessarily ignore the social development of children receiving instruction.

NORMAL DEVELOPMENT MODEL   This approach to instruction is probably familiar to everyone because it is the basic model of the public school system (Anastasiow, 1978). It focuses on traditional subject matter being taught to everyone. Conformity to the norm behavior is generally a goal of this curriculum model. It thus has limited applicability to the education of exceptional children.

In this model, the classroom has different territories for play, such as housekeeping, gross motor activities, which include tricycles and balance beams, dress-up, and a table area for fine motor tasks, such as painting and using scissors. For the greater part of the day the teacher supervises activities, as opposed to taking a

TABLE 6-2 Curricula Models

Model	Teacher-Child Interaction	Program Emphasis
Normal Development	Teacher supervised Group oriented	Social-emotional
Cognitive Development	Teacher structured Child initiated	Language Social
Behavioral	Teacher directed Small group	Academic

direct instructional role. Children circulate to the various areas and participate in group activities, such as story time. Individualized instruction is usually not associated with this model.

COGNITIVE DEVELOPMENT MODEL   The research of Jean Piaget provides the foundation for the cognitive development approach. Piaget's theory stresses that a child's development is sequential and orderly, and that stages of intellectual growth are common to all humans. The term **cognitive** refers to mental functioning, the formation of rules and hypotheses about events, which is the focus of Piaget's approach to the growth of children. Generally speaking, Piaget outlined five stages of intellectual growth (Richmond, 1970):

1. *Sensorimotor Intelligence (birth to approximately two years)*: This period is characterized by interaction of the infant and the environment in which the child learns to distinguish between "self" and "not self" in relation to objects. Exploration takes up the majority of the child's time. Achievements during this period include recognizing cause and effect and establishing object permanence (an object continues to exist whether or not the child is in contact with it).

2. *Symbolic Thought (1 ½ to approximately 5 years)*: During this period the child is able to bring forth mental images in the absence of an external event. The child creates a personal representation of the world and initially has respect solely for his or her own point of view. The use of language emerges strongly in this period; however, words often do not fit with the child's unique internal thought system.

3. *Preoperational Thought (4 to approximately 8 years)*: Language plays a major role in decentralizing the child's world. During this period the child embraces the concepts of sharing, playing with peers, and recognizes that others have thoughts different from his or her own.

4. *Concrete Operational Thought (7 to approximately 12 years)*: This period is characterized by a "learning by doing" approach to tasks. The child can deal with abstract notions (such as addition and subtraction) through active manipulation of objects.

5. *Formal Operational Thought (11 years through adolescence)*: A more "scientific" approach to thinking emerges at this stage. The child is able to mentally manipulate more than one variable at a time, and has an orderly system for organizing vast amounts of information. Arrival at the formal operations period during adolescence completes the intellectual growth stages and is equivalent to adult thinking.

An important aspect of Piaget's theory is that the child is actively involved in reorganizing mental processes (Stevenson, 1972). Children in cognitive developmental programs are encouraged to investigate their environment and to initiate learning activities.

An example of this approach is the High/Scope Cognitive Preschool Curriculum directed by Weikart. This program attempts to put Piaget's theory into practice in the preschool classroom (Banet, 1976). Teaching structure plays an important part in arranging the child's experiences to concentrate on those which promote higher cognitive functioning skills. A set of key experiences has been developed by this project. These are activities designed to reflect the child's needs at the preoperational thought stage. Some of these experiences include (Banet, 1976, pp. 10–11):

- *Representation*: Recognizing objects by sound, touch, taste, and smell
- *Language*: Describing (and listening to others describe) objects, events, and relations
- *Classification*: Investigating and labeling the attributes of things
- *Number Concepts*: Comparing numbers and amount (more/less, same amount; more/fewer, same number)
- *Temporal Relations*: Observing seasonal changes
- *Spatial Relations*: Fitting things together and taking them apart

BEHAVIORAL MODEL   This program uses a highly structured approach to teaching with emphasis on direct instruction in academic tasks. Intensive verbal interaction is the primary means of accomplishing predetermined objectives. Karnes and Teska (1975) noted that this approach differs radically from other preschool programs—the base is derived from subject matter to be taught rather than principles of child development. If the object of a week's lesson is name recognition, the teacher would directly confront the child with his or her name, have the child repeat it, trace it, find it in a list, etc. In contrast, the cognitive development program uses more subtle techniques: Name labels would be attached to the child's possessions and name charts used for daily activities to aid the child's name recognition.

The emphasis in the behavioral model is on changing behavior, accomplished through the use of reinforcers and sequenced instruction. The teacher is the initiator of activity while the child is the receptor. The behavioral model asserts that if you want a child to learn, it is necessary to delineate the subject matter and teach it directly. The teacher maintains a dominant role as opposed to the more supportive, guiding function in the cognitive approach. Teacher strategies outlined by Bereiter and Engelman (1966, p. 120) include:

- Work at different levels of difficulty at different times
- Adhere to a rigid, repetitive presentation pattern

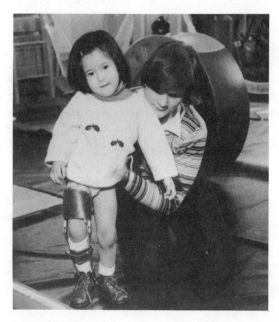

The physical therapist deliberately arranges the play environment to promote skill development.

■ Use unison responses whenever possible
■ Use questions liberally
■ Use short explanations
■ Use lots of examples
■ Prevent incorrect responses whenever possible
■ Be completely unambiguous in letting the child know when his or her response is corrent and when it is incorrect
■ Encourage thinking behavior

The cognitive and behavioral models are clearly different, but a judgment as to which is better for children cannot be made at this time. In evaluating curricular models in intervention programs, Karnes and Teska (1975) concluded that, based on the available evidence, one approach has not been shown to be superior to another. This conclusion does not mean that what you teach a child and the manner in which you teach it is unimportant. Rather, it points out the need for more systematic studies of how children develop depending upon different program methods. As a teacher, it is necessary to devote considerable time to analyzing the rationale and instructional methodology underlying each type of program and determining which will be the most effective with a particular child.

Not only do preschool programs differ in curriculum, but also in the way services are provided to the children and the target age for intervention. The following section will look at various settings in which services are delivered.

Delivery Systems

A delivery system refers to the environment in which the young child with special needs receives services. Delivery services can be categorized into (1) home-based, (2) center-based, or (3) hospital settings. The setting may be dictated by program philosophies, the child's handicap, or distance. Although many combinations are possible—for example, a combination of the center- and home-based system—each of the three systems will be separately outlined to give an idea of the differing focus each system can provide.

CENTER-BASED   Many of the programs started in the 1960s utilized a **center-based** approach, which is now the most frequently used means of reaching children in intervention projects. Children in this system spend a specified number of hours away from home on a daily or weekly basis. An advantage of bringing children to a central location is that a number of different professionals can reach a larger group of children.

The Precise Early Education of Children with Handicaps (PEECH) project at the University of Illinois uses a center-based approach (*PEECH*, 1976). Exceptional children are bused from their home school district to attend 2½-hour sessions, five days a week. In PEECH, the time before and after the children's center time is used to plan, discuss instructional strategies, and train paraprofessionals. The close working relationships among staff members is a highlight of center-based programs.

HOME-BASED   In **home-based** programs, services to the child are usually provided to the parent, who is trained so that he or she can influence other children in the home as well as the handicapped child. Although these programs require more time, staff, and funds, research suggests they tend to be somewhat more effective in stimulating development of the child than center-based programs (Karnes and Teska, 1975). A long-term, home-based program, reported by Gray and Klaus (1970), traced the achievement of children who participated in the program through fourth grade. The children who received early intervention services were superior in achievement through the end of the third-grade as compared to those who were not participants in the program. The fact that the intervention children lost the achievement edge they previously held may indicate that early intervention should not be abruptly halted at school-entrance age.

The Portage Project is an example of a home-based program. Implemented in a rural part of Wisconsin, professionals and trained paraprofessionals spend an hour and a half per week with each family in their caseload. They use this time to teach skills to parents and define goals for the next week. Using the child's natural environment, involving the entire family in the educational process, and observing all types of child behavior in the home are a few of the advantages of using the home-based approach (Shearer and Shearer, 1976).

HOSPITAL SETTINGS   Medical personnel in hospitals have recently become more aware of the preventive possibilities inherent in their facility. Educational staff members have become more prominent in hospital settings—they join forces with medical professionals to provide infant stimulation programs for children born with special needs. One program that presents evidence to support at-birth intervention has been developed by Badger (1977). Adolescent, low-income

Center-based programs provide young handicapped children with opportunities for social development.

mothers were recruited in the hospital setting and provided medical services and parenting education. Thus, their children received additional stimulation from the time they were born. Through parent education, mothers learned the value of these stimulation activities, such as cooing, babbling, visual tracking, seeing bright colors in the environment, grasping, and reaching. An analysis of mothers' pre- and post-program behavior indicated significant differences in mothers' responsiveness to infants as well as vice versa. The subjective data suggested that the mothers were enthusiastic about the value of the program (Badger, Burns, and Rhoades, 1976). The favorable results of this program add increasing weight to the argument that education should begin as early as possible.

Integration

The 1970s witnessed the integration of young handicapped children with their nonhandicapped peers. This feat has been difficult to accomplish because public school systems are not required to provide education for children younger than five or six years. As a result, unlike the elementary and secondary school, a "normal" population is not available at a young age. One encouraging sign is the 1972 legislation requiring Head Start programs to serve handicapped children.

The rationale for integration is based on arguments involving social, legal, and psychoeducational issues (Bricker, 1978). The social aspect includes the possibility of changing the negative attitudes toward people who are different by exposing young children to all different types of people. It is hoped that these children will then grow up knowing that a person is first of all an individual.

There is little research to support the practice of integration as being beneficial for either the handicapped or able-bodied students (Bricker, 1978). However, limited available research yields a direction for positive future developments. Guralnick (1976) focused on studies of the influence of modeling and peer interaction. He noted that positive behavior changes, increased language, and appropriate play behavior have been effected through interaction with nonhandicapped peers. An important point in the study is that interaction with or observation of nonhandicapped students was not enough to influence the handicapped child. The critical factor was planned interaction under the teacher's direction.

The Infant, Toddler, and Preschool Research and Intervention Project at the University of Miami (Florida) uses an integrated approach at all three age levels in their early intervention model. On top of the increased language and positive behavior effected by integration, the interaction between parents of handicapped and nonhandicapped children was an additional source of parent education, understanding, and acceptance (Bricker and Bricker, 1976).

TRENDS AND ISSUES

Early childhood special education has emerged from the 1970s as a rapidly expanding and widely accepted discipline. This growth has brought forth several issues that are important in determining future directions for early childhood programs. These issues have implications not only for the children to be served, but also for parents, teachers, administrators, and the varying professionals interested in young children with special needs.

Teacher-certification requirements are legislated by the individual state boards of education. However, most boards do not have policies governing teachers of children below mandatory school age. Obviously, when providing educational services to young handicapped children, the issue of who is qualified to work with this population is of immediate concern.

Recognizing the need for early childhood teacher education, the U.S. Office of Child Development funded a project in 1972 to evolve national standards for early education teachers (U.S. Department of Health, Education, and Welfare, 1975). This project—the Child Development Associate Consortium—developed competencies necessary for a **Child Development Associate (CDA)** certification. The CDA represents a new class of personnel whose training ranks above the paraprofessional and below the trained professional.

The emphasis of the CDA program is on-the-job training, as opposed to an academic curriculum. It was designed for individuals already responsible for young children in Head Start programs, day-care centers, and nursery schools. Certification is based on performance with children in a field setting. The candidate, who is on the certification team, is judged by a local professional trainer, community member, and consortium member. The CDA is promising, but because it is so recent, measures of its effectiveness are still unavailable.

How Early? How Long?

Weikart (1967), in reviewing early intervention programs for disadvantaged children, noted that the programs were remedial (intervention began after the problem was noted), rather than preventive. Federal legislation mandates education for the handicapped to begin at age three. Nonetheless, the question remains of whether an even earlier intervention will make the child's development conform more quickly to normal patterns. The relatively few reports available on intervention during the zero-to-three age range show some positive results. However, until long-range investigations that follow the child's progress past the early childhood stage are reported, the belief that "the earlier, the better" will remain based on common sense, not on empirical evidence.

On the other hand is the issue of how long past the early years should this intensive treatment continue. When the child enters the public school system, the special early intervention efforts (home visits, parent education, etc.) usually end. It appears that the positive effects of early intervention programs may be negated when specific service relevant to the child's education and home environment is withdrawn once he or she begins to attend public school (Caldwell, 1974; Gray and Klaus, 1970).

Who Is Responsible?

Legally speaking, the public school system is responsible for serving the needs of young handicapped children. This task, however, is too great for any one organization. Currently, there are federally funded projects, state programs, community mental health agencies, hospitals, nursery/preschools, and other organizations that in one way or another promote identification, assessment, and treatment of young handicapped children. In order to best meet the needs of exceptional children, public education must work with all these agencies and programs. Administrators and teachers must be well informed of all existing programs in order not to duplicate services or neglect areas of the child's development.

For example, in most communities public and private agencies exist to meet the mental health, social, medical, and educational needs of the population. A young child with severe emotional problems and his or her family may benefit from counseling with a clinical psychologist, but many school systems cannot afford such a person full time. Through collaboration, school personnel could call upon a mental health agency, for example, to provide the necessary psychological services. With such agreements, the public school system could coordinate various community services to supplement their own. Without such efforts, services are likely to become fragmented, losing sight of the greater well-being of the child.

It is unrealistic to believe that *only* public school educators can meet the needs of young handicapped students. It is eminently realistic to believe that cooperation on a community level can meet the complex needs of exceptional children and their families.

SUMMARY POINTS

- In the past, special education for exceptional children has focused on elementary school-age students. However, because of research and legislative mandates, programs are being provided to young handicapped persons.
- Research on the efficacy of early intervention programs for the handicapped indicated that a stimulating environment is related to positive intellectual growth.
- The federal government offers funds and incentive grants to states to develop early childhood programs for the handicapped. The Bureau of Education for the Handicapped funded 150 First Chance programs throughout the country.
- States are not obliged to comply with PL 94–142 regarding the provision of educational experience to their handicapped preschool population if such provisions are not mandated by state law.
- The development of a successful, comprehensive early identification program involves: defining the purpose and goals of the program, selecting developmental and/or medical areas to be screened and selecting related instruments, providing thorough diagnostic services by trained professionals, and implementing the program.
- Because the problems of young handicapped children are complex, it is imperative that a positive working relationship exist between parents and professionals of the multidisciplinary team.
- Various curricula models (each with its own philosophy on the teacher's role in the learning process and on program content) are utilized to teach young exceptional children. To date, no intervention model has been proved more successful than another.
- Programs for young handicapped children are center-based, home-based (or a combination of the two), or are located in a hospital environment. Regarding the former two, each environment has its advantages. A center-based program allows for more interaction with a variety of professionals and ex-

posure to structured integrated experiences. In a home-based program, the parents provide more direct services.

■ Because the field of early childhood special education is relatively new, there are several issues confronting the discipline: teacher certification requirements; determining whether intervention programs shouldn't begin earlier in children's development to include preschoolers; determining the most effective time for intervention; investigating program prototypes to identify which, if any, are more effective; and developing valid and reliable psychometric tools for assessing young children.

REVIEW QUESTIONS

1. What are the advantages of early intervention programs?
2. The concepts of least restrictive environment and mainstreaming may be applied to the young handicapped population. In order to provide quality integrated experiences for these children, what changes, if any, will your state have to make regarding regular early childhood teacher preparation and licensing standards for early childhood programs?
3. Why is it difficult to accurately assess young handicapped children?
4. You have been selected to serve on a committee responsible for developing either a center-based or a home-based early intervention program in your immediate community. Which would you choose? List the factors that influenced your decision.

TRANSDISCIPLINARY TEAMING — AN ALTERNATIVE FOR YOUNG HANDICAPPED CHILDREN

Evaluation and program development for many handicapped children is often a complex process requiring the expertise of more than one professional. Thus, there is a need for professions to team or work together. There are several teaming models to choose from: multidisciplinary, interdisciplinary, and transdisciplinary. Table 6-3 outlines the degree of interface among professionals in each model.

The multidisciplinary and interdisciplinary teaming approaches have weaknesses. These appear as the variables in the child's circumstances become more complex, and as the age range of children for which the team is responsible increases. Both of these team approaches tend to provide recommendations without due regard for the development of a consistently workable intervention program. They also tend to overlook responsibility for the critical program aspects of evaluation and monitoring.

The **transdisciplinary** approach is approriate for serving young handicapped children (birth through six years), who are often severely and multiply impaired, thus requiring direct intervention from several disciplines. It is the most effective model since "each team member assumes some of the responsibilities of other team members.

Thus, one person represents more than one discipline and is able to deliver services based on multiple disciplines" (Hart, 1977, p. 383). The Early Intervention Project at the University of Michigan utilizes the transdisciplinary approach (Schafer, 1976). This service delivery plan was adopted so a solitary professional could be the primary service provider for conducting and evaluating home visits.

To illustrate this approach, consider Anna Marshall, age 2. Anna has been diagnosed as having spina bifida (a congenital disorder characterized by failure of the spinal cord to be enclosed by vertebral arches), cleft palate and lip, and possible mental retardation. As a result of her disabilities, she is unable to control her bowels and bladder and cannot use her legs. Also, her speech is impaired. Ms. Waite, an occupational therapist, is the caseworker assigned to the Marshall family. Before making the weekly home visit, she discusses the previous visit with other professionals for their input on Anna's program: the speech and language therapist regarding Anna's speech and the child development/special educator for suggested activities to promote appropriate cognitive skills.

During the home visit, Ms. Waite discusses with the Marshall family Anna's

TABLE 6-3 Description of Three Teaming Models

Model	Professional Interaction
Multidisciplinary	Each professional independently makes a diagnosis and provides recommendations. These findings are collected by one team member who is responsible for developing a final report.
Interdisciplinary	After the child is evaluated independently by professionals, a team conference is conducted to make intervention decisions by group consensus.
Transdisciplinary	Professionals continue their involvement beyond assessment to include direct intervention, evaluation, reassessment, etc. Although one team member has the responsibility of carrying out the recommendations, this professional is supported by input from other specialists.

behavior over the past week. At this time she is able to observe family dynamics and evaluate the use of intervention strategies suggested at the last home visit. In addition, Ms. Waite demonstrates with Anna activities for continued motor, speech, and cognitive development. If she has questions regarding Anna's development, she returns to the transdisciplinary team to share her concerns and to receive additional direction from the involved professionals.

The potential impact of the transdisciplinary approach for increasing the effectiveness of individualized programs for handicapped children is great, but the process of forming transdisciplinary teams can be very painstaking. To become operational, this teaming strategy requires the unselfish sharing of knowledge and expertise of all the members. Patience and understanding are also necessary, as each member in turn attempts to learn from and act on the consulting-teacher assistance from the other professionals on the team. Transdisciplinary teaming requires a focus on the child, rather than fragmented emphasis on the specific concerns and approaches of various professional disciplines.

DISCUSSION POINTS

1. Teaming is not a common practice in many public school systems today. What are some possible reasons why teaming is not used as widely as its potential effectiveness would seem to warrant?
2. In comparison with the multidisciplinary and interdisciplinary models, why is the transdisciplinary approach more appropriate for young handicapped children? (Also discuss possible benefits to the parents and siblings.)

SUGGESTED READINGS

Caldwell, B. M. "A Decade of Early Intervention Programs: What We Have Learned." *American Journal of Orthopsychiatry* 44, 4 (1974), 491–496.

Ellis, N. E., and Cross, L., eds. *Planning Programs for Early Education of the Handicapped.* New York: Walker, 1977.

Guralnick, M. J., ed. *Early Intervention and the Integration of Handicapped and Nonhandicapped Children.* Baltimore: University Park Press, 1978.

7

EXCEPTIONAL ADOLESCENTS AND ADULTS

CONTENTS

For most adolescents, the jump from elementary school to junior and senior high school is a very exciting and also anxious time. It represents not only growing up and independence, but also a move to a somewhat foreign environment, requiring new responsibilities. Dealing with adolescent issues such as peer-group membership, sexual relationships, and physical maturation are crucial developmental tasks that have a profound impact on the way we handle ourselves as adults.

Suppose that you are a handicapped adolescent. In addition to all of the normal problems, you have a sensory, physical, learning, or emotional disability. Perhaps you were never too good at organizing, but within the confines of an elementary classroom you managed. The transition to secondary school now requires you to remember, among other things, a locker number, room assignments, several teachers, and classroom work.

NEED FOR CHANGE

The educational environment for adolescents is considerably different from that provided by elementary school. It remains, however, imperative that exceptional adolescents continue to receive support and special services beyond the elementary school years. While this need may appear to be an obvious one, the reality is that until the early 1970s, there were few programs and procedures and little teacher education and research for the exceptional adolescent population. In comparison to the preschool movement, secondary special education is in its infancy.

Participation in sports and other recreational activities is a fundamental need of all adolescents.

There are several reasons for this slow development. According to one estimate, between 65 and 75 percent of special education funds and efforts have been channeled to elementary schools (Martin, 1972). Educators either believed that concentration on the elementary-age group could "cure" the ills of exceptional children (thus negating the need for further services) or they refused to recognize that these students existed (thus denying them services). We now know that the learning disabled *continue* to have difficulties in reading, math, and social relationships; that the educable mentally retarded remain academically behind their "normal" peers; and that the visually impaired still have difficulty coping with traditional academic materials.

Besides the stresses of the academic world, the adolescent is entering a less sheltered period of life. The exceptional adolescent needs assistance in social as well as academic skills. The teen years represent a period of greater mobility and exposure to the community. The adolescent needs, for example, skills in using transportation and appropriate social behaviors in order to fit into the mainstream of society. Yet, these competencies are usually not covered in the elementary curriculum.

Appropriate secondary programs have also been slow to develop because the high school structure is different and teacher training has been inappropriate. The segmented nature of secondary schools, with each academic class being taught by a different teacher, makes it difficult to implement the flexible approach typically found at the elementary level. Also, special education teacher training programs have focused primarily on training elementary-level specialists, with few courses designed for secondary special education. Too often, high school teachers of exceptional students have had to develop their own programs on a trial-and-error basis.

IMPETUS FOR CHANGE

The vehicle for change at the secondary level has been oiled by sobering statistics on the status of post-high-school handicapped students and federal legislative mandates. Edwin Martin (1972, p. 524), Associate Commissioner for the Bureau of Education for the Handicapped, cited the following figures, which document the need for change in secondary programs:

- Only 21 percent of handicapped children will be fully employed or will continue with their education after high school
- 40 percent will be under-employed
- 26 percent will be unemployed
- 10 percent will be semi-dependent, needing a sheltered work situation or family support
- 3 percent will be totally dependent

Common Sense from a Closer Look (1978), a publication of the federally funded Parents' Campaign for Handicapped Children and Youth, stated that unemployed disabled adults outnumber the out-of-work normal population by a margin of almost three to one.

Three pieces of federal legislation provided the necessary legal power for facilitating development of concrete programs for adolescents and adults. First, Section 504 of the Rehabilitation Act of 1973 prohibits discrimination on the basis of a handicap for any federally funded program. Because public schools and many institutions of higher learning receive federal money, this law served as a door-opener for handicapped students. Second, the tenets of PL 94–142 encompass adolescents and young adults. The educational and vocational needs of this group must be dealt with and can no longer be ignored since the public schools have a legal responsibility to provide appropriate services. Third, the Vocational Education Act of 1976 (PL 94–482) broadens the range of responsibilities for appropriate education to all disabled persons, not just children. Thus, handicapped adults can also receive vocational education services. Ten percent of the funds given to states must be earmarked for the handicapped and 20 percent for the disadvantaged. The law also requires that federal funds for these programs be matched at the state and local levels (Phelps, 1977).

For many exceptional persons, high school is the last chance to prepare for adult responsibilities (Clark, 1975). Although a generally positive review was given to the mildly retarded person's ability to satisfactorily adjust to societal norms, unsatisfactory personal habits such as poor attitude, inefficiency, and irritability were cited by employers as major reasons for job failure (Robinson and Robinson, 1965). The authors suggested that extension of schooling and appropriate counseling services may help bridge the gap between the educational environment and living independently. To accomplish adequate adult preparation for the handicapped, several concepts that make high school education qualitatively different from elementary special education must be addressed by program planners.

NORMALIZATION

If there is any one term that describes the direction of the handicapped movement in the United States it is **normalization**. Normalization refers to providing opportunities for the handicapped so that they can move from marginal societal positions to more normal environments. Adolescents have the right to learn the skills necessary to survive in their community. Exceptional adults need to learn coping skills in order not to be regarded as misfits or objects of pity.

A decision must be made at the secondary level. Should normalization be realized through integration of exceptional and normal learners in the classroom? Or should it be effectuated through specialized programs focusing on preparation for adulthood that may require separate curricula? Clark (1975) cautioned that integration at this level may only be a superficial means of fulfilling legislative requirements. Speaking specifically about the educable mentally retarded population, Clark questioned whether this cosmetic approach to normalization can adequately meet the future adult needs of exceptional learners. The issue is not to ignore the mandates in the legislation, but rather to define what the least restrictive environment is for mildly educationally handicapped students.

Deinstitutionalization is one facet of the normalization movement that focuses on people institutionalized because of the degree of their retardation, mental illness, or disability. Normalizing their environment means moving them from the institution to community-based programs closer to home. Three factors provide the rationale for this trend: (1) recognition of the legal rights of all retarded citizens, (2) acceptance of the philosophy that care of the retarded should concentrate on their development—that it is better to teach the person as much as possible as opposed to providing custodial care (Payne, 1976), and (3) awareness that community care is less expensive.

This trend has brought the establishment of **community group homes** designed to care for and educate former institution residents. Such group homes have, however, met resistance not only from local communities but also from parents of institutionalized persons. Public misconceptions about the retarded fuel negative reactions to group homes. Many organizations now exist to aid the building of group homes and to reduce community resistance to them. One such agency—New York-based Community Residences Information Services Program (CRISP)—helps planners assess community attitudes and possible building sites as well as suggests solutions to potential problems (Stickney and Cupaiuolo, 1976).

The following story illustrates the unexpected success of a group home for the profoundly retarded in Oregon. This group home uses a behavioral approach to learning and emphasizes daily living skills (Fleischman, 1976).

In Oregon's Willamette Valley, rain is what falls with very little interruption from November to May. If this is October, the drizzle frosting the windshield can't be rain. Some locals put on hats for the autumn storm clouds scudding east into the Cascades, but the army surplus ponchos, the rubberized trousers, the L. L. Bean's moosehunting shoes are held in reserve. In the fall, moss gathers strength on the northern exposures.

Picking up the McKenzie River highway heading northeast out of Eugene, Dan Close is trying to reconstruct a dry July Sunday last summer when a year's work almost died on a highway bridge 48 miles up into the Cascades. Close was then the director of a new group home in Eugene for ten severely and profoundly retarded adults. He had been off that Sunday climbing Three Sisters Mountain while three of his weekend staff had taken the "folks" for a carefully planned hike along the McKenzie River. The folks were becoming accomplished walkers. Graduating from walks around town, the group-home residents were taken hiking at least every other weekend, usually along logging roads or major trails. The week before, a staff member had driven up to the tiny town of McKenzie Bridge to alert the rangers and to scout the trail.

It was a flawless summer day—so clear that when Close reached Three Sisters' summit he could see the snowy top of Mount Rainier to the north and, faintly but unmistakably, Mount Shasta over 200 miles south. He took color slides to prove it.

Tired from the day's climb, yet still exhilarated by the view, Close drove home along the river road—unaware that two of his folks had walked away from the hike. In the long July daylight, it was still bright when Close crossed the river above the little village of McKenzie Bridge and continued down the twisting valley towards home. He didn't know that less than two hours before, one of the missing residents had been struck and killed on the bridge itself by a woman motorist who told police that the man had lunged out into the roadway in front of her. When Close reached home, the phone was ringing. John Collier was dead, and Jim Clay had disappeared into the rugged woods.

Jim Clay was a strong, healthy 30-year-old with a measurable IQ below 20. He had almost no language and was wearing no coat. At about the same time that John Collier was run down on the highway bridge, Jim was spotted not very far away on the other side of the river. Crossing the McKenzie on a ramshackled log bridge, Jim encountered a local boy. The boy spoke to him, and Jim became frightened and bolted up a power-line break. The boy's father called the ranger station to report that his son had seen a strange man who looked to be on drugs.

By morning, Close was on his way back up the river road for the first of a dozen runs that July to join a search force of rangers, deputy sheriffs, group-home staffers, state police and volunteers backed by helicopters and light planes. A nearly equal force of television camerapersons and reporters—as well as the curious—turned up to watch the operation. The news media were very helpful, Close says, by emphasizing that Jim was not dangerous but only hungry and frightened. In their zeal to be of assistance, the people of McKenzie Bridge phoned in every report of an overturned garbage can or mysterious thump in the night. These false reports turned the search away from the rough hills and back towards the village.

Seven days after Jim disappeared, a man hiking up to his remote cabin spotted Jim standing in the cabin's doorway holding a jug of water. The man ran for help, and when the group-home staff came back with him, they found Jim sitting up in bed with his clothes neatly folded at the foot. He was 30 pounds lighter, spotlessly clean and very hungry.

In surviving, Jim performed skills he had never been directly taught. He selected a good path and then recognized shelter. He carried stream water back to the cabin in a jar. The water jar is a prime puzzler. Jim had filled plastic water jugs at the group home from a tap, but the connection between water from a running stream and water from a tap was his own discovery.

The river roars in the distance. Close starts back to the car. Up until the moments he lost John Collier on the trail, Jim's every waking moment had been programmed, the cues selected and presented in a uniform fashion. Then for seven days, Jim Clay ran his own life. "When he lost our cues, he found his own," says Close. (Copyright © 1976 *Human Behavior* Magazine. Reprinted by permission.)

Even though there are approximately 200,000 severely and profoundly retarded Americans, they are the most neglected of the handicapped population in terms of available appropriate services and programs (Fleishman, 1976). With emphasis shifting from institutional care to community group homes, a clear need exists for competent special educators, training programs, and community cooperation.

The process of deinstitutionalization is viewed as a humane effort to give retarded citizens the rights and privileges of all Americans. Because society has traditionally hidden the retarded, most of us have not had the opportunity to interact with them. We have preconceived stereotypes of them, spotlighting their negative characteristics with no notion of their strengths and abilities. Probably the biggest hurdle for retarded and disabled citizens to overcome is society's ignorance of their potential. If the normal adult population were tested on their knowledge of mentally retarded people, their scores would most likely reflect a "severe and profound" deficit.

CAREER EDUCATION

The realization that handicapped adolescents and adults have not been successful at finding and maintaining jobs has led to an emphasis on **career education**. Career education tries to connect material learned in school with aspects of everyday life. Some proponents view the goal of career education simply as gainful employment. For others, the concept also encompasses life skills, such as the development of social relationships, management of finances, and the handling of a household, in order to function independently within the community (Brolin and D'Alonzo, 1979; Phelps and Lutz, 1977).

Career education is a learning process that affects the individual's total lifestyle, beginning at elementary school and continuing through high school. This educational approach may be applied to all students, regardless of their level of academic functioning. It is, though, particularly relevant to handicapped students because it "brings meaning to the curriculum by making individuals more aware

An appropriate educational program with related support services assist the disabled adult in becoming a contributing member of society.

of themselves, their potentials, and their individual needs" (Brolin and D'Alonzo, 1979, p. 251). A secondary work/study coordinator referred to the concept as "motivational education" since it is necessary to show children the reason for studying certain material and how it relates to their goals.

Phelps and Lutz (1977) see career education as having three stages: (1) career awareness, which is developed at the elementary level through exposure to different career opportunities; (2) career exploration, commencing at the junior high level and stressing hands-on experiences, work values, and responsibilities; and (3) career preparation, occurring at the high school level to gain specific skills and abilities related to work and community living. From this perspective, career education pervades the entire educational system and is not limited to a separate subject or emphasis solely at the high school level.

Career education programs must provide information to students so they can choose a career that matches their interests and abilities. This means adequate student counseling must be provided. At a career-orientation stage, students are exposed to the many facets entailed in a specific career. They need to decide whether they could adapt to jobs that call for physical exertion or would rather have lighter work; whether outside jobs are more attractive than indoor work. Basic questions such as these are what students must answer at this stage.

At the end of the high school career education program is **vocational education**, which corresponds to career preparation. Although vocational education programs have existed for some time, many handicapped students have been excluded from them. Table 7-1 describes some of the barriers that confront exceptional students who wish to participate in these programs.

TABLE 7-1 Factors Interfering with the Handicapped's Participation in Vocational Education

Type of Barrier	Cause of Barrier
Societal Barriers	Tendency to focus on inabilities rather than abilities
	Apathy and indifference because of a lack of knowledge and awareness about the handicapped
	Inaccessible buildings, travelways, and public transportation
	Inadequate public leadership promoting the causes of the handicapped
	Reluctance to understand those who are different and to part with stereotypes
Professional Barriers	Competition for attention, time, money, and priority status
	Lack of knowledge of services needed on the part of program administrators, developers, and evaluators
	Lack of interagency cooperation, coordination, and planning
	Insufficient use of handicapped persons and their parents in the planning of programs and services
	Inadequate preservice and in-service personnel development
	Lack of a planned continuum of services
Personal Barriers	Tendency to foster or accept dependence rather than train independence
	Lack of knowledge about opportunities, services, and rights
	Inadequate career counseling
	Oversensitivity to criticism
	Lack of self-understanding and appreciation
	Tendency to succumb to pressure to conform to inferior roles and expectations

Adapted from a list appearing in Hull, M. E. *A Review of Vocational Education for the Handicapped*, Columbus: Center for Vocational Education, Ohio State University, 1977.

The rationale for providing more intensive preparation for handicapped learners has both an empirical and a logical base. In reviewing the research on the postschool job-success rate of retarded adults, Brolin (1976) found that while these persons can be highly successful on the job, approximately 35 to 40 percent of them experience difficulty adjusting to the work and community environments. (These adjustment problems are related to the barriers described in Table 7-1.)

Siegel (1974, p. 195) presented support for more adequate vocational education in this manner:

The ability to earn a living—if it is in one's potential to do so—is probably the single most valid indicator of an adequate adjustment to life. One need not marry, or graduate from college (or even high school, for that matter), or have many friends, or serve in the military, in order to attain a reasonable degree of personal adjustment. But the young adult who cannot support himself is a failure. He has failed for many reasons: Employment signifies financial independence at a time when one should be independent. Employment is a clear mark of adulthood, obviating the need for continuous and total parental assistance. By making it possible for him to increase the actual physical distance between himself and his parents, employment can, in effect, complete the separation process. It marks a person as "normal." It is a visible sign of achievement —by no means a picayune consideration in our achievement oriented society.

PROGRAM DEVELOPMENT

Assessment

At the elementary level, identification of exceptional students is deficit oriented; in fact, oriented toward identifying and remediating weaknesses. Assessment efforts seek to uncover weaknesses in order to provide a curriculum that helps the student keep up with his or her peers. At the secondary level, this approach may not be the most relevant. Many educators have stressed determining the student's strengths rather than concentrating on deficits (Brolin, 1976; Deshler, 1978). If we accept the notion that the end result of high school education is to produce a functionally competent adult, then dealing with an individual adolescent's strengths appears to be a concept worthy of further study. For example, normal individuals do not highlight their weaknesses when searching for a meaningful career. If one is uncomfortable with foreign languages, a liberal-arts college program that demands some expertise in language may be avoided. Exceptional students should also make use of this common-sense approach to career development.

Vocational evaluation is an approach to assessment of the handicapped adolescent that is gaining acceptance. Although developed primarily to meet the needs of educable mentally retarded students, this approach may be applied to other areas of exceptionality, such as the learning disabled. As outlined by Brolin (1976), vocational evaluation has the following components:

- Clinical assessment, which includes medical, educational, social, and psychological evaluations
- Work evaluation, involving measures of vocational interests and abilities
- Work adjustment, which centers on evaluating attitudes, social skills, and instructional needs necessary to successful work experiences
- On-the-job tryouts, which is a more pragmatic approach to assessing how an individual performs in a real-life situation

The purpose of such a comprehensive approach to assessment is to view the adolescent from several perspectives to lay the basis for proper programming. Its success requires the cooperation of many professionals, an important consideration for developers of secondary education programs.

Professional Cooperation

Brolin's concept of vocational evaluation reveals that a wide variety of people are needed in the assessment procedure as well as in the training and evaluation. At the school level, special educators, work/study coordinators, vocational trainers, rehabilitation experts, and community agencies are just a few of the needed personnel. A common problem in program implementation stems from the inadequate training of both special educators and vocational educators: the former are skilled in working with exceptional students but are more academically oriented; the latter are trained to teach work-related competencies but are geared to teaching the nonhandicapped population.

In addition to establishing a local team approach, state agencies must commit themselves to joint planning and fund sharing. The state departments of special education, vocational education, and vocational rehabilitation have the common goal of providing services to handicapped persons. Personnel of various agencies must work together to enhance training and follow-up of the handicapped worker and to avoid duplicating services. A state organization in St. Paul, Minnesota— Project Special Education, Rehabilitation, and Vocational Education (SERVE) —represents a model work/study approach to secondary education. Not only funds but also personnel are coordinated among three state agencies (Special Education, Vocational Rehabilitation, and Vocational Education) to meet student, parent, and community needs. Assistance is continued after high school if employment is not achieved. Table 7-2 outlines activities that can be funded through these three programs.

The President's Committee on Employment of the Handicapped (1976, p. 24) identified lack of interagency cooperation as a barrier to successful job training and placement of the handicapped. The problem was described in this manner:

> This deficiency in our job preparation and placement system becomes clear when we follow the path a handicapped child has to travel. First, there's special education. Next, if the handicapped child is fortunate, vocational education or industrial arts or vocational rehabilitation. And, lastly, employment security for job placement. Rarely, during this process does one agency reinforce or support the efforts of another...a handicapped child who is admitted into a vocational education class may need support (financial) from vocational rehabilitation for devices or aids that will help him to succeed. Or, that handicapped child may require program support (pre-vocational skills) from special education during the time he is with vocational education. Alone or independently, vocational education may be incapable of serving the student. Yet, there remains a reluctance for individual agencies to cooperate among themselves for fear they may lose their integrity or credit for the resources they expend.

As programs and support services for handicapped students and adults begin to take form, more cooperation among the various disciplines and agencies becomes imperative.

Secondary Options

Several options are open to exceptional pupils in high school. The general curriculum (consisting of home economics, industrial arts, general math, and general English) is still available but not regarded as the most worthwhile choice if successful adult living is a goal. Students enrolled in this type of program usually show up later in unemployment statistics because the course of study does not adequately prepare them for their futures.

Vocational Education

Figure 7-1 shows how vocational education can be broken into more distinct programs. Work/study programs, regular vocational schools, and special vocational programs are options for exceptional high school students. Although this

Activities that May Be Co-Supported by Three Programs

	Special Education	Vocational Rehabilitation	Vocational Education
Find Activities:			
1. Public awareness	X		
2. Professional awareness	X		
3. Mass screening	X		
4. Individual screening	X		
Assessment Activities:			
1. General psychological evaluations	X		
2. Social/home/peer evaluation	X		
3. Educational evaluations	X		
4. Speech and language evaluations	X		
5. General medical examinations	X		
6. Specific medical examinations	X	X	
7. Vocational interest/aptitude		X	X
8. Rehabilitation potential		X	X
Program Planning:			
1. General vocational/skill instruction	X		X
2. Vocational education and specific job preparation			X
3. Industrial arts education and home-making education	X		X
4. Modification of vocational education equipment			X
5. Academic/vocational supporting instruction	X		X
6. Counseling—academic adjustment	X		
7. Counseling—personal adjustment	X	X	
8. Counseling—vocational adjustment	X	X	X
9. Medical services other than diagnostic (restoration)		X	
10. Mental therapy (restoration)		X	
11. Hearing aids, telecommunication, and other devices	X	X	
12. Other related services, OT, PT, speech therapy, etc.	X	X	
13. Career awareness activities	X		X
14. Work-study opportunities	X	X	X
15. Job development		X	
16. Job placement		X	X
17. Occupational licenses, tools, equipment, and supplies		X	
18. Post-employment follow-up		X	X
19. Family support services	X	X	
20. Transportation	X	X	X
21. Recruiting and training services to create new employment opportunities and public service area		X	

(From "Making Better Use of Support Services," E. Gallay and G. J. Bensberg, *School Shop*, Vol. 37, No. 8, 1978, p. 56.)

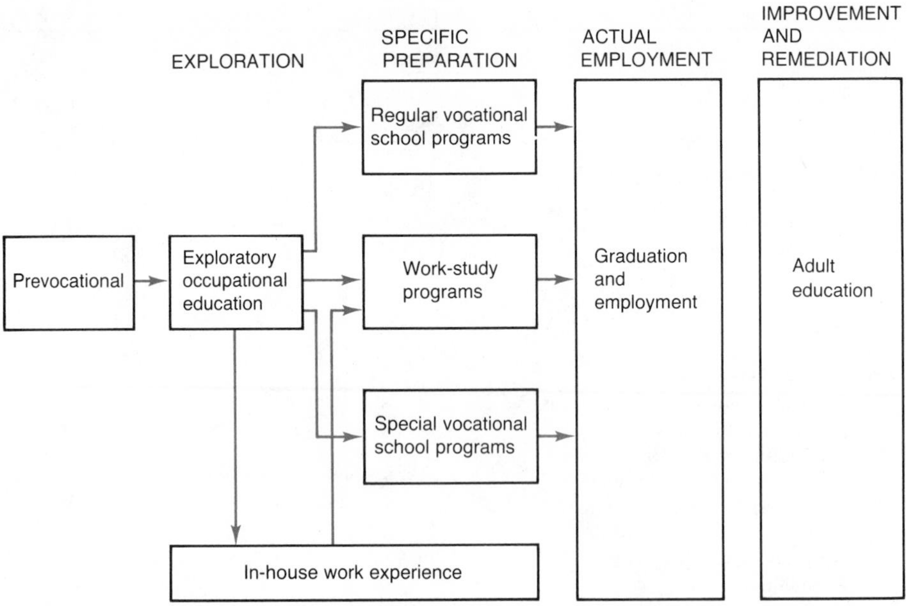

FIGURE 7-1 Occupational preparation patterns for learning-disabled youth. (From Mann-Goodman-Wiederholt: TEACHING THE LEARNING-DISABLED ADOLESCENT. Copyright © 1978 by Houghton-Mifflin Company. Used by permission.)

model was designed for learning disabled students, it also applies to other exceptional learners.

Project SERVE, mentioned earlier, is an example of a **work/study program**. Students attend their own high school for half a day to receive training in job-related academic and social activities. In this program, students are integrated with nonhandicapped students in physical education, home economics, industrial arts, and other courses. The rest of the day is spent in on-the-job training in the community or at a vocational high school (Lake, 1974).

Another program—the Career Development Center (CDC) in New York—provides a specialized environment for high school students who cannot cope with traditional high school programs. The goal of CDC is to prepare students to return to their high schools by focusing on students' affective needs (such as self-concept and attitudes) as well as on job-related skills. This program serves as an alternative to in-house high school programs for students needing the opportunity to make the transition from high school to adult responsibilities (Lake, 1974).

Project SERVE and the Career Development Center (both of which receive special funding) are two examples of the differing arrangements that can serve handicapped students. Possibilities range from a more academic program for students desiring to continue their education past high school to work/study programs to separate vocational schools.

Preprofessional Education

This course of study is the one most familiar to college students. It contains what we consider "hard-core" academic subjects. With adequate support services, many handicapped youth may find this option the most appropriate for future goals. Professionals must guard against the notion that a handicapping condition means automatic placement in a vocationally oriented curriculum.

Non-High-School Adolescents

Thus far, programs for the mildly handicapped who can function in high school have been the primary concern. There is another group of people largely removed from the public eye who also deserve a special program for adult preparation. The moderately retarded (trainable mentally retarded) usually receive separate educational services in schools financed and operated by state and county boards of mental retardation. As adolescents and adults, these people are placed in **sheltered workshops**, which provide vocational opportunities in a supportive environment without the typical demands of the world of work. Sheltered workshops have existed for a long time. There is, however, still a need for adequate vocational evaluation systems and qualified personnel to train and supervise these special workers.

Traditionally, the moderately retarded have been relegated to mundane jobs because this group is stereotyped. Marc Gold (1968) of the University of Illinois developed programs demonstrating that the retarded can perform useful functions in society. One program involves simplifying the complex task of a 15-piece bicycle-brake assembly. The severely retarded have demonstrated that they can perform this job with adequate training. Another program, also at the University of Illinois, successfully teaches moderately retarded 18- and 19-year-olds truck-driving skills. These results suggest that commonly held perceptions of retarded individuals are steeped in myth.

Workshops can provide young disabled adults with learning and earning opportunities necessary for independent living.

Educational programs for exceptional adults are sparse, but they are beginning to develop from the impetus of the 1973 Rehabilitation Act and the mandate of PL 94–142 requiring services to exceptional students through age 21. State departments of vocational rehabilitation have been the primary service providers to disabled adults. These agencies give training, materials, and assistance in job placements. As mentioned earlier, the task of vocational rehabilitation is to establish a liaison with high school vocational education programs; this link-up will provide a continuum of services to the postsecondary exceptional person. Discussed here are two postsecondary training options for adults who desire to further their education.

Technical Training

New programs are evolving with the aid of state and public education efforts. Michigan, for example, extended their public schools' responsibilities for exceptional students to age 25. As part of the state chain of vocational institutes, Minnesota created the Technical Vocational Institute for Deaf Students (TVID) in 1969 (Lake, 1974). This postsecondary program was put together in response to deaf students' educational needs, and it enrolls deaf students from across the country.

Higher Education

Colleges and unversities have also begun to respond to the needs of exceptional persons. The President's Committee on Employment of the Handicapped (1977) published a directory of 500 universities that provide services to handicapped students. Entitled *Getting through College with a Disability*, it is based on a national survey of institutions of higher education and outlines the types of college services available to disabled students. The appendices include listings of organizations in each state that aid handicapped students in making college decisions.

TRENDS AND ISSUES

Throughout this chapter, several general themes have emerged in regard to the education of exceptional adolescents and adults. The recentness of concern for this age group makes, however, the considerations tentative and without a strong research base. The issues and needed research that should be addressed are outlined in the following sections.

Program Evaluation

What constitutes the most appropriate learning situation for exceptional adolescents? Work/study, vocational high schools, and placement in regular classes with special aid have all been proposed and have been effective with some students. The difficulty arises in matching student needs and abilities with viable programs. Not only must creative programs be designed, but student progress and satisfaction with the course of study must be evaluated.

Competency standards for teachers wishing to instruct the exceptional teenager and adult need to be devised. Teacher training institutions must respond by analyzing the differences among elementary, secondary, and postsecondary populations before designing coursework and experiences for the exceptional adolescent and adult.

A more experiential approach could be used. It is one thing to be able to develop a lesson plan for a hypothetical learner and quite another to put it into practice competing with all the other considerations and pressures a teacher faces daily. Many special education teacher training programs are requiring prospective teachers to work with handicapped adults. Such experiences help student-teachers gain insight into the life problems that exceptional persons encounter (Hamalian and Ludwig, 1976).

Cooperation

The interdisciplinary teams discussed in the last chapter are certainly appropriate at the adolescent and adult levels. It is vital for exceptional individuals that the professionals who give services recognize exactly what they can and cannot accomplish. Asking for someone else's expertise is not a sign of ineptitude; it indicates true professionalism.

SUMMARY POINTS

■ Professional recognition, in conjunction with parental pressures and legislative mandates, resulted in expanding special education and related services to adolescents and young adults.

■ Among adults, approximately only one in five handicapped persons is fully employed. Handicapped adults face many economic and social barriers that prevent them from being assimilated into the mainstream of adult life and responsibilities.

■ The realization of the legal rights of handicapped adults has resulted in deinstitutionalization. In order to develop coping and daily-living skills in formerly institutionalized persons, community group homes are being developed.

■ Career education programs from kindergarten through high school are designed to assist students in seeing the relationship between school-related material and everyday living. Vocational education programs, a component of career education, are for the adolescent. In the past, handicapped students were prevented from enrolling in vocational programs.

■ Vocational evaluation includes not only the more traditional areas of assessment (e.g., medical and educational), but also includes observing and evaluating handicapped adolescents in simulated work experience and related job skills.

■ In order for vocational evaluation and vocational education to be successful, they must be planned and implemented cooperatively by the school, related professionals, and community agencies and businesses.

- The curriculum of a vocational education program can be developed using either a work/study program, regular vocational schools, or special vocational programs.
- For the more severely handicapped individual, sheltered workshops may provide an appropriate setting for developing vocational skills.
- In order for many handicapped adults to have a successful college experience, institutions of higher learning will need to develop more flexible, nontraditional approaches.

REVIEW QUESTIONS

1. How many handicapped students are enrolled at your university? What criteria, if any, do your university have regarding housing for the handicapped? Library services and materials? Peer tutors? Accessibility to buildings?
2. Define normalization and deinstitutionalization.
3. List the three stages of career education and give an example of each.
4. What barriers prevent the handicapped adult from being assimilated into society? What changes can be made to facilitate their integration into society?

VOCATIONAL REHABILITATION

A vital link to appropriate employment for handicapped persons ages 18 to 65 is the Bureau of Vocational Rehabilitation (BVR), also called the Division of Vocational Rehabilitation (DVR) in some states. These programs are funded primarily through federal allocations (80 percent) and partly through state allocations (20 percent). Organizationally, state programs are under the Rehabilitation Service Administration, affiliated with the U.S. Department of Education. Within each state are local offices regionally based to provide services for eligible persons.

The goal of BVR is to assist eligible handicapped persons in vocational adjustment by providing adaptive equipment and training and locating suitable employment. Support services can begin at age 16 or 17 for handicapped adolescents attending vocational schools. These services usually supply prosthetic devices, such as glasses, hearing aids, and artificial limbs.

Any handicapped adult may request services from BVR. Other referral sources include schools, health departments, mental health agencies, welfare departments, and physicians. Here is the usual sequence of events that occurs when a person requests services:

1. *Initial Intake*: This represents the first contact with the local BVR agency. The secretary records basic identifying information, such as name, address, age, and handicapping condition.

2. *Counselor Assignment*: The case is given to a staff counselor who will be responsible for coordinating services and planning to meet the client's needs. The minimum requirement for a counselor position is a bachelor's degree, usually in psychology, social work, counseling, or special education.

3. *Initial Interview*: The counselor meets with the client to review goals, determine the nature of the handicap, and plan for any necessary examinations. Depending on the handicap, evaluation procedures may review medical, psychological, work adjustment, hearing, dental, and speech/language status. These evaluation services are contracted by BVR from appropriate agencies or health care facilities. For example, a work evaluation may be obtained from Goodwill Industries or a sheltered workshop for the mentally retarded, while a psychological examination would be requested from a mental health agency or a psychologist in private practice.

4. *Eligibility Determination*: A three-step process determines if the applicant can receive services from BVR. First, the necessary evaluations are completed. Second, the results are reviewed by appropriate consultants on the BVR staff. The consultant's task is to decide if the evaluation report indicates that the applicant is disabled. The third step determines whether or not the disability is a work-related handicap for the applicant. (The difference between a disability and a handicap was discussed in Chapter 1.) To illustrate the BVR decision-making process, suppose two people are involved in separate car accidents and receive injuries that require the use of a prosthetic leg. One of the injured persons is a teacher and the other is employed as a dancer. While both people are disabled, only the dancer is handicapped because the teacher, when recovered, can resume employment. Of course, not all cases are clearcut. The counselor must decide if a handicap exists and, if so, to proceed to the next step.

5. *Formulating a Program*: At this stage, the counselor and the client write a rehabilitation program that includes all necessary restoration services. Training, medical intervention, physical equipment, educational tutoring, psychotherapy, and on-the-job training provided by an industry or other work site may be included in the program. A mutual decision-making process between the counselor and the client allows the client to maintain autonomy and responsibility for his or her own future.

6. *Follow-Up*: After the client is placed in a suitable employment situation, the counselor follows the client through the adjustment phase to determine if both the client and the employer are satisfied. If, after a 60-day period, the placement is judged successful by all parties, the local BVR office closes the case. If the placement is unsatisfactory, the counselor and client review the rehabilitation program and make necessary changes. One year from the closing date of the case, BVR tracks the client to determine if he or she is still working, has been promoted, or is working with a different company in a similar capacity to the one originally planned.

BVR will pay for any of the necessary services for eligible applicants that are not covered by insurance, Social Security, disability income, or other resources available to the client. As indicated in the description of the organizatonal process, BVR utilizes a great many community resources to aid handicapped adults in securing suitable work. BVR is an important resource for all handicapped persons and for the professionals who work with them.

Students interested in learning more about vocational rehabilitation programs should contact their local or state Bureau/Division of Vocational Rehabilitation (which can be found in state government listings).

1. Compare the eligibility procedures for receiving BVR services with those for determining special education placement. In what way are the types of information needed for decision-making the same? How do they differ?
2. BVR requires that the counselor and the client engage in mutual decision-making to formulate a rehabilitation program for the handicapped person. Do you think this mutual decision-making process should be required in developing IEPs for exceptional children? If yes, what advantages do you think are derived from involving exceptional children and youth in determining special education placement and planning their own IEPs?

SUGGESTED READINGS

Brolin, D. E. *Vocational Preparation of Retarded Citizens*. Columbus, Ohio: Charles E. Merrill, 1976.

Lake, T. P., ed. *Career Education: Exemplary Programs for the Handicapped*. Reston, Va.: Council for Exceptional Children, 1974.

Phelps, L. A., and Lutz, R. J. *Career Exploration and Preparation for Special Needs Learners*. Boston: Allyn and Bacon, 1977.

CONTENTS

PROFESSIONAL PREPARATION

This chapter concerns professional preparation for the modern educator. What worked 20 years ago in the classroom may not be relevant today. What once were regarded as major teacher responsibilities now may be expanded, delegated to another professional, or dropped altogether. As you read, compare the ideas presented here to your own concept of what teaching entails. Chances are that your views, molded by your past experiences as a student, may be outdated. Because teaching is a dynamic process, teachers must be willing to change; they must be willing and able to examine and evaluate their own behavior and opinions and to make modifications when needed.

ROLE CHANGES

The preceding chapters discussed the effects of legal and educational changes on the lives of exceptional people. Those charged with implementing programs for exceptional persons—special and regular teachers—are also deeply involved in the change process. A teacher's concerns were formerly centered primarily on the students in the classroom; today's teacher shares skills, students, and plans with a variety of adults, which indicates that role boundaries are now more flexible. This is a major departure from traditional instructional duties—teachers must now be as skilled in working with adults as they are in working with children. School psychologists, reading teachers, principals, speech therapists, and learning disability specialists are no longer people to send children *to*—they are colleagues to work *with* to implement individual programs for handicapped children.

In order to meet the special needs of children, new roles have been created and old ones restructured. As a result of PL 94–142, special education teachers have by far the greatest job diversification of any professional. Where once they dealt with certain exceptionalities, they now must deal also with the methods of delivering services. The two major roles that the specialist may play and the concomitant changes in the regular educator's position are discussed in the following sections.

Resource Room Teacher

This role evolved from two mainstreaming needs: (1) to directly serve more handicapped children, and (2) to provide support services to regular teachers who were instructing exceptional students. **Resource room teachers** serve students whose behavior and learning deficits inhibit success in a regular classroom. This model is appropriate for both the elementary and secondary levels.

The resource teacher provides a transition between self-contained, special placement and full-time placement in a regular classroom. Typically, a class load is between 15 and 25 children, depending upon state guidelines. Children receive individualized instruction from the resource teacher in those areas identified in the IEP and attend the regular classroom for instruction in all other subjects.

The regular classroom teacher has the major responsibility for each child's education. This situation reflects a change of duties because the self-contained special education teacher formerly provided all services to handicapped children. The resource room specialist consults with the regular teacher and helps with the educational planning and instruction for exceptional children. Table 8-1 lists activities and techniques that resource teachers can implement to initiate inter-

- Explain test results and the child's strengths and weaknesses
- Provide materials for use in the regular classroom and invite regular teachers to the resource room to observe students and to use materials
- Plan and help to implement a behavior management plan for a child having difficulty adjusting to the classroom environment
- Deliver in-service workshops to share instructional techniques and characteristics of handicapped learners
- Meet to discuss the child's progress and to plan activities
- Attend parent/teacher conferences
- Offer ideas to help classmates understand and accept their handicapped peers
- Team teach with the regular teacher to gain an appreciation of his or her responsibilities
- Ask the regular teacher for suggestions to solve problems encountered in the resource room
- Ask for specific scheduling suggestions that would help minimize interruptions of the daily routine
- Provide quick follow-up to special requests from regular teachers
- Show the regular teacher the work the student has done in the resource room

action with regular teachers (Harrison, 1976; Grotsky, Sabatino, and Ohrtman, 1976; Knight, 1976; Lott, Hudak, and Scheetz, 1975).

Both regular and special educators must make compromises. While the resource teacher may be cast as a problem-solver, it is equally important that regular teachers remain open to new ideas and develop their own innovative teaching techniques.

Consulting Teacher

The **consulting teacher** (a variation of the resource room teacher) has little, if any, direct teaching responsibility. Possible consultant roles include being a "diagnostician, remedial teacher, materials specialist, an advocate, and administrator of varied services that impinge on the entire school building's education program" (Hawisher and Calhoun, 1978, p. 141). For example, a consultant may work directly with regular classroom teachers to establish instructional goals and teaching strategies, as well as to make classroom accommodations to mainstream exceptional pupils. At the high-school level, the consulting teacher may work directly with the vocational education instructor in the design and follow-through of career education plans.

The University of Vermont maintains a graduate program for training regular elementary teachers to serve as consulting teachers (Christie, McKenzie, and Burdett, 1972). This two-year program combines university course work with classroom application to train teachers in behavior modification techniques, individualized instruction, and adaptation of materials. The consulting teacher, as a specialist, can then teach colleagues these strategies by conducting in-service training workshops.

An advantage of the consulting-teacher approach is that many exceptional learners can be served indirectly. The regular educator takes an active role in the child's learning by using the skills developed through interaction with the consulting teacher. All children in the classroom benefit from the teacher's increased skill.

THE CONSULTATION PROCESS

Consultation has thus far referred to interaction between a special educator and a regular classroom teacher. There are also others involved in consultation: principals, school psychologists, speech therapists, and parents. This expansion of adult communication is a relatively new phenomenon in educational circles and deserves more attention in teacher education.

Consulting with Professionals

Consultation contains three elements: the consultant (special teacher, school psychologist, reading specialist), the consultee (regular teacher, volunteer, paraprofessional, parent), and the child. The purpose of consultation is to assist the regular teacher or parent in meeting the needs of the student. Because it is an indirect method, consultation can frustrate special educators accustomed to working directly with handicapped children. Several factors can become potential problems, and the consultant must be aware of them before any communication begins (Parker, 1975).

- *Differences in Expertise*: The consultant has been trained to work with exceptional children; thus, he or she feels more comfortable with special programs than does the regular classroom teacher. The consultant shares information that will enable the teacher to work more confidently with the exceptional student. For example, professional terminology may lack concrete meaning to the teacher. By translating technical concepts into understandable ideas, the consultant provides an important way to overcome difficulties in training and background, which ultimately benefits the child.
- *Class Size*: The consultant and regular teacher focus on one child during a consultation, but in the daily situation the classroom teacher is responsible for 25 to 30 other children. This fact means that, in many instances, the consultant also must consider the classroom as a system. A consultant may recommend, for example, that a chapter in a social studies text be taped so a child with inadequate reading skills can more readily grasp the content. This recommendation should then include plans for having the story taped (perhaps by an older student), identification of other students who could benefit from this experience, and suggestions on how this technique can fit into the teacher's overall lesson plan.
- *Status*: Classroom teachers traditionally have taken primary responsibility for all student activity. The addition of a consultant may be a welcome relief, but it may also be viewed as a threat to the teacher's authority and expertise. To ensure a good working relationship, the consultant must be sensitive to defensive attitudes, must prove that he or she has something of value to offer, and must also be willing to explore any hostile feelings. If a consultation is a burden rather than a productive encounter, the exceptional student benefits little.

■ *Coordination*:   Professionals other than regular teachers interact with the child; it is thus important that communication among these people be smooth in order to establish a consistent approach with the child. A student may be receiving help from the school counselor to control disruptive behavior. The consultant needs to translate identifiable goals into workable classroom activities. Meetings need to be arranged so all involved can share information or change plans.

Parker (1975) identified four major abilities that consultants should possess: (1) ability to assess the child's strengths and weaknesses, (2) ability to negotiate goals, (3) ability to develop a treatment plan, and (4) ability to teach skills to the regular teacher. These competencies differentiate the task of teaching children from that of interacting with adults.

Assessing the child's strengths and weaknesses is done in conjunction with the classroom teacher. To get a complete assessment, the consultant must also be able to evaluate the teacher's strengths and weaknesses, and understand any teacher biases. This information comes from classroom observation and from an interest survey completed by the teachers. After the assessment, negotiation of goals must take place. For example, the teacher may see reducing out-of-seat behavior as the critical goal, while the consultant believes the level of difficulty of the work to be the major factor. The consultant must be willing to compromise and to help prioritize goals logically.

A treatment plan involves determining a method for accomplishing the stated goals. If the goal were to reduce the work difficulty, the plan might include using different materials, assigning a peer tutor, or restructuring lessons. To develop the treatment plan, the consultant must teach the regular educator the necessary skills. Role playing, modeling, and team teaching techniques may be employed. In adopting a mainstreaming approach for exceptional students, one special education teacher taught reading to first- and second-graders in small groups as a part of a team. The specialist helped devise plans for the handicapped readers within the context of these reading groups. This teacher then helped instruct all groups. This avoided stigmatizing the poorer readers by not singling them out. The consultant can work in a similar manner to help make suggestions meaningful.

Lott, Hudak, and Scheetz (1975) outline strategies for the consultation process of assessment, negotiation, treatment, and teaching: during the interview it is important to deal with only one or two problems and to avoid moving randomly from subject to subject; a written plan of each person's responsibilities should follow every consultation; the consultant must be consistent in following up on the status of the written plan. The classroom teacher has many other concerns and needs continued support from the consultant to achieve the agreed-upon treatment plan.

Consultation cannot just be read about and then carried out successfully. It takes practice and flexibility to become an expert consultant. An attitude of understanding and toleration is crucial. If the consultant is too task oriented without due regard for the classroom teacher's feelings, little will be accomplished. Moreover, the consultant has the responsibility to help the classroom teacher recognize that consultation is a collaborative effort. The consultant cannot wave a magic wand to make all problems vanish; meeting the needs of handicapped children is a difficult, time-consuming task.

There are several points, if agreed upon by both the consultant and classroom teacher, that help the consultation work more effectively:

■ Both persons must be willing to spend the time necessary to plan, solve problems, and resolve differences.
■ Each must believe that no one person can meet all the needs of an exceptional student.
■ Open dialogues must occur in which opinions are given freely. If the classroom teacher does not feel comfortable enough to disagree with an impractical suggestion, or if the consultant senses disagreement and does not encourage it to surface, consultation may be no more than a ritual.

Figure 8-1 contrasts the resource teacher who provides direct services and the consultant teacher's professional responsibilities for handicapped students in an integrated educational environment. Note that the latter requires interprofessional interaction whereas the former focuses on students and allows for limited, if any, interprofessional interaction.

Consulting with Parents

Parents of exceptional students are expected to play increasingly larger roles in planning the education of their children. Because they see the child in a non-academic environment, away from a large group of children, parents have valuable insights into the child's goals, strengths, weaknesses, and behavior. Teachers should be adept in gathering parental information and should consider parents allies.

Parent conferences during evaluation and placement are mandated by PL 94–142. These may be viewed as simply a formality, with the parents "signing off" so their child can receive special services, or they can be used to learn more about the child. In order to obtain new information, teachers must be sensitive to the parents' feelings and recognize the parents' priorities for their child. Parents may feel intimidated faced by a group of experts and be hesitant to volunteer their own valuable knowledge.

To establish rapport with parents, teachers should:

■ Make sure confusing education jargon is avoided
■ Explain, in understandable terms, test results and the limitations of test data
■ Offer alternatives to placement decisions and annual goals, and help parents weigh the merits of these suggestions

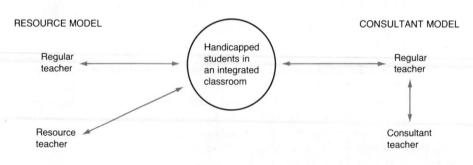

RESOURCE MODEL

CONSULTANT MODEL

Regular teacher

Handicapped students in an integrated classroom

Regular teacher

Resource teacher

Consultant teacher

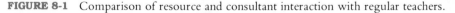

FIGURE 8-1 Comparison of resource and consultant interaction with regular teachers.

■ Solicit parental opinions on all topics discussed
■ Reinforce parental rights to obtain a second opinion, to question the goals and objectives being planned, to give their views on what they want for their child, and to suggest methods for attaining these goals

After placement, further communication between parents and school is largely controlled by the teacher and parents. Parents are required to attend meetings only when the IEP is being changed and at the time of the annual review. Thus, the teacher should devise ways to keep parents in touch with the classroom activities that occur between these meetings. One communication device for the earlier grades might be a weekly or monthly classroom newsletter of events, children's work, and teacher's tip columns for helping children at home. A teacher might, for instance, present short quizzes after a child completes a unit of instruction. The questions could be based on previous successful schoolwork. Each quiz might also contain questions for the child to ask the parent. Such activity allows the parent an excellent opportunity to interact positively with the child; it also lets the child "show off" newly acquired skills. And it gives an alternative answer to the question, What did you do in school today? Instead of shrugging or saying "nothing," the child has something tangible to show, and the parents have something concrete to go on.

Strenecky, McLoughlin, and Edge (1979) offer other suggestions for parent involvement that are appropriate at all grade levels. One is to use parents as tutors. Training and evaluation sessions should be organized to give parents feedback on their work and to ensure continuity with the teacher's goals. When parents are directly involved in school activities, not only will they increase their parenting skills, they will also appreciate the teacher's responsibilities. Another way to involve parents is to form parent groups where participants can share common frustrations and learn how others deal with parenting or child development programs. School psychologists and principals should also be invited to help plan the groups and to answer parents' questions.

If teachers wait until problems arise before contacting parents, or if they send only negative notes home ("Sally isn't doing her work," "Johnny is daydreaming again"), they should not be surprised if they receive little response. At this point, teachers are essentially asking parents to solve problems they themselves cannot handle when, instead, a collaborative relationship should be in the process of being established. In essence, every effort should be directed toward prevention, rather than waiting until intervention is necessary.

COMPONENTS OF EFFECTIVE TEACHING

To the consternation of beginners, there is no single formula for surefire success in teaching. Instructing is a blend of teacher personality, teacher strengths and weaknesses, children's unique needs, and teacher/child interaction, which varies from child to child, day to day, and class to class. These and many other factors prevent clearly defined constructs for successful teaching. There are, however, several strategies for aiding children in their learning, which, in turn, may lead to successful teaching.

The strategies to be discussed in this section originated in special education classrooms. But one need not to be a special educator to use them. It is important to keep in mind that these methods are not mutually exclusive; they can be combined and varied.

Behavioral Objectives

The first step in instructional planning is to determine what to teach. The subject matter may be obvious (math, writing, reading), but the actual process of teaching takes careful planning. The overall curriculum for a school system may dictate that children in the second grade learn to write in cursive. The instructor's task, then, is to specify a plan that will take the children from point A (manuscript writing) to point B (cursive writing).

Stating teaching goals as **behavioral objectives** is one way to facilitate the teaching/learning process. Behavioral objectives are different from other goals in that they describe, in measurable terms, exactly what is expected of the learner. Consider the following sets of objectives:

1. John will know his name.
2. Given the class roster, John will point to his name when asked on five consecutive days.

1. Ann will understand the game of basketball.
2. When viewing a basketball game, Ann will correctly state if her favorite team is using a zone or man-to-man defense for nine of ten possessions by the opposing team.

In this individualized instructional setting, the teaching goal is recognition of basic shapes.

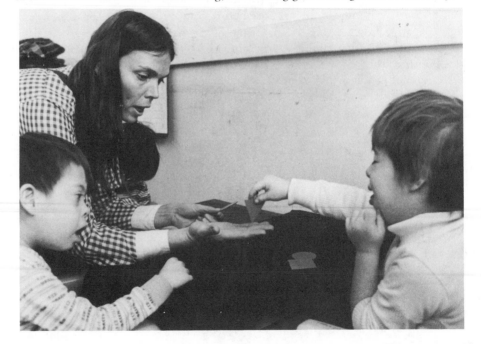

Which of these objectives would you rather teach? Which tells you what the learner is expected to accomplish? In both examples, objective 2 is stated in behavioral terms. Behavioral objectives have the following components:

- The *behavior* that the learner will demonstrate (e.g., write, state, identify, construct, list, describe)

- The *condition* under which the behavior will occur (given a list, given a true/false test, when asked, given 10 addition problems)

- The *criterion* or *standard* for judging success (100 percent accuracy, within 10 minutes, five out of six trials)

At first, including these components may seem awkward, but continued practice enhances the teacher's ability to clearly see the direction the instruction should take. The use of behavioral objectives also makes it possible to effectively evaluate student performance (was the criterion met?) and to communicate goals to the learner (Mager, 1962).

Task Analysis

Task analysis involves breaking down an educational goal into the subskills that the student must acquire to reach the terminal objective. This approach provides both the teacher and the learner with sequential stepping stones to learning and is closely tied to behavioral objectives.

We analyze tasks continually on a daily basis. Suppose you are looking for an apartment to rent. Your plan of action may include: (1) determining the maximum amount of money you can pay; (2) checking newspapers, realtors, and community bulletin boards for vacancies; (3) making appointments to see prospective apartments; (4) listing each apartment's strengths and weaknesses; and (5) deciding which apartment best suits your needs, based on your analysis. The sequence of action is important. It would be illogical to first look at rentals and then decide how much you could afford, since you would be wasting a good deal of time looking at $500 townhouses when you can only spend $250. Task analysis, whether applied to our personal lives or to planning lessons, provides a concrete, sequential method of thinking about how to reach goals.

To analyze a task, first identify the desired objective in behavioral terms. Next, identify the sequential skills one must learn to accomplish the objective. The following is a sample task analysis for learning to tell time, based on an article by Hofmeister and LeFevre (1977).

TERMINAL OBJECTIVE: Given a clock face, the student will read the time to the nearest five-minute interval with 100 percent accuracy.

TASK ANALYSIS:

1. Given a clock face with no hands and with circles in place of numerals, the student will write in the correct numerals.

2. Given a clock face with numerals and hour hand only, the student will read the hour as _____ o'clock by stating the numeral that is immediately before the hour hand.

3. Given a complete clock face (numerals, hour, and minute hand), the student will identify the hour and minute hands by drawing a circle around the hand asked for by the teacher.
4. Given a complete clock face with minute hand held constant, the student will correctly read the hour when asked.
5. Given a clock face with numerals and minute hand only, the student will count by fives starting at the top of the clock to the minute hand position and state the number of minutes indicated.
6. Given a clock face with either a minute or an hour hand, the student will orally state which hand is on the clock and then read the appropriate minutes or hour.
7. Given a complete clock face with the minute hand positioned only at five-minute intervals, the student will read the time by stating the hour first and then the minutes.

The true test of any task analysis is how it works in the actual teaching situation. You may find that the plan does not have enough detail. Task 5 in our example assumes that the student knows how to count by fives. If the student does not possess the skill, it would be necessary to teach it first. The tasks are not methods. A teacher may accomplish the different steps in a variety of ways. If a pupil has trouble differentiating between hour and minute hands, it may be necessary to color code the hands (e.g., black for hour, red for minute) until the student becomes more discriminating. If junior high school students are being taught, it may be more meaningful to use a factory-type time clock to emphasize the correlation between telling time and maintaining a job.

There are several benefits to a task analysis approach:

■ Instruction is organized.
■ Learning is simplified because only one concept is presented at a time.
■ Learning builds upon previous knowledge because it is sequential in nature.
■ Deficit or weak areas in a child's learning can be identified.

It is not necessary to analyze every task a child is asked to do. By becoming proficient at task analysis, however, it is much easier to understand the learning difficulties some children experience.

Individualized Instruction

After a task has been divided into distinct steps, the teacher can then determine the best way to present the material. Whereas task analysis provides a way to look at subject matter, **individualized instruction** refers to the process of deciding how children can accomplish each of the objectives. Some people think that individualized instruction is a different set of plans for every child in the classroom, necessitating one-to-one instruction. Individualized instruction can include one-to-one teaching, but that is not the exclusive methodology. To attain individualization, the teacher matches students' needs, interests, achievement, and abilities to appropriate teaching strategies and levels of instruction. The key is to devise systems that fit the child, rather than to fit the child into a predetermined system. Thus, individualized instruction can be one-to-one, small-group, or large-group instruction, depending on the subject matter and the students characteristics.

Kaplan, Kaplan, Madsen, and Taylor (1973) outline four characteristics of classroom individualization: (1) a wide range of materials and activities is available, (2) activities are on an appropriate level for students, (3) students participate in deciding what to learn, and (4) teachers interact with students according to their rate and style of learning. The authors point out that simply moving classroom furniture or giving students opportunities to move around the room do not constitute individualized learning. There are several methods one can use to personalize student instruction, although no one method will be appropriate for every subject or every child. It must also be realized that individualization does not occur overnight. When a teacher is responsible for 30 children, the best plan is to incorporate new ideas gradually to ensure success. Some ideas for individualizing instruction are explained in the sections that follow.

DIAGNOSTIC/PRESCRIPTIVE TEACHING **Diagnostic/prescriptive teaching** (DPT) is the process of determining the skills that a child does and does not possess (diagnosis) and, based upon that information, developing objectives and lessons (prescription) that will help the student learn unfamiliar material. DPT is a test-teach-test approach to instruction that provides continual monitoring of a student's progress. DPT uses behavioral objectives and task-analysis methods, and the focus is on what the child needs to learn in relation to what has already been learned.

The DPT approach has usually been associated with special education teachers working with small student groups in a self-contained classroom. Teachers with large groups often do not have the time to use this approach. DPT is most effective in the regular classroom for analyzing the performance of students who have failed to learn in the same way that most other students do. For example, if 6 of 25 students miss over half the problems on a multiplication assignment, a teacher might give more practice. This response can be frustrating because inadequate work must continue to be graded. A more efficient approach is to look closely at the students' papers to see what *kind* of mistakes they are making. This analysis may reveal that a pupil added instead of multiplied, does not know the basic facts, does not know place value, or even did the wrong assignment. The diagnostic/prescriptive approach aids the teacher in promoting learning and helps to objectify the learning process.

Prouty and Aiello (1975) advocate the DPT approach for mainstreaming at the elementary level. In reference to the role of consultant, these authors (p. 19) view the diagnostic/prescriptive teacher as

> a specially trained, experienced teacher who serves as a school-based, non-categorical special education consultant to classroom teachers. . . . The DPT determines the needs of children referred and develops a specific, practical, written education program for implementation by the classroom teacher. In this role, the DPT does not directly remediate children but rather functions to assist the referring teacher in modifying existing regular class practices to provide a more responsive learning environment for a greater diversity of learning and behavior styles in children. Thus, the DPT joins the classroom teacher in a partnership as change agents and child advocates.

PEER TUTORS **Peer tutors** can assist teachers with individualization. Fellow students can provide drill practice, read difficult subject matter (e.g., science, social studies, biology), help organize a student's time, and even help with instruction. Often, students can explain a difficult concept in much simpler terms

Sometimes children can be the best teachers.

than the best teacher-made plan. By listening to children's strategies, the teacher can discover new insights. In one situation, a child was helping another with addition problems. It became apparent that the child having difficulty did not know addition facts. The tutor explained his method of seeing domino patterns in his head and then counting the dots. Although this appeared to be a complex maneuver to the teacher, the student being tutored readily grasped the concept and became more efficient in her work.

It is important to ensure that the roles of tutor and tutee be reversed occasionally. Every child has something to share, whether it is magic tricks or geometric designs. Also, not only can classmates help each other, but older students can be especially useful. A cooperative arrangement among teachers and students can promote a warm, accepting climate in the classroom through respect for individual differences.

LEARNING CENTERS   **Learning centers** may be a colorful and motivating instructional device. A center contains directions, activity cards, games, and worksheets that children can do independently. It can be organized in a separate area of the classroom on a table or in a separate cubicle. Initially, such a center can be a time-consuming project for the teacher, but if constructed with care, it may have a viable lifespan of many years. Learning centers may focus on specific subjects, such as math or spelling, or on exploratory subjects, such as sample science experiments, a joke center, or creative writing experiences.

With proper organization and introduction, centers may be enjoyable supplements to other methods of classroom instruction. There are seven considerations the teacher should keep in mind when developing a learning center (Charles, 1976):

- Select a topic limited in focus so students are not overwhelmed
- Write objectives from which activities will be based
- Create activities at many different levels so all students can participate
- Collect inexpensive or free materials for the center
- Prepare materials such as task cards, worksheets, student record forms, and decorations to attract interest
- Schedule times for students to participate in the center to avoid confusion
- Prepare record forms to track student participation and results of all work

The emphasis given to learning centers will depend on the teacher's organizational skills, space available, and level of the children. Some teachers use this approach almost exclusively, while others plan a few in a year. By working together, teachers can exchange or improve many different types of centers.

COMMERCIAL PROGRAMS AND MATERIALS   Commercial programs offer many prepackaged programs, including objectives, materials, record-keeping devices, and evaluation activities in many subjects. Before committing much money to a program, make sure that it is truly individualized with a variety of activities at different levels and for different styles of learning. Many programs are on the market since individualized instruction has become widely used.

Affective Education

Thus far, we have been discussing components of effective teaching from the view of teaching subject matter or, in other words, the cognitive element of education. Another element crucial to the child is his or her affect, or emotional side of development.

Meeting the affective needs of children often requires teacher awareness and contact outside the classroom.

One's affect is composed of feelings toward self (self-concept), attitudes toward others, reactions to failure, success, fear, security, confidence, etc. By the time children reach school age, they have had many experiences that have shaped the affect. The teacher may, for instance, have to deal with a child's strong negative reactions to self or others. The child's self-concept itself is central to learning; it is difficult to teach a child who feels that he or she cannot succeed. During the preschool years, a child may have been given tasks that were too difficult or may have been constantly corrected when building new skills. This psychological history could produce a feeling of inferiority and an unwillingness to attempt new activities. On the other hand, a child may have received positive parental attention for creative uses of pots and pans or toys and, thus, have been encouraged to take risks. These two children will, with their opposite pasts, view learning situations differently—one with caution and perhaps fear, the other with excitement.

A teacher cannot be expected to compensate totally for a child's poor self-concept. However, a child's needs can be identified and experiences can be planned that will help the child to acquire a more positive self-image. Through observation, the teacher can easily pinpoint the children with potentially poor self-concepts. They are the ones who are made fun of, isolated, the last ones to be picked for a game, reluctant to try new tasks, and displaying acting-out behavior. Canfield and Wells (1976) equate self-concept with poker chips. Some children come to school with, say, 50 chips a day. They can afford to lose a few at reading group and have enough left over to take risks on new tasks. The child with only 10 chips may have a rough time getting through the morning if pushed down on the way to school and then chastised for having no homework in the classroom. As a teacher, one can add chips to a child's store and foster a climate wherein children give each other chips. The necessity of providing daily exercises in affective education is poignantly illustrated in the following true story.

Cipher in the Snow*

It started with tragedy on a biting cold February morning. I was driving behind the Milford Corners bus as I did most snowy mornings on my way to school. It veered and stopped short at the hotel, which it had no business doing, and I was annoyed as I had to come to an unexpected stop. A boy lurched out of the bus, reeled, stumbled, and collapsed on the snowbank at the curb. The bus driver and I reached him at the same moment. His thin, hollow face was white even against the snow.

"He's dead," the driver whispered.

It didn't register for a minute. I glanced quickly at the scared young faces staring down at us from the school bus. "A doctor! Quick I'll phone from the hotel...."

"No use, I tell you he's dead." The driver looked down at the boy's still form. "He never even said he felt bad," he muttered. "Just tapped me on the shoulder and said, real quiet, 'I'm sorry. I have to get off at the hotel.' That's all. Polite and apologizing like."

At school, the giggling, shuffling morning noise quieted as the news went down the halls. I passed a huddle of girls. "Who was it? Who dropped dead on the way to school?" I heard one of them half-whisper.

"Don't know his name; some kid from Milford Corners" was the reply.

It was like that in the faculty room and the principal's office. "I'd appreciate your going out to tell the parents," the principal told me. "They haven't a phone and,

Source: "Cipher in the Snow" by Jean Mizer from *Today's Education*, November 1964. Reprinted by permission of the author and publisher.

anyway, somebody from the school should go there in person. I'll cover your classes."

"Why me?" I asked. "Wouldn't it be better if you did it?"

"I didn't know the boy," the principal admitted levelly. "And, in last year's sophomore personalities column I note that you were listed as his favorite teacher."

I drove through the snow and cold down the bad canyon road to the Evans' place and thought about the boy, Cliff Evans. His favorite teacher! I thought. He hasn't spoken two words to me in two years! I could see him in my mind's eye all right, sitting back there in the last seat in my afternoon literature class. He came in the room by himself and left by himself. "Cliff Evans," I muttered to myself, "a boy who never talked." I thought a minute. "A boy who never smiled. I never saw him smile once."

The big ranch kitchen was clean and warm. I blurted out my news somehow. Mrs. Evans reached blindly toward a chair. "He never said anything about bein' ailing."

His stepfather snorted. "He ain't said nothin' about anything since I moved in here."

Mrs. Evans pushed a pan to the back of the stove and began to untie her apron. "Now hold on," her husband snapped. "'I got to have breakfast before I go to town. Nothin' we can do now anyway. If Cliff hadn't been so dumb, he'd have told us he didn't feel good."

After school I sat in the office and stared blankly at the records spread out before me. I was to close the file and write the obituary for the school paper. The almost bare sheets mocked the effort. Cliff Evans, white, never legally adopted by stepfather, five young half-brothers and sisters. These meager strands of information and the list of D grades were all the records had to offer.

Cliff Evans had silently come in the school door in the mornings and gone out the school door in the evenings, and that was all. He had never belonged to a club. He had never played on a team. He had never held an office. As far as I could tell he had never done one happy, noisy kid thing. He had never been anybody at all.

How do you go about making a boy into a zero? The grade-school records showed me. The first and second grade teachers' annotations read "sweet, shy child," "timid but eager." Then the third grade note had opened the attack. Some teacher had written in a good, firm hand, "Cliff won't talk. Uncooperative. Slow learner." The other academic sheep had followed with "dull"; "slow-witted"; "low I.Q." They became correct. The boy's I.Q. score in the ninth grade was listed at 83. But his I.Q. in the third grade had been 106. The score didn't go under 100 until the seventh grade. It takes time to break them.

I stomped to the typewriter and wrote a savage report pointing out what education had done to Cliff Evans. I slapped a copy on the principal's desk and another in the sad, dog-eared file. I banged the typewriter and slammed the file and crashed the door shut, but I didn't feel much better. A little boy kept walking after me, a little boy with a peaked, pale face; a skinny body in faded jeans; and big eyes that had looked and searched for a long time and then had become veiled.

I could guess how many times he'd been chosen last to play sides in a game, how many whispered child conversations had excluded him, how many times he hadn't been asked. I could see and hear the faces and voices that said over and over, "You're a nothing, Cliff Evans."

A child is a believing creature. Cliff undoubtedly believed them. Suddenly it seemed clear to me: When finally there was nothing left at all for Cliff Evans, he collapsed on a snowbank and went away. The doctor might list "heart failure" as the cause of death, but that wouldn't change my mind.

We couldn't find ten students in the school who had known Cliff well enough to attend the funeral as his friends. So the student body officers and a committee from the junior class went as a group to the church, being politely sad. I attended the services with them, and sat through it with a lump of cold lead in my chest and a big resolve growing through me.

I've never forgotten Cliff Evans nor that resolve. He has been my challenge year after year, class after class. I look for veiled eyes or bodies scrouged into a seat in an alien world. "Look kids," I say silently, "I may not do anything else for you this year, but not one of you is going to come out of here a nobody. I'll work or fight to the bitter end doing battle with society and the school board, but I won't have one of you coming out of here thinking himself a zero."

Most of the time—not always, but most of the time—I've succeeded.

Excellent resources for affective education can be found in Canfield and Wells (1976), Chase (1975), and Simon, Howe, and Kirschenbaum (1972).

Classroom Management

A teacher's philosophy of how children learn and how a classroom should look determine policies on structure, organization, and student activity—in other words, classroom management. Regardless of the approach selected for a classroom management system, all are committed to two phenomena: changing inappropriate behavior and maintaining appropriate behavior (Turnbull and Scheetz, 1979).

Many different approaches to classroom management exist. Two prominent schools of thought—humanism and behaviorism—have been construed as being diametrically opposed ways of relating to children in the classroom. If you belong to one camp, according to popular opinion, you certainly cannot belong to the other. A strict interpretation makes this statement accurate, but both views have much to offer to educators since they both strive to apply philosophical beliefs to teaching children.

HUMANISTIC APPROACH **Humanism** focuses on the worth of the individual, the ability to control one's own fate and decisions, and the importance of feelings and emotions. Unlike Freudian psychology (which analyzes behavior in terms of unconscious forces) and behavioral psychology (which analyzes observable behavior in relation to environmental events), humanistic psychology centers on the concept of free will—that is, a person's ability to make choices (Coons, 1977). The writings of Carl Rogers and Abraham Maslow reflect the humanistic perspective.

Successfully applying humanistic psychology to the classroom requires—like any other approach—more than a "warm, good listener." Rather, teachers must be thoroughly trained in order to be effective classroom managers. The basic premise of humanistic education is that of prevention. Specifically, proponents state that disruptive behavior is minimized when self-control is taught. Fagen, Long, and Stevens (1975) have developed a self-control curriculum that emphasizes the preventative approach at the elementary school level.

Humanistic teachers may be characterized by their propensity to recognize individual differences among students, fostering a nonthreatening atmosphere, and allowing students to choose what they want to learn as well as the most effective means of learning it. Lessons are geared to provide students with many experiences with a variety of options from which learning occurs.

BEHAVIORAL APPROACH **Behaviorism** holds that measurable observable behaviors—rather than feelings and thoughts—deserve center stage. One cannot know what a child is feeling but can only see how he or she is behaving. Behaviorists also emphasize the role of the environment, which can be systematically arranged to either maintain or change behavior (Wallace and Kauffman, 1973). Those behavioral objectives that stress the end action to be demonstrated by the student derive from behaviorism. Proponents of the behavioral approach believe that all behavior is learned and therefore can be guided and shaped by applying certain principles.

Behaviorism is regarded by some as cold and calculated, whereas humanism is regarded as empathetic and warm. The distinction is not that clear. Many important principles may be taken from the behaviorist point of view. Positive reinforcement, for example, is a behavioral technique championed by humanists. The skill resides in knowing how to employ it appropriately. The timely use of reinforcers strengthens behavior; therefore, teachers should provide warmth and praise to children *immediately* following a desirable behavior, whether it is sharing crayons, preparing a neat paper, or giving a correct answer. Some educators are reluctant to use these proven principles because a negative image comes to mind when the term *behavior modification* is used. To think of behavior modification as popping candy into a child's mouth after every correct response or to equate it with Pavlov's canine experiments is an extremely narrow view of a powerful technique.

Both humanists and behaviorists offer useful information to the classroom practitioner; to ignore one for the other reduces the teacher's repertoire of teaching strategies. The principal of the Mark Twain School for emotionally handicapped students stated that the school's teaching staff "is eclectic in its approach to behavior management. They draw from a wide variety of methods and techniques to help students modify inappropriate behavior and develop coping skills" (Laneve, 1979, p. 187). Too often the issue centers around narrowing the approach rather than developing systematic management based on sound learning theory and teaching practices.

TRENDS AND ISSUES

Teacher Certification

Currently, many states offer a variety of teacher certificates. Special education may concentrate on the visually impaired, learning disabilities, vocational education, reading specialization, the educable mentally retarded, the mildly and moderately retarded, and behavioral disorders. This multicertification fragments the services that specialists believe they can deliver. A more viable approach in light of legislative demands may be to offer only two or three specialists' certificates and require special educators to attain a broader background in the area of handicapping conditions. A logical division would be between mild handicaps and moderate-to-severe handicaps. Mild handicaps would be characteristic of students able to participate in regular classrooms with help from a consultant or resource teacher. Moderate-to-severe conditions would include children needing a highly structured or specialized environment, such as a self-contained classroom. The trend toward certifying teachers by degree of handicap, rather than generic labels, has been initiated by several states.

As special education spreads into the preschool and postsecondary environment, it becomes necessary for state boards of education to regulate teacher certification for these areas. Elementary and secondary regulations, in many instances, are not entirely appropriate when considering differences in child

Many universities require regular education majors to have experiences with the handicapped in various educational settings.

development, differing intensities of parental contact, career education, and job-adjustment factors. Competencies differ and should be reflected in teacher-certification requirements.

Teacher Education

Closely tied with certification is the issue of teacher education, including preservice and in-service levels. A major weakness of PL 94–142 is that it provides neither for a systematic plan for reeducation of practicing teachers nor for requirements for changes in colleges and universities. To make the situation worse, preservice teachers often were not getting enough exposure to principles, strategies, and practice even before the enactment of PL 94–142. For example, Corrigan (1978) noted that professional education courses may total only 13 percent of a student's undergraduate career.

A five-year undergraduate program is being implemented or considered in some states. Further, other states are encouraging a sixth-year internship under the guidance of a professional teacher. The preceding chapters point to the necessity of such a plan. All teachers must be skilled in writing and interpreting individualized education programs; in working collaboratively with parents, fellow educators, and agencies; and in adapting to meet the unique needs of all children in the classroom. New approaches and alternatives to teaching must be designed because working with 10 handicapped students is quite different from working with 30 regular students.

The training of doctors and lawyers is often compared with the training of teachers. All three professions have a powerful influence on individual lives, but only teaching allows a trial-and-error approach to becoming a professional. A five- or six-year plan is not only warranted but demanded in order for teachers to become competent before entering the practice of their profession.

SUMMARY POINTS

- The growing practice of mainstreaming handicapped children into regular classrooms requires all involved educators to recognize changes in their professional roles. If integrating handicapped students is to be successful, both regular and special educators must accept the trend toward job diversification.
- A new role for special educators is that of consultant, which requires a repertoire of skills focusing on communicating effectively with other professionals as well as with parents of handicapped students. Although the use of consultants is a trend in the public schools, few teacher-education programs have set standards for consulting competencies at the preservice and in-service levels.
- Communication between the home and school is mandated. The classroom teacher can utilize many techniques to increase parental involvement in their child's education.
- Effective teaching is based upon consistent, sound teaching strategies. Employing behavioral objectives, task analysis, individualized instruction, the recognition of affective education, and the implementation of a systematic classroom management program will benefit all students, not just exceptional learners.
- Resource room teachers have a professional responsibility to assist regular classroom teachers in developing realistic alternative teaching skills. In-service programs that are vague and general provide little practical information to individual teachers. Rather, the resource teacher must be aware of individual needs, teaching styles, available materials, and classroom organization styles of all teachers within a school.
- PL 94–142 has had its impact on higher education. Although the law does not systematically address the issue of preservice or in-service education, many regular and special teacher training programs are being reexamined or revamped in order to better prepare teachers for the mainstreamed teaching environment.
- Successfully implementing individualized instruction is contingent upon a teacher's knowledge of each student's learning strengths and weaknesses, unique needs, and interests. Although initially organizing an individualized teaching program is time-consuming, once the program is implemented, more effective learning occurs.

REVIEW QUESTIONS

1. Contrast the job responsibilities of the self-contained classroom teacher and the resource room teacher. Do they require different job-related skills? Explain?

2. Distinguish between the humanistic and behavioral approaches to classroom management. Do you think a beginning teacher would be more likely to use one approach? If yes, which one? Explain.

3. Compare your college curricula with the teacher-education issues discussed in this chapter. Would you recommend any changes? If yes, which ones?

4. Define affective education and its relationship to effective learning.

5. How do behavioral objectives and task analysis assist individualized instruction?

INDIVIDUALIZING INSTRUCTION IN THE REGULAR CLASSROOM

A major teacher concern when mainstreaming exceptional students into a regular classroom is how to meet their needs while not neglecting the other children. One approach to individualizing instruction in the regular classroom is the Workshop Way developed by Sister Grace H. Pilon, an experienced teacher of minority children. The goal of the **Workshop Way** is to instill in each student a positive attitude toward his or her learning and growing through the use of content material. Applicable to grades K through 12, Workshop Way teachers provide an individualized, positive learning environment by using an organized and structured daily schedule, materials, and teaching strategies. Following is an example of implementing the Workshop Way at the elementary level.

Mrs. Sullivan, a veteran teacher of children with learning disabilities and behavior disorders, decided to try her hand at a regular, first-grade class. She modified her techniques to organize her classroom of 29 students and maintain emphasis on individualization based on the Workshop Way system.

In order to accommodate six reading groups, Mrs. Sullivan arranged morning activities so that the children assumed responsibility for completing work. This strategy allowed her the time necessary to work with small groups of children. The morning activities are outlined on a bulletin board using short phrases and visual clues. By the end of the year, 16 different activities were included. The focus of the work is solely on pretaught skills, allowing the children to practice, in a variety of ways, lessons taught during the previous day or week. Some of the activities are:

■ *Sharpen Pencil*: This is the first on the list to get everyone ready for the coming tasks.
■ *Math Grid*: Depending on what skills the children are currently practicing, the activity card (always placed in the same area of the room) may tell the children to write numbers from 1 to 20, count backward from 70 to 50, etc. The emphasis is on numeral recognition and sequencing.

■ *Folder*: In each child's folder is a phonics paper and a directions paper. As mentioned previously, the phonics lesson has been taught before the child is asked to do the work. The direction activity tells the child to color a picture a particular color, draw shapes above, below, right, or left of a figure to practice recognition of color names, prepositions, and shapes. Folder work allows the teacher to either provide new tasks for the more advanced learner or additional skill practice for other students.

■ *Power Time*: In this activity the child must watch the second hand on the clock make a complete rotation while standing as still as possible. This task is designed to allow the child to relax, become cognizant of the length of a minute, and become familiar with the concept of clockwise and numeral order on the clock face.

■ *Command Card*: In one portion of the room is a packet of 32 cards; the child selects one and carries out the command. Emphasis here is on memory and written skills. Sample activities include "Go to the lockers and say your address," "Print your birthday on the chalkboard." When a new command card is placed in the packet, the children practice reading the words during the opening activity.

■ *Silent Reading.* The child is allowed to go anywhere in the room with the reading material of his or her choice to read silently for three minutes. An egg timer is provided for this purpose; however, the children can spend longer at this activity if they wish.

Other tasks are included, such as practicing math facts, vowel sounds, and calendar work. After a difficult task, a "breather" is given, such as Power Time (described above), the Thinking Chair (for thinking or staring out the window), or getting a drink of water. In this way, not only are the children's learning styles considered, but also their developmental needs of short activities and movement.

For afternoon activities in math, science, writing, and social studies, a unit approach is taken, which means that all chidlren are taught as a group. To individualize, Mrs. Sullivan plans activities at a variety of levels. For example, vocabulary study during a unit on the zoo included a worksheet with words given a point value of one, two, or three, according to level of difficulty. Children work in pairs practicing the words they choose and then add the point total on the teacher's calculator. A creative writing lesson includes finishing sentences such as "If I were a zookeeper . . ." Children who have difficulty expressing themselves in writing are given the opportunity to tape their stories in order to emphasize the creative aspect, which is the object of the lesson.

At the beginning of the year it takes approximately three to four hours to get ready for the next day, but as the children become accustomed to the routine and the teacher learns more about their abilities, preparation time becomes increasingly shorter. Mrs. Sullivan offers several guiding principles to help children of any age learn.

■ *Give the children responsibility*. In Mrs. Sullivan's first grade, the children virtually run classroom activities. In the system described above, the children are responsible for helping each other and checking work under a buddy system. She emphasizes that building responsibility must be a slow process, making sure all the children understand the activities. Thus, only one activity is practiced, gradually building to many.

■ *Make no distinctions among different types of learners*. Respect is a key word here and has a lot to do with the teacher's attitude. A child who speaks with no beginning or ending sounds is not made fun of, but rather his classmates translate his answers for the teacher. In fact, Mrs. Sullivan is occasionally chastised by her students for not being able to correctly understand his speech.

■ *Give credit for taking risks*. It is not a matter of being right or wrong but being willing to try. There is often group applause for a child who attempts a difficult question.

■ *Do not expect every child to master every concept*. Children have a variety of skills and, in order to group appropriately, several factors must be considered: rate of learning, ability to work independently, and frustration level. When a child is having difficulty mastering a concept, Mrs. Sullivan works with him or her on a one-to-one basis. This tells her if the child can learn the concept but needs a smaller group, or if the prerequisite skills are not mastered and different objectives need to be prepared.

Visitors to this bustling classroom often express amazement that first-graders can work so independently and also respect each other's rights. Although Mrs. Sullivan says it all just happens, it is obvious that careful planning and respect for individual differences make this room work.

For further information on individualizing instruction for students in either the regular classroom or a special education classroom, using the Workshop Way, write to:

The Workshop Way, Inc.
Box 47
7325 Palmetto Street
New Orleans, Louisiana 70125

1. Although the concept of individualized instruction is sometimes criticized for focusing on the elementary level, it can be successfully implemented at other levels. List and describe five strategies that a college professor could use to individualize classroom instruction.

2. Identify four jobs or roles that peer tutors could accomplish in Mrs. Sullivan's classroom to facilitate individualized instruction. Which students should be peer tutors and what, if any, criteria should be used in their selection?

SUGGESTED READINGS

Blackburn, J. E., and Powell, W. C. *One at a Time All at Once: The Creative Teacher's Guide to Individualized Instruction without Anarchy.* Pacific Palisades, Ca.: Goodyear, 1976.

Hawisher, M. F., and Calhoun, M. L. *The Resource Room: An Educational Asset for Children with Special Needs.* Columbus, Ohio: Charles E. Merrill, 1978.

Parker, C. A., ed. *Psychological Consultation: Helping Teachers Meet Special Needs.* Reston, Va.: Council for Exceptional Children, 1975.

Turnbull, A. P., and Scheetz, J. B. *Mainstreaming Handicapped Students: A Guide for the Classroom Teacher.* Boston, Allyn and Bacon, 1979.

II

EXCEPTIONALITIES

CONTENTS

9

THE VISUALLY IMPAIRED

For most people, the world is a visual one. Learning occurs primarily through the sense of sight. As infants, and later as children and adults, we learn to understand life through what we see. Although our other senses may reinforce vision, we tend to rely most on our sense of sight. For example, when we walk through the produce section of the grocery store, we identify vegetables by size, shape, and color, although we could feel the knubby texture of corn, the roughness of cauliflower, and the smoothness of the tomato.

Since people rely on vision to label, categorize, sequence, and understand, there is a tendency to isolate, ostracize, and pity the visually impaired. Because their impairment is obvious, they stand out. Too often, we assume they cannot succeed in what we think of as a predominantly visual world.

MARGO

Margo is a housewife, mother, and a full-time graduate student majoring in special education. Since birth she has been visually impaired due to a lack of pigmentation, commonly referred to as albinism. Although Margo usually wears contact lenses, she sometimes wears prescription glasses. Here is Margo's personal account of her feelings toward being visually impaired.

"My aunt and an older sister have the same condition. My parents knew when we were born that we were albinos. They feared that we were blind. I was taken to an eye doctor when I was three, and my parents were told the extent of my visual handicap, but they never told me or my sister. We were treated like all the rest of the children in the family. Since my parents expected me to do well in school and never made any extra fuss over me, neighbors and family also treated us like all the other children.

"Since my family never told me that I was visually impaired, I grew up not realizing the extent of my handicap. I can recall feeling shy and isolated as a child, but I was most self-conscious about my very white hair and thick glasses. I really didn't identify with being blind; I guess I simply felt 'different.' Other children would comment on my unusual hair color, and that made me feel different. I had great difficulty participating in sports, but didn't realize why things were hard for me. I thought I was just awkward.

"After high school graduation, a man from Rehabilitation Services contacted me saying that since I was legally blind, I qualified for their services. That really threw me. Though I had known I was different from other children, I had never thought of myself as blind. This idea really disturbed me. It set me apart. All I want is to be a regular person and not receive special treatment.

"With the aid of a magnifying glass and contact lenses, I can read most printed material and take notes in class. I have tried listening to texts on tape, but it is hard to concentrate, so I prefer to work from printed material. I guess I'm a visual learner! The biggest classroom problem I have always encountered is teachers writing on the blackboard. Since I can't see the words on the board, some teachers will write them on a sheet of paper for me.

"The teachers whom I have encountered have run the gamut of attitudes toward me, from those who babied, coddled, and overprotected me, to a few who have said, 'It's your problem; figure it out!' I had one teacher in junior high school who wrote an entire test on the board. When I said that I couldn't read the questions, the teacher replied, 'You'll have to decide how to solve that problem; I can't help you!' So I was forced to stand up near the board and write down the questions. I felt so humiliated. Junior high is an extremely vulnerable age and, to this day, I shudder when I think about that experience. That teacher, not my handicap, made me different.

"Teachers who were most helpful were the ones who were available for help, yet they weren't overprotective or overbearing in their attitudes. They seemed to know what I needed before I asked, and aided me without making a large project out of it. Teachers who treated me like everyone else are remembered fondly. Since I was an extremely shy child, I only wish that my teachers had made an effort to bring me out of my shell. Teachers who expected little or nothing from me because of my handicap were a disappointment. I did not like being treated as an ineffectual student.

"I am married and have spent the past four years at home caring for my two young sons. When my first child was born, I was quite worried about my ability to care for him adequately. In the hospital, a nurse grabbed the baby away from me and syringed phlegm from his throat, saying, 'He was choking! Didn't you see it?' This incident made me even more unsure of my ability to be a good mother and it took a long time for me to feel confident. Now, with two active boys, I make special efforts to compensate for my limited vision. Binoculars are useful to check on the boys when they are playing outside. Regarding my children, there are some things that worry me. I can't read a thermometer and, since I am unable to drive, would not be able to get them to a hospital in an emergency.

"My husband is helpful and supportive, but not too much so. He is ingenious at devising alternatives to hindrances that I encounter daily. I couldn't read the oven dial, so he put tape at every 100 degrees. Now that I can feel the temperature marker, our food tastes like it is supposed to—not burnt.

"Other problems for me include going into a place for the first time, especially if it is cluttered, going down a flight of cement steps, and being unable to read signs. I know people occasionally consider me unfriendly because I have a difficult time recognizing faces and responding to friendly gestures such as a wave hello from across a room. Most of all, I feel uneasy around people who don't know about my handicap, and I don't like to ask for help. People who know me accept and treat me like a regular person. That's what I want most—to be treated like everyone else!"

Points for Consideration

■ Although Margo uses special aids for performing some tasks, she is often able to function unassisted, even though she is legally blind. The visually impaired may do things differently; that does not, however, mean that their goals should be different than those of sighted people.
■ Parental support, acceptance, and commitment were critical to Margo's successful functioning in school and society.
■ Educational programs for the visually impaired must include affective as well as

cognitive components. Although Margo was successful academically, she has negative self-esteem and doubts her ability to succeed.

Common Misconceptions

Listed here are a few of the misconceptions about the blind:

■ *The Blind Cannot Work and Therefore Cannot Contribute Meaningfully to Society.* This is true to some extent; the blame is, however, on society. Because we do not think they can learn, few efforts are made to educate and train the visually handicapped to live up to their fullest potential. In essence, they adhere to our predictive notion of being helpless and dependent. Yet, if given the opportunity, blind people can become significant contributors to the work force.
■ *All Blind People See Nothing.* Ironically, very few "blind" people are totally without sight. Many have some vision, called **residual vision**, which can be improved with proper training.
■ *The Blind are Born With or Acquire an Extra Inherent Sense that Allows Them to Learn.* The blind person must develop other senses for receiving and understanding information from the environment. This feat is not done automatically, but rather through an intensive educational program.

Many of our misconceptions about the blind can be dispelled if we focus on their abilities rather than their disabilities.

Attempts to identify and categorize the visually impaired have come from two sectors: education and the law. The legal definition of **blindness**, proposed by the American Medical Association, is "...visual acuity for distant vision of 20/200 or less in the better eye, with best correction; or visual acuity of more than 20/200 if the widest diameter of field of vision subtends an angle no greater than 20 degrees" (*National Society for Prevention of Blindness Fact Book*, 1966, p. 10). **Visual acuity** is the ability of the eye to discriminate detail; normal visual acuity is identified as 20/20. If someone has visual acuity of 20/200, he or she can see at 20 feet what a nonimpaired person can see at 200 feet. Field of vision refers to the total visual area that an individual can see at any one particular time. The normal eye can see at an angle of 60 to 70 degrees. However, when the field of vision is restricted, the area of visual acuity is smaller. For persons with a limited visual field, seeing is like looking through a tunnel, thus the name tunnel vision.

The partially blind (or partially sighted) population, also recognized by the legal system, includes those who have visual acuity between 20/70 and 20/200 in the better eye with correction.

Educators argue that because the legal definition focuses primarily on visual acuity, it does not provide reliable information on how one is able to function in society. Further, the legal definition is also remiss in recognizing how effectively one might use remaining, or residual, sight. As a result, the educational definition differentiates between the blind and the partially sighted on the basis of how they learn best. The **blind** are those severely visually impaired individuals who use Braille; the **partially sighted** are, however, able to read print, even though it may have to be adapted (for example, by enlarging the print itself or by using a magnifying glass). Fonda (1970, p. 155) categorizes the partially sighted into four groups for instructional purposes:

Group I	Light perception to 1/200
Group II	2/200 to 4/200
Group III	5/200 to 20/300
Group IV	20/250 to 26/60

Braille would be used for teaching children in the first group. Although dependent upon individual circumstances, reading typed material, even if adapted, is generally appropriate for children in Group II. Fonda emphasizes that children in the remaining two groups should be taught visually. Even within the educational definition, generalizations on what is the best approach to learning should be avoided. Jones (1961) reported that of children whose visual acuity was 20/200, about 20 percent read Braille, 82 percent read print, and 6 percent read both. As visual acuity decreased, the variability among reading methods increased. Of those children with 10/200 vision, 32 percent read Braille, 59 percent read print, and 9 percent read both. These findings indicate that visual acuity cannot be the sole criterion for determining which approach should be used for learning to read. Other visual impairments unmentioned in the legal definition may affect learning, such as faulty object perception, light sensitivity, and color blindness. Any of these visual impairments, which may occur without affecting visual acuity or the visual field, can have an impact on learning.

PREVALENCE AND CAUSES OF VISUAL IMPAIRMENTS

Although a large proportion of the population has some sort of visual impairment, most defects can be corrected with prescription lenses. As a result, the prevalence of visually impaired (blind or partially sighted) children is low compared to other handicapping conditions. The U.S. Office of Education estimated in 1975 that .1 percent of the child population is visually handicapped.

Many visual impairments in children are caused by hereditary or congenital defects. It is estimated that between 64 and 70 percent of visual impairments found in children and youth can be attributed to prenatal factors (U.S. Department of Health, Education, and Welfare, 1970; Fonda, 1970). Hereditary and congenital defects are categorized into three groups: (1) refractive errors, (2) ocular motility defects, and (3) diseases and other genetically determined abnormalities. This last includes diseases contracted during pregnancy that may have a devastating effect on the fetus.

Approximately 27 percent of visual impairments are caused by trauma, disease, and injury occurring after birth. Loss of or impaired sight due to head injury, poison, excessive sunlight, or a tumor would fall within this category. Please refer to Figure 9-1, a simplistic representation of the anatomical structure of the eye, in order to better understand the following discussion of the causes of visual impairments.

Refractive Errors

The eye is an extension of the brain, which receives visual stimuli via the optic nerve. When an object in our visual field reflects light, it is seen. The visual image is focused via light rays onto the retina which transmits the image to the optic nerve. Genetically determined, refraction refers to the "physical property by which a ray of light is deflected from its course as it passes from one medium into another of different optical density" (Harley and Lawrence, 1977, p. 19). The ability of the eye to refract light rays onto the retina is related to the curvature of the lens and/or cornea. **Refractive errors** occur when the light rays are not properly focused, thus causing the visual image to blur.

FIGURE 9-1 The human eye.

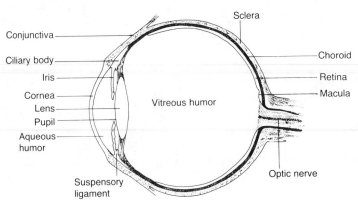

- Myopia, commonly referred to as nearsightedness, occurs when the eyeball is too long from front to back. As a result, visual acuity is affected because the visual image focus is in front of, rather than on, the retina.
- Hyperopia (farsightedness) results in the focusing of objects behind the retina because the eye is too short. In such cases, near vision, rather than far vision, is affected.
- Astigmatism results in a blurred focus of an image due to irregular or aspheric curvature of the lens and/or cornea. Corrective lenses may be required.

Ocular Motility Defects

Although each eye's retina sees a separate visual image, the brain functions to blend these two images into one meaningful perception. This fusion requires that the brain be intact and that the muscles that move each eye act simultaneously. Ocular motility problems occur when the muscles attached to the eyeballs are not synchronized. As a result, movement of the eyeball is not properly controlled and binocular vision is distorted.

- Nystagmus is characterized by involuntary, rapid, side-to-side or up-and-down movements of the eyes.
- Strabismus (heterotropia) is a muscular defect occurring when the visual axis of one eye is not aligned with the other eye. As a result, the eyes are not directed simultaneously on an object. Cross-eye occurs when the eyes converge, whereas wall-eye refers to a condition where the eyes look outward.
- Amblyopia (lazy eye) occurs in young children who are unable to use both eyes to gaze at an object. In essence, the child suppresses the use of one eye. In such cases, vision in the affected eye is restricted, thus forcing the child to use the other eye. Difficulties in simultaneously gazing at an object can also cause diplopia.
- Diplopia occurs when the child has double vision, that is, sees two images simultaneously rather than one.

Other Genetic Defects and Diseases

- Albinism is a hereditary defect that results in a lack of pigment throughout the body, including the eyes. This lack of pigmentation causes an increased sensitivity to light and can affect visual acuity.
- Retinitis pigmentosa is a hereditary disease that causes the retina to degenerate. Symptoms are night blindness and eventual loss of peripheral vision. Although retinitis pigmentosa is a progressive disease, some central vision may be retained.
- Glaucoma refers to abnormal physiology of the eye. When the intraocular fluid in the vitreous humor builds up, there is a gradual increase in pressure on the optic nerve fibers. Eventually the nerve is irreparably damaged and sight is lost. Although the exact cause and cure for glaucoma have not been identified, if caught early, it can be arrested. Glaucoma tends to be more prevalent in persons who have a family history of the disorder.

■ Cataracts, commonly found in older persons, refer to a change in the lens. Rather than being clear and responsive to the ciliary muscle, the lens becomes opaque and hard. Congenital cataracts are attributed to hereditary factors and to exposure to viral infections (such as German measles) during early fetal development.

■ Choroiditis is an inflammation of the choroid. The choroid is made up of many blood vessels and functions to provide nourishment to the inner nerve. Visual dysfunction occurs when fluid from the choroid enters the retinal area, thus impairing vision. Choroiditis is related to systemic infections such as toxoplasmosis, tuberculosis, and syphilis, which can be passed from the mother to the fetus.

Postnatal Defects

In the following discussion the more prevalent visual problems found in the school-age population are identified. Visual impairments occurring after birth can result either directly or indirectly from injury, trauma, or disease.

■ Retrolental fibroplasia (RLF) is a condition that eventually destroys the retina and is caused by administering too much oxygen to incubated infants. During the 1940s and early 1950s, a large number of premature infants were found to have RLF. However, it was not until 1952 that the cause was identified.

■ Conjunctivitis is a bacterial or viral infection resulting in inflammation of the conjunctiva. There are several types of conjunctivitis, some of which are more deadly to vision than others. A relatively nondebilitating type is "pink eye," common in school-age children. The conjunctiva area is characterized by swelling, tearing, and itching.

■ Retinoblastoma refers to tumors located on the retina. Occurring in early childhood, retinoblastoma is characterized by a grayish reflection in the pupil. These tumors tend to be linked hereditarily.

IDENTIFICATION OF THE VISUALLY IMPAIRED

The severe loss of function and the behavioral characteristics associated with blindness appear to make the diagnostic process simple. The medical label "blind," however, provides the educational specialist with little useful information. In such cases more specifics are needed, such as the presence or absence of light perception and the degree of field vision. Only when the visually impaired student's functional abilities are identified can appropriate program planning begin.

Educational Assessment

Determining the extent of the visual impairment is only one facet of the diagnostic process; a thorough assessment of all areas of development is necessary. However, the valid measurement of language, motor skills, cognition, and other functional areas is hampered because of the lack of appropriate instruments available to assess the visually impaired (Stogner, 1970). Frequently, the visually impaired child's performance is penalized because most standardized tests are visually oriented. Test items are either directly related to vision or indirectly related to experiences that depend upon normal mobility skills. Standardized achievement test scores should also be interpreted cautiously. Frequently these tests are timed, and even when the material is in Braille or large type, it still takes the visually impaired student longer to complete the tests.

Because proper diagnosis is a complex problem and the validity of test scores has been questioned, it is critical to have an interdisciplinary evaluation team. The goal of this team is to synthesize each specialist's test findings and observations into a viable educational program.

SCREENING   Not all visual impairments are readily identifiable at birth or during the preschool years. All states do, though, require routine eye examinations for school-age children. The most frequently used screening instrument is the **Snellen Test**, which consists of "objects, symbols, letters or numbers of graded sizes, drawn to a definite scale based on the portion of the arc of the visual angle" (Hathaway, 1966, p. 22). For younger children, the E symbol chart is commonly used in screening programs, whereas the letter chart is more suitable for older persons. Picture charts are effective for toddlers and preschoolers, as well as low functioning children. Too often, vision screening programs rely only on the Snellen Test for identifying potential visual defects. The Snellen, just as any screening instrument, has limitations. It tests only visual acuity, and as a result will not identify visual problems that involve other aspects of vision.

Classroom teachers should be aware of the following signs that may signal a possible visual problem (Bishop, 1971):

- Swollen or red-rimmed eyelids
- Crusts near the lashes
- Frequent sties
- Unusual discharge in the eyes or along the lids
- Reddened or watery eyes
- Eyes that do not appear straight
- Pupils of different sizes
- Eyes that move constantly
- Clouding of the pupillary opening (black center of the eye)
- Drooping eyelids
- Complaints of aches or pains in the eyes, excessive headaches, dizziness or nausea after close eye work
- Squinting, blinking, frowning, facial distortions, constant rubbing of the eyes, or attempt to brush away a blur; tilting of the head when seeing; closing or covering one eye when looking or reading
- Undue light sensitivity
- Holding reading material too close or too far away; frequently changing the distance of reading material from near to far
- Head thrust forward or body tense when viewing distant objects
- Inattentiveness during reading; cannot read for long periods without tiring; reads more poorly as time span increases
- Reversals of letters and words, or confusion of letters and numbers with similar shapes
- Constant loss of place in a sentence
- Stumbling over objects

Learning aids, such as the Braillewriter pictured here, assist severely visually impaired students in being mainstreamed successfully into regular classes.

Any child may exhibit one or more of these behaviors at times, but if any of these symptoms are *constantly* evident, the teacher should alert parents and refer the child to the school nurse. Many disorders can be arrested or corrected if identified early.

CHARACTERISTICS OF THE VISUALLY IMPAIRED

Language Skills

The visually impaired child needs not only to explore the environment physically but also to have it described and explained in detail in order for accurate concept development to occur (Lowenfeld, 1971). The blind child must be told what is being touched, heard, or seen, even if vision is distorted or limited. In addition, the opportunity to use language must be provided. One way to measure a child's understanding of a social event or academic concept is to allow the child to discuss, explain, and ask questions. The blind child's need for order and understanding of the world is no different than that of the nonimpaired child.

Vocabulary is also related to quality experiences. For example, on a trip to the beach, the blind child does not see the sailboats silently gliding over the ocean, the busy hermit crab two feet away, or the kite flying high in the sky. Because the blind child is unaware of these things, he or she cannot show curiosity, cannot ask what they are or what they do. Consequently, vocabulary will be limited, which can result in faulty understanding of the environment.

Self-Help Skills

Children learn through doing. The visually impaired child is no different in this respect. Independence may be promoted by giving the child the opportunity to learn to dress, to take care of toilet needs, to make decisions, and to take everyday risks. Yet, because parents of the visually impaired may be overprotective for fear that the child either cannot learn or will be injured, the child may not be given the necessary opportunities for such learning experiences.

Vision is used to coordinate and sequence daily events, such as dressing. However, Andrew, a visually impaired four-year-old, does not see that his shirt has four holes—two small ones for the arms, a bigger hole for the head, and a very big one for the body. Nor does he see the front or back of the shirt. Learning how to dress does not occur by watching Mom or Dad. Therefore, Andrew learns how to put on his shirt by listening to his parents instructions and feeling through the steps of pulling on his shirt. "Feel the tag at the top. This is the back of the shirt. Now find the real big hole and put your arms and head through it. Good! Now, put your head through the middle hole; feel it. See, it's bigger than the hole on either side. Now your right arm and then your left arm." In this illustration, the concepts of language (small, big, bigger), body awareness (left arm, right arm, head), and spatial relationships (top, middle, bottom) are being taught. Initially, visually impaired children may take longer to learn a task and the avenue for achieving success may be different; it is, however, possible for such children to learn.

Motor Skills

The initial development of motor skills depends largely upon vision. For example, the young infant is reinforced visually for lifting his or her head or reaching for a toy hanging above the crib. These kinds of movements develop strength for later, more complex motor patterns, such as sitting, creeping, and crawling. The visually impaired infant or child often lacks motivation to move because he or she is unaware of the exciting surrounding world. Another factor that inhibits motor development is parental fears (Campbell, 1970). Frequently, parents limit their visually impaired child's interaction with the environment because they fear for their son's or daughter's safety.

The inability to see can thwart initial motor development, which is the foundation for later exploring the home environment, for participating in peer activities, for job independence, and for overall physical health. We are stimulated by what we see. As a result, we imitate, and then learn how to move through space and act appropriately. But the visually impaired child cannot imitate visual models of appropriate social behaviors; he or she doesn't know about posture, looking at a person who is talking, or even gesturing.

Because visually impaired children do not receive visual environment stimuli, they frequently resort to **blindisms**, or primitive movements (Cratty, 1971). Excessive rubbing of the eyes, using the thumb or finger to press on the eye itself, and rocking back and forth are examples of these peculiar mannerisms. The visually impaired child finds these activities pleasurable. Unfortunately, continual stimulation can result in discoloration around the eyes and in depressed or sunken eyes. Therefore, the environment and learning must be modified so that they are stimulating, thus replacing the need for inappropriate behaviors. If the blind infant or child learns to respond to alternative stimuli, then motor development, body awareness, and understanding of spatial relationships will occur sequentially, frequently within the normal chronological range.

EDUCATIONAL PROGRAMMING

Placement

If detected early enough, many visual impairments can be corrected through the use of lenses, medication, or surgery. However, some impairments cannot be corrected; children with these impairments make up the majority of the visually impaired receiving special education services.

When deciding the least restrictive learning environment for a visually impaired student, several factors should be considered. First, the amount of functional residual vision must be evaluated. In addition to the traditional eye examination (rendered by an **ophthalmologist** or other qualified professional), the child should be carefully observed in familiar surroundings to determine the extent of visual efficiency. As a result, parents and specialists can analyze the child's performance in relation to school-related tasks.

Most visually handicapped people have partial vision and can use it in some situations. Barraga (1964) compared the functional vision of two groups of visually impaired children. After two months of using their vision in daily practice routines, the experimental group was significantly better in visual discrimination than the control group. No improvement occurred in the children's visual acuity or in their eye condition but there was significant improvement in their visual efficiency. If the child has functional visual efficiency, it is quite likely that some learning will occur through the visual modality. However, if visual efficiency is either limited or nonexistent, the child will need to learn to read and write Braille.

Another factor affecting placement is the existence of other handicapping conditions. If the only impairment is visual, the placement decision is simplified considerably. However, determining placements and teaching strategies becomes more difficult when the child has multiple handicaps (Graham, 1970). For example, Janie, although legally blind, has enough visual efficiency to allow her to be a visual learner. Yet, because she also has a severe hearing impairment, the least restrictive learning environment for her is a nearby residential day school for deaf/blind children. The decision to place a youngster in a special school is usually based upon the need for special services not found in a regular school program even if resource room support services exist.

A final consideration for placement concerns the availability of training programs for the visually impaired. More densely populated areas may be able to provide needed programs close to the family's home. Because of the low incidence of visual impairments in the population, small communities do not always have appropriate programs.

All of the above factors must be taken into account by parents and professionals to determine the best program for the visually impaired child (Scott, Jan, and Freeman, 1977).

Whether blindness is viewed as a nuisance or as a limitation will affect the visually impaired person. For example, a blind child can learn to ride a bicycle, cross the street alone, explore the neighborhood safely, and attend a regular school program. A blind teenage girl can do her homework, participate in youth clubs, choose her own clothes, and apply makeup. The visually impaired adult can properly care for an infant, be a bricklayer, psychologist, doctor, or whatever he or she desires to be. These successes at everyday, normal activities and career goals depend upon two critical factors—attitudes of parents and significant others, and proper training and learning experiences.

ORIENTATION AND MOBILITY TRAINING   Traditional teaching methods and materials can be adapted to meet the academic needs of the visually impaired. However, special instructional programs for severely impaired children and youth must be available to develop appropriate orientation and mobility skills. **Orientation** refers to the ability to understand the relationship between self and environment through intact sensory input. **Mobility** refers to one's ability to travel safely and independently through the physical environment.

The development of these skills begins with systematically teaching the visually impaired child how to discover his or her own body image. Then, awareness of near and, later, extended spatial relationships and concepts are introduced (Hare and Hare, 1977). As Foulke (1970) points out (in a discussion on the theoretical foundations, for mobility training): the visually impaired rely on perceptual systems and cognitive strategies for understanding stimuli received from the environment. Higher levels of conceptual understanding depend upon previously successful concrete, self-oriented learning tasks. Kratz (1973) has compiled a comprehensive list of activities and exercises for preschool and primary children who are visually impaired. Activities should be chosen carefully and purposefully since visually impaired children do not learn vicariously. Rather, mobility programs must be organized to ensure that the impaired students are actively stimulated and explore their environment by means of systematic instruction.

The eventual goal of such programs is to develop independent living skills. Increased freedom affects other areas of development. An outcome of a demonstration project (Bailey, 1970) on mobility training for blind adolescents was that those students not only were more independent, but also had a more positive self-concept. Depending upon each person's needs and abilities, mobility can be achieved by any one or a combination of the following approaches: sighted guide, cane, guide dog, electronic equipment, or total independent movement (Hare and Hare, 1977).

ROLE OF PARENTS   Initially, the parents are responsible for providing a normal home life for the visually impaired infant and child. However, these parents often share many societal misconceptions and stereotypical images of what the blind can and cannot do. Thus, viewing and accepting their child as normal may be quite difficult for them. Yet, because they spend a great deal of time with the child, the parents are primarily responsible for nurturing their child's positive self-concept. Here are some suggestions for parents to encourage independent social behaviors:

- Rather than leaving the infant in the crib, carry or position the baby nearby. This exposes the baby to different sounds and their meanings.
- Tell the child what you are doing. For example, for the young child, explain the vaccuum cleaner—its sound and purpose. Let the child feel what a vacuum cleaner is:
- Since visual cues of love (smiles of approval) have little or no meaning, all kinds of touches (kisses, pats, etc.) are necessary to help the child learn.
- Let other people play, hold, and care for the child. The visually impaired child needs to learn that other people are enjoyable.
- Keep talking. Auditory stimuli is the major way that the severely visually impaired child can keep track of where you are. Verbal dialogue should reflect the child's developmental level and should be rich in terms of quality and quantity.
- Allow exploring behaviors—both inside and outside the home.

All of the above activities result in the young, visually impaired child being an active and integral part of the family. Independence and a sense of belonging are thus imparted.

ROLE OF TEACHERS   When the visually impaired child is enrolled in a school program, the teacher assumes responsibility for facilitating his or her cognitive and affective development. The blind child needs alternative instructional programs to develop mobility, communication skills, and social awareness. Once these skills are mastered, the child must be allowed to use them in the regular classroom. Frequently, although not always intentionally, the teacher overprotects or excludes the blind child. The visually impaired student would probably not be in the regular classroom unless he or she is able to succeed. Frequently, failure is due to either an unwillingness to aid or to a lack of knowledge on the part of the teacher. The regular classroom teacher can help the visually impaired child into the mainstream by encouraging independence and a positive self-concept. For example, the teacher could:

- Explain and give the student the opportunity to identify the physical arrangement of the classroom and its relationship to cafeteria, bathrooms, exits, etc.
- Allow the visually impaired student to use remaining vision. This may require the teacher to readjust or invent new techniques. For example, one regular sixth-grade teacher who had a legally blind student in her class usually wrote homework and seatwork assignments on the board. With minimal disruption to the class, this student was able to get assignments unassisted by sitting next to the board.
- Have the visually impaired student be responsible for his or her own needs. Just because the eyes don't function doesn't mean that the ears, legs, and arms are impaired also. In other words, expect the student to be independent, just as the other students.
- Give nonimpaired students the opportunity to discuss blindness with the visually impaired student.
- Provide classroom experiences that allow the visually impaired student to assume a positive leadership role.
- Solicit information from parents. They frequently can answer the teacher's "how to do it best" questions.
- Repeat what is being written on the board.
- Clarify and expand visual material, such as charts or maps.

■ Since Braille, if used, takes more time than conventional methods, allow the student more time to finish assignments.
■ Encourage the student to use alternative techniques and/or technology that facilitate learning in the regular classroom.

Although each infant has a unique personality, all infants begin to develop language and body awareness during the first year of life. Learning in each developmental area does not occur in isolation; rather, each is interwoven and dependent on the others. Again, it is the responsibility of the parents and educators to work together to help the visually impaired infant, child, and adolescent succeed at each developmental stage in order to reach his or her potential as an adult.

LEARNING AIDS FOR THE VISUALLY IMPAIRED

Support services for the visually impaired focus on mobility training. They do so in order to enhance better understanding of and movement through the environment, development of all senses to their maximum, and alternative learning experiences to replace unseen or distorted visual stimuli.

Special learning devices assist the visually impaired in becoming contributing members of society. The type of adaptive material used for a particular student is

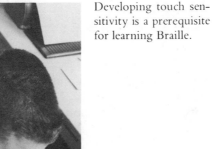

Developing touch sensitivity is a prerequisite for learning Braille.

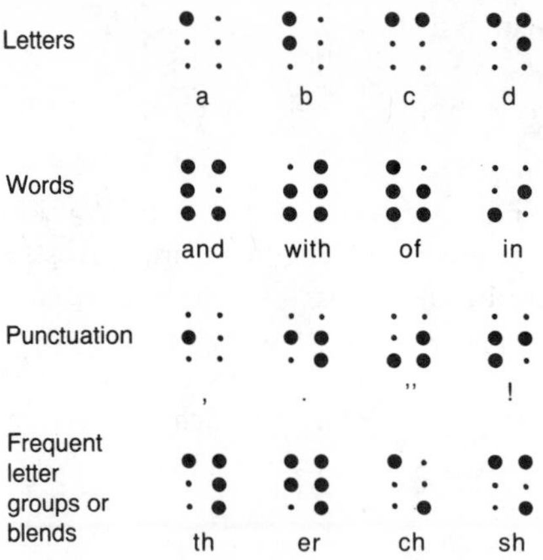

Letters	a	b	c	d
Words	and	with	of	in
Punctuation	,	.	"	!
Frequent letter groups or blends	th	er	ch	sh

FIGURE 9-2 Examples of Braille symbols.

a decision that rests with a specialist trained to teach the visually impaired. Adaptive materials for classroom use are divided into two categories: optical and nonoptical (Corn and Martinez, 1978). **Optical aids** are individually prescribed by a physician to increase visual ability. **Nonoptical aids** are not prescribed nor are they necessarily visually oriented. Rather, they include many alternative aids that assist learning through the other senses.

Optical Aids

The three most common optical aids are glasses, magnifiers, and telescopic devices. The prescription glasses category includes contact lenses, prisms, bifocals, and tinted lenses, any of which can be prescribed for use at a particular time or for a given task. Tinted lenses, for example, are worn by children whose eyes are sensitive to light. Magnifiers enlarge the size of relatively close visual images (such as the printed page), whereas telescopic aids enlarge distant visual images (such as the chalkboard).

Nonoptical Aids

For the visually impaired unable to see printed letters that are ¼-inch high, reading occurs through the use of **Braille** (Scott, Jan, and Freeman, 1977), a tactual alphabet system promoted during the nineteenth century by the Frenchman Louis Braille, who was blind. The Braille code consists of raised dots arranged in various positions within a six-dot cell to denote letters of the alphabet, numbers, musical notations, contractions, and shortened forms of words (see Figure 9-2).

Both the Braillewriter and the slate and stylus are used to write Braille. The **Braillewriter** is a six-key machine that embosses paper with the Braille code. The **slate** and **stylus** also produces the raised Braille code, and has the advantage of being lightweight and portable. It is, however, slower and more difficult to learn to use than is the Braillewriter.

Special paper products are also available to assist learning. For example, when an acetate cover is placed over the printed page, the contrast between the print and the background of the paper increases. Raised line paper tactually assists visually impaired students with writing. This special paper is manufactured for various subjects; for example, both horizontally lined paper for writing or graph paper for math assignments are available.

Academic tests and leisure reading materials recorded on cassette tapes and disks are available to eligible visually impaired persons through the Library of Congress' Talking Book program. Unlike many commercial cassettes, the speed of these special disks and tapes can be varied to meet individual listening needs. Cassette tape recorders also allow students to record class lectures and discussions.

For those visually impaired students able to read enlarged print, several other learning aids exist. The American Printing House for the Blind publishes books with enlarged print. Figure 9-3 shows the difference between 18-point type, which is most frequently found in large-print books, and 10-point type, which is usually found in regular textbooks. As with Braille texts, the major disadvantages of large-print books is that they are bulky to store and their availability is limited.

Closed-circuit television not only enlarges printed material electronically, but also allows the viewer to control the illumination and the contrast between the print and background. Also, the print can be viewed as either black on a white background or vice versa.

Another electronic reading machine is the **Optacon** which uses a camera to convert visual print images into impulses that can be read tactually. Unlike closed-circuit television, the Optacon's size and weight permit its portable use. Although expensive, portability is a major advantage of the Optacon, which permits the student to read print not only in the classroom, but elsewhere in everyday life, such as reading labels on boxes in the grocery store, recipes, and the mail. New technological advances have given the visually impaired increased opportunities to more fully enjoy life. Presently, however, the high cost of these learning aids, such as closed-circuit television or the Optacon, is prohibitive.

SPECIAL CONSIDERATIONS AND ISSUES

Educators and other related professionals recognize that although the pedagogical foundation for teaching visually impaired students has progressed in recent years, there are still areas that need attention. Curricula—from infant stimulation through high school—that promote maximum learning for blind children and youth must be developed and evaluated. Also, while successfully integrating the visually impaired into the mainstream of society depends upon their ability to work productively, there is a paucity of comprehensive, realistic vocational programs for the visually impaired (Ozias, 1970).

FIGURE 9-3 Difference in type sizes used in large-print and regular textbooks.

> This is an example of the type size used in large-print books for the visually impaired. Width of
>
> This is an example of the type size often used in books for people with normal vision. More characters fit on each line; so the width of the line

Technological advances, like the Optacon above, increase the visually impaired student's accessibility to the printed word.

Another major deterrent to independent living for the visually impaired is the physical environment. This issue is being addressed by professionals concerned with a variety of handicaps. Their efforts are directed toward developing more technologically advanced and reliable devices that will allow both the handicapped and blind to behave more freely and with more confidence.

SUMMARY POINTS

- Visual impairment is used to describe people who have defective visual acuity and/or an impaired field of vision. Definitions can be either legally or educationally based.
- Most visual impairments are attributed to congenital or hereditary factors, including structural or muscular defects as well as interferences of embryonic life due to maternal diseases.
- Periodic screening programs in the schools identify many children with visual problems that otherwise may not have been detected. Teachers should familiarize themselves with warning signals of possible visual problems.
- Most visually impaired children are capable of developing normally; language, motor, and cognitive skills may, however, be retarded if the environment is not structured to elicit and develop these skills.
- The selection of the best educational program for the visually impaired depends upon many variables. Each case must be viewed individually; not all visually impaired children require special services.

■ Critical to the visually impaired child's development is his or her ability to interact within the environment. Parents and teachers should not be over-protective or restrict activities; rather, the visually impaired child needs much stimulation and conversation. Mobility training should begin in infancy in order to develop independent functioning in the environment.

■ Teachers and parents should cooperatively plan structured learning experiences based on developmental and hierarchical skills. It cannot be assumed that the visually impaired will learn on their own. They need assistance in organizing and understanding sensory information.

■ Many learning aids are available to assist the visually impaired. Selection of appropriate learning and mobility aids should be based on the visually impaired individual's needs and abilities.

REVIEW QUESTIONS

1. Compare the legal and educational definitions of visual impairment.
2. Identify instructional and environmental modifications that a teacher could implement in the regular classroom to accommodate the visually impaired.
3. What certification requirements does your state have for teaching visually impaired children and youth?
4. How can the incidence of visual impairments be reduced?

TEACHING THE BLIND —
CONCEPTUAL LEARNING AND THE ARTS

If conceptual understanding is a goal of education, how do we teach concepts to blind children whose disabilities thwart understanding of self and environment? First, teaching must be deliberate for learning to occur (Hare and Hare, 1977). Normally, learning occurs both through direct teaching and incidental learning. However, between 80 and 90 percent of incidental learning is through the visual channel (Ozias, 1970). As a result, the blind student's learning is dependent on formal teaching.

The curricula must reflect a unified approach to instruction (Nolan, 1976), which emphasizes experiencing the wholesomeness of an object, event, etc. The visual channel affords the opportunity to synthesize not only visual stimuli but also information from other senses. The blind child does not have the advantage of seeing how different sensory stimuli are all parts of a whole. For example, the child smells gasoline, hears a whirling motor, and feels a force of air. What is not comprehended is that all these sensations are related to one object: the lawnmower. When teaching is fragmented, faulty or poor concept development is likely.

Teaching abstract concepts to the blind can be done with creativity and with planned instruction. For example, Tunkin and Kapperman (1978) discuss how blind children can be taught the concept of negative space through the arts. First the children formed their own bodies to delineate negative space by, for example, standing with their feet apart. The inside of this triangle was defined as negative space. In addition, musical activities and three-dimensional sculpture experiences related the concepts of form and space to objects in the environment. The authors stress the importance of classroom art experiences as a communication tool for conceptual learning.

Across the country there is a growing trend of providing meaningful art experiences for the handicapped population outside of the classroom. These opportunities include not only appreciating art via visits to museums, but also special arts programs that directly promote creativity, concept learning, and expression.

Harold Snider, coordinator of programs for the handicapped at the Smithsonian Institution's National Air and Space Museum, is visually impaired. He has coordinated the museum's efforts to meet the needs of the blind. Since the blind must have access to the same services provided to the nonimpaired population, the Air and Space Museum's existing procedures were modified. For example, floor plans outlining the museum are now made of plastic or plexiglass, and cassette tours replaced visual labels. Also, guide books are now available in Braille and cassettes.

Some art exhibits are designed primarily to meet the aesthetic needs of the blind. For example, the Mary Duke Beddle Gallery at the North Carolina Museum of Art is a tactile gallery that has provided successful art experiences to both the visually impaired and the sighted since 1966. Whereas most galleries draw the visitors' attention visually, materials for tactile exhibits are selected on the basis of textures.

The Junior Arts Center in Los Angeles offers hands-on arts experiences for both handicapped and nonimpaired public school students. This workshop enrichment program is geared to develop aesthetic awareness. It also allows some blind children to engage in active participation with different art media, thus providing a therapeutic experience. The emphasis of the program is to stimulate the imagination and creativity of all children involved in the Junior Arts program (Arts for Blind and Visually Impaired People, 1978).

The following guidelines will assist educators in teaching concepts (Baird and

Goldie, 1979; Woodcock, 1974; Hare and Hare, 1977):

- Use criterion-referenced assessment instruments that are developmentally based to identify the student's instructional level.
- Task-analyze the concept to be taught in order to identify a hierarchy and sequence of appropriate instructional objectives.
- Select instructional materials and activities that utilize the tactile, kinesthetic, and auditory channels.

- Sequence instruction to progress from the concrete to abstract. This can be more readily achieved by relying initially on three-dimensional materials and then introducing two-dimensional materials. Also, it is easier for a blind child to understand a concept if it is first related to the self. Later, for generalization of learning, instructional activities should emphasize self/object and then object/object relationships.

DISCUSSION POINTS

1. Identify a specific concrete and abstract concept and task-analyze how you would teach them to a blind primary-age child.
2. List equipment, materials, and related activities that might be used in a sensory stimulation room for blind children.

SUGGESTED READINGS

Cratty, B. J. *Movement and Spatial Awareness in Blind Children and Youth*. Springfield, Ill.: Charles C. Thomas, 1971.

Harley, R. K., and Lawrence, G. A. *Visual Impairment in the Schools*. Springfield, Ill.: Charles C. Thomas, 1977.

Warren, D. H., and Kocon, J. A. "Factors in the Successful Mobility of the Blind: A Review." *Research Bulletin: American Foundation for the Blind*, 28 (1974), 191–218.

10

THE SPEECH AND LANGUAGE IMPAIRED

CONTENTS

In the early 1900s the study of communication disorders focused on speech, with articulation and fluency disorders receiving considerable attention. However, the communication process is complex and goes beyond speech production. It draws on sociology, psychology, medicine, speech, and language. The contributions from these disciplines outside of speech, coupled with environmental events, such as disabled veterans returning home from war, further expanded speech pathology's field of service. Within the schools, the integration of hearing-impaired children diversified the clientele of the speech therapist. After World War II, returning soldiers diagnosed as aphasic added a new dimension to the study of speech pathology—language. Reflecting this added dimension, speech pathologists became known as **speech and language pathologists** *or* **therapists.**

The following case studies highlight the diversity of communication disorders and the complexity of treatments.

LISA

Lisa, age three, was brought to a speech clinic by her mother, Mrs. Stillman, who was concerned about Lisa's poor speech. An informal evaluation revealed that Lisa had an extensive receptive vocabulary and was able to follow complex instructions. However, her expressive vocabulary consisted of two words, "ma" and "no." Lisa's underdeveloped speech appeared to contradict her receptive skills and nonverbal expressive abilities.

Mrs. Stillman volunteered the following background information, which helped to

explain the discrepancy between Lisa's receptive and expressive language skills.

"When Lisa was about nine months old she began to talk. My husband and I did not know what to expect in the way of speech; I guess we expected too much from Lisa. When she would say 'ma,' I thought she should say 'mother' or 'mommy.' I would make Lisa sit in her high chair, sometimes for half an hour, and force her to practice saying words correctly. Each of these learning sessions would end in frustration. Lisa would cry and throw temper tantrums. Eventually, she stopped talking. Since I have never been around young children, I thought something was wrong with Lisa's speech. My husband and I thought we were doing the right thing."

Mr. and Mrs. Stillman, like many parents, did not realize that a child's first attempts to verbalize can be extremely frustrating. The young child hears adults speaking and can understand much of what is being said. However, though a baby can imitate sounds, muscular coordination is not sufficiently developed to enable an infant to talk. For this and other reasons, the child's listeners must reinforce efforts to communicate. If the frustration is too great, or the motivation or reinforcement too little, the child's speech and language may fail to develop at a normal rate. Failure to produce speech may be a defense mechanism for coping with parental anger.

RONALD

The background information on Ronald, now age 13, was furnished by his mother, Mrs. Gillmore. Ronald is similar to many other children whose communication disorders are compounded by other severe handicapping conditions and health impairments.

"When Ronald was born, we could see that something was wrong; later we were told that he had a cleft lip. But that was nothing compared to what was to come. Apparently, the doctors suspected some kind of brain damage. The neurologist said that Ronnie might have cerebral palsy, muscular dystrophy, multiple sclerosis, or mental retardation. During his first year, in addition to a temporary hearing loss, Ronnie was in and out of the hospital for collapsed lungs.

"After several years of seeing over 100 doctors and other professionals, Ronnie was diagnosed as having cerebral palsy and being mentally retarded. His cleft lip has caused considerable problems with his teeth. Twelve teeth have been pulled and each episode has been increasingly more traumatic for Ronnie and us. This has all been at our expense.

"We're not really sure what Ronnie's potential is. His teachers don't know either. When I watch Ronnie, I get upset. He tries so hard to talk. But the cerebral palsy prevents him from sounding intelligent. His speech is garbled and it takes him so much time when he does say something. For the past two years, Ronnie has been using a communication board to tell us what he wants and how he feels. Neighbors and friends think he is *really* retarded and should be put in an institution. But I know that Ronnie is thinking and feeling all the time. I can tell by looking at him; his eyes and face tell me so much."

Points for Consideration

■ Speech and language disorders are attributed to a variety of causes. Lisa's problems were related to her environment, whereas Ronald's communication deficits were congenital.

■ Since communication disorders are frequently associated with other disabilities —physical, psychological, and/or emotional trauma and deficits—it is imperative that the multidisciplinary team be utilized in planning appropriate intervention strategies that will involve the entire family.

■ Unrealistic parental expectations, such as the Stillmans', reflect an ignorance about early speech and language development. Pediatricians as well as other involved professionals can help by providing parents with realistic information about developmental milestones and behaviors.

Common Misconceptions

■ *People Who Have Little or No Intelligible Speech Are Retarded.* Although a relationship between mental retardation and communication disorders sometimes exists, many handicapped people without speech capability do have normal intelligence.

■ *Children with Speech Problems Will Outgrow Them; They're Just "Late Bloomers."* Some children might, but, many communication disordered children suffer humiliation and secondary emotional trauma because their problems were neither identified nor treated in their early years.

■ *Only a Speech and Language Therapist Can Provide Therapy.* The classroom teacher should be aware of therapeutic strategies in order to carry over therapy to the child's classroom environment. The therapist can also suggest how to develop language and speech skills in all children.

Communication is a complex, learned behavior. We can, though, think of it as a cycle that transpires between two people. The communication cycle is divided into output (expressive), integration, and input (receptive) phases. A spoken message may also be thought of as existing in three different forms as it progresses from speaker to listener. The speaker's message first originates in his or her mind at the linguistic level. Then, the oral production (pulsed code) of the message (output) exists at the physiological level, involving the muscles and organs of speech. As sound waves travel to the listener, the message exists as an acoustic signal. The listener receives the message (input) at the physiological level, through hearing. Finally, the information is processed (integration), and the reply is formulated, again at the linguistic level. In this way the cycle, or speech chain, continues (Denis and Pinson, 1963).

Many factors do not necessarily result in a deviance or disorder but do result in a difference in speech and language among a group of people. We all know people who talk "a little different," yet they are intelligible. A child's sex, intelligence, physical development, social and economic environment, emotional stability, and family constellation are all related to speech and language development. In addition, dialectal differences or a bilingual background may be influential.

Despite certain differences in speech and language development, sequential stages do occur. Table 10-1 depicts the developmental stages of early normal speech and oral language.

DEFINITION OF TERMS

Speech and language are different components of the communication process. **Speech** refers to those aspects that utilize vocal and oral symbols. In speech, the emphasis is on the production and articulation of sound. **Language**, on the other hand, is defined more broadly. It refers to the receiving, understanding, and transmission (vocal or nonvocal) of one's thoughts, beliefs, or ideas. Each language system—for example, French, Spanish, or English—has its own set of rules for transmitting knowledge. Thus, it is apparent that the concept of language includes more than just verbal expression. Without language there would be no speech.

Communication disorders is an umbrella term that covers both speech and language disorders. When any two speakers are compared, a speech difference will be noted. The central question in speech pathology is: When is that difference so great that it should be considered deviant and thus labeled a disorder? "Speech is abnormal when it deviates so far from the speech of other people that it calls attention to itself, interferes with communication, or causes the speaker or his listeners to be distressed (Van Riper, 1978, p. 43). If the listener is straining on how, rather than what, the speaker is saying, then a speech problem may exist.

Children with language disorders may have difficulty in any (or a combination of) the following areas: understanding the meaning of the linguistic message being received verbally; processing, organizing, and storing information; and using appropriate linguistic structures to express ideas and thoughts (Naremore, 1980). The scope of language disorders ranges beyond oral language production and encompasses cognitive development.

TABLE 10-1 Developmental Stages of Early Normal Speech and Oral Language

Age	General Characteristics	Usable Speaking Vocabulary (number of words)	Adequate Speech Sound Production
(months)			
1–3	*Undifferentiated crying.* Random vocalizations and cooing.		
4–6	*Babbling.* Specific vocalizations. Verbalizes in response to speech of others. Immediate responses approximate human intonational patterns.		
7–11	Tongue moves in vocalizations (lalling). Vocalizes recognition. Reduplicates sound. Echolalia (automatic repetition of words and phrases).		
12	*First word.*	1–3	all vowels
18	*One-word sentence stage.* Well-established jargon. Uses nouns primarily.	18–22	
(years)			
2	*Two-word sentence stage.* Sentences functionally complete. Uses more pronouns and verbs.	270–300	
2.5	*Three-word sentence stage.* Telegraphic speech.	450	h, w, hw
3	Complete simple-active sentence structure used. Uses sentences to tell stories which are understood by others.	900	p, b, m
3.5	*Expanded grammatical forms.* Concepts expressed with words. Speech disfluency is typical. Sentence length is 4–5 words.	1200	t, d, n
4	Excessive verbalizations. Imaginary speech.	1500	k, g, ng, j
5	*Well-developed and complex syntax.* Uses more complex forms to tell stories. Uses negation and inflexional form of verbs.	2000	f, v
6–8	*Sophisticated speech.* Skilled use of grammatical rules. Learns to read.		l, r, y, s, z sh, ch, zh, th
	Acceptable articulation by 8 years for males and females.	2600+	consonant blends

From EXCEPTIONAL CHILDREN IN THE SCHOOLS, Second Edition, edited by Lloyd M. Dunn. Copyright © 1963, 1973, by Holt, Rinehart, and Winston, Inc. Reprinted by permission of Holt, Rinehart, and Winston.

PREVALENCE

Attempts to determine the prevalence of speech and language disorders in the school population are thwarted by disagreements over definitions, variations among ages, degree of impairment, and geographic locations in population samples. Table 10-2 estimates the prevalence of specific communication disorders in children (Hull, Mielkle, Timmons, and Willeford, 1971, 1976; Irwin and Marge, 1972).

Disorder	Estimated Prevalence in School-Age Population
Voice	3% (does not include resonance disorders, which are estimated to occur in 1 to 2% of population)
Articulation	2% (refers to severe articulation disorders; does not include children with mild articulation disorders)
Fluency (Stuttering)	1%
Language	7% (includes children with no language, delayed language, or deviant language)

TYPES OF COMMUNICATION DISORDERS

Communication disorders are classified into four major groups: voice, articulation, speech flow, and language deviances.

Voice Disorders

Whereas speech is characterized as symbolic utterances, voice is defined as tones produced by vibrations of the vocal chords. **Voice disorders** may be attributed to either organic causes resulting from abnormal anatomical structures, neuromuscular disorders, or resonator mechanisms, or to functional causes such as poor modeling habits.

Voice disorders are divided into two groups. **Phonation disorders** (a dysfunction in the larynx) results in the misuse of the voice. **Resonance disorders** (difficulty in properly using the tongue, pharynx, or velum) result from an upper airway dysfunction. Correction may be necessary when there is a significant deviation in the pitch, intensity, or quality of the voice. An overview of the speech mechanism is shown in Figure 10-1.

PITCH Pitch refers to the intonation or melody of the vocal tones. For example, the voices of young children tend to be high-pitched, whereas the adult male voice is usualy low-pitched. **Pitch disorders** include voice patterns that are monotonous or tremulous. Most people with pitch disorders have normal larynxes. For these individuals, the goal of treatment is to find an optimal pitch level. Therapy begins with creating an awareness within the client that his or her pitch is indeed deviant. The next step is to locate and then develop a more acceptable pitch (Boone, 1971).

INTENSITY Intensity refers to the degree of loudness of the voice. **Intensity disorders** occur when the voice is either too loud or too soft under certain circumstances. Aphonia refers to a complete voice loss; whereas dysphonia means a partial or intermittent loss (Van Riper, 1978). For example, the young child who is always speaking in a loud voice, regardless of where he or she is or what the topic is, may have an intensity disorder. Treatment varies depending on the degree and related causes associated with each type of disorder.

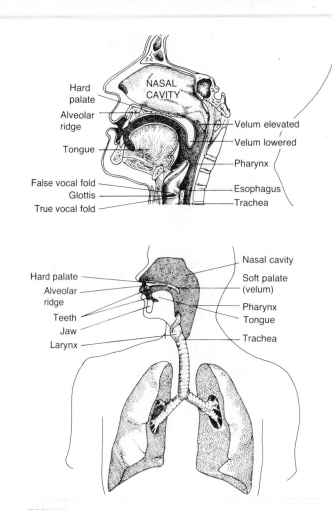

Hard palate
Alveolar ridge
Tongue
False vocal fold
Glottis
True vocal fold

NASAL CAVITY

Velum elevated
Velum lowered
Pharynx
Esophagus
Trachea

Hard palate
Alveolar ridge
Teeth
Jaw
Larynx

Nasal cavity
Soft palate (velum)
Pharynx
Tongue
Trachea

FIGURE 10-1   Mechanism for speech production. (From C. Van Riper. *Speech Correction Principles and Methods.* Englewood Cliffs, N.J.: Prentice-Hall, 1978, p. 77.)

QUALITY   Quality refers to the tone of the voice. **Quality disorders** are classified into the following five categories (Van Riper, 1978).

Hypernasality (voice identified by a high nasal quality) results from poor regulation of the airflow and acoustic energy through the velum and pharyngeal muscles. The high nasal quality occurs when too much air is passing through the nasal cavity. When the airway is constricted, thus limiting the amount of airflow and acoustic energy, voice quality is **denasal**. Speech emitted by children with enlarged adenoids or head colds is often denasal. A third type of quality deviancy is the breathy, husky voice resulting from an output of too much air during or prior to phonation. Here, speech is characteristically husky and breathy and may result in short, choppy phrases. The fourth kind of quality disorder is characterized by a harsh, strident voice, related to stress, tension, and vocalizations requiring a consistently loud volume, which is raspy and piercing in nature and causes a strain on the larynx. The fifth deviancy associated with quality disorders is the hoarse voice. Usually, it is associated with abuses such as too much yelling at a football game or a severe cold. Rest is the best cure. If any quality disorder continues for an extended period of time, a laryngologist should be consulted.

The most common speech problem found in the public schools concerns **articu-lation disorders**, which occur when children have difficulty producing speech sounds. The speech pathologist uses the International Phonetic Alphabet's (IPA) phonemic notation system for identifying and recording articulation errors. The phonetic alphabet is presented in Table 10-3.

The four types of articulation disorders are:

- Omission of a sound. Examples: "sow" instead of "slow," "gu" instead of "gum."
- Substitution of one sound for another. Examples: "tar" instead of "car," "muvver give me a tiss" instead of "mother give me a kiss."
- Distortion of a sound (the child is approximating the correct sound). Examples: child says "soup" with an initial lisping sound.
- Addition of an irrelevant sound. Examples: "helpee me" instead of "help me," "washish the doggog" instead of "wash the dog."

One role of the speech therapist is to assist hearing impaired children in producing intelligible speech.

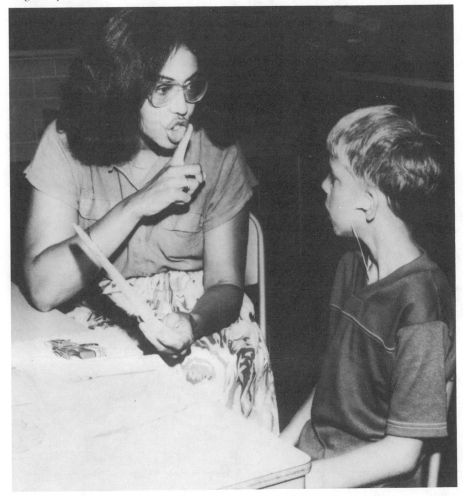

TABLE 10-3 The Phonetic Alphabet

Phonetic Symbol	Key Words English	Phonetic	Phonetic Symbol	Key Words English	Phonetics
Consonants					
b	*back, cab*	bæk kæb	p	*pig, sap*	pɪg sæp
d	*dig, red*	dɪg, rɛd	r	*rat, poor*	ræt pʊr
f	*feel, leaf*	fil lif	s	*so, miss*	so mɪs
g	*go, egg*	go ɛg	t	*to, wit*	tu wɪt
dʒ	*just, edge*	dʒʌst ɛdʒ	ʃ	*she, wish*	ʃi wɪʃ
h	*he behaves*	hi bɪhevz	tʃ	*chin, itch*	tʃɪn ɪtʃ
k	*keep, track*	kip træk	θ	*think truth*	θɪŋk truθ
l	*low, ball*	lo bɔl	ð	*then, bathe*	ðɛn beð
ḷ	*simple, fable*	sɪmpḷ febḷ	v	*vest, live*	vɛst lɪv
m	*my, aim*	maɪ em	w	*we, swim*	wi swɪm
m̩	*kingdom*	kɪŋdm̩	hw	*where, when*	hwɛr hwɛn
	madam	mæ̃dm̩	j	*yell, young*	jɛl jʌŋ
n	*not, any*	nɑt ɛnɪ	ʒ	*measure*	mɛʒɚ vɚ-ʒn
n̩	*action, mission*	ækʃn̩ mɪʃn̩		*version*	
ŋ	*sing, uncle*	sɪŋ ʌŋkḷ	z	*zebra, ozone*	zibrə ozon
ʔ	*oh oh!*	ʔo ʔo			
Vowels					
a*	*far, sad*	far sad	ɒ*	*law, wrong*	l ɒ r ɒŋ
ɑ	*father, mop*	fɑðɚ mɑp	ɝ	*early, bird*	ɝ·lɪ bɚd
e	*great, ache*	gret ek	ɝ*	*early bird*	ɝlɪ b ɝd
æ	*sad, sack*	sæd sæk	ɚ	*perhaps,*	pɚ·hæps
i	*intrigue, me*	ɪntrig mi		*never*	nɛvɚ
ɛ	*head, rest*	hɛd rɛst	u	*to, you*	tu ju
ɪ	*his, itch*	hɪz ɪtʃ	ʊ	*pudding, cook*	pʊdɪŋ kʊk
o	*own, bone*	on bon	ʌ	*mother, drug*	mʌðɚ drʌg
ɔ	*all, dog*	ɔl dɔg	ə	*above, suppose*	əbʌv səpoz
Diphthongs					
aɪ	*my, eye*	maɪ aɪ	ɔɪ	*toy, boil*	tɔɪ bɔɪl
aʊ	*cow, about*	kaʊ əbaʊt			
Centering Diphthongs					
ɛr	*wear, fair*	wɛr fɛr	ɪr	*beer, weird*	bɪr wɪrd
ɑr	*barn, far*	bɑrn fɑr	aɪr	*wire, tire*	waɪr taɪr
ʊr	*lure, moor*	lʊr mʊr	aʊr	*hour, flower*	aʊr flaʊr
ɔr	*shore, born*	ʃɔr bɔrn			

*These vowels are heard in Eastern and Southern speech.
From *Speech Correction: Principles and Methods*, 6th ed., C. Van Riper, Prentice-Hall, Inc., 1978.

In addition to looking at phonemic errors, the speech/language pathologist analyzes the child's speech to determine if there is a clustering of errors.

Infantile preservation in speech, sometimes referred to as "baby talk," is characterized by omission and substitution of sounds and frequently by immaturity in language development. However, omissions or substitutions for a particular sound tend to be inconsistent. For example, a child may say "biss" instead of "kiss," but correctly say "cup." In the latter instance, the /k/ is used correctly. The most frequent consonant errors are /s/, /r/, /l/, /ch/, /th/, /k/, /g/, /f/, and /v/ (Powers, 1971, p. 841).

Lisping occurs when there is misarticulation of at least one of the six sibilant consonants, /s/, /z/, / ʃ /, / ʒ /, / tʃ /, / dʒ / (Powers, 1971, p. 843). Inappropriate tongue placements and malocclusions (poor teeth placements) causing an improper airflow through the teeth result in the speaker lisping.

Lalling is the distortion of the /r/ or /l/ and, less commonly, the /t/ or /d/. In such instances, the child may say "wittle wed wagon," rather than "little red wagon." Cause for such distortions is failure to elevate the top of the tongue (Van Riper, 1978).

Speech Flow Disorders

Besides articulation errors, there are disorders that affect the fluency, rate, and rhythm of a speaker's speech flow. Stuttering is the most common speech flow disorder.

STUTTERING   "**Stuttering** occurs when the forward flow of speech is interrupted abnormally by repetitions or prolongations of a sound, syllable, or articulatory posture, or by avoidance and struggle behaviors" (Van Riper, 1978, p. 257). It is not uncommon to hear disfluency patterns in the young speaker. For example, omissions, inappropriate pauses, and rapid speech are typical early childhood speech behaviors. This developmental phenomenon is normal and should not be diagnosed as stuttering. Unfortunately the parent, fearful that the child is stuttering, may put pressure on the child to "talk right."

Stuttering includes a variety of symptoms, and not all of these apply to all stutterers. Following are general symptoms found at various chronological levels (Karlin, Karlin, and Gurren, 1965, pp. 97–100).

- *Preschool Age:* Simple repetitions, hesitations, mild tension of mouth and lips, mild anxiety
- *Five- to Twelve-Year-Old:* Tonic (muscular contraction) and clonic (alternating contractions and relaxation of muscle) spasms of the mouth and lips, laryngeal spasms, muscular tension, more pronounced anxiety
- *Adolescent and Young Adult:* Severe disfluency, marked respiratory disturbances, pronounced fear and anxiety

The above information indicates that with the onset of maturity actual speech errors are increasingly accompanied by inappropriate nonverbal behaviors. As the child is made aware of his or her speech difficulties, secondary behaviors, such as refusing to talk, turning from the listener, covering the mouth when talking, eye blinking, and so forth, are more evident. Because this disorder is complex, any attempts to help the stutterer in the classroom or in the home should be done in conjunction with a speech/language pathologist.

Those in the field of communication disorders disagree on the cause of stuttering, which begins in children between the ages of two and seven years. Johnson's (1955) interactional theory is based on the interaction between significant adult and child. In such cases, the adult's expectations for the child's speech are too high. The child's speech is not fluent and thus the parent's reaction is negative. This behavior results in increased pressure on the child.

Psychiatry considers stuttering from a psychodynamic perspective wherein speech is viewed as the external manifestation of repressed internal needs or conflicts. In such cases, the deviant speech flow may be attributed, for example, to extreme parental demands. As a result, the emotional stress in the child is so intense that stuttering develops.

The linguistic view proposes several theories. Bloodstein (1974) suggests that early stutterers may have difficulty encoding the syntactic structure of language. Wingate's (1976) research has focused on the relationship between rhythm of speech and disfluencies as a possible explanation. Considerable research directed at linking stuttering with a biological (genetic, neurological, metabolic, and sensory disturbances) explanation has been conducted. However, no definitive statements regarding cause and effect can be made at this time. At this point most speech/language pathologists assume an eclectic perspective, which is evident in treatment procedures (Perkins, 1980).

Perkins (1980) has identified five tactics that stutterers use as attempts to improve their fluency. Teachers should be aware of the relationship between these techniques and stuttering. If a student uses these regularly, the classroom teacher should contact the school speech and language pathologist.

- *Antiexpectancy Measures.* These result in a speech change, such as using a different pitch or speaking in a monotone.
- *Postponement Maneuvers.* Used to delay speech until the speaker thinks he or she is ready to say the word correctly. Common maneuvers are repeating words or phrases, pausing, or using stereotyped expressions, such as "you know," repeatedly. Example: "Yesterday he-he-he wanted to go."
- *Avoidance Tactics.* Ploys such as word substitution are used by the stutterer in order to avoid saying dreaded words that result in stuttering. Example: "I want the l-l (pause) big cookie." (The speaker substituted "big" for "large.")
- *Starting Devices.* These help the stutterer initiate difficult sounds at the beginning of words. Example: "The book has a uh-uh-uh-uh silly ending."
- *Escape Technique.* Attempts by the stutterer to get by the difficult sound once it has occurred. In such instances, the speaker backs up and tries again. Example: "That is w-w-w-w, that is what I need."

Language Disorders

Language disorders include those impairments that inhibit the expression of one's thoughts and ideas. Fluent verbal expression is the culmination of a hierarchy of skills. Language learning itself is related to the following sequential processes: auditory perception, memory, integration, recall, and expression in a spoken form (Myklebust, 1971). A dysfunction at one or more of these levels results in a language disorder. Language disorders, then, can be characterized by faulty

TABLE 10-4 Language Deficiencies **231**

THE SPEECH AND LANGUAGE IMPAIRED

Linguistic Structure	Associated Deficiency
Phonology	Poor discrimination of sound patterns, including the pitch, rhythm, and/or melody of sound patterns. Results in faulty understanding and expression. Example: The teacher might ask a student, "Read the second paragraph on page ten." To the student with a severe discrimination problem, the auditory reception may be garbled like a poor long distance telephone call or certain sounds may not be discriminated from others. As a result, this student does not respond at all or does so inappropriately.
Morphology	Inability to associate meaning with phonemes that are heard. Includes root words, plurals, suffixes, prefixes, etc. Example: Knows meaning of the word *cite*; however, has difficulty with *ex*cite, *re*cite.
Syntax	Inability to process, store, and organize information in order to express oneself in the accepted grammatical code. Results in faulty word order, jargon, frequent pauses, etc. Example: "They not here," in this case, a form of the verb to be is omitted. "Now to store go" illustrates incorrect word order.
Semantics	Inability to comprehend isolated word meanings and poor understanding of word combination. Results in poor comprehension of words, phrases, sentences, etc. Example: The idea that "There's a fork in the road" might be interpreted as "There's an eating utensil in the road." This faulty word meaning results from inability to use contextual meaning.

receptive, associative, and/or expressive deficiencies in regard to the phonology, morphology, syntax, and/or semantic structures of a particular language. Table 10-4 lists the more common problems associated with each of the four linguistic characteristics.

Language disorders can be divided into three categories: acquired language loss, delayed language, and deviant language.

ACQUIRED LANGUAGE LOSS   The terms **aphasia** and **dysphasia** are frequently interchanged even though, as the prefixes indicate, there is a difference (Ewanowski, 1980). Dysphasia refers to a loss of ability to use symbolic functions associated with language; whereas aphasia refers to a complete loss of ability to use language. The difference resides in the degree of loss.

Specifically, aphasics (dysphasics) have impaired functioning in the receptive, associative, and/or expressive processes related to symbolic language. Depending upon the location of cerebral dysfunction, aphasia is classified into two categories: (1) Motor aphasia, which results in the inability to express oneself in either speech or in writing; and (2) sensory aphasia, in which a person is unable to comprehend symbols received through various sensory channels. Sensory deficits can be either in the visual modality, thus affecting one's ability to read, or in the auditory modality, resulting in poor comprehension of or inability to recall the spoken word. Less common types of aphasia include amnesia characterized by the inability to recall the names of well-known objects. The child diagnosed as a semantic aphasic has expressive language skills and understands words; however, the deficit is in understanding the meaning or complete thought of what is being said (Brown, 1972).

The diagnosis of aphasia is often a difficult process (as evidenced by the complexity of the classification system). Children can have one kind in isolation or a combination of any of the above. Acquired language loss is the least prevalent type of language disorder.

DELAYED LANGUAGE   The majority of language-impaired children are language delayed. These children have language skills and can often be understood, especially by parents or siblings who are used to their simple utterances. Language for these children is "characterized as normal in all respects, except age appropriateness" (Naremore, 1980, p. 159). For example, "me eat" is a normal utterance for a two-year-old; however, a five-year-old uttering the same words would be designated language delayed. In other words, although such language production can be thought of as immature, it still corresponds to established developmental language norms.

DEVIANT LANGUAGE   Whereas children's delayed language corresponds to normal development, the child with a deviant language impairment uses language that is inappropriate regardless of his or her age (Meynuk, 1971). The language is filled with distortions, not simplifications. For example, a language-deviant six-year-old asked to repeat "the ugly little duck swims in the pond" might respond "little swims pond." A delayed child, given the same stimulus, might respond "duck swim in pond." Language deviancies are attributed to difficulties in organizing information sent and received with appropriate linguistic rules. As a result, spontaneous language production is distorted.

Language Therapy

For planning therapy, most language therapists refer to established norms on the sequential stages of normal language development. Disagreement among therapists occurs over the methods for developing these language skills. Although each perspective discussed below has ardent supporters, many language therapists use an eclectic approach (Van Riper, 1978).

The goal of the *linguistic approach* to language therapy is to help the language-disordered child discover the linguistic structure of English for better self-reception and expression (Lee, 1974). Once the child's stage of language development is identified, the therapist assumes a modeling role by providing the child with corresponding verbal input. For other children, the therapist's modeling role may not be enough of a stimulus. In these cases the therapist assists in the language discovery process by having the child use the desired constructions in his or her own speech.

Advocates of the *behavior modification approach* to language therapy view language as a learned, rather than discovered, behavior. Therapy sessions are conducted according to the principles of operant conditioning. Simplistically, the child's receipt of a reward is contingent upon his or her use of predetermined appropriate language behaviors.

COMMUNICATION DISORDERS AND RELATED DISABILITIES

Although isolated articulation disorders account for the largest number of communication-disordered children, many have speech and language problems related to other handicapping conditions. Following is a review of speech and

For the mentally retarded child, the teacher must provide structured language development activities.

language disorders associated with mental retardation, cerebral palsy, and cleft palate.

Mental Retardation

Since language and cognitive development are closely related, delayed speech and language is characteristic of mental retardation. Therefore, it is understandable that the greater the degree of retardation, the more likely would communication disorders be prevalent.

Language development may be hindered due to impaired perceptive and associative language skills, such as auditory reception, memory, comprehension, and reasoning abilities. As a result, those afflicted find it more difficult to draw conclusions or identify relationships from what is heard. Echolalic behaviors (that is, repeating what is heard) are not uncommon.

Not only is speech acquisition delayed, but there are a greater number of articulation disorders found among the mentally retarded than in the nonimpaired population. Such problems of the mentally retarded are highlighted because of increased concomitant impairments such as cleft palate and faulty dentition (arrangement of teeth). Specific speech problems are more frequently found in certain mental retardation syndromes, rather than in the general mental retardation population. For example, the incidence of stuttering is significantly higher among children with **Down's syndrome**. Also, due to an increase in musculoskeletal problems, the mentally retarded population has a higher degree of associated voice disorders. Faulty muscular development or abnormal speech mechanisms may result in a deviant pitch.

Cerebral Palsy

Cerebral Palsy is a neuromuscular disorder causing varying degrees of impairment. A diagnosis of mild cerebral palsy might indicate no speech delay. On the other hand, in severe cases there may be a complete lack of speech development. Following are the types of cerebral palsy and related speech problems:

■ **Athetosis** Involves twisting, involuntary muscular movements; affects the respiration, articulation, and voice production muscles. As a result, speech is arrhythmic and jerky.
■ **Ataxia** Involves loss of motor control, balance, and spatial orientation. Typically, speech is slurred and can be unintelligible.
■ **Spasticity** Occurs when muscles tension increases, affecting rhythmic movements. As a result, laryngeal muscles become hypertonic. Poor articulation and slow, labored speech are symptomatic of the spastic.

Due to the high incidence of respiratory deviancies and poor muscle development, voice disorders are common among the cerebral palsy population.

Cleft Palate and Lip

Cleft palate is a structural anomaly identified as a soft palate fissure which sometimes extends through the upper lip (cleft lip). This lack of separation between the oral and nasal cavities occurs during the first trimester of pregnancy. The infant born with a cleft palate is frequently subjected to secondary problems. Because the nearby ear structure may be damaged and middle ear infections are more likely, children with cleft palate abnormalities have a higher incidence of hearing loss.

Since the nose and mouth passageways are not separated, air goes from the oral cavity through the fissure into the nasal cavity. In addition, frequently accompanying lip, teeth, alveolar ridge, and soft palate anomalies cause speech and voice defects. As a result, cleft palate speech is characterized by both consonants and vowel sound distortions and by hypernasality.

Treatment of cleft palate defects involves a highly specialized team. A plastic and reconstructive surgeon and an oral orthopedist are needed in order to separate the oral cavity from the nasal cavity and to improve the cosmetic appearance. Not all surgical attempts are successful. An alternative to surgery may be a prosthetic speech device.

Emotional Disturbances

We use communication skills to interact with our environment, to socialize, and to learn about ourselves and our world. Thus, children suffering from various emotional disturbances are frequently diagnosed as having communication disorders. For example, children with autistic behaviors are initially thought to be either mentally retarded and/or hearing impaired. Some autistic children acquire limited speech while others are totally mute. The problem is not one of simply learning how to speak; rather, it is a more deeply rooted disorder requiring the expertise of a multidisciplinary team.

Historically, the speech- and language-impaired child has been especially fortunate among exceptional students in that speech difficulties (usually articulation problems) were not grounds for removal from the regular classroom. Unless the speech problem accompanied another handicap that warranted a special education program, these pupils remained in the regular class and were scheduled for speech therapy once or several times weekly.

The team approach has been common in detecting speech and language difficulties. Usually the teacher notes that a class member seems to be having speech problems and refers that student to a speech therapist. The therapist, in turn, refers the student to an audiologist to determine first if the communication problems are related to a hearing impairment.

An extensive examination by a speech and language therapist may include:

- An oral peripheral examination to make sure that the speech organs are in working order
- An evaluation of the child's motor abilities
- An estimate of general development or maturation
- An evaluation of intelligence and educational performance

In addition, if the difficulty appears to involve articulation, the therapist may administer a standardized articulation test, simply talk with the student, or ask him or her to read aloud. Then, on the basis of test findings and observations, the therapist makes a diagnosis and schedules the child for therapy, if necessary. If the problem appears to have an organic component, such as enlarged tonsils or an ear infection, the child will be referred to the family physician or to an ear, nose, and throat specialist. Any indication of an emotional problem may prompt a referral to a psychologist, psychiatrist, or social worker. Finally, of course, the teacher and speech/language therapist must confer on a therapy schedule.

Pushaw (1976) lists child behaviors that may be indicative of a speech or language disorder. Parents and professionals who identify any of these possible warning signals should contact a speech/language therapist to determine if a problem exists.

- Has no language by age two
- Language is very difficult to understand by age three
- Omits many beginning consonant sounds after age three
- Does not use two- or three-word utterances by age three
- Speech sounds are delayed by more than one year according to developmental norms
- Uses too many vowel sounds in speech
- Omits word endings after age five
- Faulty syntax still evident at age five
- Disturbed by own speech errors
- Speech errors (other than "wh") after age seven
- Voice pitch, intensity, or quality are poor or inappropriate
- Speech consistently sounds too nasal
- Speech lacks natural fluency after age five

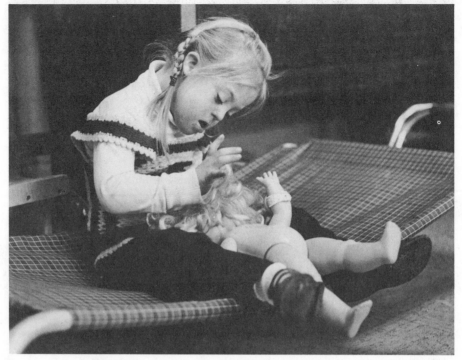

Parents and professionals can collect important speech and language information by observing a child's spontaneous play activities.

EDUCATIONAL PROGRAMMING

Because the speech- and language-impaired child generally remains in the regular classroom and attends therapy sessions on a periodic basis, success in school as well as in therapy depends on cooperation between teacher and therapist. For example, the student's schedule may call for 30 minutes every day in speech therapy. This scheduling necessitates flexibility on the parts of both therapist and teacher. To ensure that the student does not miss spelling class every day, for example, the "speech time" may alternate by day. The child may go to therapy while the rest of the class has free time or study time. Teacher and therapist must keep the student's best interests in mind when they coordinate their schedules.

The therapist should coordinate efforts with the student's parents also. Their help, cooperation, and support are necessary for several reasons. First, the child needs a supportive family. With such support, the likelihood of success is increased. Second, parental help is essential if there is a medical concern. If the student has an ear infection, for example, the parents are responsible for obtaining medical services. Third, parental involvement in therapy may bring about rapid changes. Time spent in therapy is only a fraction of the time the child spends at home. Finally, when the therapist succeeds in bringing about a change in the child's speech, that improvement must be extended to situations outside therapy. This phase of speech therapy, called *carry-over*, will be hastened if parents monitor their child's speech at home.

Because communication disorders and their causes are complex, professionals and parents should consult with the child's speech/language therapist before employing any specific intervention strategies. However, there are several general suggestions for improving speech and language in the classroom and in the home (Pushaw, 1976).

- Do not correct or criticize a child's speech. By drawing attention to errors, the child may react adversely to using speech.
- Model speech and language skills appropriate for the child's level of functioning. Use language constantly to explain daily events occurring in the environment.
- When a child has difficulty with a sound that he or she should be able to produce, try employing awareness techniques, such as exaggerating the sound (example: rrrrain) or accenting a sound (example: *r*ain).
- Recognize and accept that *different* does not necessarily mean *deviant*; for example, children displaying dialectal differences are not abnormal.

SPECIAL CONSIDERATIONS AND ISSUES

The future of the professional and clinical services in the area of communication problems depends on the progress of speech pathology and audiology. These fields may be stimulated in two ways: through research and by practitioners meeting the challenge of unsettled issues.

Issues and Trends

- *Greater Cooperation between the Speech/Language Therapist and the Classroom Teacher.* In the past, therapeutic activities were limited to the clinic and therapy sessions, with the teacher uninvolved. Opportunities for therapist/ teacher teamwork have been outlined throughout this chapter.
- *The Use of Aides in Speech and Language Therapy.* Especially in the school setting, the speech clinician is often faced with a caseload that is too large to handle effectively. In the past, the therapist found it necessary to tolerate this situation, giving as much help to as many students as was physically possible. A more effective means of dealing with this problem is the use of aides, trained to carry out therapy plans and perform duties for which the specialized training of the clinician is not necessary.

- *Early Childhood Intervention.* The success of early intervention can largely be attributed to prevention of further speech and language impairments. The speech pathologist has traditionally served to correct established communication disorders; today the trend is toward a more preventative function. For example, early childhood programs may have parent education components that focus on the prevention of speech and language difficulties. By giving parents the means to improve their youngsters' speech, therapists and educators may reduce the number of school-age children with communication difficulties. A movement is already afoot to institute speech and language appreciation programs in kindergartens and nursery schools.

■ *Improvement of the Speech of Nonimpaired Speakers*. As noted earlier, efforts to improve the speech and language of *all* children are serving to alter the traditional "fix-it" image of the speech therapist. In the regular classroom, the therapist may function as an improver of speech, not just a corrector of speech.

■ *Reduction of Caseload*. This issue is an important one in speech pathology because if the speech therapist must spend the entire working day in the clinic, he or she will not be available for teachers, parents, and nonimpaired speakers.

■ *An Understanding of the Speech of the Minority Child*. Traditionally, the black child has been at a great disadvantage in the classroom in terms of communication abilities. With the recognition that black English is a language in its own right and not a substandard form of English, the speech therapist is becoming more positively oriented toward the black speaker. Therapists are discovering that education, not remediation, is a more realistic (and effective) means of equipping the black child with what are believed to be more widely acceptable speech and language skills.

Research

The effectiveness of therapy in the remediation of disorders of speech and language depends upon the continuous evaluation of existing treatment techniques and materials, their subsequent improvement, and the invention of new methods. In addition, scientific inquiry into other facets of the communication process contributes to the body of knowledge that is speech pathology. Currently, researchers are investigating such areas as the effectiveness of behavior modification in speech therapy, auditory feedback in stuttering, and the communicative abilities of subhuman primates. By expanding our understanding of the communication process, researchers steadily improve upon current methods of treating communication disorders and language skills and may one day even approach complete prevention.

SUMMARY POINTS

■ The speech and language therapist's role is to identify communication disorders in children and to plan appropriate intervention strategies.

■ The communication process involves high-level cognitive functioning. A speech and/or language deficit interferes with one's understanding of the environment and self.

■ Although not conclusive, speech and language research has identified a normal sequence of developmental stages. Intervention strategies, regardless of the techniques used, are based on these theories of sequential developmental stages.

■ Voice disorders are identified by the location of the deficit and are related to impaired voice quality, pitch, and intensity.

■ Articulation disorders are the most common type of speech problems found in children. Articulation errors are classified as omissions, substitutions, distortions, or additions.

- The most common and controversial type of speech flow disorder is stuttering. Although various theories are available regarding etiology, information is neither conclusive nor consistent.
- Categorization of language disorders is related to the onset of the disorder (dysphasia) and the quality of language production (delayed vs. deviant).
- Language disorders affect one's ability to understand events in the environment and/or one's ability to use appropriate verbal skills for transmitting ideas.
- Language-impaired children are deficient in their abilities to use phonological, morphological, syntactic, and/or semantic linguistic structures.
- Two predominant approaches for treating language disorders are the linguistic and behavior modification approaches. They differ not only in methodology but also in theoretical perspective. The linguistic approach contends that language is acquired through a discovering process, whereas the behavior modification approach contends that language is learned.
- Communication disorders are frequently found in children who have other severe impairments (sensory, cognitive, neuromuscular, and physical).
- Classroom teachers can knowledgeably assist in screening speech- and language-disordered children when they are familiar with normal speech and language development.
- The success of therapy is enhanced when the therapist, teacher, and parents have a positive interactive relationship.
- Because of the complexity of the human communication process, research in language acquisition, development, and therapy is not only being conducted in the field of communication disorders but in allied disciplines as well.

REVIEW QUESTIONS

1. Define speech and language disorders. What is their relationship to each other?
2. What guidelines has your state or local school system established for referring a child in a regular classroom for a speech and/or language evaluation?
3. Differentiate among voice, articulation, and speech flow disorders.
4. Communication disorders can be related to other handicapping conditions and impairments. Identify these conditions and explain why the relationship with communication disorders exists.
5. Explain the difference between language-delayed and language-deviant disorders.

COMMUNICATION BOARDS — AN ALTERNATIVE TO SILENCE AND ISOLATION

There are children, such as Ronnie in the case study, who have multiple handicaps that inhibit nonverbal and verbal interaction with their environments. For many of these children, therapy to remediate speech problems is unrealistic; they need an alternative method for communicating.

Communication boards provide physically and/or verbally limited children with an opportunity to develop language and two-way communication skills (McDonald and Schultz, 1976). Selecting the most appropriate board depends upon the child's degree of impairment, present ability level, and motivation. In Figure 10-2, a beginner's communication board is contrasted with a more advanced communication board system. Regardless of the type of board, pictorial or word content should be changed as the child's vocabulary and experiences expand (McDonald, 1976).

Harris-Vanderheiden (1976) points out that electronic communication boards, such as the *Auto-Com*, develop and reinforce academic and language skills. For children excluded from interacting with their non-impaired peers due to verbal disabilities, such communication boards provide the opportunity to be contributing classroom members. Many electronic boards can be adapted to allow the child's board responses to be flashed on a TV in the classroom, thus allowing the student to communicate with anyone (or everyone) anywhere in the classroom.

With increased technology, future alternative communication systems will permit even more communication opportunities for severely communication-disordered persons. One such innovation developed by a team from Psycho-Linguistic Research Associates and Stanford University Medical School is the "talking wheelchair." The talking wheelchair permits physically disabled persons who have limited speech to "talk" by means of a computerized word processor and speech synthesizer. The disabled person "uses a keyboard, joystick or even a single switch to construct sentences on a video screen attached to the wheelchair and then directs the microprocessor to 'speak' from a box containing the synthesizer" ("A Talking Wheelchair," *Science News*, 117, 1980, p. 221). This and other technological advancements will allow handicapped persons, previously isolated and limited by their communication deficits, to function in the mainstream of society.

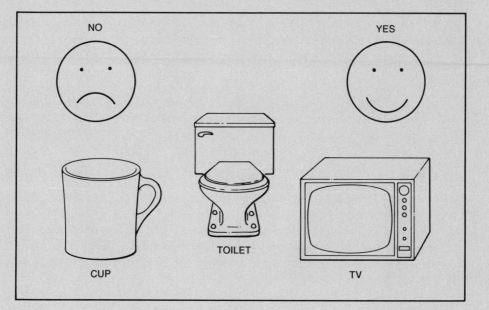

(a)

0 1 2 3 4 5 6 7 8 9 10							
YES. HI. HOW ARE YOU? I DON'T KNOW. PLEASE. THANK-YOU. GOOD-BYE. NO.							
WHO	VERB			WHAT	WHERE	WHEN	
I	HAVE	A	BIG	BALL	HOME	NIGHT	RED
MOMMY	PLAY	NOT	MY	COOKIE	PLAYROOM	YESTERDAY	YELLOW
DADDY	GO	IN	LITTLE	PRESENT	BATHROOM	TOMORROW	ORANGE
SANDY	AM	FOR		FUN	UP	WEEKEND	GREEN
LINDA	READ	THE	SICK	CAR	SCHOOL	SUMMER	BLUE
BOY	SEE	WITH	GOOD	PUZZLE	OUTSIDE	EASTER	PINK
GIRL	MAY	AT		BED	ROOM	CHRIST-	PURPLE
YOU	LOVE	TO	BAD	WORDS	P.T.	MAS	BROWN
TEACHER	LISTEN	AND	HAPPY	STORY	STORE	THANKS-	BLACK
THERAPIST	IS		SAD	LETTER	INSIDE	GIVING	WHITE
HOUSE-MOTHER	WANT			GAME	DOWN	TODAY	
	ARE			CAKE	SPEECH		
	WILL			CANDY	DINING ROOM		
	EAT			MAT			
	LIKE			BOOK			
	GET			DRINK			

(b)

FIGURE 10-2 Communication boards. ([a] from Calhoun, M. L., and Hawisher, M. *Teaching and Learning Strategies for Physically Handicapped Students*. Baltimore: University Park Press, 1979, p. 183. [b] from McDonald, E. and Schulta, A. "Communication Boards for Cerebral Palsied Children," *Journal of Speech and Hearing Disorders*, vol. 38, 1973, p. 79.

DISCUSSION POINTS

1. In order for communication-impaired children to function in the regular class, what changes, if any, need to be made regarding classroom organization?

2. Describe two activities that a regular classroom teacher could do with nonimpaired children to facilitate their awareness and acceptance of impaired children who use alternative communication devices.

SUGGESTED READINGS

Bloom, L., and Lahey, M. *Language Development and Language Disorders*. New York: Wiley, 1978.

Hixon, T. J., Shriberg, L. D., and Saxman, J. H., eds. *Introduction to Communication Disorders*. Englewood Cliffs, NJ: Prentice-Hall, 1980.

Van Riper, C. *Speech Correction: Principles and Methods*, 6th ed. Englewood Cliffs, NJ: Prentice-Hall, 1978.

Wood, B. *Children and Communication*. Englewood Cliffs, NJ: Prentice-Hall, 1976.

11

THE HEARING IMPAIRED

CONTENTS

The process of learning about ourselves and our environment depends on sensory input. Reception of auditory messages occurs constantly throughout the day, whether through listening to a speaker on the telephone, television, or radio, reacting to verbal warnings regarding safety (e.g., "watch out"), or responding to nonverbal sounds such as the car muffler dragging along the road. Our ears thus are a guide for comprehension and learning. The auditory channel also serves to monitor one's own speech, thus assisting in developing appropriate speech skills. Many hearing-impaired children are, in effect, multiply handicapped because of concomitant speech and language deficits. Too frequently, the hearing impaired are excluded from society because of their communication disorders, rather than their hearing deficits.

BRENT, JANE, AND JULIE*

For a student unable to hear a single word spoken by a professor, acceptance and understanding by friends can make the obstacle of deafness surmountable. Brent, Jane, and Julie are three deaf students who attend the same university. Here they discuss their career goals and adjustment to campus life.

Stressing the importance of friendship, Brent, who was born deaf, said, "I love being with my friends. I really do. Sometimes I go into my friends' rooms just to talk to them." Referring to his roommate, he said, "He helps me so much. He is not like some people who, when they find out I am deaf, try to get away from me. He is there all the time." A phone's ring is one sound Brent can perceive. He answers the phone by saying, "Just one minute please," and goes to find one of his friends who can come talk for him. The person acting as the go-between must relay the messages back and forth. If Brent wishes to make a call, his friends aid him by dialing and repeating what he says.

Julie has access to a teletypewriter (TTY) which she uses to type messages to people who have these typewriters connected to their phones. Jane will be getting a TTY next year, and will have one communicator located at the student union so that teachers will be able to contact her more easily. "Right now I never can get a hold of any profs. It is so hard because they have to call

and leave a message for me after I have called them. It just goes around in a circle," she said.

Classroom interaction is also enhanced by understanding friends. "I am not sure of my major," Brent said. "Some people push me into art. I really like physical education and that is my minor. Sometimes it is not necessary for me to go to class, but I think I should. I usually end up reading books during the class anyway," he said. "I often ask my friends what the teacher is talking about, and they interpret him for me."

Jane, majoring in physical education, has a notetaker go with her to classes to make a carbon copy of the notes. "I don't like to skip classes either," she said. "I would be a bad student if I skipped class."

Julie said she prepares for lectures before class by prereading and anticipating lecture material. She also asks teachers for reference materials that may help her. Majoring in nursing, Julie said that people at first discouraged her from entering the program. "After being rejected by several diploma schools offering hospital training programs, I decided to switch to a state university, only to receive harrassment and no pity. I didn't want pity and I found my determination to go to school a crisis point for me, but quite a learning experience. Overcoming these obstacles demanded much effort, assertiveness, and patience on my part. Everyone kept telling me to change my mind, but I wanted to be a nurse," she said. "I know my

*Source: Adapted from articles by Kim Van Wert and Kevin Settlage, *The BG News*, June 3, 4, and 5, 1980.

capabilities and limitations and those with less experience than I shouldn't tell me what to do with them. We all have limitations —many, once you think. People told me I should be a librarian. They insisted that my parents raised me wrong. My parents let me alone in my own motivations and self-direction.

Very much enjoying working with people, Julie said, "I love to encourage, support, and give hope. I am taking the tools I have and am refining them. I have to ask to clarify and have things repeated, but those

are tools that I have to have and no one can take them away from me. Harrassment is what upsets me the most."

Julie has made the dean's list and, after a two-year prenursing program, has a 3.4 accumulative grade point average. Adaptng to her silent class atmosphere, she said, "Should I miss anything, I guess it is the professors' jokes. I know they emit some good ones—too bad they aren't always funny the second time around. They are even worse the third time."

Brent said when he first goes to a class, he

tells the professors that he is deaf. "I like to see who takes the most notes. Girls are better notetakers than guys."

Often going to professors for help, Jane said, "They are usually willing to give me some of their spare time to work over the class discussions. To me this is a tremendous asset and one that I will cherish for a long time to come. It is often hard to read the lips of profs. Two years ago a professor of mine tried to trim his moustache so that I could read his lips better, but it didn't help and he came in the next day with it shaved off."

Classes comprise only a fraction of deaf students' days. Their activities also play an important part in their college educations.

Jane has been on the track team for three years and throws the discus and javelin. "I am going to Missouri this summer to try out for the World Olympic Games for the deaf. If I make it, I will go to Germany. I can't wait," she said. She also likes to write poetry and is trying to have a paper she wrote on deafness published in a magazine.

Agreeing that there is a lot to do on campus, Brent said, "I never had so many friends that I can go to the recreation center with or just play tennis with. I like to go uptown and make friends. There is so much to do and see. I am very happy with what I have to work with and what I am doing with my life. Making friends is the best thing that can happen to a person."

Points for Consideration

- The degree of hearing loss is only one of several variables related to successful mainstreaming into the educational, as well as community, environment. Julie's family support, for example, assisted her in pursuing her career goals.
- Although the three students have different goals and interests, all of them stressed the need for and importance of friendship and a sense of belonging.
- Too often, outsiders advise or direct hearing-impaired students toward careers on the basis of their impairment, rather than looking at individual strengths and weaknesses.

Common Misconceptions

Although limited communication skills may contribute to exclusion, society's misconceptions about the hearing impaired have also resulted in their noninvolvement with the mainstream. Some of society's erroneous generalizations about the hearing impaired are:

- *All Hearing-Impaired Persons Are Totally Deaf.* Very few hearing-impaired persons have a complete hearing loss. Most hearing impaired have some functional hearing and can be trained to use it more effectively.
- *The Hearing-Impaired Are Unable to Communicate Verbally.* Many people believe that the deaf person can learn to communicate only by sign language. While it is true that speech development is directly impeded as a result of a hearing impairment, other factors (such as the degree of hearing loss, early intervention, and age of onset) are related to successful speech development.
- *Hearing-Impaired Persons Have Limited Intellectual Capabilities.* A hearing impairment by itself does not mean that one's intellectual performance will be low. However, since language development, which can be delayed in the hearing-impaired population, is closely related to concept development, the latter may also be delayed without proper educational procedures.
- *A Corrective Device, Such as a Hearing Aid, Will Allow One to Hear Within the Normal Range.* Although hearing aids, in most cases, are used to amplify sounds, rarely, if ever, will the user of a hearing aid regain total hearing. Also, the nature of the hearing impairment, location of the impairment, type of hearing aid, the child's listening skills, and the skills of those persons working with the child are all variables related to successful learning.

Hearing impairment is a generic term used to identify anyone with a hearing loss, regardless of the degree of impairment. Within this umbrella terminology, a distinction is made between the deaf and the hard of hearing. The criteria for such differentiation depend on one's professional orientation, which may be physiological or educational.

Physiological Perspective

The physiological perspective is represented by the field of **audiology**, which is the study of hearing, both deviant and normal. Audiology focuses on measuring hearing loss in terms of one's sensitivity to hear the loudness of sounds at different frequencies. This range of sensitivity is measured by decibels, abbreviated dB. A **decibel** is a measurable unit of sound intensity. The louder the sound, the greater the intensity. For example, the sound produced by a firecracker is greater in intensity and is expressed in a greater number of decibels than is the sound of a whisper. Classification of degree of hearing impairment and related decibel loss is presented in Table 11-1 using the American National Standards Institute's (ANSI, 1969) standards for hearing threshold levels. An increase in one's hearing threshold level is related to an increase in hearing loss.

We know that sound travels at various frequencies. The more vibrations there are per second, the higher the frequency or pitch of a sound. In measurable terms,

TABLE 11-1 Degree and Classification of Impairment and Related Communication Behaviors

Hearing Threshold Levels for 500, 1000, and 2000 Hz (in better ear)	Classification of Hearing Loss	Related Communication Behaviors
Less than 25 dB	Not significant	■ Little difficulty with faint speech
26–40 dB	Slight	■ Difficulty hearing distant sounds
41–55 dB	Mild	■ Understand conversational speech at close distance
		■ May rely on visual contact for understanding speech
		■ Possible vocabulary and speech problems
56–70 dB	Marked	■ Difficulty understanding loud conversations
		■ Exhibits impaired speech
		■ Faulty receptive and expressive language
71–90 dB	Severe	■ Can hear close (one foot) loud sounds
		■ Poor speech and language development
Greater than 90 dB	Extreme	■ Unable to understand amplified speech
		■ Relies on vibrations rather than tonal patterns to hear loud sounds

EXCEPTIONALITIES

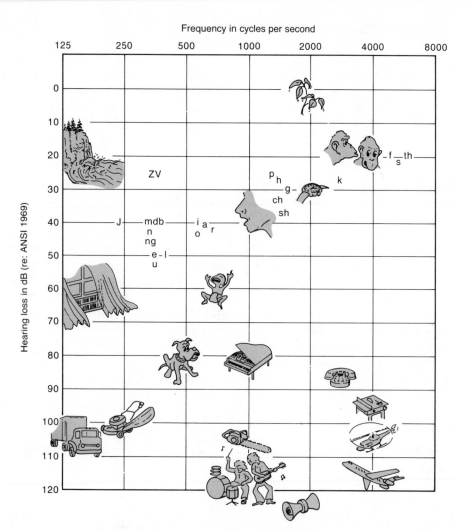

FIGURE 11-1 Frequency spectrum of familiar sounds. (From Northern, J. L., and Downs, M. P. *Hearing in Children*. Baltimore: Williams and Wilkins, 1978, p. 12.)

hertz (Hz) refers to the number of sound-wave vibrations that occur per second. A high-pitched sound will register a higher hertz than a lower pitched sound. Although we have the ability to hear sounds ranging from approximately 125 Hz (low sounds) to 8000 Hz, most speech sounds fall within the 500 Hz to 2000 Hz continuum, as indicated in Figure 11-1.

The **hard-of-hearing** population has hearing that is defective but still functional. **Deaf** persons, on the other hand, have nonfunctional hearing. A further distinction among persons with a severe or profound hearing loss is based on when the hearing loss occurred. The **congenitally deaf** are those people who were born deaf. However, if one were born with normal hearing and later became deaf due to an accident, trauma, or illness, the term **adventitiously deaf** is applied.

The educational perspective focuses on the relationship of the hearing loss to speech and language development. While the age of onset of impairment is critical to educators, they prefer to replace the congenitally or adventitiously deaf nomenclature with the terms prelingual or postlingual deafness. **Prelingual deafness** is that which was present at birth or occurred prior to speech and language development. **Postlingual deafness** refers to hearing that was lost after speech and language development.

In addition to focusing on developing the hearing-impaired child's residual hearing, educators stress the importance of early identification and intervention, the proper use of amplification devices, and appropriate educational strategies. From an educational perspective, deaf refers to those children "whose auditory channel is sufficiently damaged to preclude the *auditory* development and comprehension of speech and language, with or without sound amplification" (Ross, 1977, p. 7). The hard-of-hearing child hears sound, no matter how limited, and uses the auditory channel for developing communication skills.

PREVALENCE

Results of surveys on the prevalence of hearing impairments in children and adults appear contradictory. Estimates ranging from less than one percent to over ten percent are reported in the literature (Hull, Mielke, Willeford, and Timmons, 1976; Jordan and Eagles, 1961; National Health Survey, 1975). A comparative analysis of these studies indicates several basic differences in methodology. Whereas one study might sample the total population, others center only on school-age children who tend to have more hearing problems. Also affecting analysis is differentiation between a unilateral and a bilateral loss. Persons with a unilateral loss (only one ear affected) sometimes are not considered impaired since their ability to function normally is not disturbed. Probably the most significant issue in determining the prevalence of hearing-impaired persons concerns the lack of consistent criteria for defining hearing impairment.

STRUCTURE OF THE EAR

What is sound? Davis and Silverman (1970) point out that the answer depends upon the perspective of the answerer. The physicist views sound objectively—it has measurable qualities. To physicists, sound consists of organized molecular movement and is defined as pressure waves transmitted through the air. The psychologist, on the other hand, defines sound in terms of sensation. From the psychological perspective, sound is a subjective experience. In essence, each person's mind attaches its own attributes or interpretations to the sound experience. The study of **psychophysics**, which looks at the "relation between physical sound and the properties of human beings, particularly of their ears and their brains" (Davis and Silverman, 1970, p. 10), encompasses both the physicist's and psychologist's definitions of sound.

In order to better grasp the impact of various hearing impairments, one must

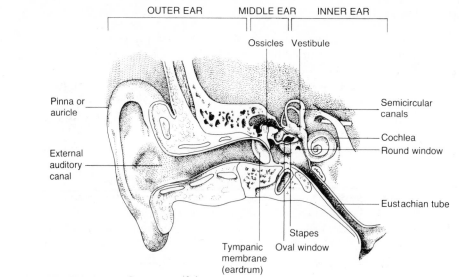

FIGURE 11-2   Structure of the ear.

understand the route of sound waves from their initial entrance into the outer ear until they are converted to impulses in the auditory nerve. Figure 11-2 illustrates the various parts of the ear.

The Outer Ear

The purpose of the outer ear is to collect sound waves and funnel them to the middle ear. The **outer ear** begins with the auricle, which is the ear that we see when we look at someone, and extends to the tympanic membrane, or eardrum. In between, the outer canal protects the more delicate inner parts of the ear by secreting cerumen (ear wax) which helps keep the canal and eardrum lubricated. An additional protector is hair that grows in the canal; hair can deter or block out dust.

The Middle Ear

The **middle ear** includes the tympanic membrane, or eardrum, the air-filled canal, and ends at the oval window. Within the air-filled canal are the ossicles (tiny bone parts), which transmit vibrations from the outer ear to the inner ear. These vibrations move through the successive three parts of the ossicles: malleus (hammer), incus (anvil), and finally to the stapes (stirrup), which is anchored to the oval window. In addition to increasing one's sensitivity for hearing airborne sounds, the middle ear acts as a compressor: it receives the light air vibrations from the outer ear and compresses the air through the ossicles. This compression of the energy or vibrations facilities their journey into the dense fluid of the inner ear.

The Inner Ear

The fluid-filled **inner ear**, frequently called a labyrinth because of its complexity and mazelike shape, is divided into two sections: the vestibule and the cochlea.

Within the vestibule are the utricle and saccule organs that are sensitive to gravity and movement. These organs are connected to three semicircular canals which house sacs filled with additional fluid and sensory cells. Any change in movement or position of the body is fed to the brain via the vestibular nerve.

The critical component for hearing is the coil-shaped cochlea which is activated by mechanical movement such as those of the ossicular chain. An oversimplified description of the function of the multifaceted cochlea is that it converts the mechanical waves into electrical impulses in the cochlear nerve, which in turn transmits the information to the brain.

HEARING IMPAIRMENTS

Proper medical attention and educational programming for any person with a hearing impairment is dependent upon a thorough examination. The examination must answer the following questions: What type of hearing loss is present? Where is the impairment located? What caused the hearing loss?

Types of Hearing Loss

Identifying the type of impairment is related to the location of the impairment. The three types of hearing loss are classified as conductive, sensorineural, or mixed.

A **conductive hearing loss** occurs when there is an interference or blockage of sound waves traveling through the auditory canal and middle ear pathways. In such incidents, the inner ear remains functional. A total air blockage results in a marked hearing loss that can be improved with a hearing aid. Fortunately, proper medical treatment or surgery can correct most conductive hearing losses (Northern and Downs, 1978). A **sensorineural hearing loss** occurs when the inner ear or auditory nerve mechanisms fail to perform properly. Damage to the sensory cells or nerve fibers is permanent and cannot be corrected surgically (Travis, 1971; Davis and Silverman, 1970). In addition to a loss in hearing sensitivity, children with a sensorineural hearing loss have difficulties in discriminating speech sounds. A **mixed hearing loss** occurs when both conductive and a sensorineural losses are present. Since hearing impairment is related to the success of treatment for only the air conduction loss, total functioning is not probable (Jordan and Eagles, 1961).

Causes of Hearing Impairments

The course of medical treatment also depends on the cause of the impairment. Table 11-2 identifies the more common hearing disorders, related causes, and the location of the hearing loss. In addition to the causes listed in the table, hearing losses can also be attributed to other factors: trauma, birth injury, anoxia, metabolic and endocrine disorders, hereditary deafness, viral infections such as mumps or measles, bacterial infections such as encephalitis or meningitis, Rh factor, drugs, and poisons. Also, an increasing cause of hearing loss is attributed to prolonged exposure to loud noises, such as excessively loud music. Truck drivers, for example, tend to have a greater incidence of hearing loss than

TABLE 11-2   Some Common Causes of Hearing Loss

Disorder	Location	Cause
Artresia	Outer ear	■ Abnormal formation of the external auditory canal ■ Usually associated with middle ear anomalies
Impacted wax	Outer ear	■ Buildup of wax that hardens or impacts the external canal ■ Prevents sound waves from reaching the eardrum
External otitis	Outer ear	■ Inflammation of the canal due to infection; may appear as a pimple ■ Hearing loss is not evident unless swelling within the canal is significant
Otitis media	Middle ear	■ Infection of the Eustachian tube, usually due to colds ■ Most common cause of conductive hearing loss
Cholesteatoma	Middle ear	■ Cyst growing within the drumhead ■ Caused by inflammation
Allergies	Middle ear	■ Reactions to food, pollen, etc., may result in blockage of the Eustachian tube or in otitis media
Otoselerosis	Middle and inner ear	■ Hereditary bone disease (hardening of the ear bones) that affects the performance of the stapes ■ Results in poor transmission of vibrations to inner ear fluid
Presbycusis	Inner ear	■ Pathological changes found in the sensory apparatus due to the aging process. Other factors such as frequent cases of otitis media earlier in life are related to presbycusis
Tinnitus	Inner ear	■ Characterized by ringing noises ■ May be symptomatic of inner ear problems
Dysacusis	Inner ear	■ Due to abnormal formation of the sense organ or to abnormal function of the brain ■ Results in poor comprehension of speech

other, less noisy occupations. It should also be pointed out that there are approx-imately 70 syndromes related to hereditary deafness (Konigsmark, 1969). How-ever, the likelihood of deaf parents passing deafness on to the next generation is small since the parents probably do not have the same genetic defect. Also, Proctor and Proctor (1967) indicate that recessive, rather than dominant, traits account for most inherited deafness.

IDENTIFICATION OF THE HEARING IMPAIRED

Annual screening programs typically organized in schools are designed to screen out those children whose hearing frequencies deviate from the normal hearing level. After a hearing-impaired child has been identified, the audiologist conducts an in-depth evaluation to determine where the problem is occurring and what is specifically wrong with the auditory system.

Assessment includes measuring one's hearing threshold or sensitivity and also the frequency of sounds that one can hear. The standard units of measurement used to analyze sensitivity and frequency are decibels (dB) and hertz (Hz), respectively. Measures used by the audiologist are classified as pure tone audiometry or speech audiometry.

Pure Tone Audiometry

The **pure tone audiometer** assesses one's ability to hear various frequencies at specified decibels. This is accomplished by converting acoustical energy into pure tones of electrical energy. In screening programs the five frequencies tested at specified decibel levels are 500 Hz, 1000 Hz, 2000 Hz, 4000 Hz, and 6000 Hz. The pure tone audiometer is also used for diagnostic purposes to categorize the impairment as either a conductive, sensorineural, or mixed hearing loss.

The location of the hearing loss is detected by comparing bone and air conduction hearing threshold levels. To determine an **air conduction loss**, a child responds to tones heard through the use of headphones. Since **bone conduction hearing losses** are associated with inner ear or nerve damage, a vibrator, placed on the child's skull, is used to transmit sounds directly to the cochlea. Test results are plotted on an **audiogram**. Children with a conductive hearing loss would have an increased air conduction threshold level. If the air and bone threshold levels are similar, a sensorineural impairment is evident. A mixed hearing loss occurs when there is a greater hearing loss registered by air conduction.

The Crib-O-Gram is a neonatal screening audiometer that detects moderately severe to profound hearing losses in high-risk infants.

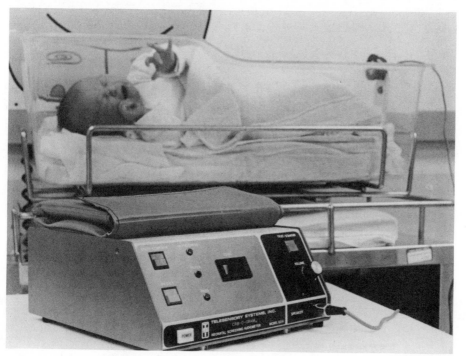

Speech Audiometry

The **speech audiometer** yields diagnostic information on how well a child understands meaningful speech sounds. A supplement to the pure tone audiometer, speech audiometry identifies impairments related to the central nervous system. Whereas the pure tone audiometer transmits nonmeaningful or abstract pure tones, the speech audiometer transmits words or sentences at alternating levels. Specifically, one's ability to hear, understand, and respond to speech can be analyzed.

CHARACTERISTICS OF THE HEARING IMPAIRED

A characteristic shared by many hearing-impaired persons is their insensitivity to speech or other sounds; there are, however, varying degrees of insensitivity. Whereas one child may be inattentive to speech, another may not respond to loud noises. As noted earlier, deviance from normal vocal production is related to the degree of impairment, early intervention, age of onset, and use of appropriate amplification devices.

Language Development

The greatest handicap resulting from a hearing impairment is retarded language development. Since language development occurs in a sequence of receptive and expressive skills, the mastery of each skill is contingent upon acquiring each preceding skill. Consequently, the hearing-impaired prelingual child is hindered since the auditory reception of language is either distorted or nonexistent. This lack of auditory feedback is critical because the child is not being reinforced adequately by self-vocal stimulation or by verbal stimulation from others.

Intelligence

The effect of hearing loss on intellectual development is difficult to determine since the hearing-impaired child's linguistic retardation adversely affects performance on verbally-oriented IQ tests. A hearing-impaired child's performance on an IQ test administered by, say, a psychologist inexperienced with the hearing impaired should be interpreted cautiously. Many psychologists are simply not aware of the relationship between the impaired child's linguistic development and test performance (Davis, 1977). A more accurate estimate of intellectual capacity can be ascertained only when a nonverbal intelligence test is administered. Research results indicate that the distribution of intelligence in deaf children compares to the nonhearing-impaired population's nonverbal IQ scores (McConnell, 1973).

Academic

The deaf child suffers retardation of educational achievement averaging three to four years below grade level. The partially hearing child (whose hearing loss occurred after spoken language was acquired) generally achieves several years below what is expected at his or her grade level (Ling, 1972; Kodman, 1963).

Regarding reading, Gentile and Di Francesca (1969) found that hearing-impaired 16-year-olds had a fifth-grade reading level and a knowledge of vocabulary similar to that of a typical child in the third grade. This poor academic showing does not mean that the deaf are less capable; rather, inferior performance may be explained by other factors, such as inappropriate learning environment and a linguistic deficiency (Streng, Krestschmer, and Kretschmer, 1978). Also, since the curricular emphasis is on the language arts, especially the reading component, the hearing-impaired child is at a disadvantage. This discrepancy between mental abilities as measured by nonverbal IQ tests and significantly poor school achievement is a dilemma to parents and educators alike.

Social/Emotional Development

A hearing impairment may also seriously affect emotional and social development due to the lack of receptive and expressive language skills. Ross (1977) points out that many environmental variables, such as language complexity, extraneous noises, and distance of the speaker, inconsistently, and thus adversely, affect the hard-of-hearing child's auditory language comprehension. These sporadic variables "make the hard-of-hearing child the recipient of behavior pressures and expectations which are completely beyond his ability to comprehend or respond to" (p. 10). Their inappropriate responses are erroneously perceived as behavioral problems, rather than as poor environmental management. As a result, self-sufficiency, social maturity, and personality development (which depend on interpersonal communications skills) may be thwarted.

The young hearing-impaired child needs a variety of learning experiences in order to promote language and cognitive development.

Green (1976) emphasizes the impact of society's perceptions toward the hearing impaired. If adults and others respond to the deaf in a condescending manner, then the impaired child will recognize his or her ineptness and dependency, which can lead to frustration and feelings of inadequacy.

COMMUNICATION APPROACHES

No unified pedagogical approach for educating the deaf exists in the United States. The methodology for teaching communication skills in each deaf education program is related to one of the following three philosophies: oral, manual, or total communication.

The **oralists** contend that the deaf child will only become a part of mainstream society if communication skills are imparted via auditory training and speech-reading methods. Within a strict oralist perspective, the use of gestures or other manual methods of communication interferes with learning and social acceptance. In 1970, Silverman and Lane pointed out that 85 percent of deaf children were being taught by oral methods; yet, ironically, few deaf persons can adroitly develop speech-reading skills. Although the education of young deaf children usually begins with the oral approach, some type of manual system is eventually introduced for two reasons. First, although classroom instruction is oral, it is not solely used outside the classroom. Also, the fact remains that oral instruction is not effective for many deaf children (Furth, 1973).

The manual communication system was introduced to the United States by Gallaudet, who concluded after his travels in Europe that this approach was best for teaching deaf children (Streng, Kretschmer, and Kretschmer, 1978). The **manualists** believe that oral teaching methods are not realistic for many deaf children and that alternative manual methods are more effective. To manualists, the goal of education is to teach the deaf child to communicate, rather than speak, effectively. They point out that sign use is not only natural, but it can be used by all people for effective communication.

Recently, an alternative to both the manual and oral approaches has appeared. This new method—**total communication**—is defined as "a philosophy incorporating the appropriate aural, manual, and oral modes of communication in order to ensure effective communication with and among hearing-impaired persons" (*Defining Total Communication*, 1976, p. 3). The rationale here is that not all children learn the same way. So, rather than fitting the hearing-impaired child into a particular communication system, the best system or combination of systems must be chosen for each child. Rather than teaching a specific language system, the goal of total communication is to develop communication as efficiently and as early as possible. As a result, auditory training, speechreading, fingerspelling, and other sign language systems are all used to maximize communication learning (Pahz and Pahz, 1978).

Oral/Aural Methods

Oral methods for teaching communication skills to the deaf emphasize residual hearing and speechreading for speech and receptive language development. From this perspective, learning occurs primarily through the auditory channel, thus the emphasis on proper amplification.

Materials, such as the game "Keep Quiet," provide integrated leisure and learning opportunities within the classroom.

AUDITORY TRAINING **Auditory training** focuses on one's functional or residual hearing in conjunction with amplification. An auditory training program begins with teaching awareness of sound, especially speech. For the severely and profoundly hearing-impaired child, the first goal is for the child to recognize that a relationship between sound and speech exists. Next, the child must be systematically taught to discriminate sounds that are grossly different. The final and most complex phase of auditory training is the teaching of speech sounds discrimination (Beebe, 1976; Sanders, 1971).

SPEECHREADING **Speechreading** (frequently referred to as lipreading) requires that the deaf child utilize visual clues emitted by the speaker in order to better understand what is being heard. A speaker's facial and lip movements become additional reinforcers to speech sounds. Although vowel sounds and some words (for example, step and stop) are not easily discriminated from facial clues, many words are. In addition to visual clues, the speechreader uses the context of what is being said to synthesize, or put closure, on those sounds that are not identifiable visually.

Manual Methods

Manual approaches utilize the visual sense for the reception and transmission of information. Unlike oral methods, the auditory channel is ignored. Although there are several manual methods, all draw on gestures of the arms, hands, and/or fingers to convey meaning.

AMERICAN SIGN LANGUAGE American Sign Language, commonly referred to as ASL or Ameslan, is a spatial language independent of the grammatical structure of English. This manual communication system uses the movement, con-

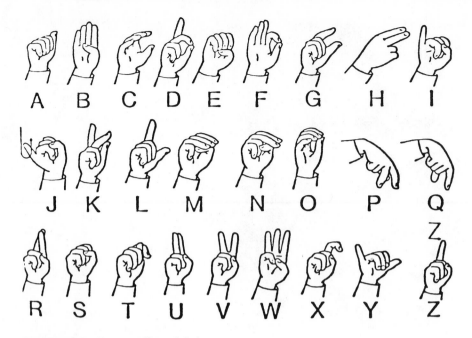

FIGURE 11-3 Fingerspelling alphabet.

figurations, and positions of the hands in relationship to each other and the body in order to convey meaning. The ASL system represents one's general thoughts or ideas rather than spelling out or signing each and every word in the mind. In doing so, articles, most verb tenses, prepositions, cases, and participles are omitted. This lack of grammatical structure has been cited as a drawback in using ASL for children, a criticism based on the fact that ASL does not follow the syntactic pattern of written English.

FINGERSPELLING   Unlike ASL, fingerspelling literally spells out one's thoughts. Figure 11-3 illustrates the one-handed symbol system. The letters of the alphabet, the ordinal numbers, and some punctuation marks each have their own sign. Although fingerspelling is comparatively easier to learn, it requires more concentration than sign language for comprehension.

Combined Methods

Combined methods for teaching the deaf fuse oral and manual approaches. An example of a combined approach is the Rochester Method, which involves the use of oral and fingerspelling techniques and excludes the use of sign language. Combined methods are not synonymous with total communication. The former refers to specified methodology, whereas the latter is a philosophical perspective that advocates the use of all approaches, one of which is the Rochester Method.

EDUCATIONAL PROGRAMMING

Because hearing is so vital to acquiring speech and language skills, educational programming for the hearing-impaired child concentrates on teaching communication skills. Early educational programming is essential while the impaired child is still an infant. This necessitates at-home parental training. Professional personnel teach parents to utilize their child's residual hearing. Parents can learn to conduct an auditory training program, which is a crucial part of early educational programming.

Early identification techniques, appropriate amplification devices, and interest in auditory training have improved nursery and kindergarten programs for the hearing-impaired. Efforts to maximize speech and language development must continue on a unified basis with the educational specialist working cooperatively with the family to ensure success. Depending upon the individual needs of the child, one program option includes both special and regular placement. For example, the child may attend the special class for half the school day and spend the remainder of that day in a regular kindergarten. This opportunity to socialize with hearing children boosts language learning. The curriculum of the special program should emphasize speech and language, intellectual, and social development. The components of each program should accommodate the age, needs, and abilities of the child. Parental involvement, counseling, and training are necessary program components.

When the hearing-impaired child reaches school age, educational placement must be decided. Ideally, the child is placed in a regular classroom. Certainly, all previous educational training has been aimed at such placement, when and if it is possible. Yater (1977, p. 43) describes the following variables as critical factors that the assessment team should weigh when considering regular class placement for the hearing impaired: "Objective child variables include intellectual capability, audiological information, achievement levels, and other test information. Observational variables include behavioral factors, use of residual hearing and amplification, communication skills, and the wishes of the child." In addition, school variables (such as classroom organization and the availability of specialized personnel) are related to successful mainstreaming efforts.

The hearing-impaired child who is not prepared for the regular classroom may attend special classes at a separate residential school, day school, or a regular school. The last integrates hearing-impaired children into regular classes when possible. For this reason, day classes are becoming more popular than day schools for many hearing-impaired children.

Although many parents prefer at-home day programs, the education of hearing-impaired children has traditionally taken place in the residential school setting. In such programs, the hearing-impaired youngsters are housed in dormitories or cottages, attend classes, and spend holidays and summers at home. Recently, however, residential programs have been changing—students are permitted to commute and the admission age has been lowered to accommodate preschoolers.

Generally, curricular objectives are identical for hearing and hearing-impaired children; however, hearing-impaired programs emphasize language development and feature different educational methods than regular programs. The special curriculum also includes hearing aids, auditory training, speech training, speechreading (or lipreading), and special media services and captioned films. The teacher must learn to work with all of these aspects of the hearing-impaired educational program in order to facilitate the student's academic, social, and personal growth.

Role of Parents

The parents of a hearing-impaired child play a vital role in their child's educational career; they must make important decisions about educational placement. Such decisions should be made only after parents have thoroughly investigated each program and observed the teachers working with children similar to their own. Of course, the child's hearing (corrected), ability to speechread, and speech and language development should also be given serious thought in deciding the most appropriate program. Parents should gather information early so that they have sufficient time to make a placement decision. Above all, they must keep their child's needs and abilities foremost in mind.

The parents' attitudes and actions toward their hearing-impaired child are also highly significant factors in the placement process. The National Easter Seal Society published a list of do's and don'ts for parents (Lehman, 1967), which may serve as a guideline for their treatment of and feelings toward their child. Here are some of these suggestions, which are valuable for educators too.

DO
- Do make a game out of playing in front of a mirror so that he can enjoy watching you in imitating facial movements.
- Do read to him and show him pictures.
- Do talk to him and ask others to do so, too.
- Do talk to him in a normal voice and in full sentences.
- Do use encouraging, positive, and specific directions to elicit desirable conduct.
- Do stress success.
- Do explain painstakingly the most vital occurrences of everyday life in the home.
- Do begin immediately to train his eyes to substitute for his ears, or at least to complement his remnant of hearing.
- Do face the light always when you are talking to him. Light on your back throws shadows on your face and makes lipreading difficult.

DON'T
- Don't keep him away from other children because he has no speech and doesn't hear as well as they do. They may be the best teachers.
- Don't talk in single words. He probably understands more than you give him credit for.
- Don't shout at him. Talk in a natural voice close to his ear. Your voice will be much louder to him than you think.
- Don't exaggerate your lip movements. This makes speech harder to understand.
- Don't correct every word he uses; accept and encourage his speech.

Role of Teachers

The hearing-impaired child placed in either a regular or special classroom becomes dependent on the teacher for academic and social success. The teacher can structure classroom activities to maximize educational benefits by following several guidelines (McConnell, 1973; Harrington, 1976).

- The hearing-impaired child is dependent on both the eyes and the ears to "hear" instructions. He or she should be seated not more than five or ten feet from the teacher in order to speechread and utilize residual hearing. Flexible classroom seating arrangements are important.

■ Encourage the child to ask for clarification when necessary. When he or she is unable to understand something, rephrase it. It may have been difficult to speechread initially.

■ Urge the child to read ahead to become familiar with new vocabulary that will be used in discussion.

■ Before discussing new material, write new key vocabulary words on the blackboard.

■ Write homework and class assignments and summaries of classroom discussions on the board.

■ Encourage hearing-impaired children to express themselves, including recitation and oral reading. Recognize that language deficits and the hearing impairment will affect vocabulary and syntax.

■ Remember that the hearing-impaired child is fatigued quickly because of intense concentration. However, require that assignments be completed on time.

■ Check child's hearing aid, if appropriate, on a regular basis.

■ Use visual aids when possible.

Since not all of the above suggestions are appropriate for each hearing-impaired student, educators should discuss program planning on an individual basis with trained professionals. With the influx of hearing-impaired students into regular classrooms, in-services on educational as well as emotional and social needs must be provided if integration is to succeed.

Educational environment for learning-impaired students should be arranged to promote multisensory learning.

Trends

Changing educational perspectives regarding the placement of hearing-impaired children have resulted in controversy over educational methods and philosophy. McConnell (1973) has identified several trends related to the education of the hearing impaired. Included are the following:

- Public schools will extend their programs to include all hearing-impaired children, beginning from birth.
- Teacher education programs will be modified to prepare teachers of the hearing impaired for all ages and grade levels. Specialists will be trained to counsel parents to aid in the education of children under three years of age.
- Day programs in regular elementary schools will be expanded to serve younger children. Integration into regular classes will take place earlier in the child's school career, and more children will eventually be placed in regular classes, receiving help in resource rooms.
- Residential and day programs will cooperate to enable the transfer of children from one to the other as necessary. Larger proportions of children will be enrolled in day programs at residential facilities.
- Work/study programs will enable students to get on-the-job experience while still in school. Vocational and technical training will be more readily available to the hearing impaired.
- Facilities for multiply handicapped children with hearing impairments will be provided for children who do not fit in any one category of exceptionality.

Research

The results of recent technological research have allowed hearing-impaired persons to be more involved in daily activities. Helpful devices include amplifiers built into telephones, an electronic device that flashes when the phone or doorbell rings or the baby cries, headphones (with volume control) for listening to the radio, television, or phonograph, and an intercom system that picks up the sound in one room and amplifies it into another.

Laboratory research projects have been designed to explore the causes of various impairments, such as otosclerosis, the hardening of ear bones. In addition, chemical and microscopic analysis of the inner ear and animal experimentation have been started to tackle the basic questions of how we hear and why we lose our hearing. Such research may also inform us as to why hearing fades with age (so that, ultimately, presbycusis may be remediated).

Sensory cells in the ear put out electrical responses relative to the loudness of the sound entering the ear. Scientists studying these impulses are beginning to understand how the ear heals itself after loss from acoustic trauma. They believe that their findings may contribute to the treatment of other hearing problems. Research indicates that the cochlear nerve is two-way: signals travel not only from the ear to the brain but also from the brain to the ear and help to regulate the ear's sensitivity to sound. This information may lead to improved remediation of hearing impairments.

Research on hearing and hearing loss will address the subjects of identifying more reliable tests, better hearing aids, alternative methods of helping individuals with sensorineural impairments, information about hearing defects that occur before and during birth, and more specific information on the extent of hearing impairments. Pure and applied research both offer hope for the hearing impaired (*Hearing Loss: Hope Through Research*, 1976).

SUMMARY POINTS

- Hearing impairment refers to those persons identified as having a hearing loss, from mild to profound.
- For educational purposes, the degree and location of hearing loss, the age of onset, family involvement, and early intervention are all important factors related to developing the hearing-impaired child's communication and learning skills.
- Hearing impairments are related to abnormalities of the outer, middle, or inner ear. Middle ear and inner ear problems result in conductive and sensorineural hearing losses, respectively.
- A hearing loss may be attributed to a variety of causes: trauma, disease, toxins, accidents, and hereditary syndromes.
- Assessment procedures identify the location (by means of air/bone conduction tests) and the hearing threshold for sound at various frequencies. The hearing-impaired child's capability for using residual hearing is an important component of the evaluation process.
- Children with a significant hearing loss frequently have poor communication, academic, and behavior skills in comparison to their nonimpaired peers. This discrepancy may be explained, in part, by inappropriate teaching in the regular class and also by rigid adherence to a particular method approach in deaf education programs.
- Special programs for the hearing impaired teach communication skills based on a particular philosophy: oral, manual, or total communication. There is a growing trend toward using a combination of methods; i.e., whatever works best for the child should be used.
- Many hearing-impaired children and youth are successfully mainstreamed into the regular classrooms. This process can be facilitated by a willing regular classroom teacher who is knowledgeable regarding alternative teaching techniques.
- Advanced technology has assisted the hearing impaired in functioning in a hearing world by providing better assessment procedures and adaptive equipment. Also, medical researchers continue to explore related causes in order to develop better preventative and intervention techniques.

REVIEW QUESTIONS

1. Why might hearing impairments associated with inner ear anomalies be more debilitating than middle ear problems?
2. Identify oral and manual methods for teaching the deaf. List the advantages and disadvantages associated with each.

3. The regular teacher can help the hearing-impaired child be more successful in the classroom. List alternative learning and teaching strategies.
4. Differentiate between a conductive and sensorineural hearing loss.
5. Why is the total communication philosophy increasingly being used in deaf education programs?
6. Identify measures that can be taken to prevent hearing impairments.

BEYOND HIGH SCHOOL — EDUCATIONAL OPPORTUNITIES FOR THE DEAF

Unlike postsecondary programs for many handicapped students, providing a college education for deaf and hearing-impaired students is not new. For over 100 years, Gallaudet College in Washington, D.C., has led the way in higher education for deaf students. This liberal arts college, specifically organized for the deaf, offers academic programs leading to 27 different baccalaureate degrees. Much of the strength of the program at Gallaudet lies in the entrance examination that is administered to students prior to college entrance. This extensive battery of admissions tests and interviews provides an analysis of the entering student's strengths and weaknesses. Since adolescent deaf students typically demonstrate general academic lags when compared to their nonhandicapped age mates, Gallaudet offers a one-year preparatory program for those whose academic skills are below the college freshman level.

Other support services offered include a tutorial center, a communications clinic, a hearing and speech clinic, a counseling and placement center, and a special program in language development. Related services and facilities available to Gallaudet students include the following: teletypewriter/telephone hookups (TTY), which enable students to communicate with other persons who have access to TTY; dormitory rooms with special warning lights to warn of emergencies or to signal the presence of messages; and a closed-circuit campus television system.

Another highly specialized postsecondary program for deaf students is available at the National Technical Institute for the Deaf (NTID) in Rochester, New York. This technical educational facility is part of the Rochester Institute of Technology and offers a wide variety of curricular opportunities to help deaf adults prepare for successful employment. Like Gallaudet, NTID provides skills and learning style assessment, individ-

ualized learning strategies, and when necessary, remedial programming.

More recently, deaf students have been integrated into regular higher education settings, as evidenced by the three college students in this chapter's case study. In these programs, such as the one at California State University in Northridge (CSUN in suburban Los Angeles), deaf students benefit from attending college classes closer to home, have a broader range of majors from which to choose, and are able to foster stronger social contacts with their nonhandicapped peers. The nonhandicapped students at CSUN seem to have benefited from this integrated program as well. Many of them enroll in classes where they learn to use sign language, which enables them to communicate better with their hearing-impaired classmates and to assist them with interpreting class lectures and discussions. The faculty at CSUN is also integrated; deaf professors and their nonhandicapped colleagues both teach integrated classes. This type of program should make great strides in removing some of the mysteries about deaf students as perceived by the nonhandicapped. It should also establish the expectation that deaf persons can and should learn and work with other students (Jones and Murphy, 1974).

Although quite different from the specialized postsecondary programs at Gallaudet and NTID, integrated programs for deaf students in universities such as CSUN and at Utah State University (Berg, 1972) also provide special instructional and curricular modifications for deaf students.

Many deaf persons, however, have graduated from institutions of higher education that are not known for their specialized programs. A follow-up 1976 study of graduates from the Central Institute for the Deaf in St. Louis, Missouri, listed over 100 universities from which deaf alumni of the Central Institute were later graduated (Gjerdingen,

1977). For capable deaf students, the availability of programs in higher education is encouraging.

As the trend toward focusing on the individual learner in higher education gains credence and acceptability, the prospects for handicapped college students will also become more expansive (Chickering and Chickering, 1978). Many of the same issues and concerns that we face in developing educational programs at the elementary and secondary level will also have to be encountered at the postsecondary level. Just as various postsecondary programs have evolved for educating deaf students (from highly specialized programs to those making very little accommodation), a continuum of services for assisting handicapped college-bound students is likely to develop. Concerns related to integration versus segregation, type of support services to be offered, and benefits to nonhandicapped college students will have to be addressed.

1. What professional standards and credentials are required for teachers of the hearing impaired in your state?
2. What alternative methods or teaching techniques might a college or university professor implement to accommodate the hearing impaired?

SUGGESTED READINGS

Furth, H. G. *Deafness and Learning: A Psychosocial Approach*. Belmont, Ca: Wadsworth, 1973.

Ling, D. "Recent Developments Affecting the Education of Hearing Impaired Children." *Public Health Reviews* 4 (1975), 117–152.

Northern, J. L., and Downs, M. P. *Hearing in Children*. Baltimore: Williams and Wilkins, 1978.

12

THE ORTHOPEDICALLY HANDICAPPED AND OTHER HEALTH IMPAIRED

CONTENTS

Of all exceptional children, those with physical handicaps possibly have the most difficulty blending into the mainstream. While their disabilities are finite, their handicaps (as measured by society's image of their limitations) have been unbounded. Often, educational placement has been decided on the basis of the disability alone.

The term physically handicapped applies to such a diverse number of people that it is impossible to characterize this group either physically or psychologically. This heterogeneous category includes individuals who are alike only in that they are below average in their physical abilities or physical strength.

JENNY

Jenny Johnson is a quiet, smiling, three-and-a-half-year-old who was born with spina bifida. This birth defect, which results from the failure of the vertebral neural arches to enclose a portion of the child's spinal cord, has deprived Jenny of the active use of her legs. Soon after her birth, doctors recommended that Jenny be allowed to die. The Johnsons had to decide whether to administer life-prolonging antibiotics and conduct the surgery necessary to prevent further impairment of Jenny's neurological system. The agony of this decision was compounded because the parents of another similarly impaired baby in the hospital nursery had elected to let their child die.

Earlier false assurances by medical personnel that everything would be all right, that Jenny's condition was only temporary, had been replaced by the harsh, cruel facts. Jenny had a severe defect requiring corrective surgery to prevent further damage to her body and mind. She would never be able to walk or run and would probably have difficulty sitting up. After the implications of this condition were discussed with the hospital's birth defects coordinator, Mr. and Mrs. Johnson spent many long, lonely hours thinking and talking. Hoping that no severe brain damage had occurred and knowing that they had the support of friends who had suffered through similar circumstances, Mr. and Mrs. Johnson elected to proceed with the medical and surgical interventions necessary to save Jenny's life.

Now, at age three and a half, Jenny is paralyzed from the waist down, unable to control her bladder, and cannot sit under her own power due to a hump on her back. She seems to have accepted her condition and often talks about her back being patched. She has begun to crawl and seems to use the strength in her arms to their fullest potential. Her grandmother, who has taken the responsibility of raising Jenny since her parents' separation, indicates that Jenny has become very verbal to compensate, she believes, for her lack of mobility.

A year ago, Jenny was enrolled in a preschool program sponsored by the Crippled Children's Center. She is in a class with seven other children. The teacher is the mother of another child with spina bifida. The necessary pre-enrollment evaluation was a traumatic experience for the family. Now, transporting Jenny to and from the class consumes a great amount of time. Despite these difficulties, Jenny's family continues to support her enrollment in this special program. They have found that this program has helped Jenny to become more outgoing and to get along better with other children and adults from outside the family. Overall, Jenny's family believes that her brief experience in the special program has been beneficial despite her frequent absences due to medical and surgical care.

Most family members have accepted Jenny and her limitations. Her older brother often plays with her, pulls her in the wagon, and pushes her on the swings. Her relatives have been extremely supportive. They have assisted her father and grandmother in providing stimulating learning experiences by taking Jenny with them on various trips around the community.

Jenny's grandmother reads to her frequently, gives her many educational toys, and tries to explain events to her as thoroughly as possible in order to help her develop her apparently normal intelligence. A main goal for Jenny's family is to teach her how to act politely. They believe that if she is polite in her interactions with others, her chances of being accepted will be appreciably increased. Because caring for Jenny is sometimes a matter of life and death, the priorities of her family members have changed—Jenny's needs often must come first.

The future for Jenny and her family remains uncertain. Her grandmother is looking forward to the time when Jenny will be able to attend a regular public school. However, she is concerned how the teachers and other pupils will react. She hopes that they will accept Jenny for what she is and what she can do. A major concern is Jenny's future welfare since she probably will never be able to live independently. Jenny's grandmother worries about what will happen to Jenny after she is gone. She wants her granddaughter to go as far as she possibly can despite her handicap and dreams of Jenny attending college. She is aware of the potential influence of others with whom Jenny will associate in her lifetime and she prays she will be accepted by society. Jenny's future, she knows, depends upon it.

Points for Consideration

■ Recent advances in medical science have made it possible for Jenny and other physically handicapped children not only to survive but also to attend school and live productive lives.

■ Many parents of children with physical handicaps and health impairments must face the serious, difficult decisions that inevitably arise in these situations. Hospitals should provide professional support systems to these families.

■ Participation in an early intervention program has helped Jenny develop appropriate social skills.

■ Jenny's family has serious concerns about her future, especially when they will no longer be here to take care of her.

Common Misconceptions

■ *The Orthopedically Handicapped Are Less Intelligent than Normal People.* A few of the physically handicapped may also be mentally retarded, but most have average intelligence and some are even gifted. Because of their physical impairments, however, casual observers may not recognize their intellectual abilities.

■ *The Physically Handicapped Learn Best in Separate, Special Schools.* Special schools with custom equipment and facilities can provide for the unique physical needs of these children. However, the physically handicapped frequently learn just as well in the regular school.

■ *The Physically Handicapped Are Unable to Care for Themselves.* Despite their disabilities, many physically handicapped persons are quite able to care for themselves through the use of special equipment and/or aids.

DEFINITION

For purposes of providing special educational services, the federal rules and regulations accompanying PL 94–142 define **orthopedically impaired** as "a severe orthopedic impairment which adversely affects a child's educational performance. The term includes impairments caused by **congenital anomaly** [an abnormality present at birth] . . . impairments caused by disease, and impairments from other causes" (*Federal Register*, August 23, 1977, p. 42478). The term **other health impaired** is defined as "limited strength, vitality, or alertness due to chronic or acute health problems such as heart condition, tuberculosis, rheumatic fever, nephritis, asthma, sickle cell anemia, hemophilia, epilepsy, lead poisoning, leukemia, or diabetes, which adversely affect a child's educational performance" (*Federal Register*, August 23, 1977, p. 42478). The list of possible medical causes relating to orthopedic impairments and the medical conditions cited in the definition of other health impaired only constitute a few examples of conditions that may impede children's functioning. Physically handicapped, physically disabled, orthopedically handicapped, crippled, and physically impaired are all terms used to refer to these persons.

PREVALENCE

In 1979, the Bureau of Education for the Handicapped counted over 177,000 pupils between the ages of 3 and 21 who were handicapped by orthopedic and other health impairments. The actual prevalence of these impairments is difficult to determine. This is so due largely to the great number and diversity of conditions existing within the general category of orthopedic and other health impairments. Numbers of children within some conditions may be increasing (e.g., spina bifida) because survival rates are much higher currently than in the past. Advances in medical science have also greatly reduced the numbers of children in some other classifications (e.g., polio).

Until quite recently, persons affected by some of the lesser known physical impairments were thought to be minimal in number. Now, as parent and professional advocacy groups prevail, the actual numbers of these persons are found to be larger. For example, prior to the late 1960s, **osteogenesis imperfecta**, commonly referred to as "brittle bone disease," was held to be extremely rare. Now, best estimates indicate that there are at least 10,000 and maybe as many as 30,000 cases in our country (Osteogenesis Imperfecta Foundation, Inc., 1970).

Environmental and societal influences are responsible for changes in the prevalence of different types of physical handicaps. The increased emphasis on prenatal care (including the use of prenatal tests) has helped to prevent some types of physically handicapping birth defects. However, the frequent abuse of alcohol and other drugs by expectant mothers continues to increase the number of congenitally impaired children. Also, accident-caused crippling conditions (motor vehicle, sports, etc.) have been increasing (Calhoun and Hawisher, 1979).

TYPES, CAUSES, AND CHARACTERISTICS

In this chapter the various impairments and conditions will be discussed under four broad categories: (1) conditions related to neurological involvement; (2) health handicaps; (3) muscular problems; and (4) orthopedic (relating to bones and joints) conditions (Calhoun and Hawisher, 1979). Some students with crippling conditions and other health impairments may be multiply handicapped. Thus, some may have additional problems related to learning and social/emotional adjustment.

Neurological Involvement

CEREBRAL PALSY **Cerebral palsy** results from brain damage or from dysfunction of those portions of the brain that control muscular function. Cerebral palsy in itself does not worsen as the child grows older. However, the child's adjustment to the disability does depend on family support, early intervention, and proper medical care.

The accompanying motor dysfunction may involve different groups of muscles of one or more limbs. Some commonly used descriptive terms involving limb paralysis are:

- Monoplegia—one limb
- Hemiplegia—both limbs on the same side
- Paraplegia—both lower limbs
- Triplegia—three limbs (two lower and one upper)
- Quadraplegia—four limbs (often head and trunk may also be involved)

Cerebral palsy may be caused by conditions occurring before, during, or after birth. Prenatal causes of cerebral palsy include severe anemia in the mother, metabolic irregularities, reduced oxygen supply, shock, and premature separation of the placenta. Problems during birth causing cerebral palsy include reduced oxygen due to problems with the placenta and the umbilical cord. Postnatal causes include head injuries, lead poisoning, and diseases such as encephalitis and meningitis.

Along with the muscle-group classification of cerebral palsy, several types of this disability are recognized with these characteristics:

■ *Spasticity*: In spasticity, injury to the brain's motor area results in loss of voluntary muscle control. Difficulties in physical coordination and increased muscle tone (tight muscles) result.

■ *Athetosis*: Athetosis is characterized by involuntary slow movements of the limbs. Frequently, the hands or arms are the most seriously affected. The muscles of the throat and diaphragm are involved, resulting in labored, and often unintelligible speech. Difficulties in controlling salivation may also be present.

■ *Ataxia*: This condition is characterized by disturbance in balance, which is reflected in posture and gait. The person sways or staggers and is dizzy and uncertain. This type of cerebral palsy does not occur as frequently as the spastic or athetoid variety.

■ *Mixed*: This type of cerebral palsy manifests some attributes of spasticity, athetosis, and ataxia.

In the classroom, students with cerebral palsy may need adaptive equipment to complete assignments, to aid with communication, and to perform such self-help activities as toileting, dressing, and eating. For some children with cerebral palsy, physical tasks may be almost impossible; however, parents and teachers should try not to overprotect these children by completing all of their tasks for them.

EPILEPSY **Epilepsy** is a seizure disorder caused by an abnormal excess of electrical discharges within the brain. There are several forms of epilepsy and some do not result in easily observed behavior changes.

Epilepsy often shocks people because of the nature of the seizures. The best known type of seizure is referred to as **grand mal**, in which the child falls and becomes unconscious with uncontrollable body movements and a marked increase in salivation. Also during the seizure the child's bowel and bladder control may be lost. Usually a grand mal seizure lasts only for a few minutes. Afterward, the child may require sleep for several hours because of the energy expended during the seizure.

Another type of epileptic seizure is termed **petit mal**. In petit mal seizures, the individual loses consciousness only for a few moments. The body does not convulse but the eyes stare and the eyelids twitch. The resulting brief lapses in concentration and attention may not even be observable to others.

In psychomotor epileptic seizures, the victim usually has short periods of amnesia. Afflicted individuals may be observed to stare, drop things, mumble, and fail to remember their actions, which may appear purposeful but actually be irrelevant to the task at hand.

The treatment of epilepsy requires medical management. Advances in medicine have made it possible for most epileptic children to remain in the regular class-

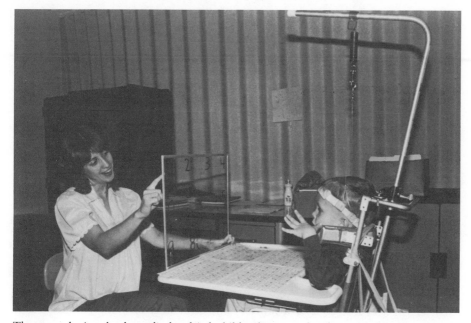

The severely involved cerebral palsied child relies on adaptive equipment to assist in accomplishing learning tasks.

room. Medication can control convulsions in 80 percent of the cases of epilepsy (Love and Walthall, 1977).

Seizure disorders may cause relatively few classroom management problems if the anti-epileptic drugs are successful and if the teacher and classmates are sensitive to the child's needs. The physician sometimes has difficulty regulating the drugs so that the child maintains attention, motivation, and learning progress, while remaining seizure-free. Thus, it is recommended that teachers record their observations of such children and relay the information to the physician. Teachers should particularly be on the alert for "more activity, less activity, complaints of headache, finger tremor, loss of appetite, drowsiness, increased tension, increased talkativeness, teeth grinding, teeth gnashing, inarticulate speech, frequent stomachache, and unexplained lapses of attention" (Calhoun and Hawisher, 1979, p. 26). During actual seizures, teachers should:

- Remain calm and attempt to set a good example for the class.
- Move furniture so that the pupil does not fall against it.
- Do not try to put any object in the child's mouth to prevent swallowing of the tongue; the child cannot swallow his or her tongue.
- Do not restrict the child's movements.
- Provide a place for the child to rest following the seizure.

Children with epilepsy seem to vary academically as much as normal children. However, heavy medication may affect the epileptic student's learning. An abrupt change in the student's academic performance should be reported to the physician for medical management.

The psychological impact of epilepsy is openly portrayed in the following statement by a 17-year-old boy with epilepsy (*Epilepsy: A Teenager's View*, 1976, p. 2):

I could put up with everything else if I just didn't have to sneak around all the time. I even think I wouldn't have so many seizures if I could just stop worrying about it and my doctor says I might be right about that. You know what I would like? I would like it if everybody could just go ahead and know I have epilepsy and not even care. I would just like to know what it feels like to be treated like everybody else, not special and not like I'm some kind of monster or even like a baby that has to be taken care of all the time, but like a person.

SPINA BIFIDA   Spina bifida means "cleft spine" and originates during the development of the embryo "when, for unknown reasons, the neural tube fails to develop completely and to close . . ." (Mullins, 1979, p. 138). Depending on the severity, it is also referred to as **meningocele** and **myelomeningocele**. In this condition, a portion of the spinal cord is not enclosed by the arches of the backbone; the protective covering of the spinal cord may be defective; or the spinal cord, its protective covering, and the back arches may be defective. Varying neurological impairments and related deformities result, depending upon the nature of the damage to the spinal cord. Impairments may vary from relatively minor motor loss to paraplegia and loss of bladder control. Frequently, children with spina bifida develop an abnormal blockage of the spinal fluid which, if left uncorrected, may lead to **hydrocephaly** and ultimately mental retardation. The excess spinal fluid and accompanying pressure on the brain can be reduced through surgery in which a **shunt**, a tube with a pressure valve, is implanted in the brain cavity.

Children with spina bifida require physical and occupational therapy to aid them in developing locomotion, usually with the use of crutches, braces or wheelchairs. The instructional program should emphasize good personal hygiene because of the odor and infections associated with problems of bladder and bowel control.

A 1979 New York State study of the educational placement of children with spina bifida discovered that 60 percent of them attended regular school classes (Lauder, Kanthar, Myers, and Resnick, 1979). One six-year-old boy with spina bifida, using crutches and changing his own diapers, readily made the transition from the special school for the handicapped where he attended kindergarten to a regular first-grade classroom. His classmates understood his special needs, and he was included in all class activities (Nelson, 1979).

SPINAL CORD INJURY   Increasing numbers of bicycle, motorcycle, automobile, and sports-related accidents have led to spinal cord injuries. These often result in paraplegia and quadraplegia for a growing number of school-age children and youths. Secondary potential problems resulting from these injuries include respiratory infections, urinary tract infections, and pressure sores from sitting or lying too long in the same position. Rehabilitation procedures are longitudinal in nature and rarely, if ever, result in total recovery of functioning. Adaptive devices, however, such as wheelchairs, hand controls in cars, and **prostheses** (artificial body parts), enable many of these persons to care for some of their needs and participate in daily activities.

The psychological trauma which accompanies spinal cord injuries and other acquired disabilities may cause problems of adjustment and depression and may interfere with the child's learning. Psychological support services are especially important to help the spinal cord disabled cope with their condition (Caywood, 1974).

The handicapping conditions discussed previously are visible to the public. Other physically handicapping conditions—known as health impairments—are usually not as evident. The relative invisibility may cause problems for this type of disabled person because the general public cannot perceive the condition or understand some of the behavioral patterns required for the individual to adapt to the disability.

DIABETES   **Juvenile diabetes mellitus** is an inherited disease that affects the body's metabolic functions. In diabetes, carbohydrates are not used properly and an excess of glucose accumulates in the blood. Concurrently, the pancreas does not produce enough **insulin**. In order for glucose to be metabolized into energy, insulin must get into the body cells. Diabetics are consequently left with no energy and cannot function properly. Diabetes is a leading cause of blindness and the third leading cause of death from disease in the United States. Currently there is only treatment for diabetes, but no cure. Teachers should be aware of the following symptoms: unusual thirst; frequent urination; loss of weight despite good eating habits; blurry vision; cuts and bruises that heal slowly; and feelings of tiredness, weakness, or drowsiness.

The classroom teacher should also know the symptoms of **insulin reaction** (too much insulin) and should notify medical personnel at the first signs of such problems. Improper identification of the symptoms and improper treatment could be fatal to the student. The symptoms of insulin reaction are headache, nausea, trembling, shallow breathing, and cold, moist skin. Reactions occur most frequently just before meals or after extreme exercise. The recommended treatment is to give orange juice or a candy bar (or anything that contains sugar) so that the insulin will have something with which to react. Also, if possible, the child's daily program should be arranged so that meals precede rather than follow heavy exercise. The symptoms of too little insulin include gradual onset of fatigue, drinking large amounts of water, frequent urination, excessive hunger, and warm, dry skin. The treatment is to provide the individual with insulin. This condition could lead to **ketoacidosis**, diabetic coma, requiring hospitalization. However, it does come on gradually. Any observed symptoms should be reported to the child's parents (Christiansen, 1975).

The Juvenile Diabetes Foundation (as its project for the International Year of the Child, 1979) promoted and distributed a recently published book designed to help children and adults dispel the many misconceptions about juvenile diabetes. The book, entitled *You Can't Catch Diabetes from a Friend*, tells about the lives of four diabetic children and how they and their families are affected by their illness (Kipnis and Adler, 1979). It can help teachers and students to better understand and accept the unique needs of diabetic classmates.

CYSTIC FIBROSIS   **Cystic fibrosis** is the most common lethal hereditary disease (Calhoun and Hawisher, 1979, p. 35). It is characterized by thick, sticky mucus that interferes with lung functioning and tends to cause chronic lung disease and deficiencies of the pancreas. These medical conditions often result in long absences from school and the use of home instruction. When in school, however, children suffering from cystic fibrosis can attend regular classes when efforts are made to de-emphasize concern for their condition. Gym, recess, and other physical activities should be encouraged because physical activity is an important aid in preventing secretions from blocking the lungs (Mullins, 1979, p. 289). Frequent coughing occurs as the body attempts to clear the lungs of the clogged mucus. Depending upon each child's needs, the teacher should let the child know that he or she may leave the room when the coughing becomes severe. The teacher should also let the child's classmates know that the cough is not contagious.

SICKLE CELL ANEMIA   **Sickle cell anemia** is a genetic disease occurring more frequently in blacks than in other races. Children with this disease experience intermittent pain crises, caused by the deprivation of blood to body tissue, which may result in heart disease, crippling, or stroke. Short stature and urination problems may also result. Crises may be brought on by infections and fever. Children suffering from this disease often have extended periods of absenteeism from school and may require home instruction.

HEART CONDITIONS   Heart conditions can be either congenital or acquired. Congenital heart disease is 20 times more common in childhood (Love and Walthall, 1977). Acquired heart conditions are usually detected by the family physician when the child is examined during routine checkups. Parents and teachers should be aware of the symptoms of possible heart difficulties. These include fatigue, shortness of breath, chest pains, fainting, and poor growth. Most children with heart conditions can be educated within the regular school program. The child's physician should recommend physical considerations and a safe level of physical activity.

Muscular Problems

MUSCULAR DYSTROPHY   **Muscular dystrophy** is an inherited disease generally caused by a recessive gene transmitted through unaffected mothers to their sons. This disability causes an increasing, progressive weakness of the voluntary skeletal muscles such as those in the arm, calf, and thigh. Muscles are replaced by fatty tissues, resulting in general weakness. Initial symptoms include difficulty in running and climbing stairs. As the disease progresses, the child may exhibit difficulties in walking, even on flat surfaces. This disease progresses fairly rapidly with death usually occurring in the late teens due to heart failure or lung infection (Bleck, 1975).

Educational programming should be conducted with the knowledge that muscular dystrophy students need special help. They may tire easily, may be easily knocked down, and may be unable to complete simple tasks such as opening doors. A positive attitude should be maintained when working with the child despite awareness of his or her terminal disability. Also, scholastic success should be encouraged with emphasis on short-term, obtainable goals. Overindulgence and overprotection should be avoided since these behaviors may cause the child to eventually develop a negative attitude toward home and school. Finally, education about death is crucial for these students, their families, peers, and teachers.

Orthopedic Problems

LIMB DEFICIENCY   The absence of one or more limbs, whether congenital or acquired, may cause difficulties with physical activity. Early intervention and rehabilitation is important for ensuring the affected person's maximum functioning. Early intervention may include training in the use of an artificial limb. (Some students may be capable of utilizing the remaining portion of the deficient limb to perform some necessary functions.) The decision whether to use an artificial limb revolves around the child's and parents' perception of such devices. An individual's motivation will determine if the limb can be more efficiently utilized with or without a prosthesis. It is recommended that the teacher of a child with an artificial limb ask the child to demonstrate the prosthesis to other classmates. This openness tends to satisfy the curiosity of other children and helps the handicapped child to be accepted (Hamilton, 1975).

Occupational therapists should be included in the educational team to teach the child to use artificial limbs or the remaining portion of the natural limb. Consistent cooperation between the classroom teacher and the occupational therapist is essential in order to generalize and carry over treatment in the classroom activities. Children who have lost arms may need adaptive devices for self-help functions such as eating. The need for psychological support services may depend on whether the limb deficiency was acquired or congenital. "In amputees below the age of sixteen, about 75 percent of the impairments are congenital, affecting boys and girls equally" (Mullins, 1979, p. 71).

OSTEOGENESIS IMPERFECTA   Osteogenesis imperfecta (OI) is commonly referred to as "brittle bone disease" because of its most common characteristic—fragility of the bone. Other characteristics include loose joints, deafness, poor teeth, and short stature due to stunted growth. OI is a hereditary disorder that in its most severe form is usually diagnosed at birth. It may not, however, become known until the affected person suffers fractures later in life. Treatment of the symptoms (i.e., deafness, poor teeth), as well as surgery to correct the deformities caused by the multiple fractures is warranted ("What Is OIF?" Osteogenesis Imperfecta Foundation, Inc., 1970).

Only a few of the crippling and other health-impairing conditions found in schoolchildren have been detailed here. Other health impairments that handicap some school-age children include asthma, juvenile arthritis, and hemophilia.

IDENTIFICATION AND PLACEMENT

Traditionally, the educational placement of physically handicapped and health-impaired children has revolved around noneducational considerations. These students were put in special classes because of their physical disabilities, despite the fact that they present as wide a range of intellectual abilities and educational needs as other children. There is, therefore, little justification for organizing these children into one category for purposes of education.

Noneducational, administrative considerations initially brought physically handicapped students together in one central location. It was more economical to transport children to one central place. Many of these children required intensive occupational, physical, and speech therapy, in addition to medical intervention and dietary supervision. Thus it was easier to bring the therapists and related health-service personnel to one location and transport the students to them rather than vice versa. Finally, considering these children's difficulties in mobility it was easier to construct one building that was barrier-free than to make all buildings in the school district barrier-free.

Today, with the passage of PL 94–142 and the adoption of the concept of least restrictive environment, many program options are available for the education of physically handicapped and other health-impaired children. Placement decisions should consider the child's ability to communicate, need for therapy and rehabilitation, level of intellectual ability, need for a limited environment for safe functioning, and degree of mobility.

EDUCATIONAL PROGRAMMING

In the classroom, the teacher should help physically handicapped children perform as independently as possible, treat them as normal members of the class, and help the nonhandicapped pupils accept and understand their physically handicapped classmates.

Curriculum Design

Traditional academic subjects are not necessarily the main curricular concerns for some physically handicapped children. Some may indeed profit from striving to achieve practical objectives in arithmetic, reading, and writing. For instance, instruction in practical mathematics may aid the student in budgeting money, balancing a checkbook, and measuring ingredients for preparing meals. Reading goals might concentrate on building a sight word vocabulary of frequently encountered words such as those on employment applications or elsewhere within the student's environment. Indeed, some physically handicapped children may have a very limited perception of the real world and of the practical skills needed

Teachers often must circumvent the orthopedically handicapped student's physical limitations in order to develop his true learning potential.

to operate successfully in places like grocery stores, restaurants, and similar community locations. If it is determined that a physically handicapped student may profit from more complex, abstract, or theoretical applications of basic academic subjects, the goals and objectives for that child should be higher. For those physically handicapped persons who are also multiply and severely impaired, however, reading, writing, and arithmetic may not be major concerns.

For those children who demonstrate some independent functioning at school or within the community, curriculum objectives should emphasize life experience skills, work skills, and related social behaviors. The idea of incorporating life experience skills into the physically handicapped student's curriculum is relatively new. Life experience skills include helping the student to find means of transportation as well as to locate and use community resources. Also, the curriculum should provide opportunities for learning about adequate and fulfilling leisure-time activities.

Another important area of instruction in working with physically handicapped students is that of self-help skills. Usually, self-help skills are defined as those that are aimed at developing self-sufficiency, including toileting, eating, dressing, homemaking, and using transportation. Some physically handicapped students may not be able to complete these tasks by themselves. In these instances, learning self-help skills may mean learning how to direct others to aid the child in completing these tasks.

Role of Teachers

COMMUNICATION Expressing basic needs is a major problem for many children with severe physical disabilities. The following suggestions will assist the teacher in helping the child communicate.

- The first priority should be to elicit from the child the manner in which he or she indicates basic wants and indicates "yes" and "no." Their wants could be communicated by signs in the room indicating "restroom," "water," and "food." The child could then point to the appropriate desired sign. "Yes" or "no" could be on cards attached to opposite sides of the child's wheelchair. The child could then glance at the appropriate card or turn his or her head indicating one card or the other.

- When questioning a child, the teacher may have to speak slowly and repeat all or parts of the question. If the child is having difficulty understanding, the teacher can say the words individually so the child can indicate which particular words are not understood.

- Some children may require special procedures in order to record their answers and ideas. Tape recorders can be used to record answers and assignments. Also, physically handicapped children can use typewriters to communicate ideas. Electric typewriters are usually the most efficient because of the convenience of the automatic carriage return. In order to prevent the child from striking more than one key, guards can be placed over the keys to individualize key selection. Also, by using special tricks, the child may be able to type with the mouth or by attaching a stick to a special headband.

PHYSICAL ACTIVITIES Studies have demonstrated that physical activities improve the motivation, self-confidence, and adjustment of many orthopedically and other health-impaired persons (Calhoun and Hawisher, 1979). With attention on the least-restrictive-environment concept, many schools attempt to provide physical education benefits to orthopedically handicapped pupils in classes with their nonimpaired peers. Some recommended programming principles include (Cathay and Jansma, 1979, pp. 9–10):

- Teach individuals how to fall correctly from crutches, wheelchairs, or from unsupported positions; e.g. use extra mats. . . .
- Modify activities where competition is involved; e.g. strike a stationary object instead of a moving one; strike a ball after bouncing it.
- Once in a while use activities and games where the regular students assume the impairment that is part of the activity; e.g. one legged relay; one/two hands behind your back relay. . . .
- Instill in all players their role in playing their own position. This will aid in preventing a play being taken away from a disabled student. . . .
- Allow a student to run or bat while a peer executes the other, depending on upper/lower body function. . . .
- In programming, include exercises which maintain function and/or remediate impairments. Include, as much as possible, the same sports, games, and other activities which are offered to regular students.

SUPPORT PERSONNEL   A classroom teacher working with orthopedically handicapped and other health-impaired children will find it necessary to remain in close contact with a variety of support personnel. Such personnel include psychologists, speech and language specialists, rehabilitation counselors, physicians, and nurses. In addition, two specialists commonly associated with the physically handicapped are **physical therapists** (PTs) and occupational therapists (OTs).

Generally, physical therapists improve postures and movement patterns and recommend various body positions for instruction within the classroom. Their therapy may include the use of massage, heat, exercise, or water. They also teach students to use rehabilitation equipment, such as braces and wheelchairs.

Occupational therapists also work on improving postures and movement. However, they traditionally concentrate on recreational and social activities as well as on the self-help skills necessary for daily living, such as eating, dressing, and grooming. Both physical and occupational therapists play major roles in teaching the handicapped individual life-experience skills, such as use of public transportation, homemaking, general mobility, and preparation for vocational pursuits.

SPECIAL CONSIDERATIONS AND ISSUES

A few areas of physical and other health impairments have been selected for special consideration and are highlighted in the following sections.

Barriers

In 1976 it was estimated that daily one of every ten Americans was prohibited from functioning usefully by architectural barriers ("Breaking Down the Barriers," 1976). Barriers to the mobility of physically handicapped persons include inaccessible parking spaces, revolving doors, steps, small restrooms lacking

Aesthetic aspects of buildings, such as steps, often become barriers for the physically handicapped, as well as for the health-impaired.

banisters, phone booths, and thick carpeting. Within the last few years, guidelines have been implemented for modifying the everyday environment to make it accessible to the handicapped. Questions such as the following allow the elements of accessibility and usability by handicapped persons to be evaluated.

■ Do toilet rooms have turning spaces of 60 inches × 60 inches to allow traffic of persons in wheelchairs?
■ Are the spouts on wall-mounted water fountains no higher than 30 inches?
■ Are the controls on elevators 40 inches or less from the floor?

Problems with architectural barriers were confronted by several special education graduate students participating in a simulation experience. They were told to confine themselves to a wheelchair, leave the classroom, and make a phone call at a pay booth (this activity necessitated going downstairs on the elevator). Comments following this exercise included the following (Glazzard, 1979, pp. 102–103):

Frustrated! The wheel of my chair got caught in the elevator. My arms were tired, and three people left me sitting on the front steps with the door closed. It seems as though my mind was always racing ahead to the "next thing"—what will happen next? How do I go to the bathroom? What if . . .? It was very draining.

Very frustrating. Elevator door shut on me. I couldn't get traction on the rug and my wheels spun. I now had to concentrate on traveling efforts, whereas before, I gave little thought to getting from point A to point B. People's reactions were the worst part. Two people went down the steps to avoid me when I was stuck on the elevator. People offered to help me in such a pitying manner that I felt humiliated and dehumanized.

People's looks of pity bothered me. I was glad to get out of the chair. I am grateful for my own health and have a new concern for the plight and frustration of others.

Psychological Adjustment

The psychological implications and other side effects of crippling conditions and health impairments vary as much as the disorders themselves. Anxiety, frustration, and poor self-concepts are symptoms common to this population. Other psychological problems may include (Sirvis, 1978, pp. 373–374):

- Unresolved dependent feelings, which may create an excessive need for affection and attention
- Excessive submissiveness, which actually may be covering a deep-seated hostility toward physical dependence on others
- Extreme egocentrism and inability to deal with being alone
- Fantasy as compensation for feelings of inferiority and/or inadequacy
- Resignation to, rather than recognition of, limits
- Superficial conscious recognition of handicap, with a subconscious rejection of self

As with other handicapping conditions, the problems of psychological adjustment relate not only to the disability itself but also to the influences of others' perceptions of the disability. Stable, psychologically supportive environments are

Opportunities to complete tasks, such as selecting his own library book, enhance the handicapped student's feelings of self-worth and independence.

necessary for enhancing positive self-image. Here, the physically handicapped child can have positive interactions with others and can receive recognition for capable performances. The complex interaction of bodily awareness, environmental settings, and self-images are depicted in the following excerpt from a story about a young, physically handicapped girl. She has come home after living for several years in a special residential school (Little, 1970, pp. 28–29):

> Sal was not used to seeing herself in a looking glass. At school she had practiced walking in front of one, but the therapist had always been telling her to watch her knees or keep her elbows in. Over the years, Sally had grown to look at herself a piece at a time. She had come to have a vague picture of herself, a girl all elbows and knees and crutches, with a face and clothes too ordinary to notice much.

The child experiencing illness is especially troubled and likely to be frightened. Psychological effects of physical illnesses may include temper tantrums, regression to immature behavior, feelings of helplessness, irritability, lowered self-confidence, fear of the dark, and changes in habits, such as bed wetting. Teachers and parents should recognize these symptoms as natural and expected in order to give appropriate support (Segal and Yahraes, 1979). General hazards to psychological adjustment in chronically ill children include the effects of medication (which may alter the child's behavior, particularly alertness); isolation caused by physical restrictions; continuous or intermittent pain; and the fear of dying (Calhoun and Hawisher, 1979). For many ill children the fear of death may not be an immediate hazard to their psychological adjustment. However, for children who have terminal illnesses such as cystic fibrosis or leukemia, the fear of death represents a realistic aspect of their everyday functioning.

Dealing with Death

Teachers must first deal with their own fears of death and feelings about the terminally ill child in order to effectively help children cope with the topic of dying. Research indicates that although young children (under six years of age) seem unaware of their condition, older children often are aware that they are dying despite their parents' desire to hide that knowledge from them (Suran and Rizzo, 1979).

The writings of Kübler-Ross (1969, 1972, 1974) have stimulated many educators' concern that schools help pupils learn about death so that they will be better prepared for their own death as well as the deaths of family members and friends. Death education in and of itself has not been accepted as an integral part of all school curricula. However, many schools are offering studies on the topic as part of the regular health education program, or else as a unit of the social studies curriculum. The content of death-and-dying courses according to one state survey frequently covers attitudes toward death, bereavement and grief, the process of dying, suicide and euthanasia, rites and rituals, and life after death (Cappiello and Trayer, 1979).

Technological Assistance

In last two decades the pace of technology applied to the problems of the handicapped has increased tremendously. The results can be seen not only in the number of new and improved physical devices but also in the very lives of the handicapped. Persons with handicapping conditions have been enabled to communicate with others and to make their way in life more independently than has ever been possible before.

Swimming pools with adjustable floors, for example, have allowed persons confined to wheelchairs to enjoy the benefits and pleasures of swimming. In such pools, the floor is raised by a hydraulic lift to the level of the surrounding deck. The wheelchair of the handicapped person is wheeled onto the pool floor, and the floor is lowered to the appropriate level, enabling the handicapped swimmer to float into the water.

Persons handicapped by limb deficiencies no longer rely on crude wooden legs and crutches. Recent developments in prosthetic devices (artificial limbs) have enabled thousands of limb-deficient children and adults to maintain a more independent, normal life. Plastics, foam rubber, and various metals have been engineered into prosthetic devices which can be fitted to simulate real limb actions. Prosthetic elbows and hands using miniature motors that can be activated by contractions of muscles have also been marketed.

Youths who have been left severely handicapped by **juvenile rheumatoid arthritis** now have a brightened outlook due to the perfecting of artificial hip joints. In the mid-1970s, 15 adolescents in Cincinnati, Ohio, underwent total hip replacement surgery. Afterward, one adolescent who had been confined to a wheelchair was able to walk without it. Others found that previously painful or impossible tasks such as climbing stairs, putting on socks, and tying their shoes could now be accomplished.

Still other devices providing the handicapped with more independence include highly sophisticated, modified vans for those confined to wheelchairs; talking calculators for the blind; and miniature electronic typewriters for those who cannot speak.

Moreover, new knowledge created from research in the behavioral sciences has the potential for being extremely helpful to the handicapped. An example is the program at Tufts-New England Medical Center in Boston, Massachusetts. There, psychologist Mary J. Willard has successfully demonstrated that monkeys can be used to assist persons with severe physical handicaps. These Capuchin monkeys have been trained to close and unlock doors, turn lights off and on, and place phonograph records on turntables. These monkeys can be taught to retrieve and place objects when guided by a beam of light. Far out? Perhaps. But just as seeing-eye dogs now commonly aid persons with visual impairments, the future may find the Capuchin monkey to be an indispensable aid to persons with severe physical handicaps.

Advocacy Organizations

Organized volunteer groups can help teachers who work with physically handicapped and other health-impaired children. There are interested citizens whose primary objective is ensuring that proper health, education, and social services are available for the physically handicapped. Many are members of organizations such as the Muscular Dystrophy Association of America, National Easter Seal Society for Crippled Children and Adults, National Epilepsy League, Osteogenesis Imperfecta Foundation, National Foundation of March of Dimes, and United Cerebral Palsy Association. These organizations carry on service and public awareness activities at the national, state, and local levels. Among their varied functions, they distribute suggestions for teachers and professionals and offer consultation to parents of handicapped children.

Perhaps the best advocates for improving public knowledge and attitudes toward the physically handicapped are those persons themselves. For instance, the recent interest in jogging and running has spawned the competition of road races and marathons across the country. News accounts often refer to a growing number of contestants who complete the races in competitive time—in wheelchairs. The winner of the wheelchair competition of the 1980 Boston Marathon bettered the winning time of the Boston footrace by 17 minutes. Such exceptional persons speak for themselves!

SUMMARY POINTS

- Children with orthopedic and other health impairments are also often referred to as physically handicapped, crippled, and physically impaired.
- Determining prevalence rates with this population is extremely difficult due to the great variety of conditions, the levels of severity within types, and cases of multiply handicapping conditions.
- Orthopedic and health-impairing conditions can be categorized under the headings of neurological involvement health handicaps, muscular problems, and orthopedic problems.
- Cerebral palsy is the most common neurological problem affecting school children. This condition can be classified as spasticity, athetosis, ataxia, or mixed. Epilepsy, spina bifida, and spinal cord injuries are among other neurological impairments.
- Diabetes, cystic fibrosis, sickle cell anemia, heart conditions and other health handicaps are relatively invisible and, therefore, difficult for the general public to readily perceive or understand.
- Educational programs for the handicapped should include nonimpaired students and teachers in order that the physically handicapped students may be better understood.
- Educational programs for physically impaired children are enhanced when there is the cooperation of such support personnel as occupational therapists, physical therapists, and speech and language therapists.

REVIEW QUESTIONS

1. What are some common misconceptions about children with orthopedic and health impairments? How do these misconceptions compare with those relating to other exceptionalities?
2. What considerations should be made when assisting cerebral palsied children in their educational efforts?
3. Describe what the classroom teacher can do to assist an epileptic child undergoing a grand mal seizure.
4. What behavioral symptoms can teachers look for to help physicians determine the optimal dose of medication for epileptics?
5. Describe the warning signs of diabetes that teachers can watch for.

6. How can the physical or occupational therapist assist the child and the teacher?

7. What are some of the problems of psychological adjustment experienced by physically handicapped children? Discuss how the teacher can help them with these adjustments.

8. What are some ways that the classroom teacher can modify physical learning activities so that all pupils can benefit? Discuss.

INTEGRATION — PREPARING ALL STUDENTS

As nonhandicapped peers have more frequent contact with the orthopedically handicapped they may display initial shock and ignorance by remarks and stares. The successful integration of exceptional pupils will depend heavily upon programs that develop the understanding of their peers.

The Meeting Street School has devised a curriculum for elementary school pupils to help them understand the reasons for and consequences of disabilities. This four-month curriculum covers each disability in two sessions. The following are included (Bookbinder, 1977):

- Simulation activities
- Work with aids and appliances
- Discussion with disabled adults
- Movies, videotapes, slides, printed material
- Group discussions in class

Open, honest classroom discussion provides a mature way for pupils to try to comprehend the problems and circumstances of their physically handicapped schoolmates. When such problems are discussed informally without teacher guidance and with less accurate information, the results will be less productive.

One teacher reports how she tried to help her nonhandicapped fifth-grade pupils understand and behave appropriately with handicapped children. The following describes an exciting event in her class (Volkmann, 1977, p. 29):

> The class was learning to play volleyball and had practiced serving and volleying for several days. One child, mildly retarded physically and mentally, had experienced momentous difficulties in learning these skills and was obviously a detriment to his team. Upon his turn to serve he miraculously was able to get it all together and serve successfully. His entire team immediately enfolded him with hugs and

cheers and the grin on his face shot around the world and back. This was the outcome of much systematic coaching with the kids to praise one another when successful and particularly the total disapproval of negative comments toward any erring student.

Perhaps the most logical manner to encourage the empathy of regular pupils for their handicapped peers is through a reading program that touches upon various disabilities. The following conversation from the book *What Do You Do When Your Wheelchair Gets a Flat Tire?* is designed to help pupils understand disabilities and their effects on children (Biklen and Sokoloff, 1978).

> QUESTION *(from curious nonhandicapped child to handicapped peer)*: What do you do when your wheelchair gets a flat tire?
> RESPONSE *(from handicapped peer, Sally* [p. 24]): I usually swear a lot. Then I go to the gas station and hope it doesn't pop when they blow it up.
> QUESTION: How do you want to be treated?
> RESPONSE *(Raymond* [p. 49]): I want to be treated as nice as my friend Jeff treats me. He never calls me a cripple, even when he gets mad at me.

An excellent source for children's and adults' books, as well as appropriate films and activities, is *Feeling Free, Activities and Stories* (Benham, 1978).

It is equally important that handicapped pupils mainstreamed from special to regular classes have experiences in anticipating and practicing the social skills they will need in order to be accepted. The role-playing process outlined below is only one of several techniques that have been implemented cooperatively by special education and regular teachers. The aim is to help children with handicaps bridge the social gap often encountered when they enter the regular classroom.

Role Playing and Rehearsal

- *Step 1* Brainstorming and Situation Clarification: handicapped pupils and regular pupils together generate a list of concerns and situations that could arise in the regular class setting.

- *Step 2* Preparing for Role Playing and Rehearsal: teacher and pupils discuss why it would be beneficial to rehearse those situations and concerns prior to actual integration.

- *Step 3* Rehearsal and Role Playing: under the direction of the regular class teacher, selected handicapped pupils pretend they are in a regular class. Other handicapped pupils and some regular class kids role play regular class pupils.

- *Step 4* Discussion and Review: pupils are asked to review what happened and to discuss alternative ways of acting and talking.

- *Step 5* Rehearsal and Role Playing: pupils role play and rehearse the same situation again. Later they again discuss what happened and what they might do differently the next time.

This process allows handicapped pupils to explore alternative social behaviors that they may need later while still having the security of the special class setting. Additionally, it allows nonhandicapped peers the opportunity to intereact positively within the integrated classroom as well as to gain practical knowledge of and insight into the handicapped student.

DISCUSSION POINTS

1. In addition to teachers and students, what other people are likely to enhance understanding and acceptance of integration? The school principal? The parents? The school guidance counselor? The school psychologist? Other school personnel? Explain how they might be involved in integration efforts.
2. In the role-playing procedure outlined in this application, who in your opinion will contribute most to the success of the technique? The special education teacher? The regular classroom teacher? The special education pupils? The regular classroom pupils? Explain your choice.

SUGGESTED READINGS

Best, G. A. *Individuals with Physical Disabilities: An Introduction for Educators*. St. Louis: C. V. Mosby, 1978.

Calhoun, M. L., and Hawisher, M. *Teaching and Learning Strategies for Physically Handicapped Students*. Baltimore: University Park Press, 1979.

Love, H., and Walthall, J. E. *A Handbook of Medical, Educational and Psychological Information for Teachers of Physically Handicapped Children*. Springfield, Ill.: Charles C. Thomas, 1977.

Mullins, J. B. *A Teacher's Guide to Management of Physically Handicapped Students*. Springfield, Ill.: Charles C. Thomas, 1979.

13

THE MENTALLY RETARDED

CONTENTS

Services to the mentally retarded have been available in the United States longer than services for any other exceptionality except blindness and deafness. In a sense, our philosophy on providing services to the mentally retarded has returned to a point similar to that which prevailed in the late nineteenth century. During that time, the first institutions for retarded persons were founded with the belief that they could be trained or cured and thus would eventually be sent home. But in following years, with the recognition that the mentally retarded could not be cured, institutional programs shifted from a training perspective to custodial care. Since the mid-twentieth century, however, society again recognizes that many retarded persons can learn to live independent or semi-independent lives. Thus services for most retarded persons now emphasize an educational perspective.

The term mentally retarded refers to an extremely heterogeneous population. Their differences in behavioral characteristics and levels of everyday functioning are described in the case studies that follow.

ANN

Ann is a severely retarded 17-year-old. She is one of about 2000 residents in a large state institution for the mentally retarded. For hours at a time, Ann can be found sitting in a chair biting her hands, which show the scars of previous bites. Her chin, neck, and hands are covered with saliva.

Ann's day is routine: up at 7, breakfast at 8, lunch at noon, dinner at 5, and bedtime in the early evening. She and her cottage mates are washed, dressed, toileted, and medicated

by attendants and teachers. In between, she goes to class, watches TV, and occasionally plays with dolls. She has few regular visitors.

After many long, hard hours of consistent effort by attendants who taught her to eat using a padded spoon, Ann is learning to feed herself. Since Ann will not voluntarily drink liquids, she is being taught to drink by attendants. The process involves holding her head, wrapping a towel around her neck to catch spillage, and pouring in the milk and stroking her throat to help her swallow. If successful, this routine will be completed before she is able to spit up the milk.

Following breakfast, Ann and her cottage mates spend the morning in class activities designed to meet a variety of educational and social goals. Ann is being taught to follow oral directions and spends much of the morning learning to knock down a block tower and to walk forward following the voice commands of her teacher. She is also being taught to substitute manipulating objects for her almost constant hand biting. Some girls are learning how to fingerpaint; others how to use underarm deodorant. Ann's teacher is faced with classroom urination, biting, eating of inappropriate objects, and many other bizarre behaviors.

HEATHER

Heather is a moderately retarded nine-year-old girl who has been diagnosed as a Down's syndrome child. Following the conclusive diagnosis, Heather and her parents were referred to the local county board of mental retardation by their pediatrician. The mental retardation program assigned a caseworker who visited with the family twice a month to check on Heather's progress, to offer suggestions for the family to follow in aiding Heather's development, and to determine the adequacy of the home environment.

At the age of three, Heather entered the county mental retardation board's preschool program on a part-day basis. She is now attending primary classes at the Mental Retardation Developmental Center where she will learn communication skills, basic word identification, counting, mobility skills, and independent living skills. Since the age of four, Heather has also been enrolled in a summer camp program sponsored by the local Association for Retarded Citizens. At camp, she engages in such typical activities as swimming, hiking, and crafts, and she continues to work on her academic skills.

Her parents' biggest concern has been for her education and the development of her potential. They are pleased that the mental retardation program offers an excellent sheltered workshop for older pupils but they are worried about the program's apparent de-emphasis on reading skills. They believe, as do most parents of exceptional children, that the main goal of Heather's educational program should be to prepare her for as great a

level of self-sufficiency in adulthood as possible. In their opinion, the ability to read plays a highly significant role in accomplishing independent living skills and should be stressed in their daughter's educational program.

They worry about her welfare after they die. Also, they hope that her older brother and sister will not have to bear the burden of constant care for her in the future. To this end they are helping to promote the establishment of additional group homes for the retarded in their community. Their fears would be alleviated if their retarded daughter learned to care for herself and lead a somewhat independent existence aside from her family.

DONNY

Donny is a "rough-and-tumble" nine-and-a-half-year-old boy who has recently entered a school program for **educable mentally retarded** pupils. His first three years of school were spent in six different elementary schools because his mother frequently moved to maintain employment. Donny's second-grade teacher suggested that he be retained but his mother felt that his poor progress was due to his frequent changes of school.

Donny's mother is aware that her son has

will take a long time before Donny will be able to accept himself.

Donny's mother is afraid that he will never be able to return to the regular classroom. He is now mainstreamed for music, art, and physical education classes. She is happy that the school is able to arrange this because she thinks it helps Donny to feel more like the other kids. Donny's mother is also concerned that he won't be able to function normally in society as he grows older. She wants him to be able to get a job and to take care of himself. Most of all, she wants her son to be happy.

Points for Consideration

■ There are extreme differences in the functioning levels of children labeled mentally retarded, but despite their differences, all mentally retarded persons can learn.
■ Parents of mentally retarded children are very concerned that their children develop skills that will enable them to live independently in the future.

Common Misconceptions

■ *Mentally Retarded Children Are Brain Damaged; That's Why They Are Mentally Retarded.* While in some cases it is known or suspected that brain damage is the cause of mental retardation, in the majority of cases the causes are unknown and are not discovered until the children enter school.
■ *Mentally Retarded Children Look Different than Normal Children.* While some cases are accompanied by physical defects, the majority are mildly retarded and look like typical children. (While Heather's physical appearance is characterized by the features of Down's syndrome, Donny is not visibly different from other boys his age.)
■ *Once a Child Is Classified as Mentally Retarded, He or She Will Always Be Mentally Retarded.* Children are classified as mentally retarded on the basis of their measured intellectual ability and ability to

entered a class for the educable mentally retarded. She does not, however, consider her son to be mentally retarded and never refers to the class in that way. She gets angry when others at school refer to it as "the class for the retarded." She doesn't want Donny to think he is mentally retarded.

Donny's mother is pleased that his class is much smaller than the ones he had been in before. A lot of individualized teaching occurs in the special class and everything appears to go much more slowly, which is better for Donny. Donny spends a lot of time in reading groups, math groups, and specific skill groups. He seems to be getting much more out of school now. He was totally lost in the regular class; now he is not forgotten or ignored. Donny's mother goes over his lessons with him every evening and helps him with his homework. He is proud of himself when he learns something new, no matter how small it is.

Donny still has a very low opinion of himself, which really worries his mother. He was constantly failing in school before he was moved to the special class and she had heard that the other children called him names and made fun of him. He didn't understand what was going on, so he often simply refused to speak to anyone. Things seem better now but his mother thinks it adapt to and interact appropriately within their social environment. Both of these abilities can be enhanced by education and training, and improved levels of either or both could remove the child from the classification of mental retardation.

■ *Persons Who Are Mentally Retarded Should Be in Institutions*. Some persons with severe or profound retardation require the custodial care of institutions. Most mentally retarded persons, however, can be educated to function successfully within the community.

■ *Persons Who Are Mentally Retarded Are Also Mentally Ill*. Mental illness occurs in persons of all levels of intelligence. Mental illness is not a condition of all who are mentally retarded any more than it is a condition of all who are intellectually average or gifted.

DEFINITION

The rules and regulations accompanying PL 94–142 define mental retardation as ". . . significantly subaverage general intelligence functioning existing concurrently with deficits in adaptive behavior and manifested during the developmental period which adversely affects a child's educational performance" (*Federal Register*, August 23, 1977, p. 42478). Many disciplines have contributed to the definition of mental retardation, including medicine, education, psychology, and sociology. Although there is some overlap among these definitions, few identified as mentally retarded meet the criteria established by all disciplines (MacMillan, 1977). In Figure 13-1 only those few persons represented by the shaded area would exhibit the problems and meet the definitional criteria of all perspectives.

FIGURE 13-1 Overlap of definitions of mental retardation from different disciplines. (Adapted from MacMillan, *Mental Retardation in School and Society.* Boston: Little, Brown, 1977,

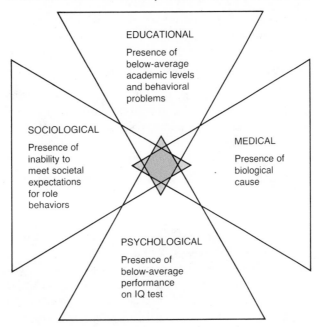

In order for children to be identified as mentally retarded their adaptive behavior as well as intellectual and academic abilities must be assessed.

The definition of mental retardation utilized in PL 94–142 is essentially the widely accepted one formulated by the American Association on Mental Deficiency (AAMD) (Grossman, 1973). It refers to three areas of concern: the psychological—"significantly subaverage general intellectual functioning"; the sociological—"deficits in adaptive behavior"; and the educational—"adversely affects a child's educational performance." It does not refer to the medical aspects nor to the suspected cause of mental retardation.

General Intellectual Functioning

Intelligence tests give a psychometric perspective of mental retardation. Whether a person performs within the gifted, normal, or mentally retarded range depends on the position of that individual's score within the normal distribution of scores. This normal distribution is derived by testing an appropriate sample of people in a given population and computing the mean score and standard deviation. In a distribution of IQ scores, the average score is referred to as the *mean*. The relative distance above or below the average score is measured in terms of a statistical concept—the *standard deviation*. Using standard deviations, one can predict what percentage of IQ scores can be found above or below a particular score. Suppose mental retardation referred to those who scored one standard deviation or more below the mean (as was, in fact, formerly the case). Then, many more people would be classified as mentally retarded (and fewer as normal) than if the IQ score requirement for mental retardation were two or more standard deviations below the mean. Figure 13-2 depicts the percentage of IQ scores falling in the classification of mental retardation using different standard deviation cutoffs.

Determination of the range of scores or categories that will define intelligence

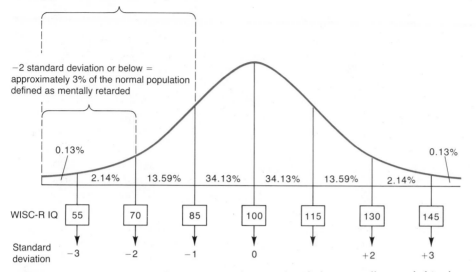

FIGURE 13-2 Comparison of percentages of scores classified as mentally retarded in the normal distribution based on WISC-R IQ cutoff scores of −1 and −2 standard deviations.

as falling within the mean average, gifted, or retarded level is thus dependent upon deciding what percentage of the population should be defined as part of the various classifications. In order to change the number of persons (percentage of the population) defined as mentally retarded, it is necessary to change the IQ score requirement.

Currently, to be classified as mentally retarded, a person must score two or more standard deviations below the mean on a standard test of intelligence. (This means a Weschler Intelligence Scale for Children-Revised (WISC-R) IQ score of 69 or below or a Stanford-Binet Intelligence Scale IQ score of 67 or below.) Also, the condition must be detected before age 18, during the developmental period, and must include below-average performance in adaptive behavior.

Adaptive Behavior

Adaptive behavior, according to the AAMD, refers to a person's ability to perform in the areas of social responsibility and self-sufficiency relative to what is expected by his or her social, cultural, and age groups. Since these expectations vary for differing age groups, deficits in adaptive behavior will vary at different ages, as follows (Grossman, 1973, pp. 11–12):

During infancy and early childhood in:

1. Sensorimotor skills development
2. Communication skills (including speech and language)
3. Self-help skills
4. Socialization (development of ability to interact with others)

During childhood and early adolescence in:

5. Application of basic academic skills in daily life activities
6. Application of appropriate reasoning and judgment in mastery of the environment

7. Social skills (participation in group activities and interpersonal relationships)

During late adolescence and adult life in:

8. Vocational and social responsibilities and performances

In order to judge skills in personal responsibility and independent functioning, several scales have been developed for measuring adaptive behavior. One of the most widely employed is the AAMD's Adaptive Behavior Scale (ABS) (Nihira, Foster, Shellhaas, and Leland, 1969).

Persons who have sufficiently impaired adaptive behavior may be classified as mentally retarded, according to the AAMD, even if they score intellectually as much as ten IQ points above the cutoff point (which is more than two standard deviations below the mean).

Most public school educators have come to recognize the fallibilities of intelligence assessment techniques and do accept the limitations of IQ scores. Relatively few, though, have had much experience with tests designed to measure adaptive behavior. In a sense, the use of adaptive behavior for determining eligibility for special education services for the mentally retarded is an idea whose time has come. Unfortunately, it yet lacks the technology to implement it adequately.

PREVALENCE

Determining the prevalence of mental retardation is hindered by lack of consensus over definition, as is the case with other exceptionalities. While 3 percent has been the traditional estimate of the number of mentally retarded persons in the United States, the actual number may be closer to 1 percent (MacMillan, 1977). If the IQ score were the sole criterion of mental retardation, using the normal distribution of test scores, 2–3 percent of the population would be counted as retarded. However, some investigators have suggested that if the additional criterion of adaptive behavior were applied, closer to 1 percent of the population would be considered mentally retarded (Mercer, 1973).

Just under one million children, ages 3 to 21, were reported to the Bureau of Education for the Handicapped (BEH) in 1978–79 as needing services for the mentally retarded. Since the figure of 915,635 is significantly less than the 1.5 million estimated in 1975, the prevalence rate, using both the IQ and adaptive behavior criteria of mental retardation, may well be under the traditionally accepted 3 percent figure.

CLASSIFICATION OF MENTAL RETARDATION

The AAMD classifies persons with mental retardation into four categories based on the degree of severity, as determined by assessments of general intellectual functioning (IQ) and level of adaptive behavior. These four are: mild, moderate, severe, and profound. The corresponding Weschler Intelligence Scale IQ score ranges are: 55 to 69 IQ for mild; 40 to 54 IQ for moderate; 25 to 39 IQ for severe; and below 25 IQ for profound. The expected levels of adaptive behavior in each category vary with the person's age and the behavior context of concern (i.e., educational, vocational, maturational). For example, at school age the mildly retarded child can be expected to learn academic skills to approximately a sixth-grade level. The profoundly retarded child, however, may require total care and be unable to profit from self-help training.

From an educational perspective, mental retardation can be classified into three degrees of severity: educable, trainable, and custodial. Although there is some overlap, the school systems' classifications correspond to the AAMD roughly as follows: educable—mild (although educable includes those persons at the upper level of AAMD's moderate category); trainable—moderate (except for the upper portion of AAMD's moderate level) and severe; and custodial—profound. Figure 13-3 compares the AAMD and the school systems' classifications based on IQ levels.

The majority of mentally retarded persons (approximately 85 percent) are only mildly retarded. Most of these cases are attributed to environmental factors related to socioeconomic status. With special education and vocational and social training such children often are able to blend into the normal population as adults, thus losing the mental retardation label. However, persons exhibiting more severe levels of mental retardation will have larger degrees of developmental delay.

Mildly Mentally Retarded

The majority of children classified as mildly or educable mentally retarded (EMR) are usually normal in appearance with no pathological signs of disease or injury. They may well be able to excel in nonacademic school activities but fail in learning academics. As all children, they are individuals with unique differences and characteristics. What they have in common is that they come to school

FIGURE 13-3 Comparison of classifications based on IQ scores used by the AAMD and school system.

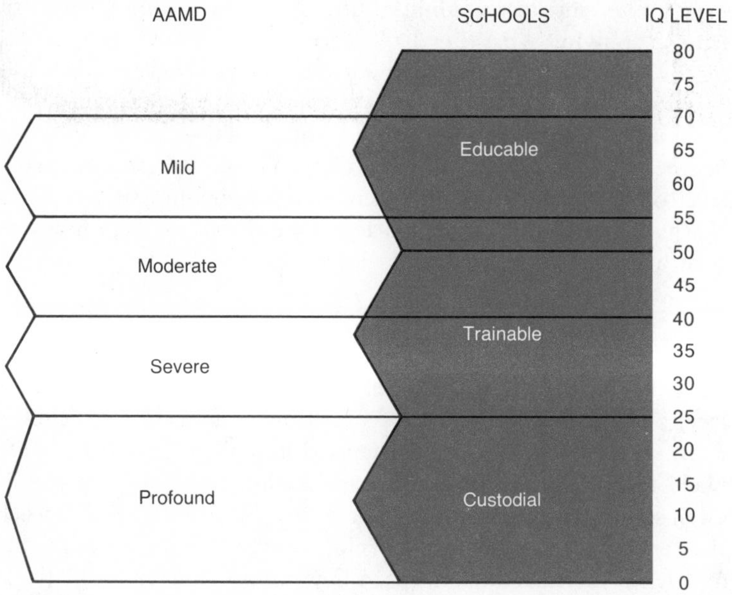

unprepared to participate successfully in learning activities. Most struggle, are retained or considered for retention, and are finally referred for assessment and possible qualification for special educational services. By that time, many of these children exhibit emotional and/or behavioral disturbances due to constant frustration and failure to live up to the expectations of teachers, parents, and peers. Although the research evidence is mixed, there does seem to be a tendency for these chidren to harbor negative self-images (Robinson and Robinson, 1976).

There is a wide diversity in the academic and behavioral performance of children classified as educable mentally retarded. Nonetheless, these children usually have a higher frequency of problems in certain areas of learning. In particular, they tend to have deficits in memory, ability to pay attention, verbal communication, motivation, ability to generalize, and in understanding similarities and differences (Smith, 1974; Neisworth and Smith, 1978).

By high school graduation time, these youth may have reached sixth- or seventh-grade level in academic subjects but some may be able to attain only a second-grade level of achievement. Most will have the skills to obtain jobs and to maintain themselves independently within the community.

Moderately Mentally Retarded

Persons with **moderate mental retardation** may score 50 or below on a standardized intelligence test and have accompanying deficits in adaptive behavior skills. Intellectual deficits or lags in short-term memory, incidental learning, and the abilities to generalize, to pay attention, and to discriminate may be present. These youngsters are not usually ready for formal academic instruction until the early teens (Litton, 1978).

In general, persons classified as moderately mentally retarded share many characteristics with those in the normal population. They have the same need for love, vary in physical appearance, have differing personality traits, and possess the potential to learn. They are, however, different in terms of learning; they have limited intellectual ability, difficulties in working with abstract ideas, problems in applying what they have learned to new situations, problems in communication, problems in establishing interpersonal relationships, problems caused by emotional immaturity and underdeveloped self-concepts. Their learning capabilities include self-help skills, social and personal skills, and, to a limited degree, academic skills. In later years, most of these youngsters can reach the level of occupational employment under noncompetitive, sheltered conditions; most will need some continued assistance with their daily living skills throughout their lives.

Severely and Profoundly Mentally Retarded

Severely and profoundly retarded persons are those functioning at an IQ level of 35 or below. They are sometimes referred to as "sub-trainable, dependent, retarded, or life-support level children" (MacMillan, 1977). They are also likely to be afflicted with additional visible handicapping conditions. They are often so limited that they may not be capable of intelligible speech, be able to use abstract concepts, be able to develop academic skills, be able to walk, or be able to care for their personal needs. They can profit from highly specific training on an individual (usually one-to-one) basis.

There are many behavioral traits unique to the severely and profoundly handicapped person. These persons often fail to respond when visually, auditorialy, or tactually stimulated. High rates of self-stimulation are prevalent (e.g., continually rolling a ball on the floor or rocking). This behavior is repetitive and seems to bear no relation to environmental stimuli. At times, self-stimulation can take the form of self-destructive behavior (e.g., biting hands and banging head).

Since these exceptional people generally fail to respond to physical or visual prompts, their development rate is often quite slow. Educational assessment is difficult because of this slow response rate; therefore, very close observations must be made if proper intervention and educational programming are to be prescribed. Another significant characteristic of this population is their limited

Learning for the severely and profoundly retarded is dependent upon the teacher's ability to individualize instruction.

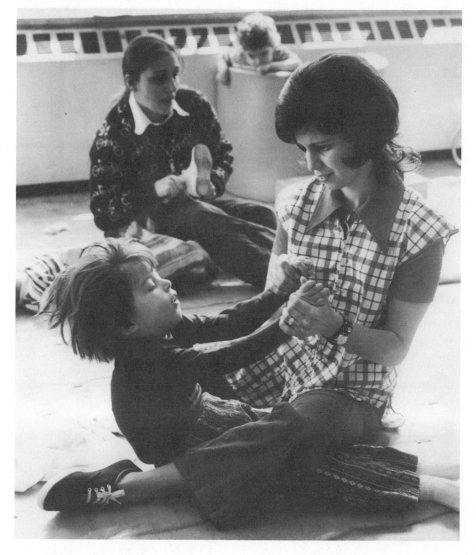

language ability. Communication is extremely difficult for them and therefore instruction in social skills and interactions with peers is hampered. Furthermore, their limited self-help skills in such areas as grooming, toilet training, and feeding restrict their social interactions.

A severely or profoundly retarded adolescent or adult may reach the level of being toilet trained, able to eat with a spoon or fork, capable of throwing a ball to hit a target, and able to hop and skip, understand simple verbal directions, and participate in simple play and games (Anderson and Greer, 1976).

Profoundly retarded persons have been defined as those with an IQ below 20 and complex physical handicaps, including poor reflexes. A degree of functional impairment distinguishes the severely mentally retarded from the profoundly retarded. At the preschool age, severely retarded youngsters demonstrate poor speech, inadequate social skills, poor motor development, and great difficulty in learning self-help skills. The profoundly retarded preschooler may not even be able to respond to stimulation from the environment and is developmentally delayed in all areas. Many profoundly retarded youngsters need constant nursing care (Neisworth and Smith, 1978).

The methods of assessing handicapped children are not as precise as they should be. Therefore, those responsible for training and educating retarded youngsters should not assume a specified degree of retardation and the accompanying specified limits to learning. Only when the instructional program has been appropriately conceived and implemented and the child has not progressed, should firmer hypotheses be made about the child's ultimate capabilities. Early training with these children has achieved remarkable success, which traditionally, under less appropriate instructional conditions, was not possible.

Additional Handicapping Conditions

The most prevalent conditions affecting the mentally retarded population in either a partial or severe form are speech disorders (55 percent), lack of fine motor control of upper limbs (44 percent), nonambulation (42 percent), lack of gross motor control of upper limbs (42 percent), and behavioral/emotional disorders (42 percent) (Conroy and Derr, 1971).

CAUSES OF MENTAL RETARDATION

The AAMD utilizes the following nine categories for grouping the causes of mental retardation: (1) brain disease; (2) infections and intoxications; (3) metabolism or nutrition; (4) trauma or physical agent; (5) unknown prenatal influence; (6) gestational disorders; (7) chromosomal abnormality; (8) environmental influence; and (9) psychiatric disorder. In this text, these causes have been grouped into three roughly distinct categories: genetic causes, physical/environmental causes, and psychosocial causes (Robinson and Robinson, 1976). There is, of course, a significant interaction among the various causes of mental retardation so that, in practice, it is often difficult to pinpoint the factor that is most responsible for the retardation, even after extensive assessment; in at least 75 percent of the cases of retardation, nothing can be confidently pinpointed as the cause of the condition (MacMillan, 1977, p. 79).

Chromosomal anomalies include having too many chromosomes, too few chromosomes (or parts of chromosomes), or the exchange of parts from different pairs of chromosomes. Estimates indicate that of every 150 to 200 children born in the United States, one has a major anomaly and a greater number have minor defects. The relationship of these errors to mental retardation is a subject for continuous genetic research.

DOWN'S SYNDROME   The most common chromosomal defect resulting in mental retardation was first described by Seguin and has been named Down's syndrome after Langdon Down, an English physician. His report in 1866 described retarded children who had facial characteristics thought to resemble those of

Although Down's syndrome children have special educational needs, their basic needs are similar to those of all children.

Mongoloid people (hence the older, less acceptable term, "mongoloid child"). Children with Down's syndrome have been identified by more than 50 characteristics. Not all of these, of course, appear in all Down's children. In addition to the facial appearances, which often include epicanthic folds at the corners of the eyes, a small, low-bridge nose, and protruding tongue, Down's syndrome children frequently are characterized by short hands, feet, and trunks. They also exhibit poor muscle tone, abnormalities of the heart, and chronic upper respiratory infections.

There are three types of Down's syndrome. The most common (occurring in 95 percent of the cases) is referred to as **Trisomy 21** and is the result of an accidental formation of an extra chromosome. These children have three number 21 chromosomes instead of the expected two. While research has not isolated the cause of Trisomy 21, the most significant factor is the mother's age when the child was conceived. As mothers reach 40 years of age and beyond, the incidence of Trisomy 21 increases dramatically. Women under the age of 30 have only a 1-in-1500 chance of giving birth to a Down's syndrome child, while the chances of those over 35 increase to 1 in 280, and those over 40 to 1 in 130.

Translocation accounts for only about 4 percent of the cases of Down's syndrome. This condition refers to an extra number 21 chromosome which has broken and become attached to another chromosome. This kind of chromosomal anomaly can be passed on from parent to child. **Mosaicism** is very rare and occurs accidentally in early cell division resulting in an extra chromosome in some cells, but not in others. These children may only have a few of the Down's syndrome characteristics because all their cells do not have the extra chromosome.

Children with Down's syndrome have widely varying intellectual levels, usually in the 30 to 50 IQ range. Sometimes, however, they score IQs in the 60s or 70s.

INHERITABILITY   Another factor contributing to mental retardation is inheritability. The combination of genes received from the child's parents may have the effect of developing a central nervous system that functions at lower ranges of normal when compared to those of the total population. The issue of how much of a child's IQ and academic performance is due to environmental factors and how much is due to hereditary was a topic of hot debate during the 1970s. It is unlikely that the complex issues involved will be completely understood within the near future. Generally, though, it is agreed that inherited abilities (nature) and environmental factors (nurture) work together in complex ways to determine children's observed abilities. The higher percentage of mildly mentally retarded children from some minority groups has caused some observers to propose theories of ethnic and racial differences in inherited intellectual ability. Others strongly disagree with this proposition and argue that inferior environments are the culprit. For a detailed review of the nature/nurture controversy related to mild mental retardation, see MacMillan (1977).

PHENYLKETONURIA (PKU)   **PKU** is a genetically transmitted metabolic disorder that results in the body's inability to metabolize phenylalanine, a necessary protein naturally found in the human body. In most states, screening programs for PKU are required shortly after birth in the hospital. Since the early 1960s, dietary treatment programs have been used to prevent brain damage and resulting severe or moderate retardation. This diet limits foods rich in protein. Recently a dietary product, Lofenalac, has been marketed to aid parents in maintaining a proper diet for their PKU children. PKU persons who go untreated will have intellectual levels below 50 IQ and may exhibit destructive and noisy psychotic episodes (Robinson and Robinson, 1976, p. 98). PKU is just one of several other metabolic disorders that have been identified as causes of mental retardation.

Physical/Environmental Causes

RUBELLA (GERMAN MEASLES) Children whose mothers contacted **rubella** early in their pregnancies have been found to be afflicted with a number of birth defects (e.g., glaucoma, congenital heart disease, hearing impairment), including retardation in all degrees, from mild to profound. Since the late 1960s researchers have discovered that the incidence of rubella and the consequent mental retardation of babies born to rubella mothers can be lowered significantly through vaccination.

Rh FACTOR Before the 1970s, conditions resulting from **Rh incompatibility** affected 20,000 infants each year. The Rh factor may be a natural component of the mother's blood, and will cause no harm to the mother. However, the antibodies that form in the mother's blood against the Rh factor destroy the red blood cells of the fetus. This condition, called erythroblastosis fetalis, can lead to the baby's mental retardation, seizures, spastic muscle movements, and death. It is not a problem with the birth of the first child unless the mother's blood has been sensitized previously. Treatment involves blood transfusion in the uterus or at birth, but prevention is possible by injection of the afflicted mothers with Rh gamma globulin after their first pregnancy. This procedure prevents formation of the dangerous antibodies and thus prevents the retardation of future children in the majority of cases.

LEAD POISONING Lead poisoning (an especial health hazard to children) can lead to seizures, cerebral palsy, mental retardation, and death. Poisoning from eating flakes of lead-based paint from the walls of older homes is a common manner in which children of urban areas contract lead poisoning. In some areas where lead pipes are used in water systems, lead has been found in the drinking water.

Other physical/environmental causes of mental retardation include severe malnutrition of the mother during pregnancy or of the baby during the first six months of life; prematurity and low birth weight; infections, such as meningitis and encephalitis; radiation; head injuries; and inappropriate use of drugs and chemical substances. Physicians and scientists have recently discovered a condition found in the babies of alcoholic mothers which has been termed "fetal alcohol syndrome." It is uncertain just how much alcohol pregnant women can drink without endangering the fetus. Nonetheless, the U.S. Food and Drug Administration (FDA) has attempted to have warning labels similar to those on cigarette packages placed on alcoholic beverage containers.

The importance of maternal nutrition to the development of healthy children was supported by the courts in the late 1970s. A young mildly retarded woman successfully brought a malpractice suit against her mother's obstetrician and was awarded several thousand dollars. The physician had placed the young woman's pregnant mother on a strict diet of polished rice and fruit, eliminating all milk and vitamins. The resultant deficiency in needed calories and proteins was found to be harmful to the normal growth of the unborn baby. Chronic malnutrition is also harmful to the normal development of young children during critical periods of brain growth.

Psychosocial Causes

Many mildly retarded pupils come from economically disadvantaged homes. Children raised in environments lacking in experiences and stimulation that promote cognitive growth are often classified as mildly mentally retarded. These children frequently lack exposure to language development models and the stimulation of the senses and perception needed for development of thinking skills. Heber's Milwaukee Project (discussed in Chapter 6) highlighted the importance of early environmental experiences on the subsequent intelligence levels of children.

Because of limitations of time and space, this section represents only a brief overview of the varied causes of mental retardation. For more detailed descriptions, the reader is referred to Robinson and Robinson (1976) and MacMillan (1977).

IDENTIFICATION

Children classified as educable mentally retarded are typically so identified due to their failure to perform academically. Their poor school performance may be accompanied by some behavioral difficulties as well. Their early development (e.g., learning to walk and talk) may have closely met normal developmental expectations. Although identified as handicapped upon reaching school age, they may well be considered normal by observers in their everyday out-of-school environment.

Moderately retarded persons are usually identified at birth or in early childhood. About 20 to 30 percent have Down's syndrome and thus may be readily identifiable by their physical appearance. The young preschool child is not ready for academic instruction and may exhibit degrees of self-stimulating and/or self-abusive behavior. Poor articulation and difficulty with oral expression are common; the moderately retarded child's speech and language development proceeds along the typical sequential path but at a slower-than-normal pace.

The severely and profoundly retarded are usually detected at birth or before the first year of life. From the beginning, the severely retarded child has interruptions in development. Possible signs of severe or profound retardation are physical abnormalities, extremely low birth weight, or a low score on the **Apgar Scale** (a test of reaction given to infants immediately after birth). Primarily, a physician, usually a pediatrician, identifies the severely and profoundly retarded.

EDUCATIONAL PROGRAMMING

Traditionally, children classified as educable mentally retarded have been served through placements in special, self-contained classes. However, because of increasing concern over program ineffectiveness and desires to avoid the stigma of the EMR label, many schools have begun exploring suitable alternative placements. These options, in keeping with the mandate to provide special educational services in the least restrictive environment, include placement in regular classes, a resource room program, a part-time special class, and a full-time special class. Selection of one or some combination of these options should ideally be based on the strengths and weaknesses of the child's academic and behavioral skills. In reality, though, situational variables must often be considered. These include the number of pupils enrolled in the class, the regular teacher's attitude toward special children, the teacher's skill in teaching exceptional children, the availability of support personnel to advise and consult with the regular teacher, and the availability of community resources (Payne, Polloway, Smith, and Payne, 1977).

The basic goal of education for the **trainable mentally retarded (TMR)** is to prepare the retarded child to live as normal a life as possible. In the past, education has stressed sensory-process training and watered-down versions of normal school curricula. Recently, however, more systematic, behaviorally oriented approaches have been used successfully. Such curricula, based on behavioral objectives, have a built-in mechanism for ongoing evaluation and assessment.

Since the goal of any education program for the mentally retarded is to enable these persons to function in society, emphasis with advanced youth is on vocational preparation. Typically, TMR programs include sheltered workshops where handicapped persons can learn job skills and be trained for employment in a protected environment. Most sheltered workshops make contracts with various local industries to complete piecework assignments. Those persons who can learn to produce in work settings at a high enough level for employment in private industries are assisted in community job placements. The State Bureau of Vocational Rehabilitation aids the mentally retarded of all levels in developing vocational skills for regular, competitive employment.

Traditionally, the severely and profoundly handicapped have been placed in institutions. A minority of this population has been kept at home, totally dependent on their families for complete care. The education of the severely retarded was generally neglected because it was assumed that they could not learn. Recently, however, it has been demonstrated that with systematic training, the severely and profoundly mentally retarded can be taught to care for their basic needs, to stop inappropriate, antisocial behaviors, and to perform basic work activities. These students make small changes slowly, and they require intensive individualized instruction and care.

Educational Groupings

Traditional groupings in a public school EMR program have followed roughly the regular school grade levels. At the primary level, readiness for learning activities predominates, while at the intermediate level, the basic skills of reading, writing, and arithmetic are the core of the curriculum. At the secondary level, personal/social adjustment and occupational skills are stressed. High school work/study programs are available in many school districts where pupils can gain on-the-job experience under supervision.

Educational programs for the moderately mentally retarded, or trainable mentally retarded, typically encompass four levels of instruction: primary, intermediate, prevocational, and vocational. The class sizes vary from 6 to 15 pupils per teacher with the smaller ratios usually at the lower age levels. Short instruction periods and frequent changes in activities are utilized in scheduling instruction at all age levels.

Many educators believe that the moderately mentally retarded are best served through special classes and separate facilities and special day schools aside from the regular public schools. This belief is based on the multiple complexity of the retardeds' handicaps (often including physical disabilities), their need for specialized services, and the large sizes of typical regular school classes (Arkans and Smith, 1974). Despite this traditional belief, integration of trainable retarded classes into public schools occurs with increasing frequency across the country. For example, in one community, an adult TMR class was integrated into the public high school. The integration was carefully planned and a group of student volunteers was trained to help orient the new students to the school and assist as aides in the classroom. Although the class remained as a segregated group within the building, the move was considered a success. In another school district, a group of TMR youngsters was moved from their special school for the retarded to a regular elementary school building. Later, the social interactions between the TMR children and the nonretarded pupils were studied (Ziegler and Hambleton, 1976). The study showed that the nonretarded children did not single out or make fun of the TMR pupils. Also, it was found that when nonretarded children were introduced into the group, less aggression and more helping behavior occurred. In still other school districts, several classes of children with severe learning problems are grouped as centers within various elementary school buildings ("Where Every Child Is Educable," 1972). This approach combines some of the benefits of the special school with those of a regular school setting. Another variation is to locate the special school near a regular public school so that some integration of activities and programs can occur.

Curriculum

Programs for the mentally retarded typically stress personal, social, and vocational skills along with the basic academic skills required to live independently in our society. One such program, called the **persisting life problems curriculum**, exemplifies this emphasis (*The Slow Learning Program in the Elementary and Secondary Schools, Cincinnati Public Schools Curriculum Bulletin #119*, 1964; *State of Ohio Curriculum Guide for Moderately Mentally Retarded Learners*, 1977). This approach recognizes that there are a large number of lifelong problems with which all persons are faced as they mature. In order to be considered successful in adjusting to the changing environment, people must be able to deal with these broad problems. The mentally retarded can benefit by special attention to these problems through education. The persisting life problems taught at each level of the program (primary through secondary) are depicted in Table 13-1. Under each of these problem area groupings, objectives have been prepared for each of six developmental levels based on mental age (from a mental age of 1½ to a mental age of 8 years and older). An example of the persisting life problem curriculum from the area, "developing the ability to travel," at level V (mental age of eight) is provided in Table 13-2.

Using this curriculum guide, or others like it, the learner's IEP can be readily developed based on comparative assessment of his or her current status and func-

Persisting Life Problem Curriculum Areas — TMR

1. Developing the ability to communicate
2. Managing one's body
3. Understanding oneself and others
4. Fulfilling home and work responsibilities
5. Developing the ability to travel
6. Developing leisure time alternatives

Persisting Life Problem Curriculum Areas — EMR

1. Learning to keep healthy
2. Learning to live safely
3. Learning to communicate ideas
4. Learning to be a responsible citizen
5. Learning homemaking and family living
6. Learning to understand oneself and to get along with others
7. Learning to understand the physical environment
8. Learning to appreciate, create, and enjoy beauty
9. Learning to use leisure time wisely
10. Learning to earn a living
11. Learning to manage money
12. Learning to travel and move about

tioning. Groupings, individualized learning activities, and regroupings can be devised based on individual students' needs in the various persisting life problem areas. In recent years, it has been found that many children classified as TMR can, with the proper instruction, advance to levels where more academic learning is possible. For example, many pupils have been placed in EMR classrooms after having developed reading and/or math skills beyond the functional academic level expected in the TMR classes. It is quite likely that as future teaching materials, techniques, and curricula become increasingly sophisticated, more and more moderately mentally retarded children will learn to read. The shift in emphasis in a child's program, however, should be done on an individual basis.

TABLE 13-2   Persisting Life Problem Curriculum

Developing the Ability to Travel

A. Getting Around
   1. Plans and goes on outings with friends (for example, makes plans to go to a movie with a friend)
   2. Requests assistance as needed when using public transportation (for example, timetables, cost, proximity to destination)
   3. Follows correct procedure for using public transportation (for example, purchases token, boards proper bus, finds own seat)
   4. Routinely extends proper courtesies when visiting another (for example, rings doorbell or knocks, arrives on time, calls before stopping by, avoids visiting during mealtime)
   5. Considers time of day and conditions in planning travel (for example, traveling during rush hour takes longer, walking in the rain requires certain clothing for protection and visibility)

Source: State of Ohio Curriculum Guide for Moderately Mentally Retarded Learners, Ohio Department of Mental Health and Retardation, 1977.

This would prevent neglect of those areas in the TMR curriculum (e.g., self-help skills) that are extremely important in preparing for the child's future well-being.

Early intervention is essential to the education of the severely and profoundly handicapped because early intervention programs have been found to lessen the effects of severe and profound handicaps later in life (Hayden and McGinness, 1977). After completion of an early intervention program, the child progresses to an intermediate level grouping. This step was not traditionally available for many youngsters due to lack of classes. Prior to recent legislation, few educational programs existed for this group of children. Their inability to communicate and absence of toilet training prohibited these children from enrollment in either special public programs for the educable mentally retarded or the county/community programs for the trainable mentally retarded. Today, however, these programs develop sensory motor skills, physical mobility, coordination, self-care skills, language, and improved social behavior in severe and profoundly retarded children. Table 13-3 presents suggested areas of program emphasis at this level.

Although more is being revealed about the potential of these children each year, current long-term goals include skill development in self-feeding, dressing, and toileting. Most of these children are not expected to achieve independence as adults.

TABLE 13-3 Areas of Program Emphasis for School-Aged Severely and Profoundly Retarded Persons

Sensorimotor Development

A. Identifying shapes, colors, sizes, locations, distances
B. Identifying sound patterns, locations, tonal qualities, rhythms
C. Identifying textures, weights, shapes, sizes, temperatures
D. Identifying familiar aversive and pleasant odors

Physical Mobility and Coordination

A. Practicing ambulation
B. Overcoming obstacles, walking on ramps and stairs, running, skipping, jumping, balancing, climbing
C. Using playground equipment
D. Participating in track and field events

Self-Care Development

A. Self-feeding with spoon and cup, eating varied diet, behaving appropriately while dining
B. Removing garments, dressing and undressing with supervision, buttoning, zipping, and snapping
C. Drying hands and face, partially bathing
D. Toilet scheduling, indicating need to eliminate, using toilet with supervision

Language Development

A. Recognizing name, names of familiar objects, and body parts
B. Responding to simple commands
C. Imitating speech and gestures
D. Using gestures, words, or phrases

Social Behavior

A. Requesting personal attention
B. Playing individually alongside other residents
C. Using basic self-protective skills
D. Playing cooperatively with other residents

Source: Adapted from Luckey, R. E., and Addison, M. R. "The Profoundly Retarded: A New Challenge for Public Education," *Education and Training of the Mentally Retarded* 9 (October 1974), 125.

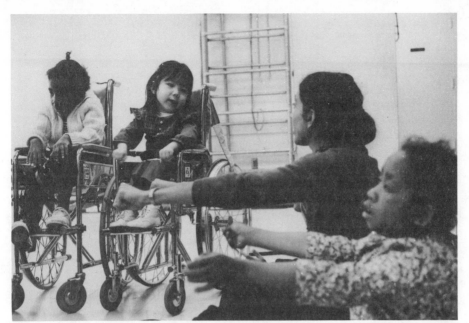

Many severely retarded children have multiple handicaps that require early intervention by a multidisciplinary team.

Limitations of the Severely and Profoundly Retarded

In recent years, determining the learning limits for the severely and profoundly retarded has been an area of considerable debate. The heterogeneity of this population has been recognized; the utilization of various systematic, precisely devised instructional programs has produced levels of learning beyond what had previously been achieved. Marc Gold, University of Illinois, has developed specific methods to teach complex tasks to severely mentally retarded persons. His technique, based on task analysis, has been used successfully to teach complex tasks to severely and profoundly retarded persons at Dixon State Hospital. His response to the question, What do you do when a learner doesn't learn? is, Try another way. This response characterizes the philosophy of his program and is the title of a series of training films currently in use to help others teach severely mentally retarded persons ("It Can Happen! Programs that Are Working Right Now," 1978).

Some maintain that ". . . the anticipated levels of learning among the severely and profoundly retarded are such that the general inclusion of academic instruction in their curriculum is unwarranted" (Burton and Hirshoren, 1979, p. 599). Others argue that our knowledge of the area is growing rapidly and it is too soon to predict what can and cannot be learned by these persons. They argue that "attempts at setting limits regarding severely and profoundly retarded handicapped learners encourages the risk of developing yet another self-fulfilling prophecy in the field of special education" (Sontag, Certo, and Button, 1979, p. 605).

Certainly the advances in language training, the exciting development of prosthetic devices, and the possibilities of using alternative means of communication

Participation by mentally retarded persons in community recreational activities is one aspect of the normalization process.

all point optimistically to new possibilities for the severely and profoundly mentally retarded. Going beyond self-help skills, behavioral analysis has been utilized successfully to develop language training programs for the severely retarded in numerous cases (Snyder, Lovitt, and Smith, 1975). Some severely retarded persons have even been taught to read using the Ball-Stick-Bird Reading Program (Fuller, 1974). With this method, persons learn to form the letters of the alphabet using three basic figures: a circle (ball), a line (stick), and an angle (bird). The formation of words with the first few letters learned provides meaning and motivation for reading; rote learning is avoided.

Role of Teachers

Teachers working with mentally retarded children should have a thorough knowledge of child development, an understanding of the theory and application of behavioral modification with children, instructional skills in the areas of self-help, and basic academic teaching skills in reading and arithmetic.

In the next few years the issue of which placement options can best serve children with mild mental retardation should become clearer. It is currently clear, however, that the majority of mildly handicapped pupils (including those identified as EMR) will find their least restrictive environment to include participation in the regular school program for at least part of each school day. Complete segregation in self-contained classrooms is recognized as inappropriate for the mildly retarded. It follows that every teacher in the school should be familiar with procedures for working with mentally retarded pupils.

As more mentally retarded are integrated into the regular public school program, it is important that "the false image of the tireless, admirable, wonderful *special education* teacher should be destroyed. Images built on false premises are damaging and destructive. We can destroy the illusion and build a true picture by remembering that we are teachers, not martyrs, that our pupils are children, not monsters" (Mays, 1972, p. 51).

SUGGESTIONS FOR TEACHERS   Currently, with a broader spectrum of program alternatives for children with mild retardation now existing, the prominent instructional method is diagnostic/prescriptive teaching (DPT). No matter what combination of administrative groupings and/or techniques are utilized, there are some basic considerations in teaching these children that cannot be ignored. Kolstoe (1976, p. 27) has outlined six principles for educators to keep in mind when presenting learning tasks to retarded pupils:

1. The tasks should be uncomplicated. The new tasks should contain the fewest possible elements, and most of the elements should be familiar so the child has very few unknowns to learn.
2. The tasks should be brief. Brevity assures that the child will attend to the most important aspects of the task and not get lost in a sequence of interrelated events.
3. The tasks should be sequentially presented. The learner should be able to proceed in a sequence of small steps, each one built upon previously learned tasks.
4. Each learning task should be the kind in which success is possible. One of the major problems to be overcome is that of failure proneness. This major deterrent to learning can be effectively reduced to success experiences.
5. Overlearning must be built into the lesson. Drills in game form seem to lessen the disinterest inherent in unimaginative drills.
6. Learning tasks should be applied to objects, problems, and situations in the learner's life environment. Unless the tasks are relevant, the learner has great difficulty in seeing their possible importance.

Special Olympics

The **Special Olympics** provides sports competition and physical training for mentally retarded persons around the world. The Special Olympics is a year-round program of physical training and competition, at the community, state, and national level. Many volunteers, nationally known sports personalities, local interested citizens, and involved college students work to implement these activities. The training and competition build physical skills, but they also help the mentally retarded participants develop self-confidence and poise. Before each game the participating athletes recite the Special Olympic oath, "Let me win, but if I cannot win, let me be brave in the attempt." Much about life is learned at Special Olympics events, by the volunteers as well as by the athletic participants themselves.

SPECIAL CONSIDERATIONS AND ISSUES

Many issues are involved in the education of mentally retarded persons. A few of these special considerations, including prevention, normalization, and sex education, are discussed in the sections that follow.

Prevention of Mental Retardation

The precise cause (or combination of causes) for particular cases of mental retardation frequently remains unknown. What is known, however, is that many preventative procedures exist for lessening the effects and prevalence of mental retardation. Some of these are:

- Provide proper nutrition to pregnant women and young children.
- Discourage pregnancy and birth during the adolescent years.
- Provide adequate prenatal medical care, including testing, immunizations, and treatment. (Rubella, iron deficiency, anemia, diabetes, Rh blood incompatibility, and overexposure to radiation are all conditions that can be treated, thus preventing possible resultant mental retardation.)
- In particular instances **amniocentesis** should be used to confirm possible disabling conditions while the child is still in the mother's womb. In this medical procedure, samples of the amniotic fluid, which surrounds the child in the mother's uterus, are analyzed. The presence of Down's syndrome and other chromosomal anomalies can be detected. Once a birth defect is determined, the parents can discuss the possibility of abortion. In the future, however, after amniocentesis confirms defects of the fetus, intrauterine surgery may be used to correct the problem in certain cases (Menolascino, 1979).

Normalization

Normalization is a concept adopted in the United States from observations of its establishment in Scandinavian countries. Normalization is the process of ". . . making available to the mentally retarded patterns and conditions of everyday life which are as close as possible to the norms and patterns of the mainstream of society" (Nirje, 1969). **Deinstitutionalization**, the removal of mentally retarded persons from large institutions and their placement in settings more akin to "normal" living conditions, is a major part of this process. A review of one study that assessed deinstitutionalization found that of 440 mentally retarded persons reintegrated into the community, 88 percent successfully adapted and 12 percent returned to the institution. The largest percentage of the successfully reintegrated persons—47 percent—lived in group homes (Gollay, 1977).

As the deinstitutionalization movement grows, it becomes less likely that the mentally retarded will be institutionalized simply because they fit a particular diagnostic category or are an embarrassment to their families. Instead, more and more mentally retarded persons will live in community-based settings.

In order to provide the reeducation necessary to ease the transition of the retarded from large public institutions, smaller regionally based institutions with cottage-type living arrangements have been developed. These regional centers also serve to prevent institutionalization, except in cases where that is most appropriate. These centers typically provide a full range of services, including occupational and physical therapy, vocational skill development, functional aca-

demic training, community socialization skill training, leisure time activity training, and mobility training. They also provide some facilities for **respite care**
when the families of the retarded need temporary assistance because of vacation,
illnesses, and so forth.

LIVING IN THE COMMUNITY   An increasing number of hostels, group homes,
halfway houses, and other similar arrangements now exist to provide 24-hour
residential services to those mentally retarded persons able to live and work with
some level of independence in the community. These facilities supplement other
community settings—such as foster homes, nursing homes, and respite care
homes—in providing the mentally retarded and developmentally disabled more
normal settings for living. Many mentally retarded persons living in these
community-based settings are classified as moderately mentally retarded.

In group homes, usually three to ten retarded persons live together under the
supervision of house parents. In some states smaller regional institutions have
been built to serve as transitional units in the deinstitutionalization process.

Despite the wider array of community-based programs, normalization has
proven to be difficult to implement. In many cases deinstitutionalization and
subsequent normalization have been unsuccessful because of too little preparation
of the community citizens, lack of enough appropriate facilities, and inadequate
follow-up. Too often, persons with moderate mental retardation were pushed
out of institutions into communities without the requisite follow-up guidance
and supervision services. Others, who had been functioning successfully in semi-
independent arrangements under the supervision of staffs from group homes or
halfway houses, were allowed to go off on their own to blend into the community in the name of normalization. In many cases, deterioration in their personal
care, work production, and general levels of living indicated that they were not
able to blend in when, in fact, they had under the previous arrangements. The
search for the least restrictive environment is not an easy one.

Sex Education

Sex education in public school curricula is a highly controversial subject. Some
educators believe that sex education is more properly a function of the family and
that teaching about sex at school only serves to further expand the school's
already enormous responsibility for children's development. Others believe that
since the family often does a poor, inaccurate job of teaching about sex, it's better
if the schools assume the responsibility.

For the mentally retarded, a thorough program of sex education is very important. Mentally retarded children are likely to have less access to accurate information about sex, are more susceptible to myths and fears about sex, are more likely
to be victimized or exploited sexually, and often require special efforts to achieve
appropriate social behavior; thus, sex education is imperative for them. Sex education programs for mentally retarded children include explanations of bodily
functioning, the mechanics of reproduction, and social behavior and responsibilities. Some suggestions for teaching about sex to mentally retarded children include the following (Kempton, 1975[b]):

■ Determine that the children are aware of their disabilities and the resultant
limitations.

- Determine the level of learning that each child is capable of and plan your teaching accordingly.
- Determine what knowledge they already have, including their emotional readiness for learning about sex.
- Determine your own level of knowledge about sex and your readiness to discuss the various subjects involved.
- Use the pupils' words until they learn the proper terminology about sex. Let them know that your words should be used as much as possible.
- Since these children may be too shy to ask many questions, don't wait for questions—give explanations.
- Make explanations direct, honest, and concrete.
- Have the pupils repeat the explanations and correct any miscommunications.
- Do not scold the children for giggling or showing other signs of anxiety or embarrassment; allow them to relieve their tension in this manner but remind them that this is a grownup subject.
- Use concrete, tangible, and visual materials whenever possible.
- Avoid lecturing and moralizing, which often blocks communication.
- Teach boys and girls together whenever possible.

In addition to these guidelines, the teacher should be aware of the importance of involving parents in the teaching of human sexuality. Because of their opportunity to observe children in social interactions, "the teacher can be a welcome ally to parents in helping them make an overall evaluation of their children's social sexual behavior" (Kempton, 1975[a], p. 534).

SUMMARY POINTS

- The AAMD definition of mental retardation specifies significantly below-average functioning in general intelligence and adaptive behavior. Adaptive behavior is defined as the person's ability to demonstrate social responsibility and self-sufficiency relative to the expectations of his or her social, cultural, and age groups.
- Although prevalence figures for mental retardation are difficult to determine (as is the case with other exceptionalities), recent counts tend to set the prevalence rate well below the traditional figure of 3 percent.
- Causes of mental retardation are many and varied. The AAMD categorizes the causes under nine headings, which in this text were abstracted into three headings: genetic causes, physical/environmental causes, and psychosocial causes.
- Down's syndrome, the most common chromosomal anomaly, usually results in moderate levels of retardation. Trisomy 21, translocation, and mosaicism are three types of Down's syndrome, which is much more prevalent in births to older women.
- Physical/environmental causes of mental retardation include rubella, Rh factor, lead poisoning, malnutrition, prematurity, and low birth weight. Psychosocial causes often stem from economically deprived environments.
- The AAMD classifies persons who are mentally retarded into four categories: mildly, moderately, severely, and profoundly. Educators have traditionally classified mentally retarded persons as educable, trainable, or custodial.

■ The majority of mentally retarded persons (85 percent) are classified as mildly retarded, with no one specific cause identified. Mildly retarded children are more like normal children than they are different and they usually are not identified as mentally retarded until they enter school.

■ While moderately retarded children have difficulties with abstract learning, problem solving, and other intellectual challenges, they are much like non-retarded people. They have different personalities, different physical appearances, different levels of learning potential, and different needs for love.

■ Severely and profoundly mentally retarded persons frequently have accompanying physical and medical problems, including poor speech and motor control and obvious physical differences. Communication and locomotion may be very difficult for them, and they are limited in self-help skills.

■ Early intervention programming is extremely important for the welfare of mentally retarded children, especially those with moderate, severe, and profound levels of retardation.

■ Educational programs for both the mildly and moderately retarded pupils often follow a curriculum similar to the persisting life problems approach, which focuses on personal, social, vocational, and basic academic skills required for living independently in society.

REVIEW QUESTIONS

1. How could common misconceptions concerning the retarded influence the manner in which people relate to them, teach them, or think about them?
2. Why is the two-part AAMD definition of mental retardation important for the identification, placement, and treatment of mentally retarded persons?
3. Describe some of the characteristics of a child with Down's syndrome.
4. What measures could be taken by individuals and/or society to prevent mental retardation?
5. Given some of the problem learning areas of mentally retarded pupils, what are some things that teachers could do to enhance their effectiveness in teaching these children?
6. What problems would be encountered if the mentally retarded persons in your hometown community were normalized? In your university community? What could you do to assist in this normalization movement?

HUMAN SEXUALITY AND MENTAL RETARDATION —
A CONTINUING CONTROVERSY

As our society becomes more aware of the rights of the individual, it also becomes more sensitive to the needs and the rights of handicapped persons. In recent years, society's responsibility of guaranteeing handicapped persons their basic human rights has become evident. This objective is not so simple, however; issues concerning individual rights and human sexuality of the mentally retarded have resulted in a controversy over sterilization. Long-held beliefs that the mentally retarded were not entirely human, and did not have human sexual needs, included the attitude that they should not be allowed to marry and have children. As late as 1979, over 30 states outlawed the marriage of mentally retarded persons.

Before the mid-twentieth century, many states permitted institutionalized mentally retarded persons to be sterilized without their consent. Using data from the University of Minnesota's Social Welfare archives, from personnel of the San Francisco Association for the Retarded, and other sources, a Richmond, Virginia, newspaper, the *Richmond Times-Dispatch*, has estimated that between 60,000 and 70,000 mentally retarded persons were sterilized in state hospitals by 1980. Some states even routinely sterilized mentally retarded persons about to be released into society. In recent years, successful litigation by and on the behalf of retarded citizens has made government officials, state institutions, physicians, and hospital staffs less willing to perform sterilizations without valid consent. Also, the federal government has excluded the use of federal Medicaid funds for sterilization of mentally retarded persons.

Historically, the mentally retarded have frequently been targets for sexual exploitation, and many are not able to adequately assess the consequences of their behavior. In addition, the capacity of many mentally retarded persons to raise children may be questioned. In a study of the marital status of 54 mentally retarded parent/couples, however, it was found that with one exception their children's physical and psychological needs were being appropriately cared for. These mentally retarded persons had previously lived at the Elwyn Institute in Philadelphia.

Many parents of mentally retarded adults argue that sterilization would permit their children to live in a less restrictive environment, since they would not have to restrict their movements to forestall sexual exploitation. Some parents have opted for institutionalization—a *more* restrictive environment—when they found it too difficult to provide the close supervision that they believed was necessary. Many parents of retarded children elect sterilization for their child after weighing their desires for their children to lead a normal family life against the ever-present concerns of victimization, the necessity of terminating pregnancies later, and their child's abilities to cope. They feel they are acting in the best lifelong interests of the child (Mills, 1977).

In the early 1970s, the National Association of Retarded Citizens (NARC) conducted a national survey of attitudes toward marriage and sterilization of the mentally retarded. Subjects of this survey were NARC members, mostly parents with retarded children. Sixty percent of those surveyed indicated their belief in the right of mentally retarded persons to marry. Most of the subjects indicated that they favored sterilization of their children upon marriage. These parents of mentally retarded persons apparently believe that "the ability to develop and sustain a meaningful marital relationship may be possible, while the ability of retarded individuals to function as parents may not be present" (President's Committee on Mental Retardation, 1975, p. 50).

Some mentally retarded couples contemplating marriage have opted for vasectomies for the husband or other sterilization procedures. Their decisions have been based on their understanding of the complexities of child raising and of the difficulty they would encounter in providing intellectual stimulation for their children.

Since the mid-1970s, federal government regulations require that the principle of informed consent be followed in sterilization procedures conducted in programs regulated by the federal government. **Informed consent** requires that the mentally retarded person ". . . voluntarily and knowingly consent to the sterilization after having been given a fair explanation of the procedure, a description of its discomforts and risks, a description of its expected benefits, an explanation of alternative methods of family planning, assurance of answers to questions and assurance of the person's freedom to change his or her mind at any time prior to the sterilization" (President's Committee on Mental Retardation, 1975, p. 50).

Some states have established review procedures to determine what action should be taken regarding sterilization of retarded persons when informed, understanding consent of the person is not possible. These procedures typically invoke the consent of the court, the permission of the parent or legal guardian, and the agreement of a group of physicians following their complete review of the case. Such methodology allows for differences in procedures to be followed under differing circumstances.

Perhaps the question, Is it a basic human right to have children?, should be answered differently depending upon the situation. Deciding whether to sterilize a mentally retarded adult capable of living independently in the community is one matter. Deciding to sterilize a severely or profoundly retarded person incapable of raising a child and perhaps even unable to be aware of the child's existence is another matter entirely. In the former case it would seem appropriate that the decision-making process take the rights and feelings of the retarded individual as the most crucial concern. In the latter case, where informed consent is impossible, the rights of the parents and/or society would seem to weigh the most heavily.

DISCUSSION POINTS

1. Think about the influence of your parents on your own sexuality. Do they in fact influence or have a right to influence your decisions regarding marriage and the possibility of sterilization? Would their influence (or decision-making role) change if you were mentally retarded?

2. Some argue that if the government or society has the authority to sterilize specific people without their consent under certain conditions, then the right to sterilize *any* member of society under certain conditions is likely in the future. What do you think?

SUGGESTED READINGS

Chinn, P. C., Drew, C. J., and Logan, D. R. *Mental Retardation—A Life Cycle Approach*. St. Louis: C. V. Mosby, 1975.

Hutt, M. L., and Gibby, R. G. *The Mentally Retarded Child, Development, Education and Treatment*, 3rd ed. Boston: Allyn and Bacon, 1976.

Kolstoe, O. P. *Mental Retardation, An Educational Viewpoint*. New York: Holt, Rinehart, and Winston, 1972.

MacMillan, D. L. *Mental Retardation in School and Society*. Boston: Little, Brown and Company, 1977.

Robinson, N. M., and Robinson, H. B. *The Mentally Retarded Child*, 2nd ed. New York: McGraw-Hill, 1976.

14

CONTENTS

THE LEARNING DISABLED

Many children and youth with learning problems have not been given the educational assistance they need to succeed in school. Many have not been identified as learning disabled and thus have not been provided with an appropriate special educational program. Instead they have been referred to as lazy, obstinate, dull, lacking confidence, or unmotivated, and have been allowed to withdraw either physically or psychologically from their school experience. For many the result has been a life of frustration, unfulfilled desires, unfulfilled potential, and continuing failure to achieve. Being unsuccessful as a learner in school leads to a lowering of self-esteem, which often carries over into adulthood.

The term learning disabilities (LD) was originally promoted by Samuel A. Kirk at a conference for persons supporting the Fund for Perceptually Handicapped Children. In his speech Kirk recommended that the use of terms like **brain damaged** *be curtailed because of their educational uselessness, but he used the term "learning disabilities" to describe children with learning problems in the areas of language, communication, and reading, and the label stuck. Those attending the convention organized the Association for Children with Learning Disabilities (ACLD) which was later changed to the Association for Children and Adults with Learning Disabilities. This group of parents and professionals dedicated itself to developing programs for children and youth with learning disabilities. Although perhaps unintentionally, a new special education category was born (Wiederholt, 1974).*

ZACHARY

Zachary's parents express a great deal of confusion, anger, and frustration when discussing their battle to understand his learning problems and the public school system. They feel guilty for not having investigated the reasons for his failure sooner.

When Zack was a preschooler, he suffered chronic ear infections and tonsillitis, which resulted in a hearing loss. Zack recovered from the loss but his language development was delayed. His nursery school teacher suggested that because of immaturity he stay one more year in the program before attending kindergarten. Zack's parents did not understand and sent him to kindergarten with his agemates. The kindergarten teacher recommended that Zack repeat kindergarten or attend a special first-grade class. The parents were surprised at this recommendation because they felt kindergarten was not challenging enough for Zack. So when the family moved to a new school district, the first-grade teacher was not informed of the recommendation.

Although the school system was new, Zack's problems remained. He repeated first grade and after a few weeks in second grade was placed in a small class for slower learning pupils. During this year, his father read a magazine article about learning disabilities and requested testing by the school psychol-ogist. Another family move to a different state interrupted the evaluation process before a diagnosis could be made.

Zack's mother arranged for testing with the mental health clinic in their new location before contacting the school. Although Zack was eligible for a third-grade learning disability placement, he was not enrolled for several months because of a waiting list. His parents were pleased with the classroom as it provided Zack with remedial help for the first time. It seemed that an answer had finally been found. Unfortunately, however, the school only provided tutors after the third grade, so the following year Zack returned to a regular classroom.

Not only was Zack suffering academically, but also socially. His only friend was a boy who, like himself, had a low self-concept. His parents were so concerned about the effects of peer pressure that they sent him to live with his grandmother who was always sympathetic and supportive. Later, they decided that Zack should be with the family and brought him back.

Zack is now in eighth grade and the family sees no relief for his learning problems. They attend the special education conferences and sign his educational program just to get him out of as many regular classes as possible. They feel they have been given many empty

promises by Zack's teachers. No one is willing to make adjustments in the curriculum. The parents fear that the school will recommend vocational high school, which neither they nor Zack want. Zack's future remains uncertain. The only thing they feel they can count on is the continued hassle with school officials over appropriate help for Zack.

In reviewing Zack's school experience, both his parents wish that the professionals had been more open with them. Even if at certain times no one knew exactly what was wrong, the parents would have appreciated a more honest appraisal of Zack's problems instead of vague recommendations. They believe Zack has a right to be happy and to be an independent person. Zack's parents feel that he needs to be made more aware of his strengths and weaknesses and that their expectations are not unrealistic.

Zack's social and educational problems are confounded by lack of communication between his parents and school. Early in Zack's school career, his teachers recognized a problem, but his parents refused to believe it. Now that Zack's parents have accepted the fact that he will not "grow out" of his learning disability, they cannot find a satisfactory educational program.

Points for Consideration

■ Zack's parents have intense feelings of frustration, anger, and guilt regarding their son's difficulties, their own role, and the role played by the schools.

- Zack's learning difficulties began at a relatively young age but intensified as time passed with no, or ineffective, intervention. As Zack became older his learning problems affected him socially and emotionally as well.
- Zack's parents seem to have resigned themselves to relating with the school in a perfunctory manner as a means of coping with the constant hassle.

Common Misconceptions

- *Learning-Disabled Children Only Have Problems in Learning.* Because of failure and frustration with school, many learning-disabled children develop poor self-concepts and other emotional problems that inhibit success in their daily lives.
- *Children with Learning Disabilities Will "Grow Out" of Them When They Reach Adolescence.* Many LD pupils need special educational services over many years; the practice of dropping these services after the elementary grades, as was the case in Zack's school, is inappropriate.
- *All Learning-Disabled Children Are Brain Damaged.* Although the behavior of some learning-disabled children demonstrates signs of possible brain damage, this diagnosis is very difficult to prove conclusively.

DEFINITION

One of the critical decisions faced by professionals and parents concerned with learning disabilities programs is in defining what learning disabilities are and which children should be so considered. To some, the term learning disabilities implies a broad range of children who, for whatever reason, exhibit difficulty in school learning. Some include children who lack motivation, who are culturally different, who are slow to learn, who are emotionally unstable, or whose learning is handicapped by conditions not classifiable under other special education categories (e.g., mental retardation, orthopedic handicaps, blindness). Such broad definitions are almost synonymous with underachievement in school. Some people believe that if a child is underachieving, he or she must be learning disabled and therefore should qualify for a special education program for learning-disabled pupils.

Others, however, believe that learning disabilities is a more specific handicapping condition. They point out that there are many reasons why children underachieve in school, with learning disabilities being only one of them. Still others believe that many school problems are caused primarily by poor teaching and instructional methods rather than some problem within the child. Pupils who have not received appropriate academic instruction should not be classified as learning disabled. If a child's learning problems can be overcome with different types of academic instruction, that child should not be considered learning disabled.

Although not completely resolving the contradiction just raised, a definition for nationwide use has been established as a result of PL 94–142 (*Federal Register*, December 29, 1977, Part 3):

"Specific learning disability" means a disorder in one or more of the basic psychological processes involved in understanding or in using language spoken or written which may manifest itself in an imperfect ability to listen, think, speak, read, write, spell or to do mathematical calculations. The term includes such conditions as perceptual handicaps, brain injury, minimum brain dysfunction, dyslexia and developmental aphasia. The term does not include children who have learning problems which are primarily the result of visual, hearing or motor handicaps, of mental retardation, of emotional disturbance, or of environmental, cultural or economic disadvantage.

The federal rules and regulations pertaining to the evaluation of children with learning disabilities further indicate that a multidisciplinary evaluation team may determine that a pupil has a learning disability. Such a determination may be made if a severe discrepancy is found between the child's actual and expected levels of achievement based on the child's age and ability. The areas in which a severe discrepancy between ability and achievement may be found are as follows (*Federal Register*, December 29, 1977, Part 3):

1. Oral expression
2. Listening comprehension
3. Written expression
4. Basic reading skill
5. Reading comprehension
6. Mathematics calculation
7. Mathematics reasoning

The multidisciplinary evaluation team can identify a learning disability by whatever method it chooses. Often, though, the deficit is based on a discrepancy between the child's performance on intelligence tests and scores on standardized achievement tests. Many professionals have cautioned against undue reliance on this discrepancy criterion. Stephens (1977) points out that the practice of using discrepancy scores in identifying learning disabilities has not yet been proven as a valid technique. He questions the predictive validity of discrepancy scores and indicates that with such a technique we are making several assumptions (p. 37):

1. Intelligence is a stable characteristic
2. Measures of intelligence and achievement are valid for that population
3. Both measures are reliable
4. The discrepancy score's reliability is high

The current definition clearly states what types of learning problems are not included as specific learning disabilities. If they are the primary reasons for the **severe discrepancy** between the pupil's achievement and ability, they cannot be used to indicate the presence of a learning disability.

In order for a child to qualify for special educational services for learning disabilities, the multidisciplinary team must find:

■ The child evidences learning difficulties in at least one of the seven previously mentioned areas
■ A severe learning achievement problem
■ The primary reason for the severe discrepancy between achievement and ability cannot be other handicapping conditions or sociological factors

PREVALENCE

Because a number of different definitions of learning disabilities exist, in the past the number of children counted as learning disabled has varied greatly. Some reports indicated that as many as 30 percent of the school-age population were learning disabled; other reports suggested only a 1 percent prevalence. Prior to PL 94–142, most special educators assumed a 3 percent prevalence of learning disabilities. Census data collected by BEH in 1978 indicated that just under 2 percent of the children from 3 to 21 years were learning disabled. (This apparent drop in prevalence, from 3 percent to under 2 percent, may be due to the implementation of PL 94–142 and is discussed later in this chapter.)

CAUSES

Determining the causes of learning disabilities is a complex and difficult task. The wide variety of conditions under the definition and the complex interactions of various suspected causes compound the problem. Research into these causes and the nature of their interaction is very much needed.

Three Types of Causes

Causes of children's learning problems are thought to fall into one of three general categories:

1. Inadequate learning environments (home and/or school); and not related to **organic problems**
2. Minor organic difficulties exaggerated because of poor environment
3. Significant inherent organic problems that handicap children's ability to learn, despite appropriate environment.

Children who fall into the first category are handicapped because of inadequate instruction, which could be the result of poor teaching, poor curricula, poor physical conditions, and/or poor attendance at school. Motivational factors associated with poor parental or professional attitudes toward education in general or toward the school or the child in particular may also play a role. Their learning problems may also be caused by family disorganization, emotional disturbance, or social adjustment difficulties. Many children in this category need specific educational and/or medical intervention to correct the inadequacies of the school program; to provide remedial education appropriate for those who are culturally, environmentally, or economically disadvantaged; to provide special education appropriate for children with emotional or behavioral disorders; or to provide them with diets of appropriate nutritional value.

Children who fall into the second category include those who are suspected to exhibit maturational lags as well as those who seem to be affected by vitamin deficiencies, allergic reactions, or too much refined sugar or additives such as artificial food coloring and flavoring in their diets. Children whose learning disorders are biochemically based could be assisted by environmental changes such as vitamin therapy, treatment for their allergies, or removal of sugar and additives from their diets. Concomitant special education programs are needed to remediate skill deficits that formed before the causative agents were recognized and removed.

Slingerland (1971) has identified a group of children having specific language disabilities as a result of lags in the normal maturational patterns of learning to use language. If left unrecognized and not provided with appropriate education, these children's problems will intensify and likely will be even more difficult to overcome as a pattern of failure in learning communication skills is established.

The third category includes children who suffer from organic damage, brain injury, neurological handicaps, or central processing disorders. Despite adequate instruction in school, proper diets, appropriate motivation, and emotional support, they continue to suffer learning problems. Problems of brain functioning may be genetically based, caused by prenatal conditions, illness, or injuries in the child's early years, a critical time in the development of the central nervous system.

Although learning disabilities have historically been closely related to the presence of neurological problems, more and more professionals are recognizing the complex interaction of causes that affect learning disabilities. The issues involved in determining whether a child is learning disabled and thereby qualifies for special educational services, are not easy to settle. Teachers, parents, and members of evaluation and placement teams must work cooperatively to resolve these issues and make the decisions that significantly improve the lives of these children.

CHARACTERISTICS

Included in the definition of specific learning disabilities is the idea that a learning disability is a disorder of one or more psychological processes involved in the understanding of, or use of, spoken or written language. Other terms commonly used to describe disorders in psychological processes (which are included as synonymous in the legal definition) include **dyslexia**, **minimum brain dysfunction**, brain injury, perceptual handicaps, and developmental aphasia.

Since the acceptance of the term learning disabilities in 1963, a variety of terms have been used by professionals from several disciplines to identify children thought to be learning disabled. A task force sponsored by the federal government and the Easter Seal Research Foundation published a report in 1966 that outlined the ten most frequently cited characteristics of learning–disabled children (Clements, 1966, p. 13). In order of frequency used, these characteristics are:

1. Hyperactivity
2. Perceptual–motor impairments
3. Emotional lability
4. General coordination deficits
5. Disorders of attention (distractability, perseveration)
6. Impulsivity
7. Disorders of memory and thinking
8. Specific learning disabilities:
   a. reading
   b. arithmetic
   c. writing
   d. spelling
9. Disorders of speech and hearing
10. Equivocal neurological signs and electroencephalographic (EEG) irregularities

Perceptual Motor Impairments

Children with perceptual motor impairments have problems identifying or reproducing information they receive through their senses. They have difficulty discriminating symbols. They may exhibit **reversals** in their printing or drawing. Their ability to accurately reproduce or copy information received visually or auditorily is poor. Examples of perceptual problems include difficulty in identifying the letters of the alphabet, reading the printed page from left to right, staying on the line when printing or writing, and copying and drawing basic shapes. Synonyms for this type of impairment include dyslexia, perceptually handicapped, and neurologically impaired. Deficits in perception are distinct from sensory deficits (e.g., blindness, deafness). The presence of sensory deficits would eliminate children from eligibility for special education for learning disabilities but would qualify them for other special education programs (e.g., programs for the visually or hearing impaired).

Disorders of Attention

Children with attention disorders have difficulty focusing and maintaining their attention for appropriate lengths of time (i.e., short **attention span**) and in changing the focus of their attention from one task to another at appropriate times. **Distractability**, or inability to concentrate on the task at hand because of extraneous stimuli, and **perseveration**, or repeating a task over and over, are related conditions. These problems can be manifested in many ways, including not being able to come to order when the class is ready to begin the lesson, inability to stay on task while completing a seatwork assignment, and continuing to do addition problems on page 2 because page 1 contained addition problems, even though the directions on page 2 call for subtracting.

Disorders of Memory and Thinking

Children with memory and thinking disorders have difficulty remembering information over long or short periods of time. Some of the many ways in which memory problems can be observed include noting children unable to remember basic information about themselves and their family (e.g., address, phone number, date of birth, etc.), children who seem to have forgotten words they learned just the day before, or children's responses to problem situations that seem to indicate an inability to generalize and apply what they have learned from other situations.

Disorders of Speech and Hearing

Children with these communication disorders may have difficulties in articulation, in organizing words and phrases in sentences, and in following standard grammatical structures. Ways in which these problems are manifested include use of incorrect sounds for letters or mispronunciation; use of the same phrases over and over, indicating a lack of breadth and variety in a child's language development; and the inability to form the plural of nouns.

Hyperactivity

Hyperactivity refers to continuous activity or involvement in some motor process. Children's hyperactivity can be displayed in many ways, including constant tapping of finger, foot, pencil, etc. on the desk, difficulty remaining seated,

Prior to planning an appropriate program for learning-disabled students, teachers must be skilled in administering and interpreting a variety of assessment tools.

or constant moving from one task or activity to another or from one part of the room to another for no apparent reason. The term for the opposite condition, **hypoactivity**, is sometimes used to refer to children who are lethargic.

Emotional Lability

Some children have not developed their social/emotional skills to levels appropriate for their ages. These children may adjust to change slowly, become frustrated easily, get upset and throw tantrums when they do not get their own way, and have very little confidence.

General Coordination Deficits

These problems may be demonstrated as clumsiness or awkwardness in activities requiring fine and/or gross motor skills. These children may have difficulty running, skipping, bouncing or throwing a ball, using a pencil or scissors, and using buttons or zippers.

Impulsivity

This characteristic refers to children's extremely quick responses or reactions made without the benefit of adequate forethought to possible consequences. Impulsive behavior includes consistently choosing the first answer from a series of response choices or running into a busy street to retrieve a ball without stopping to look.

Specific Learning Deficits in Basic Academic Subjects

Children with academic learning disorders may show a wide disparity in their achievement in various subjects (e.g., they may be a year above grade level in math and three years below grade level in reading comprehension). Terms used to describe academic learning problems include dyslexia (problems in reading), dysgraphia (problems in writing), dyscalcula (problems with arithmetic), reading disability, and word blindness.

Equivocal Neurological Signs

Questionable or uncertain indications of neurological problems are referred to as equivocal; that is, no direct evidence or proof of neurological damage is manifest. Poor concentration and attention, distractability, poor motor coordination, impulsivity, and hyperactivity may be **equivocal indicators** of neurological disorders. Recording children's brain waves with an **electroencephalogram** (EEG) has often been used to determine the normality of children's brain functioning. Irregularities in EEG profiles, however, have generally failed to discriminate between children with learning disabilities and those without and thus are used cautiously in diagnosing learning disabilities.

The variety of terms characterizing the behaviors and processes of learning disabilities reflects the multidisciplinary concern for children with these disorders. The current trend in education is to focus more on the child's observable behavior and utilize terms that describe that behavior. This trend contrasts with the application of terms that attempt to pinpoint the causes of the learning disability (e.g., brain damaged) when the causes cannot be positively identified.

IDENTIFICATION AND PLACEMENT

Federal rules and regulations outlining evaluation procedures for children suspected of having handicapping conditions require that a multidisciplinary team conduct the assessments. This team should include a teacher or other specialist knowledgeable in the field of the suspected handicap. Federal guidelines require a team evaluation for children suspected of being learning disabled. Included on the team are (*Federal Register*, December 29, 1977, p. 65083):

1. The child's regular teacher; or
2. If the child does not have a regular teacher, a regular classroom teacher qualified to teach a child of his or her age; or
3. For a child of less than school age, an individual qualified by the state educational agency to teach a child of his or her age; and
4. At least one person qualified to conduct individual diagnostic examinations of children, such as a school psychologist, speech-language pathologist, or remedial reading teacher.

Other professionals may also serve on the team when appropriate. Figure 14-1 depicts the interdisciplinary nature of the learning disabilities team.

Observations

Moran (1978) recommends that classroom teachers become keenly aware of which pupils are responding to their instructional programs and which are not.

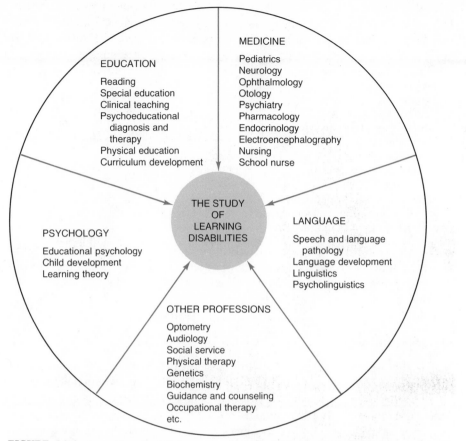

FIGURE 14-1 Learning disabilities as an interdisciplinary field. (From J. W. Lerner. *Children with Learning Disabilities*, 2nd ed. Boston: Houghton-Mifflin, 1976, p. 5.)

Those pupils not working at grade-level expectations should be investigated more thoroughly by the teacher and perhaps referred to the multidisciplinary team for further assessment. Once the child is referred, federal regulations require that another member of the team in addition to the regular classroom teacher "shall observe the child's academic performance in the regular classroom setting" (*Federal Register*, December 29, 1977, p. 65083). While observing children suspected of being learning disabled, Bryan and Bryan (1978) recommend that professionals utilize a framework that assesses at least these four areas of overall functioning:

1. General physical appearance
2. Physical movement
3. Attention, or a lack thereof, to various tasks and events
4. Interpersonal relationships with others in the class

Good practice dictates that these children be observed in other settings (e.g., the playground; the cafeteria; and physical education, art, and music classes) as well as in their relationships with a variety of adults and peers.

Many school districts are instituting screening programs to identify children who may display a high risk of developing learning or behavioral disorders. A variety of commercially prepared screening programs is available for this purpose (see Wallace and Kauffman, 1978, for detailed descriptions of these materials). Despite these programs, teachers should be aware of child development norms so that they may act on possible learning problems. Wallace and Kauffman (1978, pp. 106–110) have outlined nine areas of children's behavior that teachers can observe, assess, and use to judge whether or not children exhibit learning problems, as follows:

1. Low self-concept
2. Disturbed relations with peers
3. Inappropriate relationships to teachers, parents and other authority figures
4. Other signs of social-emotional problems
5. Deficits in speech and language
6. Disordered temporal relationships
7. Difficulties in auditory and visual perception
8. Poor quantitative reasoning and computational skill
9. Deficits in basic motor skills

For observational data to be effectively utilized by multidisciplinary teams, common agreements on the reporting of observable behaviors and on standardizing language must be reached by various professional disciplines (Stephens, 1977).

Medical Findings

Physicians, generally concerned with causes, can assist greatly in identifying children with learning problems or disabilities. While "conventional neurological examinations frequently reveal little that is clearly abnormal in children with learning disabilities" (McCarthy and McCarthy, 1969, p. 12), medical information is necessary to the multidisciplinary team. It is certainly not mandatory to label children or to hypothesize as to a medical cause in order to teach them. But the complexity of possible causes of learning disabilities requires that as many factors as possible relating to the child's condition be considered. Currently, even though "there is no precise and immediate translation of medical findings to specific teaching procedures" (Lerner, 1976, p. 66), medical treatment (e.g., drug therapy for hyperactivity) does interrelate with educational procedures. The same concept applies to a child being treated—there is not a "medical child" and a separate "educational/learning child."

Decisions and Reporting

Each member of the learning disabilities evaluation team participates in deciding the child's eligibility for special learning disabilities programs. Each signs the team's report, unless the member does not agree with the team's conclusions. In such a case, the dissenter must submit a separate report stating his or her own conclusions. The learning disabilities evaluation report must include this information (*Federal Register*, December 29, 1977, p. 65083):

1. Whether the child has a specific learning disability
2. The basis for making the determination
3. The relevant behavior noted during the observation of the child
4. The relationship of that behavior to the child's academic functioning
5. The educationally relevant medical findings, if any

6. Whether there is a severe discrepancy between achievement and ability that is not correctable without special education and related services
7. The determination of the team concerning the effects of environmental, cultural or economic disadvantage

The requirements of the report force the evaluation team to stay close to observable behavior (as opposed to using unproven hypotheses when stating a rationale for defining a child as learning disabled).

EDUCATIONAL PROGRAMMING

Recent years have witnessed a trend away from self-contained classrooms for educating children with learning disabilities and toward increases in tutorial programs, resource center programs, and consultation assistance combined with modifications of the child's program in the regular class. Most of these options attempt to offer the learning-disabled pupil a degree of both social and academic interaction with nonhandicapped peers. The ultimate aim is to reduce the time the learning-disabled child spends in the self-contained class, the resource room, or tutoring situation, and to increase the time the child spends in the regular school program. Even if the resource room teacher or the tutor provides the pupil with most of the coursework, the learning-disabled pupil will interact in the school's regular setting at some time. Therefore, teachers and administrators must be ready to modify regular school settings to more effectively serve these pupils.

Method of Instruction

There are several instructional methods currently used with learning-disabled children. The choice of method or combination of methods depends upon the teacher's or the school system's beliefs about the causes and definition of learning disabilities. Because learning problems within the current categorical definition of learning disabilities vary so widely, educational methods of preference are likely to remain diversified.

McCarthy and McCarthy (1969) describe five approaches traditional to educating children with learning disabilities: (1) perceptual/motor approaches; (2) developmental approaches in visual perception; (3) neurophysiological approaches; (4) linguistic approaches; and (5) diagnostic/remedial approaches. Historically, these provided education to children with particular types of problems.

With the rapid growth of learning disabilities research in the last 15 years, most learning disability programs can now be described as eclectic (Wiederholt, 1974). Educational personnel have, for the most part, drawn instructional ideas from a variety of traditional approaches in regular, as well as special education. The evolution of this eclecticism is not surprising in light of the fact that few school districts have the resources to operate several programs for the learning disabled, each designed for a specific condition. The use of carrels (or offices) in learning disabilities programs, for example, can be traced to the early pioneering efforts of Alfred Strauss (Strauss and Lehtinen, 1947) in teaching brain-injured pupils. Strauss recommended eliminating sights and sounds that might distract these children. Today, most rooms for instructing learning-disabled children could

The diversity of learning styles displayed by learning-disabled students requires individualized methods and materials.

certainly not be described as sparsely decorated (to reduce distractability). Many, though, have cubicles of some form available, at least as an option, for children who need a place to study with less distraction.

Many programs for learning-disabled children reflect the diagnostic/prescriptive teaching (DPT) approach, which is quite appropriate with the model used in implementing IEPs. The influence of behavioral psychology is also apparent in many learning-disability programs. Behaviorally stated objectives, target behaviors, reinforcers, behavioral management, and reward menus are common terms in the vocabulary of many teachers of the learning disabled. One highly effective application of the behavioral theory to teaching—referred to as **precision teaching**—has grown significantly over the last few years (Lovitt, 1978). This procedure utilizes direct, continuous recording of learners' behaviors to make timely decisions on introducing or modifying instructional strategies. Other programs like Stephens' (1977) Directive Teaching Instructional Management System (DTIMS) combine the principles of behavioral psychology and diagnostic/prescriptive teaching in order to teach the basic skills in arithmetic, reading, and social interaction.

Recently, Ross (1977) suggested that "learning disabilities are due to problems in the area of selective attention, and the frequently reported distractability, hyperactivity, and impulsiveness of learning disabled children are the results and not the causes of their problem" (p. 101). Various psychological research seems to indicate that children develop skills in selective attention at differing rates. Those children who lag behind in this development and thereby have difficulty learning can be helped by structured educational programs. Ross suggests that these programs be designed (1) to make the stimuli involved in learning the task more distinctive; (2) to reward the pupil for attending selectively to the appropriate learning stimuli; and (3) to teach the pupil appropriate strategies to use in responding to various learning tasks.

Ability Training versus Skill Training

Programs for learning-disabled children utilizing diagnostic/prescriptive teaching methods can be viewed as part of either of two distinct models of instruction—the **ability training** model and the task analysis model (Ysseldyke and Salvia, 1974). Those professionals advocating the use of ability training emphasize assessing weaknesses in individual abilities that serve as the underlying foundations for children's academic skills (e.g., perceptual/motor, visual perception, and psycholinguistic). Tests designed specifically to measure these underlying abilities have been constructed and the results are used to outline programs for remediation. It is anticipated that when the learning-disabled child's aptitude in the particular ability improves, his or her academic learning skills will also improve.

Those professionals advocating task analysis and **skill training** emphasize directly assessing the pupil's learning skill weaknesses (Stephens, 1977). Direct assessment methods (e.g., observation of the child performing the tasks in criterion-referenced tests) are used to pinpoint skill weaknesses. The child's sequential instructional program is then designed based on task analysis, and direct instruction to correct skill deficits follows.

Currently, the advocates of these two models conflict over the effectiveness of each other's approaches. The skill training (or task analytic) proponents seem to be proving the relative efficiency of their technique. Wiederholt (1974) reported that research conducted on the more traditional approaches (basically, the ability training models) had conflicting results. For the time being, it appears that direct skill training is the most appropriate.

Development of Secondary Programs

Parent and professional groups have recently begun to focus on the issues involved in secondary education for learning-disabled youth. For years concern has centered on detecting learning-disabled children at younger ages in order to correct their learning deficits and prevent later and possibly more severe problems. Currently the needs of these pupils, which often involve strong emotional motivational overlays and compensatory (as opposed to remedial) skill training, have been recognized.

Affective Education/Self-Concept Development

Most teachers of learning-disabled children recognize the significance of working with the social/emotional problems that often accompany school learning difficulties. Improving basic skills and increasing academic success through well-organized and implemented IEPs can go far to interrupt the failure cycle and initiate improved perception of self-worth. In addition, programs are available for heightening learning-disabled pupils' understandings of themselves and others and enhancing their social skills. The *Human Development Programs* (Palomores and Ball, 1974), *Developing Understanding of Self and Others (DUSO) I and II*

(Dinkmeyer, 1970, 1973), and *100 Ways to Enhance Self-Concept in the Classroom* (Canfield and Wells, 1976) are but a few of these resources.

Role of Teachers

Scholastic success of learning-disabled children depends upon the ability of their teachers and parents to individualize instruction to meet unique needs. The following guidelines assist teachers, parents, and administrators in working effectively to teach these children:

- Establish an atmosphere of success by looking for the positive things the child does and the progress he or she is making (no matter how small). Praise the child. Make the motto "catch the child being good" come alive in the classroom and in the school.
- Break down academic tasks and learning activities into smaller parts (task analytic approach) and then reward (praise) successful completion of each small step.
- Make learning as concrete as possible but do not assume too much. When in doubt about a choice among instruction techniques, select the more concrete rather than the abstract one.
- Encourage feelings of understanding and acceptance by recognizing that learning-disabled children do have the potential to change their behavior. Allow them to be responsible for tasks in the classroom and plan individual conferences with them to discuss their progress.

Individual conferences provide opportunities to outline and discuss academic and social goals for the day.

■ Use a variety of educational media (e.g., records, movies, tapes, television programs) to help learning-disabled students receive information, gain understandings, and produce assignments that might otherwise be impossible. Some schools have recorded various textbooks on audio-tape for pupils with reading disabilities, thus allowing them to keep up with and participate with students who can read the assignments. In secondary schools, some teachers have encouraged learning-disabled youth to tape their lectures, or they have provided an outline of the main points of the lecture. Others have permitted LD pupils to take tests orally, taping their answers or responding orally to a classroom aide.

■ Permit older LD children to help with young children's basic skill instruction in the areas in which they need strengthening. For example, an older child with difficulties in arithmetic may strengthen his or her own basic arithmetic skills by assisting with drill and practice of these skills in the first-grade class. On the other hand, avoid exposing the older child's deficits within the context of his or her own instructional setting; recognize possible feelings of embarrassment and pride.

■ Children with learning disabilities can sometimes be completely overwhelmed by homework. Teachers and parents should continually check with each other. If the amount of time consumed by homework seems unreasonable and frustration occurs, then alternative strategies should be tried. The length of writing assignments could be reduced for children with difficulties in handwriting. For children with reading problems, the amount of reading could be reduced and the major points in the reading assignments could be highlighted with a marker.

■ Adjusting LD children's programs to meet their individual needs but failing to modify the grading and report card procedure can be a grave mistake. Some children who have begun to progress academically after years of failure have been completely deflated by a report card full of "F" or "unsatisfactory" grades. Regular and special education teachers should discuss alternative methods of grading and reporting to continue motivating LD pupils (and their parents) and at the same time report their progress accurately.

Role of Parents

Raising a learning-disabled child can be confusing and frustrating. Teachers can help learning-disabled students by aiding their parents. Suggestions for parents include:

■ The most important thing that a parent can give the learning-disabled child is understanding. Remember that the child often does not comprehend, cannot remember, or can become distracted. He or she is not a bad child disobeying on purpose.

■ Since frequent failure at school can lead to rejection of certain subjects and learning in general, parents should try to provide opportunities for learning success within the home or neighborhood to build up motivation and enthusiasm for learning.

■ Remember that many learning-disabled pupils' academic behaviors are marked by erratic performance in their strong and weak areas of learning. When assisting the child, expect progress in small steps.

SPECIAL CONSIDERATIONS AND ISSUES

Many current issues relating to learning disabilities are worthy of discussion by teachers, prospective teachers, and concerned citizens. Space permits mentioning only a few such issues in this chapter.

Hyperactivity and Pharmacological Treatment

Unfortunately, the popular term "hyperactive" has come to be adopted by the public to describe a great many behaviors of children and youth, most of which are negative. The term also implies many things—such as brain damage—that are equally undesirable. Research has demonstrated that hyperactivity and brain damage are not necessarily linked. Some children displaying hyperactive behavior are not brain damaged, and some brain-damaged children are not hyperactive. The ingestion of artificial food colors and flavors has been linked to hyperactivity and learning disabilities (Feingold, 1976). Many teachers and parents are convinced that consumption of refined sugar is directly related to increased hyperactivity in children (e.g., hyperactive behavior is reported to increase dramatically at Halloween), however, research has not fully supported the biochemical causation of hyperactivity (Kauffman, 1977).

The label hyperactive carries negative connotations and frequently results in the use of medication to calm a youngster, often without adequate consideration of all the variables in the child's life. Therefore, teachers are urged to use the term with extreme caution. Renshaw (1974) lists 22 symptoms of hyperactive behavior and states that if a child exhibits half of the signs "persistently and recurrently (not occasionally)" (p. 82) after the age of five, he or she may likely be hyperactive. Guidelines for school personnel involved in this critical area have been outlined by Axelrod and Bailey (1979, pp. 547–548) as follows:

1. Physical examinations should be prerequisites to commencing and continuing drug treatment. This is necessary not only to monitor possible physiological problems, but also to determine whether physical anomalies might be causing problem behaviors.
2. Drugs should be considered only when inordinately inappropriate behavior is demonstrated. The mere claim from a parent or teacher that a child's behavior warrants drug treatment is insufficient.
3. Before drug treatment is implemented, behavior modification procedures or other remedial techniques should be attempted.
4. Children who receive drugs should be exposed to two different dosage levels: a baseline phase, and a placebo condition. Whenever possible, drug and placebo conditions should be conducted in a double-blind manner.
5. A continual, preferably daily, record of a child's behavior should be maintained. This should be done not only when attempting to determine a child's appropriate drug treatment but throughout treatment.
6. The effects of at least one behavior that should increase and one behavior that should decrease should be monitored.
7. Minimal goals for each behavior of interest should be specified in advance. Only when drug treatment meets the prespecified goals should such treatment be continued.
8. During the course of drug treatment the child should periodically be drug free. If the child's behavior again becomes disorderly, it may be concluded that the drugs were responsible for the previously noted improvement. If the child's behavior remains appropriate, it may be possible to permanently discontinue drug use.

9. Drug treatment should not be considered a permanent solution to a youngster's problems. When drug therapy is deemed necessary, it might be combined with more standard educational procedures. As the package of techniques improves a student's behavior it may then be possible to wean the student from drug treatment.

Learning Disabilities and Juvenile Delinquency

The behaviors for which young persons are labeled as **juvenile delinquents** range from very serious (e.g., murder) to the relatively minor (e.g., riding a bike on the sidewalk). While official legal definitions vary from state to state, it is generally accepted that "juvenile delinquency consists of misbehavior by children and adolescents that leads to referral to the juvenile court" (Cavan and Ferdinand, 1975, p. 2).

Many professionals in special education have recently become aware of the learning and behavioral problems of youth classified by society as juvenile delinquents (Jacobson, 1976; Ramos, 1978). Case studies of many of these youths' developmental histories indicate problems in both academic and social learning. Public institutions to which juvenile delinquents are assigned are providing increasingly more special educational services. In 1976, the Association for Children with Learning Disabilities (ACLD) was funded by the U.S. Office of Juvenile Justice and Delinquency Prevention to study the relationship between juvenile delinquency and learning disabilities. The data collected indicates that ". . . there is a preponderant number of LD juveniles caught up in a delinquency syndrome. Also, it appears that LD youth are treated differently than non-LD youth in the Juvenile Court System" (*ACLD Newsbriefs*, January/February 1980, p. 10).

A federally funded demonstration project, Operation DIVERT, in Escambia County, Florida, has reported considerable success in helping juvenile offenders. This project provides intervention services for young persons who have been labeled as juvenile delinquents and also have been identified as learning disabled. The intervention services consist of remedial educational programs, group therapy, family counseling, and individual counseling (*ACLD Newsbriefs*, March/April 1980). Working with delinquents, assisting in identification of predelinquent juveniles, and providing educational services in a preventative manner will likely be future areas of intensified concern.

Disappearance of the Learning-Disabled Population

Reflecting upon the effects of PL 94–142, one concern bears directly on special education programs for learning-disabled children. This is a discrepancy between the assumed prevalence levels and the actual numbers as reported in census reports to the Bureau of Education for the Handicapped. Meyen and Moran (1979) assume that the number of handicapped pupils reported is low and that many children are going unidentified. They believe (and many others would agree) that the majority of the unidentified children are mildly handicapped, including the learning disabled. These authors discuss several issues that raise the following questions:

■ Are regular classroom teachers failing to refer the child with relatively mild problems because they dread the time involved with special education programming?

■ Is the school district's commitment to serving the mildly handicapped pupil being reduced because of the necessity to serve the newly involved severely handicapped pupils as top priority?

■ Are the assumed negative affects of labeling a child as handicapped causing educators to opt not to label those children with mild handicaps in order to make them eligible for education services?

■ Are mildly handicapped pupils who are culturally different remaining un-identified because their cultural and/or economic differences are masking their handicaps?

■ Is the lack of advocacy for the mildly handicapped children relative to the strong parent group advocacy for the severely handicapped reducing the pressure on school districts for identifying and serving the mildly handicapped?

■ Are remedial procedures suitable for the majority of scholastic underachievers being substituted for special education services for the mildly handicapped?

How teachers, administrators, and parents answer these questions in the years ahead may well determine the fate of special education programs for children and youth with learning disabilities.

SUMMARY POINTS

■ Learning disabilities is a relatively new field in special education, although it has roots in the early nineteenth century work of scientists studying language, perceptual, and motor process disorders.

■ The current federal definition of learning disabilities indicates that it is a disorder in one or more of the basic processes of language, written or spoken, which interferes with a child's ability to listen, think, speak, read, write, spell, or do mathematical calculations. The federal definition excludes problems that are primarily due to visual, hearing, or motor handicaps; to mental retardation or emotional disturbance; or to environmental, cultural, or economic disadvantage.

■ Federal regulations require that in order for a child to be identified as learning disabled, a severe discrepancy between the actual level of achievement and ability must be found in one or more of the following areas: oral expression, listening comprehension, written expression, basic reading skill, reading comprehension, mathematic calculations, and mathematic reasoning.

■ There are three general cause-related categories of children with learning problems: children whose problems are caused by inadequate learning environments, children who have minor organic difficulties but whose problems are made worse by inappropriate environment, and children who have significant organic problems and appropriate learning environments.

■ The most frequently cited characteristics of learning disabilities are: hyperactivity; perceptual/motor impairments; emotional lability; general coordination deficits; disorders of attention; impulsivity; disorders of memory and thinking; specific deficits in reading, arithmetic, writing, or spelling; disorders of speech and hearing; and equivocal neurological signs.

■ Placement options for learning-disabled children include self-contained special classrooms, tutoring, resource room programs, and regular classroom placement with consultation and assistance to the teacher.

■ Traditional approaches to educating learning-disabled children can be categorized under perceptual/motor approaches, developmental approaches, neurophysiological approaches, linguistic approaches, and diagnostic/remedial approaches. Currently, most LD programs are eclectic, utilizing the most appropriate parts of each approach. Increasingly more attention is being given to developing educational programs at the secondary level for learning-disabled adolescents. Also, most LD programs contain an affective component to help build the pupils' self-concepts.

■ Special considerations in the field of learning disabilities today include the issues of hyperactivity and drug treatment, the relationship of learning disabilities to juvenile delinquency, and the apparent decrease in the number of LD children being served in special educational programs.

REVIEW QUESTIONS

1. What is the federal definition of learning disabilities? Discuss how it relates to the three general categories of children with learning problems discussed in this chapter.

2. What areas of a child's functioning should be evaluated in an effort to determine whether or not the child is learning disabled?

3. What are the most frequently cited characteristics of learning disabilities? Which of these apply to Zachary, the LD child in the case study?

4. What kinds of behavior should a teacher look for when observing children suspected of being learning disabled?

5. What approaches to teaching learning-disabled children are typically used in the schools?

PEER TUTORING — WHO BENEFITS THE MOST?

One of the situational variables that influences how well the least restrictive environment principle is implemented in the real world of schools concerns the presence or absence of persons to assist teachers with plans outlined in the children's IEPs. Whether or not the learning-disabled and other mildly handicapped pupils are able to succeed in school may depend on the school systems' creative abilities to revise strategies for utilizing the volunteer services of paraprofessionals, parents, and other aides, including other students.

Many school districts have recently begun using volunteer aides, a previously untapped source for helping children with learning disabilities. Some schools have been successful in utilizing students as volunteers in cross-age tutoring (i.e., high school students tutoring elementary children) and/or peer tutoring (high school students helping other high school students). A great advantage of using students as tutors is that both the tutor and the child being tutored learn from the experience. The skills and attitudes of both students are developed.

One large high school has been very successful in using a peer tutoring program as part of the school's learning disability resource room program serving approximately 30 LD high school students. Each year approximately 10 to 15 students work as peer tutors under the direction of the LD resource room teacher and the LD tutor. Peer tutors fulfill any of the following tasks within the resource room organization:

- Taping reading materials. Since many of the learning-disabled students have severe reading deficiencies, having their reading assignments on tape enables them to keep up with the class despite their handicap.
- Keeping the tape library organized and readily accessible.
- Highlighting textbooks. Some learning-disabled students can benefit by having

the major concepts in the reading assignments brought to their attention by highlighting or outlining.
- Getting LD students started on their assigned tasks in the resource room.
- Listening to students read orally and/or give oral book reports in preparation for their assignments from the regular classroom.
- Assisting in the production of instructional materials.
- Serving as messengers to regular classroom teachers and administrators.
- Assisting in the organization of learning centers.
- Helping with clerical work such as mimeographing materials, typing letters to parents, and keeping filing systems organized (personal records are kept only by the teacher).

Although many students volunteered to help when the program was begun initially, a screening process was beneficial in selecting those few students who could best meet the requirements of the peer aide/tutor task. The initial screening process followed these steps:

1. After a verbal explanation by the teacher or tutor, a signup sheet was passed around the study halls during each class period. Interested students were asked to sign up.
2. The records of students who signed up were reviewed for information on achievement levels in various subjects, personal strengths and weaknesses, and scheduling.
3. The students were then observed in a classroom and in a nonclassroom setting interacting with their peers.
4. Teachers of these student volunteers were interviewed informally.
5. The LD resource teacher and/or tutor interviewed each student volunteer personally.

The LD personnel in this high school program have found that the most successful peer tutors are those who can take directions well (they are expected to participate in a training session and are given specific instructions), and who can relate well to adults as well as peers (they are expected to work cooperatively with the LD teacher, regular classroom teachers, and administrators).

Some schools grant a specified number of academic credit hours for peer tutoring services. However, the peer tutors in this program receive academic credit reimbursement only if their work in the LD resource room program meets the requirements of a course or courses for which they are already enrolled.

Experience with peer tutoring programs has demonstrated that the tutors offer academic support to the LD students, provide valuable assistance to the teachers, and serve as positive models for the LD students. In addition, they often develop friendships extending beyond the resource room. Just how strong friendship ties can become was evidenced in a incident that occurred at the end of a school year. The teacher planned to have a small party celebrating the completion of another successful year. She wrote an invitation addressed to all teachers and administrators in the building and asked each of the LD students to join her in signing it. When the peer tutors found out that they hadn't been asked to sign they wanted to know why. They were told that they were indeed welcome to sign the invitation and that they could put the term "peer tutor" after their signature. All the tutors signed but none of them chose to distinguish themselves in any way from the LD students in the program. In this large high school many teachers received the invitation and had no way of knowing who was an LD student and who was a peer tutor. That's how the peer tutors wanted it to be!

DISCUSSION POINTS

1. In establishing the volunteer peer tutoring program, a brief initial screening process was used. In addition to those screening steps followed in this particular program, what others do you think would be important and useful? What screening procedures do you think would be necessary if the volunteers were from outside the school (i.e., adults from the community or students from another school)?

2. This peer tutoring program listed several duties that the tutors were expected to perform. Which of those duties and responsibilities do you think tutors would have the most difficulty in carrying out? Why? How could the resource room teacher and the regular class teachers help them to perform these duties?

SUGGESTED READINGS

Cruickshank, W. M. *Learning Disabilities at Home, School, and Community*. Syracuse, NY: Syracuse University, 1977.

Goodman, L., and Mann, L. *Learning Disabilities in the Secondary School, Issues and Practices*. New York: Grune and Stratton, 1976.

Johnson, D. J., and Myklebust, H. R. *Learning Disabilities, Educational Principles and Practices*. New York: Grune and Stratton, 1967.

Lerner, J. W. *Children with Learning Disabilities*, 2nd ed. Boston: Houghton-Mifflin, 1976.

Stephens, T. M. *Teaching Skills to Children with Learning and Behavior Disorders*. Columbus, Ohio: Charles E. Merrill, 1977.

Wallace, G., and Kauffman, J. M. *Teaching Children with Learning Problems*. Columbus, Ohio: Charles E. Merrill, 1978.

15

THE BEHAVIOR DISORDERED

CONTENTS

Of all handicapping conditions, perhaps the least understood, particularly from an educational perspective, is the one called behavior disordered, or emotionally disturbed. The 1950s was the first decade that focused on diagnosis and treatment of children with disturbed behavior. During that period emphasis shifted from concern mainly with the severely disturbed toward those children and youth who were less seriously disturbed. Also in the 1950s the responsibility of public schools in helping behaviorally disturbed children was recognized.

Most behaviorally disordered children have never really been identified and provided with appropriate services. Since they haven't been served, mainstreaming is nothing new to them. In the words of William Morse, pioneer in the education of emotionally disturbed children, "Most of special education for the disturbed and delinquent has been mainstream. The majority of distraught children have never been placed 'out' to be available for mainstreaming back!" (Morse, 1974, p. 208).

In the following case study, the scholastic history of a young boy, Freddy, demonstrates how quickly some behavior disordered pupils can leave the mainstream.

FREDDY

Freddy is a nine-year-old question mark to both his teachers and parents. Since kindergarten, Freddy has been in special education classes. Following an evaluation at the end of kindergarten, Freddy was placed in a class for children with learning disabilities. After an unsuccessful year, he was then placed in a severe behavior disorders (SBD) class. Unlike the LD class, the SBD class was not housed in a public school, but in the basement of a nearby church. Thus, in his brief scholastic career, Freddy has taken at least two steps away from a normal school classroom environment.

In kindergarten, Freddy's teacher reported that he was hyperactive and lacked self-control. She did not think he was ready for first grade. After referral to the school psychologist and the subsequent evaluation, it was determined that Freddy was learning disabled. His standardized test performances on both tests of intelligence and achievement were erratic. He also had trouble paying attention to the tests he was being given. His parents reported that he had been hospitalized for severe dehydration at about one year of age. An EEG completed at the end of kindergarten indicated an abnormal profile. However, no medical intervention was recommended. Even though an evaluation had been conducted, many questions remained unanswered.

During his year in the learning disabilities program, Freddy quickly gained a reputation for misbehaving. During an hour-long observation period, the building principal recorded over 70 separate occurrences of Freddy's misbehavior. These behaviors included getting out of his seat, talking or shouting (including swearing at the teacher and his classmates), pounding his feet loudly on the floor, and laughing aloud so as to interrupt others. Yet, despite his misbehaviors and extremely poor attention span, he was making progress academically. At the end of the year, however, it was decided that Freddy's behavior was causing the LD teacher to spend too much of her time with him alone. So Freddy was placed in the SBD class, which consisted of one teacher and an aide for five or six pupils. Again, however, a thorough assessment was not conducted before this placement was made.

In Freddy's first year in the SBD class, his teacher became aware that factors in Freddy's home environment might be influencing him. Freddy had shown good academic and behavioral progress after being placed in a structured program of behavioral management using contingency contracting. At the end of the first semester his progress seemed to have stopped. His homework was often not turned in and he did not use appropriate toileting habits. The teacher learned from

Freddy's parents that his home life was marked by frequent disagreements among the parents and his two older brothers and older sister. Recently, the police had been called to the home to break up an argument that had almost turned physically violent. Freddy's mother reported that since this incident Freddy had become even more bizarre and aggressive in the home. She and her husband feel that they cannot deal effectively with his behavior.

Freddy's teacher has requested a multi-factored evaluation to determine the most appropriate placement for Freddy for next year, to establish goals and objectives for his IEP, and to consider outside-of-school treat-ment interventions (i.e., therapy for Freddy, counseling for his parents and siblings, family therapy, and so forth).

Whether or not Freddy is best served through an SBD class, segregated from the rest of the school, is a question the evaluation team will have to decide. It seems vital, though, that this young, troubled child, who refers to the rain hitting the schoolroom window as "rain dancing in the wind," must be given the attention of all concerned soon.

Points for Consideration

■ Freddy has been in a progressively more segregated environment each year of his school career, going from kindergarten to an LD class in the school, and then to an SBD class outside the regular school.

■ Freddy's academic and social behaviors have been erratic since he entered school.

He can, however, achieve academically when provided with a highly structured environment and expectations.

■ Freddy's environment seems to contribute to his behavior difficulties.

A younger, more severely disordered pupil is described in the following case study.

JOHN

John is seven years old. He is one of ten children having the same chronological age but having attained various stages of mental development. These ten were grouped together for a special summer program. The principal indicated that John is mentally retarded with possible emotional disturbances. John is almost completely nonverbal. His only utterances are the names of the months. He never sits in a designated area for more than a few seconds, and often wanders around the room appearing to "tune out" whatever the teachers say. He resists their attempts to provide him with affection. John consistently opens every cupboard, drawer, and closet in the room, either throwing their contents on the floor or putting things into his mouth if they fit. John eats chalk, crayons, clay, pencils, soap, paper stars—even the plant cuttings on the window sill. John's teachers tied the cupboards and drawers shut to eliminate distractions and tried virtually every technique they knew to get through to him. John runs out of the classroom, down the hall, and out the front door of the school into the street whenever he gets close enough to the door. His teachers cannot stop him. His actions distract his classmates who eventually begin to imitate his wild movements, spitting, and biting.

The realization that John really did need professional evaluation came at the summer school picnic. John pulled the safety cap off a

can of lighter fluid and drank a few large mouthfuls as his unbelieving teachers and classmates looked on. John then proceeded to bite the doctor's hands as he attempted to pump the lighter fluid out of his stomach.

It was a long summer. Finally, after a near bout with death, John was evaluated and placed in a special, emotionally disturbed/behaviorally disordered (EDBD) program. After the first few months, he appears to exhibit some academic as well as behavioral growth.

Points for Consideration

■ John's bizarre behaviors made him stand out as unique even in a group of handicapped children who later began to imitate him.

■ John's almost complete disregard for the safety of others and himself made him a constant source of concern and anxiety to his teacher.

Common Misconceptions

■ *Teachers and Parents Cannot Really Help Pupils Who Have Behavior Disorders; Successful Treatment Depends upon Involving a Mental Health Professional, Such as a Psychiatrist or Psychologist.* Fortunately, both teachers and parents can be very helpful in improving the behavior of disturbed pupils. However, like Freddy's parents

and earlier teachers, they often *think* they cannot be effective.

■ *If a Child Is Behaviorally Disordered, It Is the Parents' Fault.* Many families of disturbed children are not different than families of normal children. In families where the parents themselves display behavioral problems, the case may be that parental troubles were caused by the presence of the disruptive child rather than vice versa.

■ *All Children Labeled as Having Behavior Disorders Are Aggressive, Acting-Out Types.* While these children are the most obviously disturbed, many behavior-disordered children are just the opposite —shy, anxious, and withdrawn.

DEFINITION OF TERMS

Terms applied to the behaviorally disordered differ depending upon the orientation of the persons using them. Educators, for instance, recently have come to prefer terms related to the improvement of learning behaviors rather than those that relate to the treatment of children medically defined as sick. The term behaviorally disordered has become generally more acceptable than emotionally disturbed.

The following two definitions reflect the educational approach to children with behavioral handicaps. Hewett (1968, p. 3) refers to this type of child as

> . . . "a socialization failure." Underlying all of the specialized terms and complex diagnostic labels used to describe him is the implication that his behavior, for whatever reason, is maladaptive according to the expectations of a society in which he lives. . . . As an individual's behavior deviates from what is expected for his age, sex and status, it is maladaptive and he may experience serious difficulties in getting along.

Kauffman (1977, p. 23) defines behavior disordered children as ". . . those who chronically and markedly respond to their environment in socially unacceptable and/or personally unsatisfying ways but who can be taught more socially acceptable and personally gratifying behavior." This definition is especially significant for educators and parents because it stresses the child's potential ability to learn more appropriate behavior.

Part of the difficulty in recognizing, understanding, and developing educational programs for behaviorally disordered children is due to the nomenclature. There is widespread use of a great variety of terms applied to the same or similar children, including maladjusted, socially maladjusted, seriously emotionally disturbed, adjustment problem children, mentally ill or sick, mentally disturbed, educationally handicapped, predelinquent, delinquent, emotionally handicapped, socially handicapped, and children in conflict (Shea, 1978, p. 6). Adding to the confusion is the use of yet other terms whose meanings vary depending upon the background and purpose of the person doing the describing. Some samples: character disorder, asocial, neurotic, personality disorder, psychopathic, schizophrenic, psychotic, and sociopathic. These all refer to specific traits or categories of behavior, and have not been particularly helpful labels in serving exceptional children. Also, these labels imply that the problem resides strictly within the child, thus ignoring the environmental interactions impinging upon the child's behavior. The term behaviorally disordered is certainly not without its drawbacks either; it has, however, become widely accepted.

PL 94–142: Issue of Definition

The rules and regulations accompanying PL 94–142 use the term seriously emotionally disturbed and define it as follows (*Federal Register*, August 23, 1977, p. 42478):

> . . . a condition exhibiting one or more of the following characteristics over a long period of time and to a marked degree, which adversely affects educational performance:
> (A) An inability to learn that cannot be explained by intellectual, sensory, or health factors;
> (B) An inability to build or maintain satisfactory interpersonal relationships with peers and teachers;
> (C) Inappropriate types of behavior or feelings under normal circumstances;

(D) A general pervasive mood of unhappiness or depression; or

(E) A tendency to develop physical symptoms or fears associated with personal or school problems.

The term includes children who are schizophrenic or autistic. The term does not include children who are socially maladjusted, unless it is determined that they are seriously emotionally disturbed.

The PL 94–142 definition essentially draws on the characteristics used by Bower (1969; Bower and Lambert, 1965) to describe children who have emotional and behavioral problems. As such, the PL 94–142 definition raises some ambiguities and causes some problems in educating these particular handicapped children. Questions arise. First, what is the difference between "an inability to learn that cannot be explained by intellectual, sensory, or health factors" and a learning disability? Secondly, a clause that was added to the Bower definition in the PL 94–142 version excludes the "socially maladjusted." Does this clause exclude those Hewett-defined (1968) children and youth who have traditionally been considered eligible for special educational services (Raiser and Van Nagel, 1980)? Kauffman (1980) has stated the dilemma, "How is one to reconcile a definition that says if a child fails to develop satisfactory relations with peers and adults or exhibits one of the other four chracteristics to a marked extent and over a period of time then he or she is disturbed, with an exclusionary clause which says that a child can be socially maladjusted but not disturbed?" (p. 524). Thirdly, the use of the term "seriously" along with the exclusionary clause just discussed is likely to have the effect of limiting the expansion of special services to children with mild or moderate disorders (Raiser and Van Nagel, 1980; Kauffman, 1980).

Clearly, then, the PL 94–142 definition that should have helped to unmuddle the definitional ambiguities has instead added to the uncertainties. Moreover, its adoption may have hindered, rather than helped, the development of services to children with behavior disorders.

PREVALENCE

Prevalence figures in the area of behavior disordered or emotionally disturbed children vary greatly as would be expected given the large number and types of definitions. "Informed estimates range from .05% to 40% of children" (Balow, 1980, p. 350). Few studies with these children precisely delineate the characteristics and behaviors used to define the population. Since the terms are so broad, we are often left with no real understanding of how well any particular group being studied compares with any other, possibly similar, groups of children (Balow, 1980).

The longitudinal nature of the studies could also be a factor. Moderate or low prevalence rates are found when the same raters rate children over a period of years as the children grow older (Rubin and Balow, 1978; Chamberlain, 1976). But these longitudinal studies indicate that there is a good chance ". . . that most children in a 5 or 6 year school career will be rated as maladjusted by at least one important adult" (Balow, 1980, p. 352). Attempting to define these children without taking into account their environments may be impossible. The prevalence rate is certain to be influenced by the rater's level of tolerance for problem behavior.

Reviews of the literature addressing this problem indicate the existence of two levels of prevalence figures. A lower level (2–3 percent) seems to apply to more serious problems that exist over a relatively long time span. The higher prevalence level (20–30 percent) seems to apply to the more transient and less severe behavioral problems (Wood and Zebel, 1978; Balow, 1980). In 1979, the number of behavior disordered children reported to BEH was 301,258, or .60 percent of the 3 to 21 age group. This figure is far below the projected number of served and unserved emotionally disturbed children (1,310,000) in 1975–1976.

CAUSES

How persons view the reasons for and causes of behavioral disorders in children is related to their own personal philosophy of life, including their beliefs about the human condition. These beliefs may be found within the five theoretical categories generally utilized to describe probable causes of emotional and behavioral disorders, namely: biophysical, psychoanalytical, behavioral, environmental (sociological/ecological), and holistic.

Biophysical

Supporters of the **biophysical model** believe that behavioral disorders are caused by the effects of biology—biochemical, biophysical, and organic factors —in a manner similar to physical illnesses. The disorder within the child's constitutional makeup may be inherited, may be congenital, or may occur later in life, such as would be the case with injuries or poor diets. Some adherents of this theory believe that while biophysical predisposition does exist, environmental factors can combine with it to trigger emotional and behavioral disorders. Considering that children with behavioral disorders come from a wide variety of cultural/social environments, ethnic groups, and types of family backgrounds, yet are subject to similar biological influences, adds to the credence of this theoretical approach.

Psychoanalytic

The **psychoanalytic** viewpoint is a traditional theory of causation originated by Sigmund Freud. This approach holds that children become behaviorally disordered because they have not successfully dealt with the problems they encounter as they progress through the five psychosexual stages of development. From the perspective of this theory, the underlying causes (problems at particular stages of development) are extremely important, more so than the demonstrated behavioral symptoms that must be dealt with if the child is to be helped. This model finds treating and changing behavior without first investigating the underlying causes inappropriate.

Behavioral

Proponents of various models under the **behavioral** category view searching for causes as a waste of time and effort. Behaviorists believe that children's maladaptive behaviors are learned through interactions with their environment. In his analysis of the patterns of behavior disorders, Quay (1972) indicates that in the main they are made up of behaviors that have been learned. Persons operating from a behavioral perspective tend to label the behavior rather than the child (i.e., "He is engaging in aggressive behavior" rather than "He is an aggressive child"). In order to change inappropriate behaviors, they believe that it is necessary to rearrange the reinforcement pattern and consequences following the behavior. This approach has more recently been utilized in education. It has been widely accepted because of teachers' abilities to successfully improve behavioral problems on their own using techniques derived from this theory, and because the theory de-emphasizes the necessity of labeling the child.

Environmental

Sociological theory stresses the influence of societal forces on children's behavior. Parents, teachers, and organizations set rules for behavior and label those who break the established rules as deviant (e.g., behavioral disorder). Behavior disorders are viewed as processes of rejection of societal/cultural norms. Children who adjust to society by rejecting both its goals and the accepted methods of reaching these goals are often labeled as rebellious or delinquent. From an **ecological** point of view, behavior disorders are caused by the complex interactive effects involving children and their environments. Analyzing either the child or the society/community alone is not appropriate. A complete analysis may indicate that in order to change the crucial interactive relationship, changes need to be made in the child, in the environment, or in both.

Holistic

Advocates of the **holistic** perspective recognize that the etiology of inappropriate behaviors may be illnesses, poor relations with others, inappropriate learning, problems in socialization, and any interaction of these factors. Since problems are often multifaceted, the holistic approach emphasizes cooperation from various disciplines (Hewett, 1974). Specifically, successful educational programs for the behaviorally disordered involve the cooperation and rehabilitative services of other allied professionals, including social workers, counselors, psychologists, juvenile court officers, physicians, and others.

Although in most cases the exact cause of a child's behavior disorder is not known, professionals

> . . . can identify conditions in the child's family, biology, and school experiences that contribute positively or negatively to the ongoing development of the child. Pinpointing the exact etiology of a behavior disorder is not usually necessary in order to provide effective intervention. Even in the few cases where the cause is unmistakable it is usually true that nothing can be done to remove the causal factor (e.g., an abused child cannot relive his earlier years and brain damage cannot be repaired) [Kauffman, 1977, p. 139].

TYPES AND CHARACTERISTICS

Vulnerable, Marginal, or Resourceful

In screening children for emotional and behavioral difficulties, Long (1974) found several levels of strengths and weaknesses relative to coping with the requirements of schools. He categorized children as either vulnerable, marginal, or resourceful pupils. Because **vulnerable pupils** have not developed a good attitude toward learning, have not mastered the academic skills, or have not learned the appropriate behavior to cope with the everyday expectations of school life, they will require special modifications in their educational program. **Marginal pupils** require a school environment that can capitalize on their strengths and build up their weaknesses. Because personalized compensation is required if school is to be a positive force for these pupils rather than an additional negative source of failure, teachers must devise individualized prescriptions for teaching them. **Resourceful pupils** are those who have demonstrated appropriate social behavior, level of academic skills, and an attitude that deals effectively with school life.

Bower's Five Behavioral Patterns

Bower and Lambert (1965) have suggested that children with emotional and behavioral problems function with a restricted set of alternative behaviors. They indicate five behavioral patterns that can be used to identify those children to whom teachers need to provide closer attention (pp. 128–129):

1. An inability to learn which cannot be adequately explained by intellectual, sensory, neurophysiological or general health factors
2. An inability to build or maintain satisfactory interpersonal relationships with peers or teachers
3. Inappropriate or immature types of behavior or feelings under normal conditions
4. A general pervasive mood of unhappiness or depression
5. A tendency to develop physical symptoms such as speech problems, pains or fears associated with personal or school problems

Bower's five behavioral patterns, although used as the basis for the PL 94–142 definition of severely emotionally disturbed children, do not focus on the unique patterns of behavioral characteristics. The ultimate purpose of differentiating among children with behavior disorders is to discover the best match between the individual child and the recommended treatment program. Currently the most widely used system of categorization is the *Diagnostic and Statistical Manual of the American Psychiatric Association*, 2nd edition (DSM-II), 1968, and the DSM-III published in 1980. Unfortunately, the descriptions of disorders are not very useful because of the low reliability of diagnoses made by individual evaluators (Beitchman, Deilman, Landis, Benson, and Kemp, 1978).

Factor analysis research done on the behavior patterns from teacher and parent rating instruments has identified two broad behavior syndromes—overcontrolled and undercontrolled. **Overcontrolled** refers to the presence of shy and anxious behavior, personality problems, internalizing, and inhibitions. **Undercontrolled** refers to acting-out, externalizing, aggressiveness, and conduct problem behaviors (Edelbrock, 1979). In a few of the instruments, evidence seems to point to the existence of more narrow syndromes describing disordered behavior in eight categories: socially withdrawn, immature, psychosomatic, hyperactive, depressed, delinquent, anxious, and aggressive. One program of research currently under way employs cluster analysis in an attempt to derive useful differentiated categories from these narrow syndromes (Edelbrock, 1979).

Dimensions

Conduct Disorder	Personality Disorder	Immaturity	Socialized Delinquency
			Life History
Behavior Traits:	*Behavior Traits:*	*Behavior Traits:*	*Characteristics:*
Disobedience	Feelings of inferiority	Preoccupation	Has bad companions
Disruptiveness	Self-consciousness	Short attention span	Engages in gang
Fighting	Social withdrawal	Clumsiness	activities
Destructiveness	Shyness	Passivity	Engages in cooperative
Temper tantrums	Anxiety	Daydreaming	stealing
Irresponsibility	Crying	Sluggish	Habitually truant from
Impertinent	Hypersensitive	Drowsiness	school
Jealous	Seldom smiles	Prefers younger	Accepted by delinquent
Shows signs of anger	Chews fingernails	playmates	subgroups
Acts bossy	Depression, chronic	Masturbation	Stays out late at night
Profanity	sadness	Giggles	Strong allegiance to
Attention seeking		Easily flustered	selected peers
Boisterous		Chews objects	
		Picked on by others	
		Plays with toys in class	

Source: Adapted from H. C. Quay, "Patterns of Aggression, Withdrawal, and Immaturity," in H. C. Quay and J. S. Werry, eds. *Psychopathological Disorders of Childhood.* New York: Wiley, 1972, pp. 10, 12, 14, and 15.

Quay's Four-Dimensional Approach

Quay (1972) has proposed a four-dimensional approach from studies utilizing teacher ratings, parent ratings, life/case histories, and responses to questionnaires by children themselves. The four dimensions are: conduct disorder, personality disorder, immaturity, and socialized delinquency.

Conduct disorder generally involves verbally and physically aggressive behavior and poor interpersonal relationships. A typical questionnaire response is "I'd do what I want whether anybody likes it or not." **Personality disorder**, on the other hand, generally involves withdrawal. Feelings of anxiety and fear characterize this dimension. A typical questionnaire response from this dimension is "I don't think I'm quite as happy as others seem to be."

Immaturity involves many traits, including daydreaming, short attention span, and passivity, and represents ". . . a persistence of these behaviors when they are inappropriate to the chronological age of the child and society's expectations of him" (Quay, 1972, p. 13).

Socialized delinquency is delineated by several life history characteristics, including having bad companions, engaging in gang activities, and being habitually truant from school.

Table 15-1 provides an overview of Quay's four dimensions and the behavioral traits categorized under each. Although this classification system is not immediately useful for designing individual treatment programs and IEPs, it is a comprehensive and research-based system for classifying behavior-disordered children.

Classification by Degree of Severity

Within the category of behavior disorders, degrees of severity exist. These can be utilized to enhance the definition as well as to arrange for the most appropriate

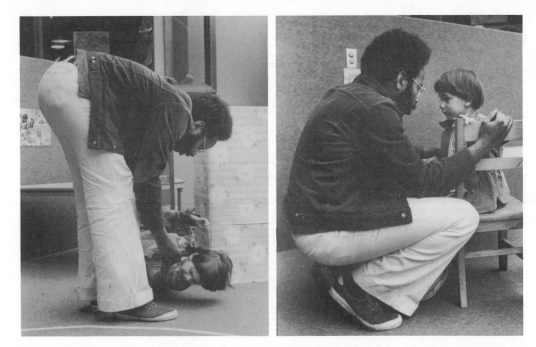

Due to the wide range of behavior disorders and varying degrees of severity, effective teachers of children in conflict must possess a variety of intervention and treatment strategies.

educational program. The terms mild, moderate, and severe are used to designate the different levels of behavioral handicaps. Educationally, children with mild behavior disorders are those who can be assisted to perform more adequately both academically and socially by the regular classroom teacher (with support and consultation from school resource personnel, such as the resource teacher or school psychologist). Those children designated as moderately disordered are in need of the intensive assistance of specialists (e.g., psychologists, therapists), even though they are able to remain in the regular school environment. Severely behaviorally handicapped pupils are those requiring placement in a special class or special school (Reinert, 1976).

Children with mild or moderate levels of behavioral disorders may require assistance through teacher consultations, resource room placement, or part-time special classes. On the other hand, the majority of children identified as severely behaviorally disordered are served through special self-contained classes in the schools, or through residential schools or clinics outside the schools.

THE AUTISTIC   In recent years, programs consisting mainly of self-contained classrooms for children diagnosed as **autistic** or autistic-like have been organized around the country. The word autism comes from the Greek word for self, *autos*. Two predominant features of autistic children are their apparent self-absorption and socially withdrawn behavior (Wing, 1972). These children, who are thought to possess average intellectual capability, nevertheless exhibit severe deficiencies in the development of appropriate behavioral patterns. Their ability to help themselves may be that of a much younger child, and they may depend greatly on others for help with eating, dressing, etc. Their self-absorption may be manifested in self-mutilation (e.g., hand biting, head banging) and/or self-stimulation (e.g., finger tapping, body rocking). Frequently they appear not to receive input through their senses and use little speech. The result is that others incorrectly think they are blind and/or deaf (Lovaas and Newsom, 1976). These children may also be resistent to change, be hyperactive, and seem to have an unusual interest in inanimate objects. Although they may be attractive, healthy, and intelligent in appearance, their behavior is bad and their academic performance is low.

The difficulties in developing the skills of language, communication, and interpersonal relationships, along with having unusual bodily movements, apparent fears, and extreme resistance to change, have traditionally placed the autistic, in the eyes of many, in the category of uneducable. Now parents who earlier could not afford the costs of private programs (if they were available) are receiving some much-needed assistance with these very special children. Despite improvements realized through behavior modification techniques (Rinconer and Tripp, 1980), the outlook for these children is bleak. Most will require institutional care as adults. However, Yahraes (1968) estimates that there are approximately 10 to 15 percent whose language and social abilities will improve to the point that as adults they may be able to function in the larger society, only appearing to be odd or immature.

IDENTIFICATION

The process of identifying children's behavioral disorders often begins with a parent, teacher, or other significant person in the child's life who expresses a feeling that something is wrong. In response to the question, What is the child doing that makes you think there is a problem?, replies from parents and teachers similar to the following are often noted: seems indifferent and inattentive, feels picked on, talks back constantly, always wants his or her own way, bullies other kids, blames others for his or her problems, picks on other children, seems moody and withdrawn. Because these and similar comments could apply to non-handicapped children as well as to behavior-disordered children, guidelines are needed to help professionals and parents make preliminary judgments about whether further evaluation is warranted.

Guidelines for Teachers

Kessler (1966) has suggested the following general guidelines and questions for screening by teachers wishing to determine whether or not a child should be referred for further assessment:

- Is the child's behavior inappropriate for his or her age? If the behavior pattern that the child is exhibiting is discrepant with those that would be expected for his or her age, there may be a problem.
- Does the behavioral problem (symptom) occur quite frequently? If inappropriate behaviors are occurring frequently they are probably occurring under conditions of relatively mild stress. This situation indicates a problem warranting further study.
- Do the problems seem to persist even though the child, parents, teacher, and others have tried repeatedly to modify or change them?

■ How would you rate the child's general adjustment? It is important to consider the child's overall behavioral adjustment in addition to specific isolated behaviors.

Pate (1963) has suggested that, from an educational viewpoint, we can perceive the effects of children's problem behaviors on others and determine:

■ Whether the child's behavior is placing too many demands on teachers and others
■ Whether the educational progress of the child's classmates is being interrupted by the child's inappropriate behavior
■ Whether the child's behavior is worsening as time passes

Use of such screening guidelines as these direct teachers in further assessment and/or in selecting educational strategies and interventions. Teachers are logically important to the identification process. They daily spend extended periods interacting with children; they have opportunities to observe both group (large and small) and individual activities in standard situations; they usually have a background in normal behavioral development; and they can observe the large variety of normal behaviors in the school by which they can gain an overall perspective of the expected range of behaviors (Reinert, 1976). Even though teachers are in a unique position to play a critical role in identifying behavior-disordered children, it does not necessarily follow that they will be effective in that role. Bower (1969) suggests that teachers' abilities to analyze themselves, to develop self-awareness, and to personally maintain emotional stability are critical variables in their effectiveness at identifying children with behavior disorders.

Screening Programs

An increasing number of school districts are adapting screening programs for behaviorally handicapped children, particularly for those in the early grades. In order for a screening program to be most effective, Long (1974) suggests six essential guidelines:

1. Negative and unproductive labeling of children, using terms such as "neurotic" and "emotionally disturbed," should be avoided
2. The information collected should relate to normal teacher/pupil/peer learning relationships
3. The teacher's time required in collecting and analyzing the information should not exceed 20 minutes per pupil
4. Pupil self-rating tests should be pleasant, interesting, and comfortable, not threatening
5. The information collected should help the teacher recognize patterns of behavior of which they might earlier have been unaware
6. For screening to be used on a mass basis, the cost per pupil must be relatively inexpensive

EDUCATIONAL PROGRAMMING

Providing special education for children with behavioral disorders in many cases calls for looking at the whole environment as well as analyzing the total child. To

successfully assist behaviorally disordered children and youth reach their goals
(both cognitively/academically and emotionally/behaviorally), educators must
involve the children's families and the broader community. Without such cooperation, the school is not likely to accomplish much.

Curriculum and Methodology

In the early 1960s, the idea was advanced that when a school program focuses on
developing a behavior-disordered child's academic skills, his or her emotional/
behavioral skills will also improve (Haring and Phillips, 1962). Programs for
these children became more concerned with observable behaviors and less with
the medical and/or psychological aspects of the problem. Doing something
directly about the problem behavior became more important than concentrating
on underlying causation. Thus, curriculum was based on instruction in the classroom and on learning sequences.

GUIDELINES FOR SUCCESS   Morse (1974) suggests that schools and teachers use
the following guidelines to assist in the development of the affective and cognitive skills of behaviorally disordered children:

- Curricula for behavior-disordered children should contain a balance of the
  cognitive and the affective. Courses that include affective as well as cognitive
  objectives, **bibliotherapy** (the reading of stories with positive role models),
  and planned affective lessons (e.g., role playing) can be used to develop the
  affective aspects of the program. More use of art, drama, music, plays, and
  dance to encourage pupils to discuss their unpleasant feelings is also valuable.
- The potent influence of the peer culture should be recognized and utilized in
  designing school programs. The teacher as a leader should use group interaction and reflection to teach group roles and codes.
- The school and classroom environment should be arranged so that concern for
  the child is evident—not the convenience of adults. The program must be
  responsive to the pupils and their participation should be valued.
- The teacher must serve as a figure for identification, a model for the pupils as
  well as a designer and provider of academic learning strategies.
- Teachers and other school personnel should not expect to handle all the needs
  of these children unassisted. Particular concerns call for specifically planned
  assistance, whether it be a Big Brother program, family counseling, crisis
  intervention services, traditional psychotherapy, or any of the many other
  possible services.

THE UNIT APPROACH   The **unit approach** of curricular design was used traditionally with pupils classified as emotionally disturbed or behaviorally disordered. This approach has the advantages of providing a beginning and an end
to learning sequences, thereby developing the feeling of successful accomplishment, much needed by most behaviorally disordered pupils. The unit approach
can provide for individual differences by allowing pupils to work on different
aspects of a topic at different levels of skill requirement (Morse, 1965). Also,
training in specific behavior and academic skills, along with group discussions,
are other teaching/learning procedures that have been used with these children
(Rhodes, 1963).

USING BEHAVIOR MODIFICATION   Many teachers have obtained positive results with various **behavior modification** procedures for children who exhibit learning and/or behavioral disorders. Some management systems may, by necessity, use **tangible rewards** (e.g., toys and food) in modifying the behavior of children exhibiting severe behavior disorders. With such children, it should be recognized that tangible rewards provide only a temporary corrective measure, a way of getting the child started on the right path. Often nothing seems to motivate these children. Recognizing that these types of rewards are only temporary and that later the child will move along to **social** and **intrinsic reinforcers** helps overcome initial, perhaps natural, feelings of repulsion toward the use of such techniques.

CONTINGENCY CONTRACTING   **Contingency contracting**, which was successful in Freddy's case, can be used in the regular classroom as well as in special education. In contingency contracting, a child first performs a task, academic or social. Then the child receives a reward, usually choosing from a predetermined set of activities agreed upon as appropriate by the child and the teacher. Sometimes these activities are posted in the classroom and are referred to as the **Reward Activity Menu**. Reward menus may have a great variety of activities (e.g., going to the book corner, completing puzzles, helping the librarian, playing chess, doing crafts) listed and usually change, with additions and deletions, over a period of time. To be effective, the listed rewards must seem important to the child.

BEHAVIOR MODIFICATION STRATEGIES FOR TEACHERS   Affleck, Lowenbraun, and Archer (1980) offer several guidelines for teachers who use behavior modification in their classes, as follows:

- Be sure that the rewards are desired and enjoyed by the pupils.
- Try to reward performances through natural reinforcement.
- Use rewards that are relatively easy to implement with your class and with which you agree.
- Rewards should be provided contingent on the completion of the appropriate behavior (as in contingency contracting).
- Rewards should follow the completion of the desired behavior as soon as possible. However, when it is not possible to provide reinforcement immediately, teachers can use **tokens**. In token systems pupils receive checkmarks, chips, pluses, happy faces, or other representations of the reward for their efforts. At some later time (end of the period, the morning, the day, the week, etc.), they exchange their tokens for the reward. Teachers interested in establishing a token system in their classroom are referred to Stainback, Stainback, Payne, and Payne's *Establishing a Token Economy in the Classroom* (1973).
- Social rewards (e.g., verbal praise, a pat on the back, a wink) should be paired with any reward offered and should eventually replace the nonsocial reward.

THE ENGINEERED CLASSROOM   In the Santa Monica Project, Hewett (1968) designed a structured classroom to teach children labeled emotionally disturbed. The **engineered classroom** structures both the physical environment of the class and the motivational system. Through the use of a variety of physical arrangements, appropriate consequences (rewards for continuous improvement), and daily progress checking, the child is constantly provided with learning situations in which success is possible. Teaching strategies are based on six levels of educational goals and tasks: (1) attention, learning to pay attention to teacher and task; (2) response, learning to respond to tasks; (3) order, learning to complete tasks with specific beginning and ending points; (4) exploratory, learning to explore the environment; (5) social, learning to work for teacher and peer approval; and (6) mastery, learning basic skills. Types of tasks and consequences differ at each level. For example, if the child is unwilling to respond in learning and is not involved, the educational task is to get the child to respond first by offering tasks which he or she likes. Then, social recognition and praise are provided as consequences for a successful response. When the child is successful at the response level, he or she is ready to proceed to the order level. There, the child will be taught to complete tasks with specific beginning and ending points.

AN ECLECTIC APPROACH   More recently, Kauffman (1974) has suggested that few programs and curricula are used with a particular child or group of children exclusively. Most educational programs for behavior-disordered children incorporate some designs of different programs in various combinations. He describes several curricular designs for use with behaviorally disordered pupils, including:

■ Curricular designs that develop a completely individualized program based on the child's specific behaviors, academic and social, and are aimed at achievement at particular skill levels. Precision teaching, **applied behavioral analysis**, programmed instructional packets, and programs utilizing teaching machines are included in this curriculum. These designs are developments in the structural behavioral approach. They fit quite well with the current requirements under Public Law 94–142 for individualized educational programs in which current levels of achievement, goals and objectives, and evaluation criteria must be specified.

■ Utilizing the school's adopted standard scope and sequence curricular offerings in modified forms. This approach emphasizes the use of texts and workbooks, or parts of them, which are already available.

■ Controlling stimuli by arranging a classroom environment to modify or eliminate visual and/or auditory distractions. Also, visual and tactile cues may be added to instructional materials to increase their hold on pupils' attention.

■ Games, exploration, novel experiences, and play activities can be implemented in an effort to help children learn and to change the child's usual negative attitudes toward school and learning.

■ The **relevant experiences curriculum** emphasizes the relationship of the skills being taught to the children's everyday lives. Children are helped to apply their developing skills to the problems they face on a daily basis. Frequently, vocational and prevocational skills are emphasized.

■ Open classroom and free schools, organizational arrangements related to **humanistic education**, recommended by some to develop behavior-disordered children's sense of purpose and self-direction. The children determine their own goals, and thereby, the content of the curriculum, with the teacher serving as facilitator or consultant.

Role of Teachers

In order to assist behavior-disordered children to reach their goals, teachers should strive to:

In this program for emotionally disturbed students, computerized learning is not only a novel instructional tool but also provides students with relevant vocational training.

■ Establish supportive interpersonal relationships with the children and create a supportive environmental atmosphere characterized by acceptance without permissiveness

■ Perceive the child on the basis of what is normal about him or her; emphasize those behaviors he or she exhibits that are appropriate; catch the child being good

■ Establish routines and clear limits and be as consistent as possible

■ Focus on academic skills and attempt to provide the child with a successful school learning experience

■ Become aware of themselves as human beings, as well as professionals, with strengths and weaknesses; it's difficult to assist children in developing self-awareness and knowledge when one is lacking these qualities oneself

■ Remove materials or objects in the environment that may be overstimulating or otherwise affecting the child; in the case of work assignments, this may mean presenting the child with tasks such as workbook pages one at a time rather than multiple or complex tasks

■ Become aware that behavioral reinforcement and interactional effects operate in the classroom among the pupils and teacher; utilize appropriate behavior management procedures

MATERIALS   Because of the wide range of individual constellations of emotional and behavioral problems typically found in groups of behaviorally disordered children, the use of commercial materials specifically prepared for them is not usually possible. However, commercial programs that aim to develop affective, social, and self-control skills are available (e.g., *DUSO Kits—Developing Understanding of Self and Others* for children in grades K through four). For the most part, teachers of children with behavioral disorders must adapt available curricular materials to meet the unique needs of these pupils. The task of developing materials is closely intertwined with the teacher's other classroom duties and activities.

An example of a creatively designed curricular material and procedure suggested for an English program for behavioral disordered children by Gallagher (1979) is the "Adopt-a-Ship Plan." With this idea, pupils contact the U.S. Coast Guard (Propeller Club of the United States, 1730 M Street, N.W., Suite 413, Washington, D.C. 20036) and request the name of a ship and the ship's captain to use in correspondence. The ship's captain contacts the pupils, sending a picture of the ship and a map outlining their voyage. After students write letters, the ship's crew members respond and correspondence is established. This idea provides opportunities for pupils to develop their skills in interpersonal relationships and knowledge of social studies/geography as well as in English composition and handwriting.

GROUPING CONCERNS   In order to be successful in working with behaviorally disordered pupils, teachers must be aware of some of the dynamics of grouping. Some suggestions for teachers are as follows:

- Be sure that the pupils' work is meaningful and relevant for them. The teacher should strive to provide a psychologically sound atmosphere encouraging a strong work orientation for the class.
- Consider having other pupils serve as models of appropriate behavior and offer support to the children in the room who exhibit behavioral disorders.
- Consider placing a child in instructional groups with slightly older pupils. This procedure may minimize some group problems caused when the inappropriate behaviors of some pupils cause anxiety or fear among their peers, but may not evoke the same reactions from older peers.
- Make agreements with teachers for visits to other classes ahead of time, so that when the teacher needs relief from the child's behavior, the child can be removed for a short time.

Role of Parents

Teachers may find it difficult to fully empathize with parents who must live with a behaviorally disordered child every day for 365 days per year. However, they must be able to provide parents with support for their feelings and assist them in learning about child development, child-raising, and behavior management (Shea, 1978).

Parents can enhance their parenting skills by observing the following guidelines suggested by Dinkmeyer and McKay (1973):

- Value the child the way he or she is
- Establish an atmosphere of mutual respect
- Be kind, yet firm in interactions with the child
- Reduce the verbalizations and follow through with action more frequently

In this section only a selected few of the many issues related to the education of behavior-disordered children are described. Positive teacher/pupil relationships, the increased use of the helping teacher model for serving the more mildly disordered, and the ambiguous nature of mental illness and abnormality concepts will be discussed.

Teacher/Pupil Relationships

Teaching and working with all schoolchildren is significantly influenced by teacher/pupil relationships. Making these relationships positive and productive is particularly critical when teaching children or youth who have emotional or behavioral problems.

Success in teaching children with behavioral disorders depends greatly on the teacher's ability to observe, to listen, and to respond; in essence such teaching depends on the teacher's ability to communicate. The following quote from a 13-year-old illustrates the importance of communication (Kavanaugh, p. 237).

> Adults in some ways aren't patient enough. They expect a kid, if he has a problem, to just come out and say it—very clear and laid out—when sometimes the kid doesn't want to do that. Kids have to say it in different ways.
>
> One thing I do when I'm trying to tell something and I'm not sure how adults will react, is I'll say it sort of slowly so that I can watch as we go along. If I get to a point where I don't like how they're reacting, then I stop. Kids act out of fear and that's why we communicate in this way—slow.

SUGGESTED TECHNIQUES   Rothman (1974) has identified several steps to be followed by teachers in establishing communication with behaviorally disordered children. They include the following:

- Teachers should separate children's feelings from their acts and accept the disturbed child's feelings and attitudes as legitimate without passing judgment.
- Teachers should present children who are behaving inappropriately with appropriate behavior alternatives.
- Teachers should help children to accept their "bad feelings." Children and adults need to know that they are not bad as persons just because they have bad feelings.

Helping Teacher/Crisis Teaching Model

Most children who have mild or moderate behavior disorders do not require placement in self-contained, special education classes. For these children, utilization of the **helping teacher concept** seems appropriate. This model was conceptualized by Morse (1976) in the early 1960s, before educating handicapped children in the regular classroom came into vogue.

Teachers who assume the helping teacher role should be trained in remedial teaching strategies as well as in curriculum design. These teachers are assigned to buildings and are not itinerant. In times of crisis involving teachers, whole classes, or individual pupils, they offer assistance based on need (e.g., difficulties in coping), not on specific categorical labels. The helping teacher may direct/assist another teacher by taking over the class or part of the class while the regular teacher focuses on a small group or an individual. At other times, the helping teacher can counsel or tutor an upset child. Thus, teachers have options to use with disturbed children that are more productive than sending them to the principal's office or excluding them by placing them in the hall. The helping teacher also assists indirectly by consulting with teachers, parents, and others involved in implementing the pupil's program.

Mental Health, Normality/Abnormality, and Stress

The concept of mental health is difficult to define. There is, in fact, no universally agreed-upon definition. All we can say is that mental health is the opposite of mental illness. We usually think of normal and mentally healthy persons as those who are: generally happy, engaged in goal-oriented behavior, able to form personal relationships with others, able to project positive self-images, able to express feelings, and able to express behavior appropriate for their age, but defining each of these traits causes much disagreement. Defining mental illness is also fraught with problems because everybody behaves in ways that could sometimes be considered characteristic of mental illness. For example, becoming overly worried about a small matter or aggressively upset over a little annoyance are behaviors that mentally healthy as well as mentally ill persons exhibit. People who are thought of as mentally ill or abnormal may act normally at times and persons thought to be mentally healthy or normal may act abnormally at times. Whether or not behavior is perceived as deviant is relative to the society and culture in which it is exhibited. Behavior labeled deviant in one society may be considered quite appropriate in another (Rhodes, 1980).

The concept of normality/abnormality may have been originated (and is being maintained) by society because of fear of deviance. Rhodes (1977) calls normality a neurosis (a state of anxiety and difficulty dealing with inner feelings) of civilization and suggests that the human ". . . uses the public myth of normality to conceal from himself his own disabilities, those crippled parts of his body or his psyche which we all possess, but do not acknowledge to ourselves or others" (p. 122).

Observers of our fast-paced, rapidly changing society, with its currently high rate of family mobility, are becoming increasingly aware of the need for education to prevent, as well as treat, children's emotional/behavioral problems. Most of today's children and youth are subject to a great number of stresses and pressures. This condition is an accepted aspect of their growth and development. Pressures to compete academically at younger ages, to develop social skills, to conform to academic and social expectations, and to select and achieve vocational goals earlier are but a few of the challenges faced by children growing up in modern America. Teachers and parents should be aware of the possibility of too much pressure and should watch for changes in the child's typical behavior pattern that may indicate an overpressured pupil.

Educators have come to realize that behavioral disturbances are not necessarily reserved for a small selected number of our children and youth. The amount and degree of stress or pressure, as well as the child's ability to cope and adjust, determine the degree of his or her need for special services. As a significant part of the lives of most children, schools and teachers play a crucial role in preventing, identifying, and treating behavioral disorders.

SUMMARY POINTS

■ It is generally believed that the prevalence rate for chronic (long-term) behavior disorders is 2–3 percent and that the rate for transitory behavior disorders (short-term) is 20–30 percent.

■ Causes of behavior disorders can be categorized as biophysical, psychoanalytical, behavioral, and environmental. Many professionals now follow a holistic approach, taking into account the various perspectives.

■ Bower and Lambert have identified five behavioral patterns of behavior-disordered children, which are the basis for the PL 94–142 definition. Quay utilizes a four-dimensional approach: conduct disorder, personality disorder, immaturity, and socialized delinquency. Quay's categorization, while not directly helpful in identifying and setting up specific intervention, does superbly describe the varied manifestations of behavior disorders in children.

■ Teachers play a critical role in the screening and identification of behavior-disordered children.

■ Most programs for behavior-disordered children select among a variety of curricular approaches and do not rely on any one methodological approach.

■ One method of working with mildly or moderately disordered pupils uses the helping teacher or crisis teacher model. The helping/crisis teacher works directly with children referred temporarily during crisis situations by the regular teacher, as well as with other teachers in a consultative relationship.

■ Behavior modification is widely used in helping behavior-disordered children to learn new academic and social skills, replacing their dysfunctional, inappropriate skills.

REVIEW QUESTIONS

1. List some guidelines that teachers can use to help identify children with behavior disorders.

2. Do you think that every teacher can be successful in working with children who are behavior disordered? Why or why not?

3. Discuss why you would (or would not) like to try behavior modification in the classroom. Why do you think these techniques would be easy (or difficult) to implement?

4. Why do you think the concept of a helping teacher will (or will not) come more frequently into use in programs for the mildly and moderately behavior disordered? Would you like to be one? Why or why not?

5. Describe Quay's four dimensions for classifying behavior-disordered children.

6. Under which of Quay's four dimensions of classification would you place Freddy, the boy in the case study? Why? Which dimension for John? Why?

CHANGING BEHAVIOR

For many pupils, a demonstration of inappropriate social behavior—among other variables—leads to their identification as handicapped. Learning how to best teach them from an academic perspective is thus not enough. If they are to be taught, and to learn, appropriate social behaviors, consideration must also be given to teaching social behavior. Research in behavioral psychology has provided teachers with a set of principles and a technology for helping pupils improve their social, as well as academic, behavior. These principles force teachers and parents to "practice what they preach" and make changes in their own behavior in order to facilitate appropriate changes on the part of their pupils.

A method of behavioral management which has come into widespread use in the last few years in special education classes as well as in regular classrooms is contingency contracting. Simply stated, contingency contracting is "Grandma's Law": first you eat your dinner, *then* you get your dessert or, in terms of school performance (for example) first you complete ten multiplication problems, then you may spend ten minutes in the activity and games corner.

Many teachers as well as parents of children with mild to severe behavioral problems have found that they can help behavior-disordered children improve their behavior by utilizing contingency contracting. In their book, *How to Use Contingency Contracting in the Classroom*, Lloyd Homme and associates suggest that teachers using this approach must be sure that the contracts they make with students are fair to both teacher and student, that they are clearly and positively stated, and that they are honestly and consistently carried out. The following five rules are suggested for using rewards in contingency contracting (Homme et al., 1970, pp. 18–19).

RULE 1 The contract payoff (reward) should be immediate. It is of particular importance that this rule be observed early in the game when the child is just learning about contracting.

RULE 2 Initial contracts should call for and reward small approximations. If the initial performance requested from the student is a small, simple-to-perform approximation to the final performance desired, no difficulties will be encountered.

RULE 3 Reward frequently with small amounts. Experience has shown (and there is considerable laboratory evidence to support this) that it is far more effective to give frequent, small reinforcements than a few large ones.

RULE 4 The contract should call for and reward accomplishment rather than obedience. Thus, the contract should say: "If you accomplish such and such, you will be rewarded with such and such," not, "If you do what I tell you to do, I will reward you with such and such."

RULE 5 Reward the performance after it occurs. At first glance, this is the most self-evident of all the rules: first some task behavior, and then some reinforcing responses or reinforcing stimuli—the old "first work, then play" rule.

Despite the simplicity of Rule 5, Homme warns that it is frequently not followed.

The five rules outlined here serve as a review of the basic principles of reinforcement. Systematically following these guidelines structures the child's behavior and also the learning environment, including the behavior of the teacher, a key ingredient.

Freddy's SBD teacher utilizes contingency contracting frequently, working on improvements in both academic and social behavior. Some contracting assignments continue over long periods of time (e.g., completion of academic tasks in the classroom) and become part of the typical school day. Other contracting situations involve shorter periods (e.g., hanging up his coat and hat appropriately upon entering the room) and the behaviors are now being performed routinely. Freddy and his teacher frequently use the class's Reward Activity Menu. One of Freddy's contracts for arithmetic reads as follows: "After you complete ten subtraction problems during arithmetic class (9:30 to 10:00 A.M.), you may have the problems checked for accuracy. For each correct answer you may have one minute of time to use an activity from the Reward Activity Menu." Initially, Freddy's teacher required only two correct problems before she checked his progress and he received the reward.

The current contract is a gradual extension of the original contract, and thus follows Rules 1 and 2. Instead of waiting until the end of the day or the morning and receiving larger amounts of time, Freddy receives smaller amounts of time more often. Thus, Rule 3 is followed. Freddy's contract does reward accomplishment and the reward was definitely provided after the accomplishment (Rules 4 and 5). The contract is also positively stated, clear, and honest (Freddy always knows what and how much is expected and what he can expect as a reward). Eventually it is hoped that Freddy can take over complete responsibility for the contracting, as self-contracting (self-control) is the ultimate goal of a contingency reward program.

Because it can be applied across settings, contingency contracting has great potential for reintegrating pupils from the more segregated settings into the regular public school environment. Learning and progress attained in the severe behavior disorder setting can be transferred to public schools. There, teachers operating under the same principles (and with knowledge gained from the special teacher's experience) can assist the pupil to appropriately phase into the less restrictive setting.

1. The most logical, simple aspect of contingency contracting is Rule 5—reward the performance after it occurs—and yet in everyday life this practice quite frequently is not followed by teachers or parents. Think of some instances in your own life or those of friends in which the reinforcement was given before the performance, breaking Rule 5. Discuss these instances with your classmates. Why do you think this happens so often?
2. Evaluate the following contingency contract in the context of Homme's five rules for using rewards as guidelines. Also, consider the desirable characteristics of fairness, clarity, honesty, and positiveness. "Your report card isn't very good this time. Here is a dollar. After the next grading period, I'll give you money for every A grade you earn." After evaluating the contract, discuss with classmates how it might be changed to have more likelihood of success. Write your ideas down in contract form and let another person review it using the guidelines.

SUGGESTED READINGS

Kauffman, J. M. *Characteristics of Children's Behavioral Disorders*. Columbus, Ohio: Charles E. Merrill, 1977.

Reinert, H. R. *Children in Conflict*. St. Louis: C. V. Mosby, 1976.

Rhodes, W. C., and Paul, J. L. *Emotionally Disturbed and Deviant Children: New Views and Approaches*. Englewood Cliffs, NJ: Prentice-Hall, 1978.

Shea, T. M. *Teaching Children and Youth with Behavior Disorders*. St. Louis: C. V. Mosby, 1978.

Swanson, H. L., and Reinert, H. R. *Teaching Strategies for Children in Conflict*. St. Louis: C. V. Mosby, 1979.

16

CONTENTS

THE GIFTED AND TALENTED

This chapter discusses exceptional people who are slightly different from others thus far considered—the gifted and the talented. This small but rather diverse group of children has long been overlooked by the schools because it has been presumed that such children are not in need of special services. Yet, the gifted and talented do qualify for special education because they will not develop to their fullest potential without intervention by the schools. These children need to be challenged, to be stimulated to think and to behave creatively, and to use their special gifts as fruitfully as possible, for their own betterment and for the betterment of society.

R. J.

The following letter was written in response to a survey of poets regarding their ideas on the nature of creativity and its place in the educational process. The author of the letter is a professional writer who is also the parent of an intellectually and creatively gifted young boy, R. J. This letter is an articulate and moving plea for attention from the schools for the gifted child.

When we began to discover the extent of the difference between our son and other children of his age, spurred by his public-school kindergarten teacher's warning that we should get him out of that school and find someone who could give him some kind of challenge, I did as much reading as I could on the subject of giftedness, including the work that's being done to define and measure creativity. I was unimpressed by most of the studies which tried to pin down creativity with the same kinds of tests, under the same kinds of pressures and time limitations as provided by intelligence tests. There was only one that seemed promising—the one that stressed a sense of fun, a nonjudgmental atmosphere, and open-ended time periods. My conclusion was that the only way to assess the creativity or creative potential of a child is to observe him/her over a long period of time in an atmosphere of sharing and trust.

The psychologist who gave R. J. the battery of tests echoed my thoughts that creativity tests had not been shown to be accurate. But she also said that anyone who works with gifted children soon learns to recognize the child whose gifts were both creative and intellectual by personality, receptivity, and humor. Perhaps because our son is an unusually happy, outgoing person, my husband and I had not suspected the degree of his intellectual potential. We were victims of the myth that the super bright are also maladjusted. But we have known of his creativity from what seems to be the beginning. Being a poet, you may understand my joy in his first "poem," said at a little under two and a half. I was explaining autumn to him because he'd noticed the leaves on the ground. He listened solemnly and said, "The leaves will fall off the tree, and they will cry. They will say, 'Mommy, Mommy, we are green and yellow and sad.'" That was the first of a series of "poems" he created before his fourth birthday. His retort, at the age of three, to a child in his carpool who had hurt his feelings was, "You don't exist. You are only in my mind." We have never doubted his creativity.

Your article set me thinking. It was when R. J. was three that we first became aware of his need for time to dream. The teacher at his Montessori preschool told me she had known immediately that R. J. was different from other children, but had needed nearly three months to decide that his difference was a positive factor in his development instead of a negative one. He would wander away from an activity he had chosen or would put away his work and wander around the room instead of choosing another activity. He spent a great deal of time looking out the window at the Ohio River, which flowed past the school's parking lot.

He would seem to "go away," to be totally unconnected with what was happening around him, though it often turned out later that he had noticed most of what had gone on in the room while he had seemed to be concentrating on the river. Finally, his teacher discovered that whenever he seemed to be finished with one of these times "away," he had taken a major step in conceptualizing. Often he would want to talk about some philosophical idea he'd had —once he explained to the class how he thought life and death and God must work.

(He had never been to church or Sunday school.) Other times he would come back and choose an activity he had never tried for himself and do it correctly, though he never had a chance to practice. It was in that quiet, dreaming time that all his "work" seemed to get done. Luckily for us and for him, his teacher was sensitive enough not to interfere before she'd had a chance to learn the value of his unusual behavior.

Like most gifted children, he never seemed to *learn* to read. Without doing the prereading activities that are supposed to be essential to reading, he simply began reading aloud to the other children one day, with proper vocal inflection and an obvious understanding of how punctuation affected the way a sentence should be read. None of us knows how or when he learned. The skill seems to have come upon him fully realized. That, too, may have grown during his quiet times.

We had no luck in trying to find special attention in the Cincinnati public schools for a child with R. J.'s capabilities and needs. In this system nothing is done for the gifted child until the upper grades. Thanks to a very generous scholarship, he is now in the first grade of a private school with an IGE (individually guided education) program, small classes, and at least a promise to try to meet him on his own ground. Your article reminded me that his creativity needs as much attention as his intellectual capabilities. I've often read that time for dreaming is essential to all gifted children, and I don't know whether that is a part of intelligence or creativity or both, but his teacher and I have discussed the dangers of trying to "keep him busy" every minute.

Do the school districts you work with provide gifted/talented programs in the primary grades? Routinely? I ask because I think I'm becoming a fanatic on the subject, and I am beginning to put together the lack of openness and freedom you describe and I have also met in poetry workshops with "honors" students on the high school level with the total lack of concern with gifted primary children.

Envision the typical primary classroom, where dreaming time is not available, where the "right" answer and the "proper" behavior are praised and all else either condemned or ignored. It has often been shown that the gifted six-year-old gradually becomes more and more "normal" as he/she progresses through the grades. It is still said by many that the others are catching up, when we know perfectly well that the bright child is simply being held back, often until the special quality which showed that child's giftedness at an early age has been systematically stifled and destroyed. . . .

It seems to me that the doubly gifted child *doesn't* disappear. That child simply learns to fear and distrust the creativity that causes trouble in the system and keeps it hidden from others for so long that it is finally unreachable, perhaps dead. You say those bright kids feel safe in the academic realm, and I agree. That's where they get their support, the validation of who they are, and the grades—the "honors" classes, are the badges without which they would be lost. A number of studies point out that the child without creativity gets along well in the system if she/he is able to use intelligence to get around the problems of creativity; the child with only creativity has the greatest problems of being only a victim. But I'm not sure I accept that. Clearly one way to use intelligence to avoid the traumas of creativity is to bury the creativity and go after academic success and achievement. While that method of coping may lead to apparent success, the important question which hasn't been answered is how much has been lost when creativity is suppressed.

Much of my own school experience is lost in the mists of forgetting—maybe repression. I never had the potential my son has, but I was brighter and more creative than most of the other children in my classes; I cannot forget the sixth-grade teacher who told me I would never amount to anything because I was interested in so many things and couldn't limit myself to one subject in which I could excel. I was truly made to believe that a general zest for living and learning was a fault I should try to remedy. I became the very academically talented child I've despaired of in poetry residencies— writing always, but writing safely, imitatively, distrustful of anything that came into my head which didn't fit a model I had read somewhere and so insecure about what I had to offer that only A's had real meaning for me. I've often yearned for a PITS (Poets in the Schools) program for the teenaged writer I was. Only now, as I approach my 36th birthday, am I beginning to trust my creativity and let go the compulsion to achieve every minute, to meet a rigid time schedule, to force my writing the way I once forced my academic tasks. . . . I've wondered a lot lately where I might be today if my creative energies hadn't had to spend more than 25 years battling their way out of the prison I'd made for them. I see my son, whose potential is so much greater, facing the same old threats, and I'm afraid for him.

What might the future hold for all of us if we were able to take the incredible wealth of our gifted children and nurture it from the beginning, letting their special qualities grow naturally from the age of three or four or five instead of looking for it at twelve or thirteen or later?

The fact that some people survive formal education with their gifts intact is a kind of miracle. But in my thinking about this problem I wonder how many are maimed by the struggle. Is it surprising that Edison, having been called retarded by the schools, went on to his astonishingly creative life at home, where his mother opened all the doors and let him follow his own paths? Or that Henry Ford had only a fifth-grade education? I wonder what 14 or 16 years in the system would have done to either of them? Is it an inevitable drying up of creative resources that afflicts a Tennessee Williams or an Edward Albee—or is it that the violent struggle to maintain their creativity through their early years was too damaging? When people point to the fragility of so many creative artists, all those who destroy themselves one way or another, I begin to wonder if that fragility could be the result of the battering they somehow had to survive as children.

I often think our priorities are backwards. It might be better to concentrate our energies on the gifted beginning at 18 months or two years, and when we've helped them along as far as we can in the elementary years, turn them loose at age 12 when they could probably fend for themselves and find their own direction instead of crushing them first and trying to help them later. . . .

I think the education of the gifted may be the single most important thing this country, world, in fact, must consider as the times get tougher and more dangerous. In every way we need the power that lies at our fingertips, not just in the sciences but in the arts and the realms of the human spirit.

Sincerely,

Stephanie

Points for Consideration

- Stephanie's feelings of frustration and, at times, futility are typical of many parents of gifted and talented children when they are unable to get schools to provide their children with a quality education.

- R. J.'s ability to achieve developmental milestones and academic skills early and in unconventional ways is a relatively common characteristic among superiorly capable children. However, not all gifted and talented children will necessarily excel in all areas of development.

- Creativity and intellectual superiority are separate, identifiable exceptionalities that may or may not be mutually exclusive. R. J.'s mother identifies specific behaviors related to R. J.'s creative efforts and intellectual accomplishments. Educational programming may require different teaching strategies for the two groups.

Common Misconceptions

As we can see, Stephanie, as a mother of an extremely gifted child, was faced with unveiling the old myths about giftedness.

- *The Educational Needs of Gifted and Talented Children Cannot and Should Not Be the Responsibility of the Public School.* Although most gifted and talented children's needs are not being met by the public schools, there are exemplary programs throughout the country.

- *Superior Children Often Have Related Emotional Problems.* Actually, the incidence of disturbed behavior is less in the gifted than the average population. The gifted are usually well adjusted and sociable, with the exception of the profoundly intellectually gifted who are so bright that they have difficulty finding peers with whom they can communicate.

■ *Gifted Means a High IQ.* There are various types of giftedness, two of which are intellectual superiority and creativity.

■ *Gifted and Talented Children Are Superior in All Pursuits and Areas of Development.* This misconception manifests itself in the schools that often adopt the philosophy, "They'll learn it on their own." There are gifted and talented youngsters who need not only guidance and nurturance, but also those who have specific learning problems.

HISTORY OF GIFTED EDUCATION

As far back as ancient Greece, there were plans for selecting and nurturing the gifted. Plato intended to take the more gifted children and educate them intellectually and morally to become the rulers of the state. Socrates even considered breeding human beings for their intellectual gifts in much the same way that hunting dogs were bred for their prowess in the field (Burt, 1975). This proposal may today seem farfetched and unthinkable but one should take into consideration that for many years it was assumed that intelligence was inherited.

Lewis Terman's *Genetic Studies of Genius*, compiled between 1925 and 1959, established a formidable case for genetic influences on intelligence. In 1921, Terman received a grant that enabled him to select 1,000 or more children with IQs over 140 from the California schools. He did, however, include 65 children whose IQs were in the 135 to 139 range. His goal was to examine the top one percent of the population. He used the Stanford-Binet intelligence test, which he had standardized in this country in 1916. His findings about these children were as follows (Terman and Oden, 1947; Gowan, 1977):

■ They were physically superior
■ They had a wide variety of interests
■ They read many books and had learned to read easily
■ They engaged in a wide range of activities
■ They knew a great deal about various games and play
■ They scored above average on tests of character; that is, they were highly moral
■ Gifted girls tended to be more masculine in their play than average girls
■ The gifted were not asocial or mentally unbalanced
■ High intelligence remained rather constant through life, and mental age increased through age 50
■ There was a disproportionate number of Jewish children in the sample
■ There were more males than females in the sample
■ One-third of the offspring of the original sample scored above 130 on the Stanford-Binet test

Terman's long-term project convinced many educators that heredity was the prime factor of intelligence. He also instilled great confidence in the reliability of the Stanford-Binet IQ test. Educators were largely content to rely upon a single figure and a single measurement of intelligence. Several criticisms of Terman's study and findings have, however, emerged (Gowan, 1977):

- Intelligence was assumed to be a single-faceted phenomenon
- Environmental factors such as socioeconomic status and environmental influences in assessing the abilities of members of minority groups were not accounted for
- There was no attempt to measure or to recognize creative ability
- Teacher nomination alone is not a very reliable method of identification

Actually, very little was done for the gifted as a group between 1925 and 1950. There were special classes in only a few states. The sparsity of such classes was due mainly to the small numbers of identified gifted children in many communities and to the fear of elitism. However, after World War II, the country recognized the need for gifted persons in the fields of science and technology. Organizations for the gifted, such as the American Association for the Gifted, began to form. In 1956, the National Merit Scholarship Corporation gave 556 awards; by 1960, some 3,000 students had started college under the auspices of Merit Scholarship funds (Witty, 1971). When Sputnik was launched by the Soviet Union in 1957, the United States was concerned why America had not been the first with a space launch. The educational system became a convenient scapegoat for our failings in science. Admiral Rickover was vociferous in his warnings that the United States would fall farther behind the Soviets militarily unless our country prepared its gifted young people for careers in science, mathematics, and technology (Tannenbaum, 1972).

Meanwhile, the civil rights movement of the 1960s began to gather momentum, and many old beliefs about the innate inferiority of blacks were attacked and disproved. IQ tests were criticized as culturally biased. Since the 1960s, a broader, more humanistic perspective of giftedness has developed. Educators began to realize that one measure, the IQ test, could not adequately identify all the gifted and talented.

DEFINITION OF TERMS AND CHARACTERISTICS

Commissioner Marland (1972) defined **giftedness** as follows:

> Gifted and talented children are those identified by professionally qualified persons, who by virtue of outstanding abilities are capable of high performance. These are children who require differentiated educational programs and/or services beyond those normally provided by the regular school program in order to realize their contribution to self and society. Children capable of high performance include those with demonstrated achievement and/or potential ability in any of the following areas, singly or in combination:
>
> 1. general intellectual ability
> 2. specific academic aptitude
> 3. creative or productive thinking
> 4. leadership ability
> 6. psychomotor ability

From the federal point of view the target population is the top 3–5 percent of the nation's school-age children (Tannenbaum, 1972).

General Intellectual Ability

General intellectual ability refers to high scores in IQ or achievement tests. An example of this type of child would be one who scores above 130 on the Stanford-Binet Intelligence Scale. This child would be expected to excel in many and varied educational settings. However, it is incorrect to believe that a child with a superior ability level would necessarily demonstrate outstanding performance in all endeavors. Yet, by the nature of the term "general intellectual ability," this is too often the expectation.

Specific Academic Ability

Specific academic ability refers to excellence in a certain subject area. For example, a child may have skills in mathematics far superior to those of his or her age group, but the child may be average or below average in other subjects.

Creative or Productive Thinking

Creative or productive thinking suggests the ability of the student to ". . . produce new forms, to conjoin elements that are customarily thought of as independent or dissimilar; not merely the propensity for seeing the bizarre but rather the aptitude for achieving new meanings having social value" (Getzels and Jackson, 1960, p. 10). This child searches for uniqueness in self and the outside world. This child may or may not also have a high IQ score. Some characteristics of the creative child are (Callahan, 1978, p. 4):

- Openness to experience
- Possession of an internal locus of evaluation
- An ability to play with ideas
- A willingness to take risks
- A preference for complexity
- A tolerance for ambiguity
- In general, a positive self-image
- The ability to lose him- or herself in a task

Torrance (1962, 1963) discusses additional characteristics of the highly creative child. By its very definition creativity demands a certain measure of nonconformity. The child must therefore learn to stand alone and trust his or her own creative impulses, or must repress them in order to be accepted by teachers and other students. Many of these students prefer to learn on their own rather than with the group. These students need a sense of purpose. They have a reputation for sometimes having wild and silly ideas. They often produce a multitude of unusual ideas in their work. They usually display a keen sense of humor and playfulness.

Leadership Ability

The Marland report also cites leadership ability as characteristic of the gifted child. Other children will look to this student as a negotiator, as a person who can help solve problems. This student is often empathetic to others. He or she may be the student who is elected president of the class, or may work more quietly behind the scenes.

Students with special talents in the arts, music, dance, drama, and other related disciplines have visual and performing arts skills. A child may be extremely talented in dance, for instance, and may not excel in academic subjects. Another child may be intellectually gifted as well as being very talented in one of the arts. This area has been grossly neglected in the schools.

Psychomotor Ability

Psychomotor skills is the final category included in the Marland report. This group includes children who are gifted in the use of their large muscles. These are the students who usually surpass other children in school sports. (Such a child may be the school track star, the skilled gymnast, the top swimmer.) This category has been deleted from the government guidelines, however, because many of these students are already being served through athletic programs.

Clearly, a child may be gifted in any one or several of the categories just cited. The main point is that in order to be considered gifted, a child does not have to exhibit a high IQ, which is no longer the sole criterion for this exceptionality.

Finding gifted and talented students often requires identification procedures that extend beyond the classroom.

IDENTIFICATION ALTERNATIVES

Identification is a complex process, and always hinges upon the particular school's definition of gifted and talented. It is important that schools define the target population in terms of either a specific number or a certain percentage. Also, schools should ensure that the instruments used for identification are appropriate and understood by the entire teaching staff. A wide variety of assessment tools should be used since no single measurement or score is accurate enough by itself.

Group IQ Tests

Group IQ tests are valuable as screening instruments but should not be used to identify children for gifted programs. They were designed for average students and therefore the ceilings for the tests are not high enough to test for giftedness. The types of questions asked usually measure the lower level cognitive skills, such as recall and comprehension, and usually require one correct answer. The highly intelligent child may see beyond the question to another possible answer. Since group tests also rely heavily upon verbal and reading skills, children who have different languages, different dialects, and/or are from different cultures might have difficulty with some of the test items because they are not familiar with English.

It is not unusual for a child's scores on the group IQ test and the individual IQ test to vary by as much as 30 points. For example, the Otis Group IQ test failed to identify nearly 50 percent of the gifted when using a cutoff score of 125. Many students who did not score 125 or higher were later found to have scores which ranged from 146 to 161 on the individual Stanford-Binet (Pegnato and Birch, 1959; Martinson, 1975).

The advantage of the group test is that it can be administered quickly and inexpensively to a large number of students, and it can be useful if combined with other screening instruments. However, the group test has many built-in biases and weaknesses and should be used with caution.

Individual IQ Tests

Individual IQ tests are more reliable in identifying gifted students. However, these tests are also more expensive and time-consuming and require trained personnel to administer and score them. Their ceiling scores are higher, the test is more comprehensive, and the items allow for a greater range of responses. The examiner can also make individual assessments of the acceptability of each response, whereas on the group test there is only one possible correct answer. Evidence shows that the individual test is quite reliable and favored by experts in identifying intellectually gifted youngsters; even the individual IQ test, however, does not identify the creative or the disadvantaged child.

Tests of other types are needed in order to identify students gifted in other than primarily cognitive areas. The possibility of broader measures of intelligence and ability is now being investigated (Kaufman, 1979). Research is being done in the neurological area of testing to better understand the brain and how it works. This area is quite new and the fascinating question of left- and right-brain functions is currently being investigated (Torrance and Mourad, 1979). Tests such as the Stanford-Binet and the Weschler measure mostly left-brain abilities and do not provide an adequate picture of the more creative right-brain abilities.

The Structure of the Intellect

The Structure of the Intellect (SOI) test (Meeker, 1969) is a viable alternative to the more traditional IQ test. Based on Guilford's three-dimensional cube representation of the human intellectual structure, the SOI measures divergent as well as convergent thought processes. A profile of a student's learning abilities in many areas provides the teacher with a detailed picture of a particular student's strengths and weaknesses. Unlike other tests, the SOI (administered by teachers) lends itself easily to lesson and individualized curriculum planning for each learner.

Behavior Rating Scales

Behavior rating scales can be useful auxiliary instruments for screening. The Renzulli-Hartman-Callahan Scale is useful because it asks the examiner to respond in terms of the child's direct behavior. Too many of the rating scales do not include this important admonition, and the consequence is that the examiner may not base responses upon observed behavior. Another important prerequisite for the success of rating scales is that the examiner be trained in their use. Too often, teachers are untrained and as a result responses are not accurate.

Teacher Nomination

Teacher nomination is one of the most frequently used screening devices but one of the least effective and reliable (Gallagher, 1966). Some teachers prefer one sex over the other. Some tend to choose the conformist high achievers and overlook the underachiever or the creative or divergent thinkers (Martinson, 1975). Jacobs (1971) found that kindergarten teachers nominated only 10 percent of the gifted. Teachers can improve their accuracy if they are properly trained in what to look for in the gifted child; many simply operate on mistaken assumptions of giftedness. Too often the teacher simply does not understand either the meaning or purpose for a gifted child's questions, or that boredom and other inappropriate classroom behaviors might be the result of a superior mind in an unstimulating environment (Tuttle, 1978).

Getzels and Jackson conducted a study in 1958 with a sample of 500 adolescents in a private, midwestern school. For the purposes of the experiment, the researchers chose the top 20 percent of students according to an IQ test and the top 20 percent of students as measured by a creativity test. Students who scored high on both tests were not included in the experiment because the purpose of the study was to examine the differentiating characteristics of each of the two groups. The findings were surprising. First, both groups were equally superior in school achievement even though there was a 23-point difference between the mean IQs of the two groups. Second, the teachers preferred the high IQ group even though both groups were achieving equally in school. Third, the creative child rated a wide range of interests, emotional stability, and a sense of humor as being more important than did the high IQ group. Fourth, it was found that the highly creative child didn't try to model him- or herself after the teacher and, in fact, was more negative toward the teacher as a model. This experiment should serve as a warning to prospective teachers of the creatively gifted. The creative may not be as easy to like as their high IQ peers, and teachers should beware of discounting their gifts simply because these children do not conform to expectations.

Parent Nomination

Parent nomination has been found much more reliable in identifying the gifted and talented than teacher nomination. Jacobs (1971) discovered that teachers accurately selected 9.5 percent of the gifted, while parents correctly identified 61 percent. The parents were also found to be more conservative in assessing their child's abilities. Parents have the advantage of having had more contact with the child and can also aid in identification by commenting on such items as (Martinson, 1975):

- Child's current hobbies or interests
- Books he or she has enjoyed
- Interests other than reading
- Special problems or needs
- Exceptional accomplishments or talents
- Special opportunities the child has had
- Leisure activity when alone

Such information is most successfully used when provided by informed and educated parents.

Peer Nomination

Peer nominations are often useful too. Students can list who they would choose to help them with a particular project or task, who is good in certain subject areas, who has the most original ideas, or whom they would go to for help in a specific situation (Martinson, 1975). Peers can be especially useful in identifying those gifted in leadership ability (Doob, 1975).

Biographical Inventories

Biographical inventories supply information about the child's background and interests and can be important to a screening committee because the instrument can easily be geared toward a specific program design. In a 1974 survey of research on such inventories, the Institute for Behavioral Research in Creativity found that biographical inventories were generally effective predictors of success in many fields.

Autobiographies

Autobiographies, or self-reporting, can be helpful in identifying gifted elementary school students. Students can talk into a tape recorder or write about themselves and offer valuable clues to giftedness. For example, a child may tell that he or she learned to read at the age of four or learned to play the violin at age three. Secondary-school students are more reluctant to be candid and may view self-reporting as an invasion of privacy or bragging.

Creativity Tests

Tests of creativity are generally rated highly by experts but have not been used widely in schools. One caution should be suggested about the use of creativity tests, however; there has been some controversy as to the validity of these measurements. One argument is that the tests do not all measure the same thing; creativity is an illusive concept to define, and the experts are not in total agreement as to what it is, or how to measure or test for its existence.

Dimensionality of creativity tests refers to the requirement of devising test items that are generally independent of other traditional cognitive measures. Too many items on creativity tests are not clearly distinct from items on other types of tests (Treffinger, Renzulli, and Feldhusen, 1975).

Since creativity tests are not as common as other types of tests, let us examine a few items that appeared on one such test (Wilson, Guilford, and Christenson, 1975).

1. Indian ——————————————— money
   Write a word on the line that associates the two words on either side.
2. tree   a   b   g   m   s   dog
   Which of the five letters is the first letter of a word that associates with both tree and dog and has a different meaning in relation to each?
3. The examinee is given two very short stories to read. In three minutes the examinee is to think of as many appropriate possible titles for the stories as he can.
4. List six uses for a newspaper besides its use to inform us of the news.

There are several possible answers to the first question. Some of the possibilities are penny, nickel, copper, wampum, etc. For the second question, the desired answer is "b" for bark. The third question also has several possible answers. The responses would be graded by a literary expert for originality. The fourth has numerous possible responses too. The originality score here would be determined by weighting each score after administering the test to a large sample and noting the frequency of certain answers. From these samples, it is not difficult to see why critics of creativity tests insist that the questions be constructed less like conventional cognitive items on other tests. Is it a test of creativity if there is one right answer?

Expert Judgment

The judgment of experts in a particular field is an especially good way to find students who have special talents. Recognition by an expert has strong motivational impact on a child and, in some cases, can encourage a child so much that he or she works much harder to achieve. An example of this phenomenon can be illustrated by the experience of a high school boy who was chosen in the late 1960s to participate in Project Prometheus, a summer enrichment program for rural Oregon children. One of David's poems was praised by an expert and subsequently published in a literary magazine that the program sponsored. David now has a Master of Fine Arts and publishing poetry has become his lifetime pursuit. He believes that his participation and recognition in the Project Prometheus was the catalyst of his commitment to becoming a writer.

Judges should be selected carefully. They should be able to differentiate between eccentricity and originality; they must also understand child development in order to know whether a particular ability indicates precocity. Often such experts are difficult to find, but when they are available the school would be wise to use them (Martinson, 1975).

Like teaching other exceptional students, providing effective learning environments for the gifted and talented requires individualized instruction.

Case Study

The case study synthesizes information from the home and school, assessing such information as the degree of intellectual stimulation at home, the interest the home shows in achievement, the nutrition provided in the home, parental attitudes, attitudes of peers toward the child, teacher attitudes toward the child's achievements and potential, and a summary of test results. The case study is especially useful for identifying gifted minority students and handicapped gifted students.

EDUCATIONAL PROGRAMMING

Delivery Services

There are many possible strategies for educating the gifted. Following is a discussion on the merits of several.

Early admission to school is usually a good idea for the gifted, particularly the intellectually gifted. There is not much evidence that early admission is harmful (Doob, 1975); the child's social and emotional development is assessed before he or she is admitted. Early admission may be especially beneficial for gifted girls since they tend to be developmentally advanced.

Acceleration is another alternative. The child may skip a grade or two, or may be enrolled in an ungraded school. Students may take more classes or may go to summer school. A good argument for acceleration is that most creative work is done early in life, between the ages of 25 and 35, and the sooner the gifted child is out of school, the sooner he or she will be equipped with the tools with which to be creative. Stanley (1976) points out that especially in mathematics, acceleration is more effective than enrichment or other means of intervention as evidenced by his accelerated math program at Johns Hopkins University.

Enrichment in the confines of the regular classroom is the most frequently used program. The child is given extra or different materials and special projects within the regular school program. The problem with this method is that the gifted child may feel isolated and the teacher may not be qualified to teach the gifted. This approach is particularly unsuited to the highly gifted child (IQ above 160).

Special classes or special schools may also be useful for the gifted. Special classes may encompass the full day or part of the day. The class may meet every day, or one or several times a week. The class may cover a subject in which the gifted child excels. It could be music or art, among many other subjects. New York City, for example, has separate high schools for students with high levels of ability in fine arts, performing arts, and the sciences. The advantages are that these schools offer smaller classes, more advanced study, and are freer to provide varied types of curricula. According to Mirman (1971), there is no data-based evidence that the self-image of the gifted is improved by interaction with average students, nor is there evidence that the academic achievement of average students improves by interacting with the gifted. In a recent survey of 250 gifted college students chosen nationally on the basis of scholastic excellence and achievement, 75 percent of the students preferred intellectual to age grouping. Ninety percent rated intellectual grouping as the best learning situation for themselves (Mirman, 1971).

Other placement alternatives for gifted children are summer programs, advanced placement, and seminars. In such programs, students can earn credits quickly and gain new experience. Advanced placement refers to college courses for advanced students. Often the student can earn college credit while still enrolled in public school. Seminars are a good idea for small or rural school systems. Several districts can be pooled to offer special programs for the gifted or talented. Itinerant teachers, in the role of consultant to the gifted, can teach special classes or can act as guides for the regular classroom teacher in such matters as curriculum.

Community sponsors, tutors, or mentors can be especially useful for creative or disadvantaged students for whom modeling is important. Usually there is not a resident poet or pianist or master mechanic in the school, and if the community has such a person who can offer his or her services, the school should take advantage of the person's expertise.

Role of Teachers

Not every teacher should teach gifted students. Gifted children are often regarded as a threat to the authority of the teacher. The child may correct the teacher, may know more than the teacher does about certain subjects, may make fun of the teacher, or may learn faster than the teacher. A teacher who is not secure emotionally may react with hostility or resentment and try to oppress the gifted child (Mirman, 1971; Maker, 1975). The child may then become hostile or bored and become a behavior problem or just "tune out" (Impellizzeri, Farrell, and Melville, 1976).

What then are the characteristics of successful teachers of the gifted? Maker (1975) suggests they have generally three basic qualities:

1. The teacher should be above average in intelligence but not *too* intelligent.
2. The teacher should have a solid ego and be emotionally mature. The insecure teacher may become authoritarian or may become embroiled in a battle of wills with the class.
3. There may be a positive correlation between creative thinking abilities on the part of the teacher and his or her effectiveness. This idea was proposed by Yamamoto in 1965.

Teachers of the high achieving gifted need extensive knowledge of the content areas in which they plan to teach. They must also know how to stimulate productive thinking, and they must have had supervised practice in working with the gifted. For low achieving gifted students, the teacher must have an understanding of advanced curriculum, be knowledgeable about children with motivational problems, have an understanding of culturally different children, and know how to work with handicapped children (Maker, 1975). Gallagher (1975) also feels that the teacher of the creatively gifted should be open and encourage a safe, permissive atmosphere. The teacher must also value the ideas and products of the child. Callahan (1978) supports this notion.

Bishop (1975) has some interesting observations regarding teachers of the high achieving gifted. He states that the teacher for these students must be intelligent (the teachers he identified had a mean score of 128 on the Weschler Adult Intelligence Scale), should have a life pattern of interest in reading and literature, should have a high achievement level and need as measured on the Edwards Personal Preference Schedule, should have an accepting attitude toward students, and should emphasize student participation rather than attentiveness.

The gifted are a complicated and fascinating group of children. They are not all alike and have as many special educational problems as does the handicapped population. Teachers must have a thorough understanding of these students and must also personally have certain gifts in order to successfully educate this group. Parents have great power to change the educational system, as was clear in the movement for providing services for the handicapped and the retarded. Now it is the turn of advocates for gifted education. We clearly cannot afford to retard gifted children any more than we already have by our benign neglect of their fine minds.

Role of Parents

Many parents are aware of their child's gifts or talents before the child enters school, especially if they know what to look for. Here are just some of the characteristics of young gifted and talented children. The child:

- Can talk and walk before other children his or her age
- Is able to categorize objects
- Has an interest in mathematics (e.g., counts objects, tells time, and can subtract or divide)
- Is highly imaginative, wears costumes of his or her own concoction, has imaginary friends
- Has a wide array of interests, reacts dynamically with the environment, asks questions about the world
- Has high powers of concentration and stays on task longer than other children the same age
- Likes to collect things
- Shows an early interest in music, art, mechanics, writing
- Has a good sense of humor
- Is very critical of him- or herself and of ideas that might be accepted by other children the same age

Once parents suspect that their child may be gifted, they should encourage the child at home and look for help from the schools and the community. Here are some suggestions for the parent (Sisk, 1977).

- Keep a journal of observations of the child to help prove that he or she is gifted or talented. Show this journal to school personnel to help them determine whether or not the child needs special services.
- Meet with the child's teacher when the child enters school and compare ideas and observations.
- Check on community resources and become involved in locating services for your child in addition to what is offered through the school.

Gowan (1964), an advocate of parental involvement in early learning, also has some practical suggestions for parents of bright and creative children.

- Parents should read to their children.
- Parents should try to find bright playmates for their children. Gifted children are often lonely if they do not have a peer with whom they can communicate.
- Parents should take their children to museums, historical sites, concerts.
- Parents should strive to answer the child's questions and not tell him or her to be quiet all the time. If parents cannot answer a question, they should make an effort to find the answer or direct the child to a source that can answer the question.
- Parents should not push the child too much or force him or her to perform for company or friends.
- Parents should not be stuffy about the child's fantasy life and should not try to overstructure the child's life.
- Parents should allow the child to make decisions.

Parents play a vital role in identifying and in serving the gifted and talented. They know the child better than anyone else and have the most vested interest in seeing that their child receives professional attention by the schools. Too often, unless the parents demand services, the child will be overlooked and will not be served because he or she is not visibly in need of special help.

EXCEPTIONALITIES

Identification of and providing more opportunities for gifted minority and handicapped children and youth are issues currently receiving more attention. Nonetheless, the gifts of these special groups have been and are still often overlooked.

GIFTED AND BICULTURAL   The bicultural student is handicapped when competing with dominant culture students on achievement and IQ tests, largely because of language and cultural interference. Often, these students are overlooked by the schools or are actively discouraged from trying to excel. Minority students seem to recognize their abilities but realistically know that they do not have an equal chance to excel in school (Raph, Goldberg, and Passow, 1966).

We need to examine what should be construed as gifted in terms of the minority culture if we are to accurately identify the gifted bicultural child. The System of Multicultural Pluralistic Assessment (SOMPA) is constructed to assess the bicultural child in terms of his or her own socioeconomic climate and norms. The Cartoon Conservation Scales can also be useful because they can be administered in Spanish. Language Assessment Scales, the Bilingual Syntax Measure, and the English and Spanish productive language tests of the Circo battery are also recommended (Bernal, 1978; Mercer and Lewis, 1978).

Torrance states that, by and large, tests of creativity do not appear to have much of a cultural bias. The Torrance Tests of Creativity have been tested for such a bias, and none appears to exist. This lack of bias plus the open-ended nature of the test allow the child to respond in terms of his or her own experience (Torrance, 1977). Torrance (1969) identifies a set of creative positives that occur frequently among creatively gifted disadvantaged children. These are: (1) high nonverbal fluency and originality; (2) high creative productivity in small groups; (3) adeptness in visual art activities; (4) high creativity in movement, dance, and other physical activities; (5) high motivation in games, music, sports, humor, and concrete objects; and (6) language rich in imagery.

We can see that certain tests do not favor the disadvantaged and that there are other measures or adjusted measurements that should be used in order to identify the gifted in this population. Also, we should bear in mind that the use of several measurements is again the wisest alternative.

GIFTED AND HANDICAPPED   The handicapped gifted are even more the victims of labeling than are the bicultural. They have been placed in an environment of special education, therapy, and remediation, and in these circumstances few teachers recognize their giftedness. These teachers are not trying to overlook gifts; they simply are not trained in what to look for. Even if the child is identified as gifted, there are still problems. It is often difficult to find a place for the handicapped in a gifted program. The special education teacher may not want to interrupt the existing program. Administrators may have problems with financial and program qualifications. In addition, testing may be difficult. The examiner must look for potential ability rather than for demonstrated ability.

There is also the question of whether it would be better to compare the gifted handicapped person to other members of the same population or compare them to their nonhandicapped peers, since that would provide a more realistic prediction of success in the mainstream. The use of the case study, biographical inventories, and several other assessment instruments, including Torrance's Checklist of Creative Positives, can aid in identification (Maker, 1977). Programs for the gifted handicapped are in the first stages of development and are being operated under the assumption that potential is worth searching for. One such program at the University of Illinois (Karnes and Bertsche, 1978), funded in 1975 by the Bureau of Education for the Handicapped, stresses the importance of exposing children to creative environments and stimulating them with a wide array of experiences before trying to screen them for special talents. This idea of long-term observation is a sound one.

Project SEARCH in Connecticut is looking for children who display complex behavior patterns, those with general creative potential, and those with potential in certain talented areas. In this project, observations of children reacting to art, music, or some other type of stimulus will be an integral part of identification (Maker, 1977). Another project at Chapel Hill, North Carolina (Blancher-Dixon and Turnbull, 1978), also funded by BEH, serves handicapped or economically disadvantaged gifted children between the ages of 2½ and 6. Structured and un-structured observations are used, as well as checklists and sociometric measures for identification purposes (Clark, 1979; Maker, 1977).

GIFTED AND LEARNING DISABLED   The gifted child who is also learning disabled presents a difficult problem in identification and in providing services. It is hard enough to ensure that the normal gifted child will be found and served, but it is even more difficult for the learning-disabled child to be identified as gifted. This special group is usually not identified on group IQ tests because they often mani-fest problems in visual perception and, as a result, cannot read well enough or with enough comprehension to do well on a group test (Elkin, 1973). If indi-vidual IQ test scores are analyzed from a diagnostic perspective, the focus is usually on the student's problem areas. Since professionals are not looking for the gifts of these learning-disabled students, their special placement is remedial in nature and their superior abilities go undetected. The gifted learning-disabled child can, however, be identified and served. It is just more difficult to identify their giftedness as it is hidden by a more visible exceptionality.

GIFTED AND FEMALE   The last subgroup to be discussed is gifted females. The general intellectual abilities of males and females are roughly the same, but there are important and puzzling differences in the specific abilities of each sex. In three years of testing mathematically gifted students, the Study of Mathematically Precocious Youth found 167 boys but only 19 girls who scored 640 or above on the SAT mathematics test as seventh and eighth graders. Attempts have been made at Johns Hopkins University to raise the mathematics scores of girls, but these attempts have been only modestly successful (Fox, 1977).

From adolescence to adulthood, boys are also better at spatial relationships. It is possible that there is a connection between spatial ability and mathematics ability. It may be the influence of the father that gives boys the edge in mathe-matics. The absence of the father in early childhood seems to correlate more with a boy's lower mathematics scores than with his verbal scores. It could be that boys learn an analytic approach from their fathers and girls do not.

Studies of creative female mathematicians show that they tend to come from homes in which the fathers were professionals and were highly dominant figures. These women were most often oldest children and had no brothers. The women

The talents of minority female students are too frequently unrecognized or undeveloped by the schools.

also identified more with their fathers than with their mothers. Problem-solving skill does appear to be related to sex-role identification. Another reason why girls do not do as well in arithmetic is because parents tend to notice and reward boys' early interest in mathematics but not girls'. Parents are more likely to purchase scientific toys for boys. Meeker suggests that little girls do not learn spatial orientation in their play and that parents should try to compensate for this. Older girls are recommended to take karate or tai chi chuan (Navarre, 1980). Generally, schools do not encourage girls to take three or four years of high school mathematics and parents do not stress the importance of such ability in girls. Girls also place more importance on being popular, being liked by boys, and not appearing too smart.

The exact reasons why girls do not perform as well as boys in certain activities are not yet known. It is safe to assume, though, that much of the reason is societal. Walberg (1969) studied the performance of gifted girls in a high school physics program and found that the girls were conforming, quiet, and did not take risks. Another finding was that the girls held back intellectual behaviors in order to gain societal approval. Gallagher, Aschner, and Jenne (1967) found that boys were eight times more likely to argue with the teacher or with peers than were girls. Highly creative girls were found to be less popular in school; not so with highly creative boys.

Teachers and screening committees should be aware of social pressures on girls; from junior high school on into adulthood, the peer pressures are greatest. Restak (1979) and Navarre (1980) suggest that because girls think and learn differently than boys, we perhaps should teach girls and boys in different ways. Parents should be aware that stereotyping can destroy potential giftedness.

393

THE GIFTED AND TALENTED

Direction of Gifted Education

The gifted are handicapped in the sense that they are being asked to perform cheerfully and effectively in an environment that is often not sufficiently stimulating. These children are often bored and many become disinterested in school. Some may even develop behavior problems. The gifted need specialized programs in order to reach their greatest potentials.

While handicapped children have been fortunate to receive money and public attention, the gifted have (except in isolated instances) largely been ignored. The attitude has been that the gifted will flourish in any classroom setting and that to indulge them with special favors is tantamount to an elitist philosophy of education. It may be true that the retarded and the handicapped warrant more attention and more services from the schools, but the gifted child should also be seen as an exceptionality and as such be entitled to the least restrictive educational environment.

Not only do people fear that education for the gifted is elitist or somehow undemocratic, some parents fear that if the gifted are recognized and nurtured, their average children will look bad by comparison. There are undercurrents of doubt about, jealousy toward, and resentment of the gifted and talented on the part of a large portion of our society. These attitudes must be modified if education for the gifted and talented is to flourish (Gallagher, 1975). The societal advantages of developing the talent and intellect of our gifted children should be recognized. Without specialized services and specialized instruction, the gifted and talented population is, in essence, being retarded because they are not being allowed to progress as quickly as they can.

SUMMARY POINTS

- Terman's comprehensive study of the gifted was among the first to list characteristics and behavior of the gifted. For many his study supported the notion that intelligence was inherited.
- Spurious efforts toward recognizing and educating the gifted are related to societal needs. There is no federal mandate to identify and teach gifted children.
- Creative children have traits that distinguish them from intellectually superior children. This does not mean that the two groups are mutually exclusive. Some children are both creatively and intellectually superior.
- Gifted and talented children and youth have superior potential in intellectual ability, specific academic aptitude, creative thinking, leadership, and/or performing and visual arts skills.
- With the expansion of the definition of giftedness to include more than a high IQ, the traditional practice of identifying gifted children and youth via standardized IQ tests was questioned. The IQ test, most frequently administered for identifying the gifted, is not reliable in identifying all gifted and talented children. Alternative and/or multiple identification procedures and practices

are recommended, such as teacher, peer, and parent nominations, rating scales, and expert judgment.

- There are gifted and talented members of society who are not identified. A child's deprived environment, sex, or a handicapping condition will frequently overshadow his or her giftedness.
- Identification of the minority gifted child is hampered by overreliance on standardized tests that are not geared towards identifying these populations.
- The identification of the learning-disabled gifted child is particularly difficult because most tests and programs for this group are designed to assess the handicapping condition rather than the giftedness.
- There are many methods for delivering educational services to the gifted and talented, each with its own advantages and disadvantages. There is no one right approach to teaching all such children.
- Research has identified teacher behaviors and teaching skills that are conducive to teaching the gifted.
- Many programs for the gifted received their impetus from parents of gifted children. Because of their personal interest, parents have turned to the courts and appealed to legislators to get a mandate for educating their children.

REVIEW QUESTIONS

1. Define gifted and talented. What are the federal guidelines for these areas?
2. Identify special problems related to the identification of the bicultural child who is gifted.
3. Why must teachers be careful in their own nomination of the creatively gifted?
4. What are some of the methods for identifying gifted and talented children? Discuss the relative strengths and weaknesses of each method of identification.
5. What can parents of gifted children do to be certain that their child will be identified and served? Explain.
6. What are the characteristics of a good teacher for the gifted?
7. Identify problems that a teacher might encounter in teaching gifted females.
8. Does your state have any legislative provision for educating the gifted and talented? If yes, explain.

DEVELOPING CREATIVITY IN THE CLASSROOM

In this chapter we have emphasized that gifted and talented children require specialized attention and instruction in our schools. Too often only cognitive areas of functioning are addressed or rewarded in these gifted children. Teachers can tap the creative resources of gifted and talented students through creative teaching techniques that assist the child in using right brain functions in the creative act. According to Kent (1977), once the child is able to learn how to utilize his or her right brain more constructively, thinking processes will become more integrated and a phenomenon called "centering" can occur.

The right side of the brain handles such information as spatial and musical processes, the artistic and symbolic modes of understanding, and the emotional and intuitive processes (see Table 16-1). It is also responsible for the perception of complex figures.

Educators cannot ignore this information in lesson and curriculum planning for the gifted. Teachers must become more aware of what creative behavior is, learn to accept creative processing in their students, and understand the basic steps in the creative process: (1) preparation; (2) incubation; (3) illumination; and (4) verification. Teachers usually spend time on preparation, but they often do not allow the student enough free time to complete the process. Students need time to daydream, to muse over an idea, to give an idea time to ripen, to incubate, to reach stage 2. Teachers should allow students this "time-out" stage. Adult scientists and artists describe this necessary incubation period that precedes great discoveries and great works. Illumination can then occur, which is the point when—according to some brain theorists—the right brain begins to dominate (Navarre, 1979).

TABLE 16-1 Some Left- and Right-Brain Hemisphere Functions

Left-Brain Functions	Right-Brain Functions
1. Control of language, both spoken and written	1. Interpretations of complex visual patterns
2. Mathematical reasoning	2. Recognition and memory of facial features
3. Reasoning required in the hard sciences	3. Memory of visual patterns, such as geometric shapes
4. Memory of names that go with a recognized face	4. Memory for information presented in diagrams, flow charts, graphic displays
5. Memory of facts, such as those that would be useful in a history or foreign language class	5. Spatial perception as required for sculpting and architecture
	6. Perception and memory of music and codes, nonverbal auditory systems
	7. Awareness of body position and perception of fine and gross motor activities
	8. Art, music, physical education, and possibly geometry
	9. Processing of many pieces of stimuli at same time
	10. Can arrive at new answers, not just the "right" ones
	11. May process unfamiliar material which is then transferred to the left hemisphere
	12. Makes aesthetic judgments

Now let us look practically at how the teacher can guide the child through these creative stages. Keeping in mind the rather solitary nature of the creative act, teachers should beware of using too many group activities in trying to generate creativity. Brainstorming can be a useful technique in the inspiration or illumination stage, but the teacher should not rely too heavily upon this technique because it can suppress inspiration or incubation if the classroom becomes too noisy or too confusing. A brainstorming session followed by a different technique might be useful.

Here is a sample lesson for a creative writing exercise. The teacher holds up an object, preferably an interesting object, that the class looks at for five minutes and then writes down as quickly as possible as many responses or associations that they can in the given amount of time. The object might be a dollar bill, an old comb, a painting, a baby bottle — nearly any object that matches the age or ability level of the child. For a small group, or a nonliterate group (such as a kindergarten class), the responses may be verbal. The class can then discuss the wide range of responses and associations and may comment on the responses that appear to have nothing to do with the original object. This activity will illustrate the uniqueness of every child's response. The class can then choose one or more of the responses and develop the idea into a story, poem, etc. Some of the students will be able to proceed toward the illumination stage and then go on to the last step, verification, when an actual product materializes, and the left brain comes back into more active play. The teacher should not expect that all of the children will proceed this far in the four-step process. Some will go no further than preparation or illumination, while others will. The teacher should not worry; this method for freeing inspiration cannot work for everyone. Some of the students will write on their own, in their own time, but the teacher must be willing to allow enough free time for students to incubate ideas.

In an art class, Kent (1977) suggests having children recall and relate their dreams and then try to produce the dream image in some other medium, such as a drawing or a painting. He also suggests that if the child dreams of some unusual object or invention, that he or she be allowed to build a model of it, regardless of how impractical it may turn out to be. Children produce art storybooks about their dreams very well. In this activity, too, we can see the four-step circuit from left to right to left hemisphere functioning — that is, integration, the utilization of the whole brain, the whole child.

In the sciences, especially in the elementary school, McCormack (1977) recommends the use of everyday materials in science lessons. For example, in one lesson a wet piece of steel wool is placed inside a glass jar that had been sealed shut with a balloon and a rubber band. As the steel wool rusted, the process of oxidation resulted in the balloon's being depressed into the jar. The class then tried to figure out what was behind the "mystery jar" and to think of a way to change the position of the balloon for themselves — in a different way. The key is to challenge the students and provide them with time to incubate ideas. It is also a good idea to just present the materials, the problem, and the challenge without presenting objectives.

These are just a few ideas for lesson planning. The four basic steps in the creative process should be kept in mind when devising exercises and learning experiences that will tap the right-hemisphere functions. Teachers must also remember that the child has to be relaxed and introspective in order for incubation to occur, and if this all-important step is not allowed to happen, the chances for creative production will be jeopardized. Rubenzer (1979) points out, furthermore, that if a child younger than the age of six or seven processes information excessively in either hemisphere, the child can suffer cognitive or affective deficits (i.e., he or she may develop thinking patterns and learning styles which are not representative of his or her true potential). Thus we see how important a wide variety of learning experiences is in early childhood education. Rubenzer (1979) also states that it has been found that "... educational experiences that were specifically designed to enhance right hemispheric processing (problem-solving skills) also improved performance on tasks considered to involve left hemispheric functions" (p. 90). It has been postulated that creative geniuses are extremely skillful in using both hemispheres of the brain appropriately in the creative process (Gilchrist and Taft, 1970).

We can see the new vistas that lie ahead in the marriage of neuroscience and educational planning, as new insights are gained into the nature of learning and creativity. We, as concerned educators, must utilize this new body of knowledge and seek to nurture our gifted students in the fullest use of their minds.

DISCUSSION POINTS

1. Using the guidelines in the preceding discussion, devise your own lesson plan. What products will you hope to have your students create?
2. What relaxation techniques can you suggest that will allow the students to incubate ideas?

SUGGESTED READINGS

Barbe, B., and Renzulli, J. S., eds. *Psychology and Education of the Gifted*. New York: Irvington, 1975.

Callahan, C. M. *Developing Creativity in the Gifted and Talented*. Reston, Va.: Council for Exceptional Children, 1978.

Doob, H. *Gifted Students: Identification Techniques and Program Organization*. Arlington, Va.: Educational Research Service, 1975.

Martinson, R. A. *The Identification of the Gifted and Talented*. Reston, Va.: Council for Exceptional Children, 1975.

17

CONTENTS

THE BICULTURAL CHILD

In America, there are three basic cultural systems — the general or dominant culture, social class cultures, and ethnic group cultures (Hurlock, 1972). The American educational system, designed and represented by the dominant culture, caters basically to the needs of white, middle-class children. However, there are many children and youth who are not members of the dominant culture. These children are unfortunately often denied academic achievement and vocational opportunities on the basis of their ethnic, racial, and/or economic background. Because these children delicately straddle two worlds — the home subculture and the dominant culture of the mainstream — they are referred to as bicultural. Dunn (1968) has eloquently pointed out that too often such minority children are overrepresented in special education programs, especially in educable mentally retarded (EMR) classes, throughout our country.

JIMMY'S SURVIVAL

Jimmy, at age eight, is a frail-looking, handsome black child. His eyes sparkle and he can talk his way either into or out of anything. He is failing second grade. Jimmy is typical of many children from poverty environments in that his childhood has been robbed by circumstances over which he had no control.

By the time Jimmy was born, his 17-year-old mother, Sherry, already had two other children. His father is unknown. Sherry lived with her three children and her mother, Mama Smith, in a small, two-room apartment with poor plumbing and heating and a stench that was overwhelming, especially during the hot, humid summers in Washington, D.C. Even though Mama Smith was employed as a washwoman, her poor health limited the family income. Sherry, a school dropout at age 13, was unable to find a job. As a result, the family received public assistance.

Until Jimmy was five years old, the small apartment and the street down below were all that he knew. Because Sherry and Mama Smith were frequently out, a woman from a neighboring apartment would periodically "check in on the kids to make sure everything was okay." Jimmy never had a mobile hanging over his crib. In fact, he never had a crib, just a large wooden box for a bed. As a toddler and preschooler Jimmy never had books to look at in order to broaden his extremely limited experiences and to de-

velop listening skills. Besides, his mother had reading skills comparable to those of a second-grader.

Sherry left her children when Jimmy was five-and-a-half years old. Because Mama Smith was unable to take care of them, Jimmy and his two brothers became wards of the court. By the time Jimmy was eight years old, he had already been shifted from one foster family to another. In fact, in 2½ years he lived with five different families. Mama Smith still sees Jimmy on a regular basis and she feels a sense of helplessness and hopelessness when discussing her grandson's future.

Because of his poor progress at the end of second grade, Jimmy was referred to a diagnostic summer program for a psychoeducational evaluation. The eight-week program included not only the typical test battery but also a daily, three-hour diagnostic classroom environment. The latter was designed to observe children in an academic setting and to assess day-to-day social interaction with peers and teachers. At the end of the evaluation, a diagnostic summary of Jimmy looked like this:

READING	Cannot identify letters of the alphabet
	Does not have sound/ symbol correspondence
	Sight vocabulary is limited to approximately 10–15 words

ARITHMETIC	Can count to 100
	Has no concept of subtraction
	Can add single-digit numbers
LANGUAGE	Poor auditory memory
	Deficit in receptive and expressive language skills
SOCIAL (PEERS)	Usually is a loner
	When group activities occur in class, has difficulty sharing and is generally a follower

| SOCIAL (ADULTS) | Appears timid |
| | Does not disturb class-room routine |

An analysis of the above information reinforces the predicted school failure for Jimmy. However, an in-depth observation of Jimmy's day-to-day behavior reveals strengths and incredible survival skills, which is characteristic of many children from poor socioeconomic urban environments. For example, he can perceive interpersonal dynamics in a social setting with incredible accuracy, makes three across-town bus transfers to get to the clinic on time, and although he can barely add two numbers, is able to make the correct change for buying pop and candy after school. However, schools often fail to recognize this kind of learning and its related significance to program planning.

Points for Consideration

■ Jimmy's early childhood years reflect a sense of neglect for his physical, emotional, and intellectual development.

■ Separation from family and constant reshuffling of foster care settings inhibited Jimmy's ability to identify as a member of a family. Frequently, children in similar positions have difficulty forming trusting relationships and positive self-images. Both are related to school success.

■ If Jimmy is seen in terms of only his academic deficits, the prognosis for school success is poor.

Common Misconceptions

■ *Bicultural Children Live in Impoverished Environments.* Although Jimmy's home life was poverty-stricken, many bicultural children have a stimulating, nourishing, and loving home life, even though it may be different from that of the dominant culture.

■ *The Purpose of Bicultural Education Programs Is To Erode the Dominant Culture's Customs, Values, and Practices.* The goal of bicultural education is to assist minority children in recognizing and adapting to the mores of the dominant culture while still valuing and maintaining the traditions and customs of their native heritage.

■ *Parents of Minority Racial, Religious, or Ethnic Groups Do Not Care about Their Children's Schooling.* Frequently, this attitude appears to be the case, especially when white, middle-class criteria are used to evaluate parental behaviors. However, effective teachers are aware that a parent's cultural heritage will influence his or her interaction with school personnel.

HISTORICAL PERSPECTIVE

The United States is frequently referred to as a "melting pot"—a country where people of any nationality could enter, settle, live peacefully, and be treated equally. Historically, many diverse cultural groups came to the "new world" to escape oppressive restrictions of the European motherland. Originally, these groups of pioneers settled in certain geographic areas. The English settled in New England and along the mid-Atlantic coast, the Dutch in New York and Pennsylvania, the Germans in Ohio and Pennsylvania, the French in Canada, and the Spanish in Florida and Mexico. For a time each culture attempted to retain certain characteristics such as language, skills, and rituals that were unique to its culture alone. However, English gradually became accepted as the standard language, and normative values, attitudes, and mores were established that reflected a merging of the colonists' varied European backgrounds and their interaction with the new environment.

During the latter part of the nineteenth century, immigration reached a peak level with the influx of Oriental laborers and the unceasing flow of European families. Several factors account for this massive immigration movement. The industrial revolution provided many jobs for these refugees as mass production and assembly lines were being quickly constructed. Also, America's political system was perceived as allowing immigrants comparatively more freedom. All of these influences tended to cause the immigrants to shed their original cultural beliefs and practices and adopt those of the dominant culture in their new land. As Gonzales and Ortiz state (1977, p. 332),

> The socio-political context of the new society was one factor that moved the immigrant along the path of assimilation. From the beginning, the immigrant was allowed considerable freedom to participate in the American political process. Citizenship and voting privileges were extended in exchange for political loyalty and commitment to a free and democratic society.
>
> As soon as the immigrants accepted the concept of "Americanism," they were well on the way to endorsing other aspects of American life, including the dominant culture and language. It is well known that as immigrants acquired English and other social and cultural behaviors, individually and collectively, they were able to move up the economic ladder to white-collar and professional levels. In most cases, acquisition of English and "deethnization" went hand in hand with upward mobility. The forces encouraging assimilation were powerful indeed.

However, some cultures did not readily assimilate because of their wide difference from the dominant Euro-American culture. For example, the ways of life in Africa, Asia, Mexico, and even on American Indian reservations were so radically foreign to European/American practices and values that anyone from those areas attempting to enter into American society was far more culturally handicapped than the European immigrant. Also, with the advent of the industrial revolution, gaps between the rich and the poor grew to immense proportions. About one-fifth of the country's population was considered to be poverty-stricken (Miller, 1978). Such extreme economic differences highlighted cultural differences as well.

IDENTIFICATION AND DEFINITION OF TERMS

In identifying the bicultural population there are two components to consider, which are not necessarily related: ethnic origin and economic level of the family. Regarding ethnic origin, the focus is on minority cultures found in America, such as African, Oriental, American Indian, and Mexican-American. The point at which the economic level identifies a child as bicultural is when his or her environment is labeled as being poverty-stricken. The bicultural environment becomes a handicapping condition when it interferes with the child's cognitive, affective, and psychomotor development.

It is critical that the blame for this handicapping condition not be placed on the minority culture; rather, the deficit is within the dominant culture for failing to recognize and accept differences between the two social systems. In the past, children from poverty-stricken families or from families retaining aspects of a minority culture were thought to be inherently less capable academically. This perception was based on their poor school performance and high dropout rate. This belief in genetic inferiority was refuted only as recently as the 1940s; many professionals felt instead that minority children were culturally deprived. They reasoned that these children were not exposed to the better way of life of middle- to upper-class children. This lack of enrichment and varied environmental influences was seen as the main cause of school failures of children from minority cultures.

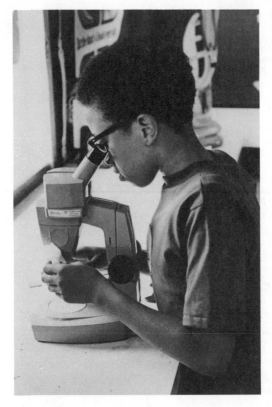

Schools have a responsibility to develop the learning potential of all students regardless of their ethnic, economic, or racial background.

Wallace (1974) states that the culturally deprived concept probably came about as a result of studies with lower animals that showed the harmful, lasting effects of nurturing in impoverished environments. However, sociologists objected to this explanation on the grounds that many of the minority cultures are complete and stimulating, not deprived. So a new label—culturally disadvantaged—was invented to explain the differences between the major and minor cultures. Culturally disadvantaged children included those from minority ethnic, economic, or geographic (rural, migrant, inner city) subcultures that differed from the dominant culture. However, this label was also rejected because the dominant culture's standards were used as criteria for comparison.

As a consequence of this controversy over labeling came the more specific "educationally disadvantaged" label, which places the blame of not providing adequate educational opportunities upon the dominant culture. This label implies that society itself is at fault and must be reformed—not the minority culture. Supporters of this notion believe the country should strive to become a more culturally pluralistic society. In such an environment, minority groups would be able to be assimilated into the dominant culture without losing their subcultural heritage.

Rodriguez (1975, p. 3) provides the following definitions of **bicultural** and **bilingual** and related educational terms.

> *Bilingualism* means, very simply, the ability to function in another language in addition to one's home language.

Biculturalism is the ability to behave on occasion according to selected patterns of culture other than one's own.

By *bilingual schooling* we mean the particular organizational scheme of instruction which is used to mediate curricula in the home language and in another language.

Bilingual Education is a process by which the learning experiences provided in the home and other educational and societal institutions enable a person to fulfill total self-development as well as to function in another language in addition to the home language.

Bilingual/Bicultural Education means a process of total self-development by which a person learns and reinforces his or her own language and culture while at the same time acquiring the ability to function in another language and behave on occasion according to patterns of the second culture.

From this perspective, the educational system becomes a major vehicle for developing effective skills in bicultural individuals so that they may function in the dominant culture while still retaining their primary cultural heritage.

CHARACTERISTICS OF THE POPULATION

In order to more fully understand the bicultural child, knowledge of the characteristics of his or her population is critical. Much of the research focusing on cultural diversity examines bicultural children in relation to their corresponding subcultural group. Also, a comparison of related research on different minority groups indicates that findings are similar: that is, the data has cross-cultural validity. For example, Puerto Rican children from poor families face many of the same pressures and problems as black children from poor families. Also, children from minority cultures who speak a language other than English will encounter parallel problems in school, depending, of course, on outside cultural pressures and the degree of difference between the spoken language and English. In an attempt to review the most salient issues of bicultural education, the following discussion will focus on the poverty-stricken child and the bilingual child.

The Poverty-Stricken Child

In his article, "The Culture of Poverty," Lewis (1966, p. 9) states, "The culture of poverty is not just a matter of deprivation or disorganization, a term signifying the absence of something. It is a culture in the traditional anthropological sense in that it provides human beings with a design for living, with a ready-made set of solutions for human problems, and so serves a significant adaptive function." Of course, for many of the poverty-stricken, there is always an accompanying feeling of futility, alienation, a sense of failure and rejection—a reaction toward being at the bottom of the labor force. These negative feelings toward self and the dominant culture are perpetuated with the increased demand for higher education and increasingly more technical prerequisite skills for entering the labor force. Thus the poor, which includes white and nonwhite families, rural immigrants, unskilled workers, and slum dwellers, have difficulty breaking out of the poverty-stricken environment (Strom, 1965).

The mother is characteristically the head of the family in the slums. In many cases, extended families join together in one large unit in order to meet economic demands. Such units tend to restrict privacy. This lack of privacy promotes mental strain since an individual is constantly having to guard his or her status. Crowding inhibits the fantasy play in which many middle-class children normally engage. Such living conditions also limit the child's ability to make decisions since there are few alternatives or choices in the slum environment. In short, "Having been denied privacy and the development of an interest in solitary pursuits, these children cannot be expected to engage easily in the kind of study habits required for success in school" (Strom, 1965, p. 5).

A comparison of middle-class and poverty-level mothers' expectations toward school and their child's school-related behaviors indicates a difference in attitudes. Mothers from lower socioeconomic environments typically tell their children to do what the teacher says, not to get into trouble, not to fight, to come home right after school, and not to get lost. Middle-class mothers, on the other hand, generally communicate that the teacher is like Mommy, you learn from her; if you have trouble go to her; you are going to learn to read and write (Hess, 1965). As can be seen from this illustration, the slum mothers are concerned with discipline; middle-class mothers are more interested in academics. Indeed, most mothers of poor families hold good discipline strategies in high regard, since, as Miller (1978) points out, most of these mothers have accepted the ideals and morals of the middle class. However, discipline strategies of the two class groups differ: middle-class families appeal to inductive reasoning, as opposed to lower-class families, who use more power-assertive strategies.

> Many slum parents feel that school is a closed system to which they are outsiders; that to be a good parent, one is expected to remain at home and not bother busy teachers. Others who experienced dissatisfaction in their own education feel that if they register a complaint to the school, their child may suffer some discriminatory action. A number feel impotent to effect change in any aspect of life and doubt whether the school would solicit their judgment in any other than [a] perfunctory way. Finally, there are those who maintain a supportive school attitude but whose behavior is an illogical concomitant. With good intent, they employ prodding, threat, physical punishment and other negative measures in the name of education. Each of these views is unfortunate in that positive home-school relations are affected [Miller, 1978, pp. 20–21].

Other factors hindering children from poverty-level families include a general lack of positive self-concepts, low teacher expectations, and poor self-assertiveness (Strom, 1964). Many lower-class children reflect the alienation of their parents and develop poor self-concepts; failure in school strengthens these self-doubts and inhibitions. Also, some of the low achievement levels of children from lower-class backgrounds can be attributed to teachers' general expectations of a poorer performance from these individuals; that is, because teachers anticipate that poverty students will achieve lower levels of academic skills, they ultimately do achieve such levels. Slum children sometimes have trouble deciding upon a specific vocation to work toward as a result of a lack of affirmation and direction. Social workers are sometimes able to interest these children in relevant subjects, course materials, and social integration strategies that ease the often harsh adjustment to classroom environments.

THE MEXICAN-AMERICAN CHILD   The mother in the poverty-stricken Mexican-American family is generally the head of the household. However, as noted by Henkin and Henkin (1977), there is less tendency for the fathers of Mexican-American families to be absent than in other subcultures since there are generally long lines of traditional families. Mexican-Americans constitute the country's second largest minority; one-third of this population lives in poverty and most working adults fill low-income jobs that require little or no formal education (Grebler, Moore, and Guzman, 1970).

Cultural influences affecting the school performance levels of Mexican-Americans have been identified. As noted by Garza (1978), most Anglo-Saxon children come from environments that emphasize efficiency, task centeredness, and individual accomplishment. Mexican-American children's backgrounds, however, are characterized by human relation concerns, person centeredness, and open acceptance of affective temperament. In other words, these children appear to have a greater sensitivity toward affective qualities in the classroom or other environments, since they perceive these affective values to be more important.

Differences in values and language are commonly related to the Mexican-American child's developing a poor self-concept. Many of these children view the white, middle-class child as having a higher status than Mexican-Americans. In one classic study, Teplin (1976) found that when shown pictures of other children and asked who they would prefer to have as friends, Mexican-American children for the most part did not choose pictures of other Mexican-Americans. Economic problems, social disadvantages, and inappropriate educational programs are all factors that contribute to poor self-concept (Henkin and Henkin, 1977). In addition to poor self-concepts, teachers should be wary of their own low expectations and stereotypic notions of Mexican-Americans. In many cases, these developments encourage delinquency and dropouts (Henkin and Henkin, 1977).

THE BLACK CHILD   Comparative studies between black and white children also indicate that social influences result in some basic differences. One study showed that black children (especially males) coming from low socioeconomic status backgrounds and large families tend to have greater behavior problems in the classroom. If these inappropriate behaviors are not corrected, they increase from one grade to the next at a faster rate than unwanted behaviors of white children (Lindholm, Touliatos, and Rich, 1978).

Some studies indicate that IQ tests, which traditionally yield lower scores to blacks than to whites, may be culturally loaded. For example, Ginsburg (1972) believes some verbal tests such as concept formation may be misinterpreted because a child understands the notion but is not able to actually label it by the test standards. Another explanation for poor test performance is that the poverty-stricken black child enters the school milieu with a depressed vocabulary and limited experiences according to the school's standards. As a result, the child is being tested on what he or she does not know. Thus, the black child may interpret school and teachers as foreign or alien. If efforts at alleviating the student's feelings of inadequacy and inferiority are not taken into account, learning will not occur.

THE AMERICAN INDIAN CHILD   Each Indian tribe has its own set of values and traditions. However, the dominant culture tends to perceive all Indians collectively, overlooking their heterogeneity. This lack of concern for each group's potential contribution to the dominant culture has had a negative effect on the education of many Indian children and youth. In general, these children tend to suffer from low teacher expectations for student performance, inadequate materials, cultural bias, and poor student self-concepts. It is also estimated that the

TABLE 17-1 A Comparison of Values

Indian	Dominant Society
Wisdom of age and experience is respected. Elders are revered by their people.	Older people are made to feel incompetent and rejected.
Excellence is related to a contribution to the group—not to personal glory.	Competition and striving to win or to gain status is emphasized.
Cooperation is necessary for group survival.	Competition is necessary for individual status and prestige.
Children participate in adult activities.	Adults participate in children's activities.
Family life includes the extended family.	Family life includes the nuclear family.
Time is present oriented—this year, this week —NOW—a resistance to planning for the future.	Time is planning and saving for the future.
Clocktime is whenever people are ready— when everyone arrives.	Clocktime is exactly that.
Work is necessary for the common good. Whatever Indian people have, they share. What is mine is ours.	Work is from 9–5 (specified time) and to obtain material possessions and to save for the future. What is mine, stays mine.
Good relationships and mutual respect are emphasized.	Success, progress, possession of property and rugged individualism are valued above mutual respect and maintaining good relationships.
People express their ideas and feelings through their actions.	People express themselves and attempt to impress others through speech.
People conform to nature.	People try to dominate and desecrate nature.
Early childhood rearing practices are the responsibility of the kin group.	Early childhood rearing practices are the responsibility of the nuclear family.
Native religion was never imposed or proselytized other groups.	Religious groups proselytize, coerce, and impose their beliefs on others.
Land gives the Indian his identity, his religion and his life. It is not to be sold or owned, but used by all.	Land is for speculation, for prestige, to be owned, sold, or torn up.
Going to school is necessary to gain knowledge. Excelling for fame is looked down upon by the Indian.	Going to school is necessary to gain knowledge and to compete for grades.
Indians have a short childhood and the male is held to be a responsible person at the age of 16.	There is an extended childhood and the male is held to be a responsible person at the age of 21.
People are usually judged by what they do.	People are usually judged by their credentials.

Reprinted from "Teaching the American Indian Child in Mainstream Settings," in R. L. Jones and F. B. Wilderson, eds. *Mainstreaming and the Minority Child* by F. C. Pepper. Reprinted by permission of the Council for Exceptional Children, 1976.

Indian dropout rate from school is twice the national average (Allen, 1976). In Table 17-1, Pepper (1976) contrasts the dominant culture's values and the Indian's values. A comparative analysis of the two value systems has serious implications for education. If curriculum content, teaching methods, and student evaluation procedures are developed and taught from the dominant culture's perspective, poor school performance in the native American Indian population should not be surprising.

THE ASIAN CHILD   Asian families generally place a high value on education. However, Asian children also have a number of difficulties to overcome that have been imposed by the dominant culture. Chen and Goon (1976) listed non-English speaking backgrounds and the lack of an Asian model in the classroom as major difficulties. Like Mexican-Americans, the Asian child's culture emphasizes different values than the dominant Euro-American culture. It is also important that the child have a positive model representing his or her culture (other than parental figures), a model who can be admired and imitated. The subculture reinforced at home (for example, by speaking the native language) is in conflict with the school and the dominant culture. As a result, the child does not easily assimilate into the school environment. It is critical that educators recognize the conflict in children whose home lives differ radically from those of the dominant culture.

BILINGUAL EDUCATION

Dealing with language differences in the classroom presents some difficulties and concerns. Children who come from families who speak other than English are at a disadvantage in American schools.

Ovando (1977, p. 231) outlined five federal programs that are available to schools interested in developing bilingual programs. However, these are optional rather than mandatory and their funding is limited.

1. The Bilingual Education Act, Title VII of the Elementary and Secondary Education Act (ESEA). This program provides the largest amount of funds for bilingual education. Essentially, it proposes a transitional model in which, ideally, the non-English language is to be dropped once English proficiency is attained.
2. Migrant programs under Title I of ESEA. These programs do not provide for full bilingual education but allow for the hiring of bilingual aides.
3. The Federal Educationally Disadvantaged Program, also under Title I of ESEA. Some bilingual services may be provided under this program, since linguistic difficulties fall under the guidelines for disadvantaged students.
4. The Emergency School Aid Act. This legislation is designed to facilitate desegregation, but 4% of the funds may be used for bilingual education as part of the desegregation process.
5. English as a Second Language (ESL), under Title I of ESEA. Obviously, this is a transitional rather than a language maintenance program.

The Bilingual Education Act prompted interested states to decree that such programs could be developed in districts with a bilingual population (Kobuck, 1972; Koln, 1974). Bilingual programs should be devised within the following guidelines. First, the child's home language should be perceived as a strength rather than a weakness to be ignored by the school. Also, the successful bilingual program integrates the linguistic and cultural background of the minority child as part of the classroom curriculum. Only when the classroom environment capitalizes upon cultural diversity will the subcultures and the dominant culture be able to mesh.

Dialectal Differences

Linguists emphasize a further dimension to bilingual education, that of the dialect. There are obvious differences between dialects and languages. The dialect-speaking child encounters problems in the classroom that accepts only standard English. These problems are similar to those of the bicultural non-English-speaking child. **Dialects** (the most often discussed is the black dialect) are often viewed as a language deficit rather than a language difference. The dialect is a product of the person's background and culture, and both verbal and/or nonverbal criticisms of such language can be damaging to the child's self-esteem. Blacks are affected most often because their language is seen by many educators to be a bastardization of English and therefore incorrect, as opposed to the Mexican-American child who is perceived as speaking a legitimate language.

Originally, it was supposed that lower-class and ethnically disadvantaged children were suffering from cultural deficits, that the existence of accents and dialects reflected a lack of cognitive development due to a debilitating environment. Such speakers were provided with remedial instruction to correct their errors and to speak standard English (Naremore, 1980). However, linguists now believe that dialectally different language is fluent, grammatical, and highly complex. In addition, although different from the dominant culture's language structure, the black dialect reflects higher level cognitive structures such as abstract thinking skills (Labov, 1972). The challenge for educators becomes tapping these resources of minority children to help them reach their maximum potential in the classroom.

The issue of dialectal differences goes beyond the classroom. Its effects can be felt in the social arena. Studies of reactions and attitudes toward spoken language indicate that: (1) teachers judge children by what and how they speak; and (2) dominant culture members tend to look down on people who exhibit different dialects (Naremore, 1971). If society evaluates potential on the basis of oral language performance, then black English speakers will be denied opportunities not on the basis of ability, but rather on a generalized perception of inability based on their dialect. Naremore (1980) believes that this practice of negative stereotypes is the "primary reason why many educators, both black and white, urge that speakers of black English vernacular become '**bi-dialectal**' (speaking both black English vernacular and a more standard form of English). A bi-dialectal speaker would be able to use black English vernacular forms or standard English forms, depending on the situation" (p. 193).

THE STATUS OF BICULTURAL EDUCATION

Although educators have spent much time debating and redefining attitudes toward bicultural children, educational systems have still failed to adequately evaluate these children in terms of their own cultural achievements. Classes for the mentally retarded have often had a disproportionately high number of bicultural children. As a result, unhappy parents turned to the courts for support. Such cases as *Arrela v. Board of Education* (1968), *Diana v. State Board of Education* (1970), *Covarrubias v. San Diego Unified School District* (1971), and *Larry P. v. Riles* (1972) led to the prohibition of discriminatory labeling and placement procedures. As a result of the court rulings, many bicultural children, previously relegated to learning disabilities classes or programs for the mentally retarded, returned to regular classrooms.

No formal programs of bicultural education have been established on a national level. The federal government has investigated bilingual issues in two pieces of legislation, the Bilingual Act of 1968 and an amendment to PL 90–247 in 1967. It has, however, only addressed the entire cultural implications to a limited extent, leaving implementation of programs to state and local authorities. Thus, the inequalities between children from dominant culture families and those from minority culture families continue in America's educational system, which purports to provide an equal opportunity for every child (Miller, 1978).

STEPS TO DEVELOPING PLURALISTIC EDUCATION

Two major conclusions can be drawn on the status of the bicultural population in America. First, although the culturally diverse population is still collectively a minority, the number of children who fit into this category is significant. Second, maintaining current educational practices will contribute to the failure syndrome of these children and youth, with many spending time in special education programs. Thus, the issue becomes not whether education should change, but rather how changes can be made to meet the needs of all of America's children. The only viable alternative for our schools and society is accepting **cultural pluralism**.

The first step toward change is to make the dominant culture aware that although minority groups' values, motives, and means of achievement are not exactly the same as the established norm, they are not inferior. The cognitive, linguistic, and educational development of children is virtually identical, regardless of their culture. Although developmental milestones occur at different times in different individuals and thus may appear deviant because of different prevailing circumstances, children among races are more similar than was once believed.

Schools must make the second step toward accepting cultural pluralism by adapting their curricula to meet the challenges of a pluralistic society. They must recognize that fundamental differences exist in the learning styles of minority groups because of their backgrounds, which are radically unlike the backgrounds of middle-class, Euro-American children. According to Epps (1974), pluralistic education must focus initially on developing programs that use the cultural context of the total population (both bicultural and dominant) in order to determine the values, goals, and content of education.

Third, appropriate assessment procedures and tests must be used in order to determine each bicultural child's needs. Before assessment begins it is imperative that the purpose of testing be examined carefully. Most of the IQ and achievement tests popular today consist of verbal and performance items. Some test authors have constructed culturally fair tests that contain items relating to a particular minority culture. However, even with the culturally fair test, educators must consider carefully their intended purpose. Wesman (1968, p. 270) cautions:

> If our purpose is to distinguish members of that subculture from their peers with respect to how much of that special culture they have assimilated, such a test might well be useful. If, as is more likely the case, we wish to predict future learnings of the content of the more general culture (e.g., the so-called white, middle-class culture such as typifies what the majority of our schools are organized to transmit), tests designed for the subculture will be less relevant than those which sample from the general culture.

Besides the tests themselves, the examiner can affect test results when he or she is a representative of the dominant culture and carries the biases characteristic of the white middle class. The examiner must attempt to prevent these variables from contaminating the test results. As Robb (1972) points out, many of the minority groups in the United States are influenced by radical, militant movements in order to gain some degree of recognition. As a result, these minority children often display some distrust while being tested.

Although awareness, curriculum modification, and alternative assessment procedures are necessary for improving the educational programs for bicultural children, each teacher of these groups must also recognize the classroom dynamics within his or her classroom. Specifically, as Sizemore (1974) notes, teachers must be aware of their own attitudes as well as those of the bicultural child. Acceptance of pluralistic societal factors must be the goal of the classroom teacher. All dialects and foreign languages, as well as standard English, must be utilized and honored in the classroom. Not only may expressive skills be diverse, but also the purpose of language may vary. Ward (1971) indicates that the purpose of language of children from low socioeconomic status environments is viewed much differently than it is for middle-class children. To middle-class parents and their children, language is a means of learning and exchanging information, but to the lower-class parent, language is for controlling behavior; the force that is used in speaking conveys authority, power, and status—not the information that is verbalized. Educators should be aware of these differences and incorporate these different attitudes into their teaching approaches to reading and language.

Teachers must recognize that all children must be appreciated equally—whether they come from extended families, partial families, families where parents encourage togetherness or independence, or where parents are authoritarian or democratic. Also, in deciding which methods of teaching facilitate

Acceptance of a student's cultural heritage promotes positive teacher-student interaction and facilitates academic progress.

learning for the individual child, learning styles should be assessed, but only for the purposes of instruction. No value should be assigned to particular styles. Lastly, the cognitive organizational patterns of all students must be taken into account when planning lessons. Emphasis should be on successful completion and positive experiences for students. Only when all of the above are considered can a teacher effectively teach a classroom of students from various cultural backgrounds.

Guinn (1977) points out that classrooms adopting attitudes of acceptance have helped bicultural children reach high levels of achievement. These bicultural children are handicapped and learning disabled, but only compared to children of the dominant culture. Once they are understood and given relevant, appropriate, stimulating materials and instruction found in bicultural-tolerant classrooms, handicaps dissolve. Guinn (1977) lists five strategies that teachers should use in order to encourage bicultural acceptance among all students.

- Individualize instruction as much as possible
- Be alert to student needs and wishes and take responsibility for helping to solve their problems
- Associate students' backgrounds with classroom instruction
- Elevate students' self-concepts by stressing security, achievement, and self-respect
- Do not restrict students' acquisition of knowledge only to the subjects traditionally taught in the classroom

A final factor related to effective bicultural education is recognition of the child's community environment. Parental involvement, or that of a surrogate parent, is extremely important in the bicultural child's school experience. The teacher should encourage parents to take an interest in their children's educational program and to interact with the school as much as possible. Parents need to understand the instructional programs in the classroom and the goals of the school; and the teacher must understand the parents' attitudes and values and foster cooperation regarding the student's success.

A teacher must be aware of the community's values, its range of cultures, acceptance of pluralistic attitudes, and basic relationships between school and community so that support of such programs will be encouraged by the community at large. Through methodical, positive, enriching programs, teachers can begin to understand and teach these children once believed to be retarded, deprived, and disadvantaged.

SUMMARY POINTS

- There are subculture groups in the United States who have been unable to assimilate into the dominant culture. One reason for failure of many of these minority members to successfully enter the mainstream of society can be attributed to poor school performance.
- Bicultural children and youth live in two worlds: the school, represented by white middle-class America, and the home, which promotes practices, values, and —at times—a language that are different from the dominant culture.
- Members of all minority groups share the common problems of lack of school success and accompanying limited vocational opportunities. Research has also

identified general characteristics and problems that relate to specific subculture groups.

■ The Bilingual Act (1968) mandated that bilingual instruction be provided for qualifying children and youth. Such programs must incorporate the student's native language and culture into the school program.

■ Education has traditionally placed a disproportionately large number of minority students in special education programs. However, recent legislation and litigation have specified procedural safeguards to prevent a student from being placed in such programs on the basis of minority membership.

■ A vehicle for establishing meaningful interaction between minority and dominant culture members is the school. In order for change to occur, schools will need to reexamine their curricula content and assessment procedures.

■ The successful implementation of a bicultural program depends upon the interactions within individual classrooms. Pre-service and in-service programs for teachers should develop not only an awareness of minority cultures' customs, traditions, heritages, and values, but also competencies for teaching bicultural students.

■ The black English dialect is a highly organized and structured language. It is not an inferior communication system.

■ Any decisions regarding the teaching of dialectally different children should consider these children's vocational and economic futures. Research repeatedly points out that users of the black English dialect are perceived negatively by dominant culture members.

■ Effective pluralistic education involves a realistic awareness and understanding of contributions made by all individuals and groups, in both majority and minority cultures.

REVIEW QUESTIONS

1. Review the cultural characteristics associated with each of the various minority groups discussed in this chapter. What influence, if any, would they have on your interaction with these students?

2. Does your state provide legislation for developing bicultural programs? If yes, identify the major tenets.

3. What activities and programs could schools, in conjunction with the local community, develop to create a more positive attitude toward its minority members?

4. Explain why special education programs have had a high percentage of minority students.

ACHIEVING BICULTURAL AWARENESS —
A TWO-WAY ENDEAVOR

There are two opposing views about including ethnic studies in a school curriculum.
Multi-ethnic advocates, labeled as cultural
pluralists, believe that such programs encourage equality for minority groups in
general and develop positive self-images for
individual minority members. On the other
hand, assimilationists argue that ethnic
studies programs undermine the foundation
of American education by distorting reality
and encouraging destructive competition
(Freedman, 1977). A moderate position
would be designing a curriculum

> whereby a social or historical event is examined
> from a variety of ethnic viewpoints, the Anglo-
> American being just one of many . . . this
> would require a reconceptualization of Amer-
> ican history and society. The result . . . would
> be a healthier and more realistic attitude toward
> ethnicity and its proper role in American life
> than currently exists [Freedman, 1977, p. 401].

Within the schools, multicultural programs
can assist students to develop a sense of cooperation and an appreciation for cultural
diversity. The key to success is to base the
curriculum on the principle that every student has skills, behaviors, and attitudes that
are valued by other students (Fruehling,
1977).

The major implication drawn from the
moderate perspective is that ethnic studies is
for all students and thus should be required
for both minority students and students of
the dominant culture. Following is a review
of two projects that attempt to preserve the
bicultural student's heritage.

THE MT. CURRIE EXPERIMENT

The Mt. Currie Indian Community School
in British Columbia was the response to a
problem facing many Indian communities: a
high dropout rate in schools whose curricula ignore and degrade the native Indian
(Wyatt, 1977). The Indian community maintained that a synthesis of traditional and
contemporary values would not inhibit
Indian students from succeeding economically within the dominant culture's mainstream. Convinced that success depended
upon Indian autonomy, the Indian community initiated the following: an all-
Indian school board was established; the
reservation school was expanded to include
junior and senior high; a field-based, native
teacher-training program was designed in
conjunction with a nearby university; and an
Indian curriculum was developed. The curriculum was expanded to include not only
the curricular guidelines established by the
British Columbia Department of Education,
but also "(1) classes in native language at all
grade levels taught by native people trained
by a linguist, (2) native songs and dances
taught by community resource people [and],
(3) social studies and literature curricula in
secondary grades which focus on vital issues
in contemporary native life" (Wyatt, 1977,
p. 407).

LA ISLA CARIBE

In 1973, the County Commissioner of Dade
County in Florida declared that because of
the influx of the Spanish-speaking population, the community was bilingual and bicultural and that Spanish was the official
second language (Beebe, 1978). Although
traditional Spanish programs were taught to
English-speaking students, there was a decrease in Spanish course enrollment at the
high-school level. As a result, Spanish-
speaking students were developing linguistic
fluency; however, the English-speaking
students were not.

To motivate participation in classes in
Spanish as a foreign language, the Caribbean
Elementary School developed *la Isla Caribe*,
an experimental, one-week simulation de-
signed to teach non-Spanish speakers the
Spanish language and to promote cultural

awareness of the Spanish community. The participants, ten English-speaking fifth- and sixth-graders, spent the school day immersed in a Latin American environment monitored and taught by three native-speaking teachers. The success of *la Isla Caribe* prompted educators to expand the program; by 1977, a two-week simulation experience had been instituted, with teachers and administrators as participants. Also, a Spanish Immersion Laboratory program was developed to supplement traditional Spanish instruction at the high-school level.

The Mt. Currie experiment and *la Isla Caribe* attack the issue of bicultural education, although from different perspectives. The first highlights a minority group's efforts toward achieving a bicultural environment, whereas the second outlines one approach taken by the major culture to bridge the gap between minority and dominant cultures.

1. Opponents of a pluralistic approach to education argue that an erosion of the dominant culture will result. Do you agree or disagree? Why?
2. Identify at least three outcomes or end results of a bicultural program that would indicate the program was a success.

SUGGESTED READINGS

Epps, E. G. "The School and Cultural Pluralism," in E. G. Epps, ed. *Cultural Pluralism*. Berkeley, Ca.: McCutchan, 1974.

Gonzales, E., and Ortiz, L. "Social Policy and Education Related to Linguistically and Culturally Different Groups." *Journal of Learning Disabilities*, 10 (June/July, 1977), 332–338.

Naremore, R. C. "Language Variation in a Multicultural Society," in T. J. Hixon, L. D. Shriberg, and J. H. Saxman, eds. *Introduction to Communication Disorders*. Englewood Cliffs, NJ: Prentice-Hall, 1980.

Strom, R. D. *Teaching in the Slum School*. Columbus, Ohio: Charles E. Merrill, 1965.

18

CONTENTS

THE ABUSED AND NEGLECTED

Why include a discussion on child abuse and neglect in an introductory text on exceptional people? Children who have been treated cruelly are considered handicapped — in the broadest sense of that word — since the damage that directly results from abuse and/or neglect is both physically and psychologically debilitating. These children's lawful rights are violated and their futures are limited (if not grim) unless schools and community agencies intercede. A second reason for including child abuse and neglect is that exceptional children are more likely to be victims of these behaviors. This is so because of the increased pressure on the family and because the handicapped child is "different" from the norm (Garbarino, 1977).

Given the daily contact with children, teachers are most likely to be in positions to identify abused children, and many commonly do suspect cases of abuse or neglect. All too frequently, though, educators ask questions such as, Should I get involved? Whom do I tell? What kind of information do I report? Will I be forced to testify in court? Such questions are raised primarily because the teacher is not familiar with the laws governing child abuse and neglect.

THE SMITHS

In cases of child abuse, attention is usually focused on the injured child. Yet, in reality, child abuse is a symptom of deeper, more complex problems related to pathological family dynamics. In essence, child abuse is family abuse since all family members are involved, either directly or indirectly.

It has been over a year since Sharon Smith left her husband, Ted, because he physically abused their daughter. Sharon, now an active member of Parents Anonymous, relates this story:

Ted and I were married after he graduated from college as a civil engineer. The first year of our marriage seemed like heaven. But things started to go wrong the second year. Soon after Susie was born, Ted lost his job. At first we were optimistic, but months slipped by and still no job. Ted, who was spending more and more time at home, became irritable over nothing. I guess I kept overlooking how bad things really were. At first he would scream and shout at me and Susie, too. But then he began to hit Susie whenever she cried or even made a noise. When Ted first began hitting Susie, he would tell me, "The only way to make her a good girl is to beat her. Kids need it to know who the boss is. My brothers and I knew what would happen to us if we didn't toe the line — we'd get the shit beat out of us." Often Ted would joke about a scar on his leg caused by his father throwing a fire poker at him because Ted was talking in church.

Susie started nursery school when she was three years old. My parents insisted on paying the tuition since Ted and I really didn't have the money. Now that I think about it, I'm pretty sure that Mrs. Guion, Susie's teacher, was suspicious of us. Once she carefully asked about Susie's frequent bruises. Quickly, I remarked that Susie was an active little tomboy. After that I made every attempt to avoid talking with Mrs. Guion.

One day, when Susie was three and a half, she and I were alone in our apartment. Ted had been gone for several days, as he had been doing lately. I kept ignoring the truth that he was seeing another woman. Anyway, Susie and I were alone. Susie was watching "Sesame Street" when I said, "Susie, let's go to the store." Apparently, she didn't hear me, so I said in a louder voice, "Susie! Listen!" Suddenly she jerked her head and looked at me with total fear. Her little body was trembling. At that moment, I realized that not only was Ted destroying our daughter, but I was too. Susie was afraid of me! It was like someone threw cold water on me. I was shocked. Shocked into action.

That day I decided things had to change. I called my parents who lived 200 miles away and said that Susie and I were coming to visit. It was difficult, but I explained everything to them. They didn't belittle me. Instead, with their support and encouragement, I contacted Parents Anonymous, an organization that helps parents who are abusing their children. That was a year ago. It seems like a lifetime. Since that time a lot of changes have occurred. I'm in a training program to become a legal secretary, Susie is in nursery school, and Ted and I are in the process of getting a divorce.

Much of this success can be attributed to Parents Anonymous. Through them I gained a lot of insight about myself. I don't like what Ted or I did to each other or to Susie, but I think I understand why things didn't work out. Also, I no longer blame only Ted for abusing Susie. I can accept that I contributed to hurting her by not helping her.

Points for Consideration

- An analysis of the Smiths' family dynamics reveals that both parents were abusive although only Ted was responsible for inflicting bodily injury. Sharon's tendency to ignore or minimize the magnitude of the problem made her a silent partner in abusive practices.

- Usually abusive parents were abused children. Ted was modeling his parents' child-rearing practices. Ted's inability to provide for his family as a breadwinner, coupled with his warped perceptions of child-rearing practices, created a climate conducive for child abuse. Either of these conditions occurring in isolation may not have necessarily resulted in child abuse.

- Sharon believed that she had little choice but to accept Ted's abusive behavior. Her refusal to recognize the deterioration of their marriage, the impact of Ted's abusive behavior on Susie, and her rationalization for staying with him since she had no marketable skills highlight Sharon's immature dependence on Ted.

- Mrs. Guion was aware that Susie's home life might be abusive. However, like other professionals involved in similar settings, she did not follow through on her suspicions.

Common Misconceptions

The Smiths' case highlights some important misconceptions about child abuse and neglect.

- *Child Abuse and Neglect Occur in Families with a Low Socioeconomic Background.* Although procedures for reporting abuse tend to pinpoint cases from poverty areas, experts believe child abuse is equally prevalent in all economic levels.

- *Abusive Parents Do Not Love Their Children.* Because of the various types of child abuse and neglect, and their related causes, it is difficult to make generalizations. However, many parents involved in child abuse practices love their children, but are unable to control their behavior.

- *The Abused or Neglected Child Is Taken Away from His or Her Parents.* Few children identified as abuse or neglect victims are removed from the family setting and placed in a protective environment.

- *Teachers Can Do Little To Help Abused Children.* On the contrary, teachers have a responsibility to report suspected cases of abuse and/or neglect.

HISTORICAL PERSPECTIVE

Although the horrors of child abuse have received increased attention within the past several decades, the problem is neither recent nor limited to the United States. Children throughout history were thought to be the property of their parents, especially their fathers. Child labor laws and children's rights did not exist. As a result, inhumane treatment of minors was neither the concern nor the jurisdiction of the state. No public welfare departments existed to protect children. This lack of jurisdiction was evident even in the 1800s when the American Society for the Prevention of Cruelty to Animals became involved in a child abuse case only because there was no other organization that had the right to deal with the case (Justice and Justice, 1976).

More recently, the general public has become concerned about the issue of child abuse. The medical profession can be credited with arousing public interest. In 1946, X-ray technicians came to public attention by stating that some brain damage as well as damage to arms and legs were often associated with early childhood beatings. Also, in 1961, Kempe publicized the "battered child syndrome" at a meeting of the American Academy of Pediatrics (Justice and Justice, 1976).

A major outcome of public interest and involvement was legislative action for the protection of children. Between 1963 and 1968, all states enacted laws governing the reporting and confirming of suspected cases of child abuse and/or neglect. In addition, protective services were created from this series of state laws (Mitchell, 1977). In 1974, Congress enacted the Child Abuse Prevention and Treatment Act, which provided agencies with money to devise strategies for preventing abuse, locating abused children, and helping parents, children, and communities deal with problems of abuse and neglect (Justice and Justice, 1976). With increasing awareness of child abuse and neglect as a major problem, guidelines and procedures were established by state and federal authorities. These attempted to cope with the growing number of cases reported and also to find methods for identifying hidden cases. Within the Department of Health, Education, and Welfare, the National Center on Child Abuse and Neglect (NCCAN) provides funds for states to develop prevention and treatment programs.

DEFINITION OF TERMS

Many people associate the term child abuse with bodily harm. For example, children with numerous broken bones, cigarette burns, severe bruises, or lacerations are recognized as possible victims of abuse. However, physical abuse is only one facet of the definition. **Child abuse** encompasses four categories: physical abuse, emotional abuse, sexual abuse, and neglect. The Draft Model Child Protective Services Act defines child abuse and child neglect as (*We Can Help*, Unit 2, 1976, pp. 12–13):

(a) "Child" means a person under the age of 18
(b) An "abused or neglected child" means a child whose physical or mental health or welfare is harmed or threatened with harm by the acts or omissions of his [or her] parents or other person responsible for his [or her] welfare
(c) "Harm" to a child's health or welfare can occur when the parent or other person responsible for his [or her] welfare:
   (i)   Inflicts, or allows to be inflicted, upon the child, physical or mental injury, including injuries sustained as a result of excessive corporal punishment; or
   (ii) Commits, or allows to be committed, against the child, a sexual offense, as defined by state law; or
   (iii) Fails to supply the child with adequate food, clothing, shelter, education (as defined by state law), or health care, though financially able to do so; for the purposes of this Act, "adequate health care" includes any medical or non-medical health care permitted or authorized under state law; or
   (iv) Abandons the child, as defined by state law; or
   (v)   Fails to provide the child with adequate care, supervision, or guardianship by specific acts or omissions of a similarly serious nature requiring the intervention of the child protective service or a court
(d) "Threatened harm" means a substantial risk of harm
(e) "A person responsible for a child's welfare" includes the child's parent; guardian; foster parent; an employee of a public or private residential home, institution, or agency; or other person responsible for the child's welfare
(f) "Physical injury" means death, disfigurement, or the impairment of any bodily organ
(g) "Mental injury" means an injury to the intellectual or psychological capacity of a child as evidenced by an observable and substantial impairment in his [or her] ability to function within a normal range of performance and behavior, with due regard for his [or her] culture.

Physical abuse is the easiest to detect. For example, a teacher notices the child who has repeated injuries that cannot be explained adequately or are located on improbable parts of the body. **Emotional abuse** is characterized by excessive yelling, belittling, teasing, and aberrant child-rearing practices, either verbal or nonverbal. Emotional abuse is just as serious in nature as physical abuse; however, detection is more difficult because outsiders do not necessarily see the actual abusive behaviors or their consequences. **Sexual abuse**, which includes rape, attempted rape, indecent exposure, sodomy, exploitation, incest, and impairing the morals of a minor, is also difficult to prove. Usually, there are no witnesses and the child is reluctant to admit the occurrence of sexual abuse. **Neglect** deals with not providing for children's needs rather than inflicting physical or psychological harm. Proving that neglect has occurred is sometimes difficult because those in authority often cannot agree upon the conditions that constitute appropriate, proper care (Mitchell, 1977).

CAUSES

In order to establish methods of preventing child abuse and intervention procedures to help the family, much attention has been devoted to determining why parents are abusive.

Parent Characteristics

One common belief is that parents who abuse their children are mentally ill; however, less than 10 percent of all abusive parents are mentally ill (Brenton, 1977; Justice and Justice, 1976). A general theme among cases of child abuse is that the parents of abused children were generally abused themselves as children. The abusive treatment that these parents underwent may not necessarily have been physical in nature, it could have been simply that they did not receive the love and attention they needed as children. As a result, they continue these abusive and neglectful child-rearing patterns because they are not prepared to provide for the needs of their own offspring (Brenton, 1977; Justice and Justice, 1976).

Another common variable in child abuse is the self-inflicted social isolation of some families. Often abusive parents do not have ongoing friendships or contacts with persons outside the family, or they are geographically distant from their extended families (Garbarino, 1977; Light, 1973). Because of this lack of established friendships and family ties, parents have no one with whom they can talk when family problems arise. Such problems might include marital, economic, or child-rearing issues. Recent studies have indicated that these difficulties often plague parents who abuse their children (Brenton, 1977; Garbarino, 1977). Stress, coupled with the lack of concerned friends or family with whom to discuss problems, inevitably leads to frustration. Unfortunately, this frustration is then channeled inward and results in misplaced anger toward the child. Social isolation prevents the family from getting the help they need to reduce stress, which can lead to eventual child abuse (Garbarino, 1977).

Another factor often observed in cases of child abuse is the kind of personality associated with abusive adults. Here are listed the four kinds of personality characteristics believed to appear in abusive parents (Justice and Justice, 1976; Light, 1973):

- Hostile and aggressive parents who are angry with everyone
- Parents who are rigid in their views, who are cold and compulsive, and therefore unable to deal with problems in a sensible, rational manner
- Parents who lack maturity, who are dependent upon others to meet their own needs, and who ignore the needs of others around them
- Fathers who remain at home and take charge of child-rearing because of unemployment

The Child

The child is another consideration in determining causes of abuse. Abuse often occurs if the parents view their child as being different from the norm. This difference could be that the child is physically or mentally handicapped, hard to control, hyperactive, has physical features that deviate from the norm, or simply that the child looks like someone whom the parent really dislikes (Garbarino, 1977; Justice and Justice, 1976). In most instances, only one child in a family receives abuse; and there is sometimes a tendency for other family members to join with the abusing parent.

The Environment

A major misconception of child abuse and neglect is that it occurs only within the lower socioeconomic bracket. However, research indicates that child abuse and neglect is pretty much equally distributed among all socioeconomic groups and all races. One reason for the misconception concerning the poor is that most identified or reported cases of child abuse come from families of low socioeconomic status. These children are often treated in a public clinic or health center which gathers highly visible data. Doctors working in these situations are more likely to report abuse cases than physicians in private practice who often know the family personally and receive payment directly from the parents (Newberger, 1977). Also, investigators have noted that professionals reporting child abuse find it much easier to call a person from a lower socioeconomic group a bad parent than to identify one of their peers or someone in a middle- to upper-income bracket as a bad parent (Davies and McEwen, 1977; Newberger, 1977). This lack of reporting among middle- and upper-income brackets inhibits preventive measures and in essence allows child abuse to continue in these groups.

PREVALENCE

Accurate statistics concerning child abuse are difficult to obtain because many cases are not reported. However, researchers believe that approximately one million children are abused or neglected annually; 100,000 to 200,000 are victims of physical abuse; 60,000 to 100,000 are sexually abused; the remainder are identified as neglected. Brenton (1977) estimates that 2000 children die annually as a result of physical abuse and that three to four million children are physically abused by being kicked, punched, or beaten. Light (1973) states that 1 out of every 100 children is either physically abused or severely neglected. Because of inaccurate reporting of child abuse, it is believed that for each reported case of abuse there are approximately 100 more unreported cases (Justice and Justice, 1976). These figures, coupled with the fact that child abuse and neglect is the number one cause of children's death in the United States, make it essential that this behavior be dealt with as a major problem confronting our society (Martenson, 1977).

CHARACTERISTICS OF THE POPULATION

Certain kinds of children are more likely to become candidates for child abuse. These include children with physical or mental handicaps, illegitimate children, premature babies, and youngsters who are often sick and demand a great deal of attention (Brenton, 1977; Mitchell, 1977). Also, family constellation is related to child abuse. For example, the youngest and oldest child in the family are more likely targets for abusive parents. Since there is a greater percentage of physical abuse to children younger than six, age appears to be a critical factor (Mitchell, 1977; Justice and Justice, 1976). This does not mean that all young, handicapped children born prematurely, for example, will be abused. There are also identifiable characteristics of abusive parents, and abusive relationships are more likely to occur when certain types of parents have children with the characteristics cited here.

Some general characteristics associated with each type of abuse and neglect can be observed within the school and classroom. Children who are physically abused by their parents are often disruptive and aggressive at school because they need to vent their frustrations and because this behavior is modeled in the home. In addition, such children and youth experience difficulties in learning to socialize with other children simply because they cannot control their emotions (Mitchell, 1977). The emotionally abused child, who may be either unusually compliant and eager to please or may be aggressive and demanding in the classroom, is characterized by a low self-concept and seems to be less competent in performing skills than he or she really is. Sexually abused children tend to have difficulty establishing positive peer relationships, have a higher incidence of delinquency and sexual promiscuity, and tend to avoid physical activities. Distinctions of the child suffering from neglect are varied. Among them are children who are malnourished, improperly clothed, poorly supervised, and noticeably medically neglected. Such children also have a high absentee rate at school.

In addition to the distinguishable behaviors associated with each type of abuse and neglect, there are several common behavioral patterns. Generally, the abused or neglected child refuses to admit that the abuse ever occurred; the child appears to be protecting the abusive parent. This denial of abuse is frequently difficult for outsiders to understand. However, an analysis of the child's perspective offers some insight for this kind of "cover-up" behavior. Regardless of the quality of parenting, the abused child may rationalize that punishment, no matter how severe, was deserved or justified, since the parent is the authority figure. Also, the child fears that if someone is told about the abuse, further and more severe abuse will result. Another factor related to the child's denial of abuse is that the child does not want to be separated from his or her parents. In essence, the child accepts the role of the abused in the family dynamics, no matter how warped or distorted his or her understanding of that position may be. By understanding the family dynamics, the professional realizes that the abused child is placed in double jeopardy—first, as a victim of abuse and, second, if reported, possibly a victim of separation from the family. From the child's perspective, it's a loss either way.

Within the identified child-abuse population there is a high incidence of deviant social, behavioral, and intellectual functioning (Gil, 1970). Yet, the cause-and-effect relationship between abuse and handicap has not been determined. In other words, did the handicap result in abuse or did abuse cause the handicap?

As mentioned earlier, many abusive parents perceive their child as being different. According to Sandgrund, Gaines, and Green (1974), there is a profile of parents who are more likely to be abusive. Such parents, in general, have a low self-image and unrealistic expectations about their child's performance. Although no conclusions can be drawn regarding the handicap as eliciting abusive behavior in parents, there is evidence to suggest that handicapped children are more likely to be high-risk candidates for child abuse.

Handicapped children have a greater risk of being abused or neglected than their non-impaired peers.

In a review of literature on child abuse and the handicapped, Soeffing (1975) concluded that the issue of abuse causing a handicap is more definitive. In a three-year follow-up study of 42 abused children, Martin (1973) found that approximately 50 percent of the abused children were developmentally delayed. Fitch (cited in Soeffing, 1975), who reported similar findings on abused children, also studied children who were neglected. Developmental test scores of neglected children obtained during a hospital stay were significantly higher than their test scores six months later. Fitch concluded that neglected children who are denied a positive, loving, and stimulating relationship with their parents may be at a greater disadvantage regarding intellectual development than abused children who tend to have a loving, although at times abusive, relationship with their parents.

IDENTIFICATION

Role of Teachers

Even though parents are sometimes aware of their tendencies to abuse and sincerely care about their child, they do not know how or do not have the courage to ask for help. The only hope for abused children and their families is outside intervention. In many instances, the only outsiders to see the children are their teachers and doctors. Unfortunately, by the time the physician sees the child, serious abuse may have occurred; even then, the physician has no way of detecting verbal or psychological abuse. On the other hand, since teachers interact with children on a daily basis, they are most likely to both observe specific behaviors that might indicate abuse and neglect and to report such incidents to the proper authorities. Since 1967, teachers in all states are required by law to report any suspected cases of abuse or neglect to the proper authorities (Martenson, 1977).

> Under the law of civil negligence, violation of a statutory duty, such as mandatory reporting of suspected child abuse and neglect, is negligence *per se*, "in itself." That means if it can be proven that a person willfully or negligently failed to report known or suspected child abuse or neglect, he or she can be sued for the injuries that occurred after the time when a report should have been made [*We Can Help*, Unit 8, 1976, p. 8].

In reference to child abuse, the concept of civil negligence was applied in *Robinson* v. *Wical, M.D., et al.* (1970). In an out-of-court settlement for $600,000, a hospital and other named defendants were accused of negligence for failure to report a case of child abuse that resulted in permanent brain injury for the young victim. Teachers are protected legally from any resulting libel that might come about if the case so reported was judged not to be an abuse case; teachers and professionals cannot be sued as long as they report all incidents in good faith (Mitchell, 1977; Frazier, 1975). Too often, teachers hesitate to report suspected cases because they do not feel they have enough proof. However, finding the proof in suspected cases of child abuse is not the job of the classroom teacher; the child protective agency will conduct an investigation.

Teachers often are reluctant to become involved because they do not want to appear in court or be responsible for removing a child from his or her parents. However, in most cases, a simple interview with the child investigator is all that

Teachers need to be informed of their role in identifying and reporting suspected cases of abuse and neglect.

is required; teachers usually do not have to appear in court. And removing a child from the family is done only in extreme cases (Mitchell, 1977).

If the teacher suspects abuse or neglect, the first step is to write notes about the situation in order to have a better perspective of what is happening. Notes should include dates and specific detailed facts, as well as impressions and feelings (Truesdell, 1977). Also, the teacher should be available to the students so they can discuss their feelings privately and candidly, without being judged. Too often the teacher is the only outsider that a child trusts to talk about such family problems. After documenting the facts and perhaps talking with parents, the teacher should move quickly, remembering that each case of child abuse is potentially terminal.

In each school a policy should be established that identifies the proper authority to whom suspected cases of abuse or neglect should be reported. One suggestion is to have a specific form on which all pertinent data could be recorded and submitted. After reporting the suspected case, the teacher should follow through to find out what action has been taken. The teacher should not try to remediate the problem alone; rather, the teacher should make the appropriate community agency aware of the situation (Mitchell, 1977; Truesdell, 1977).

Before reporting suspected cases of abuse, teachers should know the accepted definitions of abuse and neglect applicable in their states and areas (Heisner, 1978). It is also important to realize that by making the report, the teacher helps the entire family, not just the child. By helping the family, abusive tendencies in future generations might be curbed (Frazier, 1975).

Role of Social Workers

Federal law mandates that every county, parish, etc., of every state have an appropriate agency to receive reports of suspected cases of abuse and neglect. It is the responsibility of the staff at the welfare department or the children's services board (protective children's services) to identify abuse and neglect incidents and to follow through with appropriate treatment. Whereas the teacher is trained to develop children's academic skills, the juvenile social worker is an expert at identifying and intervening in the family dynamics. The social worker is responsible for verifying information received from the teacher.

In addition to direct involvement with families, local social service agencies are developing public awareness campaigns to inform the public of the law, possible signs of abuse and neglect, and the referral process.

TREATMENT

Counseling the Parents

Child abuse is a family problem. Thus it is imperative that remediation focus on the parents involved. However, getting parents into an individualized counseling program may be difficult. As Derdeyn (1977a) pointed out, since parents are often forced to seek therapy against their wills, feelings of hostility and embarrassment can be strong. An alternative to individual therapy is group therapy, which may be more successful.

In an intervention program conducted by Justice and Justice (1976), when both abusive parents were involved in group therapy with four or five other couples, the effects of counseling were greatly enhanced. Usually group therapy continued for at least four or five months and would focus on ways of handling stressful situations; it also provided the socially isolated families with other people to whom they could talk. Also discussed in group therapy was the subject of child development. Many abusive and neglectful parents are not aware of the normal developmental stages that occur in childhood and thus expected the child to have behaviors that are either physically impossible or developmentally inappropriate.

Providing Support Services

Making help available to parents on an around-the-clock basis lessens the degree of isolation surrounding the family, and thereby alleviates some stress. Assistance can be provided in many ways: parent aides, visiting nurses, homemaker services, crisis centers that offer immediate emergency child care, nursery schools where parents can work and observe children as they play and develop, transportation to therapy sessions, telephone hotlines, and parent self-help groups (Justice and Justice, 1976).

Parent aides and the homemaker services work directly in the home to help the parents handle various situations. The aides eventually form a caring relationship with parents, thereby making them feel wanted and loved. The aides are also aware of community agencies that might prove helpful to the family, such as sources of emergency funds, food, and clothing. The homemaker services provide mothers with training in child care and home maintenance. Homemaker workers make themselves available to the mother until she is more sure of her child care and home management skills. Visiting nurses also assist the family by helping them understand problems associated with child-rearing and development.

Organizations such as day care centers, child care centers, and 24-hour emergency child care furnish professional services directly to the child and family. Parents are urged to assist at these centers and observe children interacting with caregivers without the threat of physical mistreatment. Since transportation to these services is sometimes a problem for parents, many communities have established taxi or bus service. Telephone hotlines are also valuable for parents in crisis who need immediate help. Finally, parent self-help groups such as Parents Anonymous are a great aid to many families. In these structured settings families discuss common problems and appropriate coping strategies.

Removing the Child from the Parents

Once child abuse or neglect has indeed been determined, it is essential that the child involved be protected from further harm. In most instances of physical abuse, the medical problems are taken care of first (Derdeyn, 1977b). While the child is receiving medical attention (usually in the hospital or another location away from home), the home situation is investigated to determine whether or not it is safe for the child to return. If the family is found to be incompetent, alternative living arrangements must be made. Several options exist for temporary placement: foster homes, group homes, relatives, or institutional care, depending upon the circumstances of each case.

Foster home placement is not as frequently used as is commonly thought; it is usually a last resort measure (Derdeyn, 1977b). Foster care is normally a temporary intervention tactic. However, in those cases where parents are unqualified to take care of their children, long-term foster care may be appropriate.

Treatment in School

Regardless of the child's placement, therapy must be provided since the results of abuse go much deeper than bruises or lack of clothing. These children feel unloved and unwanted; they do not trust adults since they have not been provided with trustful models. Generally these children believe that they are bad and deserve such extreme punishment (Brenton, 1977). Teachers and school counselors should make every attempt to show the child that they care and are concerned for his or her welfare (Davies and McEwen, 1977). One method that seems effective in helping children to understand their feelings and family situation involves bibliotherapy, which uses books that depict similar life experiences to promote discussions. In addition, children who are having problems at home need some assurance that they are not the only ones in such situations. Through bibliotherapy, abused children can realize that their problems with family members are not theirs alone (Cocha, 1978).

The responsibility of schools must go beyond an awareness of behaviors related to abuse and procedures for reporting abuse and neglect. Alternative educational programs geared to the battered child's needs must be developed since the effects of child abuse are evident in the battered child's classroom performance. As Shanas states, "Case studies have shown a strong link between abused or neglected students and pupils who later disrupt school activities" (1975, p. 481). These battered children need an educational program that provides a curriculum focusing on trust and self-respect as well as on academic instruction.

Success Rate

Rehabilitating abusive parents is a complicated process. The success of treatment depends on two factors: client and procedure. On the basis of their research, Kempe and Kempe (1978) have concluded that 10 percent of abusive parents suffer from serious mental illness and thus do not benefit from treatment. For these parents, the most appropriate action is to remove the battered child from the home. Of the remaining 90 percent, the authors stated that 80 percent of the cases complete treatment successfully. It is Kempe and Kempe's (1978, pp. 107–108) contention that the following factors are consistently evident in those cases where the battered child is successfully returned to the home:

> First, the abusive parent's image of himself must have improved to the point where he has made at least one friend with whom he shares regular and enjoyable experiences. . . . Second, both parents must have found something attractive in their abused child and be able to show it by talking lovingly, hugging, or cuddling. Third, both parents must have learned to use lifelines in moments of crisis, so that they telephone their social worker, a friend, or another member of Parents Anonymous, or else take their child to a crisis nursery. Last, weekend reunions with their child in hospital or foster care must have gone more and more enjoyably, and increasing responsibility must not have strained family life unduly.

It is apparent that effective treatment programs should provide both crisis intervention strategies and continual long-term techniques. Also, the entire family, not just the abusive parent, requires some kind of intervention if the battered child is to return to a safe home environment.

SPECIAL CONSIDERATIONS AND ISSUES

Because of the epidemic proportions of abuse and neglect, all professionals (e.g., the clergy, medical personnel, law enforcement officials, and educators) must be informed on the topic of child abuse. Such community education programs should cover the scope of the problem, signs of possible abuse and neglect, the reporting process, and available community support agencies and organizations.

Schools must become more actively involved in not only reporting abuse and neglect but also in designing appropriate educational programs for battered children. Research is needed to identify and evaluate effective programs for these children. Since exceptional children have a higher rate of abuse and neglect, educators teaching these children should be especially attuned to identification and treatment procedures.

Further research focusing on the interrelationships between parent characteristics, child variables, and environmental factors will assist professionals in treating families who are victims of abuse and neglect. A comprehensive and thorough examination of all these issues requires schools and social agencies to work together in a cooperative, supportive, and professional manner.

SUMMARY POINTS

- Child abuse and neglect refers to aberrant child-rearing practices inflicted on children and youth by their parents or guardians. Abusive behaviors may be classified as physical, emotional, or sexual in nature.
- Adults who commit child abuse tend to have certain commonalities in their personal histories. In general, many child abusers were either abused or neglected as children; have few, if any, social contacts; are under some kind of stress; and tend to have certain personality traits.
- Within a family, child abuse usually focuses on one child. Premature children or children perceived as being different by the abusive parent are characteristically the targets of abuse.
- In addition to general characteristics, specific observable behaviors are related to each type of abuse and neglect.
- Child abuse and neglect is the number-one killer of children in America.
- Although research findings are not conclusive, they suggest that handicapped children are more likely to be victims of abuse and neglect than nonimpaired children.
- Battered children, even those who return to a safe home environment, have a greater number of learning and behavior problems. Child abuse and neglect leave long-lasting scars.
- Not only do teachers have a legal obligation to report abuse and neglect cases, but they may be held liable for not reporting suspected cases.
- School administrators and teachers must establish a process for documenting and reporting suspected cases of abuse and neglect.
- Treatment for abused children and their families is multidimensional and involves a variety of treatment techniques ranging from crisis intervention to long-term psychotherapy.
- Few battered children are removed permanently from their parents. However, many are placed in temporary settings outside the home.
- Because the battered child's school performance frequently suffers, schools need to develop special programs to better meet these children's cognitive and affective needs.

REVIEW QUESTIONS

1. Identify the school's role for reporting suspected child abuse and neglect cases in your community.
2. In your state what local social or law enforcement agency is held accountable for identifying abuse and neglect cases?

3. List those parental characteristics, child behaviors, and environmental situations that would increase the likelihood of abuse and neglect.

4. What steps can teachers take to develop an awareness of child abuse and neglect in their students at the elementary level? At the high school level?

PREVENTION — ALTERNATIVE APPROACHES

The role of parent is often a difficult, tedious, time-consuming task. Because of changes in the American family structure, today's parents do not have many of the support systems available to them for coping with their new role that their parents or grandparents had. Due to increasing mobility, many American families lack the support of an extended family living nearby. Approximately one out of five families moves each year. Also, many parents feel inadequate about being a "good" parent because of lack of knowledge and experience. If the status of the marital relationship is tentative, these feelings may be intensified.

Documentation of abuse in young children points out that the abuse occurs during a perceived crisis, no matter how trivial. For example, a mother may interpret her infant's cry from hunger as a deliberate, controllable act. Although all infants communicate through crying, the abusive parent may have unrealistic expectations. Regarding abused young children, "it is the normal development milestones, poorly understood and accepted by the parents, that account for most of the trigger crises in battering" (Kempe and Kempe, 1978, p. 28).

This lack of knowledge regarding normal child behavior and the lack of support from an extended family suggests that some type of intervention is necessary for preventing abuse and neglect. In a comprehensive study conducted at Colorado General Hospital, results indicated that trained nurses who observed parents' behaviors in the labor and delivery rooms were able to predict successful or unsuccessful parenting with 75 percent accuracy. (Kempe and Kempe, 1978). Although this area of study is still in its early stage, the implications are clear. Many potentially abusive parents can be identified prior to the initiation of abuse of their children.

The focus of prevention programs is on developing positive child-rearing practices. The Health Visitor Program, currently in practice in Great Britain, is an example of a preventative program. Trained personnel are sent to visit all new parents, providing them with any necessary help or information about child-raising and keeping a watchful eye for signs of potential child abuse.

Another approach to the prevention of child abuse is requiring a parenting course for all high school students. "Education for parenthood programs at the secondary school level must provide more information about emotional and behavioral requirements of child rearing, reasonable expectations of children, and community services" (Soeffing, 1975, p. 132). Also, practical experience requiring students to work with children in supervised settings should be included in such courses. This type of intervention would remove one factor related to child abuse—that of lack of knowledge about the child. If such a parenting course utilizing role-playing were required in all schools, many problems of child abuse could be dealt with before they occurred, and future parents would be informed of services available to help them in times of need, which would possibly curb the cyclical nature of child abuse (Brenton, 1977). In addition to a general knowledge of child development, Sefcik and Ormsby (1978) identified organized day care centers as being necessary for both intervention and prevention programs.

Since a higher incidence of abuse and neglect is found among handicapped children, it is imperative that families with handicapped children be provided with a readily available support system to promote positive family dynamics. Such services can include periodic parent group meetings or short-term respite care for the handicapped child. For example, the Children's Resource Center, a nonprofit mental health agency located in a midwestern rural county, reserves one of its six residential beds for respite care of handicapped children. This agency, in recognizing the mental health need for parents to get away for a weekend vacation without their handicapped child, offers quality supervision by trained professionals and paraprofessionals.

Although society has radically changed its attitudes toward children and their rights, many preventative programs are controversial, since they may challenge both the parent as an authoritative controlling figure and the parents' rights to privacy. Yet, in the final analysis, an informed public is the best prevention against child abuse and neglect.

DISCUSSION POINTS

1. As a teacher you would have more opportunities than other professionals to interact with your students' parents. Develop an outline of a preventative program on child abuse and neglect for parents. Identify major concepts to be covered and list local, state, and national resources (media, speakers, etc.) you would use.
2. Investigate local junior and high school programs to determine if they have a parenting course. Is the course syllabus complete? If not, explain what information you would add.

SUGGESTED READINGS

Justice, B., and Justice, R. *The Abusing Family*. New York: Human Sciences Press, 1976.

Kempe, R. S., and Kempe, C. H. *Child Abuse*. Cambridge: Harvard University, 1978.

Martin, D. L. "The Growing Horror of Child Abuse and the Undeniable Role of the Schools in Putting an End to It." *American School Board Journal*, 160 (1973), 51–55.

Soeffing, M. "Abused Children are Exceptional Children." *Exceptional Children* 42, No. 3 (1975), 126–133.

THE FUTURE

19

CONTENTS

LOOKING TO THE FUTURE

The 1980s will be a significant landmark in the history of our society's efforts to recognize the need for and to establish educational programs for exceptional persons. Education in the United States achieved cabinet-level status with the formation of the U.S. Department of Education in May of 1980. Within the department, the Office for Special Education and Rehabilitation Services was organized to include the Office of Gifted and Talented. This is a federal acknowledgement that special education is not limited to the handicapped; rather, it is directed at providing services to all exceptional children and youth.

In this chapter, several ideas and issues are presented that are likely to affect exceptional persons and professionals working with them. Few conclusions are drawn, but several challenges are discussed. Drawing conclusions and accepting the challenges is the responsibility of the individual. May it always be so.

BEYOND PL 94–142

Many educators believe that PL 94–142 was the most significant and influential piece of educational legislation in the history of our country. It has been heralded by some as a long-awaited stimulus for positive change in education. By others it has been referred to as the bearer of bad tidings, the source of turmoil and anxiety brought about by the rapidity of changes mandated.

Problems of Implementation

The continuing process of arranging for the appropriate education of America's many unserved or poorly served handicapped children in the years to come will not be easy. Finding and training competent teachers, devising and implementing IEPs, and designing appropriate physical space arrangements are tasks that carry with them contradictions, confusion, uncertainty, and anxiety.

The following letter, written by a high-school special education teacher, illustrates some of the difficulties and concerns that have resulted from attempts to implement PL 94–142.

To the Editor: An Open Letter to CEC

On the IEP my name goes on the line after "Local Education Agency Representative." I used to be called a teacher, but I don't teach much any more. Last year I was out of class the equivalent of 30 to 40 whole days because of conferences, testing, phone calls, securing confidential records, and the like. That does not count scoring tests, writing IEP's, or filling out forms because I do those at lunch or at home—when I used to do planning.

I am the model of a modern LEA representative. The only problem is, that doesn't leave anyone to teach the kids. I love teaching, and feedback from my supervisor, principal, students, and their parents tells me I am a great teacher. But I don't teach much any more.

While I was typing my posttest results (required by law), I came across several students whose reading scores showed little or no gain. I cried. Chances are, nobody will ever hold me accountable for those scores. But I teach high school. For many of these kids there is no more. When they leave, they leave formal education. They always leave with part of me; this year it wasn't enough.

The situation is similar to combat. The general makes a decision and you find yourself out on a hill somewhere surrounded by threats, firing for weeks at something nobody is sure is there. All the time you are incompetently led, ill protected, and under-equipped. Between you and the general, guess whose life is on the line?

Instead of artillery, we have legislation and litigation. Legislatures tell the state departments to provide. The departments tell the localities to provide. The localities tell the supervisors to provide. The supervisors tell the teachers to provide. What happens? Nobody can afford to pay for it so the teachers do—with their hearts.

I, and countless others, cannot learn to give only part. I cannot ask my wife and children to put up with me, depressed and tense for months each spring because I must finish my testing, must begin testing with the new kids we've identified, must get the reports in on time, must complete reams of papers (the law says so, and tells me how much time I have to do it), and *can't* teach. When I am in class, I am tense and harried because the testing isn't getting done on time. I don't have any time to plan, to diagnose, to remediate, and I can't get on top.

But it didn't begin with me. It began with litigation by people who were being treated as less than whole. The universities and CEC took up advocacy. It was so important then; it still is. There were plenty of directives, but not enough money for personnel to carry them out. So it became the province of the combat soldier to make special education better by doing more, squeezing off one more round, sleeping one hour less.

Now some of the bullets are killing our own soldiers. Kids are being dumped when they should be mainstreamed, because there just isn't time for the special education teacher to help. Teachers are falling all around me, because they are trying to do too much. Creativity is being blown apart by expediency. Good teachers are being promoted into unfulfilling administrative positions, while less qualified teachers are being hired for the classrooms. . . . [Kenneth Katzen, *Exceptional Children*, 46, 8 (1980), p. 582].

The issues raised in this commentary are legitimate and will need to be addressed by educators at all levels.

Mildly Handicapped

Education for children referred to as mildly handicapped is likely to become less distinguishable, but not ineffective, over the next 20 years. As educational systems refine their abilities to design and implement individualized, specialized programs based on children's learning needs and learning styles, the need for labeling and categorization may disappear. Noncategorical groupings based on assessments of learners' specific strengths and weaknesses will likely become the "pigeon holes" of the future. This move toward noncategorical educational programming is likely to have a limiting—and some would say negative—effect on some special education categories, especially the rapidly growing learning-disabilities movement (Forness, 1974). However, the ultimate outcome is individualized programming for all children.

Severe and Profound

Despite the more complex nature of their handicapping conditions, persons with severe and profound handicaps will move closer to the mainstream in America's educational future. Those long-forgotten but visibly different persons will be enabled to fulfill their potentials through education and training to a much greater degree than has been possible in the past. Education will more clearly come to adopt the philosophy of trying another way of teaching if success is not being achieved with particular children.

Continuing Education

If the goal of individualization and a special education for all children is to work without penalizing the children who are receiving special education services now, many resources—time, energy, and money—will have to be invested in the preparation of school personnel. Educators currently employed and those entering the profession in the near future should expect to become lifelong learners. Although the concept of **lifetime education** has been given lip service in the past, continuing education must become a reality in the future if success in providing all children with appropriate individualized educational programs is to be realized.

Litigation

Litigation is likely to continue to serve as a force for demanding the rights of children in the future. In 1979, at least one such case (*Mattie T.*) resulted in a consent decree requiring tutoring and other services for those pupils who were formerly enrolled in special education but are now in the regular classroom. These services are to be described in a written educational plan—in a sense, an IEP for non-special education pupils. Requiring IEPs for all may not be far behind (Coulter, 1979). Many educators, special and regular alike, would agree "that when it comes to educational principles, those embedded in the legislation concerning education for handicapped persons are entirely consistent with fundamentally sound principles for the education of all persons" (Chickering and Chickering, 1978, p. 95). The parents of nonexceptional children may well recognize the importance of an IEP and demand it as a right of their children as well (Kauffman, 1980).

TRENDS IN EDUCATION FOR EXCEPTIONAL PERSONS

Future educational trends related to exceptional persons include:

■ *Adoption of a Stronger Preventative Approach.* Most experts agree that in order to successfully solve the dilemmas inherent in serving exceptional persons, more resources must go into preventative programs. Research in the area of mental retardation, for example, has demonstrated that education and rehabilitation programs are effective in cutting the cost of caring for the mentally retarded by reducing the need for expensive institutionalization (Conley, 1973). Also, preventing handicapping conditions can greatly reduce society's cost relative to exceptional persons. Results of a study completed in 1969 indicated that an estimated 14 to 15 billion dollars could be saved by eliminating malnutrition in our country (President's Commission on Mental Retardation, 1975). Likewise, prenatal and preconceptual medical tests and genetic counseling combined with increased public awareness of the roles played by various environmental factors (e.g., alcohol, drugs, prenatal care of mother) are likely to gain impetus in the future.

■ *Development of Early Childhood Education and Day Care Programs.* Closely related to the future emphasis on prevention is the likely continued growth of early childhood educational programs. Research and experience have demonstrated that the earlier intervention is begun with exceptional children, the better their chances of developing to their full potential. If the least restrictive environment is going to be implemented, what better place to start than at the preschool level? Likewise, day care programs will take on increased responsibility for child development rather than simply performing the traditional child custodial role.

■ *Noncategorical Teacher Preparation.* Future teacher preparation programs in special education are likely to become oriented toward a comprehensive, noncategorical approach. In such an approach, prospective teachers are trained in the skills that they will require to meet the needs of exceptional children rather than in specific instructional techniques that apply only to particular handicapping conditions (Belch, 1979).

■ *Increased Emphasis on Career and Vocational Education.* Along with an increased emphasis on early childhood education and prevention programs in special education, there will undoubtedly be an expansion of services to older pupils as well. The development of appropriate individualized programs for exceptional pupils of all ages will require vocational and career education. At the upper levels, however, these goals become more important as we attempt to help the adolescent decide what to do with the rest of his or her life. At this transitional age, educational systems and IEPs face a stern test. To pass this test in the future, greater and more creative resources will have to be brought to bear.

■ *Increased International Sharing and Cooperation.* Special educators have long benefitted from sharing ideas with educators of other nations. The development of community-based services for mentally retarded persons during the 1970s is directly attributable to the influence of the Scandinavian countries where the principle of normalization was implemented earlier. The development of a new type of mental health professional, the educateur, in some American universities in the late 1970s was greatly influenced by French colleges (Juul, 1978). International conferences such as the Council for Exceptional Children's First World Congress and the Vienna Congress of the International League of Societies for the Mentally Handicapped marked the beginning of an increased awareness of the worldwide nature of many concerns, problems, and interventions related to exceptional children. "It is from this international fertilization of ideas that we will discover the means, the approaches, and the tools that, modified for our American settings, will enable us to serve our handicapped citizens more effectively" (Menolascino, 1979, pp. 168–169).

■ *Increased Concern with the Education of Bicultural Children.* In the years to come, more of America's schools will develop the multicultural, multilinguistic perspective used to appropriately educate youngsters from minority cultural backgrounds. Our attention will be more clearly focused on the needs of the bicultural who in the past have often been served inappropriately through special education classes for the mentally retarded.

■ *Expanded Utilization of Behavioral Analysis and Behavior Modification.* The principles of behavioral psychology, which have already made a great contribution in developing the self-care, academic, and social behavior skills of handicapped pupils, will become even more widely utilized in regular classrooms as well as in special classes.

Whether educators can follow up on ideas that have been generated to improve education for exceptional children depends, in large part, on the public's continued support of research efforts. The demand for immediate results, thereby deemphasizing the significant role of longitudinal studies, has an effect. Also, the current practice of funding agencies to decide what should be researched and how has lessened the impact of scientific research in the field and may continue to do so in the future (Gallagher, 1979).

POSSIBLE CONSIDERATIONS

Professional educators seeking to adopt a proactive stance toward change and future developments have considered some possible future events impacting on exceptional children:

- *The Concept of Year-Round Schools.* Developing a 12-month school program could aid in providing appropriate, comprehensive services to exceptional children and youth.
- *A Possible U.S. Supreme Court Decision in the Future Eliminating Compulsory School Attendance.* Many special educators believe such a future occurrence could damage the development of educational opportunities for exceptional children.

Forecasting future events, analyzing their potential impact on exceptional children, and then engaging in appropriate activities to influence these future developments are strategies required for those professionals who wish to maintain and expand services to exceptional children.

In order to adequately meet the demands of our rapidly changing society, schools of the future must attend to a broader age range of pupils. Early childhood programs aimed at preventing and ameliorating learning problems will be developed along with more sophisticated career and vocational training programs designed to more closely meet the needs of adolescents. Likewise, schools must continue to develop and expand opportunities for educating persons from minority cultural groups. Traditional educational services must be modified, expanded, and enriched in order to meet their specialized needs. Cooperation among all educators and parents concerned with the education of exceptional children will be required. Developing individual educational programs and facing the tough decisions and challenges of the future demands teamwork.

SUMMARY POINTS

- The 1980s will be a significant landmark in the history of our society's efforts to recognize the need for and establishment of educational programs for exceptional persons.
- Implementation of PL 94–142 has required many changes on the part of regular as well as special educators; as a result teachers often have felt overly pressured, anxious, and uncertain of their new role demands.
- Educational systems in the future will move toward providing individualized, personalized learning for all persons, not just those labeled exceptional.
- In the future, educational concerns about exceptional persons are likely to emphasize prevention and the development of early childhood education pro-

grams; developing career and vocational education; noncategorical teacher preparation; concern for bicultural education; expanded use of behavioral analysis and behavior modification; and increased international sharing and cooperation.

■ Future progress in special education depends upon our society's willingness to support adequate research into the needs of exceptional persons.

■ Other future possibilities relating to the education of exceptional children include year-round schooling and possible changes in compulsory attendance laws.

REVIEW QUESTIONS

1. Why will the 1980s be considered significant for the establishment of educational programs for exceptional persons?
2. Why may all children be receiving individualized educational programs in the future?
3. What areas of emphasis and considerations in the future of special education were discussed? Which of these areas do you believe to be the most important? Why?

LEARNING AND TEACHING IN THE FUTURE

Throughout, this text has emphasized the need for professionals to share their expertise; however, the classroom teacher bears the biggest responsibility for teaching pupils. Stress is now on developing the maximum learning potential of all students. Therefore, holding the teacher responsible for most of the learning of a specific number of students is not realistic considering the breadth of knowledge and skills to be taught. The expectations for acquisition of knowledge and information have increased dramatically in the recent past and will continue to expand at unprecedented rates in the future. In order to meet the demands of this trend and teach pupils how to learn rather than simply pass along information, individualized teacher roles will be required.

Several specific roles that teachers of the future may have include the following (Barnes, 1972):

- *Value Developer*. This teacher will be responsible for helping pupils identify, clarify, and develop the personal values systems that guide their everyday lives. Pupils will discover how to learn about themselves, thus facilitating their learning about others and their environment.
- *Learning Diagnostician/Prescriptive Specialist*. The teacher performing this role will assist pupils, their parents, and other educators in identifying the specific strengths and weaknesses of the pupils' academic and behavior repertoire. This specialist will also be skilled in devising educational programs to match these identified specific needs.
- *Human Relations Developer*. This teacher will utilize his or her abilities in developing interpersonal relationship skills in school pupils. Cooperation, understanding of individual differences, and self-expression skills will help pupils interact and learn with other students.
- *Career and Leisure Counselor*. This teacher/counselor will help pupils develop their interests and talents to more fully meet the potential of their future career alternatives. The appropriate use of leisure time and the interrelationship of leisure time and career activities will also be emphasized.
- *Learning Resource Consultant*. The role of this teacher will be to help pupils learn how to utilize the ever-growing number of resources available for learning. In the future, students will be able to take advantage of a broader range of persons, places, and things in their environment in order to individualize their learning experiences and learn more effectively.

A teaching tool that all teachers—especially those in the role of learning resource consultant—will utilize in the future is the computer, which has many educational applications. Both **computer-managed instruction (CMI)** and **computer-assisted instruction (CAI)** are being used to aid exceptional students. CAI is not as prevalent because of the high cost of developing the coursework software (Lance, 1977). Although the computer does not complete the work for the learner, individualized learning sequences can obviously be used to assist the pupil in making decisions and in choosing among alternatives.

Goldenberg (1979) describes three basic ways in which computers can be used in education. The first way, which he calls "computer as tutor," provides for individual assessment, planning, remedial instruction, and record-keeping, all by computer. The second educational use of computers is referred to as "computer as eyeglasses." Here, the computer does not teach or give the child information but allows the child to expand his or her own abilities with an outward focus. For example, a computer can allow a child "to experiment with musical ideas without requiring that he first gain competence with an instrument" (p. 26). The third educational use of computers is referred to as "computer as mirror"; some computers can provide very specific and sensitive feedback on various aspects of a child's performance. For example, a computer can be programmed to identify "muscular activity even before we have been able to master the strength or coordination to produce a visible movement" (p. 27), thereby telling the child when he or she is addressing the correct muscles. For handicapped children, especially those with severe learning handicaps, use of the computer provides a means of interacting with their surroundings and a means of demonstrating their creative and intellectual abilities far beyond what was previously possible. Ironically, a machine, programmed and used by knowledgeable educators, can help to personalize learning to a degree thought to be impossible only a few years ago.

DISCUSSION POINTS

1. Do you agree that individualized instruction in the future will require differentiation of individual teacher roles? Why or why not? Discuss this idea with an experienced educator and share these perceptions with your classmates.
2. Which of the future teacher roles described do you think you would like to assume? Why? Which role or roles do not appeal to you? Why?
3. What educational uses of the computer have you had experience with already? Think about the "computer as mirror" and discuss how severely handicapped persons might be helped by this means.

THE CHALLENGE

No matter what role you choose to play in the future, it is important to recognize that one person caring enough to try can make a beginning that may make the difference in everyone's future. Blatt (1978, p. 10) in his letter to "someone" on the planet, challenges all of us to do our best:

> Hardly anyone realizes that those who want to leave the world a better place are among the most powerful people on Earth. But those people don't always appreciate that the reason that they are so powerful is because they are viewed as harmless, a strength which most people believe is their weakness. Indeed, if there were not such a perception, do-gooders would be exiled or worse. But they are not exiled, they are free to do good. You can be free to improve this planet and I think you may succeed if you begin in a small way.

All of us—parents, students, and professionals—are challenged to continue the strong efforts to develop educational opportunities and the quality of life for exceptional persons. The past—both the good and the bad—is beyond our influence. The shape of the future, however, is up to us. We are the persons upon whom our futures and the futures of exceptional persons depend.

SUGGESTED READINGS

Fink, A. H., ed. *International Perspectives on Future Special Education*. Reston, Va.: Council for Exceptional Children, 1978.

Martin, E. W. "Individualism and Behaviorism as Future Trends in Educating Handicapped Children." *Exceptional Children*, 38 (March, 1972), 517–526.

Prehm, H. J., and McDonald, J. E. "The Yet to Be Served—A Perspective." *Exceptional Children*, 45 (April, 1979), 502–509.

Reynolds, M. C., ed. *Futures of Education for Exceptional Students: Emerging Structures*. Reston, Va.: Council for Exceptional Children, 1978.

Special Education Futures: A Forecast of Events Affecting the Education of Exceptional Children: 1975–2000. Washington, D.C.: National Association of State Directors of Special Education, 1975.

APPENDICES

Academic Therapy

20 Commercial Blvd.
Novato, California 94947

Five times annually. This journal is devoted to the study of causes and remediation techniques of learning disabilities. Subject matter includes case studies and current topics in the field.

American Annals of the Deaf

5034 Wisconsin Avenue, N.W.
Washington, D.C. 20016

Bimonthly. Publisher: Conference of American Instructors of the Deaf and the Conference of Executives of American Schools for the Deaf. Deals with problems and education of the hearing handicapped and the deaf.

American Association for the Education of the Severely/Profoundly Handicapped (AAESPH) Review

1600 West Armory Way
Seattle, Washington 98195

Quarterly. This review is the association's official publication. Deals with research reports related to the severely and profoundly handicapped.

American Journal of Mental Deficiency

5101 Wisconsin Avenue N.W.
Washington, D.C. 20016

Bimonthly. Articles pertain to studies and discussions of the behavioral and biological aspects of mental retardation. It is the official publication of the American Association of Mental Deficiency.

ASHA

10801 Rockville Pike
Rockville, Maryland 20852

Monthly. Publisher: American Speech and Hearing Association. Readers are mainly audiologists, teachers of the deaf, and speech and hearing therapists. Articles concern this professional organization as well as research and educational issues.

ACLD Newsbriefs

4156 Library Road
Pittsburgh, Pennsylvania 15234

Monthly. Publisher: Association for Children and Adults with Learning Disabilities. This publication has a reader audience of both parents and teachers. It contains up-to-date information about the association's activities in the field of learning disabilities, including news from local chapters around the country.

Audiology and Hearing Education

Creative Age Publications
12849 Magnolia Blvd.
North Hollywood, California 91607

Bimonthly. Contains articles pertaining to evaluation, instruction, and the rehabilitation of the deaf.

Behavioral Disorders

Council for Exceptional Children
CCBD Division
1920 Association Drive
Reston, Virginia 22091

Quarterly. Publisher: the division for children with behavioral disorders of the Council for Exceptional Children. Articles pertain to research and current issues in the field. Also included are regular columns and departmental reports.

The Deaf American:
The National Magazine for the Deaf

814 Thayer Avenue
Silver Springs, Maryland 20910

Monthly (except for a joint July/August issue). The official publication of the National Association of the Deaf.

Diagnostique

Council for Exceptional Children
Council for Educational Diagnostic Services
  (CEDS)
1920 Association Drive
Reston, Virginia 22091

Bi-annually. This professional bulletin of the CEDS contains articles and research reports relevant to professionals involved in educational diagnostic services. Available for subscription with or without membership in CEDS.

Education and Training of the Mentally Retarded

Council for Exceptional Children
1920 Association Drive
Reston, Virginia 22091

Quarterly. Publisher: Journal of the Division on Mental Retardation of the Council for Exceptional Children. This periodical deals with educational, legislative, and research issues relating to the mentally retarded. Articles urge public understanding of mental retardation through the dissemination and utilization of research findings.

Education of the Visually Handicapped

Association for Education of the
  Visually Handicapped, Inc.
919 Walnut Street
Philadelphia, Pennsylvania 19107

Quarterly. Publisher: Association for Education of the Visually Handicapped in Philadelphia, Pennsylvania. Also published in BRAILLE. A professional magazine of methods, techniques, and research for educators of visually handicapped children.

Educational Horizons

4101 East Third Street
Box A 850
Bloomington, Indiana 47401

Quarterly. Official publication of a Pi Lambda Theta, a national honor and professional association in education. A segment of each issue pertains to handicapped persons.

Exceptional Children

Council for Exceptional Children
1920 Association Drive
Reston, Virginia 22091

Eight times annually. Publisher: Council for Exceptional Children. The topics presented deal with problems, research, findings, trends, and practices in educational programs for all types of exceptional children. These represent broad problem areas that affect many handicapped children throughout many classifications.

The Exceptional Parent

P.O. Box 4944
Manchester, New Hampshire 03108

Six times annually. Reader audience includes parents and educators of exceptional children of all types. Information provided generally consists of informal reports rather than scientific research findings.

Focus on Exceptional Children

1777 South Bellaire Street
Denver, Colorado 80222

Monthly. A newsletter that deals with a single topic in each issue pertaining to some aspect of exceptional children. It also contains a short section directly related to teacher classroom practice called "Classroom Forum."

The Gifted Quarterly

217 Gregory Drive
Hot Springs, Arkansas 71901

Quarterly. The official publication of the National Association for Gifted Children.

The Journal of Applied Behavior Analysis

Department of Human Development
University of Kansas
Lawrence, Kansas 66045

Quarterly. Publisher: Society for the Experimental Analysis of Behavior. Includes reports of experimental research involving the use of behavioral analysis. This journal is not exclusively a special education publication, but it does emphasize the use of behavioral analysis with the handicapped.

Journal of Learning Disabilities

101 East Ontario Street
Chicago, Illinois 60611

Bimonthly (ten times a year). Contains articles on educational, medical, and psychological topics, as well as information on current research and curriculum material.

Journal of Rehabilitation

1522 K Street, N.W.
Washington, D.C. 20005

Bimonthly. Publisher: National Rehabilitation Association. The articles stress practical application rather than research. Areas covered are rehabilitation education, social work, employment, programs and techniques.

Journal for Special Educators

179 Sierra Vista Lane
Valley Cottage, New York 10989

Three times annually. Articles include information about the guidance, rehabilitation, psychology, and education of exceptional children, particularly the mentally retarded.

Journal of Special Education

111 5th Avenue
New York, New York 10003

Quarterly. Articles pertain to every aspect of special education with emphasis on research studies and critical issues in the field.

Journal of Speech and Hearing Disorders

10801 Rockville Pike
Rockville, Maryland 20852

Quarterly. Publisher: American Speech and Hearing Association. Articles pertain to communication disorders and include research reports.

Journal of Speech and Hearing Research

10801 Rockville Pike
Rockville, Maryland 20852

Quarterly. Publisher: American Speech-Language-Hearing Association. Articles pertain to current research in speech, language, and hearing.

Journal of Visual Impairment and Blindness

American Foundation for the Blind, Inc.
15 West 16th Street
New York, New York 10011

Monthly (September through June). Publisher: American Foundation for the Blind.

Learning Disability Quarterly

The Division for Children
  with Learning Disabilities (DCLD)
Council for Exceptional Children
1920 Association Drive
Reston, Virginia 22091

Quarterly. This journal publishes educational articles with an applied focus on learning disabilities. Includes reports of techniques in identification, assessment, remediation, and programming for LD students. Available to subscribers with or without membership in DCLD.

New Outlooks for the Blind

American Foundation for the Blind, Inc.
15 West 16th Street
New York, New York 10011

Monthly (except for July and August). Publisher: American Foundation for the Blind. Subject matter takes in all aspects of dealing with the blind of all ages.

Teacher Education and Special Education

Council for Exceptional Children
1920 Association Drive
Reston, Virginia 22091

Quarterly. Publisher: Teacher Education Division of the Council for Exceptional Children. Emphasis is on the training of teachers and other professionals who work with exceptional children.

Teaching Exceptional Children

Council for Exceptional Children
1920 Association Drive
Reston, Virginia 22091

Quarterly. Publisher: Council for Exceptional Children for classroom teachers. Articles are of a practical nature and deal with all ages of children with special needs.

Volta Review

3417 Volta Place, N.W.
Washington, D.C. 20007

Monthly (except in the summer). Publisher: Alexander Graham Bell Association for the Deaf. The review's purpose is to encourage the teaching of speech and speech reading and the use of residual hearing in deaf persons.

Behavior Disorders

American Association for the Advancement of Behavior Therapy (AABT)
305 East 45th St.
New York, New York 10017

This organization is aimed primarily at individuals interested in the research and practice of behavior modification.

American Association of Psychiatric Services for Children
1725 K St. N.W.
Washington, D.C. 20006

Membership limited to organizations and clinics that provide psychiatric services to children The association's purpose is to coordinate the activities of psychiatric clinics for children and to assure high standards of clinical practice.

American Orthopsychiatric Association, Inc.
1775 Broadway
New York, New York 10019

Designed to enhance communication among those studying and treating problems of human behavior. This professional organization also fosters research and spreads information about scientific work in the field of human behavior, including abnormal behavior. Members must have worked in the field three years, possess a master's degree, and meet the professional requirements of their discipline.

American Psychiatric Association
1700 18 St. N.W.
Washington, D.C. 20009

Membership includes psychiatrists as well as physicians with some specialized training in psychiatry. The association's purpose is to advance the study of the nature, treatment, and prevention of mental disorders. It also promotes mental health and the care of the mentally ill and advances the standards for mental facilities.

American Psychological Association
1200 17th St. N.W.
Washington, D.C. 20036

Membership is open to professionals meeting the necessary requirements of education and experience. Purpose is to promote psychology as a science and as a way of bettering human welfare. Divisions of the Association deal with specific areas of psychology.

Council for Children with Behavioral Disorders (CCBD)
(A division of the Council for Exceptional Children)
1920 Assiciation Drive
Reston, Virginia 22091

A professional organization for educators of disturbed children. Publishes the journal *Behavior Disorders*.

The National Association for Mental Health, Inc.
Suite 1300
10 Columbus Circle
New York, New York 10019

Composed of volunteers who work toward the improved care of the mentally ill and the handicapped. It strives to improve methods and services in research, prevention, detection, diagnosis, and treatment of mental illness and handicaps and promotes mental health. Membership is open to anyone.

National Consortium for Child Mental Health
   Services
1424 16th St. N.W., Suite 201A
Washington, D.C. 20036

Serves as a focal point for the exchange of information on child mental health services.

National Society for Autistic Children
1234 Massachusetts Ave. N.W., Suite 1017
Washington, D.C. 20005

Serves parents and professionals of severely disturbed children. This organization aims at improving the education, welfare, and treatment of such children.

Child Abuse

Child Welfare League of America
Center for Governmental Affairs
1346 Connecticut Ave. N.W.
Washington, D.C. 20036

Membership includes public and private child care agencies. This group accredits agencies serving children and develops both standards for the field and information on child protection.

National Center on Child Abuse and Neglect
U.S. Children's Bureau
P.O. Box 1182
Washington, D.C. 20013

Provides information to parents and professionals on various aspects of child abuse and neglect.

National Committee for Prevention
   of Child Abuse
111 E. Wacker, Suite 510
Chicago, Illinois 60601

The organization's purpose is to create a greater public awareness of the incidence, origins, nature, and effects of child abuse.

Parents Anonymous
22330 Hawthorne Blvd., Suite 208
Torrance, California 90505

This organization is for adults who have abused children. The aim is to re-educate abusers and promote the well-being of children. Provides relief in time of crisis.

Communication Disorders

American Speech-Language-Hearing Association
10801 Rockville Pike
Rockville, Maryland 20852

A professional organization for speech pathologists and audiologists as well as other interested professionals. Has established the American Board of Examiners in Speech Pathology and Audiology, which sets standards and evaluates speech pathology and audiology services. Also certifies academic training programs in these areas.

National Association of Hearing
   and Speech Action
6110 Executive Blvd., Suite 1000
Rockville, Maryland 20852

Primary purpose is to solve the problems of hearing, speech, and language handicapped persons. Members are also interested in improving both the quality and the quantity of care available for the communicatively handicapped. Membership is available to agencies, professionals, and lay persons.

Exceptional Children

Adult Education Association of the U.S.A.
810 18th St., N.W.
Washington, D.C. 20006

Provides referral services and career information.

Association for Childhood Education
   International
3615 Wisconsin Ave., N.W.
Washington, D.C. 20016

Provides information on a variety of topics by conducting workshops and maintaining an information service and library. Also publishes books, bulletins, and portfolios.

Closer Look, National Information Center
  for the Handicapped
1201 16th St., N.W.
Washington, D.C. 20036

A nonprofit organization that provides information and referral service for the handicapped.

Council for Exceptional Children (CEC)
1920 Association Drive
Reston, Virginia 22091

Primarily an organization for professionals (teachers, school administrators, and teacher educators) who deal with instruction involving special services. Has many divisions devoted to specific areas of special education and exceptionalities.

National Association of State Directors
  of Special Education
1201 16th St., N.W., Suite 610E
Washington, D.C. 20036

Promotes active leadership in educational facilities, the planning at state and local levels, and discussion forums. Considering current problems and issues, the Association provides service to exceptional children and adults. Membership limited to persons employed as directors, supervisors, or consultants in special education by a state or the national department of education.

National Therapeutic Recreation Society
%National Recreation and Park Assn.
1601 N. Kent St.
Arlington, Virginia 22209

Concerned with improving therapeutic recreation services and developing a recreation profession. The Society is a branch of the National Park and Recreation Association. Membership open to agencies and professionals.

Gifted

American Association for Gifted Children
15 Gramercy Park
New York, New York 10003

Works with community and professional groups to find gifted children. Aim is to help these children use their abilities for their own satisfaction and the benefit of others.

The National Association for Gifted Children
217 Gregory Drive
Hot Springs, Arkansas 71901

Helps schools, parents, and communities to provide for the gifted. Membership open to anyone interested.

National Clearinghouse for the Gifted
  and Talented
The Council for Exceptional Children
1920 Association Drive
Reston, Virginia 22901

The Clearinghouse is a center of information on the education of the gifted and talented. It gathers and disperses this information nationally.

National Council for the Gifted
700 Prospect Ave.
West Orange, New Jersey 07052

Promotes research in developing practical programs to educate the gifted so that American leadership in the fields of education, science, and business are assured.

National/State Leadership Training Institute
  on the Gifted and Talented
316 W. Second St., Suite PH-CA
Los Angeles, California 90012

A federally funded institute designed to provide services in the education of the gifted and talented to state agencies and local school districts.

Hearing Impaired

The Alexander Graham Bell Association
  for the Deaf
3417 Volta Place, N.W.
Washington, D.C. 20007

Membership open to anyone interested in improving the education and opportunities for the hearing impaired. Speech, speech reading, and the use of residual hearing are promoted. Organizations associated with this one are the International Parents' Organization, the Oral Deaf Adults Section, and the American Organization for the Education of the Hearing Impaired. The *Volta Review* is their official publication.

Conference of American Instructors
  of the Deaf (CAID)
5034 Wisconsin Ave., N.W.
Washington, D.C. 20016

An organization for teachers of the hearing impaired that is committed to the best results, emphasizing no particular teaching method. They publish the bimonthly journal *The American Annals of the Deaf*. Issues contain reports on research and articles related to teaching the hearing impaired. The April issue is an annual directory of programs and services for the deaf in the United States.

Conference of Executives of American Schools
  for the Deaf (CEASD)
5034 Wisconsin Ave., N.W.
Washington, D.C. 20016

A professional organization for those in management positions in schools for the deaf. Its purpose is to promote efficient management and operation of schools for the deaf as well as to enhance the welfare of the deaf and to promote professional growth of all those working with the deaf.

National Association of the Deaf
814 Thayer Avenue
Silver Springs, Maryland 20910

A national civic organization run solely by and for the deaf. Its purpose is to help insure the deaf of their rights and privileges of citizenship. Supports research concerning the deaf as well as studies of social problems of the deaf and ways of working with other associations for the hearing impaired. Tries to tell about deafness to all who are not deaf, but who must deal with those who are.

Learning Disabled

Association for Children and Adults
  with Learning Disabilities
4156 Library Road
Pittsburgh, Pennsylvania 15234

Most of the members of this organization are parents, but some teachers and other professionals also belong. ACLD aims to increase the public's awareness of the concerns of learning disabled persons and to improve services for this exceptionality.

Division for Children with Learning Disabilities
  (DCLD)
1920 Association Drive
Reston, Virginia 22091

A division of the Council for Exceptional Children. Its publication, *Learning Disability Quarterly*,

provides information concerning funding, certification, and current research in the field.

New York Institute for Child Development
205 Lexington Avenue
New York, New York 10016

A center for medical diagnosis and treatment of children who are learning disabled.

Orton Society
8415 Bellona Lane, Suite 113
Towson, Maryland 21204

Membership consists of a variety of persons from many professional disciplines ranging from special educators to the medical profession. Primary concern is developmental dyslexia. Most large cities have a chapter.

Mentally Retarded

American Association on Mental Deficiency
  (AAMD)
5101 Wisconsin Ave., N.W.
Washington, D.C. 20016

A national organization for professionals and other interested persons involved with the mentally retarded. Concerned with studying the causes, treatment, and prevention of mental retardation. Includes many divisions and subsections devoted to specific areas of study related to mental retardation.

International League of Societies
  for the Mentally Handicapped
12, Rue Forestiere
B-1050 Brussels, Belgium

The interests of the mentally handicapped are advanced by this international organization, which attempts to enhance cooperation among national organizations. Various types of membership are available to organizations working with the mentally handicapped.

Joseph P. Kennedy, Jr. Foundation
719 13th St., N.W., Suite 510
Washington, D. C. 20005

The main purposes of the Foundation are to support research on the prevention of mental retardation and to promote programs that help provide retarded persons with a better life. Has established two corporations: Flame of Hope (a sheltered workshops program) and Special Olympics, Inc.

(athletic competition for the retarded). Also sponsors an international awards competition and periodic scientific meetings.

National Association for Retarded Citizens
2709 Avenue E East
Arlington, Texas 76011

Anyone interested in mental retardation may join. This organization is aimed at promoting treatment, research, public understanding, and legislation for the mentally retarded. Various committees deal with different aspects of retardation. Its publication—*Mental Retardation News*—is primarily for parents of retarded children.

President's Committee on Mental Retardation
7th and D Sts., S.W.
Washington, D.C. 20201

This organization promotes cooperation and coordination among agencies and organizations that provide services to the mentally retarded and related groups. Also sponsors awareness of mental retardation needs, conducts surveys on programs and needs, and provides the President with advice on needed action.

Multiply, Severely, and Profoundly Handicapped

The American Association for the Education
of the Severely/Profoundly Handicapped
1600 West Armory Way
Garden View Suite
Seattle, Washington 98119

An organization composed of educational and medical professionals as well as lay people interested in the severely and profoundly handicapped.

National Committee for Multi-Handicapped
Children
239 14th St.
Niagara Falls, New York 14303

Serves as a clearinghouse for information about current programs for the handicapped and also researches literature about the blind, deaf, cerebral palsied, and brain injured. Its purpose is to create an awareness about educational, therapeutic, recreational, and social service needs of multihandicapped children. Membership is open to any interested person.

American Academy for Cerebral Palsy
and Developmental Medicine
1255 New Hampshire Ave., N.W.
Washington, D.C. 20036

Promotes professional education, research, and interest in cerebral palsy and related disorders. Also strives to correlate all aspects of these areas to benefit those with the handicap.

American Corrective Therapy Association, Inc.
%Kirk Hodges
Rt. #2, Box 199
Jonesboro, Tennessee 37659

A professional organization for those who have a physical education degree and clinical training. Its aim is to help physicians in treating the handicapped by applying the principles, tools, techniques, and psychology of medically oriented physical education.

American Physical Therapy Association
1156 15th St., N.W.
Washington, D.C. 20005

Both professional and nonprofessional memberships are available. This organization sponsors the development and improvement of physical therapy service and education by coordinating the actions of everyone involved to provide physical therapy services for those persons in need.

The Association of Rehabilitation Facilities
5530 Wisconsin Ave., Suite 955
Washington, D.C. 20015

Serves as a federation of rehabilitation centers aimed at improving rehabilitation service to handicapped and disabled persons. The Association is itself a center for unified action, for exchanging information, and for cooperating with other professional associations.

Goodwill Industries of America, Inc.
9200 Wisconsin Ave.
Washington, D.C. 20014

Serves as a halfway process for the handicapped, disabled, and disadvantaged who cannot enter the job market immediately. Provides rehabilitation services, training, employment, and opportunities for personal growth.

Human Growth Foundation
4930 W. 77th St., Suite 150
Edina, Minnesota 55435

Begun by parents and friends of children who have growth problems. The Foundation's aim is to work with the medical profession to understand more about human growth and its deviations, such as dwarfism, gigantism, and failure to thrive. Families are provided with opportunities to meet, and medical help is sought for families with limited financial resources.

Little People of America, Inc.
P.O. Box 126
Owatonna, Minnesota 55060

Provides friendship, the exchange of ideas, and moral support to little people. Offers solutions to problems unique to the group. Membership available on an individual or a family basis.

Muscular Dystrophy Association of America, Inc.
810 Seventh Ave.
New York, New York 10019

Fosters scientific research into the causes and cures of muscular dystrophy and other neuromuscular diseases. Also provides services to patients and engages in education programs among doctors and the public. Membership is open, and no dues are required.

The National Easter Seal Society
   for Crippled Children and Adults
2023 West Ogden Ave.
Chicago, Illinois 60612

A voluntary agency that provides direct services for crippled children and adults. Other services include educating the public, professional workers, and parents; research into the causes and prevention of handicapping conditions; and improving methods of care, education, and treatment of patients. Membership is held by affiliated state societies.

National Epilepsy League, Inc.
116 S. Michigan Avenue
Chicago, Illinois 60603

Promotes research in epilepsy and provides information about epilepsy, medical resources, and employment to epileptics. Also supplies epilepsy medication at a low cost, strives to increase public awareness, and tries to create more opportunities for the education and employment of epileptics.

The National Foundation—March of Dimes
1275 Mamaroneck Avenue
White Plains, New York 10605

The fight against birth defects is waged by this agency. It leads, directs, and unifies this effort by supporting programs of research, medical care, professional and public education, and community services. Volunteers, both lay and professional, are a part of programs throughout the nation. Meetings and symposia are held, publications are issued, and films and exhibits are available for loan.

National Rehabilitation Association
1522 K St., N. W.
Washington, D.C. 20005

Advances the rehabilitation of the physically and mentally handicapped. The Association attempts to create public understanding, provide information, sponsor research, encourage an interdisciplinary approach to rehabilitation, develop professional standards, and create professional training opportunities. Membership is open to professionals.

Osteogenisis Imperfecta Foundation, Inc.
1231 May Court
Burlington, North Carolina 27215

An organization of family members of persons disabled by osteogenisis imperfecta (brittle bone disease). Promotes research in the causes and treatment of O.I. and heightens public awareness through the quarterly newsletter *Breakthrough*.

The President's Committee on Employment
   of the Handicapped
1111 20th St., N.W.
U.S. Department of Labor
Washington, D.C. 20210

Full and equal employment of all handicapped persons is the main goal of this Committee, which encourages the removal of any barriers possibly impeding such employment. Members are appointed for three-year terms by the chairperson. Each state has a corresponding Governor's committee.

Rehabilitation International
432 Park Ave., South
New York, New York 10016

A federation of organizations in 59 countries that works to promote the rehabilitation of the disabled.

United Cerebral Palsy Associations, Inc.
66 E. 34th St.
New York, New York 10016

Promotes research in cerebral palsy and professional training, and provides public information about cerebral palsy. Also concerned with the care and facilities available for cerebral palsied persons. Works with governmental and private agencies involved with the welfare of the handicapped.

Visually Handicapped

American Association of Workers
   for the Blind, Inc. (AAWB)
1151 K St., N.W., Suite 637
Washington, D.C. 20005

Membership open to anyone interested in the welfare of the blind. The main purpose of the group is to promote blindness prevention programs as well as work for the blind. Its annual publication is *Blindness*.

American Foundation for the Blind
15 W. 16th St.
New York, New York 10011

A nonprofit, private agency serving as a clearinghouse for information on blindness. Promotes educational, rehabilitation, and social welfare services for the blind. Also provides several services, such as publications in many forms, manufacture and sale of special devices for the blind, and recording and sale of talking books.

American Printing House for the Blind (APH)
1839 Frankfort Ave.
P.O. Box 6085
Louisville, Kentucky 40206

APH is funded by an annual appropriation from Congress and from special funds so it can conduct research on educational material. It also provides educational materials to legally blind children in the United States. These include books in Braille, in recorded form, and in large type, as well as some aids and devices that are not commercially available. The Instructional Materials Reference Center for the Visually Handicapped is housed by APH and makes resource material available to teachers.

Association for Education of the
   Visually Handicapped (AEVH)
919 Walnut, 4th Floor
Philadelphia, Pennsylvania 19107

Serves as a clearinghouse for information on blindness and operates solely on gifts and contributions. Some of its services exist to provide a special reference library, to promote and conduct research on blindness and its accompanying problems, to consult and lobby for legislation benefitting the visually handicapped, and to publish books, pamphlets, and monographs. Publishes the *Journal of Blindness and Visual Impairments* as well as a directory of agencies serving the visually impaired.

National Association for Visual Handicapped
305 E. 24th St.
New York, New York 10010

Provides guidance to children and adults, publishes and distributes large-print books, and organizes youth activities. Also acts as a clearinghouse for public and private services available to the partially seeing.

National Library Service for the Blind
   and Physically Handicapped
Division for the Blind and Physically
   Handicapped
1291 Taylor St., N.W.
Washington, D.C. 20542

Makes available publication lists and lists of regional libraries to present more information about visual handicaps. Also provides a free library service that includes talking books, tapes, and other aids.

National Society for Low Vision People, Inc.
2346 Clermont
Denver, Colorado 80207

Training, education, and research are provided by this society to help people with low vision become more independent. Also sponsors workshops for parents of low vision children. This is not a membership organization.

National Society for Prevention of Blindness
   (NSPB)
79 Madison Ave.
New York, New York 10016

Supports research on eye diseases, distributes information about eye safety and low vision aids, surveys causes and incidence of blindness, helps in detecting glaucoma, and does vision screening. Professionals from medicine and education contribute information and help provide public service through the organization. Publishes *Sight Saving Review*.

This list of media resources (films, filmstrips, tape recordings, books, etc.) is intended for a wide range of audiences, including professionals, parents, and children. The resources are grouped by categories of exceptional children and other topics. This listing is by no means complete. It should, however, provide the reader with a starting point for examining special education concepts and facilitating an understanding of exceptional persons.

BEHAVIOR AND EMOTIONAL DISORDERS

Films

TITLE: *No Two of These Kids Are Alike*

SOURCE: United States Bureau of Education for the Handicapped
National Audiovisual Center
General Services Administration
Washington, D.C. 20409

AUDIENCE: Regular and special teachers

SYNOPSIS: Describes the daily routine of a school for emotionally disturbed children. Emphasis is placed on the role of the various members of the staff in providing a "normal" schooling for the children.

TITLE: *One Hour A Week*

SOURCE: United States Bureau of Education for the Handicapped
National Audiovisual Center
General Services Administration
Washington, D.C. 20409

AUDIENCE: Parents and professionals working in parent education

SYNOPSIS: Depicts a home training program for parents of seriously disturbed children. Parents are shown how to cope with their children's handicap by using behavior modification at home.

TITLE: *Teacher Support*

SOURCE: United States Bureau of Education for the Handicapped
National Audiovisual Center
General Services Administration
Washington, D.C. 20409

AUDIENCE: Teachers

SYNOPSIS: Emotionally handicapped children are given a full range of treatment through an elaborate teacher support system.

TITLE: *Troubled Campers*

SOURCE: International Tele-Film Enterprises   or   Wediko Films
221 Victoria Street   58 Fenwood Road
Toronto, Ontario, Canada   Boston, Massachusetts 02115

AUDIENCE: Students in education and mental health

SYNOPSIS: Behavior disordered children are shown at camp. The film is an introduction to emotional disturbance, depicting many maladaptive behaviors, fears, and feelings of emotionally disturbed children. It shows an effective camping program. The film is accompanied by a short discussion guide.

Filmstrips

TITLE: *Cindy*

SOURCE: Windmills, Ltd.
BFA Educational Media
2211 Michigan Avenue
P.O. Box 1795
Santa Monica, California 90406

AUDIENCE: Elementary grade children

SYNOPSIS: A girl handicapped by her emotions is portrayed. The filmstrip tells how she feels about her handicap and is open-ended in conclusion for discussion.

Books

TITLE: *Jordi/Lisa and David*

SOURCE: Ballantine Books
Division of Random House
Westminster, Maryland 21157

AUDIENCE: Children ages 11 to 14

SYNOPSIS: This book, which contains two stories in one volume, includes the story of Jordi, a schizophrenic child, and Lisa and David, two adolescents who are dealing with the struggle against mental illness. Written by Theodore Isaac Rubin.

TITLE: *Please Don't Say Hello*

SOURCE: Human Sciences Press
72 5th Avenue
New York, New York 10011

AUDIENCE: Children ages 9 to 12

SYNOPSIS: An introduction to autism by Phyllis Gold. This is a book that stimulates thinking about "different" people.

Video Tapes

TITLE: *Video Training Workshops on Child Variance*

SOURCE: The Council for Exceptional Children
Publication Sales
1920 Association Drive
Reston, Virginia 22091

AUDIENCE: Professionals, especially those working with behavior disordered pupils in regular classroom settings

SYNOPSIS: This training package, authored by William C. Morse and Judith M. Smith, includes a text, *Understanding Child Variance*, six self-instructional modules, six video cassettes, activity sheets, and a workshop leader's manual. Tapes include various classroom behavioral problem situations and interpretations from professionals of various disciplines.

BI-CULTURAL

Films

TITLE: *Eye of the Storm*

SOURCE: Xerox Films
245 Long Hill Road
Middletown, Connecticut 06457

AUDIENCE: Teachers and students (upper-elementary through college)

SYNOPSIS: A two-day experiment on segregation, discrimination, and prejudice is depicted in this film about a third grade class. The film is 25 minutes long and is available for sale or rental.

TITLE: *How's School Enrique?*

SOURCE: AIMS Instructional Media Services, Inc.
P.O. Box 1010
Hollywood, California 90028

AUDIENCE: Older pupils and adults concerned with problems of the bicultural student

SYNOPSIS: Presents cultural differences between the home and school lives of a Mexican-American student. Two views of educational philosophy are presented in the school setting. The major aim of this film is to increase sensitivity to the bicultural student.

TITLE: *Kindergarten: Twigs From A City Tree*

SOURCE: Coronet Instructional Media
65 East South Water Street
Chicago, Illinois 60601

AUDIENCE: Parents and teachers

SYNOPSIS: This 22-minute film depicts black ghetto children with a white teacher in a kindergarten class. A ghetto child's life is presented through activities and dialogue. The film is available for sale or rental.

Audio Tape Recordings

TITLE: *Black Dialect*

SOURCE: Southern Illinois University
Carbondale, Illinois

AUDIENCE: Professional educators

SYNOPSIS: This series of tapes (each one is about eight minutes long) combines for 10 hours of taping and includes a manual. It is designed to familiarize teachers with the various aspects of black dialect.

TITLE: *Education: Special for the Mexican-American*

SOURCE: The Council for Exceptional Children
1920 Association Drive
Reston, Virginia 22091

AUDIENCE: Teachers, psychologists, and administrators

SYNOPSIS: This 60-minute cassette tape presents bilingual education and assessment, and discusses the impact of cultural diversity. It is available for sale.

TITLE: *If You Knew Us Better*

SOURCE: The Council for Exceptional Children
1920 Association Drive
Reston, Virginia 22091

AUDIENCE: Teachers, psychologists, and administrators

SYNOPSIS: This series of eight cassette tapes and a journal deals with education, learning styles, family, culture, and social values of various cultural groups in contemporary society. Titles included are: "A Conflict of Values: Teaching Indian Children"; "Indian Gifts of Culture and Diversity"; "Cultural Diversity in Education: Teaching Spanish-Speaking Children"; "Spanish-Americans— Language and Culture"; "Barriers to Learning: Teaching Asian-American Children"; "Asian-Americans: Cultural Contrast"; and "Black Language—Black Culture." This series is available for sale.

TITLE: *The Quiet Minority— The Oriental American*

SOURCE: The Council for Exceptional Children
1920 Association Drive
Reston, Virginia 22091

AUDIENCE: Professionals and lay persons

SYNOPSIS: Asian-Americans talk about their ancestry in relation to contemporary American life. A teacher discusses problems she encounters in teaching such children.

Book

TITLE: *Helping Kids Learn Multi-Cultural Concepts: A Handbook of Strategies*

SOURCE: Research Press
Box 3177 E
Champaign, Illinois 61820

AUDIENCE: Teachers of children ages 10 to 13

SYNOPSIS: This handbook by Michael G. Pasternak presents activities that teachers can use with children from ages 10 to 13 to enhance multicultural experiences for them in the classroom.

Films

TITLE: *The Battered Child*

SOURCE: Indiana University
Audio-visual Center
Bloomington, Indiana 47401

AUDIENCE: College students, professionals, and parents

SYNOPSIS: Presents interviews with professionals and parents associated with child abuse. The causes of child abuse and treatment of abused children are discussed. Based on the book *Battered Children*. Available for rent or sale.

TITLE: *Children in Peril*

SOURCE: University of California
Extension Media Center
2223 Fulton Street
Berkeley, California 94720

AUDIENCE: Teachers and parents

SYNOPSIS: Discusses both the plight of the abused child and that of abusing parents from the perspective of providing medical, social, and legal assistance. Several treatment programs are reviewed. Available for rent.

TITLE: *Don't Give Up On Me*

SOURCE: Motorola Teleprograms, Inc.
4825 North Scott Street
Suite 26
Schiller Park, Illinois 60176

AUDIENCE: Teachers and parent groups

SYNOPSIS: The film deals with the background of abusive persons as well as causes of child abuse. It includes scenes taken from histories of an abusing mother and her caseworker.

TITLE: *The Neglected*

SOURCE: International Film Bureau
332 South Michigan Avenue
Chicago, Illinois 60604

AUDIENCE: Professionals and parents

SYNOPSIS: Describes the organization and services of child protective service agencies. The film discusses the relationship between emotional problems and poverty, which lead to child neglect and abuse. Available for sale.

TITLE: *Sexual Abuse: The Family*

SOURCE: United States National Audiovisual Center
General Services Administration
Washington, D.C. 20409

AUDIENCE: Teachers and parents

SYNOPSIS: The topic of sexual abuse and incest is dealt with honestly in this film. The methods that doctors, counselors, and police use to deal with incest are shown.

Video Tape

TITLE: *The Dynamics of Child Abuse*

SOURCE: Fort Wayne Public Library
Fort Wayne, Indiana

AUDIENCE: Parents, teachers, and medical professionals

SYNOPSIS: Raises questions about child abuse and provides answers. Recognizing child abuse, causes of child abuse, attitudes of personnel dealing with child abuse, and methods of preventing child abuse are discussed.

EXCEPTIONAL CHILDREN

Films

TITLE: *Breaking the Sound Barrier*

SOURCE: Association Films, Inc.
866 3rd Avenue
New York, New York 10022

AUDIENCE: PTA groups, service clubs, and college courses

SYNOPSIS: Nanette Fabray narrates and appears in this film, which illustrates professionals working with various types of problems involving the hearing impaired. The various types of professional services are depicted cooperating to achieve full service for individuals.

TITLE: *Looking For Me*

SOURCE: University of California
Extension Media Center
2223 Fulton Street
Berkeley, California 94720

AUDIENCE: Teachers and parents

SYNOPSIS: This film shows a dance therapist (working with normal, handicapped, and emotionally disturbed children) using movement as a means of communication.

TITLE: *People You'd Like To Know*

SOURCE: Encyclopedia Brittanica
Educational Corporation
425 North Michigan Avenue
Chicago, Illinois 60611

AUDIENCE: Professionals (preservice and in-service) and lay persons

SYNOPSIS: This series of 10 films describes the lives of 10 children and youth with different handicaps. Emphasis is on increasing awareness of and sensitivity to the needs of handicapped persons, as well as factual information about the conditions. Each film is 10 minutes long.

TITLE: *The Perkins Story —*
Adapting to Change

SOURCE: Campbell Films Incorporated
Academy Avenue
Saxtons River, Vermont 05154

AUDIENCE: Teachers

SYNOPSIS: The changes that have occurred at the Perkins School for the Blind are discussed. Services now meet the needs of multi-handicapped students, including the deaf blind, the slow learner, and the child with perceptual dysfunctions.

TITLE: *School Is For Children*

SOURCE: AIMS Instructional Media
Services, Inc.
P.O. Box 1010
Hollywood, California 90028

AUDIENCE: Teachers and parents

SYNOPSIS: The topic of this film is special education for exceptional preschool children. Young children are shown

interacting with each other in specially designed group activities.

TITLE: *Those Other Kids*

SOURCE: Leadership Training Institute
Department of Special Education
University of Minnesota
Audiovisual Library
Minneapolis, Minnesota

AUDIENCE: Professionals and lay persons

SYNOPSIS: The right to education for handicapped children clause of the 14th Amendment is emphasized.

Filmstrips

TITLE: *Hello Everybody*

SOURCE: SFA James Stanfield Film
Associates
P.O. Box 851
Pasadena, California 91102

AUDIENCE: Children and youth, grades 4 through 12

SYNOPSIS: This package of six color sound filmstrips about handicapped children is aimed at helping nonhandicapped pupils understand their handicapped peers.

TITLE: *My New Friend (Introducing*
the Special Child)

SOURCE: Eye Gate Media
146-01 Archer Avenue
Jamaica, New York 11435

AUDIENCE: Elementary pupils

SYNOPSIS: Four handicapped children are described in this series of sound filmstrips by P. J. Hancock, *et al.* The series discusses how the children can be helped in adjusting to the regular classroom.

Tapes

TITLE: *All Together Now*

SOURCE: The Council for Exceptional
Children
1920 Association Drive
Reston, Virginia 22091

AUDIENCE: Professionals

SYNOPSIS: This series of six tape recordings and a brochure describes the conference held in June 1974, which brought together a group of individuals to discuss the needs for normal peer relations among exceptional children. The conference was sponsored by the Council for Exceptional Children and brought various levels of educators together.

TITLE: *Kids Come in Special Flavors*

SOURCE: Special Flavors
Box 562
Forest Park Station
Dayton, Ohio 45405

AUDIENCE: Professionals, parents, and young adults

SYNOPSIS: This kit contains a cassette tape, a guide book, and other materials that can be used in conducting 16 simulations, which help participants to become aware of and understand children with various handicapping conditions.

Books

TITLE: *Accepting Individual Differences*

SOURCE: Developmental Learning Materials
7440 Natchez Avenue
Niles, Illinois 60648

AUDIENCE: Elementary school children

SYNOPSIS: This set of three children's books and teaching guides by Shirley Cohen is designed to teach elementary pupils about handicapped persons.

TITLE: *Biographical Sagas of Will Power*

SOURCE: Vantage Press, Inc.
516 West 34th Street
New York, New York 10001

AUDIENCE: Youth and adults

SYNOPSIS: These stories by Harry J. Boher are about the lives of 54 famous people who have overcome disabilities.

TITLE: *Deenie*

SOURCE: Bradbury Press
2 Overhill Road
Scarsdale, New York 10583

AUDIENCE: Adolescents and young adults

SYNOPSIS: This book by Judy Blume tells the story of a girl who has always been repelled by persons with handicaps, but later finds she must wear a spinal brace.

TITLE: *The Touch Mark*

SOURCE: Harcourt Brace, Jovanovich, Inc.
757 3rd Avenue
New York, New York 10017

SYNOPSIS: This historical novel written in 1973 by Mildred Lawrence focuses on a disabled girl who learns to fight against self-pity and over-protection.

Catalogue

TITLE: *National Catalogue of Films in Special Education, 2nd Edition, 1978*

SOURCE: The Ohio State University Press
The Ohio State University
Columbus, Ohio 43210

AUDIENCE: Professionals and parents

SYNOPSIS: This reference book was compiled by the National Center, Educational Media and Materials for the Handicapped (NCEMMH) to help professionals from a variety of disciplines as well as parents in gaining access to more than 900 films related to handicapped children.

FAMILIES

Films

TITLE: *Jamie: The Study of a Sibling*

SOURCE: National Film Board of Canada
1251 Avenue of the Americas,
16th Floor
New York, New York 10020

AUDIENCE: College students, professionals, and parents

SYNOPSIS: Describes sibling rivalries through the case study of an aggressive child who resents his older sister and younger brother. Available for rent or sale.

TITLE: *Chris: A Family Portrait*

SOURCE: Ithaca College
Ithaca, New York 14850

AUDIENCE: College students, professionals, and parents

SYNOPSIS: Members of a blind and retarded child's family discuss the changes and adjustments that the family has had to make. Available for rent.

TITLE: *They Are Not Expendable*

SOURCE: American Educational Films
132 Lasky Drive
Beverly Hills, California 90212

AUDIENCE: Professionals and parents

SYNOPSIS: Shows handicapped children at home in situations with their normal brothers and sisters. Available for sale.

Filmstrip

TITLE: *Families in Crisis: A Handicapped Child*

SOURCE: Coronet Instructional Media
65 East South Water Street
Chicago, Illinois 60601

AUDIENCE: Parents

SYNOPSIS: This fictional account of a family with a handicapped child is designed to show problems that may develop in the family as a result of the presence of a handicapped child.

Audio Tape Recordings

TITLE: *Discussions With Parents of Exceptional Children*

SOURCE: Affective House
P.O. Box 35321
Tulsa, Oklahoma 74135

AUDIENCE: Professionals

SYNOPSIS: This series of nine taped interviews with parents of children with different handicaps is aimed at helping professionals to communicate more effectively with parents of handicapped children.

TITLE: *The Multi-Handicapped Child*

SOURCE: Remediation Associates Inc.
Box 2067
Van Nuys, California 91404

AUDIENCE:

SYNOPSIS: A recording of the parents of a boy with cerebral palsy, aural handicap, and learning problems. Their feelings about labeling, and financial and emotional burdens in the future are discussed.

GIFTED

Films

TITLE: *The Gifted Child*

SOURCE: Indiana University
Audiovisual Center
Bloomington, Indiana 47401

AUDIENCE: College students, professionals, and parents

SYNOPSIS: Describes the special problems of the gifted child and shows how they differ in intellectual, emotional, and physical development. Negative influences on gifted children at home and at school are discussed.

TITLE: *Helping Our Exceptional Children*

SOURCE: Acme Film Laboratories, Inc.
1161 North Highland Avenue
Hollywood, California 90038

AUDIENCE: College students, professionals, and parents

SYNOPSIS: This film presents a discussion by three psychologists of gifted and handicapped children, and suggestions of how parents can help their children are made.

TITLE: *A Time For Talent*

SOURCE: National Educational Association
1201 16th Street, N.W.
Washington, D.C. 20036

AUDIENCE: College students, professionals, and parents

SYNOPSIS: This film describes and discusses three school programs designed for gifted pupils.

LP Recording

TITLE: *The Restless Mind*

SOURCE: Media Educational Materials
              P.O. Box 1355
              Vista, California 92803

AUDIENCE: Parents and teachers

SYNOPSIS: Lectures and interviews are combined to provide information on gifted and creative youth.

Book

TITLE: *On Being Gifted*

SOURCE: Walker and Company
              720 5th Avenue
              New York, New York 10019

AUDIENCE: Gifted children ages 10 to 13

SYNOPSIS: This book for children, written in 1979, is about gifted children. It was written by gifted children who tell about their joys and resentments in being gifted as well as their problems, dreams, their interactions with peers, and their social lives.

HEARING IMPAIRED

Films

TITLE: *Can You Hear Me?*

SOURCE: International Film Bureau
              332 South Michigan Avenue
              Chicago, Illinois 60604

AUDIENCE: Educational personnel, other professionals, and lay persons

SYNOPSIS: The film deals with a family's efforts to give their deaf daughter a normal life. Shows how difficult it is for deaf persons to speak words they will never hear.

TITLE: *HEAR Foundation*

SOURCE: Joyce Motion Picture Company
              8613 Yolanda
              P.O. Box 458
              Northridge, California 91324

AUDIENCE: Parents and teachers

SYNOPSIS: The basic objectives of the Hearing Education through Auditory Research (HEAR) Foundation are discussed. The main purpose of the foundation is to help children with hearing impairments achieve normal communication.

TITLE: *Lisa! Pay Attention*

SOURCE: Audiovisual Explorations, Inc.

AUDIENCE: Teachers

SYNOPSIS: A seven-year-old girl with a hearing loss is depicted in a typical school day situation. Her impairment is undetected, and the way in which it creates problems in her learning is emphasized.

Filmstrip

TITLE: *Rosa*

SOURCE: Windmills, Ltd.
              2211 Michigan Avenue
              P.O. Box 1795
              Santa Monica, California 90406

AUDIENCE: Elementary school children

SYNOPSIS: The story of a girl with a hearing impairment is presented. She describes her feelings and how she communicates.

LP Recording

TITLE: *How They Hear*

SOURCE: Gordon N. Stowe and Associates
              Northbrook, Illinois

AUDIENCE: Pupils, teachers, and parents

SYNOPSIS: This record contains simulations of various types and degrees of hearing loss. An accompanying booklet presents transcripts of the words on the recording and other information. The record jacket also has much technical information.

Books

TITLE: *Anna's Silent World*

SOURCE: J. B. Lippincott Company
              Education Publishing Division
              E. Washington Square
              Philadelphia, Pennsylvania 19105

AUDIENCE: Preschool and primary age children

SYNOPSIS: This book by Bernard Wolfe describes how Anna, who is deaf, learns to function normally with the help of persons and technology.

TITLE: *The Sand Bird*

SOURCE: Thomas Nelson, Inc.
407 South 7th Avenue
Nashville, Tennessee 37203

AUDIENCE: Intermediate and middle grade age children

SYNOPSIS: This book by Margaret Boher tells a story of the Minton children, including a deaf child, who have a sand-filled glass bird that has the power to fulfill wishes.

TITLE: *Who Am I?*

SOURCE: Hubbard
P.O. Box 104
Northbrook, Illinois 60062

AUDIENCE: Preschool and primary children

SYNOPSIS: The main character in this book is a seven-year-old hearing impaired child. The story tells about the feelings and relationships such children experience. An accompanying cassette tape sung by Mr. Rogers is available.

LEARNING DISABLED

Films

TITLE: *Adolescents and Learning Disabilities*

SOURCE: Lawren Productions, Inc.
P.O. Box 1542
Burlingame, California 94010

AUDIENCE: College students, parents, and professionals

SYNOPSIS: Young adults, their parents, and psychologists discuss the problems faced by learning disabled pupils and their teachers. Individualized instruction is described. Available for sale and rent. This is a companion film to "If a Boy Can't Learn."

TITLE: *If A Boy Can't Learn*

SOURCE: Lawren Productions, Inc.
P.O. Box 1542
Burlingame, California 94010

AUDIENCE: College students, parents, and professionals

SYNOPSIS: Tells the story of Mike, a seven-year-old boy with learning problems. A description of his problems, diagnostic testing, and subsequent teaching interventions is presented. Available for rent or sale. This is a companion film to "Adolescents and Learning Disabilities."

TITLE: *Nobody Took The Time*

SOURCE: AIMS Instructional Media
Services, Inc.
P.O. Box 1010
Hollywood, California 90028

AUDIENCE: Parents and teachers

SYNOPSIS: Deals primarily with the learning disabled child in the ghetto. Highly structured classroom and playground activities are shown that indicate a structure in everything—development of language and helping make the child aware of his surroundings is important. The child's trust in self is nurtured by love and understanding.

TITLE: *Victor*

SOURCE: Shadowstone Films

AUDIENCE: Parents and teachers

SYNOPSIS: The problems of educating students with learning disabilities are examined. The experiences of a sixth grade student whose problems are recognized and helped are presented.

Books

TITLE: *He's My Brother*

SOURCE: Albert Whitman and Company
560 West Lake Street
Chicago, Illinois 60606

AUDIENCE: Preschool and primary age children

SYNOPSIS: The characteristics of a learning disabled child are described by a sibling. The joys and frustrations of the family and child are reviewed.

TITLE: *Kelly's Creek*

SOURCE: Thomas Y. Crowell Company
666 5th Avenue
New York, New York 10019

AUDIENCE: Children grades 4 through 6

SYNOPSIS: This book by Doris B. Smith tells a story of Kelly who is able to overcome his learning disabilities and his difficulties in coordination of speech and movement.

TITLE: *The Tuned-In, Turned-On Book About Learning Problems*

SOURCE: Academic Therapy Publications
20 Commercial Blvd.
Novato, California 94947

AUDIENCE: Adolescents who are learning disabled

SYNOPSIS: This book by Marnell Hayes describes how adolescents can cope with problems of being learning disabled.

MENTALLY RETARDED

Films

TITLE: *All My Buttons*

SOURCE: Audio-visual Center
Film Rental Services
University of Kansas
Lawrence, Kansas 66044

AUDIENCE: General

SYNOPSIS: This 28-minute film focuses on the deinstitutionalization of retarded adults. Emphasis is on methods used to prepare them for integration into the mainstream of society.

TITLE: *Are You Ready?*

SOURCE: LaRue Films, Incorporated
159 East Chicago Avenue
Chicago, Illinois 60611

AUDIENCE: Parents and teachers

SYNOPSIS: Young Down's Syndrome children are engaged in the activities of a prescriptive teaching program.

TITLE: *Becky*

SOURCE: Stuart Finley, Inc.
3428 Mansfield Road
Falls Church, Virginia 22041

AUDIENCE: College students and professionals

SYNOPSIS: This movie attempts to focus on a normal day in the life of a moderately retarded person. It also focuses on the adjustments, feelings, and anxieties experienced by the family and how they receive help and support.

TITLE: *Coming Home*

SOURCE: Media Ware
12381 Wilshire Boulevard
Suite 203
Los Angeles, California 90025

AUDIENCE: Parents and teachers

SYNOPSIS: This film by the Pennsylvania Association for Retarded Citizens tells the story of a teenaged girl who moves from a state institution to a residential home for the retarded. Reactions by neighbors are explored.

TITLE: *Graduation*

SOURCE: Stanfield House
12381 Wilshire Boulevard
Suite 203
Los Angeles, California 90025

AUDIENCE: Preservice and inservice teachers and community groups

SYNOPSIS: Deals with a follow-up study of a group of moderately retarded students. Presented in a personal manner by the narration of the mother of one of the graduates. The lack of available programs and social experiences for the moderately retarded after graduation is emphasized, as well as the loneliness of the individuals.

TITLE: *Just For The Fun Of It*

SOURCE: AIMS Instructional Media Services, Inc.
P.O. Box 1010
Hollywood, California 90028

AUDIENCE: All teachers

SYNOPSIS: Demonstrates physical education activities designed for and used with moderately retarded children. These activities were planned to deal with some of the specific physical problems found with moderately retarded persons.

TITLE: *A Little Slow*

SOURCE: Association Films, Inc.

AUDIENCE: Adults

SYNOPSIS: The story of two mentally retarded persons with emphasis on the denial of their ordinary rights.

TITLE: *On Being Sexual*

SOURCE: Media Ware
12381 Wilshire Boulevard
Suite 203
Los Angeles, California 90025

AUDIENCE: Parents and teachers

SYNOPSIS: Sex education of the retarded is discussed to help parents and professionals to understand and cope with it.

TITLE: *Path To Fulfillment*

SOURCE: National Audiovisual Center
General Services Administration
Washington, D.C. 20409

AUDIENCE: Professionals

SYNOPSIS: Programs for the mentally retarded in Denmark, Sweden, and England are presented. The two major themes are that retarded people can lead normal lives and that their capabilities are functional.

TITLE: *Redin and Ritin Aint Everything*

SOURCE: Stanfield House
12381 Wilshire Boulevard
Suite 203
Los Angeles, California 90025

AUDIENCE: Parents and teachers

SYNOPSIS: Presents a view of the community-oriented approach to mental retardation, with personal accounts by a retarded adult and three families with retarded members.

TITLE: *The Step Behind Series*

SOURCE: Hallmark Films and Recordings, Inc.
1511 East North Avenue
Baltimore, Maryland 21213

AUDIENCE: Teachers and parents

SYNOPSIS: A series of three films showing adults how to train mentally retarded children in basic skills. Eating, dressing, and toileting are shown in *Genesis. Just Ask for Little Things* deals with walking, personal hygiene, and attending. *I'll Promise It To You Tomorrow* covers teaching communication, direction-following, and group participation.

Filmstrip

TITLE: *Tony*

SOURCE: Windmills, Ltd.
2211 Michigan Avenue
P.O. Box 1795
Santa Monica, California 90406

AUDIENCE: Elementary grade children

SYNOPSIS: The problems of a boy who learns slowly are covered in this filmstrip.

LP Recording

TITLE: *A Boy Is Talking*

SOURCE: Media Educational Materials
P.O. Box 1355
Vista, California 92803

AUDIENCE: Teenage students and adults

SYNOPSIS: The recording of an educable mentally retarded (EMR) teenager talking about such topics as feelings toward self, peer relationships, school, and the future.

Books

TITLE: *Like Me*

SOURCE: Little, Brown and Company
34 Beacon Street
Boston, Massachusetts 02106

AUDIENCE: Preschool and primary age children

SYNOPSIS: This photo-story by Alan Brightman tells of a mentally retarded boy who desires very much to be accepted despite his awareness that he learns slower than others.

TITLE: *Me Too*

SOURCE: J. B. Lippincott Company
Education Publishing Division
East Washington Square
Philadelphia, Pennsylvania 19105

AUDIENCE: Adolescents and young adults

SYNOPSIS: This story by Vera and Bill Cleaver describes the affective relationship between twin sisters, one of whom is mentally retarded.

MULTIHANDICAPPED

Films

TITLE: *Children Of The Silent Night*

SOURCE: Campbell Films, Inc.
Academy Avenue
Saxtons River, Vermont 05154

AUDIENCE: Parents and teachers

SYNOPSIS: The deaf and blind children of Perkins School and of Massachusetts are featured in this documentary.

TITLE: *Deaf-Blind Circus*

SOURCE: Campbell Films, Inc.
Academy Avenue
Saxtons River, Vermont 05154

AUDIENCE: Parents and teachers

SYNOPSIS: The need for social and group activity for deaf-blind children is emphasized. The background for the film is a circus produced by the Deaf-Blind Department at the Perkins School for the Blind.

TITLE: *Legacy of Anne Sullivan*

SOURCE: Campbell Films, Inc.
Academy Avenue
Saxtons River, Vermont 05154

AUDIENCE: Children and adults

SYNOPSIS: The problems of deaf-blind persons throughout life are presented. The contributions of Anne Sullivan and children of the Perkins School are emphasized. Tells the story of eight successful deaf-blind students.

TITLE: *Special Children's Special Needs*

SOURCE: Campus Films Productions, Inc.
2 Overhill Road
Scarsdale, New York 10583

AUDIENCE: Parents and teachers

SYNOPSIS: The early education of multihandicapped children is studied comprehensively in this film. Emphasis is placed on providing experiences relative to individual strengths and handicaps in a variety of situations.

TITLE: *Splash!*

SOURCE: Documentary Films
3217 Trout Gulch Road
Aptos, California 95003

AUDIENCE: Special education teachers

SYNOPSIS: Physically and mentally handicapped children are presented in a pool setting. They are engaged in activities designed to strengthen their listening, coordination, balance, and visual discrimination. The film offers many different ideas for water recreation in addition to swimming.

Video Tape Recording

TITLE: *Up the Dressing: Steps to Independence*

SOURCE: United States Bureau of Education for the Handicapped
National Audiovisual Center
General Services Administration
Washington, D.C. 20409

AUDIENCE: Teachers and parents

SYNOPSIS: This video tape shows ways young multihandicapped children can be helped to become independent in dressing themselves.

Books

TITLE: *About Handicaps*

SOURCE: Walter and Company
720 Fifth Avenue
New York, New York 10019

AUDIENCE: Children

SYNOPSIS: This book by Sara B. Stein is written for children about physical and mental handicaps, and is designed to overcome attitudinal barriers.

TITLE: *Child of the Silent Night*

SOURCE: Dell Publishing Company
245 East 47th Street
New York, New York 10017

AUDIENCE: Children ages 7 to 10

SYNOPSIS: The biography of Laura Bridgman who was deaf, mute, and blind. Describes the way she was taught to communicate.

TITLE: *The Story of Helen Keller*

SOURCE: Tempo Books
Grosset & Dunlap, Inc.
51 Madison Avenue
New York, New York 10010

AUDIENCE: Children ages 9 to 12

SYNOPSIS: This well-known story of Helen Keller written by Lorena A. Hickok describes how Helen, a deaf, mute, and blind person developed under the guidance of Anne Sullivan.

ORTHOPEDICALLY HANDICAPPED AND OTHER HEALTH IMPAIRED

Films

TITLE: *Being*

SOURCE: Paramount Communications
5451 Marathon Street
Hollywood, California 90038

AUDIENCE: Children of upper elementary and high school age level

SYNOPSIS: The story of a crippled young man who cannot accept friendship or love for fear of being pitied. The feelings of handicapped persons are emphasized.

TITLE: *Crip-Trips*

SOURCE: The President's Committee
on Employment of
the Handicapped
Washington, D.C.

AUDIENCE: Parents and teachers

SYNOPSIS: Preconceptions about physically disabled persons are confronted in this film. Three individuals are pre-sented who have dealt with the problems of being handicapped. The film is designed to raise questions, and to help overcome fears and anxieties about disability.

TITLE: *Fitting In*

SOURCE: Photographic Media Center
University of Wisconsin
1327 University Avenue
P.O. Box 2093
Madison, Wisconsin 53701

AUDIENCE: Older children

SYNOPSIS: Three disabled persons are followed through a typical day. The way in which they have managed to fit into society despite their disabilities is shown.

TITLE: *Nicky: One of My Best Friends*

SOURCE: McGraw-Hill Films
110 15th Street
Del Mar, California 92014

AUDIENCE: Elementary school children

SYNOPSIS: The story of a twelve-year-old multiply handicapped boy and his integration into a regular public school. His friends tell about his needs and his similarities to them.

TITLE: *Problems of Self-Help Task Performance*

SOURCE: National Audiovisual Center
General Services Administration
Washington, D.C. 20409

AUDIENCE: Teachers

SYNOPSIS: By watching handicapped children perform certain self-help tasks, the viewer can create a teaching strategy based on observation and analysis.

TITLE: *The Promise of Play*

SOURCE: Bradley Wright Films
1 Oak Hill Drive
San Anselmo, California 94960

AUDIENCE: All teachers

SYNOPSIS: A physical education program for orthopedically handicapped children is the main theme of this film. Students are shown participating in their individualized physical education program. The film ends with a "play day" when the students demonstrate their new skills to other members of the school.

TITLE: *Public School Programs for the Physically Handicapped*

SOURCE: Continental Film Group
Elk Grove, Illinois 60070

AUDIENCE: Educators and college students

SYNOPSIS: The various causes of physical handicaps are explained and then several illustrations are provided. Various preschool and school activities for handicapped children are shown.

TITLE: *They Can Be Helped*

SOURCE: DMDP Media Business Services
West 164th Stadium Street
Provo, Utah 84602

AUDIENCE: Teachers and parents

SYNOPSIS: The methods used to help four severely handicapped children are dealt with in this film. The procedures and the progress over a six month period are revealed.

Filmstrip

TITLE: *Mark*

SOURCE: Windmills, Ltd.
2211 Michigan Avenue
P.O. Box 1795
Santa Monica, California 90406

AUDIENCE: Elementary grade children

SYNOPSIS: This filmstrip describes a day in the life of an orthopedically handicapped boy who uses a wheelchair. He tells his feelings about his handicap.

Audio Tape Recordings

TITLE: *Danny's Song*

SOURCE: Hubbard
P.O. Box 104
Northbrook, Illinois 60062

AUDIENCE: Preschool and primary age children

SYNOPSIS: A short story about an eight-year-old physically handicapped boy, with a song sung by Mr. Rogers.

TITLE: *Josephine, The Short-Necked Giraffe*

SOURCE: Hubbard
P.O. Box 104
Northbrook, Illinois 60062

AUDIENCE: Preschool and primary age children

SYNOPSIS: The story of a giraffe who is different outside and finds out about herself inside. Accompanied by a song by Mr. Rogers.

TITLE: *Where Do I Go From Here?*

SOURCE: Media, A Division of Remediation Associates, Inc.
Box 2067
Van Nuys, California 91404

AUDIENCE: Teenage students, parents, and teachers

SYNOPSIS: An interview with a teenage cerebral palsy boy who attends a regular classroom environment. He discusses his feelings toward himself, his peers, and his parents.

Books

TITLE: *Epilepsy*

SOURCE: J. B. Lippincott
East Washington Square
Philadelphia, Pennsylvania 19105

AUDIENCE: Intermediate, elementary school children, and teenagers

SYNOPSIS: This book, written by Alvin and Virginia Silverstein, explains epilepsy to teenagers. It includes what epilepsy is, misconceptions about epilepsy, and discusses needed research and treatment.

TITLE: *Howie Helps Himself*

SOURCE: Whitman, Albert & Company
560 West Lake Street
Chicago, Illinois 60606

AUDIENCE: Children ages 3 to 8

SYNOPSIS: A boy confined to a wheelchair makes his wish come true. The frustration and the triumph of living with a handicap are dealt with.

TITLE: *Mine for Keeps*

SOURCE: Little, Brown and Company
34 Beacon Street
Boston, Massachusetts 02114

AUDIENCE: Children ages 9 to 12

SYNOPSIS: This book by Little is about a cerebral palsy girl who adjusts to life in a normal setting after living for years at a school for the handicapped.

TITLE: *You Can't Catch Diabetes From A Friend*

SOURCE: Triad Publishing Company
P.O. Box 80
Gainesville, Florida 32602

AUDIENCE: Children, youth, and adults

SYNOPSIS: This book by Lynne Kipnis and Susan Adler is illustrated with many photos. It tells about four children ages 7 through 14 who have diabetes, and is aimed at providing accurate information on diabetes and dispelling misconceptions about this disease.

SPEECH AND LANGUAGE IMPAIRED

Films

TITLE: *Broken Bridge*

SOURCE: Time-Life Films
100 Eisenhower Drive
Paramus, New Jersey 07652

AUDIENCE: Professionals

SYNOPSIS: Focuses on beginning speech therapy for three mute children. These therapy sessions take place in the children's homes.

TITLE: *Song for Michael*

SOURCE: Creative Arts Rehabilitation Center
251 West 51st Street
New York, New York 10019

AUDIENCE: General

SYNOPSIS: The history of Michael, a fourteen-year-old autistic youth, is described. The focus is on his participation in a music therapy program.

TITLE: *Time for Georgia*

SOURCE: New York Film Library
26 Washington Place
New York, New York 10003

AUDIENCE: General

SYNOPSIS: This award-winning film features Georgia, a preschool child identified as autistic.

Books

TITLE: *Burnish Me Bright*

SOURCE: Pantheon Books
Division of Random House, Inc.
201 East 50th Street
New York, New York 10022

AUDIENCE: Children ages 9 to 12

SYNOPSIS: A once-famous mime adopts a homeless mute boy and teaches him his art. Insights about "different" people are presented as well as peoples' reaction to them.

TITLE: *The Skating Rink*

SOURCE: Dell Publishing Company
245 East 47th Street
New York, New York 10017

AUDIENCE: Children ages 11 to 14

SYNOPSIS: A fifteen-year-old boy who stammers isolates himself from others. He breaks out of his isolation with the help of the owner of the new skating rink.

VISUALLY IMPAIRED

Films

TITLE: *Blindness . . . It's No Big Deal*

SOURCE: Stevenfeldt Educational Films
4080 23rd Street
San Francisco, California 94114

AUDIENCE: Teachers and college students

SYNOPSIS: This film depicts blind students functioning in a public school setting. It emphasizes their ability to learn in a relatively normal school situation. The ability of the teachers to make slight adaptations for the presence of blind students and the ability of nonblind peers to consider the visually impaired as individuals like themselves is described.

TITLE: *Children Without Sight*

SOURCE: Campbell Films, Inc.
Academy Avenue
Saxtons River, Vermont 05154

AUDIENCE: Parents and teachers

SYNOPSIS: The many aspects of an educational program for blind children are explored.

TITLE: *Penny and Anne*

SOURCE: AIMS Instructional Media Services, Inc.
626 Justin Avenue
Glendale, California 91201

AUDIENCE: Teachers of the blind

SYNOPSIS: The life of a blind girl, Penny, is depicted as she learns how to move about confidently in the seeing world. Her relationship with her occupational therapist, Anne, is discussed.

TITLE: *What Color Is The Wind*

SOURCE: Alan Grant
808 Lockearn Street
Los Angeles, California 90049

AUDIENCE: Parents and teachers

SYNOPSIS: The story of two four-year-old twin boys, one of whom is blind. The parents attempt to give the blind boy a sense of visual beauty. Both boys learn to share the worlds of darkness and light. The film is 27 minutes long and is available for rental or purchase.

Audio Tape Recording

TITLE: *Growing Up Without Sight*

SOURCE: Hubbard
P.O. Box 104
Northbrook, Illinois 60062

AUDIENCE: Preschool and primary age children

SYNOPSIS: These cassette tapes increase awareness of persons not having sight. They emphasize that the person is more important than the handicap and tell what visually impaired

people can do. Accompanying song is sung by Mr. Rogers.

LP Recording

TITLE: *Days of Shadow*

SOURCE: Media Educational Materials
P.O. Box 1355
Vista, California 92803

AUDIENCE: Special education teachers

SYNOPSIS: The characteristic problems and needs of visually handicapped children are discussed. Excerpts from children, parents, and professionals are included.

Books

TITLE: *A Cane in Her Hands*

SOURCE: Child Craft Education Corporation
20 Kilmer Road
Edison, New Jersey 08817

AUDIENCE: Elementary school children

SYNOPSIS: This story, written by Ada Litchfield, tells about a young girl who learns to do things without being able to see. Readers gain an understanding of blindness and handicapped vision.

TITLE: *Connie's New Eyes*

SOURCE: J. B. Lippincott
Education Publishing Division
East Washington Square
Philadelphia, Pennsylvania 19105

AUDIENCE: Children grades 4 through 6

SYNOPSIS: This story by Bernard Wolf follows the growth and development of Blythe, a seeing-eye dog, from puppyhood to life with her blind mistress, Connie.

TITLE: *Gift of Gold*

SOURCE: Dodd, Mead and Company, Inc.
79 Madison Avenue
New York, New York 10016

AUDIENCE: Adolescents and young adults

SYNOPSIS: This book by Beverly Butler tells the story of a blind girl, Cathy, who wants to become a speech therapist but is opposed by the head of her college's speech department.

Ability training A teaching approach emphasizing the identification and remediation of underlying abilities or processes that seem to cause poor academic performances. Proponents of this approach believe that by correcting the problems with the specific aptitudes, academic performance itself can be corrected.

Acceleration The practice wherein pupils with high academic ability can complete more than one school grade during a single year. Acceleration is used to provide more appropriate educational placements for gifted pupils.

Adaptive behavior A concept that refers to a person's ability to adjust to the environment, displaying adequate levels of independence and responsibility in daily life. Along with intelligence, adaptive behavior is now considered to be a major criterion for defining mental retardation.

Adaptive devices Devices modified to enable a physically disabled person to engage in the activities of everyday life.

Adventitiously deaf Phrase referring to a person of normal hearing made deaf through accident or disease.

Affect That part of a person's being having to do with feelings, emotions, and attitudes.

Air conduction hearing loss A hearing loss caused by irregularities in the transmission process (wherein sound waves enter the ear, hit the eardrum, and cause the eardrum to vibrate, initiating the procedure that results in hearing).

Amniocentesis A medical procedure in which a sample of the amniotic fluid of the uterus is withdrawn and analyzed, permitting physicians to assess aspects of fetus development prior to birth. Congenital defects such as spina bifida and Down's syndrome can be detected in this manner.

Annual goals That part of the Individualized Education Program (IEP) required by PL 94–142 which specifies the academic and/or behavioral achievements to be reached within the next year.

Apgar scale A widely used screening test for newborn infants that measures the degree of oxygen deprivation experienced by an infant during birth.

Aphasia A language disorder. Aphasia is caused by brain injury and results in the partial or complete loss of the ability to comprehend or to produce language, spoken or written.

Applied behavioral analysis A method of systematically studying behaviors by selecting target behaviors, developing intervention strategies, and measuring the behavior changes daily. This method is based on the principles of behavioral psychology and includes experimental controls.

Articulation disorders Problems in the production of speech sounds through the use of jaw, lips, tongue, etc.

Ataxia A type of cerebral palsy characterized by poor muscle coordination, difficulty in movement, and poor balance.

Athetosis A type of cerebral palsy characterized by involuntary motions of the arms, legs, head, and tongue resulting in difficulties with tasks that require motor skills (including speech).

Attention span The period of time during which persons are able to focus their attention on an activity or topic without attending to other internal or external activities or objects.

Audiogram A graph that indicates the threshold levels of hearing for each ear for the different frequencies measured by the audiometer.

Audiology The study of hearing; the professional discipline that engages in research, identification of problems, and the development of treatment programs for hearing-impaired persons.

Auditory training Instructional process that helps people with hearing losses to use their residual hearing to the maximum level.

Autistic A term developed from the Greek word for "self" and applied to children who exhibit the characteristics of autism, a severe disorder of childhood. Autism is characterized by the inability to communicate through meaningful speech and the inability to develop relationships with other persons due to withdrawal.

Behaviorism A field of psychology established on the belief that all behavior is learned through previous experiences.

Behavioral objectives A precise measurable statement of what the pupil is expected to achieve, including the conditions under which the pupil will achieve, and the criteria for measuring the achievement.

Behavioral theory A psychological theory holding that a person's present behavior is caused by past learning experiences.

Behavior modification The process of eliminating inappropriate behaviors and/or encouraging appropriate behaviors through the application of learning principles.

Bibliotherapy A technique to help socially or emotionally maladjusted persons through the reading of books or stories that portray characters or circumstances with which the reader can identify.

Bicultural A term referring to those who identify with two cultures, sharing the differing language, values, beliefs, attitudes, and mores of each.

Bi-dialectal Communicating in more than one dialectal form of a language (e.g., black children who may use non-standard English at home and in the community but are required to use standard English in school).

Bilateral loss A hearing loss in both ears.

Bilingual The ability to speak more than one language.

Biophysical A theoretical model of the causation of learning and behavior disorders that postulates that these problems occur through biochemical imbalances, genetic abnormalities, and/or neurological insult.

Blind (blindness) A disability characterized by a level of vision insufficient for carrying out daily life. In many states blind is legally defined as visual acuity of 20/200 or less in the better eye with correction or peripheral vision that allows for the visual field to cover the angular distance of no more than 20 degrees.

Blindisms Behaviors, such as the moving of the head back and forth, from side to side, that characterize the movements of persons who are blind.

Bone conduction hearing loss A hearing loss resulting from difficulties that occur in the process whereby sound waves are transmitted to the inner ear through vibrations of bones in the middle ear.

Braille An approach (named after its originator, Louis Braille) used by blind persons to read and write. This technique relies on touch to recognize letters formed by raised dots.

Braille writer A machine used to type Braille.

Brain damaged A term describing children who have—or are thought to have—suffered injury to brain tissues, leading to central nervous system impairment.

Career education An educational program that emphasizes the teaching of the work ethic and job familiarity early in life, with follow-up vocational training throughout the school years.

Center-based program Educational services provided for handicapped young children through day care centers, neighborhood group centers, or nursery schools.

Cerebral palsy An abnormal alteration of human movement or motor function steming from defect, injury, or disease of tissues of the central nervous system. Major types usually identified are: spastic, athetoid, and ataxic.

Child abuse The negligent or harmful treatment—physical or mental—or sexual abuse of a child under age eighteen by the parent or guardian.

Child Development Associate (CDA) A highly trained specialist in educational child development who identifies young children requiring special educational services and who implements home or center-based programs to meet their needs.

Child Find Process by which each state devised strategies for identifying all handicapped children in order to provide them with an appropriate education.

Child Health Assessment Program (CHAP) A federally proposed program aimed at providing physical and developmental screening, diagnosis, and treatment services (including speech and language therapy, physical therapy, and occupational therapy) for children of low income families. This program emphasizes interagency cooperation and coordination.

Chromosomal anomalies Defects in chromosomal material that can result in birth of an abnormal child.

Cleft palate A condition characterized by an opening in the roof of the mouth, involving the hard or soft palate (or both), and often going through the upper lip. Causes include faulty development before birth, injury, or disease.

Cognitive A term used to refer to the mental processes of reasoning, comprehension, judgment, and memory.

Communication boards Nonoral communication systems using pictures or symbols. Individuals with little or no speech are taught to communicate by pointing to symbols on a special board.

Community group home A planned living environment for handicapped persons where they can live a more normal life within the community setting rather than remain in an institution. In recent years, group homes have become more prevalent as increasing numbers of mentally retarded and mentally ill persons leave institutions and return to local communities.

Computer assisted instruction (CAI) A process in which a computer assists the teacher and/or pupil in the teaching/learning process by serving as a source of readily available information and feedback.

Computer managed instruction (CMI) A process in which the computer guides the learning interaction between it and the pupil and selects courses of action based on the pupil's responses.

Conduct disorder A pattern of behavior characterized by attention-seeking, hyperactivity, and aggression (verbal and/or physical).

Conductive hearing loss A hearing loss caused by an obstruction in the auditory canal; partially or totally prevents sound waves from reaching the inner ear.

Congenital anomaly A condition or characteristic present in an individual at birth.

Congenitally deaf Any form of deafness present at birth; of concern because much of this type of deafness is hereditary and can be passed on to offspring.

Consent agreement A court agreement between two parties that recognizes equitable remedies in solving legal problems.

Consulting teacher A resource person who provides diagnostic and other support services to other teachers.

Contingency contracting A contract in which a

teacher and a pupil (or a parent and child) develop an agreement stating positive results of certain behaviors. It may be signed by all involved.

Cultural pluralism A philosophy wherein a society recognizes, embraces, and promotes various cultures with their accompanying languages, values, and beliefs.

Curriculum A logical, systematic arrangement of learning activities, courses and content of instruction, and instructional materials toward the goal of providing education.

Cystic fibrosis A congenital, degenerative disease that affects the mucous glands in the body resulting in damage to the lungs and pancreas.

Deaf A condition in which the auditory channel is not the primary sensory means by which speech and language are learned.

Decibel A measurement of the intensity of sound.

Deinstitutionalization The movement of mentally retarded or emotionally disturbed persons from large institutions to alternative living arrangements in local communities. This concept follows along with the principles of "normalization" and "least restrictive environment."

Denasal A speech condition characterized by a lack of resonance in the voice caused by blockage of airflow through the nose such as occurs with the common cold.

Diagnostic/prescriptive teacing (DPT) Individualized instruction that recognizes the student's strengths and weaknesses and prescribes instruction to remediate the weaknesses and develop the strengths.

Dialects Variations in language that differ from the traditional or standard form in pronunciation, inflection, or word choice.

Dimensionality The quality of having scope and proportion; items on creativity tests should be independent from traditional measures of intelligence, having their own proportions.

Disability A deviation from the norm in an individual's physical, psychological, or neurological make-up that inhibits the person's ability to function normally.

Distractibility Behavior typified by the tendency to respond to inappropriate and/or unnecessary stimuli in the environment rather than attend to the appropriate stimuli; often a characteristic of children thought to be brain damaged.

Down's syndrome A medical condition resulting from chromosomal abnormality and involving mental retardation of various degrees. Persons with Down's syndrome are recognizable by several physical characteristics (including slanting eyes, broad skull, and depressed nose). These attributes led to use of the term "mongoloid" because of their similarity to some physical characteristics of persons of the Mongoloid race. This syndrome is found in three forms: trisomy 21, translocation, mosaicism.

Due process A principle of law that guarantees the rights of handicapped children and their parents to have a hearing prior to placement in special educational programs.

Dysphasia Aphasia; inability to produce or understand language (written and/or spoken) caused by injury or disease of the brain.

Dyslexia Full or partial inability to read. Pupils with this problem are often classified under the broader category of learning disabilities.

Early admission A method of accelerating young gifted children by admitting them to formal schooling before they reach the age normally expected for beginning school.

Early childhood period Developmental period of a child's life from birth to age six. This period is critical for establishing the foundation for the child's future learning.

Early and Periodic Screening, Diagnosis, and Treatment (EPSDT) A federally funded program aimed at providing physical and developmental screening, diagnostic, and treatment services for children of families receiving welfare assistance.

Ecological An approach to psychology and education that perceives a child's academic and social behavior to be influenced by all the many factors in the environment; this approach emphasizes factors external to the child rather than internal.

Ecological assessment Assessment that stresses analyzing all the environmental factors that influence the child's academic and/or social behavior.

Educable mentally retarded The term used by educators to refer to pupils with a mild level of intellectual retardation (usually defined as functioning within an IQ range of 50-75 with concurrent below normal adaptive behavior).

Electroencephalogram (EEG) A recording produced by a machine that measures "brain work;" electrical discharges of the brain; it is often part of the assessment of persons suspected to be epileptic or suffering from brain injury.

Elusive grieving process The developmental process whereby persons adjust to the loss of a loved one. Originally described by Dr. Kübler-Ross in her studies of death, this concept has been used by Dr. Ken Moses to describe what the par-

ents of handicapped children go through in adjusting to their circumstances.

Emotional abuse Harmful treatment of children or adults that damages feelings and emotional development rather than the body.

Engineered classroom A highly structured classroom management system utilizing a developmental sequence of educational goals and reinforcement for task completion; originated by Frank Hewett to teach pupils with learning and behavior problems.

Enrichment An approach to teaching gifted children that emphasizes the expansion of the curriculum to greater depths through creative projects, additional reading, and other methods.

Epilepsy A nervous disease characterized by convulsions (grand mal type), momentary loss of consciousness (petit mal type), and irrational reactions such as temper tantrums (psychomotor type).

Equivocal indicators Factors that seem to be related to the presence of brain damage in children but are not considered as direct evidence. These indicators include hyperactivity, distractibility, and a short attention span; this indirect evidence is often referred to as "soft" signs of neurological impairment.

Exceptional Persons who deviate from the norm either because of superior ability or because of disabilities.

Field of vision The total area that a person can see without changing his or her gaze.

First Chance Network Programs designed to provide services to children from birth to age five. These services include prenatal instruction and technical assistance to parents and members of the family.

Formal norm-referenced tests Tests used to make educational placement decisions. Formal tests have norms for comparison of scores and require the test administrator to follow standardized procedures.

Giftedness The state of unusually high demonstrated performance and/or potential ability in any one or combination of the following areas of achievement: general intellectual ability, specific academic aptitude, creative or productive thinking, leadership ability, visual and performing arts ability and psychomotor ability.

Grand mal A type of epileptic seizure resulting in convulsions of the body and loss of consciousness.

Handicapped Refers to the result of a disability that inhibits functioning, achievement, or acceptance of everyday life activities.

Hard of hearing A disability characterized by a low level of hearing ability; often requires services and/or adaptations for successful education.

Helping teacher concept A teacher role requiring a teacher to work with other on-site teachers as well as directly with children in order to facilitate the educational program of emotionally disturbed or behaviorally disordered pupils.

Hertz A measurement of the frequency of sound waves (vibrations per second).

Holistic An approach to teaching children with learning and behavior disorders that incorporates the strengths of various theoretical positions and diverse professionals in the planning and implementing of appropriate treatment programs.

Home-based program The provision of educational services to young children by child development specialists who make home visits and help the parents to understand and to work with the child's handicapping condition.

Humanism A philosophy that emphasizes interest in and a strong concern for the dignity and worth of individual persons and their capacities to achieve self-realization through reason.

Hydracephaly A medical condition characterized by the accumulation of excess fluid in the cranial cavity causing pressure on the brain and an enlarged head. If the fluid is not reduced surgically, the condition usually results in mental retardation.

Hyperactivity A behavioral state characterized by high degrees of activity, frequent and quick movements; often observed as a symptom of children with learning and/or behavior disorders.

Hypernasality A speech condition characterized by high nasal voice quality resulting from excessive airflow through the nasal passages.

Hypoactivity Behavioral state characterized by very low levels of activity; infrequent and slow movement.

Immaturity A level of development in physical or psychological attributes below the levels that are normally expected for the child's age.

Impulsivity The tendency to respond to stimuli immediately, without reflection.

Individualized Education Program (IEP) A major requirement of PL 94–142; requires a plan of instruction to be written by an educational team to include the following information: (1) statement of the child's current level of educational achievements; (2) annual goals; (3) short-term objectives; (4) specific services required for the child to be educated; (5) dates when the services will begin; and (6) methods for evaluating the effectiveness of the planned services.

Individualized instruction Instruction aimed at achieving the individually established goals and objectives stated in the IEP; does not necessarily require the provision of individual, one-on-one instruction.

Individualized Instructional Plan (IIP) The teaching plan that specifies the objectives and activities outlined more broadly in the Individualized Education Program (IEP).

Informal tests Teacher-made tests used to specify academic skill levels and abilities prior to or during instruction. These tests are not based on group norms and do not typically require following standardized procedures during their administration.

Informed consent Provision of consent after having been informed of all rights and of possible consequences of such consent.

Inner ear The innermost part of the 3-part human ear. Here, the mechanical sound waves received from the middle ear are converted into electrical impulses by the cochlear nerve and transmitted to the brain.

Insulin A hormone used in treating diabetes; taken from the pancreatic glands of animals or produced synthetically.

Insulin reaction A state of shock characterized by perspiration, trembling, and muscular contractions that results when the body needs sugar due to an excess of insulin in the body. A person with diabetes may suffer from insulin reactions because of over exercise or insufficient food.

Intensity disorders Disorders of speech that relate to the degree of loudness or softness (intensity) of the person's voice when speaking.

Interdisciplinary A method characterized by the interaction and cooperation of professionals from various disciplines or areas of expertise.

Intrinsic reinforcers Rewards for behavior that are found within the behavior itself (e.g., a pupil who likes math and enjoys working math problems is rewarded by intrinsic reinforcers for completion of math problems).

Juvenile delinquency Legal term for illegal behavior engaged in by young persons who are—by law—considered to be children, not adults.

Juvenile diabetes mellitus A disease marked by the inability of the pancreas to produce insulin thus raising the level of sugar in the blood, which enables sugar to be burned up. If left untreated, this disease may result in coma and death.

Juvenile rheumatoid arthritis A medical condition of unknown cause found in young children and characterized by severe inflammation of the body joints (similar to rheumatoid arthritis in adults).

Ketoacidosis A condition of untreated or under-treated diabetes wherein not enough insulin is present in the body to utilize the sugar. Subsequently, body fat is converted to energy at high levels producing a rising level of ketone bodies that in turn causes an excess of acid leading to a diabetic coma and possibly death.

Lalling The production of sounds by a baby of about six months of age, caused by the ear-voice reflex (sound production stimulates the ear which stimulates sound production again in a cyclical fashion).

Language A system for communication among persons in a group. Language consists of words and/or symbols and a set of rules for putting them together.

Learning centers An instructional part of a classroom, organized at a table or booth, in which a teacher arranges learning materials (i.e., activities, games, worksheets) that children can complete independently to supplement their other classroom learning experiences.

Learning disabilities A disorder in one or more of the basic psychological processes involved in understanding or in using spoken or written language. Such a disability may manifest itself in an imperfect ability to listen, think, speak, read, write, spell, or do mathematical calculations.

Least restrictive environment That place where the handicapped pupil can be educated with no more segregation or restriction than is absolutely necessary. This concept (required by PL 94–142) has led to mainstreaming—serving handicapped children in regular school programs.

Legislation Laws that are officially enacted at the local, state, or federal level by vote of the appropriate law-making bodies.

Lifetime education A philosophy of education proposing that learning need not be restricted to specified periods in one's life (e.g., during public school years). Lifetime education stresses that people should engage in learning activities all through their lifetimes. Demands of the future will require that our society apply this philosophy more widely than has been the case in the past.

Lisping A speech articulation defect evidenced in the improper production of the "s" and "z" sounds such as in pronouncing "saw" as "thaw."

Litigation A legal process involving the settling of differences (law suits) on questions of law within the court system.

Mainstreaming The procedure of providing a regular school program for the handicapped rather than placing them in a self-contained special classroom. This process provides a "least restrictive environment" in many instances.

Manualists Deaf persons who communicate with fingerspelling and/or sign language instead of speech.

Marginal pupils Young children (as described by Nicholas Long) who appear to require individualized teaching prescriptions if the school is going to capitalize on their strengths and build up their weaknesses, making school a positive force in their life, rather than an additional negative force.

Meningocele A sac that contains cerebral-spinal fluid and coverings of the spinal cord but no spinal nerves, and protrudes through an open area in the spinal column. This condition is a form of spina bifida, a congenital malformation of the back arches of the vertebral column.

Middle ear The middle portion of the 3-part human ear. Here, sound wave vibrations are transmitted from the outer ear to the inner ear via tiny bones.

Mildly mentally retarded Individuals assessed to be in the IQ score range of 55 to 70.

Minimum brain dysfunction This term refers to persons of average, near average, or above average intelligence who exhibit learning or behavioral disorders as a result of suspected or diagnosed changes in functions of the central nervous system.

Mixed cerebral palsy A term used to describe cerebral palsy when characteristics of spasticity, athetosis, and ataxia are present.

Mixed hearing loss A loss of hearing resulting from both conductive and sensorineural hearing losses.

Mobility The ability to move about safely and effectively within one's environment.

Moderately mentally retarded Individuals assessed to be in the IQ score range of 40 to 55.

Mosaicism A type of Down's syndrome with an unusual pattern of chromosomes in which not all the cells are abnormally composed.

Muscular dystrophy A progressive hereditary disease in which the body deteriorates as a result of atrophy or wasting of muscle tissue.

Myelomeningocele A sac, protruding through an open area of the spinal column, that contains cerebral-spinal fluid, coverings of the spinal cord, and the spinal cord itself. This condition is the most severe form of spina bifida, a congenital malformation of the back arches of the spinal column.

Neglect The act of a parent or guardian giving little or no respect or attention to the care of a child for whose welfare they are responsible; any disregarding of parent or guardian responsibility that endangers the child.

Nondiscriminatory evaluation Evaluating measures that are not prejudicial against minority groups or individuals.

Nonoptical aids Adaptive aids for person with visual impairments that are usually designed to assist learning through the other senses. Examples include Braille, special high contrast overlay paper, raised line paper for writing, cassette and disk recordings of reading materials, and enlarged print books.

Normalization The procedure of placing handicapped persons in situations as nearly like normal ones as possible. For example, the placement of a retarded person in a group home rather than in an institution.

Occupational therapists Upon the referral of a physician, the occupational therapist develops educational, recreational, and creative activities for the treatment of disabled persons.

Ophthamologist A medical doctor that specializes in treatment of the eye.

Optacon A device that allows blind persons to read by converting print into vibrations that can be read tactually with the finger.

Optical aids Aids that enhance visual ability for persons with visual impairments, including glasses, magnifiers, and telescopic aids (for enlarging visual images in the distance).

Oralists Those persons who teach the hearing impaired through speech reading (lip reading), listening, and writing without the use of sign language.

Organic problems A condition that results from disease, damage, or dysfunction of a body part.

Orientation A blind person's ability to use his or her functional senses to determine position in the environment relative to other persons, places, or things.

Orthopedically handicapped Persons disabled by physical impairments related to the joints, bones, and muscles.

Osteogenesis imperfecta An inherited disease resulting in the formation of fragile bones; sometimes referred to as "brittle bone" disease.

Other health impaired Persons with physical impairments related to chronic or acute health problems which cause limited strength, vitality, or alertness and adversely affect a person's educational performance.

Outer ear The outermost part of the 3-part human ear. Here, sound waves are collected and funneled into the middle ear.

Overcontrolled A general classification of behavior disorders referring to behaviors that limit and narrow the child's range of social interaction (e.g., failure to relate to adults or other children, withdrawal).

Paraprofessionals Persons who are not professionals but who are trained to perform as teachers' aides or handle nonteaching duties in order to free the teacher for other responsibilities.

Parent advocacy groups Groups of parents who support and represent the welfare of others. Several parent advocacy groups have been responsible for developing public understanding and support for various types of handicapped children.

Partially sighted Seriously impaired vision generally defined as being between 20/200 and 20/70 visual acuity in the better eye with correction. The terms "visually impaired" and "visually handicapped" are now more frequently used.

Peer tutors School pupils who work individually or in small groups with other pupils to help them progress academically.

Permissive legislation Laws that permit or enable programs to begin but do not require—or mandate—that the programs be started.

Perseveration The continued, persistent repetition of a behavior regardless of the result.

Persisting life problems curriculum A curricular design for mentally retarded pupils that stresses the teaching and learning of those skills that will enable the retarded person ultimately to function in adulthood as independently as possible. Areas of study include health care, safety, use of money, transportation, communication, and citizenship.

Personality disorder Any disorder that interferes in rapport building with people or in adjusting to society but is not enough of a problem to be considered a serious mental illness.

Petit mal A mild seizure taking place in epileptic conditions. These seizures can occur from one to 200 times a day and can last from 5 to 20 seconds each. They may be identified by dizziness and momentary lapse of consciousness.

Phonation disorders Problems of the functioning of the larynx to produce vocal sounds and voice.

Physical abuse The negligent or maltreatment actions of a parent or guardian that result in physical harm to a child under 18 years of age.

Physical therapists (PT) Persons trained to treat disabilities by using massage, exercise, water, light, heat, and certain forms of electricity. These methods are mechanical rather than medical.

Phenylketonuria (PKU) A hereditary condition that results in a gradual buildup of toxic substances in the blood and urine of infants; an absence of an essential enzyme for digesting protein affects the metabolism of the body, which interferes with the normal development and function of the brain; an abnormality of metabolism that causes mental retardation.

Pitch disorders Disorders in the highness or lowness of speech that can be too high, too low, monotoned, stereotyped, inflectuous, or has pitch breaks.

Postlingual deafness Deafness that happens after speech and language have been developed.

Precision teaching This procedure entails the continuous and direct recording of academic and/ or social behavior; employs the techniques of task analysis and behavior modification to teach academic and social skills.

Prelingual deafness Deafness occurring before speech and language are acquired; deafness that is present at birth or early in life.

Prevalence Frequency of occurrence that is often reported in percentages.

Prosthesis An artificial part (such as an arm or leg) attached to one's body; enables the person to regain partial or full function of the limb.

Prosthetic device A prosthesis. An artificial part (arm or leg, for instance) attached to one's body; enables the person to regain partial or full function of the limb.

Psychoanalytic A psychological point of view proposing that behavior disorders are caused by children's failures to proceed successfully through the psychosexual stages of development. Psychoanalytic theory holds that, in order to correct behavior problems, the underlying cause (problem with development) must be uncovered and dealt with—dealing with the observable behavior (symptom) is not enough.

Psychophysics A science that studies the relationship of human abilities, particularly those related to the brain and the ears, and sound production, from a psychologist's as well as a physicist's perspective.

Public Law 94-142 The Education of All Handicapped Children Act of 1975. This law specifies that all handicapped children must be provided with a free appropriate education, have a right to a nondiscriminatory evaluation to determine the need for special educational services, and have the right to due process of law in making the special education placement decision.

Pure tone audiometer Testing instrument used for measuring the acuity of hearing at selected frequencies, usually in 5-decibel steps.

Quality disorders A voice disorder that may be termed as nasal, strident, breathy, falsetto, or hoarse.

Refracture errors Genetically determined vision problems resulting in difficulties with the eye's ability to refract light rays properly; included are myopia (nearsightedness), hyperopia (farsightedness), and astigmatism (blurred focus).

Rehabilitation counselor A counselor who aids a deviant or nonproductive person through education or retraining toward the desired standard.

Related services Services such as speech therapy, audiology, and physical education that are supportive of but may not be part of classroom instruction; described in PL 94-142.

Relevant experiences curriculum Method of teaching children with behavior disorders that emphasizes learning from the relationship between the pupils' everyday lives and their school subjects; pupils are directly taught how to apply what they are learning to solve problems in their daily lives.

Residual vision The degree of visual acuity that remains for a visually handicapped person to learn how to use.

Resonance disorders A voice disorder related to the quality of sound produced by the organs of the vocal tract; the varying sound quality influenced by the organs' size, shape, and texture.

Resource teacher A special teacher who works in a resource room where handicapped pupils come for specific individualized instruction. This specialist also serves as a consultant to regular classroom teachers and suggests methods and materials to those working with children who have learning problems.

Resourceful pupils Young children (as described by Nicholas Long) who appear to have developed the appropriate attitudes and levels of social and academic skills to adjust effectively to school, and to be successful pupils.

Respite care Temporary service providing a period of rest from one day to two weeks for the parents of handicapped children. Community agencies, group homes, foster homes, and other institutions often provide this service.

Reversals A problem in reading or writing where the pupil confuses letters with each other, the order of letters, or mixes the order of letters in words.

Reward activity menu A classroom listing of rewarding and reinforcing activities and events, chosen by the pupils, from which pupils select activities to engage in after they have completed their assigned tasks.

Rewards A reinforcer; anything that follows a behavior (is a consequence of the behavior) and increases the probability that the behavior will occur again in the future.

Rh incompatibility The incompatibility of the mother's blood and the blood of the fetus during the prenatal period; an allergic reaction caused by incompatibility results in the breakdown of red blood cells which can later result in severe handicaps including mental retardation.

Rubella A communicable disease transmitted by virus and after called German measles. Children born to women who were infected by rubella early in their pregnancies are often affected by severe handicaps, including mental retardation.

Screening A variety of procedures used to test large groups of children in order to find those who will need more detailed evaluation and/or special training.

Self-concept People's perceptions of and feelings about themselves; related to people's perceptions of how others view them and to their level of self-confidence.

Self-fulfilling prophecy The theory stating that, if people are labeled something, others will treat them in the manner designated by that label. The marked group thus comes to believe the label does in fact belong to them and behaves accordingly.

Sensorineural hearing loss A physical condition involving a disorder of the inner ear and/or the central nervous system; sometimes called nerve deafness.

Severe discrepancy The degree of difference between a pupil's actual and potential achievement; used as a criterion in determining whether a child is learning disabled. The multidisciplinary team decides whether any existing discrepancies are severe or not.

Severely and profoundly mentally retarded A term used to describe those mentally retarded persons who have intellectual levels of 35 IQ or less and similar subaverage levels of adaptive behavior. These persons may be able to live in a community group home but the intensity of their handicap require extensive supervision.

Sexual abuse The negligent or maltreatment actions of a parent or guardian that results in sexual harm or insult to a child under 18 years of age.

Sheltered workshop A controlled, supervised work environment where persons who cannot work in competitive, everyday employment can learn the skills leading to competitive employment and can develop a healthy self-concept through participation in productive work activities. Many sheltered workshops include work on jobs under contract to private industries.

Short term objectives A required part of the Individual Educational Program (IEP) that lists the objectives (measurable statement of what the pupil is to achieve) leading to the selected annual goals.

Shunt A permanent drainage system developed through neurosurgery to relieve hydrocephaly; it consists of a plastic tube with a valve and allows excess fluid in the brain cavities to be drained into the heart or abdomen.

Sickle cell anemia A genetic condition of the blood mainly found among persons of the black race. The red blood cells become sickle in shape and do not carry oxygen properly. The result is pain, low vitality, and the blocking of proper nutrition for the brain. Severe cases may result in mental retardation or death.

Six-hour retarded Term applied to those children (largely from disadvantaged and minority backgrounds) labeled as mentally retarded by the schools but who function capably in their home, neighborhood, and community environments.

Skill training A teaching approach that emphasizes the identification of specific errors in academic performances and direct teaching to correct the difficulties. Proponents of this approach believe that assumptions regarding possible underlying cause of the problem(s) are unnecessary.

Slate and stylus A method of writing the Braille code of raised dots by embossing paper held in a slate with openings for the indentations to be made by the stylus.

Snellen test A test of distant visual acuity that uses a chart with black letters or symbols of different size on a white background to screen for vision problems.

Social reinforcers Rewards (reinforcers) that

take the forms of social responses to children's behavior (e.g., a smile, a wink, a pat on the back, an activity, words such as "good job," etc.).

Socialized delinquency One of four categories (dimensions) of behavior disorders in children, identified by Quay. Characteristics include: stealing, truancy, fighting, having bad companions.

Socioemotional problems Problems related to poor social development and adjustment involving unusual feelings, attitudes, or reactions to environmental stimuli.

Sociological Relating to the forces and institutions of cultures and societies.

Spasticity Term that refers to muscular incoordination caused by muscle spasms, opposing contractions of muscles, and paralytic effects.

Special Olympics A program of physical training and sports competition for mentally retarded persons. Founded in 1968 by the Joseph P. Kennedy, Jr. Foundation to help expand the opportunities of mentally retarded persons to develop self-confidence and poise as well as physical skills.

Speech Sound articulated as vocal and oral symbols in the communication process.

Speech audiometer A device used for measuring hearing and to determine when the testee can identify the spoken words rather than voice sounds at set levels of intensity.

Speech/language pathologist A person who diagnoses and treats speech and language problems and the lack of their development. Methods of treatment include individual testings, instruction, and work with small groups.

Speechreading Instruction given to the deaf and hard of hearing in which they understand what is said by observing the context of the situation and the visual cues, such as lip and facial movements.

Spina bifida A congenital malformation of the spine that often allows a protrusion of the spinal cord into a sac at the base of the spine; caused by an opening of the vertebrae column. This condition has varying degrees of severity and may also be referred to as meningocele or myelomeningocele, its most severe form.

Stuttering Blocking, hesitation, repetition of single sounds, words, and sometimes sentences in speech.

Tangible rewards Reinforcers (rewards) that are obvious and manipulatible (e.g., checkmarks, points, pluses, candy, toys, etc.).

Task analysis The breaking down of a task into its smallest elements in the proper sequence. Instruction using task analysis involves systematic teaching of the elements in sequence.

Tokens Tangible secondary reinforcers that may be accumulated and exchanged for reinforcers at a later time.

Total communication A combination of language systems (manual signs and fingerspelling are coupled with speechreading and listening) that are used to benefit the language development of the hearing impaired.

Trainable mentally retarded Those individuals assessed at the 25 to 50 IQ range. Such people are defined as not being able to profit suitably from regular class or classes for the educable mentally retarded. They are capable of learning self-help skills, programs in social adjustment, and controlled work settings.

Transdisciplinary A type of multidisciplinary team where various members share the knowledge and skills of their particular discipline with other members of the team. With this teaming arrangement one member can act as the primary source provider for a family, avoiding possible confusion, and developing firmer relationships and trust.

Translocation A type of Down's syndrome. Here, a portion of a chromosome of one group attaches to another, causing an excess of genetic material in one cell and a lack of it in another.

Trisomy 21 The most common form of Down's syndrome. Three chromosomes are present rather than two in a pair, and the individual cell contains 47 chromosomes rather than the normal 46.

Undercontrolled A general classification of behavior disorders which refers to excessive social responses and/or antisocial behavior (e.g., constant talking, hitting, arguing, teasing).

Unit approach Learning activities that are centered around a major topic. The activities span several subject matter areas.

Visual acuity The accuracy of a person's eyesight.

Visual efficiency The effectiveness of a person's use of their eyesight.

Vocational education A program aimed at preparing pupils for jobs in their chosen area of work.

Voice disorders Unusual volume, pitch, or voice; a sound quality resulting in abnormal spoken language.

Vulnerable pupils Young children (as described by Nicholas Long) who appear not to have developed the attitudes toward learning, or have learned the appropriate behaviors, that would enable them to cope successfully with everyday school life. Such children require special modifications in their school program if they are to be successful.

Workshop Way An approach to individualizing instruction in the regular classroom which utilizes an organized, structured daily schedule, teaching strategies, and prepared materials.

Work study program An educational program for mildly handicapped secondary pupils in which participants work part-time under the school's supervision and go to school part-time.

"A Talking Wheelchair." *Science News*, 117, 5 (1980), 221.

Abeson, A., and Ballard, J. "State and Federal Policy for Exceptional Children." In F. J. Weintraub, A. Abeson, J. Ballard, and M. Lavor, eds. *Public Policy and the Education of Exceptional Children*. Reston, Va.: Council for Exceptional Children, 1976, 83–95.

Abeson, A., Bolick, N., and Hass, J. *A Primer on Due Process*. Reston, Va.: Council for Exceptional Children, 1976.

Abeson, A., and Weintraub, F. "Understanding the Individualized Education Program." In S. Torres, ed., *A Primer on Individualized Education Programs for Handicapped Children*. Reston, Va.: Foundation for Exceptional Children, 1977.

Abeson, A., and Zettel, J. "The End of the Quiet Revolution: The Education of All Handicapped Children Act of 1975." *Exceptional Children*, 44 (October 1977), 114–128.

ACLD Newsbriefs, January/February 1980.

ACLD Newsbriefs, March/April 1980.

Affleck, J. Q., Lowenbraun, S., and Archer, A. *Teaching the Mildly Handicapped in the Regular Classroom*. Columbus, Ohio: Charles E. Merrill, 1980.

Alcorn, D. A. "Parental Views of Sexual Development and Education of the Trainable Mentally Retarded." *Journal of Special Education*, 8, 2 (1974), 119–130.

Allen, S. V. "On Educating Indians." *Compact*, 10 (Autumn 1976), 19–21.

American National Standards Institute. *Specifications for Audiometers*. ANSI S3.6–1969. New York: American National Standards Institute.

American Orthopsychiatric Association. "Developmental Assessment in EPSDT." *American Journal of Orthopsychiatry*, 48, 1 (1978), 7–21.

Anastasiow, N. J. "Strategies and Models for Early Childhood Intervention Programs in Integrated Settings." In M. J. Guralnick, ed. *Early Intervention and the Integration of Handicapped and Nonhandicapped Children*. Baltimore: University Park Press, 1978.

Anderson, R. M., and Greer, J. G., eds. *Educating the Severely and Profoundly Retarded*. Baltimore: University Park Press, 1976.

Arkans, J. R., and Smith, J. O. "Now More Than Ever: A Case for the Special Class." *Exceptional Children*, 40, 7 (1974), 497–502.

Arts for Blind and Visually Impaired People. New York: National Arts and the Handicapped Information Service, 1978.

Axelrod, S., and Bailey, S. L. "Drug Treatment for Hyperactivity: Controversies, Alternatives, and Guidelines." *Exceptional Children*, 47 (April 1979), 547–548.

Badger, E. "The Infant Stimulation/Mother Training Project." In B. Caldwell, ed. *Infant Education*. New York: Walker, 1977.

Badger, E., Burns, D., and Rhoades, B. "Education for Adolescent Mothers in a Hospital Setting." *American Journal of Public Health*, 66 (1976), 469–472.

Bailey, M. J. "Orientation and Mobility Research at California State College." In *Selected Papers: Fiftieth Biennial Conference*. Philadelpia: Association for Education of the Visually Handicapped, 1970.

Baird, A. S., and Goldie, D. "Activities and Experiences Develop Spatial and Sensory Understanding." *Teaching Exceptional Children*, 11, 3 (1979), 116–119.

Ballard, J., and Zettel, J. J. "The Managerial Aspects of Public Law 94–142." *Exceptional Children*, 44 (March 1978), 457–462.

Balow, B. "Definitional and Prevalence Problems in Behavior Disorders of Children." *School Psychology Digest*, 8 (Fall 1979), 348–354.

Banet, B. "Toward a Developmentally Valid Preschool Curriculum." *High/Scope Educational Research Foundation Report 1975–76* (1976).

Barnes, R. *Learning Systems for the Future*. Bloomington, Ind.: Phi Delta Kappa Educational Foundation, Library of Congress Catalogue #72–90559, PDK Fastback #9.

Barraga, N. *Increased Visual Behavior in Low Vision Children*. New York: American Foundation for the Blind, 1964.

Beebe, H. H. "Deaf Children Can Learn to Hear." In G. W. Nix, ed. *Mainstream Education for Hearing Impaired Children and Youth*. New York: Grune and Stratton, 1976.

Beebe, V. N. "Spanish Comes Alive in *la Isla Caribe*." *Phi Delta Kappan*, 60 (1978), 95–98.

Beitchman, J. H., Deilman, T. E., Landis, J. R., Benson, R. M., and Kemp, P. L. "Reliability of the Group for the Advancement of Psychiatry, Diagnostic Categories in Child Psychiatry." *Archives of General Psychiatry*, 35 (1978), 1461–1466.

Belch, P. J. "Toward Noncategorical Teacher Certification in Special Education—Myth or Reality?" *Exceptional Children*, 46 (October 1979), 129–131.

Benham, H. *Feeling Free, Activities and Stories*. New York: Scholastic Book Services, 1978.

Bereiter, C., and Engelman, S. *Teaching Disadvantaged Children in the Preschool*. Englewood Cliffs, N.J.: Prentice-Hall, 1966.

Berg, F. S. "A Model for a Facilitating Program for Hearing Impaired College Students." *Volta Review*, 74 (September 1972), 370–375.

Bernal, E. M., Jr. "The Identification of Gifted Chicano Children." In A. Baldwin, G. H. Gear, and L. J.

Lucito, eds. *Educational Planning for the Gifted: Overcoming Cultural, Geographic, and Socioeconomic Barriers.* Reston, Va.: Council for Exceptional Children, 1978.

Biklen, D., and Sokoloff, M., eds. *What Do You Do When Your Wheelchair Gets a Flat Tire? Questions and Answers About Disabilities.* New York: Scholastic Book Services, 1978.

Birch, J. W. *Mainstreaming Educable Mentally Retarded Children in Regular Classes.* Minneapolis: Leadership Training Institute/Special Education, University of Minnesota, 1974.

Bishop, V. E. *Teaching the Visually Limited Child.* Springfield, Ill.: Charles C. Thomas, 1971.

Bishop, W. "Characteristics of Teachers Judged Successful by Intellectually Gifted High Achieving High School Students." In B. Barbe and J. S. Renzulli, eds. *Psychology and Education of the Gifted.* New York: Irvington, 1975.

Blancher-Dixon, J., and Turnbull, A. "A Preschool Program for Gifted Handicapped Children." *Journal for the Education of the Gifted,* 1 (1978), 15–22.

Blatt, B. "Introduction: The Threatened Planet." In A. P. Turnbull and H. R. Turnbull, eds. *Parents Speak Out.* Columbus, Ohio: Charles E. Merrill, 1978.

Bleck, E. "Muscular Dystrophy—Ducheme Type." In E. E. Bleck and D. A. Nagle, eds., *Physically Handicapped Children: A Medical Atlas for Teachers.* New York: Grune and Stratton, 1975.

Bloodstein, O. "The Rules of Early Stuttering." *Journal of Speech and Hearing Disorders,* 39 (1974), 379–394.

Bloom, B. S. *Stability and Change in Human Characteristics.* New York: John Wiley & Sons, 1964.

Blumberg, L. "The Case for Integrated Schooling." *Exceptional Parent,* 3 (September/October 1973), 15–17.

Bonham, S. J., Jr. "Public Law 93–380: A Bill of Rights for the Handicapped." *Focus on Exceptional Children,* 7 (September 1975), 1–8.

Bookbinder, S. "What Every Child Needs to Know." *Exceptional Parent,* 7 (August 1977).

Boone, D. R. *The Voice and Voice Therapy.* Englewood Cliffs, N.J.: Prentice-Hall, 1971.

Bower, E. M. *Early Identification of Emotionally Handicapped Children in School,* 2nd ed. Springfield, Ill.: Charles C. Thomas, 1969.

Bower, E. M., and Lambert, N. M. "In-Schooling Screening of Children with Emotional Handicaps." In Long, Morse, and Newman, eds. *Conflict in the Classroom.* Belmont, Calif.: Wadsworth, 1965.

Bradfield, R. H., Brown, J., Kaplan, P., Rickert, E., and Stannard, R. "The Special Child in the Regular Classroom." *Exceptional Children,* 35 (1973), 384–390.

"Breaking Down the Barriers." *Readings in Physically Handicapped Education,* Guilford, Connecticut: Special Learning Corporation, 1978.

Brenton, M. "What Can Be Done about Child Abuse?" *Today's Education,* 66 (September/October 1977), 51–53.

Bricker, D. D. "A Rationale for the Integration of Handicapped and Nonhandicapped Preschool Children." In M. J. Guralnick, ed. *Early Intervention and the Integration of Handicapped and Nonhandicapped Children.* Baltimore: University Park Press, 1978.

Bricker, W. A., and Bricker, D. D. "The Infant, Toddler, and Preschool Research and Intervention Project." In T. D. Tjossem, ed. *Intervention Strategies for High Risk Infants and Young Children.* Baltimore: University Park Press, 1976.

Brolin, D. E. *Vocational Preparation of Retarded Citizens.* Columbus, Ohio: Charles E. Merrill, 1976.

Brolin, D. E., and D'Alonzo, B. J. "Critical Issues in Career Education for Handicapped Students." *Exceptional Children,* 45, 4 (1979), 246–253.

Brown v. Board of Education of Topeka. 347 U.S. 483, 493, 1954.

Brown, J. W. *Aphasia, Apraxia, and Agnosia.* Springfield, Ill.: Charles C. Thomas, 1972.

Bryan, T. H., and Bryan, J. H. *Understanding Learning Disabilities.* Sherman Oaks, Calif.: Alfred, 1978.

Burt, C. *The Gifted Child.* New York: John Wiley, 1975.

Burton, T. A., and Hirshoren, A. "The Education of Severely and Profoundly Retarded Children: Are We Sacrificing the Child to the Concept?" *Exceptional Children,* 45 (May 1979a), 598–602.

Burton, T. A., and Hirshoren, A. "Some Further Thoughts and Clarifications on the Education of Severely and Profoundly Retarded Children." *Exceptional Children,* 45 (May 1979b), 618–625.

Cain, L. F. "Parent Groups: Their Role in a Better Life for the Handicapped." *Exceptional Children,* 42 (May 1976), 432–437.

Caldwell, B. M. "A Decade of Early Intervention Programs: What We Have Learned." *American Journal of Orthopsychiatry,* 44, 4 (1974), 491–496.

Calhoun, M. L., and Hawisher, M. *Teaching and Learning Strategies for Physically Handicapped Students.* Baltimore: University Park Press, 1979.

Callahan, C. M. *Developing Creativity in the Gifted and Talented.* Reston, Va.: Council for Exceptional Children, 1978.

Calvert, D. R. "Dimensions of Family Involvement in Early Childhood Education." *Exceptional Children,* 37 (May 1971), 655–659.

Campbell, L. F. "Mobility for Young Blind Children." In *Selected Papers: Fiftieth Biennial Conference.* Philadelphia: Association for Education of the Visually Handicapped, 1970.

Canfield, J., and Wells, H. C. *100 Ways to Enhance Self-Concept in the Classroom.* Englewood Cliffs, N.J.: Prentice-Hall, 1976.

Cansler, D. P., Martin, G. H., and Voland, M. C. *Working with Families.* Winston-Salem, N.C.: Kaplan, 1975.

Cappiello, L. A., and Trayer, R. E. "A Study of the Role of Health Educators in Teaching about Death and Dying." *Journal of School Health*, 49 (September 1979), 397–399.

Carey, H. L. "Educational Services for the Handicapped: Federal Role." *Compact*, 5 (August 1971), 8–13.

Carroll, A. W. "The Classroom as an Ecosystem." *Focus on Exceptional Children*, 6 (September 1974).

Cartwright, C. A., and Cartwright, A. P. *Developing Observational Skills*. New York: McGraw-Hill, 1974.

"Case History: I'm Driving Everybody Crazy." *Exceptional Parent*, 4 (January/February 1974), 40–43.

"Case History: Who Shall We Sacrifice?" *Exceptional Parent*, 5 (October 1975), 17–22.

Cathey, M. L., and Jansma, P. "Mainstreaming Orthopedically Disabled Individuals in Various Activities." *Directive Teacher*, 2 (Fall 1979), 9.

Cavan, R. S., and Ferdinand, T. N. *Juvenile Delinquency*. Philadelphia: J. B. Lippincott, 1975.

Caywood, T. "A Quadraplegic Man Looks at Treatment." *Journal of Rehabilitation*, 40 (November/December 1974), 22–25.

Charles, C. M. *Individualizing Instruction*. St. Louis: C. V. Mosby, 1976.

Chase, L. *The Other Side of the Report Card: A How-To-Do-It Program for Affective Education*. Santa Monica, Calif.: Goodyear, 1975.

Chen, J., and Goon, S. W. "Recognition of the Gifted from among Disadvantaged Asian Children." *Gifted Child Quarterly*, 20 (Summer 1976), 157.

Chickering, A. W., and Chickering, J. N. "Life-Long Learning for Handicapped Persons." In M. C. Reynolds, ed. *Futures of Education for Exceptional Students: Emerging Strategies*. Reston, Va.: Council for Exceptional Children, 1978.

Christiansen, R. O. "Juvenile Diabetes Mellitus." In E. E. Bleck and D. A. Nagle, eds., *Physically Handicapped Children: A Medical Atlas for Teachers*. New York: Grune and Stratton, 1975, 123–131.

Christie, L. S., McKenzie, H. S., and Burdett, C. S. "The Consulting Teacher Approach to Special Education: Inservice Training for Regular Classroom Teachers." *Focus on Exceptional Children*, 4 (1972), 1–10.

Clark, B. *Growing Up Gifted*. Columbus, Ohio: Charles E. Merrill, 1979.

Clark, G. M. "Mainstreaming for the Secondary Educable Mentally Retarded: Is It Defensible?" *Focus on Exceptional Children*, 7, 2 (1975), 1–5.

Clements, S. D. *Minimal Brain Dysfunction in Children: Terminology and Identification, Phase I of a Three Phase Project*. Washington, D.C.: U.S. Department of Health, Education, and Welfare, 1966, Public Health Service Bulletin no. 1415.

Closer Look (a project of the Parents Committee for Handicapped Children and Youth). Box 1492, Washington, D.C. 20013 (Summer 1978).

Cocha, F. B. "Book Therapy for Abused Children." *Language Arts*, 55 (February 1978), 199–202.

Cohen, J. S., and DeYoung, H. "The Role of Litigation in the Improvement of Programming for the Handicapped." In L. Mann and D. Sabatino, eds. *The First Review of Special Education*, Vol. 2. Philadelphia: Journal of Special Education, 1973.

Combs, R. H., and Harper, H. L. "Effects of Labels on Attitudes of Educators Toward Handicapped Children." *Exceptional Children*, 33 (1967), 399–403.

Conley, R. *The Economics of Mental Retardation*. Baltimore: Johns Hopkins, 1973.

Conroy, J. W., and Derr, K. E. *Survey and Analysis of the Habilitation and Rehabilitation Status of the Mentally Retarded with Associated Handicapping Conditions*. Washington, D.C.: Department of Health, Education, and Welfare, 1971.

Coon, D. *Introduction to Psychology*. St. Paul, Minn.: West, 1977.

Corn, A., and Martinez, I. *When You Have a Visually Impaired Child in Your Classroom: Suggestions for Teachers*. New York: American Foundation for the Blind, 1978.

Corrigan, D. "The Present State of Teacher Education and Needed Reforms." In M. C. Reynolds, ed. *Futures of Exceptional Students: Emerging Structures*. Reston, Va.: Council for Exceptional Children, 1978.

Coulter, W. A. "Mattie T. and the Prescience of Individual Plans for All." *National Association of School Psychologists Communique*, 8 (August/September 1979).

Cramer, W. *How to Conduct an Effective Parent-Teacher Conference*. Portland, Maine: J. Weston Walsch, 1978.

Cratty, B. J. *Movement and Spatial Awareness in Blind Children and Youth*. Springfield, Ill.: Charles C. Thomas, 1971.

Crawford, W. L. *New Help for the Handicapped*. Toledo, Ohio: Lake State Printing, 1978.

Cross, L. "Identification of Young Children with Handicaps: An Overview." In N. E. Ellis and L. Cross, eds. *Planning Programs for Early Education of the Handicapped*. New York: Walker, 1977.

Crozier, J. "Project P.A.C.E.: Parent Action in Childhood Education, Ages 0–6." *Exceptional Parent*, 6 (August 1976), 11–14.

Davies, L. G., and McEwen, M. K. "Child Abuse and the Role of the School Counselor." *The School Counselor*, 25 (November 1977), 92–97.

Davis, H., and Silverman, S. R. *Hearing and Deafness*. New York: Holt, Rinehart and Winston, 1970.

Davis, J. "Personnel and Services." In J. Davis, ed. *Our Forgotten Children: Hard of Hearing Pupils in the Schools*. Minneapolis: University of Minnesota, 1977.

Defining Total Communication. A committee report presented at Conference of Executives of American Schools for the Deaf. Rochester, N.Y., 1976.

Denis, P. B., and Pinson, E. N. *The Speech Chain: The Physics and Biology of Spoken Language*. Garden City, N.Y.: Anchor Press/Doubleday, 1963.

Derdeyn, A. "A Case for Permanent Foster Placement of Dependent, Neglected, and Abused Children."

498

American Journal of Orthopsychiatry, 46 (October 1977a), 604–612.

Derdeyn, A. "Child Abuse and Neglect: The Rights of Parents and the Needs of Their Children." *American Journal of Orthopsychiatry*, 47 (July 1977b), 377–387.

Deshler, D. D. "Issues Related to the Education of Learning Disabled Adolescents." *Learning Disability Quarterly*, 1, 4 (1978), 2–10.

Diagnostic and Statistical Manual of Mental Disorders, 2nd ed. Washington, D.C.: American Psychiatric Association, 1968.

Diagnostic and Statistical Manual of Mental Disorders, 3rd ed. Washington, D.C.: American Psychiatric Association, 1980.

Dinkmeyer, D. *Developing Understanding of Self and Others, D-I.* Circle Pines, Minn.: American Guidance Services, 1970.

Dinkmeyer, D. *Developing Understanding of Self and Others, D-II.* Circle Pines, Minn.: American Guidance Services, 1973.

Dinkmeyer, D., and McKay, G. *Raising a Responsible Child: Practical Steps to Successful Family Relationships.* New York: Simon and Schuster, 1973.

Doob, H. *Gifted Students: Identification Techniques and Program Organization.* Arlington, Va.: Educational Research Service, 1975.

Dunn, L. M. "Special Education for the Mildly Retarded: Is Much of it Justifiable?" *Exceptional Children*, 35 (1968), 5–22.

Edelbrock, C. "Empirical Classification of Children's Behavior Disorders: Progress Based on Parent and Teacher Ratings." *School Psychology Digest*, 8 (Fall 1979), 355–369.

Edge, D., Strenecky, B. J., and Mour, S. I. *Parenting Learning Problem Children: The Professional Educator's Perspective.* Columbus, Ohio: National Center, Educational Media and Materials for the Handicapped, 1978.

Elkind, J. "The Gifted Child with Learning Disabilities." *Gifted Child Quarterly*, 17, 2 (1973).

"Epilepsy: A Teenager's View." The Epilepsy Association of Franklin County, Columbus, Ohio, 1976, 2.

Epps, E. G. "The School and Cultural Pluralism." In E. G. Epps, ed. *Cultural Pluralism.* Berkeley, Calif.: McCutchan, 1974.

Ewanowski, S. J. "Dysphasia in Adults." In T. J. Hixon, L. D. Shriberg, and J. H. Saxman, eds. *Introduction to Communication Disorders.* Englewood Cliffs, N.J.: Prentice-Hall, 1980.

Fagen, S. A., Long, N. J., and Stevens, D. J. *Teaching Children Self-Control: Preventing Emotional and Learning Problems in the Elementary School.* Columbus, Ohio: Charles E. Merrill, 1975.

Federal Register, 42 (May 4, 1977), 22682.

Federal Register, 42, 163 (August 23, 1977).

Federal Register, 42 (August 23, 1977), 42478.

Federal Register, 42 (December 29, 1977), 65083.

Federal Register, 42 (December 29, 1977), 65083.

Feingold, B. F. "Hyperkinesis and Learning Disabilities Linked to the Ingestion of Artificial Food Colors and Flavors." *Journal of Learning Disabilities*, 9, (1976), 551–559.

Fleischman, J. "Teaching the Unteachables." *Human Behavior*, 5, 5 (1976), 40–47.

Fonda, G. "Use of Eyes in Partially Sighted Children." In *Selected Papers: Fiftieth Biennial Conference.* Philadelphia: Association for Education of the Visually Handicapped, 1970.

Forness, S. R. "Implications of Recent Trends in Labeling." *Journal of Learning Disabilities*, 8 (August/September 1974).

Foster, G. G., Ysseldyke, J. E., and Reese, J. H. "I Wouldn't Have Seen It If I Hadn't Believed It." *Exceptional Children*, 41 (1975), 469–473.

Fox, L. H. "Sex Differences: Implications for Program Planning for the Academically Gifted." In J. C. Stanley, W. C. George, and C. H. Solano, eds. *The Gifted and Creative: A Fifty-Year Perspective.* Baltimore: Johns Hopkins, 1977.

Foulke, E. "The Perceptual Basis for Mobility." In *Selected Papers: Fiftieth Biennial Conference.* Philadelphia: Association for Education of the Visually Handicapped, 1970.

Frankenburg, W. K. "Considerations for Screening." In N. E. Ellis and L. Cross, eds. *Planning Programs for Early Education of the Handicapped.* New York: Walker, 1977.

Frazier, B. G. "Child Abuse: A Growing National Concern." *Dimensions: A Journal of the Southern Association on Children Under Six*, 4 (1975), 9–11.

Freedman, P. I. "Multi-ethnic Studies: Proceed with Caution." *Phi Delta Kappan*, 58 (1977), 401–402.

Fruehling, R. T. "Multicultural Education as Social Exchange." *Phi Delta Kappan*, 58 (1977), 398–400.

Fuller, R. "Breaking Down the IQ Walls: Severely Retarded People Can Learn to Read." *Psychology Today*, 8 (October 1974).

Furth, H. G. *Deafness and Learning: A Psychosocial Approach.* Belmont, Calif.: Wadsworth, 1973.

Gallagher, J. "The Special Education Contract for Mildly Handicapped Children." *Exceptional Children*, 38 (March 1972), 527–535.

Gallagher, J. J. *Research Summary on Gifted Child Education.* Springfield, Ill.: State Department of Public Instruction, 1966.

Gallagher, J. J. "Rights of the Next Generation of Children." *Exceptional Children*, 46 (October 1979), 98–107.

Gallagher, J. J., ed. *Teaching Gifted Students.* Boston: Allyn and Bacon, 1965.

Gallagher, J. J. *Teaching the Gifted Child.* Boston: Allyn and Bacon, 1975.

Gallagher, J. J., Aschner, M. J., and Jenne, W. *Productive Thinking of Gifted Children in Classroom Interaction.* CEC NEA Research Monograph Series B, No. B–5, 1967.

Gallagher, P. A. *Teaching Students with Behavioral Disorders: Techniques for Classroom Instruction*. Denver: Love, 1979.

Garber, H., and Heber, R. "The Milwaukee Project: Early Intervention as a Technique to Prevent Mental Retardation." *National Leadership Institute — Teacher Education/Early Childhood*. University of Connecticut Technical Paper, March 1973.

Garbarino, J. "The Price of Privacy in the Social Dynamics of Child Abuse." *Child Welfare*, 56 (November 1977), 565–575.

Garza, R. T. "Affective and Associative Qualities in the Learning Styles of Chicanos and Anglos." *Psychology in the Schools*, 15 (January 1978), 111–115.

Gath, A. "Sibling Reactions to Mental Handicap: A Comparison of the Brothers and Sisters of Mongol Children." *Journal of Child Psychology and Psychiatry*, 15 (July 1974), 187–198.

Gentile, A., and DiFrancesca, S. *Academic Achievement Tests Performances of Hearing Impaired Students, United States, Spring, 1969*. Washington, D.C.: Gallaudet College, 1969.

Getzels, J. W., and Jackson, P. W. "The Meaning of 'Giftedness' — An Examination of an Expanding Concept." *Phi Delta Kappan*, 40 (November 1958), 75–77.

Getzels, J. W., and Jackson, P. W. "The Study of Giftedness: A Multidimensional Approach." *The Gifted Student*. OE–35016, Cooperative Research Monograph No. 2, 6–18.

Gil, D. G. *Violence Against Children: Physical Child Abuse in the United States*. Cambridge, Mass.: Harvard University, 1970.

Gilchrist, M., and Taft, R. "Creative Attitudes and Creative Productivity: A Comparison of Two Aspects of Creativity Among Students." *Journal of Educational Psychology*, 62 (April 1970).

Ginsburg, H. *The Myth of the Deprived Child*. Englewood Cliffs, N.J.: Prentice-Hall, 1972.

Gjerdingen, D. B. "What Colleges and Universities Can Deaf Students Successfully Attend?" *Volta Review*, 79 (February/March 1977), 112–113.

Glazzard, Peggy. "Simulation of Handicaps as a Teaching Strategy for Preservice and Inservice Training." *Teaching Exceptional Children*, 2 (Spring 1979), 102–103.

Gold, M. N. "The Acquisition of a Complex Assembly Task by Retarded Adolescents." Urbana: University of Illinois, Children's Resource Center, 1968.

Goldenberg, E. P. *Special Technology for Special Children*. Baltimore: University Park Press, 1979.

Goldstein, H., Moss, J., and Jordan, L. J. *The Efficacy of Special Class Training on the Development of Mentally Retarded Children*. Urbana: University of Illinois, 1965.

Gollay, E. "Deinstitutionalized Mentally Retarded People: A Closer Look." *Education and Training of the Mentally Retarded*, (April 1977), 137–144.

Gonzales, E., and Ortiz, L. "Social Policy and Education Related to Linguistically and Culturally Different Groups." *Journal of Learning Disabilities*, 10 (June/July 1977), 332–338.

Goslin, D. A. *The Search for Ability*. New York: Russell Sage Foundation, 1963, 130.

Gowan, J. C. "How to Identify Students for a Gifted Child Program." *Gifted Child Quarterly*, 19, 3 (1977).

Gowan, J. C. "Twenty-Five Suggestions for Parents of Able Children." *Gifted Child Quarterly*, 8 (1964).

Graham, M. D. "Multiply Impaired Children: A National Study." In *Selected Papers: Fiftieth Biennial Conference*. Philadelphia: Association for Education of the Visually Handicapped, 1970.

Gray, B., and Fygetakis, L. "The Development of Language as a Function of Programmed Conditioning." *Behavior Research and Therapy*, 6 (1968), 455–460.

Gray, S. W., and Klaus, R. A. "The Early Training Project: A Seventh Year Report." *Child Development*, 41 (1970), 909–924.

Grebler, L., Moore, J. W., and Guzman, R. C. *The Mexican American People: The Nation's Second Largest Minority*. New York: Free Press, 1970.

Green, R. R. "Psycho Social Aspects of Mainstreaming for the Child and Family." In G. W. Nix, ed. *Mainstream Education for Hearing Impaired Children and Youth*. New York: Grune and Stratton, 1976.

Grossman, H. J., ed. *Manual in Terminology and Classification in Mental Retardation*. Washington, D.C.: American Association for Mental Deficiency, 1973.

Grotsky, J. N., Sabatino, D. A., Ohrtman, W. F., eds. *The Concept of Mainstreaming: A Resource Guide for Regular Classroom Teachers*. Harrisburg: Pennsylvania State Department of Education, 1976 (ERIC Document Reproduction Service, No. ED 132 784).

Guinn, R. "Value Clarification in the Bi-Cultural Classroom." *Journal of Teacher Education*, 28 (January 1977), 46–47.

Guralnick, M. J. "The Value of Integrating Handicapped and Nonhandicapped Preschool Children." *American Journal of Orthopsychiatry*, 46, 2 (1976), 236–245.

Hall, J. E., Morris, H. L., Barker, H. R. "Sexual Knowledge and Attitudes of Mentally Retarded Adolescents." *American Journal of Mental Deficiency*, 77, 6 (1973), 707–709.

Hamalian, C. S., and Ludwig, A. J. "Practicum in Normalization and Advocacy: A Neglected Component in Teacher Training." *Education and Training of the Mentally Retarded*, 11, 20 (1976), 172–175.

Hamilton, Andrew. "The Remarkable New Prosthetics, " *American Education*, 11 (January/February 1975).

Hare, B. A., and Hare, J. M. *Teaching Young Handicapped Children: A Guide for Preschool and the Primary Grades*. New York: Grune and Stratton, 1977.

Haring, N., and Phillips, E. L. *Educating Emotionally Disturbed Children*. New York: McGraw-Hill, 1962.

Harley, R. K., and Lawrence, G. A. *Visual Impairment in the Schools*. Springfield, Ill.: Charles C. Thomas, 1977.

Harrington, J. D. "Hard of Hearing Pupils in the Mainstream: Educational Needs and Services." In *Serving Hard-of-Hearing Pupils: Alternatives and Strategies for Personnel Preparation.* Minneapolis: University of Minnesota, 1976.

Harrison, D. B. "The Resource Teacher." In J. Jordan, ed. *Teacher, Please Don't Close the Door: The Exceptional Child in the Mainstream.* Reston, Va.: Council for Exceptional Children, 1976.

Harris-Vanderheiden, D. "Field Evaluation of the Auto-Com." In G. C. Vanderheiden and K. Grilley, eds. *Non-Vocal Communication Techniques and Aids for the Severely Physically Handicapped.* Baltimore: University Park Press, 1976.

Hart, V. "The Use of Many Disciplines with the Severely and Profoundly Handicapped." In E. Sontag, ed. *Educational Programming for the Severely and Profoundly Handicapped.* Reston, Va.: Council for Exceptional Children, 1977.

Hathaway, W. *Education and Health of the Partially Seeing Child.* New York: National Society for the Prevention of Blindness, 1966.

Hawisher, M. F., and Calhoun, M. L. *The Resource Room: An Educational Asset for Children with Special Needs.* Columbus, Ohio: Charles E. Merrill, 1978.

Hayden, A. H., and McGinness, G. D. "Bases for Early Intervention." In E. Sontag, ed. *Educational Programming for the Severely and Profoundly Handicapped.* Reston, Va.: Council for Exceptional Children, 1977.

Hayes, J. "Annual Goals and Short Term Objectives." In S. Torres, ed. *A Primer on Individualized Education Programs for Handicapped Children.* Reston, Va.: Foundation for Exceptional Children, 1977.

Hearing Loss: Hope Through Research, Publication No. (NIH) 77–157. Bethesda, Md.: Department of Health, Education, and Welfare, 1976.

Heisner, J. D. "What Are You Going to Do about Your Abused Child?" *Instructor*, 87 (February 1978), 22–23.

Henkin, C. S., and Henkin, A. B. "Culture, Poverty, and Educational Problems of Mexican Americans." *Clearing House*, 50 (March 1977), 316–319.

Hess, R. D. "Maternal Teaching Styles and Educational Retardation." In P. Torrance and R. D. Strom, eds. *Mental Health Deficiency.* New York: John Wiley, 1965.

Heward, W. L., Dardig, J. C., and Rossett, A. *Working with Parents of Handicapped Children.* Columbus: Ohio: Charles E. Merrill, 1979.

Hewett, F. M. *The Emotionally Disturbed Child in the Classroom.* Boston: Allyn and Bacon, 1968.

Hewett, F. M. In J. Kauffman and C. Lewis, eds. *Teaching Children with Behavioral Disorders: Personal Perspectives.* Columbus, Ohio: Charles E. Merrill, 1974.

Hixon, T. J., Shriberg, L. D., and Saxman, J. H., eds. *Introduction to Communication Disorders.* Englewood Cliffs, N.J.: Prentice-Hall, 1980.

Hofmeister, A., and Le Fevre, D. "The Tool Chest." *Teaching Exceptional Children*, Spring 1977, 82–83.

Holdsworth, L., and Whitmore, K. A. "A Study of Children with Epilepsy Attending Ordinary Schools, 1: Their Seizure Patterns, Progress and Behavior in School." *Developmental Medicine and Child Neurology* (1974), 16.

Homme, L., Csanyi, A. P., Gonzales, M. A., and Rechs, J. R. *How to Use Contingency Contracting in the Classroom.* Champaign, Ill.: Research Press, 1971.

Hull, F., and Hull, M. "Children with Oral Communication Disabilities." In L. Dunn, ed. *Exceptional Children in the Schools: Special Education in Transition.* New York: Holt, Rinehart and Winston, 1973.

Hull, F., Mielke, P., Timmons, R., and Willeford, J. "The National Speech and Hearing Survey: Preliminary Results," *ASHA*, 13 (1971), 501–509.

Hull, F., Mielke, P., Willeford, J., and Timmons, R. *National Speech and Hearing Survey*, Project No. 50978. Washington, D.C.: Bureau of Education for the Handicapped, U.S. Office of Education, 1976.

Hurlock, E. *Child Development.* New York: McGraw-Hill, 1972.

Impellizziri, A. E., Farrel, M. J., and Melville, W. G. "Psychological and Emotional Needs of Gifted Youngsters." *NASSP Bulletin*, March 1976.

Irwin, J. V., and Marge, M. *Principles of Childhood Language Disabilities.* Englewood Cliffs, N.J.: Prentice-Hall, 1972.

Jacobs, J. C. "Effectiveness of Teachers and Parent Identification of Gifted Children as a Function of School Level." *Psychology in the Schools*, 8 (1971), 140–142.

Jacobson, F. N. *The Juvenile Court Judge and Learning Disabilities.* Reno: National Council of Juvenile Court Judges, University of Nevada, 1976.

Jensen, A. R. "How Biased Are Culture Loaded Tests?" *Genetic Psychology Monographs*, 90 (1974), 185–244.

Johnson, C. A., and Katz, R. C. "Using Parents as Change Agents for Their Children." *Journal of Child Psychology and Psychiatry*, 14 (1973), 181–200.

Johnson, W., ed. *Stuttering in Children and Adults.* Minneapolis: University of Minnesota, 1955.

Johnston, W. *A Study to Determine Teacher Attitude Toward Teaching Special Children with Regular Children.* DeKalb: Northern Illinois University, 1972 (ERIC Document Reproduction Service No. ED 065–950).

Jones, J. W. *Blind Children: Degree of Vision, Mode of Reading.* Washington, D.C.: U.S. Department of Health, Education, and Welfare, 1961.

Jones, R. L., and Murphy, H. J. "Integrated Education for Deaf College Students." *Phi Delta Kappan*, 55 (April 1974), 542.

Jordan, R. E., and Eagles, E. L. "The Relation of Air Conduction Audiometry to Otologic Abnormalities." *Annals of Otology Rhinology and Laryngology*, 70 (1961), 819–827.

Justice, B., and Justice, R. *The Abusing Family.* New York: Human Sciences Press, 1976.

Juul, K. D. "European Approaches and Innovations in

Serving the Handicapped." *Exceptional Children*, 44 (February 1978), 322–332.

Kaplan, S. N., Kaplan, J. A. B., Madsen, S. K., and Taylor, B. K. *Change for Children*. Pacific Palisades, Calif.: Goodyear, 1973.

Karlin, I. W., Karlin, D. B., and Gurren, L. *Development and Disorders of Speech in Childhood*. Springfield, Ill.: Charles C. Thomas, 1965.

Karnes, M., and Bertschi, J. "Identifying and Educating Gifted/Talented Nonhandicapped and Handicapped Preschoolers." *Teaching Exceptional Children*, 10, 4 (1978), 114–119.

Karnes, M. B. "Mainstreaming Parents of the Handicapped." *Teacher*, 95 (October 1977), 90–91.

Karnes, M. B., and Teska, J. A. "Children's Responses to Intervention Programs." In J. J. Gallagher, ed. *The Application of Child Development Research to Exceptional Children*. Reston, Va.: Council for Exceptional Children, 1975.

Kauffman, J. M. *Characteristics of Children's Behavioral Disorders*. Columbus, Ohio: Charles E. Merrill, 1977.

Kauffman, J. M. In J. Kauffman, and C. Lewis, eds. *Teaching Children with Behavioral Disorders: Personal Perspectives*. Columbus, Ohio: Charles E. Merrill, 1974.

Kauffman, J. M. "Where Special Education for Disturbed Children is Going: A Personal View." *Exceptional Children*, 46 (April 1980), 522–527.

Kaufman, A. S. "Cerebral Specialization and Intelligence Testing." *Journal of Research and Development in Education*, 12, 2 (1979).

Kavanaugh, D., ed. *Listen to Us! The Children's Express Report*. New York: Workman, 1979.

Kempe, R. S., and Kempe, C. H. *Child Abuse*. Cambridge: Harvard University, 1978.

Kempton, W. *Sex Education for Persons with Disabilities that Hinder Learning*. N. Scituate, Mass.: Duxbury, 1975a.

Kempton, W. "Sex Education—A Cooperative Effort of Parent and Teacher." *Exceptional Children*, 41 (May 1975b), 531–535.

Kent, R. "Centering as a Process for Children's Imaging." *School Arts*, 77 (November 1977).

Keogh, B. K., and Kopp, C. B. "From Assessment to Intervention: An Elusive Bridge." In F. D. Minifie and L. L. Lloyd, eds. *Communicative and Cognitive Abilities: Early Behavioral Assessment*. Baltimore: University Park Press, 1978.

Kessler, J. W. *Psychopathology of Childhood*. Englewood Cliffs, N.J.: Prentice-Hall, 1966.

Kipnis, L., and Adler, S. *You Can't Catch Diabetes from a Friend*. Gainesville, Fla.: Triad, 1979.

Kirk, S. A. *Early Education of the Mentally Retarded: An Experimental Study*. Urbana: University of Illinois, 1958.

Kirk, S. A. "The Educability of Intelligence: Start with Young Children." In J. B. Jordan and R. F. Dailey, eds. *Not All Little Wagons Are Red*. Arlington, Va.: Council for Exceptional Children, 1973.

Kirk, S. A. "General and Historical Rationale for Early Education of the Handicapped." In N. E. Ellis and L. Cross, eds. *Planning Programs for Early Education of the Handicapped*. New York: Walker, 1977.

Knight, N. "Working Relationships that Work." *Teaching Exceptional Children*, 8 (1976), 113–115.

Kobuck, J. W. "The Compelling Case for Bilingual Education." *Saturday Review*, April 29, 1972, 54–58.

Kodman, F. "Educational Status of Hard of Hearing Children in the Classroom." *Journal of Speech and Hearing Disorders*, 28 (1963), 297–299.

Koln, R. "Ethnic Studies and Equality." In A. Kopan and H. Walbert, eds. *Rethinking Educational Equality*. Berkeley, Calif.: McCutchan, 1974.

Kolstoe, O. P. *Teaching Educable Mentally Retarded Children*, 2nd ed. New York: Holt, Rinehart and Winston, 1976.

Konigsmark, B. W. "Hereditary Deafness in Man." *New England Journal of Medicine* (1969), 281.

Kratz, L. E. *Movement Without Sight*. Palo Alto, Calif.: Peek, 1973.

Kübler-Ross, E. *On Death and Dying*. New York: MacMillan, 1969.

Kübler-Ross, E. "The Searching Mind." *Today's Education*, 61, 1 (1972), 30–32.

Kübler-Ross, E. *Questions and Answers on Death and Dying*. New York: MacMillan, 1974.

Labov, W. *Language in the Inner City*. Philadelphia: University of Pennsylvania, 1972.

Lake, T. P., ed. *Career Education: Exemplary Programs for the Handicapped*. Reston, Va.: Council for Exceptional Children, 1974.

Lance, W. D. "Technology and Media for Exceptional Learners: Looking Ahead." *Exceptional Children*, 44 (October 1977), 92–99.

Laneve, R. S. "Mark Twain School: A Therapeutic Educational Environment for Emotionally Disturbed Students." *Behavioral Disorders*, 3 (May 1979), 183–192.

Lauder, C., Kanthar, H., Myers, G., and Resnick, J. "Educational Placement of Children with Spina Bifida." *Exceptional Children*, 45 (March 1979), 432–437.

LaVor, M. "Economic Opportunity Amendments of 1972, Public Law 94–424." *Exceptional Children*, 39 (November 1972), 249–253.

Lee, L. L. "Linguistic Approaches to Developmental Language Disorders." *Folia Phoniatrica*, 26 (1974), 33–67.

Lehman, J. U. *Do's and Don'ts for Parents of Pre-School Deaf and Hard of Hearing Children*. Chicago: National Easter Seal Society, 1967.

Lerner, J. W. *Children with Learning Disabilities*, 2nd ed. Boston: Houghton-Mifflin, 1976.

Lewis, O. "The Culture of Poverty." *Scientific American*, October 1966, 9.

Light, R. J. "Abused and Neglected Child in America: A Study of Alternate Policies." *Harvard Educational Review*, 43 (1973), 556–598.

REFERENCES

Lindholm, B. W., Touliatos, J., and Rich, A. "Racial Differences in Behavior Disorders of Children." *Journal of School Psychology*, 16 (Spring 1978), 42–48.

Ling, D. "Rehabilitation of Cases with Deafness Secondary to Otitis Media." In A. Glorig and K. S. Gerwin, eds. *Otitis Media*. Springfield, Ill.: Charles C. Thomas, 1972.

Little, J. *Mine for Keeps*. Boston: Little, Brown, and Co., 1970.

Litton, F. E. W. *Education of the Trainable Mentally Retarded*. St. Louis: C. V. Mosby, 1978.

Long, N. In J. Kauffman and C. Lewis, eds. *Teaching Children with Behavioral Disorders: Personal Perspectives*. Columbus, Ohio: Charles E. Merrill, 1974.

Looft, W. R. "Sex Education for Parents." *Journal of School Health*, 41 (October 1971), 433–437.

Lott, L. A., Hudak, B. J., and Scheetz, J. A. *Strategies and Techniques for Mainstreaming: A Resource Room Handbook*. Monroe, Minn.: Monroe County Intermediate School District, 1975.

Lovaas, O. I., and Newsom, C. D. "Behavior Modification with Psychotic Children." In H. Leitenberg, ed. *Handbook of Behavior Modification and Behavior Therapy*. Englewood Cliffs, N.J.: Prentice-Hall, 1976.

Love, H., and Walthall, J. E. *A Handbook of Medical, Educational and Psychological Information for Teachers of Physically Handicapped Children*. Springfield, Ill.: Charles C. Thomas, 1977.

Lovitt, T. C. "The Learning Disabled." In N. G. Haring, ed. *Behavior of Exceptional Children*. Columbus, Ohio: Charles E. Merrill, 1978.

Lowenfeld, B. *Our Blind Children*. Springfield, Ill.: Charles C. Thomas, 1971.

MacMillan, D. L. *Mental Retardation in School and Society*. Boston: Little, Brown, and Co., 1977.

MacMillan, D. L., Jones, R., and Aloia, C. "The Mentally Retarded Label: A Theoretical Analysis and Review of the Research." *American Journal of Mental Deficiency*, 79 (1974), 241–261.

Mager, R. *Preparing Instructional Objectives*. Belmont, Ca.: Fearon, 1962.

Maker, J. C. *Providing Programs for the Gifted Handicapped*. Reston, Va.: Council for Exceptional Children, 1977.

Mandell, C., and Strain, P. "An Analysis of Factors Related to the Attitudes of Regular Classroom Teachers Toward Mainstreaming Mildly Handicapped Children." *Contemporary Educational Psychology*, 3 (1978), 154–162.

Mann, M. "What Does Ability Grouping Do to the Self-Concept?" *Childhood Education*, 36, 8 (1960), 357–360.

Marland, S. P. *Education of the Gifted and Talented*. Washington, D.C.: U.S. Office of Education, 1972.

Martenson, J. H. "Child Abuse: How Caregivers Fight Back." *Day Care and Early Education*, 4 (May/June 1977), 26–27.

Martin, D. L. "The Growing Horror of Child Abuse and the Undeniable Role of the Schools in Putting an End to It." *American School Board Journal*, 160 (1973), 51–55.

Martin, E. N. "Individualism and Behaviorism as Future Trends in Educating Handicapped Children." *Exceptional Children*, 38 (1972), 517–525.

Martinson, R. A. *The Identification of the Gifted and Talented*. Reston, Va.: Council for Exceptional Children, 1975.

Mays, M. "No Stars Please for Teaching the Retarded." *Today's Education* (March 1972), 50–51.

McCarthy, J. J., and McCarthy, J. F. *Learning Disabilities*. Boston: Allyn and Bacon, 1969.

McConnell, F. "Children with Hearing Disabilities." In L. M. Dunn, ed. *Exceptional Children in the Schools: Special Education in Transition*, 2nd ed. New York: Holt, Rinehart and Winston, 1973.

McCormack, A. J. "Science with Everyday Things." *Instructor*, 87 (October 1977).

McDonald, E. T. "Design and Application of Communication Boards." In G. C. Vanderheiden and K. Grilley, eds. *Non-Vocal Communication Techniques and Aids for the Severely Physically Handicapped*. Baltimore: University Park Press, 1976.

McDonald, E. T., and Schultz, A. R. "Communication Boards for Cerebral Palsied Children." *Journal of Speech and Hearing Disorders*, 38 (1976), 73–88.

Meeker, M. N. *The Structure of the Intellect: Its Implications and Uses*. Columbus, Ohio: Charles E. Merrill, 1969.

Menolascino, F. J. "Handicapped Children and Youth: Current-Future International Perspectives and Challenges." *Exceptional Children*, 46 (November 1979), 168–175.

Menyuk, P. *The Acquisition and Development of Language*. Englewood Cliffs, N.J.: Prentice-Hall, 1971.

Mercer, J. R. *Labeling the Mentally Retarded*. Berkeley: University of California, 1973.

Mercer, J. R. *System of Multicultural Pluralistic Assessment Conceptual and Technical Manual*. New York: Psychological Corporation, 1979.

Mercer, J. R., and Lewis, J. E. "Using the System of Multicultural Pluralistic Assessment (SOMPA) to Identify the Gifted Minority Child." In A. Baldwin, G. H. Gear, and L. J. Lucito, eds. *Educational Planning for the Gifted: Overcoming Cultural, Geographic, and Socioeconomic Barriers*. Reston, Va.: Council for Exceptional Children, 1978.

Meyen, E. L., and Moran, M. R. "A Perspective on the Unserved Mildly Handicapped." *Exceptional Children*, 45 (April 1979), 526–530.

Michaelis, C. T. "Chip on My Shoulder." *Exceptional Parent*, 4 (January/February 1974), 30–35.

Miller, H. L. *Social Foundations of Education*. New York: Holt, Rinehart and Winston, 1978.

Mills, N. "Our Daughter's Happiness Depends on Her Being Sterile." *Exceptional Parent*, April 1977, M2–M4.

Mirman, N. J. "Education of the Gifted in the 70's." *Gifted Child Quarterly*, Autumn 1971.

Mitchell, K. L. "What You Can Do About Child Abuse." *Early Years*, 8 (November 1977), 40–41.

Mizer, J. "Cipher in the Snow." *Today's Education*, November 1964.

Moore, B. D. "Implementing the Developmental Component of EPSDT Programs." *American Journal of Orthopsychiatry*, 48, 1 (1978), 22–32.

Moran, M. R. *Assessment of the Exceptional Learner in the Regular Classroom*. Denver: Love, 1978.

Morse, W. C. "The Helping Teacher/Crisis Teacher Concept." *Focus on Exceptional Children*, 8 (September 1976).

Morse, W. C. "Education of Maladjusted and Disturbed Children." In J. Kauffman and C. Lewis, eds. *Teaching Children with Behavioral Disorders: Personal Perspectives*. Columbus, Ohio: Charles E. Merrill, 1974.

Moses, K. L. "Dealing with Your Feelings." In E. McCleary, ed. *You Are Not Alone*. Chicago: National Easter Seal Society, 1978.

Moses, K. L. "Effects of Developmental Disability on Parenting the Handicapped Child." In M. L. Reiff, ed. *Patterns of Emotional Growth in the Developmental Disabled Child*. Morton Grove, Ill.: Julia S. Mollay Education Center, 1977.

Moses, K. L. *The Elusive Grieving Process*. Personal presentation to the Maumee Valley School Psychologists Association, Toledo, Ohio, April 20, 1979.

Mullins, J. B. *A Teacher's Guide to Management of Physically Handicapped Students*. Springfield, Ill.: Charles C. Thomas, 1979.

Myklebust, H. R. "Childhood Aphasia: An Evolving Concept." In L. E. Travis, ed. *Handbook of Speech Pathology and Audiology*. Englewood Cliffs, N.J.: Prentice-Hall, 1971.

Naremore, R. "Teachers' Judgments of Children's Speech: A Factor Analytic Study of Attitudes." *Speech Monographs*, 38 (1971), 17–27.

Naremore, R. C. "Language Disorders in Children." In T. J. Hixon, L. D. Shriberg, and J. H. Saxman, eds. *Introduction to Communication Disorders*. Englewood Cliffs, N.J.: Prentice-Hall, 1980.

Naremore, R. C. "Language Variation in a Multicultural Society." In T. J. Hixon, L. D. Shriberg, and J. H. Saxman, eds. *Introduction to Communication Disorders*. Englewood Cliffs, N.J.: Prentice-Hall, 1980.

National Advisory Committee of the Handicapped. *The Unfinished Revolution: Education for the Handicapped, 1976 Annual Report*. Washington, D.C.: U.S. Government Printing Office, 1976.

National Health Survey: Prevalence of Selected Impairments. Rockville, Md.: U.S. Department of Health, Education, and Welfare, 1975.

National Society for Prevention of Blindness Fact Book. New York: National Society for Prevention of Blindness, Inc., 1966.

Navarre, J. "Incubation as Fostering the Creative Process." *Gifted Child Quarterly*, 23 (Winter 1979).

Navarre, J. "Is What is Good for the Gander, Good for the Goose: Should Gifted Girls Receive Differential Treatment?" *Roeper Review*, Winter 1980.

Nedler, S. E., and Oralie, D. M. *Working with Parents:*

Guidelines for Early Childhood and Elementary Teachers. Belmont, Calif.: Wadsworth, 1979.

Neisworth, J. T., and Smith, R. M. *Retardation, Issues, Assessment, Intervention*. New York: McGraw-Hill, 1978.

Nelson, D. H. "Mainstreaming a Child with Spina Bifida." *Instructor*, 88 (March 1979).

Newberger, E. "Child Abuse and Neglect: Toward a Firmer Foundation for Practice and Policy." *American Journal of Orthopsychiatry*, 47 (July 1977), 374–376.

Nihira, K., Foster, R., Shellhaas, M., and Leland, H. *AAMD Adaptive Behavior Scale*. Washington, D.C.: American Association on Mental Deficiency, 1969.

Nirje, B. "The Normalization Principle and its Human Management Implications." In R. B. Cugel and W. Wolfesberger, eds. *Changing Patterns in Residential Services for the Mentally Retarded*. Washington, D.C.: President's Committee on Mental Retardation, 1969.

Nolan, C. Y. "Implications from Education of the Visually Handicapped for Early Childhood Education." In H. H. Spicker, N. J. Anastasiow, and W. L. Hodges, eds. *Children with Special Needs: Early Development and Education*. Minneapolis: University of Minnesota, 1976.

Northern, J. L., and Downs, M. P. *Hearing in Children*. Baltimore: Williams and Wilkins, 1978.

"What Is OIF?" Osteogenesis Imperfecta Foundation, Inc., 632 Center Street, Van Wert, Ohio, 1970.

"Osteogenesis Imperfecta Foundation (OI)." *Exceptional Parent*, January/February 1974, 22–23.

Ovando, C. J. "School Implications of the Peaceful Latino Invasion." *Phi Delta Kappan*, 59 (1977), 230–234.

Ozias, D. K. "Prevocational Continuum: A Step Towards Conceptualization." In *Selected Papers: Fiftieth Biennial Conference*. Philadelphia: Association for Education of the Visually Handicapped, 1970.

Pahz, J. A., and Pahz, C. S. *Total Communication*. Springfield, Ill.: Charles C. Thomas, 1978.

Palomares, V. H., and Ball, G. *Human Development Program*. La Mesa, Calif.: Human Development Training Institute, 1974.

Parker, C. A., ed. *Psychological Consultation: Helping Teachers Meet Special Needs*. Reston, Va.: Council for Exceptional Children, 1975.

Pate, J. E. "Emotionally Disturbed and Socially Maladjusted Children." In L. Dunn, ed. *Exceptional Children in the Schools*. New York: Holt, Rinehart and Winston, 1963.

Payne, J. E. "The Deinstitutional Backlash." *Mental Retardation*, 11, 2 (1976), 43–45.

Payne, J. S., Polloway, E. A., Smith, J. E., and Payne, R. A. *Strategies for Teaching the Mentally Retarded*. Columbus, Ohio: Charles E. Merrill, 1977.

PEECH: Precise Early Education for Children with Handicaps. Urbana-Champaign: University of Illinois, 1976.

Pegnato, C. W., and Birch, J. W. "Locating Gifted Children in Junior High Schools: A Comparison of

Methods." *Exceptional Children*, 25 (March 1959), 300–304.

Pepper, F. C. "Teaching the American Indian Child in Mainstream Settings." In R. L. Jones, ed. *Mainstreaming and the Minority Child*. Reston, Va.: Council for Exceptional Children, 1976.

Perkins, W. H. "Disorders of Speech Flow." In T. J. Hixon, L. D. Shriberg, and J. H. Saxman, eds. *Introduction to Communication Disorders*. Englewood, Cliffs, N.J.: Prentice-Hall, 1980.

Phelps, L. A. "Vocational Education for Special Needs Learners: Past, Present, and Future." *School Psychology Digest*, 7 (1977), 18–34.

Phelps, L. A., and Lutz, R. J. *Career Exploration and Preparation for Special Needs Learners*. Boston: Allyn and Bacon, 1977.

Powers, M. H. "Functional Disorders of Articulation: Symptometology and Etiology." In L. E. Travis, ed. *Handbook of Speech Pathology and Audiology*. Englewood Cliffs, N.J.: Prentice-Hall, 1971.

President's Committee on Employment of the Handicapped. *Getting Through College with a Disability*. Washington, D.C.: U.S. Government Printing Office, 1977.

President's Committee on Employment of the Handicapped. *Pathways to Employment*. Washington, D.C.: U.S. Government Printing Office, 1978.

President's Committee on Mental Retardation. *Mental Retardation: The Known and the Unknown*, DHEW Publication No. (OHD) 76–21008. Washington, D.C.: Department of Health, Education, and Welfare, 1975.

President's Committee on Mental Retardation. *Mental Retardation: The Known and the Unknown*, OHD 76–21008. Washington, D.C.: Department of Health, Education, and Welfare, 1975.

Proctor, C. A., and Proctor, B. "Understanding Hereditary Nerve Deafness." *Archives of Otolaryngology*, 85 (1967), 23–40.

Prouty, R. W., and Aiello, B. "The Diagnostic/Prescriptive Teacher: An Elementary School Mainstream Model." In B. Aiello, ed. *Making it Work*. Reston, Va.: Council for Exceptional Children, 1975.

Public Law 93–112, Section 504, 1973.

Public Law 94–142, Education for All Handicapped Children Act, November 29, 1975.

Pushaw, D. R. *Teach Your Child to Talk*. Fairfield, N.J.: CEBCO Standard, 1976.

Quay, H. C. "Patterns of Aggression, Withdrawal, and Immaturity." In H. C. Quay and J. S. Werry, eds. *Psychopathological Disorders of Childhood*. New York: John Wiley, 1972.

Raiser, L., and Van Nagel, C. "The Loophole in PL 94–142." *Exceptional Children*, 46 (April 1980), 516–520.

Ramos, N. T., ed. *Delinquent Youth and Learning Disabilities*. San Rafael, Calif.: Academic Therapy, 1978.

Raph, J. B., Goldberg, M. L., and Passow, A. H. *Bright Underachievers*. New York: Columbia University, 1966.

Rapier, J., Adelson, R., Carey, R., and Croke, K. "Changes in Children's Attitudes Toward the Physically Handicapped." In G. J. Warfield, ed. *Mainstream Currents*. Reston, Va.: Council for Exceptional Children, 1974.

Reinert, H. R. *Children in Conflict*. St. Louis: C. V. Mosby, 1976.

Renshaw, D. C. *The Hyperactive Child*. Chicago: Nelson-Hall, 1974.

Reschly, D., and Lamprecht, M. "Expectancy Effects of Labels: Fact or Artifact?" *Exceptional Children*, 46 (September 1979), 55–58.

Restak, R. M. *The Brain: The Last Frontier*. Garden City, N.Y.: Doubleday, 1979.

Reynolds, M., and Rosen, S. "Special Education: Past, Present, and Future." *Educational Forum*, May 1976, 551–562.

Rhoades, E. A. "Grandparents' Workshop." *Volta Review*, 77 (December 1975), 557–560.

Rhodes, W. C. "Curriculum and Disordered Behavior." *Exceptional Children*, 30 (1963), 61–66.

Rhodes, W. C. "The Illusion of Normality." *Behavior Disorders*, 2 (February 1977), 122–129.

Rhodes, W. C. "Beyond Theory and Practice: Implications for Programming for Children with Emotional Disabilities." *Behavior Disorders*, 5, August 1980, 254–262.

Richmond, P. G. *An Introduction to Piaget*. New York: Basic Books, 1970.

Rinconer, A., and Tripp, J. K. "Management and Education of Autistic Children." *School Psychology Digest*, 8 (Fall 1979), 397–411.

Rioux, J. W. "Parents and Educators—A Forced or Natural Partnership." *The Directive Teacher*, 1 (Fall 1978).

Robb, G. P., Bernardoni, L. C., and Johnson, R. W. *Assessment of Individual Mental Ability*. New York: Intext, 1972.

Robinson, N. M., and Robinson, H. B. *The Mentally Retarded Child: A Psychological Approach*. New York: McGraw-Hill, 1965.

Robinson, N. M., and Robinson, H. B. *The Mentally Retarded Child*, 2nd ed. New York: McGraw-Hill, 1976.

Robinson v. Wical, M.D., et al. (Civil No. 37607, California Superior Court, San Luis Obispo, filed September 4, 1970).

Rodriguez, A. "Introduction." *Inequality in Education*, February 1975, 3.

Roos, P. "Parents of Mentally Retarded Children: Misunderstood and Mistreated." In A. P. Turnbull and H. Rutherford Turnbull III, eds. *Parents Speak Out: Views from the Other Side of the Two-Way Mirror*. Columbus, Ohio: Charles E. Merrill, 1978.

Rosenthal, R., and Jacobsen, L. *Pygmalion in the Classroom: Teacher Expectations and Pupils' Intellectual Development*. New York: Holt, Rinehart and Winston, 1968.

Ross, A. O. *The Unrealized Potential.* New York: McGraw-Hill, 1977.

Ross, M. "Definitions and Descriptions." In J. Davis, ed. *Our Forgotten Children: Hard-of-Hearing Pupils in the Schools.* Minneapolis: University of Minnesota, 1977.

Rothman, E. P. In J. Kauffman and C. Lewis, eds. *Teaching Children with Behavior Disorders: Personal Perspectives.* Columbus, Ohio: Charles E. Merrill, 1974.

Rubenzer, R. "The Role of the Right Hemisphere in Learning of Creativity Implications for Enhancing Problem Solving Ability." *Gifted Child Quarterly,* 23 (Spring 1979), 78–100.

Rubin, L. "Jackson Passes Ball to Teachers . . ." *The Ohio State University College of Education News,* 3 (December 1978), 1–2.

Rubin, R. A., and Balow, B. "Prevalence of Teacher Identified Behavior Problems: A Longitudinal Study." *Exceptional Children,* 45 (1978), 102–113.

Russell, F., Shoemaker, S., McGuigan, C., and Bevis, D. *I.E.P. Individual Education Programming.* Boise, Ind.: State Department of Public Instruction, 1976.

Safford, P. L. *Teaching Young Children with Special Needs.* St. Louis: C. V. Mosby, 1978.

Salvia, J., and Ysseldyke, J. E. *Assessment in Special and Remedial Education.* Boston: Houghton-Mifflin, 1978.

Sanders, D. A. *Aural Rehabilitation.* Englewood Cliffs, N.J.: Prentice-Hall, 1971.

Sandgrund, A., Gaines, R. W., and Green, A. H. "Child Abuse and Mental Retardation: A Problem of Cause and Effect." *American Journal of Mental Deficiency,* 79 (1974), 327–330.

Schafer, D. S. "Early Intervention Developmental Profile: Application in a Transdisciplinary Program." In M. S. Moersch and T. Y. Wilson, eds. *Early Intervention Project.* Ann Arbor: University of Michigan, 1976.

Schoening, B. "P.E.E.R.S.: Parents Are Effective Early Education Resources." *Exceptional Parent,* 8 (February 1978), D8–D12.

Schult, M. "I'll Never Do That!" *Exceptional Parent,* 5 (October 1975), 6–10.

Scott, E., Jan, J., and Freeman, R. *Can't Your Child See?* Baltimore: University Park Press, 1977.

Sefcik, T. R., and Ormsby, N. J. "Establishing a Rural Child Abuse/Neglect Treatment Program." *Child Welfare,* 57 (March 1978), 187–195.

Segal, J., and Yahraes, H. "The Psychological Fallout of Physical Illness." *Parenting,* 2 (August 1979).

Segal, S. A. "On the Road with Charles Kuralt." *Reader's Digest,* 113 (December 1978), 132–135.

Shanas, B. "Child Abuse: A Killer Teachers Can Help Control." *Phi Delta Kappan,* (March 1975), 479–482.

Shea, T. M. *Teaching Children and Youth with Behavior Disorders.* St. Louis: C. V. Mosby, 1978.

Shearer, D. E., and Shearer, M. S. "The Portage Project: A Model for Early Childhood Intervention." In

T. D. Tjossem, ed. *Intervention Strategies for High Risk Infants and Young Children.* Baltimore: University Park Press, 1976.

Siegel, E. *The Exceptional Child Grows Up.* New York: E. P. Dutton, 1974.

Silverman, S. R., and Lane, H. S. "Deaf Children." In H. Davis and S. R. Silverman, eds. *Hearing and Deafness.* New York: Holt, Rinehart and Winston, 1970.

Simon, S. B., Howe, L. W., and Kirschenbaum, H. *Values Clarification.* New York: Hart, 1972.

Sirvis, B. "The Physically Handicapped." In E. L. Meyen, ed. *Exceptional Children and Youth.* Denver: Love, 1978.

Sisk, D. "What if Your Child is Gifted?" *American Education,* 13 (October 1977).

Sizemore, B. A. "Making Schools a Vehicle for Cultural Pluralism." In E. G. Epps, ed. *Cultural Pluralism.* Berkeley, Calif.: McCutchan, 1974.

Skeels, H. M. "Adult Status of Children with Contrasting Early Life Experiences: A Follow-Up Study." *Monographs of the Society for Research in Child Development,* 31, 3 (1966).

Skeels, H. M., and Dye, H. B. "A Study of the Effects of Differential Stimulation on Mentally Retarded Children." *Proceedings and Addresses of the 63rd Annual Session of the American Association of Mental Deficiency,* 44, 1 (1939), 114–136.

Slingerland, B. H. *A Multi-Sensory Approach to Language Arts for Specific Language Disability Children: A Guide for Primary Teachers.* Cambridge, Mass.: Educators Publishing Series, 1971.

The Slow Learning Program in the Elementary and Secondary Schools, Curriculum Bulletin No. 119. Cincinnati, Ohio: Cincinnati Public Schools, 1964.

Smith, H. W., and Kennedy, W. A. "Effects of Three Educational Programs on Mentally Retarded Children." *Perceptual and Motor Skills,* 24 (1967), 174.

Smith, R. M. *Clinical Teaching Methods of Instruction for the Retarded,* 2nd ed. New York: McGraw-Hill, 1974.

Snyder, L. K., Lovitt, T., and Smith, J. O. "Language Training for the Severely Retarded." *Exceptional Children,* 42 (September 1975).

Soeffing, M. "Abused Children are Exceptional Children." *Exceptional Children,* 42, 3 (1975), 126–133.

Soeffing, M. Y. "BEH Officials Identify and Discuss Significant Federal Programs for the Handicapped." *Exceptional Children,* 40 (March 1974), 437–442.

Sontag, E., Certo, N., and Button, J. E. "On a Distinction Between the Education of the Severely and Profoundly Handicapped and a Doctrine of Limitations." *Exceptional Children,* 45 (May 1979).

Speece, D. L., and Mandell, C. J. "An Analysis of Resource Room Support Services for Regular Teachers." *Learning Disability Quarterly,* 3 (Winter 1980), 49–53.

Spencer, T. L. "Parent Involvement in Education." *Practical Applications of Research,* Phi Delta Kappa, Bloomington, Ind., 1 (March 1979).

Stainback, W. C., Stainback, S. B., Payne, J. S., and

Payne, R. A. *Establishing a Token Economy in the Classroom.* Columbus, Ohio: Charles E. Merrill, 1973.

Stanley, J. "Identifying and Nurturing the Intellectually Gifted." *Phi Delta Kappan,* 58 (November 1976).

State of Ohio Curriculum Guide for Moderately Mentally Retarded Learners. Ohio Department of Mental Health and Mental Retardation, 1977.

Stephens, T. M. *Teaching Skills to Children with Learning and Behavior Disorders.* Columbus, Ohio: Charles E. Merrill, 1977.

Stevenson, H. W. *Children's Learning.* Englewood Cliffs, N.J.: Prentice-Hall, 1972.

Stewart, J. C. *Counseling Parents of Exceptional Children.* Columbus, Ohio: Charles E. Merrill, 1978.

Stickney, P., and Cupaiuolo, A. "From CRISP: Strategies for Community Residences." *Child Welfare,* 55, 1 (1976), 54–58.

Stogner, P. C. "Evaluation of Intelligence, Academic Aptitude and Achievement of the Visually Impaired." In *Selected Papers: Fiftieth Biennial Conference.* Philadelphia: Association for Education of the Visually Handicapped, 1970.

Strauss, A. A., and Lehtinen, L. *Psychopathology and Education of the Brain Injured Child.* New York: Grune and Stratton, 1947.

Strenecky, B. J., McLoughlin, J. A., and Edge, D. "Parental Involvement: A Consumer Perspective in the Schools." *Education and Training of the Mentally Retarded,* 14 (1979), 54–56.

Streng, A. H., Kretschmer, R. R., and Kretschmer, L. W. *Language, Learning, and Deafness.* New York: Grune and Stratton, 1978.

Strom, R. D. "The School Dropout and the Family." *School and Society,* 92 (April 1964), 191–192.

Strom, R. D. *Teaching in the Slum School.* Columbus, Ohio: Charles E. Merrill, 1965.

Suran, B. G., and Rizzo, J. V. *Special Children: An Integrative Approach.* Glenview, Ill.: Scott, Foresman, and Co., 1979.

Tannenbaum, A. J. "A Backward and Forward Glance at the Gifted." *National Elementary Principal,* 51 (February 1972), 14–23.

Teplin, L. A. "A Comparison of Racial/Ethnic Preferences among Anglo, Black and Latino Children." *American Journal of Orthopsychiatry,* 46 (October 1976), 702–709.

Terman, L. "Mental and Physical Traits of a Thousand Gifted Children." In L. Terman, ed. *Genetic Studies of Genius,* Vol. 1. Stanford, Calif.: Stanford University, 1925.

Terman, L., and Oden, M. *The Gifted Child Grows Up.* Stanford, Calif.: Stanford University, 1947.

Torrance, E. P. "Creative Positives of Disadvantaged Children and Youth." *Gifted Child Quarterly,* 13 (1969).

Torrance, E. P. *Discovery and Nurturance of Giftedness in the Culturally Different.* Reston, Va.: Council for Exceptional Children, 1977.

Torrance, E. P. *Education and the Creative Potential.* Minneapolis: University of Minnesota, 1963.

Torrance, E. P. *Guiding Creative Talent.* Englewood Cliffs, N.J.: Prentice-Hall, 1962.

Torrance, E. P., and Mourad, S. "Role of Hemisphericity in Performance and Selected Measures of Creativity." *Gifted Child Quarterly,* 33 (Spring 1979).

Torres, S., ed. *A Primer on Individualized Education Programs for Handicapped Children.* Reston, Va.: Foundation for Exceptional Children, 1977.

Travis, L. E., ed. *Handbook of Speech Pathology and Audiology.* New York: Appleton-Century-Crofts, 1971.

Treffinger, D. J., Renzulli, J. S., and Feldhusen, J. F. "Problems in the Assessment of Creative Thinking." In W. B. Barbe and J. S. Renzulli, eds. *Psychology and Education of the Gifted,* 2nd ed. New York: Irvington, 1975.

Truesdell, W. H. "Child Abuse: Shadow on the Classroom." *Teacher,* 95 (December 1977), 52–53.

Tunkin, M., and Kapperman, G. "Teaching the Concept of Negative Space to Blind Children: An Experience in Art." *Teaching Exceptional Children,* 10, 4 (1978), 119–120.

Turnbull, A. P., and Schultz, J. B. *Mainstreaming Handicapped Students: A Guide for the Classroom Teacher.* Boston, Allyn and Bacon, 1979.

Turnbull, A. P., Strickland, B. B., and Brantley, J. C. *Developing and Implementing Individualized Education Programs.* Columbus, Ohio: Charles E. Merrill, 1978.

Turnbull, A. P., and Turnbull, H. R. III, eds. *Parents Speak Out: Views from the Other Side of the Two-Way Mirror.* Columbus, Ohio: Charles E. Merrill, 1978.

Turner, E. T. "Attitudes of Parents of Deficient Children Toward their Child's Sexual Behavior." *Journal of School Health,* 40 (December 1970), 548–549.

Tuttle, F. B., Jr. "What Research Says to the Teacher— Gifted and Talented Students." National Education Association Publication, 1978.

U.S. Department of Health, Education, and Welfare. "Competency Standards." *The Child Development Associate Consortium.* Washington, D.C.: U.S. Government Printing Office, 1975.

U.S. Department of Health, Education, and Welfare. *Statistics for 1966 on Blindness in the Model Reporting Area.* Washington, D.C.: U.S. Government Printing Office, 1970.

U.S. Office of Education. *Estimated Number of Handicapped Children in the United States, 1974-75.* Washington, D.C.: Bureau of Education for the Handicapped, 1975.

Van der Veen, F., and Novak, A. C. "The Family Concept of the Disturbed Child." *American Journal of Orthopsychiatry,* 44 (October 1974), 763–772.

Van Riper, C. *Speech Correction: Principles and Methods,* 6th ed. Englewood Cliffs, N.J.: Prentice-Hall, 1978.

Volkmann, C. "Integrating the Physically Handicapped Student into the Elementary School." *Education,* 99 (1977).

Walberg, H. "Physics, Femininity, and Creativity." *Developmental Psychology,* 1 (1969), 47–54.

Wallace, G., and Kauffman, J. M. *Teaching Children with Learning Problems*. Columbus, Ohio: Charles E. Merrill, 1978.

Wallace, G., and Larsen, S. C. *Educational Assessment of Learning Problems: Testing for Teaching*. Boston: Allyn and Bacon, 1978.

Wallace, P. "Complex Environment: Effects on Brain Development." *Science*, 185 (1974), 1035–1037.

Ward, M. *Them Children*. New York: Holt, Rinehart and Winston, 1971.

Ward, S., and Reale, G. "The Exceptional Parent Survey." *Exceptional Parent*, 2 (August/September 1972), 28–29.

We Can Help: A Curriculum on the Identification, Reporting, Referral, and Case Management of Child Abuse and Neglect. Washington, D.C.: National Center on Child Abuse and Neglect, U.S. Department of Health, Education, and Welfare, 1976.

Weikart, D. P. "Preschool Programs: Preliminary Findings." *Journal of Special Education*, 1 (1967), 163–181.

Wesman, D. "Intelligent Testing." *American Psychologist*, 23 (1968), 267–274.

"What is OIF?" Osteogenisis Imperfecta Foundation, Inc., 632 Center Street, Van Wert, Ohio, 1970.

"Where Every Child is Educable." *Instructor*, 81 (March 1972), 66–68.

Wiederholt, J. L. "Historical Perspectives on the Education of the Learning Disabled." In L. Mann and D. Sabatino, eds. *The Second Review of Special Education*. Philadelphis: Journal of Special Education, 1974.

Wilson, R. C., Guilford, J. P., and Christensen, P. R. "The Measurement of Individual Differences in Originality." In W. B. Barbe and J. S. Renzulli, eds. *Psychology and Education of the Gifted*. New York: Irvington, 1975.

Wing, L. *Autistic Children*. Secaucus, N.J.: Citadel, 1972.

Wingate, M. *Stuttering: Theory and Treatment*. New York: Irvington, 1976.

Witty, P. A. "The Education of the Gifted and the Creative in the U.S.A." *Gifted Child Quarterly*, 15 (Summer 1971).

Wood, F. H., and Zabel, R. H. "Making Sense of Reports on the Incidence of Behavior Disorders/Emotional Disturbance in School Aged Populations." *Psychology in the Schools*, 15 (1978), 45–51.

Woodcock, C. C. "A Sensory Stimulation Center for Blind Children." *Phi Delta Kappan*, 55 (April 1974), 541.

Wyatt, J. D. "Self-Determination Through Education: Canadian Indian Example." *Phi Delta Kappan*, 58 (1977), 405–411.

Yahraes, H. "New Light on Autism and Other Puzzling Disorders of Childhood." Rockville, Md.: National Institute of Mental Health, U.S. Government Printing Office, 1978.

Yamamoto, K. "Creativity: A Blind Man's Report on the Elephant." *Journal of Counseling Psychology*, 12 (1965), 428–434.

Ysseldyke, J., and Salvia, J. "Diagnostic-Prescriptive Teaching: Two Models." *Exceptional Children*, (1974), 41.

Yater, V. U. *Mainstreaming of Children with a Hearing Loss*. Springfield, Ill.: Charles C. Thomas, 1977.

Zehrbach, R. R. "Determining a Preschool Handicapped Population." *Exceptional Children*, October 1975, 76–83.

Ziegler, S., and Hambleton, D. "Integration of Young TMR Children into Regular Elementary School." *Exceptional Children*, 42, 8 (1976), 459–461.

(credits continued from p. iv)

page 408 Reprinted from "Teaching the American Indian Child in Main Stream Settings" by F. Pepper in *Mainstreaming and the Minority Child*, R. L. Jones, editor, 1976, by permission of the Council for Exceptional Children.

pages 442-443 Reprinted from *Exceptional Children*, May, 1980, by Kenneth Katzen by permission of the Council for Exceptional Children.

PHOTO CREDITS

pages 35, 57, 61, 73, 92, 98, 105, 118, 143, 182, 183, 255, 305, 314, 364, 386, 392 Elizabeth Crews; **2** Sybil Shelton, Monkmeyer Press Photo Service; **9** B. Kliewe, © 1979 Jeroboam, Inc.; **15** Association for Retarded Citizens; **19** Special Olympics created and sponsored by the Joseph P. Kennedy, Jr. Foundation; **31** Toledo Public Schools; **41** Mitchell Payne, © 1978, Jeroboam, Inc.; **113** Eric Kroll, Taurus Photos; **125** Toledo Public Schools; **138, 141, 152, 163** Photos courtesy of the National Easter Seal Society; **157** Jane Scherr, © 1980 Jeroboam, Inc.; **178** Mimi Forsyth, Monkmeyer Press Photo Service; **188** Photo courtesy of the National Easter Seal Society; **206** Jean-Claude Lejeune, Stock, Boston, Inc.; **211** © Guy Gillette, 1973, Photo Researchers, Inc.; **214** Photo Courtesy of Telesensory Systems, Inc., Palo Alto, California; **227** Photo courtesy of the National Easter Seal Society; **233, 236** Sybil Shelton, Monkmeyer Press Photo Service; **253** Photo courtesy of Telesensory Systems, Inc.; **257** Photo courtesy of Kopptronix Company; **261** Photo courtesy of BG News; **275** Larry LaBonte; **280** George Bellerose, Stock, Boston, Inc.; **283** Larry LaBonte; **284** © Hanna Schreiber, Photo Researchers, Inc.; **298** C. Capa, Magnum; **303** Bayer, Monkmeyer Press Photo Service; **313** Anna Dorfman, © 1980 Jeroboam, Inc.; **331** Larry LaBonte; **336** Teri Lee Stratford, Monkmeyer Press Service; **338** Don Getsug, Rapho/Photo Researchers, Inc.; **358** Elizabeth Hamlin, Stock, Boston, Inc.: **381** Jeff Albertson, Stock, Boston, Inc.; **404** Patricia Hollander Gross, Stock, Boston, Inc.; **412** © Susan Ruklin, Photo Researchers, Inc.; **427** Larry LaBonte; **429** Hap Stewart, © 1978, Jeroboam, Inc.; **450** Susan Meiselas, Magnum.